Praise for
THE REAL SPECIAL RELATIONSHIP

"A remarkably good read . . . Michael Smith has written a fascinating, meticulously researched, and deeply insightful book on what truly has been a 'real special relationship' between British and American intelligence services over the past eighty years. Smith expertly chronicles the many secret conversations, decisions, and joint activities that shaped not only the breadth and depth of the US-UK security relationship but also the course of major world events."

—John Brennan, former CIA director

"As NSA director for six years, I participated firsthand in this special relationship. So special in fact that in the early days of the War on Terror, I told my British counterpart that in the event of a catastrophic loss at NSA Headquarters we would entrust management of the US SIGINT system to him. There is an unprecedented level of trust, and this book is an excellent chronicle of the critical junctures that created this relationship, tested it, and kept it strong."

—Michael Hayden, former director of both NSA and the CIA

"A well-written and gripping overview of one of the closest intelligence and security relationships in the world—one that has served both the UK and the US incredibly well over the past eighty-plus years and that continues to make a true difference today to each nation and their friends and allies. Amazing to see the twists and turns in the relationship laid out before the reader in such a compelling story."

—Admiral Mike Rogers, former NSA director

"As former director of the CIA, it became very clear to me that there is no more critical intelligence partnership than that between the US and the British secret services. . . . Michael Smith has done a remarkable job in this book detailing the sheer depth of that historic collaboration. It is truly a 'special relationship' built on trust and shared values and one that has been absolutely essential to protecting the national security of the US, Britain, and the world."
—Leon E. Panetta, former CIA director and Secretary of Defense

"This excellent book gives a detailed, highly professional account of the unique intelligence relationship, originally between the US and UK, now including Canada, Australia, and New Zealand—the Five Eyes. For more than eighty years this 'special relationship' has been fundamental to the security of our countries and of liberal democracy. As the story makes clear, we certainly need each other now."
—Sir John Scarlett, former MI6 chief

"The US/UK intelligence relationship has quietly shaped world events over the last eighty years. Michael Smith convincingly explains how and why this unique partnership of trust came into being. He does not shy away from illuminating the difficulties and personality clashes in its early years, but it is the account of the subsequent extraordinary joint successes that provide the most riveting read, successes that will ensure that the relationship will continue to be essential to our national security."
—Professor Sir David Omand, former director of GCHQ and UK security and intelligence coordinator

"The pre-eminent historian of Bletchley Park cuts through the hype about the Special Relationship to tell the gripping stories of what has been achieved in secret through the ups and downs of this enduring eighty-year partnership. His account reminds us why it is worth preserving."
—Robert Hannigan, former director of GCHQ and Prime Minister's security adviser

THE REAL SPECIAL RELATIONSHIP

THE REAL SPECIAL RELATIONSHIP

The True Story of How MI6 and the CIA Work Together

MICHAEL SMITH

FOREWORD BY MICHAEL HAYDEN
INTRODUCTION BY SIR JOHN SCARLETT

ARCADE PUBLISHING • NEW YORK

First North American Edition

Arcade Publishing books may be purchased in bulk at special discounts for sales promotion, corporate gifts, fund-raising, or educational purposes. Special editions can also be created to specifications. For details, contact the Special Sales Department, Arcade Publishing, 307 West 36th Street, 11th Floor, New York, NY 10018 or arcade@skyhorsepublishing.com.

Arcade Publishing® is a registered trademark of Skyhorse Publishing, Inc.®, a Delaware corporation.

Published by arrangement with Simon & Schuster UK Ltd, 1st Floor, 222 Gray's Inn Road, London, WC1X 8HB, A CBS Company

The author and publishers have made all reasonable efforts to contact copyright holders for permission and apologize for any omissions or errors in the form of credits given. Corrections may be made to future printings.

Visit our website at www.arcadepub.com.
Visit the author's site at michealsmithauthor.com.

10 9 8 7 6 5 4 3 2 1

Library of Congress Cataloging-in-Publication Data is available on file.
Library of Congress Control Number: 2023930366

Cover design by Erin Seaward-Hiatt
Cover illustration: Pete Sherrard/Getty Images (figure); Simon2579/
Getty Images (flags)

ISBN: 978-1-956763-68-3
Ebook ISBN: 978-1-956763-70-6

Printed in the United States of America

In memory of my good friend and mentor
Thomas Ralph Erskine, 1933–2021

CONTENTS

AUTHOR'S NOTE

I have taken a number of measures throughout this book to avoid the inevitable problems caused by a large number of similar names, abbreviations and titles. For the sake of simplicity, I have referred to the Soviet intelligence service as the KGB, ignoring the various titles that preceded it, to the British Secret Intelligence Service as MI6, and to the head of the CIA as the CIA Director, although for most of the period covered by this book, the correct title was Director of Central Intelligence.

I am extremely grateful to all those who helped me in the research and writing of this book, some of whom have understandably declined to be named. I am particularly grateful to Michael Hayden and Sir John Scarlett for their generous yet authoritative foreword and introduction to this book. I would also like to thank David Abrutat; Jonathan Bush; Ali Chokri; Tony Comer; Martyn Cox; Linda Eberst; Ralph Erskine; Helen Fry; Tony Insall; Bruce Jones; Alan Judge; Graeme Lamb; Dan Lomas; Kevin Moore; Dan Mulvenna; Henry Pavlovich; Hayden Peake; Meta Ramsay; Maria Robson Murrow; Rod Saar; John Sipher; John Stubbington; Andy Thomas; Philip Tomaselli and Dermot Turing.

I would also like to thank my my editor at Arcade Publishing, Cal Barksdale, and my agent, Tom Cull. I must also thank my family and friends for their support as the manuscript struggled through the pandemic, most particularly of course my wife, Hayley.

FOREWORD

As a senior leader in the US Intelligence community between 1999 and 2009, I developed a deep understanding of the Special Relationship involving US, UK, Canada, Australia and New Zealand, which grew out of the remarkable meeting at Bletchley Park in February 1941, described in detail by Michael Smith in *The Real Special Relationship*. At this 1941 meeting, Britain and the United States shared their most crucial (codebreaking) secrets ten months before the US entered the war.

In the nearly eighty years since the end of the Second World War, the Special Relationship has been much discussed, its high and low points recorded, especially at the senior political level. In this discussion, there has been a persistent inclination to question its real value and ability to survive especially from the US point of view. The British are widely perceived as playing up the relationship to emphasize their continuing global role which in reality has been in decline. I have always found this frustrating, knowing as I do from my personal experience the reality of what the Relationship has brought and continues to bring to the five countries now involved.

I am therefore especially pleased to have the opportunity to draw attention to, and to highlight the quality of, this detailed history by Michael Smith. As Michael makes clear, the Special Relationship has been a major and continuing feature of global politics for over eighty years. As he also explains, the foundation lies in the profound collaboration which spreads across all the security and intelligence services and special forces commands. The nature and the strength of the relationship can only be understood by close and careful study of the detail, starting, of course, with the Second World War. The story continues, encompassing major events across the decades, many, but not all, linked to the Cold War: Suez 1956; Cuban Missile crisis 1962; further conflicts across the Middle East; the Falklands War; the end of the Cold War; 9/11 and the aftermath, notably Afghanistan; the invasion of Iraq 2003; now, currently, growing tensions with China and the Russian invasion of Ukraine, so clearly and publicly anticipated by US and British intelligence.

As Michael makes clear, and as I can confirm, the exceptional value of the Relationship is fully understood and supported by the United States and the leadership of the US intelligence community as well as by my colleagues on the British side. Indeed, Michael demonstrates how the mutual and fundamental trust which is essential to a relationship of this kind has grown over the years through the personal connections and experiences of the generations of individual officers involved.

I will end by highlighting one of many meaningful episodes recorded by Michael Smith. In early April 1982, the Falklands War broke out. There was serious discussion in parts of the US administration as to whether the US should become directly involved in support of Britain or seek to maintain a neutral position given the importance in South America of Argentina. At a meeting in the White House Situation Room, Bobby Ray Inman, deputy director of CIA and former director of NSA, gave an impassioned speech on the need to "back our British allies to the hilt. I am not evoking just the historic ties of bloodlines, language, law, alliance, culture and tradition, central as these are. I want you to remember the overwhelming importance of our shared interest in the strategic stakes, the depth and breadth of our intelligence cooperation, the whole gamut of global Cold War concerns we have riding on the close interaction with the UK."

As a final and personal comment, as NSA director for six years, I participated first-hand in the special relationship, so special in fact, that in the early years of War on Terror, I told my British counterpart that in the event of a catastrophic loss at NSA headquarters, we would entrust management of the US SIGINT system to him. There is an unprecedented level of trust, and this book is an excellent chronicle of the critical junctures that created this relationship, tested it and kept it strong. Even on the rare occasions when our governments are at odds, the intelligence relationship remains strong.

MICHAEL HAYDEN, FORMER NSA DIRECTOR (1999–2005)
AND CIA DIRECTOR (2006–2009)

INTRODUCTION

On 8 February 2016, I had the privilege, as chairman of the Bletchley Park Trust, to attend a ceremony in the office of Commander Alastair Denniston, the wartime head of Bletchley Park, to mark the 75th anniversary of the effective beginning of the 'Special Relationship' alongside the then GCHQ director Robert Hannigan and his NSA counterpart Admiral Mike Rogers.

Seventy-five years previously, just before midnight, 8 February 1941, Denniston had received two US Army officers, Captain Abe Sinkov and Lieutenant Leo Rosen, and two US Navy counterparts, Lieutenant Robert Weeks and Ensign Prescott Currier, in the same office. They had brought with them the top secret analogue device 'Purple Machine' they were using to decipher sensitive Japanese communications, such as ambassadorial communications to Tokyo. This success was arguably the US's biggest secret.

Over the following month the US officers were given a complete briefing on activities at Bletchley Park, including full details of British success at breaking the German Enigma cipher. Without doubt, this was Britain's biggest secret. The two countries were exchanging their biggest secrets. This denoted an extraordinary level of trust. As noted to the BBC in 2016, there was at that time no treaty between them. There was no formal commitment to each other. The United States would not join the war for another ten months. The exchange was simply unprecedented.

A particular feature of the occasion was provided by nineteen-year-old Barbara Abernethy, assistant to Commander Denniston.

She handed out sherry from the Army and Navy Stores. It was her first encounter with Americans. There was a romantic aftermath. Barbara was to marry one of the American officers subsequently posted to Bletchley Park. Their marriage lasted until his death in 2003. Barbara died in the US in 2012.

This is a romantic story in many respects. But it is fair to say that the meeting was the beginning of the unique 'Special Relationship', which continues to this day. It is appropriate for the story to begin at Bletchley Park. The relationship has from the beginning been rooted in broad-ranging, cutting-edge intelligence work, an aspect which has been better understood since the Five Eyes partnership has become publicly acknowledged and discussed in recent years.

As Michael Smith demonstrates, it goes much wider than that. There is a widespread view that the relationship is more appreciated and talked up by the British as a means of promoting their global role, which has visibly declined since 1941. In my experience, the relationship is highly valued by all participants in the Five Eyes, not just the US and UK, but also Canada, Australia and New Zealand, who, as 'British Dominions', were brought into the BRUSA (UKUSA since 1953) intelligence collaboration agreement in March 1946.

The relationship is still going strong after more than eighty years. It is based on an exceptional degree of trust between five independent nation states. As noted in the prologue, this may have been best described by Prescott Currier, one of the four American visitors, commenting in the late 1960s. The Special Relationship 'is still on a personal friendly basis, without any regard to what the politics of the moment may be. It doesn't seem to make any difference at all. We've never faltered and we've never lost out and we've never become very disenchanted with one another. It's something which will probably continue indefinitely.' That was said over fifty years ago. It is still true. The commitment, trust and personal emotion still apply.

Smith describes the very beginning and early years of the relationship in detail. His account is well informed, balanced and well judged. He puts the story into its historical and political context. For me, at least, some key aspects stand out.

A long-lasting and structural achievement on this scale can only take place on the basis of exceptional political leadership. This was certainly provided in the 1940s by Winston Churchill and Franklin D. Roosevelt. Notwithstanding the friendship and the emotion described above, there were many differences and misunderstandings between the British and American individuals involved.

The story reminds us how little we knew each other before the age of global travel and 24-hour communications. After 1941, Americans came in large numbers to wartime Britain. Everyone had to adapt quickly. We did not know each other well. Jean Howard from Bletchley Park summed it up forcefully. 'They were different animals and the English they spoke had different meanings. They were fat, we were emaciated. They were smart (eleven different sorts of uniform). We were almost in rags. They were rich, we were poor . . . We were overworked and exhausted and having to teach people who barely knew where Europe was, was the last straw.'

The Americans saw the British as overcautious and overprotective of their strengths and assets, including their intelligence achievements and experience. For them, the British were truly defensive. For their part, the British worried about US assertiveness, including taking unnecessary risks with their operational planning and seemingly endless resources. The Americans seemed careless, including on occasions with their secrets, which had a habit of leaking into the frontline US media.

The British security and intelligence services had been in place since before the First World War and by the early 1940s were well structured and essentially confident. There were rivalries, but they were used to working with each other. The US services were still underdeveloped. Until the Office of Strategic Services (OSS) was formed during the war, they did not have a separate human intelligence agency. Indeed, OSS did not survive the end of the war and the CIA was not formed until September 1947. Until the formation of the National Security Agency (NSA) in 1952, communications intercept was conducted within the navy and army.

There was intense rivalry and manoeuvring throughout the US system not just during the war, but, as Smith demonstrates, up to and including Korea. The British were keen to encourage the development of the OSS and subsequently the CIA. Indeed, these US agencies were often seen within the US system as British nominees and lackeys. At the same time, the British were only too aware of the growing disparity in resources and the risk of being outmatched on the global scale in the post-war world. This book captures well the speed with which independent US activity took off across Europe in the aftermath of D-Day and liberation.

Throughout the story told we find some notable and well-known spies, mainly but not exclusively on the British side (Philby, Burgess, Maclean, Fuchs, Weisband, Cairncross, Blake, Ames). Their stories are well described. They are not exaggerated.

The Special Relationship was founded in the exceptional circumstances of the Second World War. After May 1945, it was tested and developed in the confrontation with the Soviet Union, most notably in the complex and collaborative intelligence work against Operation Borodino, the Soviet programme to develop atomic weaponry, the conflicts and tensions in the Balkans (notably the joint operations in Albania) and then Korea.

The Korean War was a major test in east Asia where the US had a dominant role but depended significantly on the resources offered by Hong Kong. Smith highlights the achievements but also the tensions and misjudgements of this war. There were intelligence failures, most notably over the large-scale Chinese military intervention in late 1950, but as the book makes clear, there was also impressive intelligence reporting on the Chinese build-up before the intervention. The key misjudgements were at the top political and military level. The policy makers found it difficult to understand and anticipate Chinese strategic thinking and objectives. This leaves us something to think about today.

Smith describes the intense collaboration in the Cold War, including the developing (and dangerous) air reconnaissance of eastern Europe and the Soviet Union, operations in East Germany and Vienna and, of course, the Berlin Tunnel. The overthrow of Mossadeq in Iran in 1953 is of particular interest in the context of the Special Relationship. US awareness of the capabilities and assets of the United Kingdom comes through clearly. But the US was determined, including at the top level, to assert US interests, objectives and leadership.

The year 1956 was exceptional and testing with the Hungary and Suez crises reaching a climax at the very same time in the autumn. The year was certainly testing for the Special Relationship. The US and UK were in basic disagreement over the British–French–Israeli intervention to overthrow Gamal Abdel Nasser in Egypt. The CIA and the NSA were well aware of British (and French and Israeli) plans. Smith shows, however, how they continued to share their intelligence with the British.

President Eisenhower had long personal experience of the Special Relationship and UK-USA intelligence sharing. In late November 1956, in a personal message to Lord Ismay, NATO secretary-general, he noted: 'I have never lost sight of the importance of Anglo-American friendship and the absolute necessity of keeping it strong and healthy in the face of the continuing Soviet threat.' He then told *Newsweek* that 'Our friendship with the people of Great Britain and Western Europe must be maintained and must be strengthened.' In March 1957, and at Eisenhower's suggestion, a successful conference took place in Bermuda 'to restore confidence in the Anglo-American relationship'. Suez had been a test. The Special Relationship survived wholly intact. But British global influence and prestige was significantly reduced.

Eisenhower's commitment carried through to John F. Kennedy, whom, as Smith shows, he briefed carefully on the intelligence relationship during the transition period before Kennedy took office in January 1961. This briefing justified itself to an exceptional degree at the international high point of the Kennedy presidency, the Cuban missile crisis of October 1962. Smith explains in detail the key role in the crisis played by intelligence from GRU colonel Oleg Penkovsky on Soviet missile development and capability. The intelligence not only helped the US to identify the significance of the missiles as they were installed, but critically, also allowed Kennedy to judge 'how much time he might have to negotiate before taking action to destroy the missiles'. Penkovsky was an MI6 agent, run in close coordination with the CIA.

In a broader sense, Smith's account demonstrates the close and mutually supportive personal relationship enjoyed by President Kennedy and Prime Minister Macmillan. Indeed, he describes this as one of the undoubted high points of the Special Relationship, a high point which came to an end with Macmillan's resignation on 18 October 1963 and Kennedy's assassination just over one month later. But at least one achievement of their close collaboration was the continuation of 'the independent British nuclear deterrent and the close nuclear relationship between Britain and America, which has remained in place until the current day'. Smith demonstrates how this was not an easy achievement in terms of the US–UK relationship. Interestingly, in the early 1960s, the US was taking increasing account of continental European positions, especially French (de Gaulle) resentment over the Special Relationship and the risk as they saw it that US support for the UK deterrent would become a key factor in the blocking of UK membership of the EEC (a membership which the US strongly supported).

Smith also reveals interesting (and for some, perhaps, surprising) details on British influence on US policy in the early years of US involvement in Vietnam. This influence was based on British success in countering the Malayan insurgency in the 1950s, in particular through the development of strategic hamlets across sensitive rural areas of the country. The British example suggested this was the route to follow in combating the Việt Cộng, not a more conventional military approach. Some senior British advisers sought to oppose the military overthrow of President Ngô Đình Diệm on 1 November 1963. Their advice was not followed. President Diệm was killed in the coup. The US had advance knowledge of the operation, even if they were not actively involved. President Kennedy was visibly shocked by the president's death. Just over three weeks later, he was dead himself.

Kennedy's assassination was followed in October 1964 by the arrival of a new British Labour prime minister, Harold Wilson. The increasingly complex conflict in Vietnam led to significant early tension between Prime Minister Wilson and President Johnson. Famously, Wilson resisted intense pressure from Johnson to commit British troops to the campaign. But underlying support for US objectives continued through military means, in particular the deployment of Royal Navy submarines, signals intelligence operations and RAF support in Europe, to ease the pressure on USAF.

An especially interesting and significant aspect of the support is explained by Smith's account of the work of successive British consuls general in Hanoi as the conflict developed from 1964 onwards. Most of these consuls general, who followed each other in quick succession, were career MI6 officers, including Brian Stewart and Daphne Park, both of whom went on to senior positions in the service. Classic secret agent running was very difficult in the wartime circumstances of Hanoi. But these British intelligence officers were on the ground, well trained and well motivated to report on the impact of US military operations, most especially bombing raids on targets in Hanoi. Slightly to their surprise their reports landed regularly on the president's desk. Their work will certainly have contributed to the much-improved relationship between Wilson and Johnson, even though the prime minister kept Britain out of direct involvement in the conflict.

At this point, the story begins to move into the current era. From 1966 the Special Relationship was required to adapt to the changing balance of power, most especially the continuing decline in Britain's global role, influence and capabilities. In reality, this process of global retreat was more complicated than might at first appear. In any event, the Special Relationship continued to function with deep effect, most notably in intelligence, but also in political cooperation.

On the intelligence side, Smith highlights success in the tracking of Soviet submarines in the Atlantic, monitoring of Soviet warships, including (intriguingly) through the deployment of British trawler skippers, and the capturing of the latest radar technology in a sophisticated short notice operation in Berlin. Notably, in the 1967 Arab–Israeli War, the key intelligence role was played by the British military intercept site at Ayios Nikolaos near Famagusta in Cyprus. Intelligence coverage monitored the build-up to war, highlighting Israel's critical advantage in air combat capability. This allowed the JIC to give a remarkably accurate prediction that the war would be short, 'a week plus'. (The head of Mossad made a very similar prediction to President Johnson.) Special Relationship collaboration was not confined to intelligence-gathering, as confirmed by the British proposal for a joint US–UK naval task force to guarantee freedom of navigation in the Gulf of Aqaba. This proposal drew especially warm praise for Harold Wilson from President Johnson.

In 1968, attention moved from the Middle East to Europe with the Soviet and Warsaw Pact intervention in Czechoslovakia on 20 August. As tension mounted following the start of Dubček's reforms, the movements and activities of Soviet and other Warsaw Pact forces were followed in the closest detail by shared US and UK military signals intelligence. This formed the basis for continual policy dialogue characterised in the early part of the year at least by a shared US–UK instinct to question whether Moscow would take the risk to its international reputation by military intervention. This political judgement, that Moscow would build up pressure but refrain from the final act, persisted in London at least within the JIC, to the last moment.

By mid-July, assessment in Washington had hardened that 'the chances of a violent Soviet intervention had sharply increased'. Subsequent reflection in the UK following the invasion focused on the risk of 'mirror imaging' and 'persevering' with an established view, recognised risks for intelligence assessment. Significantly, the limitations of reliance on signals intercepts began to be acknowledged. Perhaps the only way of knowing in advance of the decision to invade was to have an agent in or near the Politburo. This would become increasingly relevant as the Cold War dragged on.

As Smith points out, the early 1970s marked a low point in the Special Relationship, the consequence of a combination of politics and personalities on both sides of the Atlantic. The UK was under serious economic pressure. The top priority for Prime Minister Edward Heath was to secure membership of the European Economic Community (EEC). From a personal point of view, Heath also seemed less inclined to focus on the US. In Washington, Henry Kissinger was dominant in formulating foreign policy and quick to take offence if US interests were not met.

The resulting tensions and occasional formal interruptions in intelligence exchange prompted concern about the long-term implications for the relationship. But it soon became apparent that the relationship had become exceptionally deep and meaningful, at the levels both of intelligence exchange and of personal commitment. A series of personal comments from those involved at the time demonstrate the point. 'The relationship between the NSA and its British counterparts was founded on far more than just an exchange of intelligence. It was a joint intelligence production programme.' Also, as noted by an internal NSA history, 'collaboration remained almost total'. Each side brought additional access and assessment capability to their relationship. For example, the 1970s was a time of rapid technological change and a big increase, especially on the US side, in computer capacity. This was a major benefit for the UK.

On the global scene, 1973 saw the build-up to the Yom Kippur War in October that year, a major intelligence challenge not met with total success. British signals intelligence facilities in Cyprus were a major source of UK–US insight as Egyptian and wider Arab attack planning developed. As of May–June, the JIC seemed to understand that Sadat was prepared to launch an attack even against the virtual certainty this would lead to defeat. But during the summer it became increasingly hard for Washington and London to believe that Egypt would take such a risk. Up to the last moment, and in spite of continuous reporting from the NSA and GCHQ, US and UK assessments did not predict the outbreak of war. In retrospect, this came to be seen as another example of 'perseveration'.

By the end of the 1970s, we are moving towards the end of the Cold War and the global tensions, at least some of which took place in this context. Smith's account of the differing British and US approach to countering the Soviet invasion of Afghanistan in late 1979 is of particular interest, given the relevance to recent and current events (a good example of the importance of understanding history). His account of the Falkland Islands, an episode not directly connected to the Cold War, is deeply illuminating regarding the complexity, depth and sheer importance of the Special Relationship. Britain was a direct participant in the conflict. At the political level, at least in the early stages, the US was potentially neutral and possibly a mediator. There was some conflict within the Reagan administration about who to support. In practice, and as the conflict developed, the role of intelligence collaboration became central to the outcome.

Smith gives a lot of detail concerning the effective US role in the recapture of the islands, including the final surrender of Port Stanley. He also brings out the emotional commitment of the US policy and intelligence leadership to the British alliance. He draws particular attention to the comments of Bobby Ray Inman, CIA deputy director and a former director of the NSA. Inman knew the value of the relationship better than anyone else in the White House Situation Room and explained bluntly but eloquently, in one of the most memorable quotes in the book, why it was far more important to America's strategic interests to support Britain rather than Argentina.

To return to the Cold War, we are reminded that no one on the US or British side expected 'the swift end to communist rule which followed Gorbachev's attempts to reform the system'. Among the multiple consequences of the collapse came major defections from the Soviet side, notably to MI6, including Vladimir Pasechnik, the microbiologist, and, famously, Vasili Mitrokhin, who brought over an extraordinary archive of Soviet operational activity in the West. All of this was shared with the US.

A persistent theme throughout this story is that, whatever the ups and downs in the US–UK political relationship at different times, the foundation and underlying strength of the Special Relationship has continued to lie in the unique and exceptionally close security and intelligence collaboration between them. This collaboration has, of course, been at its most developed in the work of the NSA and GCHQ. But as we approach the final stages of the Cold War, we see the key role played by the sharing of human source intelligence between MI6 and the CIA. Smith discusses in detail the work of Oleg Gordievsky, the MI6 agent within the KGB, and Ryszard Kukliński, the CIA agent within the Polish Army and Warsaw Pact Command. Intelligence from these two agents played an especially

important role in helping to avoid military, even nuclear, confrontation between NATO and the Warsaw Pact in the early 1980s.

In recent years, the Soviet leadership's misunderstanding of US intentions, in particular during the NATO exercise Able Archer in November 1983, has been the subject of extensive analysis and debate. At the time, and as Smith points out, well-qualified experts, especially in the US, found it difficult to accept that the Soviet leadership believed the US was ready to launch a nuclear first strike against the USSR. Gordievsky's insight into their thinking is a powerful demonstration of the value of intelligence. It is important to note that, as of 2022, the risks of misunderstanding have not gone away.

The final two chapters cover the last twenty years of an eighty-year story (so far). They describe a period of exceptional turbulence and rising uncertainty in global affairs. We begin, of course, with 9/11, the overthrow of the Taliban and the occupation of Afghanistan. We then encounter the invasion of Iraq, ongoing counter-terrorist operations and terrorist attacks, including 7/7 in London 2005, Gaddafi's renunciation of nuclear weapons capability and, seven years later, the British–French–US operation to overthrow him. Now, in early 2022, we have continued tension with China and, as the most immediate threat, a major confrontation with Russia over Ukraine and NATO expansion. It is fitting to note that a particular feature of the run-up to the Russian invasion of Ukraine has been the public demonstration of NATO intelligence cooperation and capability, most notably that between the US and the UK, who have been speaking throughout with one voice. The world of intelligence has been constantly changing and adapting to the technology revolution. Increasingly, the special intelligence relationship has public visibility. It also continues to play a central role in decision-making and the development of events on the ground.

These are very demanding issues. Smith has researched them carefully and, where appropriate, goes into the detail. This helps him to illustrate the sheer depth of collaboration between the US and the UK in terms of the political relationship and policy formulation and the extent to which this almost certainly rests upon the intensity of the intelligence relationship, with an increasing focus on the role of other members of the Five Eyes, most recently and notably the announcement of AUKUS. But, as Smith demonstrates, collaboration has rarely been free of tension, most especially given different US and UK approaches to judicial issues and their human rights consequences in the field of counter-terrorism.

A key final comment for this foreword. Throughout the story, going back to the Second World War, we see the relative decline of Britain's global role and capability and the ever more obvious contrast in the resources available to the United States. As anyone who has worked in this area knows, those resources are vast. But whatever media coverage might imply, the Special Relationship is alive and well. Readers will have their own assessment as to why this might be. Undoubtedly, key factors are: shared interests and values; shared capabilities; a very long history of intimate collaboration at the personal as well as the national level; and, most crucially, mutual trust. Trust is the word.

SIR JOHN SCARLETT, FORMER CHIEF OF THE
SECRET INTELLIGENCE SERVICE, ALSO KNOWN AS MI6

MARCH 2022

THE REAL SPECIAL RELATIONSHIP

PROLOGUE

Barbara Abernethy had never seen an American before, except in Hollywood films, and none of them had ever seemed quite as exciting as this. The arrival of these four mysterious Americans in the dead of night was so secret that she was one of only a handful of people who knew they were there. The stuff you saw in the cinema was make-believe. Those Americans were actors. These were the real thing, US Army and Navy officers, in uniform. It was shortly before midnight on 8 February 1941. The attack on Pearl Harbor that would bring America into the war was still ten months away. She knew this must be a very important moment—although she could never have guessed quite how important—and she had her very own role in it all.

Barbara was only nineteen. She had been recruited into the Government Code and Cypher School three years earlier because of her ability to speak several languages, but when the British codebreakers moved to an old country estate at Bletchley Park in Buckinghamshire at the start of the war, she was reassigned as personal assistant to the boss, Commander Alastair Denniston RN. Earlier that day, the commander had called her in. 'He had something important to tell me. "There are going to be four Americans who are coming to see me at twelve o'clock tonight," he said. "I require you to come in with the sherry. You are not to tell anybody who they are or what they will be doing."'

A few minutes before Denniston called Barbara into his office, he had received a telephone call to inform him that the 'packages' he was expecting had landed at Sheerness in Kent, on board HMS *Neptune*. John Tiltman, Denniston's top codebreaker, was at the dockside to meet the four Americans, US Army officers Captain Abe Sinkov and Lieutenant Leo Rosen, and their US Navy counterparts Lieutenants Robert Weeks and Prescott Currier. The crates of equipment they had brought with them were loaded onto lorries, then they climbed into a car and drove off into the night towards Bletchley.

'It soon became dark and the countryside was pitch black with rarely a light showing except for the faint glow emanating from a small hole scraped in the blacked-out headlight lens of the cars,' Currier said. 'When we arrived, the large brick mansion was barely visible; not a glimmer of light showed through the blackout curtains. We were led through the main doors and, after passing through a blacked-out vestibule, into a dimly lit hallway, then into the office of Commander Denniston. He and his senior staff were standing in a semi-circle around his desk and we were introduced to and greeted by each in turn. It was truly a memorable moment.'

Denniston rang a bell for Barbara to bring in the sherry. 'It was from the Army & Navy Stores and was in a great big cask which I could hardly lift,' she said. 'But I struggled in and somehow managed to pour glasses of sherry for these poor Americans, who I kept looking at. I'd never seen Americans before, except in the films. I just plied them with sherry. I hadn't the faintest idea what they were doing there, I wasn't told. But it was very exciting and hushed voices. I couldn't hear anything of what was said but I was told not to tell anybody about it.'

Barbara had no idea at the time, but the meeting with the four mysterious Americans would lead to a very personal special relationship. She fell in love with Joe Eachus, one of the US codebreakers sent to Bletchley as a result, and their marriage would last until his death in 2003. But there was another special relationship which began on that day, one that in its own way was even closer, a relationship between Britain's and America's spies and codebreakers that has remained so tight that, no matter the many and various ups and downs in the political relationships between their two countries, the US president and the British prime minister have always been able to respond to any international crisis buoyed by the same detailed background knowledge the other side enjoyed, intelligence produced by a comprehensive alliance that, ever since that meeting at Bletchley Park, has been and remains the real basis for what commentators and politicians alike continue to refer to as the 'Special Relationship' between Britain and America.

The reality of that 'Special Relationship' is often questioned, frequently even derided, but Pres Currier, one of those four Americans who sipped sherry with Denniston that night and went on to a long and highly successful career in US intelligence, was in no doubt whatsoever of its importance. 'That was the beginning of our "Special Relationship" which has existed from that time to this and is probably the most radical one ever in intelligence terms between any two countries in the world,' he later recalled. 'It's still on a personal friendly basis, without any regard to what the politics of the moment may be. It doesn't seem to make any difference at all. We've never faltered and we've never lost out and we've never become very disenchanted with one another. It's something which will probably continue indefinitely.'[1]

I

TWO MONGRELS MEET

The extraordinary level of intelligence cooperation between Britain and America that has lain at the heart of the so-called 'Special Relationship' ever since that first meeting at Bletchley Park has given the governments of both countries an unprecedented advantage in both peace and war, but it has often been conducted in an atmosphere of deep mutual suspicion, never more so than during its genesis, a process memorably described by Ted Hilles, one of the first US Army codebreakers to work at Bletchley Park, as the two sides 'walking around and eyeing each other like two mongrels who have just met'.[1]

The first tentative approaches on intelligence exchange were made by the British through Captain Alan Kirk, the US naval attaché in London, in early 1940 and again that June, just weeks after Winston Churchill became prime minister. They were roundly rejected by senior US Navy officers convinced it was an attempt by the British to secure details of the Americans' own top secret cipher systems.[2]

Fortunately, a far more significant discussion was in play. Three days after taking office on 10 May 1940, Churchill sent a personal message to President Franklin D. Roosevelt asking for US material and financial assistance.[3] The president's response was positive but he faced staunch resistance from an isolationist Congress opposed to US troops taking part in another European war. There was a general assumption that the Second World War would be a rerun of the first, with Britain and France eventually pushing Germany towards defeat with little need for American assistance. Why spend US money or sacrifice US lives? The German invasion of France ended that illusion

and while a substantial number of Americans maintained an isolationist stance, many began to realise, as their president already had,
that at some point the United States would be forced to intervene.

Roosevelt and his chief foreign policy adviser, Sumner Welles,
devised a plan that would ensure that the American people would
support the US president's determination to provide much-needed
assistance to Britain. Suggestions from within Churchill's cabinet of
a direct appeal to the American people by the British prime minister
and French president Albert Lebrun were rejected as likely to be
counter-productive for a US audience. Welles instead proposed that
Churchill himself make a radio broadcast to the Empire in which
he spelled out in stark terms the position in which Britain now
found itself, standing alone against the Nazi menace. America was
a multicultural nation but its Anglo-Saxon origins still had a very
strong resonance for many US citizens.[4] The result was the British
prime minister's now famous 'Fight them on the beaches' speech
of 3 June 1940.

That most inspirational part of the speech, broadcast live by radio
stations across the USA, was inevitably the focus of attention both
at home and abroad. 'We shall defend our island, whatever the cost
may be,' Churchill declared. 'We shall fight on the beaches, we shall
fight on the landing grounds, we shall fight in the fields and in the
streets, we shall fight in the hills; we shall never surrender.'

The prime minister's powerful rhetoric provoked sympathy and
support for Britain across America, but while at the time his next
few words did not grab the attention in the same way, Churchill's
prediction of a point where 'in God's good time, the New World,
with all its power and might, steps forth to the rescue and the liberation of the old', and the faith it demonstrated in America's sense
of what was right, and all that was wrong about Nazi Germany, was
arguably in terms of the choreography the most important part of
the speech.

Exactly a week later, on the day Italy joined the war on Germany's
side, Roosevelt used an address at his son's graduation ceremony
at the University of Virginia to dismiss the isolationists' position
that America could stand alone untouched by the Nazi threat as a

'somewhat obvious delusion'. What America's next move should be was clear, he said. 'We will extend to the opponents of force the material resources of this nation; and, at the same time, we will harness and speed up the use of those resources in order that we ourselves in the Americas may have equipment and training equal to the task of any emergency and every defence.'[5]

The reaction from the audience, shared widely across America, reflected what was a tipping point in US public opinion. Opposition to becoming embroiled in another European war did not by any means disappear completely but the majority of Americans had clearly swung behind Roosevelt's determination that at the very least America should do what it could to help Britain and its Empire in their lone stand against Hitler. The *New York Times* reported that when the president declared that his administration would go 'full steam ahead' in providing the 'opponents of force' with material aid, the audience 'broke into the wildest applause, cheering, and rebel yells. As the President neared the end of his speech the cheering became general and members of the faculty stamped their feet and applauded . . . those on the platform and in the audience forgot academic decorum in spontaneous approbation.'[6]

Malcolm Kennedy, a Bletchley Park Japanese specialist whose work had been stymied by a complex new Japanese diplomatic cipher the British had failed to break, sat listening to Roosevelt on the other side of the Atlantic on the wireless. He was elated by what he heard. 'He did not mince his words,' the British code-breaker noted in his diary, 'but referred outright to Italy's action as a cowardly stab in the back and, amidst terrific cheers promised the full material resources of the US for "the opponents of force". The change that has come over public opinion in the US during the past two or three weeks is immense.'[7]

A few days later, Roosevelt nominated Henry L. Stimson as secretary of war and the latter's fellow Republican Frank Knox as secretary of the navy. Both men were staunch advocates of providing Britain with any material assistance it needed. They were also as determined as Roosevelt that America itself should be preparing for war. Once they were confirmed, Lord Lothian, the British ambassador in Washington, passed the president an 'aide-memoire' in which the British offered to share their latest radar and scientific research as part of 'an immediate and general interchange of secret technical information'. The British proposal was approved by Roosevelt, Stimson and Knox three days later. It was Knox's first day in office, and Stimson had only taken up his post the previous day.[8]

Brigadier-General George Strong, then head of the US Army's war plans division, travelled to London in August 1940, along with the US Navy's assistant chief of naval operations, Rear-Admiral Robert Ghormley, in order to find out what the British had to exchange. On 5 September, having been briefed by a British side anxious for cooperation on what he regarded as a 'gold mine' of material, Strong sent a cable to Washington asking the US Army chief of staff, General George Marshall: 'Are you prepared to exchange full information on German, Italian and Japanese code and cryptographic information therewith? Are you prepared to agree to a continuous exchange of intercept in connection with the above? Please expedite reply.'[9]

Strong's willingness to accept the British offer of an intelligence exchange appeared to come out of the blue, but shortly before his departure for Britain, Colonel Spencer Akin, the head of the army's Signals Intelligence Service (SIS), and his most senior codebreaker, Bill Friedman, had proposed just such an exchange in remarkably similar language to that used by Strong. The 'gold mine' of intelligence produced by the breaking of the Enigma ciphers had been shared with Strong by Stewart Menzies, the 'Chief' of MI6, who controlled the British codebreakers, in a deliberate and highly successful attempt to persuade him to back such a deal.* Having seen what Bletchley Park had produced, only a fool would not have agreed. Four days later, under orders from Roosevelt, Stimson told the US Army to share intelligence, including 'cryptanalytic information', with the British. Meanwhile, Menzies set about persuading

---

* The use of the term 'Chief of the Secret Service', CSS or 'C', which continues to the present day, was adopted by Mansfield Cumming, the founder of the British Secret Intelligence Service or MI6, to formalise the title of 'C', which had originally been derived from the first letter of his surname in order to disguise his identity.

Admiral Ghormley that the US Navy's concerns were ill-founded, helped no doubt by the fact that both Roosevelt and Knox had already backed the deal.[10]

This was the context in which the four Americans arrived at Bletchley Park shortly before midnight on 8 February 1941. The problem for the British was that the Americans, who had only been working on a limited number of Japanese diplomatic codes and ciphers, were keen to exchange what they had achieved for as much detail as possible on German, Italian, Japanese and even Russian systems. So keen that—to the evident astonishment of their hosts they had brought with them a 'Purple Machine', an analogue device designed by Leo Rosen to unravel the ciphers used by Japanese ambassadors in their dispatches to Tokyo, solving precisely the problem Malcolm Kennedy's team faced.[11] The British had broken many of the key Axis ciphers, but they had failed to crack Purple, which had been broken a few months earlier by a US Army team led by Frank Rowlett, a former maths teacher. The significance of the gift the Americans brought with them was immense, reflecting Strong's realisation that the British had something extremely valuable in the breaking of the top German ciphers that the US needed in return.

'It was a wonderful gesture of the American Party that they handed over the Purple Machine,' John Tiltman said. 'I always thought it was especially important as the first gesture. Somebody had to make the first step and the Americans made it.' The problem for the British was an adequate reciprocation. The only logical secret that they could provide the Americans in response was their success against the German high-grade Enigma ciphers. But the entire future of the British war effort rested upon the ability of Bletchley Park to break the Enigma ciphers. How could they trust the Americans? 'We were in the war, they were not in the war, and we weren't that ready,' said Tiltman, who was put in charge of the four Americans and what they could see. 'We hadn't really been fully consulted about what the exchange meant, and we weren't originally prepared to reciprocate by handing over our Enigma results.'[12]

The British had set out from the very first to exchange intercepted and decoded German and Japanese messages but having been rejected twice they were totally unprepared for the extent to which the Americans were now ready to share this valuable material. Menzies initially insisted that it was impossible to disclose the fact that the British were breaking the Enigma ciphers without it 'becoming known in a wide circle in America' with the certainty that the Germans would find out and change the system to make it unbreakable.[13]

Alastair Denniston was also concerned that the Enigma secret might leak and he did not have the initiative to consider an alternative, but Tiltman felt that, given what the Americans had put into the pot, in terms of the Purple Machine—providing details of conversations between Hitler and the Japanese ambassador in Berlin, General Hiroshi Ōshima, on the former's future plans—it would be untenable to try to hide the fact that the British had broken the German Enigma ciphers. The Americans were being shown all over Bletchley Park. They could not help but notice that they were refused access to key areas, like Hut 6 and Hut 8, where the Enigma ciphers were broken.

'I tried to get the Director [Menzies] to give way on this, but he wouldn't do it,' Tiltman recalled. 'So, I went up to see Menzies. I said to him: "Unless you give way over this and allow them to see all our work on the Enigma, I don't see how we are going to have any kind of successful collaboration." General Menzies agreed with me. He said: "All right, but if you disclose it to them, they must sign a document which lists all the people to whom they'll make the disclosure when they get back to Washington, otherwise we won't do it."'[14]

Menzies was not making the decision on his own; he had asked Churchill for permission to share the details of Enigma and the prime minister had agreed that there must be 'complete cooperation' with the Americans.[15] Sinkov, Rosen, Weeks and Currier were shown everything. They were taken into both Hut 6 and Hut 8, provided with details of the Bombes, the electro-mechanical device designed by Alan Turing to speed up the process of breaking Enigma, and given access to all of the work on lower-level German and Japanese systems.

'All of us were permitted to come and go freely and to visit and talk with anyone in any area that interested us,' Currier said. They were not given an actual Enigma machine. The British had none to spare. But they were given 'a paper Enigma', a full description and diagrams of the machine including details of the various contacts on the rotors and how it worked. 'We were thoroughly briefed on the latest techniques applied to its solution and in the operation of the Bombes,' Currier said. 'We had ample opportunity to take as many notes as we wanted and to watch first-hand all operations involved.'[16]

The British codebreakers did everything they could to make the Americans feel at home. They were put up in nearby Shenley Park, the home of Lord Cadman, chairman of the Anglo-Iranian Oil Company, invited to drinks and generally integrated into the Bletchley Park social life. 'During lunch hour on one of the many days at Bletchley, we were introduced to "rounders", a game resembling baseball played with a broomstick and a tennis ball,' Currier recalled. 'It was not long before I could hit "home runs" almost at will and soon wore myself out running around the bases. Many of our evenings were spent at the home of one or another of our British colleagues. Food and liquor were both rationed and it was not easy for them to entertain. Whisky and gin were generally unavailable in the pubs and most people had to be satisfied with sherry.'

Currier in particular was to become very close to Tiltman, who was the perfect choice to deal with the Americans. Tiltman, the head of Bletchley Park's military section, was arguably one of the best codebreakers working during this period. As a child, he was so brilliant that at the age of thirteen he was offered a place at Oxford. He served with the King's Own Scottish Borderers in France during the First World War, winning the Military Cross for bravery, but was badly wounded and withdrawn from frontline fighting to become a codebreaker. A tall, rangy man, whose clipped moustache and tartan regimental trews gave him the false air of a martinet, he in fact had a very casual approach to discipline. His only military interest was in codebreaking, a role in which he was quite brilliant.[17]

Tiltman's many achievements included breaking the most important Japanese military and navy systems, complex enciphered codes

that were extraordinarily difficult to untangle. Prior to the attack
on Pearl Harbor, both the US Navy codebreaking organisation, Op-
20-G, and its military counterpart, SIS, had focused on breaking
Japanese diplomatic ciphers and had made very little progress on
Japanese naval and army systems, so Tiltman had something very
tangible, where he was the real expert, to offer his American guests
in return for the gift of the Purple Machine.[18]

Two days after the four Americans arrived, Admiral John
Godfrey, the director of Naval Intelligence, sanctioned a complete exchange between the Far East Combined Bureau (FECB) in
Singapore, the main British outpost working on the Japanese codes
broken by Tiltman, and its US counterpart, which was based on the
rocky island fortress of Corregidor in the Philippines. Lieutenant
Rudi Fabian, the commanding officer of the US codebreakers, sent
Jeff Dennis, one of his intelligence analysts, to Singapore to see what
the British had to offer. The FECB codebreaking section had around
forty people working solely on the JN-25 code and for the past ten
months they had been able to recover enough of the code groups to
read simple messages.

Dennis returned to Corregidor laden with invaluable gifts. 'He
brought back the solution [to JN-25], how to recover the keys, the
daily keys, how the code was made up and a lot of code values,'
Fabian recalled. 'And since it was the heaviest volume system on the
air, I talked with my people and I went back to the CNO [chief of
naval operations] and requested permission to drop everything else
and go to work on this system. And we did pretty well on it. We
couldn't do any solid reading, no. But we could pick up step phrases
like "enemy", "enemy submarine" or "enemy aircraft". But we were
coming along pretty fast.'[19]

Although, in response to the pressure from Tiltman, the decision was made to allow 'full cooperation', the British still sought
to limit it by pressing for the Americans to concentrate on the
Japanese codes and ciphers while leaving Bletchley Park to deal
with the German and Italian systems. This was an entirely rational
approach albeit, amid doubts over US security, firmly anchored in
British desperation to prevent the Enigma secret leaking out. As a

Pacific nation, America was more threatened by the expansion of the Imperial Japanese Navy than by the fighting in Europe. It was not yet at war and it might never go to war.

The British had the only intercept stations capable of picking up the German radio traffic and far greater experience, including possession of the Bombe. To them, it made obvious sense that they concentrate on German and Italian codes while the Americans took the lead on Japanese. But despite the evident satisfaction of both Currier and Fabian with the material the British had handed over, the limitations imposed on the number of people in Washington who could be told about the Enigma breaks led to claims that the British codebreakers were holding out on their US counterparts, claims that would continue to hamper the vital development of trust between the two sides.

The main problems at this early stage were caused not by the US Army codebreakers, who understood the point the British were making, and in any event had shared the Enigma material more widely among their top codebreakers, but by the two central person-alities among the US Navy codebreakers. Lieutenant-Commander Laurance Safford, the head of Op-20-G, and his chief codebreaker, Agnes Driscoll, had worked together closely since the mid-1920s.[20]

Driscoll took the view that she had no need of help from anyone to break codes while Safford, whose speciality was creating rather than breaking codes, still believed cooperation was a British 'back-door' attempt to obtain the US Navy's cipher systems. It was on Safford's advice that US Navy chiefs had initially been so reluctant to cooperate with the UK; indeed, he had vigorously opposed the exchanges with the British. In October 1940, no doubt irritated that his advice had been overruled, he set Driscoll to work breaking the German naval Enigma. She had achieved a fearsome reputation among senior naval officers following her pre-war successes against Japanese codes and ciphers, and she soon convinced Safford that they had no need of British assistance in breaking the main naval Enigma system: she could do it all herself by the old-fashioned methods of pencil and paper.[21]

All Driscoll had to help her at this stage was a commercial Enigma machine and she set about working out how to break it by hand, using methods similar to those devised by the British codebreaker Hugh Foss back in the 1920s.[22] The ease with which Foss broke the original commercial Enigma machine had led the British to decide it was insufficiently secure for their use. The German Navy had taken a completely different view, dramatically increasing the complexity of the machine in order to ensure that it was secure. The pencil and paper methods used by Driscoll were never going to break the far more sophisticated naval system. Although the British, with the help of the Poles, had broken some of the German Army and Air Force Enigma systems by hand, the naval ciphers had appeared initially to be completely unbreakable, leading Alan Turing to opt to deal with the problem because 'no one else was doing anything about it and I could have it to myself'.[23]

Breaking the naval Enigma was not simply an intellectual challenge that would keep Turing happy. The fall of France had given the German U-boats new bases on the French Atlantic coast that allowed them easy access to the convoys bringing vital supplies of food, oil, machinery and weapons from America to Britain. Every day, the U-boats radioed in their locations, enciphered in an Enigma system which Bletchley codenamed Dolphin. They then lay in wait in so-called 'wolf packs', lined up north to south across the shipping routes ready to pounce en masse on the convoys. Dolphin needed to be solved quickly to allow the Admiralty to reroute the convoys around the U-boats. Between June and October 1940, the U-boats sent several hundred Allied ships to the bottom of the Atlantic. The need to find a sustained break into Dolphin had become vital to Britain's survival.

It was not until early March 1941, shortly before Currier and his US colleagues returned home, that Turing and his fellow codebreakers in Bletchley Park's Hut 8, where naval Enigma was broken, could make any substantial progress, the result of the capture, or 'pinches', of German cipher material. British commandos found key tables for February 1941 on a German armed trawler off Norway's Lofoten Islands. This allowed Turing and his team to break into the Dolphin cipher. They read the U-boat messages for most of February and part of April, giving them a better understanding of how the cipher worked. The discovery a few weeks later that weather messages sent in an easily broken weather system were being relayed to the U-boats using Enigma, together with 'pinches' of keys from two German weather ships and from the *U-110*, which had been forced to the surface off Iceland, ensured that from June 1941 onwards Turing and his team could read Dolphin, and that the Admiralty could reroute the Atlantic supply convoys around the 'wolf packs'.[24]

When Currier and Weeks went back to Washington in mid-March, they took the paper description of Enigma and other material and notes provided by Turing with them, handing it to Safford personally and, as agreed with Stewart Menzies, briefing him alone on Bletchley's work on Enigma. Safford passed the material on to Driscoll to assist her in her attempts to break the U-boat cipher. Nevertheless, she continued to insist that she did not need the help of the British or their Bombe. She could break Enigma on her own.

On 10 August 1941, Roosevelt and Churchill met on board USS *Augusta*, anchored off Newfoundland, to sign the Atlantic Charter, which laid out America's and Britain's ambitions for post-war peace. More importantly at the time, the US president committed the US Navy to escorting the Atlantic convoys on the first leg of their crossing to Iceland, making it even more imperative that the issues surrounding the U-boat cipher be resolved.[25]

Two days later, Alastair Denniston travelled to Washington, preparing a series of exchanges with both the US Navy and the Army, not just on codebreaking but also on technical intercept systems which helped to identify different radio stations, an area where the British were ahead of the Americans. He met Driscoll, who claimed to be 'evolving a method by which she can attain solution' of the U-boat Enigma by hand and asked a number of questions about how it worked. Denniston also set up a liaison system through Captain Eddie Hastings, an MI6 officer who had been sent by Menzies to Washington as his personal representative.[26]

Turing and his colleagues were highly sceptical that Driscoll might be able to read the naval messages without the Bombe but

replied fully to all of her questions. They also sent her all the captured keys that had allowed them to break the system plus copies
of all the U-boat messages intercepted for 1941. The problem was
that Hut 8 could only break the U-boat messages using the Bombe
while Driscoll was adamant she could break them by hand. In terms
of the intelligence itself, whether she could or could not break the
U-boat Enigma was to an extent immaterial because with US vessels increasingly under threat from the U-boats, the British were
passing any relevant deciphered U-boat messages to Admiral Harold
Stark, the US Navy's chief of naval operations. But Safford and
his Op-20-G team were only interested in breaking the German
ciphers themselves. If US commanders were being provided with
the intelligence, as a matter of personal pride, they wanted to be
the ones providing it.[27]

Notwithstanding her failure to break the U-boat Enigma,
Driscoll had a long-established reputation to maintain. She convinced Safford that the only reason she could not break the cipher
was because the British were holding out on her. The two of them
persuaded Vice-Admiral Leigh Noyes, the US Navy's director of
communications, that when it came to German naval Enigma, the
British had 'double-crossed' them and, despite the generous US
gift of the Purple Machine, were refusing to provide them with the
solutions to German ciphers. Noyes in turn persuaded senior US
Army officers that the British were holding out on the Americans. It
was nonsense. The British had provided Agnes Driscoll with everything she had asked for and Admiral Stark with all of the relevant
intelligence. But Driscoll insisted that the only reason she had not
broken the naval Enigma was because the British were deliberately
'balking' her efforts. Hastings warned Menzies of 'grave unrest',
with Safford 'in a mood to withhold further information unless he
receives full reciprocal information on European work'.[28]

The timing of the row, erupting as it did at the beginning of
December 1941, could not have been worse. Throughout the
summer, the Purple telegrams between Tokyo and its embassies in
Berlin, London and Washington had revealed increasing signs that
the Japanese were planning to go to war with Britain and America.

Ōshima had reported negotiating a secret deal with Hitler and Mussolini under which 'should a state of war arise between Japan and the United States, Germany and Italy for their part will consider themselves at war with the United States'.

The Japanese Foreign Ministry informed its embassies in London and Washington that they would receive a coded signal, disguised as a weather report, when war was about to start. '*Higashi no kaze, ame*', 'Easterly wind, rain', would indicate war with America and '*Nishi no kaze, hare*', 'Westerly wind, fine', war with Britain. Malcolm Kennedy, whose team were on continuous watch for what became known as the 'winds messages', recorded in his diary that Churchill was continually calling Bletchley to find out what was happening: 'From now on, for the time being, we are to take turns about at night in case anything calling for immediate action comes in. Incidentally, the All Highest [Churchill] is all over himself at the moment for latest information and indications re Japan's intentions and rings up at all hours of day and night, except for the four hours in each 24 when he sleeps.'

The next day, Tokyo sent the 'Westerly wind, fine' message, signalling the expected Japanese attack on the British colony of Malaya. 'A message received just before leaving the office this evening had indicated that the outbreak of war was probably only a matter of hours,' Kennedy noted in his diary. 'But the news on the 9 p.m. wireless that Japan had opened hostilities with an air raid on Pearl Harbor more than 3,000 miles out in the Pacific came as a complete surprise.' It left eighteen ships, including seven battleships, destroyed or badly damaged, 164 aircraft destroyed and 2,341 US servicemen dead. Roosevelt denounced it as 'infamy' and promptly declared war on Japan. Four days later, Hitler declared war on America.

The British had been genuinely bemused by the claims from Noyes that they were withholding information on the breaking of Enigma. Certainly, they had not given the Americans the detailed plans for the Bombes, but they had given the US Navy everything they had on naval Enigma. 'I still cannot understand what Noyes wants and am disappointed at my apparent failure as far as the

Navy Department is concerned,' Denniston told Hastings. 'Noyes is wrong in thinking we are withholding captured material which might assist in reading current telegrams.'[29]

Menzies and Denniston sent Hastings details of everything that the British had shared, including the intelligence reports to Admiral Stark, enabling Hastings to persuade Noyes that Bletchley had given Agnes Driscoll as much as they had.[30] With her excuse for not having broken the U-boat Enigma removed, she suddenly declared success and Frank Raven, a young German-speaking US Navy codebreaker, was ordered to head up a twenty-strong team to work alongside her deciphering the messages. It did not take Raven long to realise there was a serious problem.

Raven was an expert on the German Navy. His family was of German origin and the main language spoken at home was German. He had studied mathematics at Yale and then took a reserve commission with the US Navy codebreaking organisation where he was taught codebreaking before being told that, with war with Germany inevitable, he should go off and read every book he could find on the German Navy. He was called up in 1940 and put to work in Op-20-G, initially on the Japanese Purple cipher, with such success that his bosses decided he was the right man to lead the team reading the U-boat messages.

Within days of being tasked, in mid-December 1941, to lead a group that included Pres Currier in using Driscoll's methods to break the U-boat Enigma, Raven realised something was wrong and, after Driscoll left the office that night, he opened her safe. It contained the full correspondence with the British which showed that they had held nothing back from her. It also revealed that she had completely misunderstood a key aspect of the machine. Her claims that the U-boat Enigma could be broken by hand were nonsense. It would require the use of machines like the British Bombe. Raven realised that he would have to tell his bosses that Driscoll had not broken the U-boat Enigma at all and was 'just spinning her wheels'.

He was warned by close colleagues of the dangers of going up against the all-powerful Agnes Driscoll. 'Currier was very nervous about my getting Aggie's hackles up,' Raven said. 'He gave me considerable advice: whatever you do, handle with kid gloves.' By now, Safford had been eased out, replaced by Commander Jack Redman, brother of Rear-Admiral Joe Redman, the new director of naval communications. Raven went to Redman's deputy Joe Wenger, a long-standing and highly respected codebreaker. 'I laid out the whole thing to Wenger, laid it right on the deck. She [Driscoll] had refused to tell the senior officials what the solution was because it was too sensitive. I respectfully pointed out in my opinion I didn't think she had a solution, and as far as I'm concerned it's going to take special purpose machinery and five million dollars and probably an all-out drive to build equipment to bring this thing under control.'

Wenger's reaction was one of consternation and suspicion. Raven was relatively new and inexperienced. Driscoll was a well-respected codebreaker with a superb record. Why would she have got it wrong? He kept Driscoll in place—leading Raven to insist he went back to working on Japanese codes—and appointed Howard Engstrom, a newly arrived mathematics professor from Yale, to investigate the use of machinery like the British Bombe to break Enigma. Engstrom knew Raven from Yale and sought his advice. 'He heard me out, became convinced and he went to bat, practically over Wenger's head, to get the money to [solve] the problem,' Raven said. 'Engstrom walked in and really set that thing up. To me the father of the American Navy Enigma is Howard Engstrom.'[31]

Meanwhile, the British had run into their own problems with the U-boat Enigma system. On 1 February 1942, the U-boats operating in the Atlantic introduced a new, far more complex Enigma machine, making their messages unreadable. Bletchley codenamed the new cipher Shark. The vital intelligence used to reroute the Atlantic convoys around the 'wolf packs' disappeared and the supply of messages to Admiral Stark dried up, reinforcing the view in Washington that the British were holding back on them and Op-20-G needed to push ahead with its own plans to break the U-boat Enigma.

Joe Redman, the new director of naval communications, was an Anglophobe. A conversation with one senior British officer revealed that his 'hostility' to the British codebreakers was 'based on Irish memory for grievances real and imaginary'.[32] He insisted that his codebreakers must be able to break the Enigma cipher themselves to provide the information the US ships escorting the Atlantic convoys needed to avoid the U-boats. It was clear that the relationship between Bletchley Park and its US counterparts would have to be recalibrated.

Menzies had just reorganised the British codebreaking operation, moving Denniston to London to take charge of the diplomatic sections while the far more businesslike Commander Edward 'Jumbo' Travis took charge of Bletchley Park, focusing on the German, Italian and Japanese armed forces. John Tiltman was given responsibility for liaison with the US codebreakers. He was told to go to Washington and do everything in his power to persuade the Americans that they should not get involved in the breaking of Enigma. It was a ridiculously unrealistic and foolishly optimistic brief.

Tiltman arrived in Washington at the end of March, shortly before a freak snowstorm which deposited more than a foot of snow on the US capital. The next day he was called to a meeting with the US Navy codebreakers and their US Army counterparts in Op-20-G's offices in the US Navy Department Building on Constitution Avenue.

> I can remember walking down to the Main Navy Complex in a deep snow. They had a meeting at which for the first time, I met Wenger, and Friedman, and probably Rowlett and the others. This was an introductory session. I told them what I brought with me and what we were doing. My instructions and my own feeling was that I was trying to implement our orders which were for a complete exchange. I brought over every bit of paper I could when I came over . . . sacks of it. Everything, all of our recoveries. The Enigma story, I'm sure, was discussed, but in very hushed terms, because of the security rules that had been established.

His orders from Menzies were to hold the line very firmly against either the US Army or Navy breaking Enigma on American soil. The dangers of a leak were too great, particularly since building the necessary Bombe-type machinery would involve commercial companies, significantly increasing the risk. The restrictions on discussion of Enigma were so strict that in his conversations with Op-20-G, Tiltman was not even allowed to discuss the problems the British were having with the new Shark U-boat cipher.[33]

This was a ludicrous position to take, putting Tiltman in an impossible situation. The issue that was always going to dominate his visit was the breaking of the U-boat cipher. The German submarines were focusing their attacks on America's eastern seaboard, picking off the merchant ships before they crossed the Atlantic. Thirty-four US ships had been sunk since 'the Shark Blackout' began, with the loss of 718 crew. Thirty-three of the ships were merchantmen but they included the destroyer USS *Jacob Jones*, torpedoed off the Delaware coast with the loss of 138 men just four weeks before Tiltman arrived. With no U-boat messages being passed to the US Navy and the lives of hundreds of US seamen lost, Rear-Admiral Redman tore into Tiltman.

'I had a bad time with Redman,' Tiltman recalled. 'Redman would ride roughshod over anybody. He was pretty rough with me, saying German submarines were operating on the east coast of the United States, and we were withholding life and death information. I sent a telegram home to the Chief [Menzies] and explained this situation and said that they would simply have to come clean, otherwise, any future cooperation could go wrong, and they [Menzies and Travis] gave way.'[34]

A full explanation of the problems breaking Shark, a promise to share any information the British had on the naval Enigma and— after some persuasion by Tiltman—a recognition by Menzies that the Americans had to be allowed to investigate their own ways of breaking Enigma, eased the situation.[35] But Driscoll was still insisting she could break the U-boat cipher by hand. With Laurance Safford gone and her limitations now widely recognised by senior members of Op-20-G, Tiltman was able to back her into a corner. 'After several disappointments, she was forced to disclose the details of her methods to myself and to the senior cryptographers of the War and Navy Departments,' he said. 'I was obliged to tell her quite bluntly that her methods had been known to our experts for the past two years and could not be expected to succeed.'

During his first visit to Washington, Tiltman had very little problem with the US Army's SIS, where 'some very excellent work is done'. The US Army codebreakers were extremely grateful for the material he gave them, which included the solution to half a dozen systems they had struggled with, and in his final report he made clear that although at the higher levels there was considerable rivalry between the US Army and Navy—some of which he suggested was due to 'the dislike of Jews prevalent in the US Navy' given that many of the army codebreakers were Jewish—there were far fewer problems between the individual codebreakers themselves and indeed Wenger and Friedman were good friends. Nevertheless, the lack of experience in both Op-20-G and the SIS made it clear that they needed as much help as the British could provide.

'There are a number of good men in each of the service sections,' Tiltman said. 'But their approach is necessarily theoretical, and the best of them are aware that they are somewhat lacking in that varied experience of our best experts which is so important in the early diagnosis of unknown ciphers. While I was in Washington, the responsible cryptographers of the Navy/War Departments met continually to pool their views with regard to the investigation of 'E' [Enigma]. Both Services are quite satisfied to leave the exploitation in our hands. They are determined, however, to equip themselves to deal with this type of investigation should it ever become necessary. They feel strongly that they have a vital contribution to offer in that they have been carrying out experiments for years towards the construction of high-speed scanning machinery by use of electronic methods.'[36]

It was clear to Tiltman that his main problems dealing with the Americans would revolve around the British reluctance to allow them to work on the Enigma ciphers—which was difficult to justify on the US Navy side as a result of the American involvement in the Atlantic convoys and would become impossible to justify once the US Army was involved in the war in Europe. The only way to deal with it would be through formal agreements providing for total cooperation, with each side sharing all of its knowledge and intelligence with the other.

2

'HAVE A RYE, SISTER'

Although the British work on the main Japanese naval code, JN-25, had provided a vital contribution to the US Navy's efforts, the Americans had surged ahead on Japanese naval codes and were reading far more material than their British counterparts. The US Navy codebreaking unit at Pearl Harbor, under Commander Joe Rochefort, enjoyed good reception of Japanese Navy messages and was breaking JN-25 with ease. As a result, the Americans were able to read the complete Japanese operational orders for Admiral Yamamoto's attempt to draw the US Pacific Fleet into an ambush off the island of Midway, 1,000 miles west of Hawaii. Having obtained the full details of its opponent's plans in advance, the US Navy inflicted a crushing defeat on the Japanese in early June 1942, destroying four irreplaceable aircraft carriers and putting the Japanese Navy on the defensive for the rest of the war. But the stunning victory had an unfortunate consequence in that it only reinforced the British concerns over US security.

On Sunday 7 June, the last day of the battle, a dispatch by the *Chicago Tribune* reporter Stanley Johnston, who was with the US fleet, revealed that the 'US Navy knew in advance all about Jap Fleet'. Johnston's report was syndicated to a number of newspapers, most notably the *Washington Times-Herald*. Admiral Ernest J. King, the chief of naval operations, apparently 'in a white fury while his staff frantically tried to discover the source of the leak', called an immediate press conference to deflect suggestions that the US Navy had known the detailed dispositions of the Japanese invasion force heading for Midway. But Johnston had published them in his article. The Japanese only had to read it to know that the information was right. It seemed the cat was well and truly out of the bag. The British, whose worst fears about American security had been realised, protested to Washington. Fortunately, the Japanese persuaded themselves that the Americans could not have broken JN-25 and must have captured a codebook. They simply issued a new codebook and continued using the same system.[1]

Meanwhile, Major Solomon Kullback, the head of the US Army's German codebreaking team, and two US Navy codebreakers, one of them Lieutenant Joe Eachus, were visiting Bletchley Park and looking in detail at how the British broke the Enigma ciphers, with particular attention to Alan Turing's Bombe. Eachus stayed for more than four months, spending most of his time with Hut 8 and the Bombe team and sending back two sets of blueprints for the Bombe. Kullback spent two months talking to the British codebreakers. He returned with a recently captured Enigma machine and full details of its internal wiring, as well as the keys for the German Tunny teleprinter cipher used for high-level discussions between Hitler and his generals on the frontline, which had been broken by John Tiltman and his colleague Bill Tutte.[2]

'I really had no formal piece of paper which said do this, that and the other things,' Kullback said. 'It was essentially really, go over there, see all you can about the way in which the British were functioning, learn as much as you can, pick up as much as you can in the way of documents, captured code books, copies of these things, and come on back. And I went through that place. There was no door that I couldn't go into. Nothing was kept from me. They told me everything and gave me a lot of material. I brought back a hell of a lot of stuff, also the tricks that were being used on the Enigma. I saw the Bombes, [they] explained everything to me, they gave me a lot of information—in fact, when I came back in August, I had a duffle bag just jammed with things.'[3]

The British, still fearful that American production of the Bombe would inevitably lead to a leak of the Enigma secret, were desperate to limit US production. But their apparent inability to produce a four-rotor Bombe capable of breaking Shark led Redman and

Wenger to push ahead with Howard Engstrom's multi-million-dollar Bombe programme. The signing of a contract with the National Cash Register Company of Dayton, Ohio, in September 1942 forced the British into a written agreement with Op-20-G, the first of a number of such deals that would eventually become the BRUSA agreement, which formed the initial basis for the real Special Relationship between British and American intelligence. Most importantly, the first formal agreement with the US Navy set the terms for a situation in which America and not Britain, which given its dominance at the time ought to have held the whip hand, was the senior partner.

The US Navy was to take control of work on Japanese naval codes and ciphers while work on German Navy systems was to be a collaborative effort between the two sides involving full exchange of all material and technical expertise. At least some of the problems faced by the British in securing a better deal arose from the fact that the US Navy's director of communications, Captain Carl Holden, who led the negotiations on the US side, outranked his UK counterparts, Edward Travis, the new head of Bletchley Park, who was only a Royal Navy commander, and the head of the Bletchley naval section, Frank Birch, who was a civilian. After what Birch described as 'some stickiness' on the second day of the conference, Travis took a 'tactful' decision not to press too hard on a full exchange, which unfortunately left the British dependent on American goodwill in all of its future links with the US Navy codebreakers.[4]

One positive outcome of the Holden agreement was the posting of Joe Eachus to Bletchley as a liaison officer. He worked alongside the Hut 8 codebreakers as they struggled to break the Shark cipher. 'My official duty was to report back to Washington what was happening at Bletchley,' Eachus recalled. 'But that was not a full-time job, so I undertook to be a cryptanalyst while I was there.' Eventually in December 1942, the British managed to break back into the U-boat messages, but still there were times when messages were unreadable. 'Often-times we were reading stuff currently,' Eachus said. 'Other times, something would happen and we were not and there was just a feeling of gloom around when we would go for a week without reading things, very downhearted. Then it got going again and you would see the smiles in the corridors. That was very noticeable that people there took a personal interest in the work.'

Cooperation between Bletchley Park and the US Army had always seemed to be on a much firmer basis than with Op-20-G. The breaking of the German Enigma ciphers and the Italian Navy's Hagelin machine cipher was turning the tide in north Africa where the British and their Commonwealth allies had previously struggled against Lieutenant-General Erwin Rommel's Afrika Korps. The deciphered messages not only provided the British commander Major-General Bernard Montgomery with details of Rommel's battle plans, they also provided details of his supply convoys crossing the Mediterranean from Italy, allowing the Royal Air Force and the Royal Navy to intercept them, at times imposing a near stranglehold on Rommel's supplies.

The Enigma decrypts allowed Montgomery to win the Battle of Alam Halfa, shortly after his arrival in August 1942, and push on to win the crucial Battle of El Alamein, while the interdiction of the German supply convoys left Rommel with too few tanks and insufficient fuel. The British advance prepared the way for Operation Torch, the Anglo-American invasion of French North Africa which took place in November 1942, with MI6 Special Liaison Units (SLUs) providing General Dwight D. Eisenhower, the Allied supreme commander, with exactly the same intelligence they were handing over to the British generals.

But the arrival of US troops on the frontline put pressure on George Strong, who was now in charge of US military intelligence. The argument that the British were providing Eisenhower and his generals in north Africa with everything that there was to be got from breaking the German codes simply did not wash. How could he as a professional reconcile himself with the fact that the British were providing intelligence to a US commander that his own people were incapable of producing? His codebreakers were blocked from breaking the German Enigma ciphers by the British. Yet they were allowing the US Navy to break the U-boat Enigma. Strong saw no reason why his codebreakers should not be breaking the German Army's Enigma systems.

The situation came to the boil around a seemingly innocuous visit to Washington by Alan Turing. He was to visit Op-20-G and Dayton to discuss the US Navy's Bombe programme, where his advice resulted in significant cuts in the number of machines the Americans needed to produce.[5] He was also expecting to visit the Bell Laboratories in New Jersey where the army was developing the 'X-System' radio telephone scrambler device—to be used on transatlantic conversations that would inevitably mention intelligence gained from the breaking of Enigma—and a teleprinter cipher system to be used for communications between Bletchley Park and Arlington Hall, a former girls' school five miles north of Washington to which the army codebreakers had moved a few months earlier. For the British, this new equipment raised important communications security issues and Bletchley Park had agreed with the US Army's chief signal officer, Major-General Dawson Olmstead, that they could send an expert to the Bell Laboratories to ensure it was secure.[6]

But in an apparent lack of communication, senior US Army officers decided that this was just a 'back-door' way of the British trying to break into US encryption systems.[7] John Tiltman happened to be visiting America at the time. Checking that the X-System scrambler was secure was regarded as one of Turing's key briefs during his trip to the US. 'While he was on the high seas, General Strong heard about it and said he couldn't see it,' Tiltman recalled. 'And I had a telegram from England, I should think in December of 1942, telling me not to come back until General Strong changed his mind.'

The issue was so important that Field Marshal Sir John Dill, the chief of the British Joint Staff Mission in Washington, intervened directly with General George C. Marshall, the US Army chief of staff. Strong nevertheless refused to allow Turing into the Bell Laboratories. In an extraordinarily blunt intervention, given that he was talking to a senior officer who clearly felt the British had a point, Strong told Marshall the request to allow Turing to visit the Bell Laboratories 'constitutes one more pain in the neck resulting from the consistent practice of British representatives using back-door practices to gain information'.

Marshall suggested to Dill that the difficulties surrounding Turing's visit would be 'eliminated' if the British provided intelligence derived from German Army field operations, Russian communications and German agent traffic, which Strong believed was being withheld from the Americans.[8] The claim that they were holding back on German Army operations appeared bizarre to the British. Eisenhower was receiving precisely the same information on German operations in north Africa as the British generals, while a US Army officer, Captain Roy Johnson, and four senior NCOs had been based at Bletchley Park analysing German military communications for the previous two months. But Strong was furious that the British were receiving the credit for the intelligence and determined to control it himself.[9]

That said, there were undoubtedly problems with Russian and German secret agent traffic. The British had stopped intercepting most Russian material once Germany invaded the Soviet Union and Stalin became an ally, contracting the work out to Polish codebreakers in a highly secret operation controlled by MI6.[10] As for German agent traffic, some of it was being shared with the FBI, who were working with the British Security Service MI5 to turn captured agents back against the Germans as double agents, feeding false intelligence to Berlin. The problem was that one of the few things the senior army and navy officers controlling the US codebreakers were agreed on was that they would not work with the FBI, leaving the British in an impossible position.[11]

They got round the problem with a rather nebulous assurance from Dill to Marshall that 'all our Most Secret information, including the items quoted in your letter, are available to a duly authorised United States representative, indeed US officers are already working with our authorities in London on these matters'. Tiltman meanwhile was sent off to try to convince Strong that the British were holding nothing back. 'I had a two-hour conversation alone with General Strong during which he talked again about everything under the sun and in the middle of it, he looked directly at me and said: "I know that you think that I have horns and cloven hooves." And I thought to myself, My God, do I say: Yes Sir, or No Sir?'[12]

Tiltman managed to persuade Strong that the Americans were receiving all the intelligence they needed and suggested that posting a US Army intelligence officer to Bletchley to work in Hut 3, where the intelligence reports from German military and air force Enigma messages were produced, might reassure him, a proposal blocked by Menzies. The MI6 Chief's concerns only increased when it emerged during the talks that the US Army was building its own Bombe and that its codebreakers had told the US Coast Guard the British had broken the Enigma cipher used by the German secret service. The Coast Guard had then told the FBI, who had not been briefed on the break into the Enigma ciphers, complicating the British relationship with the Bureau and further increasing the risk that the secret would leak out and lead the Germans to introduce changes to the Enigma systems that would remove the vital intelligence at a stroke.[13]

Against Strong's very firm advice, Turing was given permission to visit the Bell Laboratories,[14] but the row forced the British to realise they needed a formal agreement with the US Army spelling out a complete exchange of Axis military codes and ciphers, with Britain controlling the breaking of German systems and the Americans in charge of Japanese. By now, Menzies had accepted Tiltman's idea that having US Army officers break Enigma at Bletchley was the only way to build confidence. But before that could happen, Strong ramped up the pressure by announcing that the US Army Bombe would be ready to start operating by April and insisting the British provide all the material his codebreakers needed to break Enigma at Arlington.[15]

Menzies, backed by Churchill, stood firm. The Americans were welcome to have liaison officers inside Hut 6 breaking Enigma and with access to everything, but for security reasons the British were not prepared to allow the US Army to work on Enigma in America. Strong sent his deputy Brigadier-General Hayes W. Kroner to London to negotiate with Menzies. US forces in north Africa were coming up against German forces in combat for the first time in the war, and struggling, and the British were supplying Eisenhower with intelligence far superior to any that Strong's own people could provide. Friedman was telling him that Arlington Hall would take two years to break Enigma without British help. Now Kroner reported back that Churchill himself was adamant the Americans should not break Enigma at Arlington. Strong's frustration and anger boiled over.[16]

At this point, Strong came as close as any senior US officer during the war to making what would have been a disastrous break in relations with Bletchley Park. The situation became so bad that at one point Churchill was prepared to send Menzies out to America to deal directly with Strong.[17] Fortunately, wiser heads held sway. Lieutenant-Colonel Telford Taylor, a young Harvard-trained lawyer who had recently joined US military intelligence, was asked to look into the situation.

Taylor got Strong on side by enthusiastically embracing his view of 'perfidious Albion' before rightly pointing out that talk of breaking off ties would never get past the Combined Chiefs of Staff and, even if it did, would ultimately be vetoed by both Roosevelt and Churchill. The US military had no choice but to piggyback on the greater British codebreaking expertise in order to achieve their ultimate aim of being in a position to do what they wanted without having to kowtow to their British allies. The essence of Taylor's message was that Bill Friedman was right about Arlington's inability to match Bletchley Park's ability to break Enigma. It would take far too long to get there without British help.

'In working on European traffic, we are suffering from lack of cryptanalytic continuity, inadequate intercept facilities, and a shortage of fully trained personnel,' Taylor said. 'British assistance can greatly expedite our progress. What we really want at this time is to gain a foothold in Enigma and develop technical competence. What we ultimately want is independence, but if we get the foothold, and develop our technique, independence will come anyhow.'[18]

Colonel Al McCormack, the deputy head of US Army Special Branch, flew to Britain to assess whether the US Army should work on Enigma at Arlington 'or whether more satisfactory results could be achieved by combining with the GC&CS personnel at Bletchley Park'.[19] Taylor and Friedman travelled with him. They spent seven weeks examining the Enigma problems and were struck by the sheer scale and efficiency of the British operation. The degree to which they were impressed by the Bletchley Park operations—and the challenge that presented to Strong's belief that Arlington might match them—is best summed up in Friedman's report on the visit.

'British success in this field represents, without question, the most astounding and the most important cryptanalytic and intelligence achievement in all history,' said the man then widely regarded as America's leading codebreaker. 'Their achievement is astounding not only because of the breadth of the concept upon which the operations are based and of the directness with which they are prosecuted, but also because of the manner in which the British tackled and successfully solved a cryptographic system which apparently presents insurmountable and impenetrable bulwarks against attack by pure cryptanalysis. Dogged British persistence, extremely painstaking attention to minute details, and brilliance in coordinating and integrating into one vast picture the many small operations involved, have brought about a success beyond the wild est expectations of any cryptanalyst's fancy.'[20]

Meanwhile, Edward Travis was in Washington negotiating a deal with Colonel Preston Corderman, the head of Arlington Hall. He was assisted by a blunt assessment sent back from Bletchley by McCormack, a Wall Street lawyer who had been brought in to sort out US Army signals intelligence (SIGINT) operations in the wake of the Pearl Harbor attack. In a no-nonsense report to Washington from Bletchley, McCormack warned that 'if Corderman wants his people to learn what makes this operation tick, he had better send them here to learn it, because they never on God's green earth will learn it from anything Arlington will be able to do in any foreseeable future'.[21]

The German forces in north Africa had surrendered a week earlier. The Allies were already preparing for the invasion of Italy. Corderman and Travis were under pressure to get a deal done that allowed US intelligence officers to process the intelligence derived from German Army and Air Force Enigma messages. McCormack's unequivocal statement eased the way to the agreement of a complete exchange of information on Axis military codes and ciphers with Arlington taking responsibility for Japanese and the British for German and Italian. The existing British security regulations on the use of the highest-grade Bletchley intelligence, codenamed ULTRA, would be adhered to by both sides, with British-controlled SLUs providing frontline US generals with all the ULTRA relevant to their respective operations. Importantly, it was agreed that 'where an American officer is Commander-in-Chief, an American officer, properly trained and indoctrinated at Bletchley Park, will be attached to the unit to advise and act as liaison officer to overcome difficulties that may arise in regard to differences in language'.[22]

Arlington would be free to carry out research on Enigma, but the main US Army contribution to breaking German high-level ciphers would be carried out by a party of eighty-five Americans based at Bletchley and working alongside their British counterparts in Hut 6, where German Army and Air Force Enigma was broken; in the Newmanry and Testery, where the German teleprinter ciphers were broken; and in the Hut 3 intelligence reporting section. A week later on 17 May 1943, the agreement was signed off by Travis and Strong.[23]

While McCormack and Friedman returned to the US, Telford Taylor stayed at Bletchley to head up the US Army team. He persuaded Travis to send someone from Hut 3 to America to select US intelligence officers who would fit into the Hut's somewhat rarefied atmosphere. The man chosen for this task was Jim Rose, a Hut 3 air adviser who became close friends with Taylor for life.

'When Telford came over in 1943, he asked me to go out to Washington to interview candidates for Bletchley,' Rose said. 'Most of the officers who came to Bletchley, I chose. There were some very bright people. One of them was Lewis Powell, who became a judge of the US Supreme Court. There was a man who became managing editor of the *Washington Post*, Al Friendly. There were quite a lot of lawyers and their reception in Hut 3 was extremely friendly. They all felt integrated.'

While the Hut 3 reporters selected by Rose came, like Taylor, from US Army Special Branch, the codebreakers came from Arlington Hall and were under the command of Captain Bill

Bundy, whose father was a close personal friend of Roosevelt's War Secretary, Henry L. Stimson. Bundy was an alumnus of both Yale and Harvard, where he studied law.

> I went to Arlington Hall in the spring of '43. And I remember vividly, a group of us, a very small group, were convened in a room there and told: 'What you're going to hear today is something you will not discuss.' After considerable sparring back and forth an agreement had been reached between the American and the British governments that the Americans would keep the major role on Japanese material and the British would maintain the major role on German, but as a sort of codicil to that it was agreed that a small American contingent, thirty to fifty, should go to Bletchley Park to integrate right into the organisation there and I was picked to be the commanding officer of that outfit.

Amid conditions of great secrecy, they were sent to England on board the SS *Aquitania*. 'I think we were twenty in our advance contingent and on the way over we had to bunk with other services,' Bundy recalled. 'Our cover story was that we were pigeon experts in the Signal Corps. I don't think we used it very often, Lord knows it would have broken down very quickly, but that was the cover story we used.'

Art Levenson, a young mathematician, was one of Bundy's advance party. 'We were a somewhat select group,' he said. 'But this was the first experiment in cooperating in the codebreaking business between any two countries in history and I don't know if you want to put your best foot forward, but you want to put one of your better feet forward. I don't think I'd ever met an Englishman in my life until that point. We were introduced to Brigadier Tiltman and they treated us like visiting generals.'

Despite the VIP treatment, there was a continuing mutual distrust. 'I remember with horror the American invasion when every section had an American,' said Jean Howard, who worked in Hut 3. 'We believed they had no sense of security and were terrified that material they took out of the hut would go astray. We felt strongly that they

34

THE REAL SPECIAL RELATIONSHIP

would never have come into the war but for Pearl Harbor. They were different animals, and the English they spoke had different meanings. They were fat, we were emaciated. They were smart (eleven different sorts of uniform), we were almost in rags. They were rich, we were poor. They brought in alcohol: "Have a rye, sister." "We don't drink here." We were overworked and exhausted and having to teach people who barely knew where Europe was, was the last straw.'

The mutual mistrust came to a head during celebrations to mark Independence Day on 4 July. 'We were challenged by the Americans to a game of rounders,' Barbara Abernethy recalled. 'They nearly went home. Now in the United States, you don't need to get all the way home in one go to score. As long as you get all the way home eventually you score. Now our rules for rounders of course were very tough. You had to go all the way round in one go. It was a lovely day, we all played well, and at the end of the game we all sort of clapped each other on the back and the Americans said: "Well, we're sorry we beat you," and the British captain said: "I'm sorry, but we beat you." The Americans were a little touchy. They were convinced that they'd won, and it took a bit of explanation on somebody's part to soothe ruffled feathers. It all ended with drinks all round, actually we agreed we'd won by our rules and they'd won by their rules. So that was all right. But they never asked us to play again.'

They might never have played rounders again, but both sides swiftly got over their prejudices. If some of the British codebreakers had assumed the Americans would be brash and careless about security, the Americans imagined the British would be too 'stiff upper-lipped' to get on with. 'We thought they'd be aloof, hard to reach. That it would be very hard to get to know them and that they'd probably be rather cold,' Bundy recalled. 'Well, that broke down, I should say, in the first forty-eight hours and certainly the first time that you had a mug of beer with a Britisher. If we're talking original stereotypes, they didn't last.'

Gradually as the two sides got to know each other, a level of mutual respect replaced the suspicion and relationships between the two sides became very much closer. Stuart Milner-Barry, the head of Hut 6, who had viewed the prospect of integrating Americans into his team 'with some consternation', would later describe their arrival as 'one of the luckiest things that happened to us', with the Americans bringing fresh ideas and a different approach which helped to improve the already highly efficient Hut 6 production line. Bundy on the other hand could not speak highly enough of the way the Americans were treated. 'We were integrated on an individual basis in the various offices of Hut 6, or on the translation and exploitation side in Hut 3,' he said. 'It was, from the standpoint of personal relations, a terribly good relationship, taking people as they came, as they were, laughing about the national differences and customs, a very relaxed, very giving and taking relationship.'

Inevitably, given that the majority of people working at Bletchley were young women, and the immediacy of war, there were a number of liaisons and even marriages. Art Levenson recalled having a 'pretty heavy' social life.

> We were a handful of Americans and we were, I guess, somewhat exotic. There were lots of Wrens around. They invited us to lots of parties and we had a great time. I made many friends that I still have. It was great fun, they were wonderful people, a great crowd. I had been full of stereotypes about the English. "They're distant and have no sense of humour, they won't speak to you unless you're introduced" and all kinds of nonsense. But these were the most outgoing people, who invited us to their homes and fed us when it was quite a sacrifice, and with a delightful sense of humour. Maybe there were some English that fitted the stereotype, but there were none at Bletchley, they were all a delight and just enough screwballs to be real fun.[24]

If the relationship with the US Army had been transformed by the arrival of more than eighty of its codebreakers and intelligence officers at Bletchley, liaison with the US Navy was more complicated. Op-20-G's Bombes were more reliable than their UK counterparts and from late June, as they began to come on stream, they helped break Shark. Hugh Alexander, the head of Hut 8, later recalled that the transatlantic cable connections were so good that he and his team could use the more sophisticated US Navy Bombes 'almost as conveniently as if they had been one of our outstations 20 or 30 miles away'.

By the middle of September 1943, when there were only a dozen US Bombes operational, they were being used to break the Shark U-boat ciphers, eventually allowing Op-20-G to take over the breaking of Shark from Hut 8 completely. Indeed, having initially resisted any American Bombes, the British were now welcoming their use not just against the German U-boats but also against German Army and Air Force Enigma, ensuring that Bletchley was able to break Enigma keys that would otherwise have remained unbroken. The U-boat losses rose exponentially as a result of the addition of the US Bombes, forcing their withdrawal from the Atlantic in May 1944, just two weeks before D-Day.[25]

'Toward the end of the war, we got to competing with the British pretty successfully,' said Howie Campaigne, one of the leading US Navy codebreakers. 'The British were always a little bit more ingenious than we are. They had a head start. But it got to where we could do more than they because our resources were greater. Mechanically, our Bombes were better and more reliable. They'd done it first so we could see their mistakes. But yes, our Bombes were more reliable devices than theirs.'[26]

Unfortunately, Bletchley Park's relationship with the US Navy codebreakers on Japanese codes was nowhere near as cordial. The Japanese invasion of Malaya had forced the British codebreakers working on Japanese naval codes to retreat from Singapore, first to Colombo and then to Kilindini, near Mombasa in Kenya, while those working on Japanese Army and Air Force codes moved to the newly formed Wireless Experimental Centre at Delhi. The army codebreakers would be based in the Indian capital for the remainder of the war and enjoyed a highly productive relationship with their colleagues at Bletchley and their US counterparts at Arlington Hall and Brisbane, Australia. But the departure from Singapore was disastrous for the naval codebreakers, leaving the British struggling to keep up and heavily reliant on the American codebreakers now operating from Melbourne and Pearl Harbor.

The dominance of the American position in the 1942 agreement between Bletchley Park and Op-20-G, and the fact that US forces were only interested in intelligence on the Pacific area of operations, left Admiral Sir James Somerville, commander-in-chief of the Royal Navy's Eastern Fleet, without the intelligence he needed to cover the Indian Ocean and the Japanese supply routes between Singapore and Burma. One senior British officer said that the most notable feature of a visit he made to the US codebreakers in Melbourne was 'the inability of the Americans to appreciate the full meaning of the word "co-operation". The atmosphere was "What is yours is mine, and what is mine is my own".'[27]

The belligerent US director of communications, Joe Redman—who was himself under pressure from the commander-in-chief of the US fleet, Admiral Ernest King, another Anglophobe, to focus solely on assisting US operations in the Pacific—deliberately fostered this approach among his officers. Harry Hinsley, Bletchley's most senior naval intelligence analyst, was sent to America in December 1943 to try to sort out the problems. He reported back that Redman was 'chock-full of grievances largely because he likes grievances for their own sake'.[28]

Regardless of the reasons for Redman's behaviour, the British had to find a way around it. Having given the Americans the help they needed to get into JN-25 before the start of the war against Japan, the British were now denied the technical assistance they desperately needed to get back on top of it. With Redman determined that all his resources should be focused on the Pacific, leaving Somerville's ships in the Indian Ocean without the intelligence they required, the Admiralty considered the most drastic of measures.

'The lack of US intelligence supply to C-in-C Eastern Fleet led the British to consider ditching the Americans on the Japanese side,' said Frank Birch. 'Admiralty was not willing to be dependent on such small scraps as US were willing to provide and the only alternative to sharing all available intelligence between the two countries was for this country to build up independently an organisation big enough to provide, without American help, as much intelligence as could be got.'[29] As a result, the British were forced to compromise on their previous 'Europe first' approach and throw substantial resources into breaking Japanese codes, moving the Kilindini codebreakers back to Colombo and building their operation there up to the point where it became so successful that Redman tried to take it over and break its link with Bletchley.[30] Eventually, with the creation of a communications network connecting all of the US and British naval codebreaking bases, the problem was reduced to manageable levels.

The issues the UK codebreakers faced in dealing with their US counterparts on the Japanese codes demonstrated the problems Britain's intelligence agencies would continue to face in dealing with their US counterparts where the British had nothing, or very little, to offer. But the war in Europe was completely different. Here the British held the whip hand and the relationship with the Americans was extremely strong, perhaps best demonstrated by the way in which the US Navy was willing to use its superior Bombes to help break German Army and Air Force Enigma ciphers as well as the Shark U-boat cipher. The good liaison forged by the US Navy and Army codebreakers attached to Bletchley and their British counterparts based in Op-20-G and Arlington Hall ensured that during the D-Day landings and the invasion of Europe, Eisenhower and his generals had better real-time intelligence, on a far greater scale, than any commander had previously enjoyed. By no means all of it came from the breaking of Enigma.

The break into the German Lorenz SZ-42 teleprinter cipher, which Bletchley codenamed Tunny, was one of the most productive of the many British cryptanalytical successes, producing telex conversations between Hitler and the German High Command and the German commanders on all of the major fronts, an invaluable source of intelligence on German intentions and on the friction between Hitler and his generals. For Britain and the US, the most important of these teleprinter links were those between Berlin and Field Marshal Albert Kesselring in Italy, and Field Marshals Gerd von Rundstedt and Rommel in France.

The first breaks into Tunny came in a triumph of instinctive codebreaking from John Tiltman, and as a result of his initial break into the system, the machine was patiently and methodically

reconstructed by one of his research team, the mathematician Bill
Tutte. One of the academics brought in to work on the cipher, Max
Newman, who had been Alan Turing's supervisor at Cambridge,
soon realised that a key part of the decipherment could be carried
out by the kind of computing machine that his former student had
proposed. The result was Colossus, the world's first electronic,
digital, programmable computer.

Art Levenson was one of a number of Americans who worked on
the Tunny cipher. 'Colossus was the one warm spot in the British
Empire,' he recalled. 'It gave off a lot of heat and everybody wanted
to be next to Colossus, particularly on the night shift. It was more
fun to work on because it was more analytic. You had to make these
runs on Colossus. In a sense it was a predecessor of the modern
computer and you could program it by setting switches.'

The intelligence produced by the Tunny material was unprece-
dented in modern warfare, Levenson said. 'Rommel was appointed
Inspector-General of the West, and he inspected all the defences
along the Normandy beaches and sent a very detailed message that
I think was 70,000 characters and we decrypted it as a small pam-
phlet. It was a report of the whole Western defences. How wide the
V-shaped trenches were to stop tanks, and how much barbed wire.
It was everything and we decrypted that before D-Day.'[31]

Hiroshi Ōshima, the Japanese ambassador in Berlin, also toured
the German defences in northern France, sending back his own
detailed report to Tokyo which was deciphered using the Purple
Machine. The Japanese military attaché, whose cypher had been
broken by Tiltman in 1942, then made his own tour of the defences,
sending an even more comprehensive account of every installation,
itemising every weapon right down to the smallest collection of
flamethrowers. Anything missed by these two accounts was filled
in by the Japanese naval attaché in Berlin, whose Coral machine
cipher had been broken just weeks earlier by a US Navy team led
by Frank Raven, with assistance from Hugh Alexander, who flew
to Washington to contribute to the final elements of the break,
a dramatic example of how close cooperation had become ahead
of D-Day. The Japanese naval attaché also included his personal

discussions with Rommel on how the German commander intended to respond to an Allied invasion, invaluable intelligence for Eisenhower and his planning staff.

There were numerous examples of intelligence produced from Enigma messages that fed into the success of the invasion of Europe but the most important in terms of the actual landings was the 1941 break into the Abwehr Enigma cipher by the veteran codebreaker Dilly Knox. From the start of the war, British intelligence had captured the majority of the German spies sent to Britain and had been using them to feed false information to German commanders. The problem for the intelligence officers in charge of the so-called Double Cross system was that they could not be certain that the Germans believed these false reports. The breaking of the Abwehr Enigma told the British that they had fallen for the fake intelligence, allowing them to use it to persuade Hitler that the Normandy landings were a feint to draw attention away from the main Allied attack, which was to be on the Pas-de-Calais, thereby ensuring the Germans kept most of their forces there and giving the Allied forces a far better chance of building a bridgehead in Normandy.

At Telford Taylor's request, the American intelligence officers who were to join the British SLUs attached to the top US commanders involved in the invasion spent six weeks at Bletchley Park, working in Hut 3, or its naval equivalent, Hut 4, so they understood how the intelligence was produced and just as importantly the strict security limitations surrounding its use.[32]

Bill Bundy's brother Mac was one of the US Army officers trained in the use of the Enigma material, providing the ULTRA intelligence for Rear-Admiral Alan Kirk, who as US naval attaché in London in 1940 had received that first British exchange proposal and was now commander of the combined navies' Western Task Force, based in the English Channel for the D-Day invasion.

The spectacular triumphs of both Bletchley Park and the US codebreakers, pooling their resources to break German, Italian and Japanese ciphers more efficiently than each could have done on their own, and the game-changing impact this had on virtually every front in the war, ensured that nobody involved, certainly not the politicians and military leaders who had seen the impact—not just on the war but on their own reputations—wanted to see it disappear from a post-war world that was unlikely to be any less dangerous than the past. Just as importantly, within the intelligence agencies producing those reports, the prejudices on both sides had been swept aside. Transatlantic trust and friendship had been created that would never die. Many of those involved would go on to hold prominent positions in the Cold War world, not just in intelligence but also in government.

The sheer value of the codebreaking alliance was priceless, with some historians suggesting, based on the number of ships saved during the Battle of the Atlantic, at a time when how long it took to move equipment and men from the US to Britain was vital to the point at which the D-Day landings could take place, that it cut more than two years off the length of the war. While such claims are too simplistic, taking no account of the influence of a large number of other factors, the battle against the U-boats was by no means the only period of the war in which the Allied codebreakers played a crucial part. The truth is that the impact on the war of the intelligence they produced is impossible to calculate, not just in terms of the war itself but also in terms of the post-war continuation of the Special Relationship between Britain and America.

Bill Bundy went on to serve in the Kennedy and Johnson administrations and, along with his brother Mac, became one of the so-called 'Wise Men' who during the second half of the twentieth century advised successive presidents on foreign policy. Yet he would later say that he never worked with 'a group of people that was more thoroughly dedicated and with a range of skills, insight and imagination' than those at Bletchley.*

It was a terrific human experience and I've never matched it since. I had other jobs with superb people, important and worthwhile

---

* The Bundy brothers' mother Kay and Bill's wife Mary were both codebreakers during the Second World War. Kay initially worked for Op-20-G and later worked for Arlington Hall, where Mary also worked.

pursuits but certainly for me personally this was the high point. This was a totally dedicated group working together in absolutely remarkable teamwork. Their whole structure was one where you might readily find a major working under a lieutenant or under a civilian, somewhat younger. Whoever was in charge was the person who had been judged to be more effective at doing it. It was an extraordinary group, and that was true right across the board in Bletchley, whatever system of selection they used, and I've heard lots of narratives and lots of colourful stories about it, the result was an extraordinary group of people in an extraordinary organisation.[33]

3

'WILD BILL' ENTERS THE RING

The teething problems that bedevilled the early relationships between the British and American codebreakers were as nothing compared to those between the British and US secret intelligence and special operations agencies, not least because far more mongrels were involved, all circling their national rivals with a great deal more suspicion than they did their transatlantic allies.

While espionage had played a major role at various points in America's history, the country had no central organisation tasked with intelligence-gathering. The army and the navy both had their own intelligence organisations, but the only body that came close to human intelligence (HUMINT) operations on a regular basis was the FBI, which was much more focused on countering major crime than threats to national security. Nevertheless, the FBI had collaborated with both MI6 and MI5 against communist and Indian subversives. So, despite being a notoriously difficult man to deal with, FBI director J. Edgar Hoover was the first and most obvious point of contact.

MI6 Chief Stewart Menzies was to play the same leading role in setting up the links between US and British human intelligence organisations as he had with the formation of the codebreaking alliance, making a very good choice in selecting William Stephenson, a Canadian millionaire businessman in his early forties, as the man to lead the way. Stephenson had approached MI6 in 1939 with the offer of his own private intelligence network, which had been collecting information on German imports. Although his intelligence was not particularly useful—his best sources were MI6 officers providing him with information they had already sent to 'head office'—Stephenson himself made a very good impression and in the spring of 1940, Menzies sent him to America to try to establish a much closer relationship between MI6 and the FBI.[1]

Stephenson returned to London having set up a personal channel between Hoover and Menzies using codenames based on the initial letters of their first names—SCOTT for Menzies and JONES for Hoover—and claiming that the FBI director had specifically requested that he, Stephenson, be based in New York as Menzies's personal representative. Whether it was Hoover himself or Stephenson who actually first suggested this remains uncertain but there is no doubt that Menzies believed the millionaire's exceptional social skills, his widespread US contacts and his experience of industrial intelligence would make him an ideal go-between not just with US intelligence organisations but also with the administration. Nor can there be any reasonable doubt that the MI6 Chief was right. Stephenson was to be a key player in the relationship which developed between Britain's secret service and what would eventually become the CIA.

Menzies sent him to New York in June as his principal passport control officer, the cover for MI6 heads of station abroad. Although his ostensible role was to take charge of all MI6 operations in the United States and Mexico, Stephenson and Menzies had agreed a much wider brief aimed at providing a direct line into the White House. The MI6 Chief told the Foreign Office—rather optimistically as it turned out—that his new US representative's close links with Hoover, who saw Roosevelt on a daily basis, were likely to prove 'of great value' on a much wider basis than simply issues relating to the FBI, and he asked that a close link also be set up between Stephenson and the British ambassador in Washington.[2] At the same time, Menzies was working to persuade the Americans to create their own equivalent of MI6 and the Special Operations Executive (SOE), which had been set up the previous July with orders from Churchill to coordinate sabotage and subversion in Nazi-occupied areas and, in the prime minister's own words, 'set Europe ablaze'.

In the wake of his 'Stab in the Back' announcement that the USA would do everything it could to assist Britain to fight Nazi Germany, Roosevelt decided to send his own personal observer to the UK to determine whether Britain was capable of holding off the Germans. Stephenson informed Menzies on 15 July 1940 that Bill Donovan, a leading Wall Street lawyer and celebrated First World War hero, popularly known as 'Wild Bill', was being sent to London as the president's personal representative.

Despite his Irish Catholic background, Donovan was an Anglophile who had long argued publicly against isolationism, pointing out in a number of speeches that it was inevitable that the United States would eventually be forced to go to war to stop Hitler. As early as November 1939, Donovan had warned against giving the Nazi dictator the impression there were no circumstances in which America would join the war. 'In an age of bullies,' he said, 'we cannot afford to be a sissy.'[3]

Donovan was a close friend of Roosevelt's navy secretary, Frank Knox, who initially suggested him to the president as a possible secretary of war. Roosevelt rejected the idea but described Donovan, who had been in his class at Columbia Law School, as 'an old friend' whom he would be happy to have in his cabinet. So, when the president was looking for someone to travel to the UK to ascertain whether the British were capable of sustaining what, in the wake of the fall of France, had become a lone fight against the Nazis, it was perhaps unsurprising that Donovan's name came up. He was called to the White House, where Roosevelt, secretary of state Cordell Hull, Henry L. Stimson and Knox were assembled in the Oval Office, and asked to go to England, on the face of it to examine how the UK was dealing with 'the Fifth Column problem', but in reality to answer the key question of whether Britain could hold off a German invasion. In short, would US assistance be wasted on a nation which, according to the US ambassador in London, Joe Kennedy, was already staring defeat in the face, a claim the Anglophobic Irish-American Kennedy had made repeatedly in dispatches and telephone calls to Washington monitored by the British with the transcripts passed directly to Churchill.[4]

Menzies personally ensured that Donovan saw as many key

people as possible. He met Churchill, the King and Queen, members of the war cabinet and just as importantly both Menzies himself—on an almost daily basis—and the highly influential director of naval intelligence, Rear-Admiral John Godfrey. Menzies and Godfrey went out of their way to persuade Donovan of the need for a US equivalent of MI6, most emphatically perhaps during a long conversation at Godfrey's country home on the night before Donovan's return to Washington, leading the latter to describe the London trip as 'the real start' of the Office of Strategic Services, or OSS, the organisation he would eventually create to work with MI6 and the SOE.[5]

On his return from London, Donovan worked extremely hard to persuade Roosevelt that Britain had 'excellent prospects of pulling through' and should be supported, telling a British friend that prior to his visit the mood in Washington had been one of 'extreme depression' to which Kennedy had 'largely contributed'.

Stephenson would later claim that it was he who suggested the trip to the UK to Donovan, a statement which, like many he subsequently made—including having been appointed personally by Churchill—embroidered reality in order to enhance his own reputation. They had never even met until Donovan returned from London. But under orders from Menzies, Stephenson contacted him and they went on to become firm friends and collaborators, with Stephenson working very hard to push Donovan's credentials as the head of an American equivalent of MI6.

He swiftly developed a very strong relationship with Donovan, built up over evenings spent in New York's infamous former speakeasy, the 21 Club, during which the Canadian repeatedly outlined the arguments in favour of an overarching American intelligence agency that could liaise with MI6 in order to ensure that Roosevelt and Churchill would see the best possible intelligence, thereby ensuring that they and their generals in the field were working from the same script. Donovan, having already heard the same arguments from Menzies and Godfrey, needed little convincing, but later credited Stephenson with being 'largely instrumental in bringing about a clearer conception of the need for a properly coordinated American intelligence service'. Their relationship became so strong that British officials referred to Stephenson as 'Little Bill' to Donovan's 'Big Bill'.[6]

In December, Donovan was sent on a second reconnaissance mission for Roosevelt to London and around the Mediterranean, visiting Cairo, the north African front, the Balkans, Greece, Turkey, Palestine and Iraq. Stephenson accompanied him on the plane to London and handed him over to Menzies, telling the MI6 Chief that Donovan had 'a vast degree of influence' over Roosevelt and if Churchill were to be completely frank with him 'he would contribute very largely to our obtaining all that we want of the United States'.[7]

Menzies not only arranged for Donovan to have lunch with the British prime minister, where they discussed intelligence and the need for common practices on both sides of the Atlantic, he also agreed to fund Donovan's tour of the Mediterranean out of secret service funds. Churchill meanwhile ordered that the American, 'who has been taken fully into our confidence', should be given every assistance possible wherever he went on his trip. While he was in the UK, he was given a thorough briefing on the SOE – which was split into two branches, SO1 disseminating propaganda and SO2 carrying out operations in enemy territory – while Menzies and Godfrey took every opportunity to impress on him again the need for a US equivalent of MI6.

Shortly after returning to Washington, Donovan had a meeting with the president in which he reported back on his tour around the Mediterranean before going on to suggest the creation of 'a new agency' to carry out intelligence, guerrilla warfare and strategic planning. A few weeks later, Donovan wrote a four-page report outlining in more detail how British intelligence operated and laying down the basic principles under which a similar US system should work. It should be independent and controlled only by the president. Its funding should be secret. It should have sole charge of all human intelligence collected from abroad and of all intelligence that was to be passed to the president.[8]

At the beginning of 1941, Stephenson was appointed director

of British Security Coordination (BSC), an organisation which already worked with the FBI and US port authorities to prevent German sabotage operations against goods purchased by Britain. This umbrella allowed him to act as the US representative not just of MI6, which continued to control his activities, but all British secret organisations, including the SOE and MI5.

Stephenson continued to encourage Donovan to see himself as the potential head of a US secret intelligence service and word soon began to leak out of proposals 'fostered by Col. Donovan, to establish a super agency controlling all intelligence'. The process of doing so was to be severely hampered by yet more jealousy and in-fighting between the various US intelligence organisations, who regarded Donovan as a competitor and rival rather than a potentially helpful colleague. In an early indication of the opposition Donovan would face, the then head of US Army intelligence, Brigadier-General Sherman Miles, told the army chief of staff that the agency Donovan wanted to set up 'would collect, collate and possibly even evaluate all military intelligence which we now gather from foreign countries', adding that 'from the point of view of the War Department, such a move would appear to be very disadvantageous, if not calamitous'.[9]

It was not just the army and navy that were concerned by the threat of Donovan's new agency. J. Edgar Hoover, who saw his relationship with Stephenson as being exclusive and a means of keeping control of as much intelligence as possible, was extremely concerned that the BSC chief had developed such a strong relationship with Donovan and proceeded to stir the waters behind the scenes. The operations of the main US intelligence organisations – Hoover's FBI, the army and navy intelligence services and the State Department's own internal intelligence service – were coordinated in theory through the Interdepartmental Intelligence Conference. The State Department's representative on the conference, Assistant Secretary of State Adolf Berle, was no friend of the British, regarding them all as full of 'rank impertinence'.[10]

In typically mendacious fashion, Hoover welcomed the intelligence Stephenson provided him from the BCS's rapidly expanding organisation in the United States and Latin America, while at the same time suggesting to Berle that he should look into the activities of British intelligence officers in New York, Baltimore, Seattle, San Francisco, Los Angeles and Houston. The FBI director also tipped off his bosses in the Justice Department, who sent a second letter to Berle asking what the State Department's position was on 'the very large increase of the British intelligence service which has recently taken place'. Berle responded by demanding an investigation into why Stephenson was running 'a full-size secret police and intelligence service' across America using agents and informers none of whom were registered as foreign agents, in breach of the law. While keeping his own hands clean, Hoover had skilfully created major problems behind the scenes for Donovan's biggest backers.

Encouraged by Menzies, Godfrey flew to Washington intent on ensuring that regardless of the opposition Donovan would become head of a US equivalent to MI6. He was accompanied on the trip by his personal assistant Ian Fleming, who, hearing during a stopover in Lisbon that German intelligence officers based in the Portuguese capital frequented the local casino at Estoril, persuaded Godfrey to go there with him and watch as he played the Germans at baccarat, an incident which saw Fleming lose his entire £50 expenses, but did at least provide part of the inspiration for the first James Bond novel, *Casino Royale*. Godfrey and Fleming stayed in Donovan's New York apartment with Fleming in particular coming up with ideas for the prospectus the American was putting together for the new American secret intelligence service.

Godfrey also engineered a dinner at the White House with Roosevelt, during which he put the case for the new organisation, carefully avoiding mentioning Donovan's name lest it be seen as a British attempt to place their own man in charge. Godfrey flew home shortly afterwards, leaving Fleming behind to help Donovan complete the prospectus. The creator of James Bond later claimed to have written 'the original charter of the OSS', which overstated his role, although his two memoranda on how to set up an intelligence service undoubtedly fed into Donovan's recommendation to Roosevelt, in a paper of 10 June 1941, for the creation of 'a central enemy intelligence organisation which would itself collect, either directly or through existing departments of Government, at home and abroad, pertinent information' on the armed forces, economies and foreign policies of potential enemies.[11]

The US president accepted Donovan's proposals and a delighted Stephenson signalled Menzies on 19 June 1941 to pass on the good news that 'our man' had been appointed coordinator of information (COI) with a mission to create the intelligence service he had proposed.

> Bill saw President today and after long discussion wherein all points were agreed he accepted appointment. He will be coordinator of all forms intelligence and will control all departments including offensive operations equivalent SO2. He will ... be responsible only to President. Bill accuses me of having 'intrigued and driven' him into appointment. You can imagine how relieved I am after three months of battle and jockeying for position at Washington that 'our man' is in a position of such importance to our efforts.[12]

There were, however, obvious problems with the idea that Donovan was 'our man'. The close relationship between him and Stephenson had not gone unnoticed among Donovan's rival intelligence services, not just in the army and the navy but also by the State Department and of course Hoover. Fleming, who was Godfrey's main liaison with MI6, and subsequently with the OSS London office, wrote to Menzies on the day Donovan was appointed warning that while Roosevelt was 'very enthusiastic' and Donovan had his full support, there were already rumours in Washington that the new COI was 'a British nominee' and a 'hireling' of MI6.[13]

A report in the New York Times, which described Donovan's new role as 'Coordinator of Intelligence Information', took the official line that his appointment had met with 'the approval and general cooperation of the various intelligence agencies which will feed reports into it'. The reality was somewhat different, as recalled by Bill Casey, one of Donovan's recruits and a future CIA director.

'It is no exaggeration to say that Donovan created OSS against the fiercest kind of opposition from everybody—the army, navy and State Department, the joint chiefs of staff, the regular army brass, the whole Pentagon bureaucracy, and, perhaps most devastatingly, the White House staff,' Casey said. 'Everyone in Washington was trying to walk off with a slice of Donovan's franchise. J. Edgar Hoover resented a rival and fought for as much intelligence turf as he could get. He grabbed control of secret intelligence operations in Latin America, an area from which the OSS was totally excluded.'[14]

Godfrey returned from Washington with an extraordinarily pessimistic picture of the potential ability of the various US intelligence agencies, telling the Joint Intelligence Committee (JIC), which coordinated the intelligence produced by all the British intelligence services, that the Americans had no secret intelligence service and no counterpart to the SOE that would carry out sabotage operations in enemy territory. Even if they entered the war against Germany they were 'unlikely to be of much assistance for many months to come'.

Too many 'amateurs' were running around 'playing at spy', Godfrey said.

Cooperation between the various organisations is inadequate and sources are not coordinated to the mutual benefit of the departments concerned. There is little contact between intelligence officers of the different departments and the desire to obtain a 'scoop' is fairly general. Even the more senior US Navy, Military and State Department officials are credulous and prefer their intelligence to be highly coloured. This predilection for sensationalism hinders the reasoned evaluation of intelligence reports.

Donovan's appointment as COI was the one positive note, Godfrey said. If he accepted 'a full measure of advice and co-operation from British Intelligence', he would certainly improve the situation. 'I feel that, if we play our cards properly, we can exploit to the full, the money and enthusiasm that Donovan, with the backing of the president, will throw into his new Service.'[15]

Meanwhile, Donovan set to work building up his new agency,

then known simply as COI, into a large organisation, doing so as swiftly as possible in order to stymic his rivals' attempts to strangle it at birth. He selected people he knew and trusted, tapping into his wide circle of friends for recommendations and not just lawyers and academics, and went out of his way to recruit people with influence, picking the president's son James, a US marine, to liaise with the other intelligence agencies, and William D. Whitney, an Anglophile lawyer and former British Army officer whose wife was British, to head up the COI London office that was to be central to liaison with MI6 and the SOE.

He persuaded Archie MacLeish, the head of the Library of Congress, to help him recruit academic experts and provide the resources and offices for a Research and Analysis (R&A) branch, which would compile 'analyses of policy issues over the whole area to be covered by the intelligence service'. Godfrey and Menzies ensured that Eddie Hastings and Stephenson passed Donovan all the intelligence they received, including all of the JIC reports, helping to enhance the R&A branch assessments and the president's regard for Donovan's work, while at the same time infuriating Hoover. The FBI director caused so much trouble for Stephenson that MI5 decided to liaise directly with the FBI office at the US embassy in London rather than risk becoming embroiled in Hoover's turf wars.

Donovan's problems with rivals were exacerbated by his attempts to create a propaganda and subversion section, which he saw occupying a very wide brief, from portraying America's role in the best possible light, using prominent Hollywood figures like multi-award-winning director John Ford, to producing black propaganda aimed at destabilising the Nazi regime. This set him against a number of government departments already working in the field, creating even more tension.[16]

On 7 December 1941, Donovan was at a baseball game watching the Brooklyn Dodgers hammer the New York Giants when his name was called out on the public address system. A phone call summoned him to the White House for urgent discussions with Roosevelt. The Japanese had just attacked Pearl Harbor, bringing America into the war. When Donovan outlined his plans for a secret intelligence service and special operations forces to match those of the British, the president nodded his assent, adding: 'It's a good thing that you got me started on all this.'[17]

Finally, Donovan set up the departments that the British had wanted to work alongside MI6 and the SOE, creating a Secret Intelligence (SI) branch under David Bruce, a Baltimore lawyer turned diplomat who was head of the US Red Cross in London, and a Special Operations (SO) branch, briefly under Robert Solberg, a Russian émigré who had worked for MI6, but from February 1942 under Preston Goodfellow, a former newspaper proprietor.

Despite the added urgency caused by America's entry into the war, Hoover and Berle continued to try to discredit not just Donovan but Stephenson as well, collaborating with isolationist opponents of the war and Anglophobic members of the Senate to draft a bill to force Stephenson to reveal the names of anyone BSC employed, including its MI6 agents.

Stephenson sought help from the embassy but had not assisted his cause by warning Menzies a few weeks earlier that the State Department was 'prepared, willing and even anxious to assume that the British Empire must emerge from this war as a definitely second-class power' compared to the US, and Britain would 'have to face the patent fact that her position in the world has changed and that hegemony has passed into other hands'.[18]

Although Stephenson's report was undoubtedly accurate, not to say prescient in its warning, it ruffled feathers in the embassy, leading one senior and very pompous diplomat to accuse Stephenson of having 'strayed wide beyond his province into realms with which he is not familiar'. The BSC chief had brought the whole thing down on himself, the official claimed. The State Department was indeed waging 'a private war' against Donovan but 'in the long run the State Department are of more importance to us than the impetuous and ambitious Colonel'.[19]

With embassy officials unwilling to intervene, Stephenson sent Dick Ellis, his MI6 deputy, to talk to Adolf Berle, 'who was extremely unpleasant [and] accused BSC of having 3,000 agents in America and bumping off people in Baltimore'. Ellis categorically denied the claims and went to see Donovan, who persuaded Roosevelt to veto the bill. Meanwhile, Stephenson accused Hoover of orchestrating the entire affair, pointing out that he had provided the FBI director with thousands of intelligence reports on Nazi activities in the US and telling him bluntly 'exactly what he thought of him'. Hoover allegedly left with his tail between his legs, 'rather apologetically' promising to sort things out.[20]

Stephenson told Menzies that Berle was 'intensely hostile to British activity generally in this hemisphere and is the driving force of intrigues against COI'. Meanwhile Peter Loxley, the Foreign Office official dealing most directly with MI6, sought to mend fences for Stephenson, explaining in a long memorandum to his boss, Alexander Cadogan, the permanent under-secretary at the Foreign Office, 'how exceedingly difficult it is for the SIS [MI6] to collaborate with the Americans when the latter have so many different organisations in the field each one of whom is exceedingly jealous of its rivals'.[21]

With strong support from Menzies, Stephenson continued to back the 'impetuous and ambitious Colonel' to the hilt, passing on large amounts of intelligence to Bruce, who aided by Ellis 'rapidly set to building up a very workmanlike organisation'. But Goodfellow struggled to recruit the necessary military talent for his SO branch, leading Donovan to approach General Marshall with the idea of recruiting servicemen from émigré communities across America who retained their cultural identities and continued to speak their old languages among themselves. He proposed setting up a 2,000-strong Special Service Command of US-Greeks, US-Poles, US-Yugoslavs and US-Norwegians as guerrilla groups in enemy-occupied territory.[22]

This rang alarm bells within the newly created Joint Chiefs of Staff over the existence of an independent organisation, not only led by a man who was still widely regarded across government as 'Wild Bill' but carrying out military action over which they had no control. They argued that they should take the COI under their control in order to restrain the 'aggressive, ambitious and very much action-minded' Donovan.

The COI's opponents were exultant at the move, seeing it as a way of finishing Donovan off for good, and were poised like vultures to pick off the various parts of his organisation. The State Department saw it as a way of absorbing, and taming, COI's R&A branch. The navy thought Donovan's 'commandos' might be taken over by the US Marines, while the Office of Naval Intelligence could appropriate Bruce's SI branch. The army's military intelligence chief General Strong, as belligerent as ever, began sketching out how COI's various functions could be split apart in order to neuter the entire operation while enhancing those of both the army and the navy.

Despite these behind-the-scenes machinations, Donovan was convinced that coming under the direct control of the Joint Chiefs offered the most secure way forward. Not only did he believe he could persuade them to protect his operation against those who were desperately trying to kill it off, he knew that with their support he could be sure of receiving all the manpower and military equipment his special operations forces required. Given the power that men like Strong held, it was a high-risk strategy, but Donovan saw it as the most sensible way forward.

'When I told Roosevelt, he said we'd be better [to] stay clear of the Joint Chiefs. They'll absorb you,' Donovan recalled. 'I said: "You leave that to me, Mr. President!" I knew the rumours that were going around that the Joint Chiefs wanted to get us under their control and then tear the agency apart piece by piece and scuttle me, but I explained to Roosevelt that the Joint Chiefs were the ones who would win the war, so that was the place for the agency to be.'[23]

Donovan seems to have seen himself as a heavyweight boxer who despite being battered in the early rounds remained supremely confident he would win the fight. When Ellery Huntington, a New York lawyer and former squash partner of Donovan's, wrote to him in early April 1942, commiserating over the 'tough time' he had been going through, he added that 'I'm sure for anyone less rugged the results would have been far worse. Please let me know if there is anything anywhere which I can contribute.' Donovan's immediate response, by Western Union telegram, was: 'Thank you very much. We are still in the ring.'

Huntington, who was forty-nine, had enjoyed a successful career as an American college football player and coach before serving, like Donovan, with distinction in the First World War. He had worked as a corporate lawyer not just in New York but across Europe, spoke French, Spanish, Italian and German, and was described by the officer who interviewed him for COI as 'a very high-class type . . . a lawyer, a gentleman, has a fine appearance and mental capacity'. Huntington was soon to play a defining role in getting Donovan's special operations and intelligence teams to the point where they could work successfully alongside their British counterparts.[24]

Donovan flew to London on 9 June 1942 with Bill Stephenson to meet up with the SOE chiefs and work out an agreement under which they could work together. Four days later, Roosevelt announced the creation of the Office of Strategic Services, run by Donovan under the control of the Joint Chiefs, and focusing solely on intelligence collection and special operations.[25]

The London agreement, drafted out over a week between Donovan and Sir Charles Hambro, the head of the SOE, split the world into spheres of influence where one side or the other would take the lead, which would become a key feature of the post-war intelligence relationship. This was not really a problem in the Far East. But the British presence on the ground in occupied Europe and the Middle East left the Americans frustrated that they could only operate in key areas like Yugoslavia, Greece and Norway—where they had high hopes of infiltrating their émigré guerrilla forces— with the permission of the local British commander, which in reality would often not be forthcoming.

British defence chiefs had in fact pushed the SOE to create joint units but the idea was not raised because Hambro knew that the Americans, who were desperately trying to find the success that would prove the value of their new organisation to the Joint Chiefs, would never accept 'the loss of identity' involved. The two sides also set up liaison offices in London and Washington, which in essence already existed in the COI London office and BSC, and confirmed arrangements already in place for training US special operations personnel in SOE training camps in Canada and the UK as well as agreeing on US supply of equipment to SOE operations.[26]

While accepting that the British were already in the field across occupied Europe, not just in terms of special operations but also intelligence networks, and that there had to be measures in place to avoid either side compromising the other, Donovan was never happy with the extent to which this allowed the SOE to dominate OSS operations and would soon attempt to row back on the agreement in a number of fields. But even so there remained many areas where the Americans simply could not operate without British permission.

There were also severe problems in the relationship with MI6, which was very happy to share a great deal of intelligence with the SI section of the OSS's London office, run by Whitney Shepardson, but constantly placed barriers in the way of any independent American activity, even to the extent of trying to control OSS contacts with the intelligence branches of the European governments-in-exile, such as the highly productive Poles and Free French.

Bill Maddox, deputy head of the SI London section, noted that while the relationship with MI6 was 'cordial and cooperative', there was a blunt refusal to allow independent OSS intelligence agents to operate into occupied western Europe, and suggestions from Shepardson or Maddox that joint OSS–MI6 intelligence teams be sent into France, Belgium or Holland were 'met with a disinterested and non-committal response'. This was undoubtedly due in large part to Claude Dansey, the MI6 assistant chief who controlled its operations against the Germans and saw the Americans as inexperienced and gullible. He claimed that they were too willing to pay large sums to agents for dubious intelligence, had a tendency to 'swallow easily and are not critical'.

Although Maddox got on reasonably well with Dansey, finding him 'in his fashion a genial friend of SI officers', there was little doubt that his 'obstructionist' behaviour prevented any independent US intelligence operations into France and the Low Countries. The OSS found itself caught in a trap. Unable to produce any evidence for the Joint Chiefs that it was making a difference, it was unable to call on the funding and logistical support that was the principal reason the SOE saw any advantage in working with the Americans.[27]

'Donovan soon regretted his commitment not to send American agents into Europe from Britain without British approval, but he could not change it,' Bill Casey recalled. 'Moreover, even without such an explicit agreement, the British could easily have stopped any independent effort whenever they felt it risked their own operations. They controlled the air and the sea and all movements in and out of Britain. We were the new boys on the team and the British were reluctant to risk what they had built up to let us show our stuff and develop our talents in areas where they were already active and successful.'[28]

But there were some areas where the OSS could make a start on persuading the Joint Chiefs that it had a vital role to perform and that they should not 'tear the agency apart piece by piece' as still desired by powerful opponents such as George Strong, who had even persuaded the head of British military intelligence to stop sharing intelligence reports with the OSS London office.[29]

Donovan had long believed that the OSS's main opportunity to prove its worth was in French North Africa. In the immediate aftermath of Pearl Harbor, Churchill and Roosevelt had agreed an Allied invasion of north Africa—what would become Operation Torch—focused on the French colonies of Morocco, Algeria and Tunisia, which were controlled by the Vichy government. The Joint Chiefs were initially opposed, in part because of anti-British prejudice. They believed that the campaign in north Africa was more about protecting the Empire than defeating Hitler. But in intelligence terms, the invasion offered more opportunities to the Americans. Although the British could operate in the international city of Tangier, they were *personae non gratae* elsewhere in Vichy territory because of attacks in 1940 on the French fleet at Mers-el-Kébir in Algeria and on Dakar, in French West Africa (now Senegal). This left the OSS free to carry out completely independent special operations and intelligence-gathering there.

An economic agreement with the Vichy French authorities in north Africa under which the US would supply them with cotton, sugar, tea and petroleum had allowed twelve US officials to check that none of these goods were being passed on to the Germans. The vice-consuls, who became known as the Twelve Apostles, were in fact selected and briefed by US naval and military intelligence and from January 1942 their work was supervised by one of Donovan's men. Colonel Bill Eddy, a US Marine who had been born and raised in Lebanon, where his parents were missionaries, spoke Arabic so well that he could recite from the Koran in several different Arabic dialects and had been the head of the English Department at the American University in Cairo. Yet another First World War hero, he was the recipient of a Navy Cross, the Distinguished Service Cross and two Silver Stars. Eddy walked with a limp as a result of a severe injury to a hip suffered at the Battle of Belleau Wood.[30]

Eddy was sent to Tangier under cover of naval attaché and began immediately organising the most efficient of the vice-consuls, based in Tunis, Oran, Algiers and Casablanca, into an intelligence network. All reports were to be sent to him rather than Washington, giving him direct control of the intelligence. He set up a radio network allowing communication between the vice-consuls. The US entry into the war had led to a crackdown on the Americans, with Gestapo and Abwehr officers watching their movements, so the radio network had to be set up in total secrecy. French radio operators were equipped and trained by the British. The control station was operated out of a wine press overlooking Tangier airport. The network had an impressive number of agents who included a police commissioner, members of the French intelligence service the Deuxième Bureau, a wealthy French industrialist, French Army officers and large numbers of other well-placed French and Arab contacts. It also included 190 Spanish communists who were in exile in French Morocco.[31]

OSS Algiers assisted a number of MI6 operations in Vichy North Africa, providing an MI6 coast watcher with a radio that allowed him to report on the movement of German and Italian warships in the Mediterranean, while US vice-consuls in Oran and Casablanca serviced two separate MI6 networks. The MI6 station in Malta was also running a moderately successful, if dangerously maverick, intelligence network in Tunisia, with results shared with Whitney Shepardson in the OSS London office.[32] Yet the most successful cooperation between MI6 and the OSS on secret intelligence in north Africa was surreptitious, the man responsible not even realising he was being controlled by the British.

Mieczysław Zygfryd Słowikowski was a Polish intelligence officer who believed he was working for his country's government-in-exile but was in fact controlled, via the Poles, by MI6 officer Wilfred 'Biffy' Dunderdale. Słowikowski operated initially as an intelligence officer in occupied France, but in July 1941 moved to Algiers where he set up Agency Afrika, a widespread network of around a hundred primary agents, and many more secondary agents, based in all the main ports and administrative centres of Vichy North Africa. Under the codename RYGOR, he assumed the role of proprietor of the highly successful Floc-Av factory processing oatmeal for breakfast cereal, which not only provided his cover but also helped to fund his operations. While he was able to supply his bosses in London, whom he assumed to be the Polish intelligence service but were in fact MI6, with intelligence reports by radio, he was not able to back it up with the large amount of documentary evidence his agents collected.

When the United States entered the war, Słowikowski approached John Knox, the US vice-consul in Algiers and one of the Twelve Apostles, asking him if there was a way the Americans could transmit his reports to London in the US diplomatic bags. Knox and his colleague John Boyd met Słowikowski and, stunned by the amount of intelligence he was producing, immediately agreed.

'They were very bewildered at such a substantial package and I unpacked it to show them that it contained nothing dangerous,' Słowikowski recalled. 'As they ransacked the plans and reports, which were in French, they became increasingly amazed. After satisfying their curiosity, they agreed that we were doing a great job and that our material was invaluable.'

He was not happy when Knox and Boyd came back to him and told him that due to 'State Department rules' his reports must remain unsealed so the Americans could read them. But

having no alternative, I was compelled to agree. I realised that, by handing the Vice-Consuls our unsealed pouch, we would enable them to exploit the fruits of our labour by copying our information and sending it directly to Washington. I resigned myself to writing it off as a payment to the Americans for the service they were more than willing to perform for us. I took it for granted that they were drawing essential information from Agency Afrika's pouches for themselves.[33]

MI6 were undoubtedly aware that the Americans were using their man's intelligence, but Stewart Menzies would have been very happy to see the US Joint Chiefs receiving exactly the same intelligence the British were seeing. Small wonder, given that so much of the US intelligence derived from MI6's own agent in the field, that the British Foreign Office considered Bill Eddy to be 'a reliable observer' whose assessment 'accords with our own'.[34] From July 1941 to November 1942, Słowikowski sent 1,244 highly detailed intelligence reports to London. As a result of the access to Agency Afrika's reports, both Menzies and Eddy had virtually every detail of the Axis defences. At the end of September 1942, with just over a month to go before the invasion, Słowikowski was confident that he had provided every detail the Allies needed to carry out Operation Torch.

'When, as was my habit at the end of the month,' Słowikowski said, 'I studied my tracing paper showing the disposition of army divisions and the defence fortifications in North Africa, I concluded happily that we had information on all the military units, batteries and coastal fortifications, and the exact amounts of ammunition stored, bombs and military equipment. I was now convinced that London, being in possession of all this data, was familiar with the exact military situation in French North Africa.'

As a result of his contribution to the Allied intelligence picture ahead of Operation Torch, Słowikowski was awarded the OBE by the British and the Legion of Merit by the Americans with the citation commending him for risking his life to provide 'information of inestimable value . . . of vital importance to military operations'.[35]

The role of the OSS station in Tangier was not limited to collecting intelligence. Two OSS special operations officers, Arthur

Roseborough, a New York corporate lawyer, and Warwick Potter, an investment broker, arrived a few months after Eddy to set up resistance groups among the local population. Both had been trained in sabotage by the SOE training facility at 'Camp X' on the north-western coast of Lake Ontario in Canada. The curriculum included lessons in hand-to-hand combat by Bill Fairbairn, the SOE's much-feared specialist in the field. 'Colonel Fairbairn, once of the Shanghai police, trainer of the famed British commandos, taught us the deadly arts, mostly in hand-to-hand combat,' one OSS officer recalled. 'Within fifteen seconds, I came to realise that my private parts were in constant jeopardy. I will not describe the unpleasant techniques taught. In short, the good Colonel's theory was that gentlemanly combatants tended to end up dead, and he persuaded us that this was the proper attitude in the area of self-defence.'

Shortly after arriving in Tangier, Roseborough and Potter recruited two charismatic personalities, one an influential tribal leader in the Rif Valley, codenamed TASSELS, and the other the head of the most powerful religious brotherhood in northern Morocco, codenamed STRINGS, the spiritual leader of tens of thousands of Moroccans who would follow him unquestioningly. TASSELS's tribe were cut-throat Berber adventurers whose way of life left them oblivious to danger, skilled in handling weapons and adept at fighting across tough terrain while avoiding the attention of the authorities. Both groups were not only primed to prepare for resistance, under Roseborough's direction, they also reported intelligence, with imams from STRINGS's group able to enter areas forbidden to the general population. The two groups were armed with machine-guns, pistols and explosives smuggled in the British diplomatic bags shipped across from Gibraltar.[36]

'Squads of friendly Frenchmen, Moors and Rifs were instructed to cut telegraph and telephone lines and to obstruct public utilities generally,' Bill Casey recalled. 'Still others were to go just before H-hour to detonate mines on roads and beaches which the allies would have to use. Groups were assigned to beachheads and landing and parachute fields, with flares to signal troops in from ships and guide them inland. Bill Donovan's OSS had successfully prepared the way and almost entirely eliminated resistance to the landing of only 110,000 American and British troops along 1,200 miles of Atlantic and Mediterranean beaches.'[37]

Eddy's extensive preparation for Operation Torch was widely acclaimed for paving the way for the successful Allied invasion. It was the ideal OSS showpiece operation which Donovan had been looking for to persuade the Joint Chiefs of its value. The months leading up to the invasion had seen Adolf Berle, George Strong and Hoover all continuing their attacks on the OSS, with Strong in particular fighting hard to try to absorb R&A into military intelligence and to prevent the Joint Chiefs giving it the go-ahead as an independent intelligence agency. Arguing the OSS case to the Joint Chiefs, Donovan's deputy James Grafton Rogers, a Yale law professor in peacetime, said that it had been 'almost stopped in its tracks' after becoming 'entangled in the rivalries of several government agencies'. The official OSS war report concluded that the success of Eddy's operation was 'the main reason OSS survived', adding that 'without this evidence to the Joint Chiefs of its value it most probably would have been dismembered'.[38]

The Joint Chiefs' directive on 'The Functions of the Office of Strategic Services' was hammered out only two days before Christmas 1942 after the intervention of General Marshall, who was clearly irritated by Strong's continued attempts to get rid of Donovan. The directive, heavily caveated to sideline the OSS's opponents, prevented it from operating anywhere in the Americas, a clear attempt to pacify Hoover. But, despite that caveat and others aimed at keeping army and navy intelligence happy, the directive left the OSS free to carry out propaganda, special operations and intelligence collection in all occupied enemy territory.

In a Christmas message to Donovan, Marshall expressed his personal regret that, after voluntarily putting the OSS under the direction of the Joint Chiefs, Donovan had been forced to go through 'the trying times of the past year', and he paid tribute to the OSS's 'invaluable service' in the north African campaign. Donovan thanked him for his 'very cordial note', adding: 'I recognise that due to your intervention the present directive is a revolutionary and courageous document and that it imposes upon us a very serious obligation.' Although the directive was followed by a few minor skirmishes, caused by Donovan's continued determination to keep control of some elements of propaganda, and a very dangerous moment in which Strong briefly persuaded Roosevelt over lunch in the White House that the OSS should be subordinate to him, the Joint Chiefs stood firm. Donovan's OSS was at last safe, able to get on with doing its job and, combining as it did the roles of MI6 and the SOE, perfectly placed to work alongside the British.[39]

4

SHARING THE TRICKS
OF THE TRADE

Ellery Huntington, Bill Donovan's former squash partner, was appointed to head the OSS Special Operations branch at the end of July 1942 and began an immediate revamp of the way it worked. He travelled to London for discussions with SOE chiefs a couple of months later convinced that the use of recruits from within America's, and Canada's, Greek, Norwegian, Yugoslav and Italian émigré communities offered the best way in which the OSS could make a unique contribution to Allied special operations.

It was soon clear the British were keener on obtaining American funding, radio sets, weaponry and small boats to infiltrate enemy territory than allowing inexperienced US operators with questionable accents to join their networks in occupied Europe, but Sir Charles Hambro, the head of the SOE, had made clear that he was happy for the OSS to operate in southern France, where the SOE was weak, and backed OSS ambitions to make a substantial effort in Norway, using recruits from America's large ethnic Norwegian community. Huntington returned to Washington frustrated at being prevented from operating in Greece or Yugoslavia, two of the areas where he felt the OSS was most able to make a contribution, but it was pointless doing anything, and impossible to recruit trained military men, until the Joint Chiefs had issued a directive confirming the roles they wanted the OSS to take.[1]

No sooner was the directive announced, confirming the special operations and secret intelligence roles, than Huntington left on a three-month trip to London, Algiers and Cairo, determined to kick-start OSS operations in Europe, Africa and the Middle East and to negotiate liaison arrangements with the SOE, and to a lesser extent MI6, that 'would demonstrate more clearly to the Joint Chiefs that those operations were independent and not simply an adjunct to the British'.

He was blunt about the lack of progress the OSS had made so far and the problems it faced even if the British relaxed the rules agreed in the original deal. The OSS had done a superb job in north Africa but had been 'pretty much liquidated' after the invasion. In the Middle East, the OSS had only 'meagre' personnel and 'practically nothing' in terms of operations. There was a tiny OSS presence in Cairo, processing intelligence from MI6, but no special operations personnel, even though this was where SOE missions into Greece and Yugoslavia were run. As for western Europe, OSS special operations were 'non-existent' and the secret intelligence operations merely processed reports produced by the British, the Poles, the Free French and other Allied agencies. 'This is valuable work, of course,' Huntington said, 'but is not the conduct of "Secret Intelligence" in any sense of the word.'[2]

After stopping off briefly in Algiers, Huntington spent the second week of January in London explaining to Hambro and his military deputy, Major-General Colin Gubbins, that the OSS had to be seen to be operating independently to get the support both it and the SOE needed from the Joint Chiefs.

'SOE wished, at first, to absorb our operations department,' Huntington recalled. 'Hambro was quick to see that this would not work. We were able, even in the short period I was there, to demonstrate that it was obvious that much of value would be lost to both organisations unless we [were] permitted to function separately, in addition it became clear that only by "dividing territory" would we receive air transport and other facilities.'[3]

From the very start, Huntington's mission was focused on increased flexibility for the OSS to deploy into its own areas by the introduction of 'spheres of influence' where one side or the other could operate best, a key element of the way in which the British and American intelligence agencies were to operate together right up to the present day. He saw the best way in which the OSS could play to its strengths as the deployment of operational groups (OGs) made up of fifteen to twenty native speakers recruited from among the US émigré communities, with Norway his first target. Hambro and Gubbins were largely supportive of the OG concept, with the former suggesting that Huntington discuss 'the Norwegian project' with General Wilhelm Hansteen, head of the Norwegian armed forces. Huntington had a number of meetings with Hansteen, who was keen on the idea of dispatching a group of Americans of Norwegian extraction to Norway and offered to attach some of his men to the groups.

Hambro and Gubbins pushed for the OSS to take over operations from north Africa, which would allow the Americans to infiltrate officers into southern France and Italy, leaving the SOE to run operations into northern Europe from London, and continue controlling those in the Balkans from Cairo. But given that a key part of the OSS gameplan was to deploy members of the US Greek and Yugoslav émigré communities into their homelands, with a couple of dozen Yugoslavs already trained by the SOE specialists at Camp X, Huntington insisted from the start on an independent OSS operation in the Middle East and the Balkans.[4]

The result was a broad agreement between Huntington and both Hambro and Gubbins that the spheres of influence agreed in July should largely continue but with both the SOE and the OSS allowed to operate independently in each other's territories. Huntington told Gubbins that he did not want to restrict the SOE from operating in US-controlled areas. 'I was convinced that both of us should strive to infiltrate as many individuals and groups as possible.' But the OSS must have exactly the same rights inside British 'spheres of influence'. Coordination of operations would be laid down by a joint policy committee chaired by an officer from whichever country 'owned' that area.[5]

'We were particularly concerned with Greece, Yugoslavia, Turkey and Albania where because of commitments already made as a result of British foreign policy, we would be severely handicapped if our association with SOE appeared to be too close,' Huntington told Gubbins. 'In the Balkans and in certain spots on the Continent, nationalistic cooperation will come to us much more readily than to the British. Unless we maintain a semblance of independence only British contacts will be available to either of us. In many places, because of their recognised post-war ambitions, Englishmen will be under suspicion.' This view of British post-war ambition, although undoubtedly exaggerated through the lens of US perspectives, was not altogether inaccurate and was a persistent theme of early US attempts to take over SOE operations.

Huntington softened his bluntness with a frank admission to Gubbins that the OSS would not be able to carry out the independent operations it craved without leaning heavily on its SOE colleagues.

> It would take many months for us to build an organisation comparable in size and experience to his own. It is necessary, however, that we give the appearance here, as elsewhere, of being able to 'walk by ourselves'. Actually, I expected and hoped he would 'lead us by the hand'. In six or eight months, our boys will be able to run things and our air force and navy (perhaps) will have learned the rudiments of cooperation. Meanwhile, we must be realistic. We need SOE assistance all along the line.[6]

Huntington and Gubbins flew to Algiers in February 1943 for discussions with Bill Eddy and General Walter Bedell Smith, Eisenhower's chief of staff, and an even firmer consensus emerged. 'We in effect decided that independence of operations could be maintained without sacrificing cooperation in the higher echelons,' Huntington said. 'While there might be territories where one of us could work more advantageously than the other (as SO might in Italy or the SOE in France), neither party was to be barred from any so-called "sphere of influence" of the other. It was in the interests of everyone to get as many operatives behind enemy lines as possible.'[7]

There is no doubt that Gubbins and Hambro admired Huntington's hard-nosed realism and were keen to give the OSS as much assistance as possible in demonstrating an independent capability, not least to get their hands on US money and equipment. But even the Americans accepted they could do little to help in northern and central France at that stage. North Africa was different; the OSS had demonstrated its worth there and the SOE was happy to let Eddy send men into southern France and Italy. However, the Balkans, where Donovan and Huntington had high hopes of demonstrating the value of the émigré teams, were a major problem since SOE London had far less control over operations there. SOE operations in the Balkans were run from Egypt by the local SOE representative, Lord Glenconner, in coordination with the British minister of state in Cairo, Richard Casey.

After the successful meetings in Algiers, Huntington flew to Egypt knowing he had a tough job on his hands. He had held discussions in London with Glenconner on how OSS–SOE special operations in the Balkans might work and while he thought the British aristocrat 'a pleasing chap' it was clear he was going to be a problem. On the face of it, the approach was the same as in north Africa, with operations coordinated by a policy committee. It would be chaired by Glenconner and comprise his chief of staff, Colonel Mervyn 'Bolo' Keble, and Ulius Amoss, the head of the OSS special operations team in Cairo. But Keble would direct all operations. Huntington said that while that was fine initially, once the OSS had appointed its own chief of staff, he must be allowed to direct all OSS operations.

Glenconner appeared to accept this. But for all his apparent agreement to the idea of independent US operations, he remained determined to keep control of all OSS activity in the Balkans, including intelligence operations, a move that reflected a Foreign Office fear that the OSS could insert intelligence officers into Greece or Yugoslavia and then switch their roles to special operations. This was not an unreasonable concern. Stewart Menzies was much more relaxed about the OSS inserting secret intelligence officers into Yugoslavia and Huntington was keen for OSS officers in the field to be capable of running both special operations and secret intelligence networks.[8]

Shortly before Huntington left Cairo, a memo from Glenconner laying out how the relationship would work arrived at the OSS officer's hotel. 'It was a blatant attempt to make OSS operations of all kinds subject to SOE control' and treated the Americans as 'a mere appendage of SOE', Huntingdon complained. Glenconner was to control all OSS operations in the Balkans, including intelligence operations. Huntington wrote back rejecting any proposal that did not see the OSS operating as an independent entity and flew back to London where he went into immediate discussions with Hambro and David Bruce, who had just taken over as head of the OSS London office, briefing them on the discussions in Algiers and the unacceptable nature of Glenconner's position. Huntington noted in his diary that they all agreed that independent OSS operations were 'the only way we will get the recognition we need from our own forces and the consequent aid that we both badly need'.[9]

Huntington returned to Washington with the backing of both Hambro and Gubbins for OSS units to have independent operational status. 'Without this we would be an adjunct of SOE,' Huntington noted, 'and as such would not only not receive the facilities and aid we need from our own military/services but would be compelled, for political reasons, to confine our dealings with national groups to those who are now willing to play with the British.'

His report to Donovan emphasised the need to speed up the formation of OSS teams behind enemy lines and to leave no stone unturned in the fight to get resources and manpower into the field. 'SOE feels that we have let them down completely and the beginning of "bad relationships" is at hand unless something happens soon,' Huntington said. He also made clear that one of the biggest problems the OSS faced was that very few US commanders knew what it was or what it was supposed to do, so it was difficult to get high-level support for its operations. 'With the exception of General [Bedell] Smith, I dealt with no officer who had the remotest idea of what we're trying to do and very few who had ever before heard of OSS except in the vaguest sort of way,' he said. 'This was upsetting but I concluded it was not unnatural since we had never had organisations in the field working with the military authorities there. We must bear in mind, however, that ours is a never-ending selling job.'[10]

The need for the OSS to sell itself hard was to be a key driver for the aggressive expansion of its operations throughout 1943, and indeed the rest of the war. Although Huntington had been critical of the lack of intelligence operations from OSS London and Cairo, the SI branch was running valuable intelligence operations from the neutral European cities of Lisbon, Madrid, Stockholm, Istanbul, and Berne, which controlled by far the most productive of those operations.

Allen Dulles, a lawyer and diplomat, and another future CIA director, was sent to head up the Berne station in November 1942, recruiting a number of useful agents who were allowed to travel between Germany and Switzerland or who had access to information from inside Germany. His most prestigious agent was Fritz Kolbe, a German Foreign Ministry official whom the British had previously rebuffed after he attempted to contact them via a go between.

The Dulles decision to recruit 'an obvious plant' infuriated Claude Dansey at MI6 and there was a succession of rows but the OSS officer's willingness to take a gamble on Kolbe, whom he code-named GEORGE WOOD, was ultimately proven correct. The value of most of his reports, largely based on telegrams from German embassies abroad, is probably overstated, not least because a substantial number of them were being read in real time by the British and US codebreakers. Nevertheless, embarrassingly for the British, Kolbe revealed that the valet of Sir Hughe Knatchbull-Hugessen, the British ambassador to Turkey, was a German agent, codenamed CICERO, and was passing the ambassador's secret correspondence to the German Sicherheitsdienst.[11]

'Dulles took great risks that paid off,' one of his OSS colleagues said. 'While the British schooled us that great intelligence officers should be low profile, dealing with agents only through intermediaries, or "cut-outs", Dulles quickly let out the word that he was American intelligence and left his light on, so to speak. He met directly with several top agents, which shocked MI6. Germans hoping to help the West flocked to Dulles rather than to the hidden British agents in Switzerland.'[12]

The contacts between Dulles and German intelligence officer Hans-Bernd Gisevius, the Abwehr head of station in Zurich, were far less helpful to the British than the CICERO revelation since they were themselves in contact with him via Halina Szymańska, whose husband, a Polish Army officer, was a close personal friend of Admiral Wilhelm Canaris, the head of the Abwehr. Canaris had placed Szymańska in Switzerland and visited her on at least five occasions, staying with her in her flat and giving her intelligence to pass to the British. His last known visit was in March 1942 and from then on the intelligence provided by Szymańska, codenamed WARLOCK, came largely from Gisevius.

One of the biggest problems for the British was doubts over US cipher security, as Claude Dansey made clear in a short-tempered telegram to Frederick Van den Heuvel, the veteran MI6 head of station in Zurich, which fully reflected the tensions between the two sides: 'Could you report to the fool who knows his code was compromised [Dulles] if he has used that code to report meetings with anyone, Germans probably identified persons concerned and use them for stuffing. He swallows easily.' Fortunately, Van den Heuvel realised working closely with Dulles to ease the concerns was a better option and conceived a scheme codenamed Unison, under which the Gisevius intelligence was shared with MI6 and only reported after consultation between both sides.[13]

MI6 concerns with OSS security, or lack of it, had led in mid-1943 to what was one of the best examples of cooperation between the two sides during the war. It allowed OSS London complete access to all of the files of Section V, its counter-espionage section, a treasure trove of detailed information on Axis and Soviet intelligence agencies which had been built up over many decades. It also offered to train the staff of X-2, the OSS counter-espionage section formed as a result, in counter-espionage techniques, an offer that was gratefully taken up, with X-2 officers sitting and working alongside their MI6 and MI5 counterparts for the rest of the war. Kim Roosevelt, grandson of US president Teddy Roosevelt and an OSS intelligence officer, noted in the official OSS war report that the importance of the British agreement to share its information on

German and Soviet intelligence agencies was impossible to over-state. 'Starting at a late date, X-2 developed a counter-espionage organisation for wartime service which could take its place among the major security services of the world,' Roosevelt said. 'No small part of the credit for making this achievement possible was due to the records and experience made available by the British.'[14]

One X-2 officer went further in his assessment of how important this was, not just for the OSS but for its successor organisation, the CIA: 'For even an ally to be admitted to a full access to most secret files and to a knowledge of their sources; to information on most secret methods and procedures; and to a knowledge of the personnel and the system of organisation and of its operations . . . in short, to the inner-most arcana of perhaps the world's most experienced and efficient, and therefore most carefully safeguarded security system, was beyond precedent or any expectation,' he said. 'Yet the British did it. That they did it is one of the incontestable, diamond-hard facts of the Anglo-American alliance. The value to the future of US security in trained and experienced personnel and in the enormous registry of counter-espionage intelligence thus rapidly accumulated by this liaison is almost literally beyond reckoning.'[15]

The rows over OSS teams carrying out independent operations in Greece and Yugoslavia continued through the summer of 1943 and, by June, in a reflection of the frustration felt by Bill Donovan and his senior staff, David Bruce was bluntly warning SOE officers in London that 'some people held the view that the Balkans was at the moment nobody's sphere of influence' and that the Americans should just send their people in whatever the British said.[16]

A small number of OSS officers were inserted into Greece, where the SOE's Monty Woodhouse found them of mixed quality. The first senior US officer to arrive at his mission to the ELAS communist resistance in September was Captain Winston Ehrgott from the 7th US Cavalry. 'Ehrgott was a brave and thoroughly professional cavalryman,' Woodhouse recalled. 'But when he was not dealing with horses, he was soon out of his depth. He had his own ciphers to communicate with his Cairo headquarters, but he used my wireless sets. He became convinced that I was delaying his messages and, when his headquarters were unable to decipher them, he was sure that I had sabotaged them. In the end I had to do his ciphering for him, which naturally increased his suspicions. It was a relief when he was superseded a few months later by a more senior officer, Major Gerry Wines, a level-headed Texan. A much older man than myself, he had served in the First World War and should by rights have been my senior in rank. But he was devotedly loyal and made sure that there were no more visible divisions between British and American officers in the field.'

Several individual OSS officers were infiltrated into Yugoslavia to serve with the British missions to the main resistance leaders, the communist Partisan Tito and the Serb royalist General Draža Mihailović, but with the British leaning towards backing Tito, largely based on evidence from Enigma decrypts, the Foreign Office remained resistant to US involvement, a concern that in their own terms was justified given that the first OSS officer attached to Mihailović was highly critical of the British willingness to drop him in favour of Tito.[17]

It was not until October, following the forced resignation of Glenconner (and Hambro) over a botched conference with Greek resistance leaders, that the issue was resolved. The OSS was already playing a strong role in the invasion of Italy—where crucially there was no formal arrangement for cooperation with the SOE. It included a much more aggressive and highly successful OSS intelligence-collection operation led by Ellery Huntington. He set about correcting the failings he had railed against earlier, sending locally recruited agents through the lines to collect intelligence on the German forces and even dispatching one agent to Rome, where he discovered details of the German plans for a counter-attack against the Allied forces who had landed at Anzio.

This appears to have provided far more effective support for the Allied advance than No. 1 Intelligence Unit, the MI6 intelligence team based at Bari, which failed to achieve anything substantial until it was revamped by John Bruce Lockhart later in the campaign. Meanwhile, Bill Eddy was conducting extensive intelligence and special operations into southern France and Corsica. Glenconner's departure removed the main obstacle to cooperation in the Balkans, while Gubbins, who had taken over from Hambro, was convinced that, with the Americans coming of age, full-scale collaboration was the only way forward.[18]

The Foreign Office still objected to OSS operations in the Balkans on the basis that post-war considerations might lead it to work against the British policy of backing Tito. But Lord Selborne, who as minister of economic warfare had political responsibility for the SOE, told Foreign Secretary Anthony Eden that while he agreed that the political problems in the Balkans and the potential for post-war problems were acute and would only be made more difficult by American interference, it was impossible for the SOE to continue to block OSS involvement. If the Foreign Office were to continue to do so, it must do so in its own name.

'Gubbins's view is that since OSS are now established in southern Italy and Cairo and ready to work in the Balkans, the only basis upon which it is wise or safe for them to do so is one of whole-hearted and ungrudging collaboration,' Selborne said. 'If SOE fail to work on such a basis the result will be to impair their relations with OSS in all other parts of the world and encourage OSS to pursue their own policy and carry out all sorts of wild operations without our knowledge. I do not see how they can be excluded from operating in these territories now that they are beginning to grow up and stand on their own feet.'[19]

The Foreign Office concerns were in any event misplaced, with OSS officers on the ground reporting 'well substantiated evidence of close collaboration' between Mihailović and the Germans and backing Tito's Partisans. Louis Huot, the OSS officer most trusted by SOE Cairo, held discussions with Partisan representatives in Algiers before travelling to Bari from where he crossed the Adriatic and, unknown to Fitzroy Maclean, the British officer in charge of the Allied mission to Tito, met with the Partisan leader. Huot had secured a number of small ships to ferry supplies to the Partisans, including Italian weapons captured in the invasion. When Maclean found out, he was incandescent and had Huot and his team placed under house arrest.[20]

The situation was exacerbated by Maclean warning an OSS SI officer that he and his colleagues would be 'arrested or flung out' of Yugoslavia if they did not show him all of their intelligence reports. Bill Donovan's response was immediate. At a two-hour meeting in Cairo, he bluntly informed Gubbins and a senior Foreign Office representative that he was 'not prepared to accept any situation in Yugoslavia, Albania or Greece where OSS was subordinate to SOE'.

In his account of the meeting for Selborne, Gubbins said that although it was cordial, Donovan 'commenced with violent attack on SOE particularly Fitz for obstructing OSS efforts in the Balkans'. The OSS director insisted that Maclean, being in charge of an SOE mission, had no authority whatsoever to interfere with OSS intelligence operations. Nor did Donovan care what the Foreign Office thought. He did not work for the Foreign Office, or indeed the State Department, he worked for the Joint Chiefs, who had just taken the shackles from the OSS in a new directive giving it a free hand to mount special operations and carry out espionage.

Gubbins told Selborne it was clear that independent OSS operations in the Balkans 'figure largest in his [Donovan's] war aims and he will stick at nothing to obtain them'. The OSS chief had 'made it perfectly clear that he regarded OSS as being definitely on equal terms with SOE in these countries and was prepared to accept nothing more than minimum operational control in Cairo'. Gubbins also made it clear that he thought it 'absurd' for the British to demand control over OSS intelligence operations, not least because Donovan 'could undoubtedly establish a separate direct link with Tito and persuade him to accept hordes of SI men'.

The simple truth was that the extent of their operations in north Africa, Italy, southern France and the Far East meant that the OSS were no longer the junior partner, Gubbins said. 'All above is the natural development of OSS finding their feet and demanding consequent increased participation,' he told London. 'I do not rate their motives as differently to previously but as we must work with them, we must do so wholeheartedly and not grudgingly. Latter brings us nothing, not even knowledge of their actions which former will at least help in doing.'[21]

Maclean was told he had no choice but to accept that OSS intelligence officers were not under his control. The SOE left arrangements on intelligence networks to Stewart Menzies and agreed that the Americans could send around 150 special operations officers into Yugoslavia and Greece, with one fifteen-man OG going immediately to Greece, another to Mihailović and a third to Tito. More than a dozen OGs went into Yugoslavia and Greece over the next twelve months, attacking enemy garrisons and destroying vehicles and infrastructure, including railway lines and bridges.[22]

The OSS sent the Hollywood star Sterling Hayden, who before becoming an actor had skippered schooners across the Caribbean for a living, to Bari where, in a very clear demonstration of the US 'can-do' approach and with access to unlimited resources, he created and commanded a small fleet of schooners and fishing boats that ferried 6,500 tons of weapons, explosives, medicines and uniforms across the Adriatic to the Partisans in the space of a few months, far more than the British had managed in two years.[23]

Meanwhile, Donovan flew on from one row in Cairo to another in Delhi where the head of SOE India, Colonel Colin Mackenzie, a pre-war director of yarn company J. & P. Coats, was engaged in a bitter feud with Lieutenant-Colonel Dick Heppner, the senior OSS officer on the staff of General 'Vinegar Joe' Stilwell, the commander of US forces in China. Heppner, a member of Donovan's law firm with a brief to gather intelligence across south-east Asia, was fighting attempts by the British to control OSS operations in the region.

The July 1942 agreement had made it very clear that the British were in charge of all operations based in India but, even before it was agreed, Donovan had persuaded Roosevelt of the importance of holding northern Burma in order to maintain supplies to Stilwell and recruited a hard-bitten army officer, Major Carl Eifler, to lead what would become Detachment 101, renowned for its heroic operations against the Japanese. The only sensible base for operations into Burma was in India. Eifler's team set up their headquarters at Nazira in north-eastern India, where they began recruiting Anglo-Burmese fighters to operate inside Burma.[24]

Despite its breach of the agreement, the activities of Detachment

101 were far less of a problem for the British than the OSS propaganda specialists. The Americans were extremely wary of being tied too closely to the colonialist British in the eyes of native populations across south-east Asia. It was an OSS anti-British propaganda campaign which had infuriated Mackenzie and sparked his attempts to take control of all OSS operations in the Indian sub-continent. In a memo to Donovan, Heppner denounced Mackenzie as 'a thoroughly unscrupulous behind-the-scenes manipulator'. SOE India had taken 'an invariably hostile attitude' to the OSS. By contrast, OSS officers reported that the MI6 willingness to cooperate in south-east Asia was 'characterised by frankness and friendliness and we seem to be operating to our mutual benefit'.[25]

The colonialist nature of British rule in India was a real problem for the Americans. Bonner Fellers, a senior OSS officer, warned Donovan that 'justly or not, the British are bitterly disliked by the Orientals. To identify our agencies with those of the British simply means we shall immediately inherit all the antipathy which the Oriental holds for the British.' Fellers, who was described by one OSS colleague as 'the most violent Anglophobe I have ever met', was well known to the British as a result of bitterly acerbic assessments of British operational planning in north Africa when he was US military attaché in Cairo, assessments which due to weak US cipher security were read by Rommel. But Vinegar Joe's political adviser was even more critical.

'In so far as the British are fighting the Japanese enemy and seeking to punish aggression, we are united with them,' he said. 'But we are not to the same extent united with the British in their attempt to regain their colonial empire—unless American foreign policy and public sentiment have undergone a revolutionary change yet unannounced in these distant parts. The reacquisition and perhaps extension of the Empire is an essential undertaking if Britain is to be fully restored to the position of a first-class power. Therefore, reconquest of empire is a paramount task in British eyes. The raising of the Union Jack over Singapore is more important to the British than any victory parade through Tokyo. There still exist at home highly vocal and influential publishers and men in public life who will be ready to brand our collaboration with the British in Burma, Malaya, Indochina and Sumatra as snatching British, French and Dutch colonial chestnuts out of the Japanese fire. The question will be asked: "Why should American boys die to repossess colonies for the British and their Dutch and French satellites?"[26]

The problem would dominate relations between the OSS and the SOE in the Far East, although Admiral Lord Louis Mountbatten, Supreme Allied Commander, South-East Asia Command, later professed to having preferred the OSS to both MI6 and the SOE. The OSS might not have been joined 'at the roots' to official policy but it was very good at a whole range of 'nefarious' activities.[27]

The reality was that by the end of 1943, the OSS was operating on its own into southern Europe and the Far East and there was little that the SOE could do about it other than to accept the informal coordination the Americans were prepared to concede. In any event, the main attention was now focused on the impending invasion of north-west Europe. Gubbins was as determined as Donovan to ensure that the relationship between OSS special operations and the SOE was one of equals and at the beginning of 1944 it was decided that the two should 'substitute partnership for liaison'. A joint organisation of independent equals, Special Force Headquarters, was set up incorporating the SOE, OSS Special Operations and the British SAS.[28]

By this time, plans were already well advanced for joint SOE–OSS–French operations into France as part of the invasion of Europe. All 144 of the OSS personnel due to take part had already been selected and were undergoing training for the three-man Jedburgh teams which were to parachute in ahead of D-Day to coordinate and organise resistance operations. Each of the teams was to consist of one US or British officer, one French officer, and a wireless operator from any one of the three countries.

They were given parachute training at Ringway in Manchester or, in the case of the Americans, at Fort Benning in Georgia, and paramilitary training at the SOE training centre at Arisaig in Inverness-shire before undergoing more specific mission training at Milton Hall near Peterborough. There, Daphne Park taught the

Jedburgh teams to encipher and decipher their messages, making a number of friendships among the Americans that would last into her subsequent Cold War service in MI6, most notably with Bill Colby, one of her trainees who would go on to become CIA director.

'The Americans were mixed,' she recalled. 'Some had been fighting in the Pacific, and Hod Fuller who commanded them was a brilliant marine colonel of the utmost courage and competence. But half his lot were green, young men who'd done their jumps at Fort Benning and absolutely nothing else and they were very, very green.'

The first of the ninety-two Jedburgh teams were parachuted into France the night before D-Day with the rest following over the next three months. A total of 83 OSS, 90 SOE and 103 French personnel took part, organising the destruction by communist Maquis resistance groups of fuel and ammunition dumps and communication links and attacking pockets of German troops who had been cut off by the Allied advance. They also provided liaison between the Maquis and Allied commanders to coordinate their attacks with the needs of the Allied advance.

While most of the Jedburghs were dispatched from RAF Tempsford in Bedfordshire, a couple of dozen were sent in from Algiers, and struggled with the competition to get aircraft to take them in. Two of them, the SOE officer Major Ossie Grenfell and OSS lieutenant Lucien 'Lou' Conein, were frustrated by their inability to get the air transport they needed. Conein had been born in France, emigrating to the US as a child before returning to France to enlist in the Foreign Legion at the start of the war. After the fall of France, he returned to America, joined the US Army and was assigned to the OSS. A gregarious, natural fighter, he was not one to be kept long from the action. He and Grenfell smuggled themselves onto the aircraft of a US general who was flying to London in order to plead with Gubbins to send a 'briefing officer' out to Algiers to organise the Jedburgh flights and ensure their teams were allocated aircraft to take them in.

'Gubbins said: "I simply haven't any, everybody's flat out, it's impossible. Very sorry but you know that's it, that's how it is,"' Park recalled. 'So, then they took me out to lunch and in the middle of lunch they looked at each other and they said, "what about it". They didn't say anything more and went back and they saw General Gubbins and they said: "We've found our Briefing Officer", and he said "Who?" and they said: "Daffers, Daphne Park".' Park was commissioned and sent out to Algiers to organise their flights. By early September, both Conein and Grenfell had been dropped into France.[29]

The Americans also sent nineteen OGs into France, some of them ethnic Norwegians who had been training for operations into Norway that never took place. Seven were dispatched from the UK and a dozen from Algiers. They were mostly around fifteen men strong but ranged in size from the seven-man Mission Union II team put into the Les Saisies Pass in the French Alps in early August to the 57-man Christopher group dropped north of Dijon a month later. It would not be until March 1945 that the only OG to operate in Norway was deployed, with Colby, having returned from his Jedburgh operation, leading a 36-man team which dropped into central Norway to cut the Nordland railway line between Trondheim and Bodø. It was a 'disastrous' failure, one senior OSS officer recalled. 'Two planes crashed, men were killed and many supplies were dropped irretrievably off target.'[30]

Although relations between MI6 and OSS London were generally good throughout the war, with Walter Bell, the MI6 liaison officer, visiting on a day-to-day basis to advise Bill Maddox and his colleagues and iron out any problems, Claude Dansey's continued restriction of attempts by Maddox's SI team in London to run agents into Norway and France remained a significant frustration. The team's only real function for much of the war was the provision of OSS intelligence reports to MI6 and the dispatch of MI6 reports to Washington, the same basic role that Ellery Huntington had railed against in early 1943. But in the summer of that year, the situation changed. OSS London approached MI6 in May 1943 with the idea of preparing for joint operations to take place during the invasion of Europe and at last received a positive response. Stewart Menzies suggested to David Bruce that MI6, OSS's SI branch and the Free French intelligence service use small two-person French teams to infiltrate ahead of the Allied forces and collect intelligence on strategic sites along the invasion route.[31]

The Sussex plan, which was to become the first major joint operation between the British and American secret services, stumbled briefly when the incoming commander of the US Army European Theatre of Operations, General Jake Devers, was briefed that MI6 was unhappy with the 'slick' way in which the OSS operated. It is clear that Bruce regarded the 'crusty old curmudgeon' Dansey as the chief suspect for this briefing. Bill Donovan flew to London and persuaded Menzies to talk to Devers and explain that he was not at all unhappy with the OSS and very much wanted it to take part. They also agreed a substantial increase in staff for the OSS London office ahead of the invasion. Dansey was diverted to focus on other issues with Menzies making clear to his officers the 'necessity for harmonious collaboration' with the OSS.[32]

The Sussex plan was led by a triumvirate of MI6 officer Commander Kenneth Cohen, Colonel Francis Miller of the OSS and Free French officer Gilbert Renault-Roulier, who had adopted the pseudonym 'Colonel Rémy'. It initially aimed to drop the teams in 'blind', with no one to meet them, but this was deemed too much of a risk and two teams were sent in ahead to prepare the way, setting up reception parties and safe houses for each of the teams. The joint OSS–MI6 operational team was based at Glenalmond, an MI6 outstation in the small city of St Albans, in Hertfordshire. It was led by Colonel Malcolm Henderson, a pre-war opera singer whose great advantage was that he had also served in the French Foreign Legion.

He was not the only member of the Sussex staff with an unusual CV. The staff in nearby Praewood House, where the training took place, included an instructor who before the war had been a circus acrobat in the Balkans. The more than fifty teams were divided equally between OSS 'Ossex' and MI6 'Brissex'. Their targets, for intelligence collection, not sabotage, were located in a broad sweep from Brittany across to the Belgian border. The targets were selected by the invasion planners and included enemy headquarters, airfields, strategic railway junctions, communications sites, vehicle storage sites, ammunition dumps and bridges over the Seine and the Loire.

'Authority for Sussex was given in November 1943, although by then it was becoming clear that it would not be easy to find agents with sufficient knowledge of current conditions in France,' recalled Pat Hawker, one MI6 officer involved in the operations. 'Attempts to recruit French exiles in the United States failed, and the search then switched to North Africa. By March 1944, some 90 Frenchmen had been recruited in North Africa for Sussex, largely from French Army and military reservists.

'Each team was assigned to a specific town or city, with care taken to ensure that they were not known there. They were dropped well away from Normandy and several teams given the address of a French woman who ran a café to whom the agents would make themselves known using a password. She would look after them and provide a safe house in the days immediately after they arrived in France and before they made their way to their target area. Ossex teams were dropped to the rear of areas allocated to American forces while the Brissex team operated in the rear areas of British, Canadian and French Forces.' MI6 sent its own military-style unit, 2 Intelligence (Underground) Section, to Saint-Gabriel-Brécy in Normandy to control the Brissex agents and infiltrated others through the enemy lines, some accompanied by donkeys carrying the team's radio equipment concealed in their saddles.[33]

A total of fifty-six Sussex teams were sent into France between early April and the end of August 1944, with the OSS dispatching twenty-six and MI6 a total of thirty. The operation produced a wealth of intelligence far in excess of what the planners had expected. One of the American teams, Ossex 6, was the first to identify the Panzerlehrdivision, the strongest German armoured division, ensuring that the British and Canadian forces it was about to attack were prepared and able to inflict heavy damage on it. Brigadier Bill Williams, who was General Montgomery's chief intelligence adviser, told one of his US colleagues that 'the value of this piece of information alone was sufficient to justify all the work that had been put into the Sussex project, even if nothing else were accomplished'.[34]

The invasion of Europe freed OSS London to carry out

intelligence operations on its own and, in the wake of Sussex, it sent out half a dozen joint intelligence missions with the French, codenamed Proust, which were completely independent of MI6. It also mounted operations into Germany that were much bigger than those contemplated by the more cautious British. OSS London put forward plans for widespread penetration of Germany, an operation they codenamed Kent, a few weeks after D-Day, but MI6 declined to take part, fearing that OSS handlers would be too keen to take risks that would compromise MI6 agents. Although the British did drop a number of agents and pushed others through the lines into Germany they were nowhere near as aggressive as the Americans. Bill Casey, then a senior member of David Bruce's management team, devised and took charge of the operations, assisted by another future CIA director, Dick Helms.

'Our British partners and tutors had decided long ago that odds against agents sent to Germany were stacked too high,' Casey recalled. 'This shook me, but we had to try. Between October 1944 and April 1945, we sent more than 150 agents, mostly Belgians, Dutchmen, Frenchmen and Poles, into Germany with identification as foreign workers, together with anti-Nazi prisoners of war in German uniform. These brave men went into Germany blind and it was remarkable that over 95 per cent of them came out alive. In the few months, some of them only weeks, these agents had to operate inside Germany, with the war drawing to a close, the intelligence produced was of marginal value. But the experience and confidence it gave us was invaluable.'

The risks the OSS was prepared to take with its agents, as opposed to the more cautious approach of MI6, were encouraged by US military commanders, with Brigadier-General Eugene Harrison, the intelligence chief for the 6th US Army Group, warning against 'excessive caution' on the basis that the Allies 'should not hesitate to take risks with our agents while a thousand men a day were being killed along the front.' This was anathema to the British. Who knew how many lives the intelligence from an agent might save if he or she were allowed to survive? On Menzies's recommendation, Churchill authorised a series of measures to protect MI6 agents in the field, including introducing the codeword GUARD to be stamped on any files that were not under any circumstances to be shared with the Americans and—amid concern over the extent to which the Americans were intercepting British communications—an instruction that all GUARD reporting should be sent using one-time pad cipher systems.[35]

Although the British tuition and a competitive drive towards independence had turned the OSS into a highly professional organisation, with a few notable exceptions—in Switzerland, France, Italy and north Africa—there were still serious questions to be asked over how successful it actually was. A number of films in the immediate aftermath of the war, including Jimmy Cagney in *13 Rue Madeleine*, Alan Ladd's *OSS* and *Cloak and Dagger*, starring Gary Cooper, seemed designed to demonstrate its importance in terms of winning the war. The truth, as Helms pointed out, was not quite so impressive.

'If you look it straight in the eye you have remarkable talent, but the things it contributed were really not all that large in the scale of things,' he said. 'There were an awful lot of brainy people running around, and there were a lot of able people and so forth, but if you really look honestly at what OSS contributed to the winning of the Second World War, it really isn't all that much. I think probably the element of OSS that made the most consistent contribution was the research and analysis branch, where a lot of these academics were brought together and refugees, émigrés and so forth from Europe, that area. It was a very brainy bunch who really did some remarkable studies on various aspects of the economy of Europe and so on, which really did contribute to the war effort. But I think most of the "derring-do" of OSS reads better in books than it does if you were a general wondering about how you're going to win the war.'[36]

At the end of the war, the relationship between the OSS and its British partners was still far from stable, in part because of the differences of approach, but also in terms of where and how each was happy for the other to work. Both the Foreign Office and the State Department had been determined throughout the war to ensure that the wartime intelligence liaisons with the exiled governments, and the work of the special operations forces helping the resistance on the ground, shaped the post-war world in the way that best suited their immensely different perspectives.

The British had managed to rein the Americans in on both the special operations and secret intelligence fronts for much of the war—in large part because Bill Donovan was having to spend so much time fighting for backing in Washington. But the invasion of Europe, the need for the OSS to prove itself to its military masters, and the more aggressive US 'can-do' attitude allowed it to surge ahead of the under-resourced and far more cautious SOE and MI6 in terms of operational presence, if not necessarily actual impact. But this surge was soon to come to an abrupt halt.

5

THE COLD WAR BEGINS

The OSS had been grateful to its British tutors for the start they had given it but hard-headed in its belief that once the war was over it should move on, using superior US resources, in terms of both money and manpower, to create its own organisations which it anticipated would be far more capable than those of its under-resourced British 'cousins'. OSS London was unequivocal about 'the desire to establish and maintain an independent American secret intelligence service . . . free of British control at the earliest possible moment'. While it accepted that 'too great or too soon a cleavage from close collaboration with the British would certainly not be to the interest of SI, which had learned an enormous amount about secret intelligence work from its vastly more experienced cousins', the view was that, once the OSS had obtained what it could from the British, the split would come.[1]

Similar views were being expressed in Whitehall, where a Foreign Office report into the future of MI6 was pointing out that although cooperation with the allied intelligence services, includ-ing the OSS, had yielded 'excellent results' and officials did 'not by any means wish to see such collaboration come to an end as soon as the war is over', once the OSS stopped operating out of London 'a new danger creeps in'. MI6 had been fully aware of everything the allied intelligence services were doing 'through their control of communications and by other means . . . and the Allies could have but few secrets from us'. But once the Americans and the European Allies were operating on their own, MI6 would no longer have any control over their activities or reports.[2]

Such concerns would not have come as a surprise in the OSS London office where it was clear that MI6 policy towards its US counterparts was 'consistently directed towards preventing, in so far as they are able, the development of an effective American secret intelligence service in Europe'. Senior OSS officers in London stressed that 'no moral stigma' needed to be attached to MI6 over this 'for if positions were reversed, we might do the same'.[3]

Bill Donovan had been pushing Roosevelt for some time to create a post-war equivalent of the OSS, what he described as a 'Central Intelligence Service', which would report direct to the president, collecting and coordinating the intelligence needed by government to determine how best to pursue its policies. He gave Roosevelt written proposals in November 1944, which were circulated by the Joint Chiefs, and it was not long before J. Edgar Hoover and Donovan's other enemies within the State Department and armed forces intelligence were plotting to use them to get rid of him.

Selective elements from the proposals were leaked to the press and, despite an insistence that the new central intelligence service would have 'no police or law-enforcement functions, either at home or abroad', Donovan's proposed body was portrayed as an American 'Gestapo'. The *Chicago Tribune* announced in banner headlines that the new agency's 'sleuths would snoop on US and the world', while the *Washington Times-Herald* claimed Donovan wanted to create 'an all-powerful intelligence service to spy on the post-war world and to pry into the lives of citizens at home'.[4]

Stewart Menzies, meanwhile, was steadfastly working for post-war cooperation with the OSS or its successor, sending Jack Easton, his director of intelligence requirements, and Christopher Arnold-Forster, his chief personal assistant, to America in February 1945 to discuss the way forward.[5] But Donovan's enemies decided to weaponise the links between the OSS and MI6 to attack him. Roosevelt responded to the press criticism by asking his military adviser, Colonel Richard Park, to carry out an investigation into the OSS. The move gave Hoover, and Donovan's enemies in the military, the opportunity to destroy him and they took full advantage. Park's report, which carefully conceded that none of its sources could be checked because they were 'confidential', was highly damning, dismissing the OSS as 'incompetent', completely lacking in any sense of security and penetrated by a 'dangerously large proportion' of communists.

'It appears probable that many improper persons have penetrated into OSS, some who cannot handle themselves, some with questionable backgrounds, and some who may be plants for foreign intelligence,' Park said. 'If OSS is permitted to continue, it may do further serious harm to citizens, business interests, and national interests of the United States.'

The report was a parade of unsubstantiated tittle-tattle and obvious nonsense, a great deal of which had evidently been supplied by the FBI. But in many ways, its most damning criticism was that the OSS was 'hopelessly compromised' by its association with the British, 'rendering it useless' as a prospective independent post-war espionage agency. 'The British, in particular, have always worked closely and cleverly with the OSS,' Park said, 'and while OSS knows details about normal British intelligence, it knows very little about British secret intelligence. On the other hand, the British are believed to know everything about OSS and exercise quite a good deal of control over OSS.' Park and his allies insured themselves against any fact-checking by adding that 'questioning of British intelligence authorities will evince nothing but praise because OSS is like putty in their hands and they would be reluctant to forfeit a good tool'.

The Park report described the proposals for a post-war intelligence service as having 'all the earmarks of a Gestapo scheme' and recommended that Donovan be replaced 'at the earliest possible moment'. Only two elements of OSS should be retained. The Research and Analysis Branch should be absorbed by the State Department while, in a proposal which gave a good indication of the real authors of the report, the X-2 Counter-Espionage Branch should be retained under the control of 'the agencies who have always done an excellent job in this field both in war and in peace, namely, the FBI, the Army and the Navy'.[6]

Roosevelt would almost certainly have seen through the report but on 12 April 1945 he had a stroke and died. Park passed the report to new president Harry Truman, who had known nothing about intelligence until he succeeded to the presidency but would have read the negative press reports. He only had those reports and Park's tendentious 'investigation' to go on. Nor was he a fan of the British. Shortly after becoming president, he told a group of Democratic Party colleagues: 'It is not Soviet communism I fear, but rather British imperialism.' When Donovan went to see him to discuss the proposals for a post-war central intelligence service, he was shown the door within a quarter of an hour. A few weeks later, the *Washington Times-Herald* carried another article, clearly based on the Park report, which denounced the OSS as 'scarcely more than an arm of the British intelligence service'. It was clear that it was in trouble.[7]

Shortly before the German surrender on 8 May 1945, Allen Dulles had been sent to Germany with 200 OSS staff to set up an intelligence organisation with bases in Berlin, Heidelberg and Karlsruhe. 'We relished hearing tales of Dulles's success as America's outstanding spymaster in World War Two,' said Dick Cutler, one of his senior intelligence officers. 'He enjoyed retelling accounts of his cases, interspersed with hearty laughter and dramatic gestures. All espionage tales are exciting, and his were especially so. They reflected the importance, glamour, and skill of our new espionage service. We were all starved of recognition, having been a "hush-hush" agency, and now with the war finished, we could tell of how "we" had outwitted the Germans, citing Dulles's achievements as our own.'

Dulles ran a separate mission in Czechoslovakia and controlled all US reporting on Germany. The focus was initially on hunting down Nazis and gathering political, economic and sociological intelligence on Germany itself. The US military governor, Lucius Clay, was anxious not to upset the Russians and opposed intelligence operations against them. 'Clay had voluntarily assured his Soviet counterpart, that the United States would not engage in espionage against them,' Cutler recalled. 'He thought the Soviets were overly suspicious about American espionage and disbelieved reports that the Soviets were already spying on Americans.' This presented the OSS with a problem. So it decided to keep spying on the Russians but not informing Clay, Cutler said, 'no doubt feeling that the naïvety of a general should not block its mission to protect America from rampant espionage by a new, hostile, heavily armed force'.

Ultimately, the Russian clampdown on the Soviet sectors of Berlin and East Germany forced Clay to rely on intelligence provided by OSS sources for information on what was happening there. Dulles was soon replaced by Dick Helms, who under Dulles had run the US secret intelligence operations across Germany and Czechoslovakia. 'He exuded the warm friendliness of a Midwesterner and had a disarming smile,' Cutler said. Before joining the OSS, Helms had been a newspaper reporter with the United Press in Europe and had interviewed Hitler. 'He had a journalist's keen nose for facts, as well as an admirable management and training style. Whenever I proposed to Helms how to solve a particular espionage problem, such as deciding an agent's next move, he was courteous, crisp, imaginative, and above all, sensible.'

Other ex-OSS men were spread around Europe: first Bill Casey and then Phil Horton took charge of the Paris station. Al Ulmer covered Austria and the Balkans from Vienna. Jim Angleton was in Rome and Jim Kellis in China.[8]

Amid uncertainty over the future of the OSS and US intelligence in general, MI6 was initially tentative on continuing liaison relationships with its US colleagues, particularly on Soviet material. Approached by a US naval intelligence liaison officer in May 1945, Tim Milne, the head of Section V, 'agreed the whole problem of continued liaison should be raised soon', while Kim Philby, who was in charge of the new Soviet counter-espionage unit, Section IX, put the Americans off, saying policy on exchange of Russian material had yet to be decided.

'The question at issue with the British, according to Philby, is— in view of present relations between Great Britain and Russia—can the former afford to follow the same policy of exchange with her American ally as on Germany,' the US naval intelligence officer told his boss. 'Philby further remarked that he was unsympathetic toward the OSS attitude of seeking to extend its prerogatives with MI6 merely for the sake of prestige without having any organisation to back up or implement its claims for wider relationships with MI6.' The best Philby would offer was that 'from time to time there was no reason why unofficial discussions on the subject of Russia could not be held'.[9]

Given Philby's position as a Soviet 'agent-in-place' at the heart of MI6, it is tempting to see this as deliberate obfuscation designed to prevent the Americans obtaining intelligence on Russia, and as one of the key players in the decision-making that was probably his intention, but it was the same position taken by Stewart Menzies two weeks later over lunch with the same US intelligence officer and his boss. The MI6 Chief made it clear that, so far as he was concerned, the uncertainty over the future of the OSS was at the heart of the issue. The US record of the meeting noted that Menzies 'stressed his conviction strongly that there should be continued cooperation between the British and Americans and expressed the hope that the United States would soon decide whether it could support a secret intelligence service'.

It was nothing to do with not wanting to share intelligence with the Americans, Menzies said. Russia was a common problem for both countries and he was determined to continue some form of cooperation between MI6 and its US counterpart, whoever that might be. But he refused to go into 'the longer-term aspects of liaison in view of the need to know with whom he should deal and the absolute necessity for security'. Indeed, the only interesting piece of information the Americans learned over lunch was that Menzies occasionally saw the King, 'to whom he always tried to give a good spy story', and that as a result senior MI6 officers had a brief to watch out for operations that might keep the monarch in awe of his secret service.[10]

A few weeks later, Victor Cavendish-Bentinck, the chairman of the JIC, visited Washington and during talks with Eisenhower, now military governor of the US Occupation Zone in Germany, agreed that there should be collaboration between British and US intelligence on Russia. As a result, Philby called the London representatives of US military and naval intelligence to an informal meeting along with the OSS X-2 representative. Philby said the intelligence exchange would be directly between him and them alone and absolutely ruled out any collaboration in the field between MI6 and X-2 representatives until such time as the US organised a post-war secret intelligence service.[11]

It was left to Dunderdale to sweeten the pill during a visit to the OSS Paris station. A veteran MI6 Russian specialist, who spoke the language perfectly – his mother was a Tsarist countess – he had operated in Ukraine, where he was born, before being sent to Paris, because so many Russian émigrés with access to intelligence were living there. He discussed the Soviet problem at length with OSS station chief Phil Horton, teasing him by revealing the outlines of ideas he had for various operations while clearly also trying to work out what material Horton might have to offer in any exchange. He reiterated the Menzies message that the uncertainty over the future of the OSS was the only thing delaying cooperation plans and suggested he go to Washington in October to discuss the issue with Horton's bosses, flattering his host by suggesting that it might be helpful if he were also there.

'He is extremely interested of course in the problem of intelligence work on Russia, both from the positive viewpoint of the procurement of intelligence and the counter-espionage viewpoint of the protection of the British and American services against agents provocateurs and penetration,' Horton told Washington. 'He is convinced that it will not be possible to produce any regular and reliable flow of intelligence on Russia by agent penetration. He feels that the only technique which will produce results is that supplied by the technical services.'[12]

Bill Donovan's response was to send John Bross, a lawyer turned special operations officer, to London to head the OSS office there, with a specific brief to find out what the British were hiding and improve the liaison relationship to the point where MI6 was prepared to share its intelligence. The OSS desperately needed to up its game in order to survive and the only way to do that was to take control of the circulation to US customers of the

MI6 reports. From now on 'working' MI6 would be the London station's main role.

'The job is to re-invigorate the British–American relationship here, step up the exchange of intelligence and experience and keep ourselves broadly informed of our friends' activities, plans and methods of operation,' one senior OSS official in London said, adding that they also needed to gather intelligence on MI6 to work out its post-war structure and how it operated. 'It should make for greater flexibility in dealing with our friends who, as you know, are not always as straightforward in their approach to mutual problems as we might like them to be.' MI6 political and economic reports and assessments from behind the Iron Curtain were of a 'very high calibre'. They were regarded in Washington as 'unequalled' and most customers would not know the reports they were receiving came not from the OSS but from MI6. 'It is true that at the moment our intake is not heavy. But there is reason to believe that we can step up the quantity.'[13]

Bross's efforts were in vain. On 20 September 1945, Truman disbanded the OSS, ordering the Research and Analysis branch to be handed to the State Department while the War Department was to take charge of X-2 and the Secret Intelligence branch, which together were to be reconstituted as the Strategic Services Unit (SSU) under Donovan's deputy, Brigadier-General John Magruder.[14]

Donovan and his OSS may have gone, but MI6 continued to cooperate with its much-reduced successor. At its peak more than 2,000 people worked at OSS London. The SSU maintained the London office and its close links to MI6 but with only seventy-three staff. 'Biffy' Dunderdale, whose Special Liaison Controllerate had taken over liaison with OSS, continued to discuss operations and targets, and share intelligence. But with the SSU ostensibly only a temporary fix for America's intelligence requirements, it was a tenuous existence, known to those like Dick Helms who went on to serve in the CIA as 'the dark days'. Paradoxically, thanks to the efforts of the London office, the number of reports it received from MI6 doubled. There was also local liaison between MI6 and SSU field stations in Europe, but this was never formalised and depended largely on individual relationships between the respective heads of station, a position that remained the case throughout the Cold War and indeed continues to the present day.[15]

Dick Cutler recalled that MI6 officers on the ground in Berlin were always willing to talk to their OSS counterparts. 'Especially helpful were frequent, long sessions in which the head of British MI6 counter-espionage in Berlin, Major James Brydon, and I shared our recent operations involving Soviet intelligence,' he said. 'A bachelor like me, he offset the loneliness of his secret work with a pet dog, a distinct rarity in food-short Berlin. Brydon was a quiet operative who had considerable experience with counter-espionage. In the fall of 1945, he was already working with the first defectors from the Soviet intelligence system. I admired British skill in attracting those defectors and hoped I could do the same. MI6 also explained that they had obtained extensive intelligence from Russian slave labourers in Germany.'[16]

Yet despite the OSS/SSU enthusiasm for extensive cooperation on Russian material in particular, and the improved reporting it produced, the anti-British attitudes that surrounded the demise of Donovan's OSS were pervasive. The defection in September 1945 of Igor Guzenko, an official at the Soviet embassy in Ottawa, had revealed that Alan Nunn May, a British scientist on the Allied atomic weapons programme, the Manhattan Project, was a Soviet agent. Congress was already debating a bill which, despite the start the British had given America in creating the atomic bomb, banned the exchange of atomic information with the UK.

When Dick Ellis went to Washington for talks with Magruder on cooperation in May 1946, he was told there was opposition in some quarters to any liaison with MI6 on the basis that it might feed the SSU intelligence specifically designed to promote British post-war policy objectives. Two months later, Colonel 'Buffalo Bill' Quinn, who had replaced Magruder as SSU director, told a gathering in Heidelberg of SSU European station chiefs that 'in dealing with foreign liaison people or groups the basic aim is to get everything and give nothing. That is the target.'[17]

The SSU in Berlin and Karlsruhe used Henry Sutton, a pre-war Austrian Social Democrat politician, and Peter Sichel, a German wine maker whose family had created the bestselling Blue Nun brand, to set up an impressive if overly ambitious network of more than 250 agents throughout the Soviet zone of eastern Germany. This moved in March 1946, under direct orders from Washington, to focusing more on the Soviet military.

'Washington required that we elevate military intelligence, especially the Order of Battle of the Soviet Armed Forces, to the highest priority, at no matter what cost to our other operations,' one senior SSU representative in Germany noted. 'Operations had to be greatly expanded, and with great speed. In retrospect it is easy to criticise this free and easy period, but at the time everyone—our customers, Heidelberg, Washington—was immensely pleased and kept on demanding more. There was a certain gratification in being able to pinpoint a target anywhere in the Russian Zone and dispatch an agent to cover it at a moment's notice.'

The networks were put together far too quickly with widespread use of inexperienced agents running their own sub-agents and, with the focus now almost entirely on Soviet targets, it did not take long for the Russians to detect the networks and find their way in. The main blow came over Christmas 1946, with other networks being picked off throughout the following year.[18]

Liaison with British intelligence 'followed a pattern of continuing friendliness and cooperation' but was quite badly hit in 1947 when material provided by MI6 was leaked to the US press, including a speech by Vasili Sokolovsky, the military governor of the Soviet zone, to East German industrialists threatening dire consequences if they did not increase production. Sokolovsky announced that, amid widespread vandalism and black-marketeering, political officers were to be placed in factories to uncover 'inefficiency, slackness, or incorrect political orientation'. But relations were not damaged for long and one SSU report back to Washington noted that 'mutual favours'—like the exchange of currencies between members of the MI6 and SSU Berlin stations, and the British willingness to secure thirty Volkswagens to replace the SSU's battered wartime jeeps—were 'a small but significant item in operational goodwill', ensuring that informal exchanges of secret intelligence between the UK and US missions continued.[19]

The creation in September 1947 of the Central Intelligence Agency (CIA) led to much closer relationships and joint operations in the field. One remarkable operation in post-war Berlin was aimed at obtaining the roubles needed to pay agents and fund operations inside the Soviet Union, a perennial problem for both MI6 and the CIA. MI6 took over a smuggling operation carried out by railwaymen on trains transporting industrial equipment to the Soviet Union.

The Russians were stripping German industry in the Soviet zone of all useful machinery and sending it back home by rail as 'war reparations'. Trains would leave Berlin and travel around the Soviet zone picking up wagons loaded with industrial equipment, and then make their way across Poland to Brest-Litovsk on the Soviet border to be unloaded. A number of East European Jews who had survived the concentration camps, led by a Pole who shared the surname of one of James Bond's most famous villains, Mandel Goldfinger, were now making a living on the black market. They were based around the Bahnhof Zoo, West Berlin's main railway station, flitting between the eastern and western sectors of Berlin.

Goldfinger bought gold jewellery cheaply from straitened Germans and sold it on to the occupying forces. His main interest in the smuggling ring was in Swiss gold watches, which were in high demand in the Soviet Union, particularly ladies' watches, which were known to the Russians as 'Damskis'. He and four other black-marketeers were recruited by MI6 officer Tony Divall, who operated under the work-name of 'Herr Stephan', to run a vastly expanded smuggling ring. Each of the five then enlisted their own railwaymen to smuggle the watches along the line. Goldfinger and his colleagues, who became known within MI6 as the 'Godfathers', bought the men's watches for around £18 each and the Damskis for just £4, selling them on to the railwaymen for £24 and £8 respectively. The Russians paid 1,000 roubles per watch and when the railwaymen returned from Brest-Litovsk with their roubles the Godfathers gave them £50 per 1,000 roubles, more than doubling the smugglers' money. As the official exchange rate was £100 per 1,000 roubles, and 'Herr Stephan' paid £70 per 1,000 roubles, everybody, MI6 included, was left in profit.

The railwaymen earned their money. The trains were regularly searched by border guards and the railway crews were riddled with informers. Initially the watches and roubles were concealed inside condoms suspended in a water tank, a piece of MI6 tradecraft that dated back to the Russian Revolution, but this limited the numbers that could be smuggled. So, MI6 recruited a railway engineer to hollow out various parts of the train to hide the contraband. The operation, which ran from 1946 to 1955, was so successful that the CIA tried to copy it, but this only led Goldfinger and his fellow Godfathers to play the two sides off against each other to demand more money, so MI6 turned it into a joint operation, keeping the prices at the original rates and producing large sums of roubles for itself and the Americans.[20]

While that level of collaboration between the CIA and MI6 took time to develop, there was far less debate over post-war cooperation with the British within the US signals intelligence community, which was all too aware of the debt it owed to its wartime counterparts at Bletchley Park. In the wake of the D-Day landings, with victory against the Nazis effectively guaranteed, the Allied codebreakers were already looking to the future. Despite orders from Roosevelt not to intercept the communications of their Russian ally, both the US Navy and US Army codebreakers had been running small-scale programmes on Russian codes and ciphers, the army with more success than the navy. By June 1944, there was increasing interest in Washington in any work the British had been doing on Russian communications. Bletchley swiftly agreed to share Russian material obtained from the interception of German signals intelligence communications networks, but this was nowhere near as much as the British had at their disposal.[21]

John Tiltman, who spoke fluent Russian, had done a lot of work on Soviet codes and ciphers between the wars, including liaison relationships with the Estonian and Finnish codebreakers which he personally established in the run-up to the Second World War and which produced a number of captured Soviet codebooks. He subsequently passed some of these on to the US codebreakers who visited Bletchley Park in February 1941. When Germany invaded the Soviet

Union in June 1941, Churchill ordered all work on Russian codes and ciphers to stop, but in fact it merely paused briefly, with a Polish signals intelligence team which had fled to Britain tasked to continue work on Soviet systems for the rest of the war.

During the autumn of 1944, the British had begun to intercept the high-level teleprinter network used by senior Soviet armed forces and Communist Party officials. A highly secret, fifty-strong joint section of Russian specialists from MI6 and the Government Code and Cipher School (GC&CS) was set up under Richard Pritchard, one of Tiltman's leading Soviet experts, to work on Russian material, codenamed Taper. Based in an anonymous office overlooking London's Sloane Square, it included Hugh Alexander and Gerry Morgan, two of the leading Bletchley codebreakers, as well as Bill Bonsall, a future director of GCHQ.[22]

GC&CS director 'Jumbo' Travis and Harry Hinsley, one of his key intelligence aides, toured the various signals intelligence centres around the world, from the Indian sub-continent to Australia and Pearl Harbor, in the spring of 1945 to discuss work on Japanese targets before arriving in Washington where, along with Clive Loehnis, a senior naval intelligence officer who would subsequently go on to head GCHQ, they hoped to discuss post-war cooperation.[23] Although an already ongoing but informal exchange of Russian, French and Dutch material was discussed, there was no attempt by either side to talk about what precisely would happen once the war was over. Nor did Travis tell the Americans the extent to which the British were working on Soviet material. He and his colleagues had assumed the Americans would want to discuss post-war cooperation but were reluctant to raise the issue themselves. It was clear both sides wanted it to continue, but neither was prepared to mention it first. This curious dance continued through the summer of 1945. Eric Jones, the highly influential head of Bletchley Park's Hut 3 intelligence section and another future director of GCHQ, was sent to Washington as senior liaison officer with the Americans, in a clear sign of how important the British saw a future relationship, but it was a result of a top secret joint mission to Germany which finally brought the two sides together.[24]

The Allied codebreakers had decided to send teams into Germany to discover what the German signals intelligence teams had uncovered about the Allies, and in particular the Russians. The most important of these Target Intelligence Committee (TICOM) missions, led by the US Navy codebreaker Howie Campaigne, was sent into Bavaria where, in late May 1945, in the small city of Rosenheim, it found a team of German codebreakers who had been working with a great deal of success on Russian communications and who had a cache of cryptographic machinery designed to decipher high-level Soviet military and civilian communications.

Soviet technicians had devised a system of encrypting teleprinter communications which split each message into nine different elements, each of which was sent on a separate radio channel. The message was then reassembled by the receiving station. The German codebreakers had developed equipment to intercept and decipher these transmissions and hoped the Allies might allow them to remain free in return for continuing to monitor the Russians on their behalf.

Selmer Norland, a US officer based at Bletchley, and Major Edward Rushworth, one of the senior British officers in Hut 3, were ordered to take the equipment and its operators back to England. 'I'll never forget leaving Rosenheim fairly early one morning,' said Norland. 'Major Rushworth was riding up in the front of the convoy of five lorries and I had the dubious honour of riding in the fifth lorry. That turned out to be slower than all the others. So, with a very sinking feeling, I saw the other four lorries disappear out of sight. I felt very much alone because the four ahead had all of the equipment and all of the German personnel were riding in my lorry. I was surrounded. I had a German driver and assistant driver in the cab with me and all of the other German personnel, I don't remember how many, fifteen or twenty, in the back of the lorry.

'I didn't realise then, I only discovered later, that neither hell nor high water would have kept them from following their equipment, they were so devoted to it. But I did have some very uneasy moments. Most of the overpasses on the autobahn had been blown up. So, there was a detour every time you came to an intersection and that would run down through German villages and as soon as the population, mostly women of course, saw there were German prisoners on the back of this truck, they came rushing out with food and coffee and things of that sort. So, I felt very much alone and very insecure, I can tell you.'

The capture of the German equipment to decipher the Russian teleprinter ciphers was probably the most important success of the TICOM missions. By the beginning of July, high-level Soviet tele-printer traffic from army staffs and Soviet Communist Party officials was being intercepted and deciphered in the UK, including messages to Stalin himself. Since it was a joint UK–US mission, both sides were involved in the interrogation of the German codebreakers and both saw the material produced once the equipment arrived back in the UK.

The British efforts to break Soviet codes and ciphers were assisted by an MI6 operation to purchase the expertise of Finnish codebreakers who had worked on Russian codes and ciphers from the earliest days and throughout the war. Believing that Moscow's peace terms for ending its war with the Soviet Union would lead to Soviet annexation of their country, the Finnish codebreakers fled en masse to Sweden, taking their families and equipment with them. The Finns had spent the past seventeen years attacking Soviet codes and ciphers. They not only provided assistance to the Swedish codebreakers, but also sold the details of 120 reconstructed Soviet codebooks and cipher systems to MI6.

Then, in late 1945, in a joint British–French operation organised by 'Biffy' Dunderdale, four of the Finnish codebreakers were taken to France, under the pretence that they were joining the Foreign Legion, even travelling via the Foreign Legion's training base at Sidi Bel Abbès in Algeria. They were based in the Château de Belloy just outside Paris, producing detailed reports from their archives on Soviet order of battle. Known as Source-267, the reports were passed on to the British codebreakers via the MI6 station in Paris.[25]

President Roosevelt had banned US codebreakers from working on the Russian ciphers, Howie Campaigne said. 'There were people down the line who thought that was very unwise. But when we uncovered these Germans there at Rosenheim, we got quite a lot of back traffic. They had some and they knew how to read some of it. So, they told us what they knew. That was a big step up. We enlarged on our Russian effort, which was still a deep secret as it was undercover sort of thing, and eventually the prohibition against working on Russian was relaxed.'[26]

The fact that the Americans had the full details of the German work on Russian codes forced the British to share all of their Russian material with the US codebreakers and led to discussion on how they might cooperate in breaking Soviet codes and ciphers in the future. 'Existing agreements between US and British SIGINT organisations governing the exploitation and disposal of captured equipment have made it unavoidable that the operation of the inter-cept gear should be undertaken under joint supervision,' one British official wrote, explaining why it was pointless trying to hide the British work on Soviet systems from the Americans. 'Such Russian traffic as is being intercepted is being seen by both US and British personnel. Joint exploitation of other Russian information (mainly medium-grade Russian cryptographic information) obtained from German captured SIGINT personnel has been unavoidable.'[27]

The following month, the US Navy and US Army codebreakers dropped the intense wartime rivalry and worked together in the post-war world. They would cooperate to intercept and read Soviet communications, which they codenamed Bourbon, and perhaps most importantly of all agreed that continued collaboration with the British was in the 'best US interests'.

The first complete exchanges between the US codebreakers and their British counterparts on Russian systems began in August 1945 and, according to the officer leading the US Army's work on Russian codes, the British material 'gave a much extended picture of the Bourbon traffic of every sort, since their intercept covers an area hitherto unattained by US sources'.[28]

Impressed by what the British were sending them, the US codebreakers sought agreement from the president to continue the wartime relationship into what became the Cold War. On 12 September, Truman authorised the US Army and US Navy to continue collaborating with the British on communications intelligence and 'to extend, modify or discontinue this collaboration, as determined to be in the best interests of the United States'.

A few weeks later, Travis, Hinsley and Tiltman flew to Washington for a month of discussions. Some of these were made more difficult by Admiral Redman's refusal to amend the American draft agreement in any way and by the belief among many of the US delegates that the British, now known as GCHQ, would use their superior codebreaking skills to collect economic data that would enable British industry to outperform its US competitors. But eventually a way forward was agreed that allowed both sides to cooperate, not just with each other but with Canada, Australia and New Zealand, if the other side agreed. Although New Zealand was not specifically mentioned in the discussions, it was covered by the use of the term 'British Dominions' in the text.

The details of the agreement took nearly six months to nail down but at a conference in London in March there was finally agreement not on 'complete' cooperation but on 'unrestricted' cooperation on communications intelligence (COMINT). Stewart Menzies told the delegates at the conference that it was difficult to exaggerate the seriousness of the international situation. He stressed the importance of what became known as the BRUSA agreement 'both in ensuring cooperation in the SIGINT field and in its effect in cementing the relations between the two countries generally'. The MI6 Chief also told the delegates that, at a separate Commonwealth conference a few weeks earlier, Canada, Australia and New Zealand had accepted the terms under which they would be invited to take part, effectively laying the ground for what more than fifty years later would become known as the Five Eyes intelligence alliance.[29]

There was another Anglo-American intelligence exchange which continued after the Second World War. The OSS-controlled Foreign Broadcast Intelligence Service (FBIS),* which monitored radio broadcasts around the world, had leaned heavily on the BBC

---

* Subsequently renamed the Foreign Broadcast Information Service.

Monitoring Service, based at Caversham Park, north of Reading, for its wartime coverage of public broadcasting from Germany, Italy and occupied Europe. In July 1947, the FBIS, now part of the CIA and relying just as heavily on the BBC for reporting of Soviet radio stations, was anxious to extend the cooperation into the post-war period. It agreed to exchange BBC reporting from Europe and the Soviet Union for the areas in the Far East and Latin America where its own operations were strongest, replicating the process of dividing the world into areas where one or other side led the coverage that was being worked out between GCHQ and its US counterparts.

Throughout the Cold War, in a good example of the importance of open-source intelligence (OSINT), news of what was going on in the closed societies of the Soviet Union and its eastern European satellites, from the Soviet test of its first atomic bomb in 1949 to the nuclear accident at Chernobyl in 1986, was picked up first by the BBC Monitoring Service. Its interception of Soviet and eastern European radio was so valuable to the CIA that it had its own staff based at Caversham Park in a little-known area of transatlantic intelligence cooperation.[30]

The most important reason the intelligence liaison between Britain and America continued into the Cold War was that both sides recognised the other could make a vital contribution to the collection of intelligence, which, as a result of the wartime successes, senior decision makers on both sides of the Atlantic now saw as the norm. The spectacular triumphs of both Bletchley Park and the US codebreakers, pooling their resources to break Japanese and German ciphers more efficiently than either could have done alone, and the game-changing impact this had on every front of the war, shaped the way the relationship worked in a post-war world where Russia was now the main threat, controlling much of Europe and pushing an alien creed which challenged America's view of the world. Britain not only shared US antipathy to Soviet-style communism, it had a proven capability, and far greater experience than the US agencies, in both codebreaking and the gathering of human intelligence, with the considerable bonus of overseas bases across the

Empire that enabled the Americans and British intelligence agencies to cover the entire world.

By September 1945, GCHQ was sending the Americans material produced from a Russian enciphered teleprinter system known as Caviar, which was almost certainly broken as a result of the Norland–Rushworth TICOM mission. A few months later, Arlington Hall broke the machine cipher in use by Red Army command units in the Soviet Far East, codenaming it Sauterne. The most important success against Soviet armed forces machine ciphers of the early Cold War came at the beginning of 1946 when GCHQ, now based at Eastcote in north London, broke the first of several mainline Soviet armed forces machine ciphers which it dubbed the 'Poets Systems'.

The initial break came with a cipher codenamed Coleridge, which was used on the Soviet Army, Navy and Air Force mainline circuits inside the Soviet Union. The Coleridge operation was led by Hugh Alexander. The Soviet circuits using the machine were largely concerned with administrative matters, but this nevertheless produced a great deal of intelligence on the Soviet armed forces' order of battle and their peacetime activities. The ability to read Coleridge was a very important success. Soviet military strengths, capabilities and dislocations were second only to the extent of Soviet atomic capabilities in the wishlist handed to Britain's intelligence agencies by the post-war JIC. GCHQ was also working on another Soviet cipher machine, Albatross, a name that suggests that it may have been associated in some way with Coleridge.

The British ability to make the initial breaks into new systems, which had been one of the key foundations of the wartime alliance, was an important factor in ensuring the Americans overcame their concerns about maintaining the relationship with the British. The US Navy liaison officer at Eastcote reported back to Washington in April 1947 that Coleridge was 'the most important, high-level system from which current intelligence may be produced and is so in fact regarded here'. There was a further break into a 'Poets' system in February 1947, when in what appears to have been the first joint attack of the Cold War, GCHQ cryptanalysts led by Gerry Morgan, working in tandem with a team of US Navy codebreakers led by Howie Campaigne, solved and began to exploit a system which they codenamed Longfellow.[31]

But disaster was about to strike. The KGB had a long-term agent-in-place inside the US Army's Russian section at Arlington Hall. William Weisband had been born in Odessa, then part of Russia, in 1908. He had emigrated with his parents to the US in the 1920s and become a US citizen in 1938. But he had already been recruited as a KGB agent. Called up in 1942, he became a codebreaker, working in north Africa and Italy before being brought back to Arlington Hall because he could speak Russian. As a result, the Soviet armed forces knew precisely how many codes and ciphers the British and Americans were breaking and had plenty of time to ensure that when they changed their systems the Western codebreakers would be unable to get back in any time soon.

For the first three years of the post-war period, Allied intercept operators and intelligence analysts had enjoyed a relatively easy time tracking the Soviet armed forces radio networks. On 29 October 1948, 'Black Friday' as it became known, things began to change. Soviet networks that had been tracked, and their ciphers broken, began dropping off the air. Over the following weekend more and more networks disappeared as the Soviet authorities switched their most important links to landline communications, sending only dummy messages on the networks that remained.

It was not until the real traffic began reappearing in early 1949 that the full scale of the changes emerged. Soviet signal security had been completely revamped. Only the Soviet armed forces machine cipher Albatross, which GCHQ's greatest talents had failed to break, remained in place. The broken ciphers had been dropped and replaced, leaving them virtually unreadable for around five years. It would not be until the mid-1970s that the US and British codebreakers would get back to anything like the capability they had on the day before 'Black Friday', and that would be in no small way the result of a remarkably generous decision by the British codebreakers to send their leading codebreaker and top Russian expert to America to help their US colleagues.

John Tiltman, now the GCHQ assistant director in charge of codebreaking, was sent to Washington 'urgently' on 19 March 1949. Ostensibly he was simply the new senior British liaison officer. In reality, he was there to provide the experience and expertise the Americans would need if they were to get back into the Soviet codes and ciphers.[32]

6

PLAYING MOSCOW AT
ITS OWN GAME

Truman may have begun his presidency by underestimating the Soviet threat, referring to Stalin as 'Uncle Joe' and describing him as 'honest', but he soon realised the reality of Moscow's quest to dominate the countries around its borders, imposing communist regimes across eastern Europe, demanding chunks of Turkish and Iranian territory and making aggressive attempts to influence the political situation in Italy and Greece.

The defection of Igor Guzenko in September 1945 and the decision two months later by Soviet spy Elizabeth Bentley to go to the FBI, together with their revelations of spies inside the Manhattan Project and the US government, coincided with an influential telegram from George Kennan, the US chargé d'affaires in Moscow, outlining the view that the Russians were intent on subverting capitalism by means of 'an underground operating directorate of world communism, a concealed Comintern tightly coordinated and directed by Moscow'. The US response to this aggressive Soviet policy 'must be that of long-term, patient but firm and vigilant containment of Russian expansive tendencies . . . with unalterable counter-force at every point where they show signs of encroaching upon the interests of a peaceful and stable world'.

The British position was outlined by the JIC, which noted that 'Communism is the most important external political menace confronting the British Commonwealth and is likely to remain so in the foreseeable future' and that 'Russian policy will be aggressive by all measures short of war'. Stalin was unlikely to start a major war unless he unwittingly pushed America or Britain too far, but 'we cannot exclude the possibility that Russia may pursue a policy, which will present the West with local *faits accomplis*'.[1]

The Kennan telegram was immensely influential, ultimately leading to the 'Truman doctrine', a combination of containment of Soviet expansionism and, where possible, 'rollback' of communist control. Kennan was not alone in flagging up the advent of the Cold War. In many ways, the more public, rhetorical flourish of Britain's wartime leader was even more significant. On 5 March 1946, Churchill, now out of office but still well briefed on intelligence matters, made a speech at Fulton, Missouri, that was to herald a radical sea change in the public perception of the Soviet Union, both in Britain and America.

'From Stettin in the Baltic to Trieste in the Adriatic, an iron curtain has descended across the continent,' Churchill said. 'Behind that line lie all the capitals of the ancient states of central and eastern Europe. Warsaw, Berlin, Prague, Vienna, Budapest, Bucharest and Sofia, all these famous cities and the populations around them lie in the Soviet sphere and all are subject, in one form or another, not only to Soviet influence but to a very high and in some cases increasing measure of control from Moscow.'

As the Russians sought to subvert Greece, Italy and France, imposed a communist government on Czechoslovakia and blockaded Berlin, trying unsuccessfully to force the British, American and French Allies to leave, and Mao Zedong's communist guerrillas swept across China, creating a bamboo curtain on the other side of the world, it merely confirmed what the US and British intelligence services had known since long before the Second World War came to an end. For the foreseeable future their main role would be dealing with the Soviet Union, China and their respective communist satellite states.

If American human intelligence operations against the Soviet Union were initially hampered by the lack of a clear successor to the OSS, their UK equivalents were continually hamstrung by officialdom in the shape of the Foreign Office. At the end of the war,

Stewart Menzies had been told by Alexander Cadogan that he was banned from running any operations from the British embassy in Moscow. All MI6 intelligence operations against Moscow would have to be penetration operations from outside the Soviet Union.[2]

Even before the end of the war, MI6 had begun drawing up plans whereby its officers and agents would be sent into a post-war Soviet Union either under 'official cover' as members of trade delegations or under 'natural cover' as businessmen, engineers and industrialists. There were even suggestions in a 1943 report into the future of MI6 in the post-war world that it might set up its own companies carrying out genuine business to offer a vehicle for espionage.

But the main plans focused on the long-standing MI6 practice of recruiting agents among businessmen visiting the Soviet Union. Agents could also be recruited among cultural organisations that organised exchanges with the Russians on music, ballet, drama and sport, one MI6 officer suggested. 'A start could be made now by preparing the ground with the Football Association to get them to be prepared to start work straight away,' he added.

Commercial companies doing legitimate business in the Soviet Union that were to be used as vehicles for espionage included the Hudson's Bay Company, which had performed that role before the war; the Sir Henry Lunn Travel company;* Harland and Wolff, who were about to start talks on the construction of icebreakers for the Russian merchant fleet; and Johnson Matthey, who 'have entered into preliminary talks with the Russian Trade Mission on the processing and distribution of Russian platinum and other rare metals'. Given that Kim Philby was a member of the committee drawing up these plans, it is unsurprising that they were passed to the KGB before anyone in MI6 had begun to enact them.[3]

The other long-standing MI6 practice which would allow the collection of intelligence without any action taken from inside the British embassy was the use of anti-Soviet émigré organisations. The first MI6 attempt to set up an intelligence network in Latvia had taken place shortly after that country was annexed by Moscow

---

* The company subsequently became Lunn Poly, then Thomson Travel, and is now part of TUI.

in June 1940. Kenneth Benton and his wife, Peggy, then posted to the service's Riga station, trained a stay-behind agent to use a small wireless, but after sending three messages detailing Russian activities he disappeared. 'There were no more messages from our agent and we concluded that the Soviet police or NKVD [a KGB predecessor] had traced his signals and located him,' Kenneth Benton said.[4]

MI6 resumed its attempts to set up networks in the Baltic republics in 1945. Anthony Cavendish was one of the officers charged with sending Latvian émigrés back into their homeland to produce intelligence on the Russians. 'Youngish men were recruited,' Cavendish recalled. 'Those who were, firstly, ideologically sound; secondly, who were prepared to return to their homelands and for whom a fitting cover story could be produced; and, thirdly, who could successfully complete our training course, which involved instruction in radio, weapons, explosives and subjects essential to secret communication such as codes, ciphers and the use of secret inks.'

The agents were quietly flown to the UK for training. About a week before they were due to set off, they were returned to an RAF airfield in Germany accompanied by their conducting officer. The émigré agents were smuggled in on a former Wehrmacht patrol boat, the *S-208*, skippered by one of the most successful of the German wartime S-boat captains, Lieutenant-Commander Hans Helmut Klose. 'My job was to liaise with the naval intelligence officers involved in supervising Klose and his vessel, and to see that, from the time the agents arrived in Germany to the time they boarded the *S-208*, they were securely housed and adequately protected,' Cavendish said. 'After they had boarded the *S-208*, my job was to liaise with Naval Intelligence during the progress of the boat's mission, since she would keep radio silence until she had dropped our agents and was on her return voyage.'[5]

But the émigrés had little idea of security, often getting drunk and bragging to friends and relatives about their mission to save their homeland even before they went in. They were very swiftly rounded up by the authorities. Major Jānis Lukaševics, a Latvian KGB officer, organised a deception operation to convince the British that their agents were in place. 'We had to know the MI6 plans and the only way we could do that was by successfully infiltrating our men into the MI6 networks,' Lukaševics said. Once the networks were infiltrated, the KGB men were to be left in place, feeding back false information to London and providing Soviet intelligence with details of what the British were trying to do. 'There was a decision not to touch them, to continue finding out what their specific tasks were. Well, we quite quickly found out that their job was not just spying but also to prepare the way for other spies, to set up a link and new points of support and to establish contact with resistance groups.'[6]

A substantial number of British agents, most of them émigrés, were dispatched to Lithuania, Estonia and Latvia, but Soviet penetration of the émigré groups meant that many of the operations were blown before they even began and those that were successful in setting up intelligence networks produced very little information of any real value.[7]

'We were underfunded from the start,' recalled Benton. 'The KGB was streets ahead of us in almost every way. They were extremely well trained and well manned, and they had absolutely unlimited money. We had none. We had very, very little. The only way we could have got penetration agents right into Russia would have been a long-term process. It would have been putting in sleepers over a long period of years costing money. We never got the money from the Foreign Office. They had a stranglehold over us, not only on our finances, but over the way we went about our work. Every time we produced a scheme that looked promising, the Foreign Office wouldn't agree.'[8]

The attempts by the SSU to use émigrés to penetrate the Soviet Union fared little better. It focused on Ukraine, sending in agents to set up intelligence networks among opponents of the regime in an operation codenamed Belladonna. It was run from Munich by SSU station chief Bill Holtsman, and from Vienna through a Hungarian SSU agent, Zsolt Aradi, but the results were at best 'minimal'. By early 1947, SSU headquarters in Washington was complaining that 'intelligence derived from such Ukrainian groups is not worth the time and effort'. The information the émigrés provided was 'low-grade and ideologically biased' and they were so defensive of their 'sub-sources' that it was impossible to verify the quality of the intelligence. The headquarters' assessment was unequivocal. 'It is seriously recommended that this contact be severed completely.' The operations lingered on briefly but when the CIA took over, they were abruptly closed down. Harry Rositzke, who would go on to lead successful penetration operations into the Soviet Union, was highly critical of the 'hasty exploitation' of Ukrainian, Georgian and Baltic émigrés who were sent in regardless of the 'dangerous security and political hazards'.[9]

None of this would have surprised those British and American intelligence officers who had been based in displaced-persons camps in Germany at the end of the war. As they interrogated Soviet defectors and line crossers, it became clear that most of the Russian, Ukrainian and Baltic émigré groups had been penetrated by Soviet agents. Arnold Silver, a US Army intelligence officer who worked as an interrogator in the camps before going on to join the CIA, described the evidence of such penetration as 'staggeringly convincing'. Silver found it 'astonishing' that both MI6 and the CIA nevertheless decided to use the émigré groups to set up networks inside the Soviet Union. 'Given the scale of Soviet penetration of the groups, it could not be expected that such operations would benefit anybody but the KGB, and of course the CIA and MI6 suffered one disaster after another,' Silver later recalled. 'There was not one successful operation. The mass of information militating against this kind of blindness on the part of those responsible for the decision to operate with émigré groups was simply ignored, resulting in many lost lives of émigré agents.'[10]

As Stewart Menzies negotiated with the services over their post-war intelligence requirements, MI6 was told that its most urgent priority was information on the Soviet Union's attempts to produce an atomic bomb. US intelligence officers were given the same 'number one' priority. MI6 officers in Germany began recruiting low-level scientists in the Russian zone. 'We are convinced', one British official said, 'there is an opportunity now to obtain high-grade intelligence from these men which will enable us to build up an almost complete picture of Russian scientific and technical activities in Germany and so make it possible to forecast more accurately than we can at present the progress of Russian development of weapons during future years.'[11]

The Allied efforts to keep track of the Soviet atomic weapons programme, which the Russians codenamed Operation Borodino, were among the closest joint operations between MI6 and its US counterparts, the OSS, the SSU and finally the CIA, in the immediate post-war period. They evolved from those created during the war to track the German atomic weapons programme, when an Anglo-American Intelligence Committee was based in London under the control of Michael Perrin, the Ministry of Supply's deputy controller atomic energy, and with MI6 officer Eric Welsh as the senior intelligence officer.

A Combined Anglo-American Intelligence Unit was set up in the immediate aftermath of the US atomic bomb attacks on the Japanese cities of Hiroshima and Nagasaki to focus on the Soviet atomic weapons programme, which unbeknown to the British or Americans had been based in substantial part on British research passed to Moscow by John Cairncross, the so-called 'Fifth Man' in the Cambridge spy ring, who throughout 1941 was private secretary to Lord Hankey.

As minister without portfolio in the Churchill government, Hankey was in charge of investigating a wide range of top secret projects, including Tube Alloys, the British atomic weapons programme, which at the time was ahead of its US counterpart, the Manhattan Project. Hankey was chairman of a committee known as the Scientific Advisory Committee, which reviewed two reports summarising British research into the potential of the atomic bomb. These reports, 'Use of Uranium for a Bomb' and 'Use of Uranium as a Source of Power', were passed to the Americans in August 1941, a transfer of information that helped to kick-start the Manhattan Project.

A few weeks later, Cairncross, who was the committee's joint secretary, passed them to the Russians, and according to Igor Kurchatov, the so-called 'father of the Soviet atomic bomb', they formed the basis for the Soviet atomic weapons programme. Hankey was also a member of the Tube Alloys Consultative Committee, which subsequently oversaw the British atomic weapons programme. His boss's position gave Cairncross extensive access to information that was as invaluable to the Russians as it was to the Americans.[12]

The British effort to obtain intelligence on the Soviet atomic weapons programme, led by Perrin and Welsh, was located in Shell-Mex House, overlooking the Thames in central London, with Welsh reporting directly to Menzies. The US intelligence efforts were originally led by the US Army and then by the Manhattan Engineering Department (MED) of the US Atomic Energy Commission. While the limits of the McMahon Act restricted how much technical information the Americans could share with the British, ways were found round the problem, not least because much of the intelligence was being supplied by MI6 sources in Germany. Welsh was not the scientific expert he purported to be but he was adept at 'schmoozing' the US scientists, using them as 'unwitting agents' to obtain information to fill the gaps in what the Americans were providing. Arnold Kramish, the MED's intelligence liaison officer with the British, recalled that Malcolm Henderson, the deputy head of the MED, was 'one of Eric's best American spies', regularly taking top secret files home to share with Welsh.

As the Allied forces invaded Germany, the US and British intelligence services had not only seized scientists in their own zones of occupation, they had snatched others from the French and Soviet zones and launched a bomb attack on the Auer company's uranium oxide plant at Oranienburg, 15 miles north of Berlin in the Soviet zone, in order to reduce its usefulness to the Russians, who nevertheless transferred everything that was left back to the USSR.

The early intelligence on the Russian efforts to build a bomb came from British and US agents in the Soviet zone and from the interception of the letters home from German scientists taken to the Soviet Union to work on the programme. MI6 tracked the movement of leading German scientists who had been involved in the German weapons programme to Russia. They included Gustav Hertz, a Nobel Prize winner in physics who had devised the gaseous diffusion method of separating isotopes, and Nikolaus Riehl, the chief scientific director of the Auer plant.

The interception of the scientists' letters allowed the Combined Anglo-American Intelligence Unit to work out where each was based, while their individual specialities indicated what role that particular location had in the overall Soviet programme. As Henry Lowenhaupt, one of the scientists working in the CIA team, recalled, MI6 agents inside Czechoslovakia were able to report that one 10-ton rail truck full of uranium ore was sent from the Jáchymov mine in the Ore Mountains on the border with Germany to Elektrostal, to the east of Moscow, every ten days. 'The UK had also learned that the Russians were requiring the former Bitterfeld plant of IG Farben to set up the production of highly pure metallic calcium at 30 tons a month, enough for the manufacture (by oxide reduction) of 60 tons of uranium metal,' Lowenhaupt said. 'Several Bitterfeld chemical engineers chose to resettle at IG Farben plants in British-occupied Germany, thoughtfully taking with them copies of reports on calcium production written for the Russian management. Penetration sources had furnished the specifications on the amounts of impurities allowable in the calcium. These conclusively indicated that it was for atomic use.'

An SSU agent inside the Bitterfeld plant reported in early 1946 that some of the German scientists, including Hertz, were at 'Institute A' at Sukhumi on the eastern coast of the Black Sea, a little more than 100 miles north of the Turkish border. Meanwhile, Riehl's former secretary defected to the British, telling MI6 that his last letter was postmarked from Elektrostal. It was quite a moment for Lowenhaupt and the rest of the US and British analysts working on the Soviet atomic weapons programme. 'The circumstantial evidence that Elektrostal was the site of the Russian uranium metal plant was becoming impressive,' Lowenhaupt recalled. Nevertheless, at the end of October 1946, the US–UK assessment of the capability of the Soviet Union to produce an atomic bomb was that while the information available to the Allies was 'meagre', the Russian atomic weapons programme was limited so that they would not be able to produce an atomic bomb until 'sometime between 1950 and 1953'.

At the beginning of 1947, Adolf Krebs, a German scientist who had been approached by the Russians to join the programme, spoke to the Americans after returning to Germany. He corroborated much of what the British and Americans had worked out. Krebs confirmed that the Hertz group at Sukhumi was working on isotope separation problems and revealed that research was also taking place there on different ways of producing heavy water. The Russians had taken Krebs to Elektrostal in the hope that Riehl would be able to persuade him to take part in the programme, so he was able to tell the Americans that the former Auer scientists were 'segregating uranium on a production scale using a new process which utilised electric furnaces'. He also reported that Kurt Patzschke, the former director of the Jáchymov mine, was in charge of a group prospecting for uranium ore in the Fergana Valley near Tashkent in central Asia.

Meanwhile, Welsh mounted a major operation to penetrate the Bitterfeld plant in more depth. He tried to persuade the Americans to drop their source inside the plant, fearing that he or she would compromise the MI6 operation, but the SSU refused. 'Welsh's fear of American "clumsiness" was misplaced,' Lowenhaupt said. 'Welsh's confidence in his Bitterfeld penetration, however, was not misplaced at all. From its inception it produced long sheets of monthly shipment statistics on a box-by-box basis. Selected product analyses were received periodically, and Russian specifications and requirements as they occurred. These data were interpreted in the light of the design reports which the British (and to a lesser extent we ourselves) had already received. In addition, the agent usually added comments as needed for understanding. Indeed, it is fair to say that as far as the technical side of the Bitterfeld calcium operation was concerned, by 1948 the British (and in turn we ourselves) knew as much about it as the Russians did.'

Despite the SSU's initial refusal to put its agent on hold, he was subsequently stood down. Perrin told the JIC in August 1947 that 'by agreement with our American colleagues, who incidentally uncovered this line, they have not been making special efforts to follow it up, nor will they now do so. It was agreed that the British agencies would be in a better position to do this. There is, therefore, no danger of the wires being crossed between the Americans and ourselves in the collecting field.'

The US change of heart may have been because the extent of the intelligence being produced by Welsh's agent was so comprehensive or because by now the MED intelligence section had been absorbed into the CIA, becoming the Nuclear Energy Group in the Office of Scientific Intelligence. Whatever the reason, the information provided by the MI6 agent left little doubt that the purity of the calcium was so high it could only be required for the Soviet atomic weapons programme and that the aim was to produce a plutonium bomb.

A CIA source in the Soviet zone revealed in late 1948 or early 1949 that the Russians were extracting far more uranium from mines in the Ore Mountains than the British and the Americans had thought possible, which led to a revision of the joint US–UK assessment of how many bombs the Russians would be able to produce. Nevertheless, the persistent Allied position was that Moscow would not be able to produce an atomic bomb before January 1950 at the very earliest. Indeed, the JIC was even more cautious, pushing that date back a year to January 1951. It was a shock when the Russians successfully tested their first nuclear device, codenamed First Lightning, at Semipalatinsk in Kazakhstan on 29 August 1949.[13]

The fact that the Russian test came as a complete surprise was undoubtedly a major intelligence failure. But ironically, the MI6 intelligence from Bitterfeld, which showed that the Russians were producing a plutonium bomb rather than using uranium, almost certainly fed into the belief that it would take the Russians far longer to achieve. A few weeks after the Soviet test, it emerged that Klaus Fuchs, a German physicist working for the British Tube Alloys atomic weapons programme, was a KGB spy. In January 1950, as part of the British investigation into Fuchs, Perrin interviewed him on what he had given the Russians.

While Fuchs's own work, which focused largely on the gaseous diffusion method of separating isotopes, was described by the KGB's Moscow Centre in early 1945 as having been of 'great value' to Borodino, it was no longer needed once Hertz, who had pioneered the process, joined the Soviet atomic weapons programme a few months later. It was the information Fuchs learned during his two years with the Manhattan Project at Los Alamos, New Mexico, from August 1944 to the summer of 1946, which was crucial to Igor Kurchatov and his team, cutting as much as eighteen months off the time it took for the Russians to build a successful plutonium bomb.

'While there he learnt the details of the design and method of operation of the alternative type of atomic bomb using plutonium, produced in an atomic pile, instead of U.235,' Perrin said. 'The use of this materiel requires the solution of much more difficult technical problems and Fuchs stated that he had passed to the Russian agent a full account of the make-up of the first bomb that was successfully tested in New Mexico in July 1945. This information would undoubtedly save a long period of research and development that must otherwise elapse between the first large-scale production of plutonium and its use as the explosive ingredient in an atomic bomb.'[14]

The Bitterfeld mission was one of a number of joint British–American intelligence operations taking place in the Soviet satellites in eastern Europe, although, as with any intelligence operation, they tended to emerge only when something went wrong, as it did in Romania in late 1947. Careless tradecraft by two CIA officers based in the US embassy in Bucharest led to the arrests of a number of Romanian opponents of the regime who had been approached in a joint CIA–MI6 operation. The two CIA officers were swiftly withdrawn but not before secret police had held one senior US diplomat at gunpoint and searched one of the CIA officers' homes.

The resultant trial of twelve Romanians, who were handed long prison sentences for 'high treason, espionage conspiracy, subversive activities and economic sabotage in complicity with United States and British agents', would not have encouraged other Romanians to work for either the CIA or MI6. Opponents of the CIA in Washington were not slow to leak news of the intelligence disaster, with one *New York Times* commentator referring to the two CIA officers dismissively as 'carry-overs from the OSS' who had carelessly carried a list of the names of the agents 'and even the minutes of the "secret" meetings held—apparently in order to impress their superiors'.[15]

At the beginning of 1946, the SOE had been absorbed into MI6 as the Special Operations Branch, retaining some of its most valuable agents in Germany and Austria as well as a number of experts on eastern Europe. The branch was led by Harold 'Perks' Perkins, the former head of the SOE's Polish section, who had already handed over many of his former agents behind the Iron Curtain to MI6 to protect his networks from being closed down on the orders of the Foreign Office, which at the time was determined to appease the Russians.

'Perks' was described by one colleague as 'the only man I have ever seen bend a poker in his hands'. He was given the title of Adviser, Special Operations, and put in charge of operations already in place to protect Iran from Soviet influence. The refusal of the Soviet Union to withdraw, as agreed, from those areas of northern Iran it had occupied during the war (in a joint operation with the British, who had dispatched troops to take control of the south) led the Foreign Office to order Stewart Menzies to prepare 'a detailed plan for immediate action' to support resistance operations. In the event, Soviet troops withdrew that May, but the plans stayed in place.

Perkins also used his contacts in Poland to cause problems for the communists in the run-up to the fraudulent elections of January 1947, which confirmed the Soviet control of the country with falsified results, electing the communist Polish Workers' Party to power. He sent former SOE officer David Smiley to Warsaw under cover of assistant military attaché to carry out subversive operations designed to put the communists in a bad light. 'I had not only been under the orders of Perks for certain operations but he insisted on joining me for the more hazardous and exciting missions,' Smiley recalled. 'Perks was a big man, full of fun and not only a brave and congenial companion on operations, but a leader for whom it was a pleasure to work.'

The Foreign Office, and Sir Archibald Clark Kerr, the British ambassador in Moscow, continued their ban on any MI6 operations being carried out from within the Soviet Union. Instead, Perkins was ordered to prepare plans for aggressive special operations, stay-behind forces and potential resistance forces inside a number of countries that might be the first to be overrun in the event of a Soviet attack on the West. They included Afghanistan, Iran, Iraq, Turkey, Greece, Czechoslovakia (which at the time had not been absorbed into the Soviet Bloc), Italy, Austria, Germany, Denmark, Sweden, Norway and Finland.[16]

When a conference of the foreign ministers of Britain, the United States, France and the Soviet Union, held in London in late 1947, broke down in acrimony, with British foreign secretary Ernest Bevin accusing his Russian counterpart, Vyacheslav Molotov, of 'duplicity' over the future of Germany, influential voices in London and Washington decided enough was enough. They were beginning to see special operations as the most effective way of responding to the aggressive approach the Russians were taking in Europe and the Middle East, fitting as they did with the Truman doctrine of a combination of containment and rollback.

Shortly before Christmas, the British Chiefs of Staff asked the Foreign Office to consider whether, given that 'Russia has forced upon us a state of conflict which might be termed the "cold war"', Britain in tandem with America should not 'unleash political warfare against the Soviet [Union] of the same ruthless type that the Soviet [Union] employs against the Americans and ourselves'. They suggested that Britain agree a joint political warfare plan with the Americans to 'play the Russians at their own game'.

By now Clark Kerr had moved to Washington, and his successor, Sir Maurice Peterson, frustrated by the Soviet attitude, welcomed a change in policy. The Foreign Office asked Menzies to put together a list of covert special operations that Perkins and his team might carry out around the world. The paper specifically suggested using underground opposition networks to mount special operations inside Russian-controlled territory. It stressed that such operations must be absolutely deniable—'HMG must in no way be implicated'. The suggested operations ranged from infiltrating factories and trade unions to promote strikes, through the framing of party officials with planted evidence, to sabotage, arson, bombings, the kidnapping of senior officials to give the appearance that they had defected, and even the 'liquidation of selected individuals'.

Bevin, a bluff, no-nonsense former trade unionist who was an ardent advocate of British support for America against the Soviet Union, gave Menzies and Perkins 'a free hand to carry out such special operations as are possible in peace time in the Soviet Union itself and in the Soviet Zones of Germany and Austria'. He also ordered the encouragement of organisations inside the Soviet satellite states that 'would form the basis for a resistance movement if that became necessary later' and, with the ambassador's backing, authorised Menzies to place a senior officer in the embassy with a mandate to resume limited operations against the Russians.[17]

At the same time as this debate was going on in London, Frank Wisner, a former OSS officer now working for the State Department, produced an influential paper which argued that the US was 'ill-equipped to engage in the political and psychological conflict with the Soviet Union now forced upon us'. Despite the earlier British and US failures in the Baltic republics and Ukraine, Wisner advocated that the CIA make more use of the 'mass of refugees' who had fled the Soviet Union and eastern Europe for the West and included members of their countries' political elites. 'The government is inadequately informed regarding the Soviet World, even in official intelligence there are large and vitally important gaps,' Wisner said. He urged that the CIA consider using the émigrés to provide intelligence and take part in 'politico-psychological' operations that would 'further US interests in the current struggle with the USSR and whatever may eventuate therefrom'.[18]

The calls for more use of refugees from the Eastern Bloc were raised in London a few weeks later by Denis Healey, then a senior Labour foreign affairs adviser, who suggested that Britain should ask the Americans 'what their intentions were about supporting the efforts of some of the prominent political refugees from the Iron Curtain countries in their efforts to keep anti-Communist movements going inside their countries'. Healey referred to the US debate on the subject and said that while Britain should shy away from encouraging 'active insurrection', the refugees could provide valuable intelligence. But he warned that, without British involvement, 'the Americans would very likely go further and make a mess of it' by using 'irresponsible people of the OSS-type'.

Junior foreign minister Hector McNeil argued rather optimistically that if the British were involved 'we might be able to make their plans wiser than they would otherwise be, and perhaps even reach agreement that they would supply the bulk of the funds which might be required, and we undertake the main direction'. George Kennan reassured one of his British counterparts that while some of the US plans for 'subversive actions' behind the Iron Curtain had 'made his hair stand on end' those ideas had been 'sat on'.[19] Nevertheless, the momentum in Washington was such that when Jack Easton, now assistant chief of MI6, flew to the US capital in early May for discussions with CIA boss Admiral Roscoe H. Hillenkoetter on the agenda for a joint MI6–CIA conference to be held in London a few weeks later, the subject of special operations dominated his meetings.[20]

Hillenkoetter was understandably reluctant to repeat the previous failures with émigré organisations, telling the National Security Council (NSC) that

these groups are highly unstable and undependable, split by personal rivalries and ideological differences, and primarily concerned with developing a secure position for themselves in the Western world. They have been completely unable to provide intelligence of real value since they are rarely able to tap useful sources of information within the USSR, and generally concentrate on producing highly biased propaganda materials in place of objective intelligence. They immediately capitalise upon any assistance which they receive to advertise the fact of official support to their colleagues and to other governments in order to advance their own personal or organisational interests. CIA has sufficient evidence at this time to indicate that many of these groups have already been successfully penetrated by Soviet and satellite intelligence agencies.[21]

He was wasting his breath. To make matters worse, the KGB were already receiving detailed briefings on the British discussions with their American colleagues from McNeil's private secretary, Guy Burgess, another member of the Cambridge spy ring. The homosexual Burgess, codenamed MÄDCHEN, German for 'young girl', by his KGB handlers, told Moscow that 'the basic dilemma for British foreign policy . . . is this: a desire and determination to confront the Soviet Union everywhere—in Germany, in south-east Europe and in the Middle-East—but without causing a military conflict with Russia, and how is this to be reconciled with policy designed to secure the support of the USA without being drawn into an American war with Russia.'[22]

In early June 1948, the NSC, in response to Moscow's 'vicious covert activities', agreed the creation by the State Department of a special operations organisation to counter the Soviet threat, to be hidden inside the CIA. At the time of the NSC discussions it was designated the Office for Special Services, which reflected a rather extravagant disregard for the dangers inherent—far more in Washington than Moscow—in the use of the initials OSS. By the time the NSC published the directive authorising its formation, it had become the Office for Special Projects. Its eventual title, the Office of Policy Coordination (OPC), was sensibly anonymous.

Whatever its name, it was clearly a cuckoo in the CIA nest. Hillenkoetter would have little control over the OPC, which would be an independent division within the CIA that was effectively under the control of George Kennan, as head of policy planning at the State Department, in tandem with the NSC and the Pentagon. Hillenkoetter was supposed to prevent any conflict between the OPC and the CIA's clandestine intelligence operations in the Office of Special Operations, but with two secretive, rival organisations this was impossible—a problem that ought to have raised serious concerns over the potential for one to inadvertently prejudice the other's operations. Nor did Hillenkoetter have any say over who was in charge. The head of the OPC was to be nominated by the State Department and approved by the NSC.

When the NSC directive which set up the OPC was published,

on 18 June 1948, Hillenkoetter was not even in the country, having sailed to Britain on the *Queen Mary* for talks in London with Menzies on future cooperation between the CIA and MI6. The issues discussed included joint intelligence operations in the field, stay-behind units, special operations and, amid continued British concerns over US tradecraft, common training. It was the Americans who raised the issue of special operations behind the Iron Curtain, and it was clearly the main thrust of the debate.

With much of the planning still up in the air on both sides of the Atlantic, they agreed to come back to the subject a week later when Hillenkoetter would return to London after a brief tour of CIA stations in Europe. On 18 June, he took the Golden Arrow to Paris, going on to The Hague, Brussels, Berlin, Vienna, Berne and Rome before returning to London for more discussions with Menzies and Easton on joint special operations.

When Hillenkoetter returned to Washington, he was given a role in the appointment of the head of the OPC and, albeit probably only for form, he offered the job to Frank Wisner, the former OSS officer who had drafted the original proposals. Wisner, like Bill Donovan, was a well-heeled former Wall Street lawyer, and a member of a group of former OSS officers who were unimpressed with Hillenkoetter's leadership and felt they had a mission to ensure the CIA followed Donovan's combination of extensive clandestine operations combined with good intelligence research and analysis. Wisner took over the job on 1 September 1948.[23]

Perkins and Easton, who as assistant chief had the brief to oversee special operations, were by now busy planning operations inside the Soviet Bloc. With the ban on MI6 operating inside the Soviet Union lifted, and a head of station sent to Moscow, they placed former SOE officer Ernest van Maurik in the embassy to work out what might be done in the event of a war. They were also working with the Americans to organise the stay-behind systems they had been specifically tasked by Bevin to set up in countries that might be overrun by the Russians, such as Iran, Turkey, Greece, Finland, Sweden and Norway. Several of these had already approached MI6 for assistance in creating the basis for resistance organisations in the event of war.[24]

Throughout the late 1940s and early 1950s, the CIA and MI6 worked together setting up stay-behind units in western Europe in preparation for the expected Soviet invasion, with the programme accelerating during the latter half of 1951. The extensive stay-behind network in France, set up several years earlier and based largely on former members of the resistance, was a matter of some concern to the CIA head of station in Paris because the French government had no idea it existed. He suggested to Washington that in order 'to provide against political repercussions' it might be best to disclose its existence to General Eisenhower's Supreme Headquarters Allied Powers in Europe (SHAPE), which was based at Rocquencourt, just west of Paris, although not to the French government itself. Daphne Park, now a junior officer in MI6, was put in charge of running the British-led operation. 'Up until then I was on the fringes of SIS and I was very unhappy,' she later recalled. 'Then all of a sudden I was in. Of course, meeting all those members of the Resistance and working with them was such an honour.'

The British Treasury drew the line at the idea that MI6 should run a stay-behind operation in Spain, forcing the MI6 head of station to suggest to his CIA counterpart that the Americans finance it. The Greek general staff took some persuading that there was no sense in them having operational control of the stay-behind network in their own country while, despite the close cooperation between the British and Norwegian secret services during the Second World War, the Norwegian Social Democratic Party was happy to help the CIA, but reluctant to assist if the British were also involved.

Shortages of CIA trainers led MI6 to take charge of the important joint CIA–MI6 stay-behind network in Italy, which subsequently became known by the infamous codename of Gladio. Seven officers from the Italian intelligence service, the Servizio Informazioni Forze Armate (SIFAR), who were to play the key roles in running the network, were brought to the UK in October 1951 for initial evaluation. MI6 had stressed to the Italians that this was to be a joint Italian–British–American operation and insisted on 'absolute secrecy'. Nevertheless, General Umberto Broccoli, the director of Italian intelligence, took the precaution of keeping the CIA head of station in Rome fully informed and explaining to him, on the officers' return, that 'a more concrete form of operational collaboration in stay-behind matters' was being planned.[25]

Simon Preston and Michael Giles, who as young Royal Marines officers were attached to MI6 in the immediate post-war period, were among those selected to take part in the operations and were sent to Fort Monckton, the MI6 training base on the Solent, where they were given instruction in codes, weapons-handling and covert special operations. 'We were made to do exercises, going out in the dead of night and pretending to blow up trains in the railway stations without the stationmaster or the porters seeing you,' Preston said. 'We crept about and pretended to lay charges on the right part of the railway engine with a view to blowing it up.'

Not all the sabotage was simulated. Giles took part in an exercise at the Eastleigh marshalling yards, near Southampton, part of the Southern Railway. 'We laid bricks inside railway engines to simulate plastic explosives,' he recalled. 'I remember rows and rows of steam engines all under thick snow, standing there in clouds of vapour. There were troops out with dogs. The guards came past and I was actually hiding among the cylinder blocks of these engines as they went past. We were also opening up the lubricating tops of the axle boxes and pouring in sand. What happens is that after about 50 miles the sand in the axle box starts to turn them red hot and they all overheat.' Preston was dispatched to London for an additional course on tradecraft. 'I had to do a ten-day course in Greenwich, learning about following people in the street and shaking off people following me—the practicalities of being in the intelligence world.'

They were then sent to Austria, where MI6 and the CIA had set up a number of underground bunkers, filled with weapons, clothing and supplies. 'We spent a lot of our time up in the mountains, learning all about the terrain, learning German, meeting other potential agents, recruiting agents if possible, identifying and plotting dropping zones,' Preston said. 'The whole object was that we would form the nucleus of a partisan or a guerrilla army should the Russians invade. It was thought that within five years there would be a conventional war. We would be dropped back into the area we knew and immediately we would be among friends. The food, arms and explosives would be all there in the bunkers. It doesn't take much imagination to work out that the Russian army would have hunted us from pillar to post. It would have been a short but interesting life, I suspect. But I can't remember ever worrying about that.

'There was one nasty moment. We'd been up in the mountains for about a week, when early one morning there was an enormous number of explosions down in the valley which sounded like the beginning of something. It turned out to be some kind of saint's day, and the villagers were just letting off fireworks.'[26]

7

VALUABLE OR WORTHLESS?

Operation Valuable, the much-maligned attempt to run agents into Albania with the ultimate intention of overthrowing the communist regime of Enver Hoxha, had been under consideration by 'Perks' Perkins since the MI6 Special Operations branch was set up in early 1946, although its original aim was not to get rid of Hoxha. It was originally a straightforward special operations mission to deny the Greek communist Dimokratikos Stratos Elladas (DSE) rebels the use of camps inside Albania from which they were making hit-and-run attacks across the border against the Hellenic Army. Those raids had begun in March 1946, in response to the election of Prime Minister Konstantinos Tsaldaris, a right-wing populist.[1]

The Foreign Office's Russia Committee, which advised on policy towards the Soviet Union, was briefed on the possibility of special operations behind the Iron Curtain in cooperation with the Americans. During a meeting in late November 1948, Sir Ivone Kirkpatrick, the Foreign Office official responsible for secret service activity, raised the idea of insurrection in Albania, using émigrés to link up with opponents of the regime, in what he suggested should be a joint operation between MI6 and the CIA. Albania was seen as small enough to be the easiest country to detach from the Soviet orbit, thereby demonstrating to the populations of other eastern European countries that it was possible to overthrow a Moscow-backed communist dictatorship. Both Ernest Bevin and Hector McNeil were kept informed of the committee's discussions, ensuring that its minutes were passed to the KGB by Guy Burgess and read in Moscow.[2]

The State Department was consulted and Frank Wisner's OPC, which had been formulating its own plan to detach Albania from the Soviet orbit, agreed to discuss a joint operation. JIC chairman William Hayter and Jack Easton, MI6 assistant chief, flew to Washington in March 1949, accompanied by Gladwyn Jebb, the chairman of the Russia Committee, for talks with Wisner and Bob Joyce of the State Department, who reported directly to George Kennan. The Americans agreed to fund it, with MI6 tasked to make the preparations. The British were the ones with the idea and the expertise to set up such an operation. They should put a plan together.[3]

Operation Valuable began at a defining moment in the Cold War, in a year which reinforced the stark divisions between communism and democracy that would last for more than forty years. In January 1949, the Soviet Union strengthened its control over eastern Europe with the formation of the Council for Mutual Economic Assistance (COMECON). Three months later, with the Soviet threat firmly established in the eyes of America and most western European countries, the North Atlantic Treaty Organisation (NATO) was created. Moscow finally gave up on its brazen attempt to blockade the Allies out of Berlin that May and by September the western zones of Germany were combined into the Federal Republic of Germany. Within a month, the Soviet Union had tested its first atomic bomb, the Chinese Communists had founded the People's Republic of China and the Soviet zone of Germany had become the German Democratic Republic.

There have been suggestions that the MI6 plan for special operations inside Albania was amateurish. In fact, it was devised by experts with considerable experience in special operations inside Albania and was sensibly conservative in its aims. The operation was not designed to overthrow the Albanian government. Its primary aim remained simply to deny the Soviet-backed DSE rebels the ability to use southern Albania as a base to mount operations into northern Greece as part of the Greek Civil War. The communist rebels were much stronger and better organised than at the beginning of 1946 and they frequently controlled substantial tracts of land inside Greece itself. They were a genuine threat.

The plan for Operation Valuable envisaged an initial reconnaissance mission to determine how much support there was for resistance to the Hoxha regime. The British would focus on southern Albania, using the nationalist, anti-communist Balli Kombëtar (National Front), the strongest anti-communist organisation in the south, to make contact with potential resistance forces who might be able to deny the support of the local population to the DSE guerrillas. The aim was to 'ascertain their willingness to engage in special operations and test the degree of substance behind their assurances by mounting preliminary operations on a very small scale'. The main British objective was special operations against Greek communist forces to 'limit, if not entirely deny, the refuge and facilities which the guerrillas have hitherto enjoyed on Albanian soil'.

No more than six small teams of Albanians, who had been brought up in the area to the north of the Greek border and therefore had local contacts, were to be sent into the south, where the Balli Kombëtar had operated during the war. Each team was to be equipped with gold sovereigns, a number of captured German weapons, like those the wartime resistance groups might have used and stashed after the war, and a wireless set. They would be infiltrated by boat at night.

The British special operations team overseeing the project was made up of former SOE officers who had worked with the Albanian resistance groups during the war. But the need for credible deniability meant that this time they could not risk going into Albania themselves. David Smiley was asked to control operations in the field from Malta where he would also be in charge of training the Albanians. Julian Amery and Billy McLean were to negotiate with the Albanian leaders in order to put together a coalition that could be portrayed as a government-in-waiting, while Alan Hare, another SOE Albania veteran now in MI6 working for Perkins, manned the forward operations and communications base in a former royal villa on Corfu, a few miles across the Straits of Corfu from southern Albania.

Such was Perks's loyalty to members of his team that he even sent Robin Zaehner, a hard-drinking Oxford academic who had spent the war with the SOE in Iran, to take part in the operation. 'Doc Zaehner, as we called him, was a brilliant scholar in classical Persian,' Smiley recalled. 'And although he was sent out as an interpreter, his own speciality and Albanian had little in common, but he was a most useful and entertaining member of the staff.' In fact, Zaehner's linguistic ability ensured he learned Albanian within the space of a few months. The schooner that would land the guerrillas on the Albanian coast, the *Stormie Seas*, was skippered by John Leatham and Sam Barclay, two former Royal Navy officers who had run operations between the Greek islands for MI6 during the war.

The guerrillas were to tell potential resistance members that they were emissaries of the British, 'who are willing to supply local bands of guerrillas with money and arms if in return those guerrillas will carry out attacks on the facilities and communications which the communist Greeks enjoy in southern Albania. As evidence of their good faith and intentions, the British have supplied them with gold for the initial stages and a token supply of arms which the emissaries have either brought with them or cached near their point of landing.'

The teams would then report back on the success, or failure, of their meetings with potential resistance members as well as any intelligence on the DSE bases and operations. If possible, they should stay in country for around two months, gathering intelligence and talking to people who might lead potential resistance groups. Anyone who fitted that bill was to be persuaded to be exfiltrated along with the MI6 team so they could 'receive the necessary instructions and hold discussions with the British regarding his requirements'. In these original plans, there was no mention of overthrowing the regime. That would only come if the initial objectives succeeded.[4]

The plan was put to the Americans, who liked it. 'They had obviously given a lot of thought to the planning,' said Bob Low, one of the OPC officers involved. 'At that stage it was entirely up to the British "cousins" to provide local knowledge and political guidance. Their secret service with its men who had served in the SOE during the war were the world's experts in this kind of thing. The various papers were well done. They made sense and they were feasible. I never thought it was going to be a "cinch" but I certainly thought it was worth a try. If I hadn't, I'd have said so at the time.'

Wisner and Kennan clearly had more ambition for the operation than the British, with expectations of swiftly building up a resistance and then bolstering it by sending in a 1,000-strong armed force of Albanian émigrés. MI6 thought these American plans 'grandiose'. But the British plan was seen by all as an initial reconnaissance, 'the first phase in a joint operation', and the changes the Americans suggested did not affect the operational detail. For political reasons, the CIA wanted the preliminary objective to be 'denial to the Soviets of a base for air, land and naval forces in the Mediterranean' and, in order to bring the plan into line with State Department policy, wanted more emphasis on the ultimate objective, which to their minds was very firmly 'the restoration of Albanian independence through the overthrow of the Moscow-controlled regime and its replacement by an enlightened government acceptable to the people of Albania'.

It was agreed that Operation Valuable, or as the CIA dubbed it, Project Fiend, was to be overseen and coordinated at the higher levels by a joint policy committee in Washington. The senior MI6 liaison officer, then Peter Dwyer, would represent the British position. The early operations in the field were to be British and run from Europe by Perkins in London and Smiley in Malta. Subsequent US and British operations would follow the same formula as SOE–OSS operations during the war of 'closely integrated policy control' by joint committee with no engagement between the two sides at an operational level. The head of the OPC's Southeastern Europe Division, Jim McCargar, was the main US contact, largely to ensure the politics of the operation fitted with State Department policy rather than for any involvement in the operational control.

'I was chiefly concerned with organising the political side of the operation,' McCargar said. 'The expertise in the affair was 99 per cent British. They had so many people there who had been there during the war, most of them young and intelligent. We only had American citizens of Albanian origin, none of them specialist in what we were trying to achieve.' The publication in the US in 1949 of *Sons of the Eagle*, Amery's account of his, Smiley's, McLean's and Hare's wartime exploits in Albania, reinforced that impression, McCargar said. 'It became our bible.'[5]

Amery and McLean spent a lot of time in Rome over the summer of 1949, talking to the various Albanian opposition leaders who were living in the West, attempting to put together a National Committee for Free Albania that would be as broad-based as possible. It was a near-impossible task but Amery was highly persuasive and eventually, after some marathon discussions, a format was devised which included the main anti-communist factions. The initial front men were Balli Kombëtar leader Mithat Frashëri, and two of Amery's closest wartime associates, Abas Kupi of the royalist Legaliteti party and Kosovo Albanian leader Said Kryeziu. Frashëri, the nominal head of the committee, died a few months after it was formed and was replaced as chairman by Hasan Dosti, another Balli Kombëtar leader. McCargar sent Michael Burke, an OSS Italy veteran, to Rome to attempt to babysit, if not actively control, the committee and to recruit potential agents. His UK liaison in Rome was with Peter Kemp and John Hibberdine, two other former SOE Albanian men now working for Perkins.[6]

Thirty potential Albanian guerrillas, or 'pixies' as they were known as a result of their typically short, wiry stature, were selected from the refugee camps at Bari in Italy, where the bulk of the wartime anti-communist resistance were living, and sent to the operational base at the nineteenth-century Fort Bin Jema on Malta for training by Smiley. He focused on guerrilla tactics and weapons training, Signals instructors seconded from the British Army taught the 'pixies' how to use the radio and communications procedure while Smiley's wife Moy, who had worked with the SOE during the war, was the codes and ciphers specialist.[7]

Meanwhile in Greece, the DSE rebels had begun a major offensive from their bases in southern Albania. Russian and Bulgarian ships ferried arms and equipment, including artillery, into the Albanian ports of Valona and Durrës for the rebels to use. Ten thousand communist guerrillas swarmed across the Greek border, initially gaining a substantial foothold. The Greek Army's response was brutal and unremitting. Throughout the summer it poured troops into the battle, focusing on the roads and tracks across the Albanian border with the Royal Hellenic Air Force carrying out missile and bomb attacks on rebel escape routes to prevent them reaching the safety of their camps. Under heavy attack from the air, the DSE guerrillas were pushed back but frequently found themselves without any means of retreat across the border.[8]

To all intents and purposes, the communist rebels had already been beaten by the time the first two MI6 teams were infiltrated on board the *Stormie Seas* at 'Seaview', the name that Smiley and McLean had given to the promontory beside a small creek from where they had been exfiltrated by motor torpedo boat back in late 1943. It was chosen as the first point of insertion for Valuable because the two of them had spent so much time there waiting for the boat that the detail of the surroundings was engraved on Smiley's mind, allowing him to brief the teams on what to expect. But the Albanian security forces, heavily bolstered by Soviet advisers, also knew what to expect. In October 1949, Kim Philby was posted to Washington to replace Dwyer as the senior MI6 liaison officer. He was briefed on Operation Valuable before he went, and no doubt delivered the details of the briefing to his Soviet controllers. This will have been passed on to the Soviet 'technical advisers' who effectively controlled the Albanian security forces and intensified patrols along the coastal areas opposite Corfu in the days before the initial landings.[9]

Four of the 'pixies' headed north towards Valona but were soon intercepted by Albanian security forces who clearly knew they were coming. Three of them were shot dead and the other managed to flee. The other team of five, who had headed south towards their home town of Nivica, survived. They made contact with Hare in Corfu on 12 October by radio to report they were fine but the team headed for Valona had not fared so well and the Albanians appeared to have been expecting them.

It is easy to blame Philby's role in providing his KGB handlers with as much as he knew of Operation Valuable—although that would have been unlikely to include much in the way of frontline operational detail—but far too many other people knew about the operations anyway. The Russian head of the Sigurimi, the Albanian secret police, was reported to believe as early as July—even before Philby was briefed—that MI6 was running agents into Albania from a base in Corfu. Since the fall-back exfiltration for the MI6 teams was across the Greek border, Pat Whinney, the MI6 head of station in Athens, who himself had served with the SOE, also informed the Greek authorities.

The Italians, who were running their own intelligence operations into Albania, were also briefed, although they were doubtless already well informed because the National Committee for Free Albania (NCFA) leaked like a sieve and the Albanian émigrés in Rome and in the camps in Bari, where many were disappointed not to have been among the thirty selected, talked of nothing else but how Britain and America would help them overthrow Enver Hoxha and liberate their country from the Soviet yoke.

On 10 October, the day Kim Philby started his new job in Washington, two more teams were landed, this time on a beach north of Valona, with orders to contact friends and relatives in their home districts of Korçë and Gjirokastër in southern Albania. All of the teams that survived found the same response: considerable opposition to the Hoxha regime but extreme scepticism that the Valuable teams were evidence that there could be change. The teams had brought in gold sovereigns but no weapons with which to arm opposition forces. The only weapons they had were their own. The need to keep the operation deniable meant there were no British officers on the ground inside Albania, as there had been during the war, to plan attacks on government forces or call in weapons drops. It did not inspire confidence.

Two more teams were sent into other locations; one of the men was shot dead by the Albanian security forces. With informers thought to be everywhere, the teams lived off the land, moving through remote country by night and sleeping by day, and as the cold weather began to set in, they headed south across the border into Greece, losing one further man, shot dead in a clash with security forces, along the way.

The reconnaissance teams had produced disappointing results in terms of responses from the local population and ten men had been lost, at least four of whom were dead, out of a total of twenty-nine sent in. It was not great but nor was it a total disaster. The losses would have been factored into the equation as an inevitable result of sending special operations troops into an autocratic police state. Nevertheless, given the unenthusiastic response from the local population and the Greek government's victory over the communist rebels, which removed the principal British objective, it was clear that there needed to be a reappraisal of the mission.

At a meeting of the Joint Policy Committee in Washington on 15 November, led by Frank Wisner and Kim Roosevelt on the American side and by Philby on the British, the problems they faced with the low quality of the Albanian émigrés they were working with were examined in detail. Wisner said they should look at other methods of achieving their aims, including economic warfare and propaganda. Philby said MI6 shared Wisner's concerns but since he had only been given permission from London to hold exploratory talks he could not agree to any changes to the approach. London was sending Jack Easton to Washington for talks with Wisner within the next week or so. The proposals on economic and psychological warfare should be examined then.

It was Philby himself who raised the issue of security. The British were worried about the security of the operation since it was clear that the French, Italian and Greek intelligence services were 'obviously well informed', Philby said. 'The chief sources of information available to other powers' were the Albanians themselves and they had to find a way to keep the NCFA 'generally informed' without giving them details of the operations that might leak out. Wisner agreed. Philby said that, despite the leaks, MI6 would be very reluctant to stop reconnaissance at this stage. There was then a general discussion as to what the Russians knew about the operation. Philby, perhaps unsurprisingly, dismissed this as unimportant. The Soviet satellite states had 'plenty of proof of British SIS [MI6] operations, but in none of the trials to date in which espionage has been an issue were any genuine cases ever brought to light'. Some of the Americans questioned whether the British really wanted to overthrow the Hoxha government. Wisner shut the argument down, saying that the objective was not up for debate, it was the method of achieving that objective which had to be resolved. He wanted 'concrete proposals, views and recommendations on alternative methods' by the next meeting.[10]

Wisner asked Kim Roosevelt to carry out an assessment of the reconnaissance phase of Operation Valuable/Project Fiend and recommend a way forward. Roosevelt saw only one way to cure the lack of confidence in the idea of insurgency among the local population. The operations had to be far more aggressive, with stronger teams backed up by weapons drops to give potential rebels confidence they would get the support they needed. His report concluded that the British and the Americans had three choices: the abandonment of the project completely; the adoption of 'a more time-consuming non-paramilitary type of operation backed up by a propaganda campaign . . . almost certainly excluding the possibility of revolt in the foreseeable future'; or sending in tougher, better-armed Albanian guerrillas to ramp up 'the US–UK-inspired operation aimed at overthrowing the Kremlin-dominated Hoxha regime'.

No one reading Roosevelt's assessment could have been in any doubt even before he disclosed his recommendations as to what they would be. If the operations were to be successful, they needed to ditch the cautious British approach. The lack of success enjoyed so far was entirely due to the poor quality of the Albanian recruits, their small numbers and their lack of firepower. The Allies needed to drop weapons into Albania as soon as possible to demonstrate their commitment.

'The teams should have higher grade personnel and capable leadership and should operate as small guerrilla bands which would "shoot their way out" of difficult situations,' Roosevelt said. 'This guerrilla band concept visualises a two-fold mission—the organising of nuclei of resistance and operational intelligence nets. The resistance nuclei will help the reconnaissance teams to survive and lay the groundwork for an insurrectionary apparatus. The organising of resistance nuclei will involve the dropping in immediately of limited quantities of arms and ammunition for distribution to these resistance centres. Without this tangible evidence of the seriousness of the reconnaissance teams' intentions, indigenous elements will not actively support the teams or take part in the development of the necessary underground apparatus.'[11]

The Foreign Office took a completely different stance. It was happy to drop the project completely—against the inclination of Perkins and his officers—not least because it feared that any precipitate action in Albania might give the Kremlin an excuse to invade Tito's Yugoslavia and drag it back into the Soviet orbit. If it were to continue, the British role should be limited to propaganda. Ernest Bevin was initially persuaded but his determination to tie British action against the Soviet Union to that of the Americans ensured that if Washington wanted to keep going the Foreign Office felt obliged to allow MI6 to continue to take part, if only on a small scale.

From this point on, the Foreign Office, and its inability to agree a joint position with the State Department, would severely limit the MI6 role. There was agreement on a propaganda campaign of leaflet drops to prepare the population for the idea of resistance, but the best that could be agreed on operations inside Albania was for the British to take a support role, mounting low-level intelligence operations 'at a very slow tempo' and leaving the more aggressive special operations to the Americans. The previous agreement that while there should be coordination on policy in the Washington committee, there should be 'operational disengagement' on the ground covered any differences between what each side's missions sought to achieve.

A joint meeting in Washington on 6 December 1949 agreed that the new objectives would be:

1. To reduce the value of Albania to the Soviets by persistently and constantly undermining Communist authority and by harassing the Hoxha regime with domestic difficulties.
2. To encourage and assist the Albanian people in their resistance to the Hoxha regime; to maintain hope of eventual liberation; and to prepare the people psychologically for eventual action to free them from Communist tyranny.

3. To create, foster and support a skeleton resistance organisation which could be used as the foundation of a liberation movement if and when such an active operation should seem politically and strategically desirable.

The Americans continued to focus on building up the resistance 'skeleton', making plans for weapons drops and recruiting several hundred Albanians who were to be held in a 'labour battalion' at Wächterhof, south-east of Munich, and trained there and at several other wooded estates nearby to provide a pool of agents for US 'armed reconnaissance' missions into northern Albania, leaving the south to the British.[12]

MI6 concerns over American security resurfaced in March 1950, when over lunch with the prominent *New York Times* journalist Cyrus L. Sulzberger, a US diplomat disclosed the details of the first British mission. Sulzberger promptly reported that two teams of Albanian émigrés who were trained 'in Malta and Corfu' had been landed on the Albanian coast the previous November. 'Their assignment was to take radio equipment into the hinterland and to establish communications between the anti-Hoxha resistance movement and the émigré committees,' Sulzberger wrote. While he did not mention that it was a British operation, the fury in MI6 was exacerbated by the diplomat's claim that all of the Albanians were rounded up and shot. Jim McCargar was so angry at the diplomat's stupidity and the journalist's willingness to reveal a secret operation that he resigned.[13]

The Americans dropped their first teams into northern Albania in November 1950, by which time Wisner's OPC was fully under the control of the CIA. Nine men in three teams who had been trained in a wooded estate at Mornay, 30 miles south of Munich, were parachuted into three areas of northern Albania. Four of them were dropped on the border with Kosovo in the far north-east, two near Krujë and three near Dibër. They were flown in by Polish aircrew who had served with the RAF during the war and stayed in the UK. By now, the British had downgraded their operations to several teams a year doing nothing more than collecting intelligence, but the US-controlled teams had much more aggressive goals, very much in line with Kim Roosevelt's proposals.

Their mission was 'to lay a foundation for and form the nucleus of resistance groups in these areas, to establish safe houses, and to prepare facilities for eventual covert air supply of limited guerrilla groups'. Like the British they suffered losses, but the majority of agents were extracted safely, and a number went back in repeatedly. At the beginning of 1951, the joint MI6–CIA view remained that, in the words of one of the US officers involved, 'operations into Albania had produced definite tangible results and the venture had been also of great value in providing the British and ourselves with a mass of experience and knowledge obtainable in no other way'.[14]

Inevitably, sending armed guerrillas into a police state brought problems with agents killed in firefights or captured by the Sigurimi. The worst year by far was 1951, a turning point in the operation. That summer an American team and a British team were mistakenly dropped too close to each other. The CIA team were looking for food when they stumbled upon a group of communist officials and felt they had no choice but to shoot them. They evaded the resultant manhunt but the MI6 team did not.

Both operations were now run from Athens and the CIA officer in charge there accepted that his team were technically in the wrong but argued that they had been 'justified by necessity in operating outside their route and, under the circumstances, killing the communist officials was done for self-preservation'. He saw 'the whole incident as an unfortunate case of uncontrollable circumstances whereby British intelligence was the loser' and expressed the hope that MI6 shared his desire 'to let bygones be bygones and that nothing will occur to change excellent . . . relations now existing in Athens'.[15]

Things only got worse in October that year, undoubtedly the operation's worst month, with six British agents and the same number of US agents killed in two separate missions. This led to a change of policy in which both MI6 and the OPC adopted a much more selective process in terms of recruiting agents, using former members of the Albanian armed forces linked to King Zog's entourage rather than émigrés selected by the opposition politicians. It worked. The following year, four British teams and four US teams were infiltrated into Albania. No agents died, none was captured, and none went missing.[16]

In the three years between November 1950, when the Americans sent in their first mission, and the end of 1953, the CIA sent in 27 teams, a total of 104 agent missions, a number of the agents having been inserted on multiple occasions. Just twelve agents were killed. Ten were captured, five went missing and two defected to Yugoslavia. There were more than fifty supply drops and enough weapons and ammunition were stockpiled in Greece to supply a small army of 6,000 men for two months.[17]

The CIA remained fixated throughout on plans to liberate Albania, including its original proposal—which terrified the Foreign Office—of sending in a substantial guerrilla force. At a conference in Rome in October 1951, MI6 had been enthusiastic about the idea, but its hopes of a 'more aggressive' approach from the Foreign Office were overly optimistic. At a meeting with the CIA in London in the spring of 1952, the MI6 officers were forced to admit that while they had thought in Rome that renewing the idea of a plan to liberate Albania was worth pursuing, 'the definite directive which they had received from the Foreign Office [was that it] would never accept a plan which involved a follow-up-force'. Frustrated by the limitations the British were imposing on operations, Allen Dulles, now CIA deputy director, told his British opposite number, John Sinclair, that the Albanian operations were 'now on trial'.[18]

Despite the completely different emphasis each side put on the operational objectives, and the undoubted losses for both the CIA and MI6 in terms of agents killed or put on trial by the Albanian authorities, MI6 continued with Operation Valuable until the spring of 1955, by which time both sides were sending in teams of agents on a regular basis and carrying out leaflet drops, with the Americans also making clandestine radio broadcasts from a ship based in the Adriatic.

At his 'farewell party' in the opulent Hotel Grande Bretagne in Athens in March 1955, an MI6 officer told his CIA opposite number that he was going back to London for 'consultations' on the project. He assured him he would be back, and that MI6 was planning to drop a team of agents into north-central Albania in May and to have another team make a quick, in-and-out, cross-border infiltration into the south-west around Kakavia in late June. Within weeks both operations had been suspended indefinitely. The Foreign Office had decided that the risks associated with Operation Valuable out-weighed any benefits.[19]

The CIA briefly continued its own operations, inserting a two-man team in June to service a dead drop for an intelligence network. But plans for a follow-up operation in October were turned down by Washington and by the end of 1955 the US operation was confined to leaflet drops and propaganda broadcasts. No longer required, the NCFA was dissolved. The operation was at an end.[20]

Operation Valuable could scarcely be described as a major success, but nor was it the catalogue of disasters it is often portrayed as being. It would simply not have continued for six years with such basic objectives on the British side if that were the case. But equally it was far more important to MI6 for the way in which it ironed out differences and demonstrated how joint operations with the Americans could be carried out—despite the concerns in London that the CIA was too aggressive in its approach—than it was for the intelligence and results it produced.

During the war, the British had held the Americans back, their control of the ground inside occupied Europe, and OSS acceptance of its own inexperience, giving them the lead role. Until the invasion of Europe, first in Italy and then in France, the Americans had only been able to exert their independence in the Far East and with espionage operations from neutral countries, some of which enjoyed a good deal of success. But the dynamic had changed. America was a true superpower. Britain might still retain influence but only in the shadow of its ally. Some within the CIA, but by no means all, were still willing to accept that the British had more experience in the special operations field, but they were determined to take the lead. With Valuable, or Fiend, they had allowed the British to use their experience to set up the operation before effectively taking it over. It might irritate MI6 when rash US behaviour betrayed a lack of experience, but held back by a hesitant Foreign Office, it had no choice but to accept reality.

The principle, hammered out with the British by OSS special operations chief Ellery Huntington during the war, of coordination of strategy by committee but complete operational disengagement on the ground, had been shown to work in a Cold War framework. Indeed, the only major problem in relations between the two sides throughout the operation came when the CIA discovered that the MI6 representative on the Joint Policy Committee, a man privy to every secret it shared with its British colleagues, was a KGB agent-in-place.[21]

The US realisation that Kim Philby was a Soviet agent came as an indirect result of what was one of the most important codebreaking operations of the Cold War, revealing as it did, both directly and as in Philby's case indirectly, the full extent of Soviet penetration of many secret US and British organisations. The Venona project began in 1943 when the US Army codebreakers first started looking at what were thought at the time to be low-level trade and diplomatic messages of relatively little importance; the diplomatic messages were believed to concentrate solely on consular issues. The messages had been sent via the international cable system and copies were provided to the US codebreakers under an arrangement with the cable companies, which had also supplied the Japanese and German diplomatic telegrams.

The Russian messages were encoded using a codebook which produced a series of numerical code groups. The encoded message was then itself enciphered using a one-time pad additive system. The pad contained a number of sheets providing streams of figures which were placed under the figures in the code groups. The two sets of figures were then added together using non-carrying arithmetic to produce the enciphered message. Since each sheet on the pad was used only once, it should in theory have been an unbreakable system. But the Americans discovered that for a very brief period between 1942 and 1946, the pressures of war had led to the Russians making the mistake of using duplicate pads on a number of messages, thereby allowing the codebreakers to strip off the additive to expose the code groups underneath.[22]

It was not until 1946 that Meredith Gardner, the expert cryptana-lyst and Russian linguist attempting to rebuild the codebook from behind the strings of additive, finally broke his first messages. Like Dilly Knox, working on the more difficult German Enigma systems at Bletchley Park, Gardner was assisted by a group mainly made up of young women. The codes could only be broken slowly, in small batches of groups, so the messages were mostly only partially readable, but what lay beneath demonstrated beyond a shadow of a doubt that the messages, initially thought to be low-level trade and consular communications, included several thousand between Soviet intelligence officers based in various American cities and their headquarters in Moscow.

The three messages Gardner and his team managed to partially decode in 1946 included one, sent from the KGB *rezidentura* in New York to Moscow Centre in December 1944, which listed a number of scientists working on the Manhattan Project. The messages soon began to produce more details of the Soviet agents operating in America and the British were brought into the project. During 1945 and 1946, Cecil Phillips, one of the US Army codebreakers working on the project, kept the British fully briefed on Bride, as the operation was then known. GCHQ was brought in full-time in 1947, basing a number of its Russian linguists at Arlington Hall to assist Gardner, with Joan Malone, a leading US Army codebreaker, travelling the other way to Eastcote to assist the GCHQ Bride section, which was led by Wilfred Bodsworth, a white-haired veteran of the 'First Cold War' between Britain and the Soviet Union during the twenties and thirties when he had worked on Russian Navy codes and ciphers.[23]

The FBI was also brought into the project to help track down the Soviet agents, with FBI agent Robert Lamphere working closely with Gardner to identify the Soviet agents behind the various codenames. Lamphere's habit of assiduously polishing his spectacles might have given him the air of a thinking man but he was a former lumberjack with scant regard for the British intelligence officers, whom he viewed as 'a bunch of skilful horse-traders with whom you trafficked at your peril'. The Soviet agents he and Gardner uncov-ered included Klaus Fuchs, who was caught after Gardner's team decoded a message revealing that he had passed his KGB handler a paper on gaseous diffusion which he had himself written, the same report that Moscow Centre had described as being of 'great value' to the Soviet atomic weapons programme.[24]

Kim Philby had been introduced to Gardner and the Bride project by Peter Dwyer shortly after arriving in Washington in October 1949. By now, the US Navy and Army codebreakers had been amalgamated into the Armed Forces Security Agency. Philby himself barely appeared in the messages the US and British codebreakers managed to read, and where he did a confusion over codenames would have led the investigators away from him. But Donald Maclean, his fellow member of the Cambridge spy ring, who between May 1944 and August 1948 had been first secretary in the British embassy in Washington, received repeated mentions under the codename HOMER.

The messages were easier to spot and decipher because they began with an introduction that was always the same: 'To the 8th Section. Materials of "G".' There is no equivalent of H in the Russian alphabet so HOMER was rendered GOMER in Russian, and 'Materials of "G"' was simply an indication that the message referred to intelligence produced by HOMER. At the time Philby was first briefed on the problem, HOMER was as yet unidentified. But the fact that all of his or her intelligence went to the 8th Section, the political section, and the contents of what could be decoded, made it clear that whoever it was had access to an extensive range of British Foreign Office documents, including a number of secret conversations between Churchill and Roosevelt.

The only reason someone with that sort of access would be handled from Washington was that they were working inside the British embassy. In August 1950, one of the young women in Gardner's team made a breakthrough, decoding a message that stated that HOMER had himself been entrusted with deciphering a personal message from BOAR (Churchill) to CAPTAIN (Roosevelt). It was now clear that the Soviet agent was a senior embassy official.[25]

Meanwhile, Guy Burgess had arrived in Washington as a second secretary in the embassy and, to the dismay of Philby's wife Aileen, was lodging with his friend during his stay in Washington, firmly associating the two of them together. But for Philby, it was not his association with Burgess that bothered him, it was his links to Maclean. He had not only recommended Maclean to Otto Deutsch, their initial KGB contact, he had actually made the first approach, receiving an instantly positive response. If Maclean were to be uncovered and interrogated, he too would soon be blown, his career for both MI6 and the KGB destroyed. Then in April 1951, Gardner's team found the vital clue to HOMER's identity. For part of 1944 he had had regular contacts with his Soviet control in New York, using the fact that his wife was pregnant and staying there with her mother as an excuse. There was only one member of the wartime British embassy who fitted that profile. The search for HOMER had been narrowed down to one man, Donald Maclean.[26]

Philby was one of the first people to hear of the breakthrough. Maclean was now based in London as head of the Foreign Office's American Department. MI5's 'watchers' were already mounting surveillance on him, albeit far too limited. Philby could not risk allowing Maclean to be interviewed by either MI5 or the FBI. But by chance, Burgess was suspended and ordered home following a series of complaints about multiple instances of poor behaviour which had culminated in his being booked for speeding on three separate occasions in one day.

Philby told Burgess that Maclean's treachery had been uncovered and that as soon as he got to London, he must tell their friend that he had no choice but to flee to Moscow. Philby stressed that it was vital that Burgess did not give himself away by associating too obviously with Maclean, since that would point straight back to him. Burgess crossed the Atlantic on the *Queen Mary* with his friend's warning 'Don't you go too' ringing in his ears. On arrival in the UK, he went straight to Anthony Blunt, who passed the news to the KGB. Burgess had dinner with Maclean at the Reform Club and told him he had no choice but to defect. Maclean was reluctant. But the Centre ordered him to go to Moscow and, to make sure he did, Burgess went with him in a move that would ultimately damn Philby.

The MI5 report on the HOMER affair was due to be sent to London by Wednesday 23 May, which meant that Maclean's interrogation might be expected to begin as early as the following Monday. Blunt suggested using one of the ships making mini-cruises across the English Channel. They sailed on Fridays, put in at several French ports, and returned on Sunday night or Monday morning. Passenger papers were not checked on the cruises. Maclean could disembark at the first French port and fail to return to the boat, and no one would be any the wiser until the ship returned to England.

On Friday 25 May, the two men drove from Maclean's house at Tatsfield, in Surrey, to Southampton and boarded a ship that would call at Saint-Malo, where they disembarked. Once in France, they were given false documents by Soviet intelligence officers and made their way to Moscow via Berne, where they took a flight to Stockholm which was stopping off in Prague. When it landed in the Czechoslovak capital, they were met by KGB officers who whisked them away to Moscow. GCHQ monitored heavy increases in KGB communications between Moscow and Paris, Berne and Prague ahead of and during their flight, but there was nothing that could have been done in response. Burgess and Maclean had gone.[27]

The realisation that Burgess was also a Soviet spy came as a complete shock to British intelligence and, combined with the fact that their defection occurred shortly before Maclean was due to be interrogated, threw immediate suspicion on Philby. MI5 was convinced that Philby was the so-called 'Third Man' who was assumed to have tipped Maclean off. Perhaps more importantly, there were those in the CIA and the FBI who were absolutely certain that a man with whom they had shared some of their most valued intelligence, and in doing so endangered some of their very best sources, was a Soviet agent-in-place.

Walter Bedell Smith, always known as 'Beetle' Smith, who as Eisenhower's chief of staff during the war had been a key champion of the OSS, was now CIA director. He insisted that Philby be recalled to London immediately. Once there, he was questioned by Dick White, the then head of MI5, who clearly did not believe a word he said. Stewart Menzies told him with a great deal of regret that the Americans had insisted that he could not return to Washington. His close association with Burgess had damned him, Menzies felt unfairly. But the service had no choice but to ask for his resignation—much to the disappointment of some of his fellow officers, who, like Menzies, found it impossible to believe he was a Soviet spy.[28]

The impact on relations between the British and US agencies is easily overemphasised but certainly in the short term there was an undoubted impact; and longer term, for those who had no affection for the British, it was a useful stick with which to beat them. No doubt there were some within the CIA who saw the lack of deaths in the Albanian operations in 1952 compared to the earlier failures as being a direct result of Philby's departure. But in reality, the better success rate was the result of more considered recruitment methods and a conscious decision not to inform the NCFA of impending operations—a reaction to the October 1951 disasters, which could scarcely be laid at Philby's door given that he had resigned three months earlier. One CIA officer working on the Albanian operations felt the need to warn against any precipitous action in terms of cooperation in reaction to the news about Philby. Cooperation was a two-way street and the Americans benefited from it just as much as the British did.

'It is quite possible that Fiend/Valuable is unique among OPC projects in regard to the close liaison which is required with the British and the fact that certain phases of the operation have depended to some degree on British good will,' the CIA officer said. 'If it is proposed to restrict access, it is strongly recommended that this be done in such a manner as to avoid retaliatory treatment in London. It is naturally desirable to maintain close control over OPC contacts with the SIS representative in Washington. The object of this memo is merely to point out that if a new system is introduced which suggests an abrupt change in attitude toward working with the SIS representative, it may have repercussions.'[29]

Nevertheless, the realisation, in Washington at least, that Philby was a traitor led inevitably to attempts by the CIA to impose limitations on MI6 access, bypassing Philby's deputy Mac

Silverwood-Cope, who had temporarily taken over liaison when his boss was ordered home, and only liaising with MI6 via the CIA head of station in London. When MI6 responded to the crisis in relations by informing the Agency that it planned to send John Bruce Lockhart to Washington to take the chief liaison post, there was immediate concern among the former OSS contingent within the CIA. Bruce Lockhart had run MI6 operations in Italy during the war and in post-war Germany, tutoring the Americans. He was not only a very experienced officer, he represented an era when the OSS and the SSU relied far more heavily on the British and were very definitely the junior partners. The Americans regarded that dynamic as having changed. They were the dominant force in the relationship now and Silverwood-Cope was precisely the sort of officer they wanted in Washington, someone relatively junior in status with very little clout.

Frank Wisner, who was informed of the MI6 plans during a visit to London, was clearly concerned to hear that someone with Bruce Lockhart's authority was being sent over. His many relationships with CIA officers would ensure he had far more reach inside the Agency than someone like Silverwood-Cope. Wisner suggested that since he was in London he should speak to Menzies to 'reaffirm CIA's view that London should remain the chief point of liaison between the two services' and that Smith contact the MI6 Chief to express his full confidence in Silverwood-Cope. Wisner also suggested the CIA build up Silverwood-Cope's reputation in London 'possibly by allowing him greater access and increasing the importance of his position'.

The British response to this resistance was to send Major-General Kenneth Strong, who had been Eisenhower's chief intelligence officer when Smith was his chief of staff, to Washington in late October 1951 to inform his wartime colleague of wholesale changes to the leadership of British intelligence. Menzies was to be replaced by MI6 vice-chief Major-General John Sinclair, with Jack Easton, whom the Americans knew well and trusted, as his vice-chief. Sir Percy Sillitoe, the MI5 director-general, was to be replaced in early 1952, and for good measure, although he had no responsibility for anything related to Philby, Sir Edward Travis, the head of GCHQ, was stepping down. The UK government would also overrule council planners holding up construction of a CIA European analysis and communications station at RAF Croughton in Oxfordshire. But at the same time, MI6 made it very clear that the new chief liaison officer to the CIA was John Bruce Lockhart. He would be arriving in one month's time.[30]

8

THE KOREAN WAR

The Korean War was the first major test for the CIA and one it is widely seen as having failed. In particular, the lack of any warning that North Korean troops were about to invade South Korea led to claims of a 'new Pearl Harbor'. As ever, the truth was much more nuanced. The situation in Korea at the start of the Cold War reflected the same stark contrasts between East and West that were present in occupied Germany. At the end of the Second World War, it was divided into two zones, split along the circle of latitude 38 degrees north of the equator, the 38th Parallel. The Soviet Union controlled the area north of that line and the Americans the south. The United Nations set up a special commission to oversee elections, but North Korea declined to take part and they were only held in the south, which in August 1949, with negotiations to create a single Korea having failed, became the Republic of Korea (ROK). Shortly afterwards the Democratic People's Republic of Korea was set up in the north under the communist former resistance leader Kim Il-Sung.

The CIA had in fact warned very clearly in February 1949 that if US troops were withdrawn from South Korea, this 'would probably, in time, be followed by an invasion' by the North Korean People's Army, possibly assisted by small battle-trained Chinese communist units and 'backed by Soviet aid and advice'. The decision the previous month to pull all US troops back from the 38th Parallel had already led to a number of probing attacks by North Korean forces testing the South's defence, often leading to exaggerated press reports of impending invasion.

But the impact of the CIA assessment that invasion was likely was severely limited by a dissenting view from US Army intelligence, which in the Far East came under the autocratic control of Major-General Charles Willoughby, chief intelligence officer to General Douglas MacArthur, the Supreme Commander Far East Command. MacArthur opposed anything the CIA said on principle and with defence cuts biting into his forces was adamant that US troops in Korea were not needed there and should be withdrawn. Willoughby shaped his intelligence assessments to fit what his master wanted to hear. In a response to the CIA assessment, he dismissed its arguments. The People's Army, although well trained, was far too small to defeat even South Korea's limited forces, Willoughby said, with an extraordinary disregard for reality. By the end of June 1949, all but a few hundred US Army trainers had left.[1]

A couple of months after warning that the withdrawal of those troops would almost certainly lead to an invasion, the CIA issued a series of reports detailing a deal with Stalin that Kim had signed during a three-week visit to Moscow that March. The result was ostensibly a 'cultural and economic' agreement, but this was just cover for a military pact which involved the provision of substantial amounts of arms and weaponry to allow a significant increase in the size of the People's Army, plus an influx of Soviet military advisers to assist in training, in return for which Pyongyang would provide bases for thirty Russian submarines, a dozen destroyers and frigates, and more than 120 combat aircraft.

The three weeks Kim was in Moscow appear to have been spent persuading Stalin that he should allow North Korea to invade the south. The following month, the CIA reported a military pact between North Korea and communist China that would allow the 60,000 Korean volunteers serving with the People's Liberation Army (PLA) to return to North Korea that July. By September, the CIA was issuing reports of Soviet tanks and artillery being unloaded at North Korean ports and transported to the 38th Parallel.[2]

The creation of the People's Republic of China (PRC), and continuing US support for Chiang Kai-shek's Nationalists, forced the CIA officers operating under official cover to leave China, leading to the death of Douglas Mackiernan, who was under cover as vice-consul in Urumqi, the capital of the north-western province of Xinjiang. He was ordered out by Washington in late 1949, after the Communists took control of Xinjiang. Mackiernan decided to go south via Tibet to avoid contact with the Communists, but he was shot dead by Tibetan border guards who had not received a message from Lhasa ordering them to let him through, the first CIA officer to be killed on active duty.

Robert Boull, chief operations officer of Civil Air Transport, a US company financially controlled by the CIA, was captured by the Communists in December 1949 when Nationalist forces he was supplying defected en masse. Despite the forced departures, there were at least four CIA officers operating under non-official cover inside China who did not leave and apparently, initially at least, went undetected.[3]

The loss of its stations inside China forced the CIA to expand its already strong presence at the US consulate-general in Hong Kong, taking full advantage of a major base overlooking China offered by the close cooperation with the UK. With thousands of refugees fleeing the Communists, both the MI6 station in the British colony and the CIA had a ready supply of sources of intelligence and indeed potential agents who might be sent back into China.

The US consulate-general grew so much that it included forty-two vice-consuls, the vast majority of them CIA officers under official cover, and thousands of staff. Bill Colby, who had served with the OSS before joining the Agency, would later look back fondly to the days when CIA officers or agents would 'slink out of Hong Kong and sneak through China to see what was going on in Manchuria'. British colonies might be anathema to many Americans for purely historical reasons, but they were yet another advantage in favour of the close intelligence alliance with the British. As OPC chief Frank Wisner remarked: 'Whenever we're in trouble, the British always have a little piece of territory that's very useful.'[4]

Britain took a different stance on the Communist takeover, recognising the PRC and maintaining its embassy in Beijing with its MI6 presence, largely in order to retain lucrative trading links. It was a policy which would continue to present problems for relations between Britain and America right up until the US recognition of communist China in the early 1970s. A JIC delegation which visited Washington in the aftermath of the Communist takeover, at a point when British recognition of the PRC had yet to be confirmed, asked their US counterparts for information on Korea and were told that, notwithstanding the close cooperation implicit in the BRUSA agreement, any intelligence on Korea and Taiwan was deemed not to be part of the Anglo-American intelligence exchange.[5]

Yet despite British recognition, the Chinese Communists ordered most British officials to leave and downgraded the status of the most senior diplomat at the British embassy in Beijing to that of a 'negotiator', simply there to agree diplomatic relations once the UK had earned that right by breaking its ties with Taiwan. MI6 had enjoyed extensive success against communism in China in the 1930s and during the war, when its man in Chongqing was 'in close personal touch' with future Chinese Communist premier Zhou Enlai. But despite a continued presence at the embassy, and good reporting on the presence of a large number of Korean volunteers in the PLA, it had less success in the post-war period. Following its failure to provide any warning of a Chinese communist attack on the British consulate-general in Guangzhou in early 1948, Menzies was forced to admit that his intelligence operations in China were 'barely underway'.[6]

As for signals intelligence, under the terms of the 1946 BRUSA agreement, updated in 1948 in order to iron out a number of problems that had arisen, the British and American codebreakers carved up the world between them. America dominated south-east Asia, albeit with a substantial amount of the coverage of Chinese and Soviet targets coming from two British intercept sites in Hong Kong, an RAF unit at Little Sai Wan at the eastern end of Hong Kong island, and an army unit in Kowloon Tong on the mainland.[7]

The Korean peninsula was very much in America's fold, both politically and in terms of signals intelligence collection. But US signals intelligence operations against North Korea were virtually non-existent. There were just two intercept positions in Japan monitoring a single North Korean communications network and without any qualified Korean linguists. The US Army had two Korean interpreters, but neither worked in signals intelligence. They were attached to the US Army Language School in Monterey, California. North Korea itself was not even on the official US signals intelligence main requirements lists, although anything on relations between North Korea and the Soviet Union or China was—albeit low down the secondary list and only from the basis of Soviet or Chinese communications.[8]

The CIA and MI6 both had a presence in Tokyo, but General MacArthur tried to limit their operations, specifically banning anyone bar Charles Willoughby's military intelligence organisation from collecting intelligence there. MI6 operations were overseen by a Far East controller based in Singapore with a relatively large staff of eight. The service sent a newly recruited Canadian academic to Japan in August 1947 under cover as a member of the British liaison mission to MacArthur's military government. A year later, George Blake was sent to head up a new station in the South Korean capital, Seoul, with a brief to target north-east China and South Korean communists, but he had little success. The best intelligence MI6 could obtain came from the Nationalists, who agreed to supply all of their intelligence to the British on a contract basis, receiving £3,000 a month (equivalent to more than £100,000 in today's terms) for information which was clearly politically tarnished. Appropriately codenamed Salvage, the cooperation received mixed reviews from customers and required an additional station in the Taiwanese capital, Taipei, to run it.

The CIA station in Seoul continued throughout the early months of 1950 to report on the build-up of North Korean forces, with Kim Il-Sung ordering nationwide conscription for all males aged eighteen to thirty, leading a number of young North Koreans to flee to the south where they were debriefed by the CIA. By early 1950, the State Department was beginning to take notice of the increasing threat. Amid what it described as 'fragmentary' intelligence, it asked for a fresh integrated analysis of the military, political and economic situation in North Korea. Were these reports merely symptomatic of a newly created nation building its defences or concerted preparations for war? What were 'the current capabilities' of North Korea? As the CIA analysts struggled to persuade Willoughby to provide them with the latest data, the Seoul and Hong Kong stations reported thousands of Korean volunteers returning from China to bolster the People's Army and even an unconfirmed report that Kim had flown to Changchun in China for secret talks with Soviet deputy premier Vyacheslav Molotov to request yet more Soviet weaponry.[9]

Despite the lack of specific signals intelligence targeting of North Korea, there was one diplomatic intercept which confirmed that war was imminent. On 11 April 1950, Kim Il-Sung informed the Soviet ambassador in Pyongyang that his troops would invade South Korea in June, a message that was immediately passed to Moscow and intercepted by a US Army signals intelligence unit in Japan which reported directly to Willoughby. It was the best kind of intelligence: the prime decision maker laying out his decision in no uncertain terms, received via an impeccable source. Willoughby's failure to ensure it was sent out as a flash signal to leading decision makers in Washington is only explicable as a continuation of his refusal to accept any intelligence that contradicted his master's pronouncements.[10]

The North Korean People's Army was now 127,000 strong, with a large proportion of its soldiers battle-hardened former volunteers in the PLA. The military assistance pacts with Moscow and Beijing had provided it with substantial weaponry and equipment, including Russian artillery, 150 tanks and 200 combat aircraft, and it was bolstered by a large number of Soviet military advisers. Much of this would have appeared in the CIA's State Department-ordered assessment of North Korea's current capabilities, which was due to be published in April but was delayed by various departments failing to provide the necessary data and was yet to be finished on 25 June 1950 when North Korean troops poured across the border and the Korean War began.

Two days later, the UN Security Council called on its members to 'furnish such assistance to the Republic of Korea as may be necessary to repel the armed attack and to restore international peace and security in the area'. President Truman ordered MacArthur to rush US troops from Japan to Korea. The following day Seoul fell, with MI6 head of station George Blake taken prisoner, and Britain placed its Singapore-based East Indies Fleet under MacArthur's command. The British fleet had an integral albeit limited signals intelligence capability which had been targeting the Soviet and Chinese threats and, like its US counterparts, had virtually no Korean capability.

Despite committing British warships to the UN coalition, which soon included elements of the Australian, Canadian, Dutch and New Zealand navies, the British Chiefs of Staff baulked at offering any ground forces. They were concerned that Stalin's willingness to allow the North Korean invasion might portend military threats elsewhere across the world, such as in Iran. But intense pressure from Dean Acheson, Truman's secretary of state, delivered with 'obscurely worded menace'—and outrage in Congress, where the British recognition of the PRC, largely to preserve trade, infuriated many US politicians—persuaded the British government that it had no choice if it were not to see a break in 'the Special Relationship'.[11]

Guy Burgess, at the time still Hector McNeil's private secretary, had warned Moscow that 'under political and military pressure from the USA' Clement Attlee's cabinet were planning to send a British Army brigade to Korea. Burgess also disclosed the deep concerns in London over how far the Americans, and MacArthur in particular, were prepared to go. Would they simply retake the occupied areas of South Korea or go further and invade the North?

'The British government intends to give the Americans firm support while the American aim is to prevent the "capture" of South Korea,' Burgess told the KGB. 'It is persistently, but as yet unsuccessfully, trying to find out from the Americans just how far they are prepared to go.'[12]

As Burgess had predicted, the British government dispatched an infantry brigade from Hong Kong to Korea in August 1950 and two months later sent another to Korea from the UK. The two brigades were combined with Australian, Canadian and New Zealand units to form the 1st Commonwealth Division, which included a British

Army signals intelligence unit, Intelligence School No. 9, with Chinese- and Russian-speaking linguists carrying out intercept operations.[13]

The US codebreakers had rushed the two Korean linguists from the Monterey language school to Korea, even though neither of them had the necessary security clearance for such highly classified work. 'Until their clearances came through, they worked in a locked and guarded room every day,' an internal NSA history records. 'Intercepted messages were brought in periodically. They would translate the traffic and then pass it through a slot in the wall to the communications centre.' The US codebreakers also enlisted a number of South Korean signals intelligence specialists and recruited Korean linguists from among the US expatriate community in South Korea—including a Catholic priest, who turned out to be a more than capable codebreaker, producing the first decrypts of enciphered North Korean air force traffic.[14]

While the shortage of Korean linguists and background on North Korean communications networks was a major disadvantage, the US codebreakers had a lucky break. The Soviet military advisers might have trained the North Koreans well in terms of military tactics, but their communications security was appalling. They transmitted large amounts of highly classified information on troop locations and tactics in clear, not only providing a wealth of intelligence for UN military commanders but also giving the codebreakers a large number of 'cribs', streams of plain text to search for in the messages that were encrypted. By the end of July, the US codebreakers were reading around a third of all enciphered North Korean messages as well as the many plain text messages. The deciphered messages included the main battle plan for a major assault by five North Korean divisions on the South Korean city of Daegu, which was defended by Lieutenant-General Walton Walker's US 8th Army and South Korean troops.

By now, the North Korean advances had pushed the UN and South Korean forces back into a small corner of South Korea around the southern port of Busan. If Daegu were lost, it was likely that Korea would fall completely into North Korean hands. But the intelligence provided by the codebreakers allowed Walker to shift his troops and successfully fight off the attack. One US officer recalled that allied intercept operations had supplied Walker and his staff with 'perfect intelligence'. It all went straight to the people who needed it, he said. 'They knew exactly where each platoon of North Koreans was going, and they'd move to meet it. That was amazing, absolutely amazing.'[15]

The successful defence of Daegu allowed MacArthur to launch an amphibious landing of 75,000 troops at Incheon on the north-western coast of South Korea, way behind the North Korean lines, turning the war in favour of the UN forces. The North Koreans retreated in disarray, allowing Walker's 8th Army to break out of the Busan Perimeter and push on towards the 38th Parallel. Seoul was recaptured and the North Koreans were forced to retreat towards the border. As UN forces advanced north, concerns mounted in Beijing and London, and indeed among many in Washington, over where this was leading. The concerns were not so much over how far Truman was prepared to go, but how far MacArthur would go regardless of what the president told him to do. The UN commander gave every indication of being both out of touch and out of control, having already had to be reined in by the White House over 'sabre-rattling' claims hyping up the potential for all-out war between America and China.[16]

MacArthur's aggression towards China and his suggestion in a message to the Veterans of Foreign Wars that America would go to war to defend Taiwan had scarcely failed to allay concerns in London that he was, in the words of Sir Gladwyn Jebb, now Britain's ambassador to the UN, 'a mad satrap'. Guy Burgess told the KGB that 'the British regard with suspicion the position taken by MacArthur on defending Formosa [Taiwan]. In the opinion of the British, defending Formosa could lead the Chinese to use their trained troops against Hong Kong.' Burgess also reported continuing confusion in London and Washington over the extent to which Stalin was controlling what was happening in Korea, and how Moscow might react to UN troops invading the north. 'Neither the British nor, it seems, the Americans have any intelligence on the position the

Soviet government might take,' Burgess said. 'The British have no information that could be viewed as confirming direct assistance to the North Korean government.'[17]

In fact, unlike the Chinese, Stalin had from the start distanced himself from the war, acceding to Kim's plea to allow him to invade the south, but making it clear to the North Korean leader that aside from military advisers, logistics, weaponry and equipment, Soviet support would be limited and that if things went badly he would be on his own. There would be no Soviet ground troops, only covert air support to help to level out a crucial area of US dominance. As MacArthur's forces moved north of the 38th Parallel, Stalin told Kim he was evacuating many of the Soviet military personnel. He was not prepared to allow a defeat in Korea to weaken Moscow's hardline image in Europe, thereby suggesting that the Soviet Union could be defeated by the West. Nikita Khrushchev, the future Soviet leader, said Stalin was surprisingly relaxed about the idea of the Korean peninsula coming under US control. 'So what?' he said. 'Let it be. Let the Americans be our neighbours.' That was not the Chinese position.

The British and US signals intelligence operations in Hong Kong, Japan and Hawaii were monitoring Chinese Communist communications. Reporting from Chinese military communications relied heavily on traffic analysis, which despite the understandable obsession over whether codes and ciphers could be broken, provided a considerable amount of intelligence in its own right. But the Chinese commercial communications network, intercepted by the British in Hong Kong and the US Army in Hawaii, transmitted both personal communications and official messages in plain text, albeit using high-speed Morse, and was in fact providing far more intelligence on the Chinese military than their own communications. Milton Zaslow, who was in charge of the section at Arlington that was working on PLA material at the time, said the plain text messages on the commercial network had provided almost 80 per cent of the very detailed knowledge his section had of the Chinese armed forces.

'From the standpoint of both quality and amount, virtually all of this information has been derived from an analysis of plain text messages,' Zaslow said. 'Virtually all identifications of Chinese Communist Ground Force tactical units in China proper are derived exclusively from plain text, [which] provides extensive COMINT information on Chinese Communist military units and organisations—in many cases most or all of that information.'

The other advantage of the plain text messages was that the North Korean ones were formatted in the exact same way as the encrypted messages. The knowledge that a named officer was signing all of a unit's messages going out on the Chinese commercial network on a particular day, for example, could be used as a 'crib' for the signature at the end of the unit's enciphered messages, allowing the cryptanalyst to break into the cipher and read all of the messages encrypted using that system.[18]

Both the British and US signals intelligence operators had been reporting the movement of many thousands of Chinese troops to the border with Korea for months. Analysis of several dozen messages sent in plain text on the commercial network in July showed that elements of the 4th Field Army, seen as the PLA's most effective fighting force, were also moving north. The US intelligence Watch Committee, chaired by the CIA, but heavily skewed by the US Army's recycling of Charles Willoughby's assessments, ruled that the 'concentration of Chinese Communist troops in Manchuria might be intended for use in Korea' although at the time, with North Korean troops in full control of the situation on the ground, 'there was no indication as to when or under what circumstances they might be committed'.[19]

Diplomats based in Beijing and the CIA's reports suggested as late as 7 September that there was opposition within the Chinese leadership to intervening in Korea. They would support the North Koreans 'by all means short of armed intervention', the CIA and diplomatic reports maintained, even though throughout August there was evidence on the commercial network of thousands more Chinese troops moving towards the border. By early September it was clear that a major command headquarters, the 13th Army Group, had moved to the Chinese city of Dandong on the Sino-Korean border, while other elements of the 4th Field Army which had been moving east were now heading north.[20]

The success of the Incheon landings and MacArthur's known ambitions removed the Chinese hesitation over whether to intervene. In the second half of September, Chinese premier Zhou Enlai repeatedly sought to use Dr Kavalam Madhava Panikkar, the Indian ambassador in Beijing, to warn that China would intervene if UN forces crossed the 38th Parallel, knowing that India would pass the message on to London and hauling him out of bed twice in one week to do so. In fact, Panikkar's diplomatic communications with Delhi were intercepted and read by GCHQ, so the warnings were immediately available to both the British and US governments.[21]

On 1 October, South Korean troops crossed the 38th Parallel. The following day, the Chinese Communist Party Politburo agreed to intervene if US forces pushed north of the parallel. Zhou, still hoping that the moment of crisis could be averted, once more dragged Panikkar out of bed in the early hours of 3 October to reinforce his point that if US forces crossed into North Korea, China would attack.

At a meeting in the immediate aftermath of the Incheon landings, the Watch Committee agreed that Chinese forces could cross the Yalu River into Korea 'with little advance notice' and, throughout October, that view should only have been reinforced by the increasing number of major units being sent personal messages addressed to Dandong.[22] A British-sponsored UN resolution, deliberately reworked in a vain attempt to give MacArthur as little justification as possible to use it as an excuse to invade the North, called for 'all appropriate steps to be taken to ensure conditions of stability throughout Korea' and free elections leading to the creation of a unified democratic state.[23] MacArthur simply interpreted it the way he wanted to, as a green light to push north towards the Chinese border.

President Truman, who had decided to meet MacArthur on Wake Island in the central Pacific in order to reinforce his authority over the course of the war, called CIA director 'Beetle' Smith and told him he wanted to take intelligence estimates of six different questions: the threat of full Communist Chinese intervention in Korea; the threat of Soviet intervention; the threat of Communist

Chinese intervention in Taiwan; the threat of full Communist Chinese intervention in Indo-China; communist capabilities and threat in the Philippines; and Soviet and Communist Chinese intentions and capabilities in the Far East.[24]

With Truman due to fly out twenty-four hours later, Smith summoned the five members of the Intelligence Advisory Committee, representing the State Department, the navy, army and air force intelligence departments and the Joint Chiefs, to his office. A former CIA historian later noted that when one of them suggested he was not about to interrupt his dinner to be in Smith's office within the hour 'he was straightened out in the language of a drill sergeant addressing a lackadaisical recruit'. The president needed these estimates within twenty-four hours. If the committee member cared to question that, then perhaps he would like to tell the president himself that work on the estimates he needed could wait until one of his subordinates had finished his dinner.[25]

The estimates were produced in a timely fashion but, in the key areas, positions were predictably hedged. The PLA was capable of intervening effectively in Korea but did not have the necessary air support to win a war. Despite Zhou Enlai's repeated warnings and the massing of troops on China's border with North Korea, there were 'no convincing indications of an actual Chinese intention to resort to full-scale intervention'. Having laid out all the reasons for and against Chinese intervention, the paper concluded: 'While full-scale Chinese Communist intervention in Korea must be regarded as a continuing possibility, a consideration of all known factors leads to the conclusion that barring a Soviet decision for global war such action is not probable in 1950.'

Chinese involvement would probably be restricted to covert support for North Korea, the paper said. The Soviet Union was capable of intervening overwhelmingly in Korea virtually without warning, but despite its support in terms of training and materiel, Moscow had consistently distanced itself from the action in Korea and was unlikely to risk the global war that would be likely to ensue if Soviet troops openly attacked US and British troops in Korea. Smith added a seventh paper on the Soviet position with regard to war with the

West, making clear that the Soviet leaders were already achieving many of their aims without resorting to such a war, but it remained a possibility and would do so for the next three years at least. As for Taiwan, MacArthur's obsession was a side issue. There was little likelihood of Communist China attacking Taiwan at that time and even if there were 'success would be improbable'.[26]

During the Wake Island meeting, which was attended by a number of presidential advisers, including army secretary Frank Pace, assistant secretary of state for far eastern affairs Dean Rusk and chairman of the joint chiefs General Omar Bradley, Truman told MacArthur that he was concerned about the threat of Chinese intervention. 'I have been worried about that,' the president was reported as saying. 'What are the chances for Chinese . . . interference?' MacArthur insisted there was little chance of the Chinese intervening and even if they did, they would not be successful. 'Had they intervened in the first or second months, it would have been decisive,' MacArthur said. 'We are no longer fearful of their intervention.' No one, it seemed, not even Truman himself, had the grasp of the situation, or more likely perhaps, the temerity to disillusion MacArthur, and his intelligence adviser Willoughby was scarcely likely to do so.[27]

The conclusions in London were nowhere near as reassuring. The Chiefs of Staff, led intellectually by Marshal of the Royal Air Force Sir John Slessor, the chief of air staff, argued very strongly that Zhou's persistent private warnings and the dispatch of several hundred thousand Chinese troops to the border painted a very clear picture. Slessor was in no doubt that if MacArthur crossed the 38th Parallel, the Chinese would intervene and he made this point with some force. Surprisingly, the JIC thought it unlikely, while Ernest Bevin cautioned against interfering too much in the US conduct of the war. He and Clement Attlee decided on balance that the Americans were right and that Moscow would hold the Chinese back. They were wrong.[28]

When Chinese troops intervened to prevent the North Korean forces from being overwhelmed, the allied intelligence services were inevitably blamed for yet another 'Pearl Harbor moment'.

CIA reporting and estimates had certainly underestimated the situation, but the Agency did report that Chinese troops were preparing to cross the Yalu River to protect the Suiho hydroelectric plant, on which much of north-east China depended for electricity. A week later, the first Chinese troops entered Korea and they did indeed throw a defensive cordon around Suiho, but there were far more troops—in excess of 100,000—than were needed for that task alone. They moved forward to meet the initial South Korean advance, destroying the South Korean 2nd Corps together with a US cavalry regiment before falling back into the mountains and waiting for the UN response.[29]

Signals intelligence was prevented from warning of this initial Chinese incursion by the PLA's rigorously observed radio silence. But up to that point, and beyond, it provided plenty of evidence of what was to come. Messages on the commercial network over several months showing thousands of Chinese troops moving towards the Chinese border with Korea, and GCHQ decryption of diplomatic telegrams reporting repeated warnings from Zhou and other senior Communist Party officials, were extremely clear and ought to have left no room for doubt.

The day after the CIA reported on the possibility of Chinese troops entering Korea to protect the Suiho plant, intercepts of Chinese military communications provided even more evidence of troops being moved into place, reporting that the entire railway network in the north-east had been taken over by the military and that twenty trains carrying troops from the 3rd Field Army had been sent from Shanghai to the North Korean border with more on the way.[30] They also showed that many more Chinese troops, previously held some distance from the border, were moving forward to the banks of the Yalu and preparing to cross it.

Certainly, the CIA had not covered itself in glory, although its warning back in February 1949 that if US troops left there would be a North Korean invasion supported openly by Chinese troops and covertly by Moscow had proven correct. But the signals intelligence bodies monitoring Chinese civil and military communications intercepted from Hong Kong, Japan and Hawaii had more than made up for any failure in human intelligence. The refusal to recognise what was about to happen—and the twin assumptions that Zhou's repeated warnings were a bluff and that even if they were not Stalin would not allow China to intervene—were the result of a flawed mindset among those in government in Washington and London. The failure to predict the Chinese intervention was the result of poor decision-making, not a failure of intelligence.[31]

Even after the first Chinese troops crossed the Yalu, both the CIA and MacArthur remained in denial. One senior US intelligence officer working with Willoughby in Tokyo recalled that 'the great fault over there was poor evaluation of the intelligence that was obtained. They knew the facts, but they were poorly evaluated. I don't know just why that was. It was probably in good part because of MacArthur's personality. If he didn't want to believe something, he wouldn't.'[32]

'Beetle' Smith sent Truman a personally signed report, dated 1 November, on the initial Chinese incursion. It seriously under-estimated the number of Chinese troops already in Korea, putting the figure at only around 20,000. The report hinted at the future shape of communist forces in Korea, pointing out that the Soviet Air Force appeared to be providing air support to the Chinese troops, but Smith remained focused on the CIA assumption that they had crossed the border to protect the Suiho plant, which while true up to a point scarcely justified the 200,000 potential reinforcements now waiting on the other side of the Yalu. 'This pattern of events and reports indicates that Communist China has decided, regardless of the increased risk of general war, to provide increased support and assistance to North Korean forces,' he told the president. 'Although the possibility cannot be excluded that the Chinese Communists, under Soviet direction, are committing themselves to full-scale intervention in Korea, their main motivation at present appears to be to establish a limited "cordon sanitaire" south of the Yalu River.'

The CIA still clung to the illusion that the Chinese were taking their orders from Moscow and argued that rather than being an indication of a readiness to intervene with overwhelming force, the Chinese troops were probably massed on the other side of the border because Beijing feared a US invasion of China. 'The reported evacuation of industrial machinery and civilian personnel . . . could be the consequence of such a fear,' Smith said. 'Although the possibility exists that this evacuation has been undertaken in an effort to anticipate possible retaliatory action by UN forces following the Chinese Communist intervention in Korea.'[33]

During the first three weeks of November, the authorities in Beijing enforced a state of emergency, with mass demonstrations demanding intervention. The Americans had no diplomatic representation in Beijing, but the British still did, and they, together with intercepted diplomatic communications between other countries' ambassadors and their governments, gave a very clear picture of a nation preparing for war, with air defence systems being put in place and calls for volunteers to serve in Korea. Meanwhile, the commercial network revealed that the Chinese soldiers lined up along the Yalu were being immunised against smallpox, cholera and typhoid fever, all of which were prevalent in North Korea, and that tens of thousands of maps of Korea had been sent to the waiting troops.[34]

Despite the multiple warning signs, MacArthur planned a 'final offensive' for 24 November that would take UN forces up to the Chinese border, occupying the entire Korean peninsula and allowing democratic elections to take place. The day after the offensive began, 200,000 additional Chinese troops swept into Korea to bolster those already there, throwing the UN forces into disarray and pushing them back across the 38th Parallel. Lieutenant-Colonel James H. Polk, one of Willoughby's deputies, said the intelligence they received had shown very clearly that MacArthur's offensive risked a massive Chinese retaliation. 'We had the dope,' Polk said. 'But Willoughby bowed to the superior wisdom of his beloved boss.'

Seoul was retaken by North Korean and Chinese forces in early January 1951, but within weeks they had been pushed back across the 38th Parallel, raising renewed concern in London that MacArthur might again advance into North Korea. The British government was assured by the US administration that it agreed with the UK that holding to a line just north of the 38th Parallel offered the best chance of bringing the Chinese to the negotiating table, but if its assessment changed in any way Washington would discuss it with its allies before making any moves.[35]

Signals intelligence now threw up two separate, dramatic developments that were to have a major impact on the war. The first was the interception of communications between Soviet air defence ground control and Soviet fighter pilots in aerial combat with their US counterparts—MiG-15s ranged against the US F-86 Sabre fighter aircraft in the air over Korea—sparking an urgent US request to post a unit of US Air Force signals intelligence operators at the British intercept site in Hong Kong. A US Russian linguist recalled intercepting the dogfights between the Russian and American pilots. 'We were actually monitoring the Soviet Air Force fighting the American air force and we were listening to the Soviet pilots being directed by Soviet ground control people to fight the Americans. We were fighting our own little war with the Soviets.'[36]

The second development was intercepted in diplomatic communications between the Brazilian, Portuguese and Spanish ambassadors in Tokyo and their foreign ministries, which the British codebreakers were reading. They revealed that both MacArthur and Willoughby, who was a great admirer of the Spanish fascist dictator General Franco and close to the Spanish ambassador to Japan, Francisco José del Castillo, had briefed the diplomats on MacArthur's ambitions to expand the war. Among the many comments the general himself made in private conversations with the diplomats was that the war was the perfect opportunity to destroy Mao Zedong's Communists and install a Nationalist government amenable to America. He also said he hoped the Soviet Union would intervene in Korea. War with the Soviet Union was inevitable, MacArthur said, and it would be a very good thing if the West were given the opportunity to fight that war now.

Paul Nitze, then head of the State Department's Policy Planning Staff, said it was clear from the intercepts that the reason MacArthur had been willing to take the risk of advancing north—even after the initial Chinese intervention had given a clear signal to stop—was that, despite knowing that Truman's policy was to limit the extent of the conflict, he was quite happy to provoke a third world war. 'It was perfectly clear', Nitze said, 'that what MacArthur had in mind was that either he would have complete victory in North Korea or, if the Chinese communists got involved, then the war would be spread to the Chinese mainland as a whole and the object of the game would then be the unseating of Mao Zedong and the restoration of Chiang Kai-shek. In the course of doing that you had your nuclear weapons if you needed them.'

Truman could not act immediately to sack MacArthur for fear of revealing that the British and American codebreakers were reading the Spanish, Portuguese and Brazilian diplomatic ciphers. But a few weeks later, a letter from MacArthur to House Republican leader Joe Martin, sharply criticising US policy, gave Truman cover to fire him. MacArthur later made clear that he blamed the British and the US State Department for this 'great betrayal'. He claimed the British vetoed his plans to win the war. 'The perfidy of the British' and 'constant harassment and interference from the State Department' had robbed him of the victory which was 'in the palm of my hand'.[37]

Aerial reconnaissance producing photographic and radar imagery of what was happening behind the communist lines was severely lacking early on in the war and although the US Air Force (USAF) gradually built up the RB-29 Superfortress reconnaissance aircraft of the Okinawa-based 91st Strategic Reconnaissance Squadron, they were vulnerable to the MiG-15s. So, RB-45 Tornado jet reconnaissance aircraft, which could outrun the MiG-15s, were introduced for daylight operations. The RAF's Far East Flying Boat Wing patrolled the west coast of Korea in Sunderlands taking sideways-looking photographs across the peninsula while a detachment of 81 Squadron was sent to RAF Kai Tak in Hong Kong from where it flew Spitfire Mk XIX reconnaissance aircraft over China, along more than 600 miles of coastline from Hainan in the west to Shantou in the east. Flight Lieutenant Ted Powles, who led the detachment, flew as far south as the Paracel Islands and up to 100 miles inland photographing military establishments and airfields, pushing his aircraft so close to its limits that he frequently returned to Kai Tak with fuel levels exhausted. His determination to carry out his missions whatever the cost led in June 1952, after more than a hundred missions constantly in danger of being shot down by Chinese aircraft or air defences, to the award of the Air Force Cross.[38]

The CIA's intelligence operations behind the lines in Korea were under the control of Colonel Benjamin 'Vandy' Vandervoort, a Second World War hero whose role during the D-Day landings was played by John Wayne in the film *The Longest Day*. Vandervoort rubbed so many colleagues up the wrong way that he eventually had to be withdrawn. His replacement, John L. Hart, became immediately suspicious of the way in which the Seoul station was run. With none of the CIA officers fluent in Korean, they were relying on Korean lead agents to control the agents going through the lines.

An investigation ordered by Hart discovered that the Korean agents were in fact swapping information on what was going on in the south with North Korean and Chinese intelligence officers who in return supplied them with detailed intelligence on the north, the vast majority of which was deliberate deception designed to confuse the Americans. Nevertheless, Vandervoort had at least one major success, ensuring that a covert CIA agent was appointed special assistant to South Korean president Syngman Rhee. 'Beetle' Smith was told in September 1951 that the agent had been 'instrumental in the change of attitude of the ROK Government toward the US Government'. It was anticipated that 'with careful control this agent will develop into an outstanding deep-cover agent in the Far East'.[39]

The OPC did far better with special operations mounted behind the communist lines. Most were small-scale raids aimed more at disruption and damaging morale than any major impact but they also directed UN air strikes on a number of targets behind enemy lines and rescued a number of US pilots who had been shot down over enemy territory. A couple of dozen pilots were recovered in this way, leading to the gratitude of the USAF. It was also extremely grateful for the acquisition by one of the OPC-controlled fishing boats of a discarded wing tank from a MiG-15, which allowed the Americans to work out the aircraft's range. There were inevitably losses, the most serious of which was the capture by Chinese troops of two CIA officers, Jack Downey and Dick Fecteau, whose aircraft was shot down in late 1952 while on a mission to retrieve documents lost in an earlier operation.[40]

Possibly the most important of the CIA special operations missions was carried out by an OPC-controlled fishing boat, the *Sea Wolf*, which targeted a submarine cable across the Yellow Sea between the Chinese ports of Dalian and Zhifu. The cable carried high-level communications between Beijing and the Chinese commander Peng Dehuai. The *Sea Wolf* cut the cable in the early hours of 2 December 1951, dragging up a length of approximately 120 yards from the bottom of the ocean.

On its way back to South Korea, the *Sea Wolf* was intercepted by four Chinese patrol boats, one of which challenged the CIA boat with a shot across its bow. When the patrol boat came alongside the *Sea Wolf*, the CIA team scrambled aboard the Chinese boat and attacked its crew, killing all seven of them. They then reboarded the *Sea Wolf*, sinking the Chinese patrol boat with the CIA boat's M-18 57mm recoilless gun. The other Chinese patrol boats tried to close in but were held off by the M-18 gunfire. The *Sea Wolf* escaped in the darkness, taking shelter in a harbour on the South Korean island of Daecheongdo. The CIA team lost one man and suffered four wounded. The *Sea Wolf* returned to its home port of Busan four days later bringing the length of cable it had cut out. The removal of the submarine cable forced the Chinese to transmit their communications over the air, allowing allied signals intelligence teams to intercept them.[41]

The US Army had two separate units carrying out special operations behind enemy lines. The 8086th Army Unit and the 8240th Army Unit specialised in training and organising Korean nationals into guerrilla units. They carried out attacks on enemy units, destroyed bridges, roads and railways and set up a number of agent networks sometimes in tandem with the British. Eventually all the UN special operations units were coordinated under Covert, Clandestine and Related Activities in Korea (CCRAK), which operated under the less threatening covername of Combined Command for Reconnaissance Activities Korea. The OPC missions, carried out under the covername Joint Activities Commission Korea

(JACK), were ostensibly part of CCRAK, but inevitably operated independently, with air support provided by Civil Air Transport.[42]

The CIA continued to have a number of officers operating under non-official cover in China during the war. One of those officers, Hugh Redmond, had been recruited by the SSU to operate in Shanghai. His cover was as a salesman for the US ice cream manufacturer Henningsen's. Redmond was arrested in April 1951 as he attempted to board a flight to the United States, suggesting that the Chinese might have known about his existence for some time. Two months later, Robert McCann, a US businessman who had set up China's first car factory, was also arrested as a spy. McCann was not a CIA officer, but he was a trusted agent who had taken part in a number of CIA operations in the Tianjin region south-east of Beijing. 'Beetle' Smith was warned that although the Chinese had arrested McCann for breaches of foreign exchange laws, they were subjecting him to 'severe and intensive interrogation aimed at establishing his involvement in espionage'. There was particular concern because McCann knew the identity of several CIA officers operating under non-official cover.[43]

While the OPC's special operations behind the lines in Korea were largely successful, those mounted into mainland China from the CIA station in Hong Kong caused extensive problems. Its cooperation with the nationalist Chinese Kuomintang led to repeated disputes with the governor, Sir Alexander Grantham—who had vetoed, but not entirely prevented, the USAF stationing signals intelligence specialists at the RAF's Little Sai Wan intercept site on Hong Kong Island. Grantham openly accused the CIA of being 'extremely ham-handed' and claimed that he had been forced 'to take a very strong line to stop them being so stupid'.

The issues that led to his intervention included several cases where Chinese arrested under suspicion of breaking Hong Kong's law banning flagrant action against the PRC turned out to be nationalist guerrillas carrying out CIA sabotage missions inside China. Under orders from the governor, the Hong Kong police deliberately thwarted CIA operations, at one point seizing two OPC-controlled junks which were infiltrating communications teams into China to work with nationalist guerrillas and towing them back into Hong Kong harbour.[44]

There was concern in both London and Washington that the governor and his police chief, Duncan MacIntosh, might damage cooperation between the Americans and British intelligence. Two weeks before the Korean War broke out, Guy Liddell, the director of MI5's counter-espionage operations, noted in his diary that 'MacIntosh has apparently written a long diatribe against the CIA, suggesting that they be banned from the colony and this is supported in a covering letter by Grantham, the suggestion being that they would in due course withdraw'. MI5 needed to present a joint front with MI6 and the JIC to prevent the situation getting out of hand. 'Hong Kong seemed to be regarding this whole business in rather a parochial way, not realising that relations existed with CIA all over the world,' Liddell said. 'There is no doubt that CIA have been in the wrong, but it would be the greatest mistake to antagonise them permanently.'[45]

Liddell was right to be concerned. The issue, threatening disclosure of multiple US agents and the identification of CIA officers, caused such alarm that it was raised with Smith. The CIA head of station in Hong Kong told Washington that the British authorities appeared to be 'making a determined bid to reduce the scope of CIA activities' there. It was not clear if this was Grantham and MacIntosh acting on their own initiative or, more worryingly, if it was being directed from London, and the station head asked Washington to carry out 'a review of our Hong Kong liaison arrangements with the British in order to protect our intelligence assets'. Stewart Menzies sent Jack Easton to Hong Kong in November 1951 to sort out the issues and to create a firm alliance on the ground between the CIA head of station, his MI6 counterpart and the colony's MI5 defence security officer that would bypass the governor. Easton returned to the UK via Washington to report back on his efforts, but Grantham and MacIntosh continued to cause difficulties.[46]

UK operations behind the lines were originally expected to be carried out by a squadron of SAS raised specially for the war, the regiment having been disbanded after the Second World War. But the

Chinese intervention, and the need for special forces to counter the insurgency in Malaya, changed that and special operations behind the lines were controlled by the British Army's Intelligence Corps. A unit previously based in the Burmese capital of Rangoon, 904 Field Security Section, was moved to Korea as part of the British 29th Brigade in October 1950. Running agents behind enemy lines was just one of its tasks, which also included military and civil security, and the vetting and screening of refugees. But assisted by Canadian and Australian colleagues, it appears to have been successful in persuading agents to go through the lines and ensuring that they collected genuine intelligence or carried out specific sabotage briefs before returning alive. Given the climate of fear in North Korea, and the problems faced by the CIA in keeping their agents on track, this was no easy task.[47]

Such 'special reconnaissance' operations were also carried out by the Divisional Agent Detachment run by the Australian Sergeant Alf Harris, who accompanied a number of his agents through the lines himself to ensure they got through. Harris made eleven trips into enemy territory either to show new agents the routes or on special reconnaissance missions of his own. He was awarded the Military Medal for an operation which followed a period when several new agent groups had been unable to cross the enemy lines.

Harris decided that the only way to get them through was to take them himself. Late in the evening of 2 July 1953, he led a group of three new agents into no man's land. They moved forward to the Samichon River, which was heavily flooded and fast-flowing. Harris swam the river, taking one end of a guide rope with him, and then helped the agents across on the rope. He split them into two groups, two of the agents going off on their own and the other staying with him. The two groups then made for an anti-tank ditch just under a mile behind the enemy forward defences where previous agent groups had run into trouble. As they approached the ditch, Harris and his agent came under sustained small-arms fire. The agent was killed instantly and Harris was hit in the hand and thigh. Realising that the other two agents had not been detected, he drew enemy attention to himself by returning fire with his pistol. When he ran out of ammunition, he dived into the river and let the current carry him away, drawing the enemy fire and further diverting attention away from the other agents, who as a result managed to get through, 'eventually returning with much useful information'.[48]

Signals intelligence was undoubtedly the most reliable source of intelligence, although during a war that is generally the case. Unless a human intelligence organisation has an agent-in-place at the heart of the decision-making process, as the CIA did have with Syngman Rhee's special assistant, it is rarely going to match the ability of signals intelligence during a full-scale conflict. The signals intelligence was not always perfect, in large part because of a lack of linguists. Even the Americans, with large numbers of ethnic Chinese living in America as US citizens and continuing to speak their native language at home, struggled to find enough Chinese speakers, largely because most spoke Cantonese rather than Mandarin, which was uniformly used by the PLA.

There were also problems of coordination. The creation of the Armed Forces Security Agency had failed to remove the lack of cooperation between the US Army and US Navy—with the former complaining in 1949 that its liaison with the British still 'ran with greater smoothness than that with the Navy'. The formation of the US Air Force with its own signals intelligence organisation had only made matters worse. An investigation led in November 1952 to the creation of the National Security Agency (NSA), forcing all three service organisations together.[49]

'Beetle' Smith eventually insisted he must have complete control over Frank Wisner's OPC and in 1952 merged it with the Office of Special Operations to form a single Directorate of Plans. An investigation into CIA operations in the Far East noted 'many excellences' but conceded that there was little appreciation among its customers of what the Agency could and could not do. 'There is widespread lack of knowledge among important armed services officers of the capabilities and, more importantly, the limitations of CIA intelligence procurement,' the investigation concluded. 'This leads almost inexorably to blaming CIA for every intelligence lack without too much critical examination of their own shortcomings.'

Wisner pointed out that the CIA had only been in existence for a few years. It would take time to get things right. 'We are all aware that our operations in the Far East are far from what we would like to have them, and in some cases stand in need of drastic action to accomplish improvement,' he said. 'This Agency is still in its extreme youth, and we simply have not had the time to develop the quantity and kind of people we must have if we are to successfully carry out the heavy burdens which have been placed upon us.' The dynamic between the British and the Americans might have changed, with political realities making the CIA and NSA the senior partners, but in many areas they still relied heavily on the material produced by their UK opposite numbers, and while that was not lacking in the British reporting from Hong Kong, its absence in Korea was keenly felt.[50]

9

THE IRAN COUP

During the early years of the Cold War, America's political dominance over Britain, so obvious in the Far East and emerging more slowly but undeniably in Europe, had seemed—to the Foreign Office at least—to have no great impact on its position in the Middle East. The British still retained a large degree of influence, in particular in Egypt, Iraq, the Gulf States and Iran. Dean Acheson had gone out of his way to recognise Britain as 'the senior partner' in the region.

Britain had dominated the situation in Iran in the first half of the twentieth century. It remained a major force there, partly for historical reasons, but also as a result of the UK government's part-ownership of the Anglo-Iranian Oil Company (AIOC), which, due to a concession dating back to 1901, controlled the Iranian oil reserves. Both Britain and America saw Iran as a vital barrier to Soviet expansion into the Middle East, but while the Truman administration recognised that US policy in the region needed to be allied with that of the UK, there was increasing frustration at what it saw as Britain's continuing 'colonialist' approach.[1]

The British had always enjoyed a curious relationship with the Iranians, most of whom, including the Shah, saw Britain's 'hidden hand' behind virtually everything bad that happened to their country. The way in which the division of the proceeds from Iran's oil was weighted heavily in favour of the AIOC only exacerbated the widespread mistrust of the British. Throughout 1950, there were increasing demands from the nationalists, led by veteran politician Mohammad Mossadeq, and the outlawed Soviet-backed Tudeh Party, for the country's oil industry, including the AIOC refinery at

Abadan, to be nationalised. These demands were resisted by prime minister Haj Ali Razmara for fear of the likely British reaction and the inevitable damage to Iran's economy, but when the US company ARAMCO agreed to split its profits on a similar Saudi concession equally with Riyadh, the pressure became unstoppable. After an initial hesitation, the AIOC offered the Iranian government an equal share of the income from its concession, but it was no longer enough. Mossadeq and his supporters wanted nothing less than full ownership of the oil.

On 7 March 1951, Razmara was assassinated by a member of an Islamist nationalist group, Fada'iyan-e-Islam. The Shah replaced him with Hossein Ala, who also favoured compromise with the British. A few days later, the Iranian parliament, the Majlis, unanimously approved the nationalisation of the country's oil industry. Both the nationalists and the communists took to the streets for a series of protests against Ala's government and, on 27 April, he resigned. The Shah bowed to the inevitable and appointed Mossadeq prime minister. The same day, the Majlis passed a bill nationalising the AIOC and on 1 May the Shah signed it into law.

The British response was to impose economic sanctions on Iran, to withdraw key British experts from the oilfields and the Abadan refinery and to lay off 20,000 Iranian workers. A British airborne brigade was moved to Cyprus and Royal Navy warships prevented any movement of Iranian oil in the Persian Gulf. Intercept operators on board the British warships listened in to the radio messages of the Iranian military, whose ciphers had been broken by GCHQ. Meanwhile, pressure was brought on the Shah, who while sympathetic to British concerns was too scared to act against Mossadeq, and a long series of fruitless negotiations began in which the AIOC stuck to a 50–50 split of profits, which the Iranian prime minister persistently refused to accept.[2]

The US position was heavily influenced by the fear of Iran falling into the Soviet orbit. Both the State Department and the CIA saw Razmara's assassination as bringing that situation much closer, with Kim Roosevelt, now head of the CIA's Near East and Africa Division, arguing that 'Iran's loss under Cold War conditions would be disastrous and that unless something is done to stem the tide it is a strong possibility'. The State Department saw Mossadeq as the last man standing between an Iran aligned with the West and a major Middle East player under Soviet control, and pushed the Attlee government into ever more concessions. Meanwhile, Mossadeq skilfully played Britain and America off against each other, constantly suggesting to the US ambassador that this or that concession might get negotiations up and running again, only to reject it once the Americans had persuaded the reluctant British to offer it. The Attlee government became increasingly frustrated with the Truman administration, which seemed to expect it to make whatever concessions Mossadeq required.[3]

By the summer of 1951, the British had decided Mossadeq must go and if the Shah would not remove him, they would. Monty Woodhouse, whose time running wartime SOE operations in Greece alongside the OSS was seen as essential experience for the kind of political action needed in Iran, was dispatched to head up the MI6 station in Tehran and work out how to get rid of Mossadeq. 'Doc' Zaehner was already there contacting the Iranian agents he had developed during the war. Norman Darbyshire, a former SOE officer who had worked alongside Zaehner in wartime Iran and was now Woodhouse's deputy, said the academic's brief was very simple: 'Go out, don't inform the ambassador, use the intelligence services to provide you with any money you might need and secure the overthrow of Mossadeq by legal or quasi-legal means. Vast sums of money were being spent.'

Woodhouse said that his own objectives as MI6 head of station were very clear: 'to forestall a Soviet-backed takeover by the Communists, to remove Mossadeq from power, to establish a pro-Western government and to undo so far as possible the damage done to the UK's oil interests'. The unusual aspect of the Foreign Office pushing for such action, rather than attempting to restrain MI6, was not lost on Woodhouse, who acerbically recalled that the diplomats tended to refer to Britain's spies 'politely but not very sincerely as "the Friends"'.

His new station was relatively large by post-war standards. 'My own assets when I took up a nominal post in our embassy were considerable, but demoralised by the setbacks of the past year,' he wrote. 'Three or four able young men in the embassy specialised in intelligence on Iran and the communists. Another cultivated leading Iranians hostile to Mossadeq. Another conducted a useful liaison, approved by the Shah, with the chief of the security police, who was well informed about the Tudeh Party.' There was also a signals intelligence unit at RAF Habbaniya in Iraq, 50 miles west of Baghdad. It was originally sent there in the late 1940s to monitor Soviet radio communications, but it also monitored Iranian Army and police networks.[4]

The MI6 station had a number of useful agents, including Assadollah Rashidian, and his two brothers Seyfollah and Qodratollah, well-placed businessmen who had been cultivated by Zaehner during the Second World War. The eldest brother, Assadollah, was a Godfather-like figure, with widespread business interests which gave him enormous influence—he regularly held open house where people paid their respects to him and asked for his assistance in solving their problems. He was very close to the Shah and his sister Princess Ashraf, and was highly influential among the wealthy merchants in the bazaar, senior army officers, politicians and the mullahs, including Mossadeq's political ally Ayatollah Sayyed Abul-Qassem Kashani.

The brothers were confirmed Anglophiles who had sent their children to school in England and owned expensive property in London. Zaehner and Woodhouse set them to work buying up key members of the ruling National Front coalition, to split them off from Mossadeq, a campaign that proved extremely productive. The bribes, which amounted to around £10,000 a month (£300,000 in today's terms), were funded by MI6 via a company set up to import British films to Iran. They were paid out to politicians across the political spectrum, to mullahs, businessmen and tribal leaders in order to undermine Mossadeq. The MI6 station also had agents inside the Tudeh Party who were used to manipulate the normally well-organised communist protests and provide intelligence that helped the Rashidians arrange for gangs of youths to disrupt the protests with violent clashes.[5]

Meanwhile, the British ramped up the pressure, breaking off negotiations with Mossadeq and, when he responded by expelling the remaining British workers from Abadan, moving troops to the region in preparation for Operation Buccaneer, a planned occupation of the oilfields and the Abadan refinery to take back control of the AIOC's operations. Darbyshire was sent to Abadan as 'vice-consul' and persuaded the Iranian commander-in-chief at Khorramshahr to give him details of all the Iranian forces and their plans to take over the refinery. 'That cost HMG the princely sum of 2lbs of Liptons tea, because he couldn't get it in Persia and I got it for him and that is precisely what I paid him,' Darbyshire recalled. He persuaded the Iranian commander not to offer more than token resistance to the British forces. But with the CIA warning that any British military action might lead to a response from the Soviet Union under the 1921 Soviet–Iranian Treaty of Friendship, Truman made very clear to Attlee that he was not prepared to support armed intervention, insisting negotiation was the only way forward.[6]

Behind the scenes, the CIA was also manipulating the situation, albeit focusing on discrediting the Soviet Union and the Tudeh Party. Two young anti-communist journalists, Ali Jalali and Farrokh Keyvani, had approached the CIA station in Tehran in early 1951. Jalali had been the editor-in-chief of the conservative newspaper *Ettela'at* and Keyvani was one of the newspaper's best-known reporters. The pair had subsequently worked for *Tehran Mossavar*, a weekly newspaper controlled by Iranian military intelligence.[7]

They told Roger Goiran, the CIA station chief, that the US policy of backing Mossadeq as a barrier to a communist takeover was a mistake. Almost certainly pushing the views of Iranian military intelligence, they argued that the prime minister's willingness to conspire with the Tudeh Party to organise street demonstrations in order to get his own way was a dangerous ploy which risked leaving Iran vulnerable to a pro-Moscow coup. Kim Roosevelt met them and was impressed with their potential, not least their understanding of covert intelligence operations, and recruited them as the CIA's 'principal agents' in Iran, giving them the codenames NERREN and CILLY. They were to become the main driving force for a long-term

CIA political action programme codenamed Operation Bedamn in which they planted anti-communist articles and cartoons in Iranian newspapers, wrote articles exposing links between prominent nationalist politicians and Moscow and, as with MI6, infiltrated agents provocateurs into the Tudeh Party to turn demonstrations violent and discredit the party among the wider population.[8]

Their operations, which like those of the Rashidians included bribing key politicians and influential mullahs, were funded at around a million dollars a year ($10 million in today's terms). This begged the question as to how two young journalists could possibly have access to such large sums of money. In an interesting echo of the British arrangements for funding the Rashidians, Louis de Rochemont, who had produced *13 Rue Madeleine*, one of the post-war films designed to show the OSS in a good light, and was working on a CIA-funded film of George Orwell's *Animal Farm*, announced that he had bought the rights to 'an original story dealing with the current oil crisis in Iran' which had been written by two young up-and-coming Iranian journalists.

'The CIA's two principal agents in Iran have received a letter from Louis de Rochemont, informing them that their recently submitted scenarios have been accepted by Hollywood,' the CIA director's morning meeting was told. 'Arrangements have been made to release this information to the press and Voice of America will beam the story to Iran and the UK. The scenarios do not exist. The intent of the letter and the attendant publicity is to cover the substantial expenditures being made by the agents in Iran who, ostensibly, are politically active newspapermen of nominal means.' A few days later, the *New York Times* carried the story of two young Iranian newspapermen, Ali Jalali and Farrokh Keyvani, who had hit the jackpot with their screenplay, the story of an American journalist searching for the 'news behind the news' in Iran.[9]

Meanwhile, the Truman administration continued to push for British concessions, every one of which Mossadeq inevitably rejected as not enough. The US embassy in London left the State Department in no doubt that the British felt very badly let down by the Americans' approach to the negotiations. Feelings were running high not just at government level but in the country at large. The British government, as America's 'friendliest and staunchest ally', was 'hurt and bewildered' that their main ally should insist they make concession after concession to appease Mossadeq when it was clear that nothing short of complete capitulation would satisfy him.[10]

Robert Cecil, who had been Foreign Office adviser to Stewart Menzies during the war and was now head of the Foreign Office's American Department, noted a growing determination in Washington that 'if the Americans have to go on paying the piper, they will call the tune'. Britain was increasingly anxious—not least given the existence of US nuclear bombers on British soil—that 'impetuous all-or-nothing tendencies in the United States will prematurely expose this country to the first onslaught of Communist aggression'. Yet contrary to the impression often given of a bullying United States oblivious to UK interests, the Americans were keenly aware that the British remained 'the most resolute and effective of our allies and through their commonwealth ties and influence with other areas represent an element of strength in the Free World second only to the US'. They were very anxious not to damage the relationship with Britain in any way.[11]

Britain took the issue to the UN in October 1951 with Mossadeq flying to New York to argue the Iranian case personally. While there, he was treated for a long-standing intestinal problem by Dr Claude Forkner, a CIA contract agent who had also treated other foreign dignitaries, including King Faisal of Saudi Arabia and the Shah. Forkner carefully steered his supposedly confidential conversations with his patients to obtain whatever information his CIA handler required.

'Arrangements are being made to debrief Dr Forkner daily during his contact with Mossadeq,' the CIA morning meeting was told a few days before the Iranian premier arrived in New York. Given that Mossadeq would be having talks in Washington with US and World Bank officials, the Agency also had high hopes of surreptitiously placing their own man inside the Iranian delegation to update them on Mossadeq's intentions. The Iranian embassy in Washington had reportedly recommended that the Iranian prime minister should employ an expert adviser who, unbeknown to the Iranians, was a CIA agent, the meeting was told. The agent was being briefed on what he would be required to find out if his employment was confirmed.[12]

While the Rashidians worked to undermine Mossadeq, Monty Woodhouse focused on developing a plan to remove him. The former SOE officer realised that it would have to be carried out in conjunction with the Americans, so like most British intelligence officers abroad he made it his business to get close to his CIA counterpart. The British embassy had a summer camp beside a trout stream in the mountains north of Tehran where Woodhouse and Goiran spent a week fly-fishing. 'I was convinced from the first that any effort to forestall a Soviet coup in Iran would require a joint Anglo-American effort,' Woodhouse said. 'The CIA was still a youthful organisation with a high regard for its British counterpart, liaison with my CIA colleague could be the key to success. He was a second-generation American of French descent, so he was both bilingual and quick to grasp a European viewpoint.'[13]

The British general election on 25 October 1951 brought Winston Churchill back to power, with Anthony Eden as his foreign secretary. Following discussions with Eden in Paris—prior to which Churchill insisted the UK must 'not yield an inch'—Dean Acheson warned his closest colleagues in the State Department that they should expect no change in the British position. The new Conservative government started from the same basis as its Labour predecessor, with the only change being the addition of 'a certain truculent braggadocio'.

'This attitude extends all through the government from the Prime Minister to the civil servants,' Acheson said. 'It starts from Churchill, with the roar of a wounded lion, becomes more articulate with Eden . . . and is fully rationalised by the civil servants.' The Second World War had brought Britain to the verge of bankruptcy and it was not willing to jeopardise commercial relationships with other countries which might be tempted to follow the Iranian lead. Nor was it prepared to cause lasting damage to its reputation by giving in to Mossadeq simply because the Americans wanted to keep him on side.[14]

Nevertheless, Churchill knew nothing could be done to solve the Mossadeq issue without the Americans. He went to Washington in January 1952 determined to use his personal reputation to pull Anglo-American relations back to something like the close wartime alliance. The British prime minister concluded a historic third address to a joint session of Congress by pointing out to wild applause that while the world had changed substantially since he last made such an address midway through the war 'there is one thing that is exactly the same as when I was here last—Britain and the United States are working for the same high cause. Let us make sure that the supreme fact of the twentieth century is that they tread the same path.'[15]

Over the next six months, the British and American attempts to solve the oil crisis by diplomatic means were repeatedly frustrated by Mossadeq's endless intrigues. MI6 used 'parallel diplomacy', setting up secret talks in Paris between Julian Amery, by now a Conservative MP, and Ahmad Ghavam, a former prime minister who was being lined up as a possible replacement for Mossadeq. He assured Amery that he was keen to reinstitute the 'traditionally cordial' relations with the British and get the oil supplies flowing again.[16]

By the summer of 1952, the Americans were beginning to believe that the British were right and that they should start looking for an alternative figure to keep the Soviet Union at bay. This view was considerably hardened by an attempt by Mossadeq to appoint himself war minister, supplanting the Shah's control over the armed forces. When the Shah refused to allow it, Mossadeq resigned. He was replaced by Ghavam. Acheson prepared to bolster the new government with a $26 million aid payment and the British had high hopes that the new prime minister would fulfil his promises, bringing the crisis to an end. But Mossadeq and his National Front allies, in worryingly close collaboration with the Tudeh Party, brought tens of thousands of protestors out onto the streets three days in a row, leading to riots that left sixty-nine dead and hundreds injured. Ghavam resigned and Mossadeq returned to power.[17]

The obvious close cooperation between Mossadeq and the Tudeh Party, suggesting that the Iranian prime minister was not quite the barrier to Soviet expansion the State Department imagined him to be, led to urgent consideration in Washington of whether to get rid of him and, if so, how. The CIA began to discuss 'a coup d'état type of action' using local tribes in the south. Kim Roosevelt had developed close links with the Qashqai tribes of southern Iran who were violently anti-communist, but they were ardent supporters of Mossadeq and would never support action against him. The British had far closer ties to the rival Bakhtiari tribe and their leader, Abul Qasim Bakhtiari, which had been developed by 'Doc' Zaehner during the war. 'Beetle' Smith ordered close CIA coordination with MI6 on contingency plans in case of a Soviet occupation of Iran.[18]

Both the CIA and MI6 were authorised to begin stockpiling weapons close to the tribal areas as a matter of urgency, although the Foreign Office, now backtracking from its initial aggressive approach, ruled it was too early for any joint planning. Woodhouse set up arms caches in a number of areas accessible to the Bakhtiaris. The CIA were already stockpiling enough explosives and weaponry 'to support a 10,000-man guerrilla organisation for six months'.[19]

The Americans were not the only ones worried by Mossadeq's collaboration with the Tudeh Party. In London, the JIC expressed grave concern that 'their influence must be expected to increase'. Mossadeq was only exacerbating the situation. The most effective way of stopping the Tudeh Party's advances was a regime led by 'a strong Shah' backed by a powerful army. Unsurprisingly, that view was shared by senior Iranian Army officers. The Rashidian brothers approached Fazlollah Zahedi, a retired general and a member of the Iranian Senate, who had served in one of Mossadeq's governments and was seen by the British as a potential coup leader. As head of the Iranian Army's Retired Officers Association, Zahedi had considerable support within the military and would make an ideal anti-communist prime minister.[20]

At this point, Woodhouse recruited a new agent, to whom he gave the pseudonym OMAR. A senior Iranian civil servant, he offered to provide the British with information that would help them act in the best interests of both Britain and Iran. 'He came so openly that he clearly thought he was doing nothing wrong,' Woodhouse recalled.

From his position as Director-General of an important department, he had become convinced that Mossadeq was ruining his
country. Like most Iranians, even men as highly educated as himself, he believed that nothing happened in Iran except at the will
of the British. Since we were all-powerful in Iran, he reasoned
that if we were regularly and accurately informed about what was
going on inside Mossadeq's government, we would be able to act
more effectively in the common interest of both our countries.

Although Omar was in many respects naïve, his reports were
another matter. They were objective and evidently accurate. He
attended meetings of Mossadeq's Council of Ministers. Two or
three times a week, he and I met privately, and I heard intimate
details from within the Iranian administration. Mossadeq held
the Council of Ministers' meetings usually at his own house and
conducted the meetings from his bed. All the major decisions
were imposed by himself. We learned of them instantly.[21]

By now, Churchill was chomping at the bit. He reminded Eden that
he had asked him previously 'whether our embassies in Tehran and
Cairo had pistols and tommy-guns', adding: 'I think they ought to
have them.' When Eden, suffering from ill health, went on a brief
holiday to Portugal, Churchill seized the opportunity to propose
to Truman that they make a joint proposal to Mossadeq. If it were
accepted, he would be hard put to go back on it later, while the
public rejection of a reasonable proposal from the US president and
the British prime minister would expose his perverse behaviour
both internationally and in Iran itself.[22]

'I thought it might do good if we have a gallop together such as I
often had with FDR,' the British prime minister said in a personal
message to Truman. 'There is little doubt that a brief, cogent, joint
telegram would be far more effective than a continuance of the
futile parleying which has got us no further in all these months.
I believe that your name and mine at the foot of a joint telegram
would be an effective assertion of right over wrong.'[23] The joint
proposal called for the International Court of Justice to decide the
issue of compensation to the AIOC for the nationalisation of the

company's property in Iran. In return, Britain would ease sanctions, relax restrictions on Iran's access to its UK bank accounts and have the AIOC send in experts to help the Iranians ensure that the oil began flowing again. The Americans would also make an immediate grant of $10 million to help Mossadeq balance the country's budget. But Mossadeq rejected it as a 'nefarious snare'. He demanded that Britain pay Iran £49 million, £20 million of it within seven days, and warned that he would break off diplomatic relations if the UK refused. Churchill had already made it very clear that he was not prepared to pay Mossadeq a penny.[24]

OMAR told Woodhouse at the beginning of October that the decision to expel the British had been taken, although it would not be announced for another two weeks. This gave the MI6 station chief time to work out how to keep in touch with the key MI6 agents inside Iran. Ostensibly, he handed control of the Rashidian brothers and others who might be useful in the event of a coup to Roger Goiran. But he decided to 'extemporise' in the cases of several others, including OMAR, using the few remaining members of the British community to keep the lines of communication open, ensuring OMAR could keep MI6 informed of Mossadeq's decisions.[25]

Meanwhile, Mossadeq had learned of Zahedi's plotting and the role of the Rashidians. Zahedi and other politicians had parliamentary immunity, but the Rashidians were arrested, along with a pro-coup general, for 'plotting and inciting on behalf of a foreign embassy'. The general was swiftly released but the Rashidians remained in jail for six weeks before being freed. Shortly after the arrests, Mossadeq broke off relations with the UK, expelling the ambassador and his staff, including the members of the MI6 station.[26]

Woodhouse briefed Eden on the MI6 proposals for a coup, taking Zaehner with him in the mistaken belief that the academic's experience in Iran would add weight to his arguments. To his horror, Zaehner said he could not see any chance of a coup succeeding. 'As I had asked for him to be present as the leading authority on Iran, I was quite unable to counter his gloomy advice,' Woodhouse said. 'That seemed likely to terminate the whole project. But Eden left one loophole open. He remarked that an operation such as we contemplated would have no chance of success without American support. I took his words as tantamount to pursue the idea further with the CIA. As I already had a good relationship with the CIA representative in Tehran, who was now the channel for most of our communications, I thought I might be able to make progress with the CIA in Washington.'[27]

Woodhouse and one of his officers flew to Washington to brief the CIA on Operation Boot, his aptly named plan to get rid of Mossadeq. He focused on US fears over the Iranian prime minister's close relationship with the communist Tudeh Party, and their obvious interest in using him while they waited for their moment to get rid of him and seize power themselves. 'Two separate components were dovetailed into the plan, because we had two distinct kinds of resources: an urban organisation run by the brothers and a number of tribal leaders in the south,' Woodhouse said. 'We intended to activate both simultaneously. The urban organisation included senior officers of the army and police, deputies and senators, mullahs, merchants, newspaper editors and elder statesmen, as well as mob-leaders. These forces, directed by the brothers, were to seize control of Tehran, preferably with the support of the Shah but, if necessary, without it and to arrest Mossadeq and his ministers. At the same time, the tribal leaders were to make a show of force in the direction of the major cities of the south. If there were resistance by the Tudeh Party, the tribes would occupy key towns such as Isfahan and Abadan.'[28]

Frank Wisner, now deputy director plans, the head of the CIA operations division, was extremely receptive to the idea. He and Kim Roosevelt were itching to use unconventional measures to sort out the Iranian crisis and were well aware that the British had many more useful agents than they did in Iran. They included senior army and police officers worried about communism, and the politicians and mullahs who had been bought by the Rashidians. But MI6 did not have access to the funding required to sustain a long-term operation and, having been expelled, they had no one on the ground with the experience and ability to orchestrate Operation Boot.

The Americans did have the ability to put someone into Tehran to take charge of the operation, with both MI6 and the CIA seeing Roosevelt as the obvious candidate, but they would need the British assets, and in particular the Rashidians, to make it work. The CIA had plenty of agents prepared to help keep the Iranian prime minister in power to prevent the communists taking over but very few who would help to get rid of him.

'CIA has no group in Iran which could effectively promote riots demonstrating against Mossadeq,' a candid internal CIA assessment admitted in March 1953. 'It could provide fairly effective pro-Shah demonstrations on the condition that these demonstrations not be in effect anti-Mossadeq demonstrations.' Using Ali Jalali and Farrokh Keyvani, it did have a proven ability to produce anti-Tudeh demonstrations, but could do so 'only under favourable conditions, and provided that the central government does not strongly object'.[29]

While Woodhouse was in Washington, Roosevelt had been in London talking to his British counterpart, George Kennedy Young, and other senior MI6 officers. They shared the Woodhouse plan with him. Although they did not name the British agents that were lined up to help overthrow Mossadeq, they did discuss the attitude of the Shah, pointing out that a number of their agents were close to him and could help persuade him to back a coup. Aside from the Rashidians, these included Soleiman Behdudi, the Shah's chief of court protocol; Ernest Perron, the Shah's Swiss private tutor and lifelong friend; and Shapoor Reporter, another close friend of the Shah who had been recruited by Zaehner during the war. Although Reporter was now political adviser to US ambassador Loy Henderson, he retained his close contacts with MI6, providing them with a useful agent of influence inside the US embassy. The British were anxious to get moving, but Roosevelt pointed out that with the Truman administration coming to an end, there was little chance of getting the political go-ahead until Eisenhower took over.[30]

Paradoxically, at the same time that the British were pushing for a coup, the pressure was building in Washington for the administration to sideline its allies and take control of the situation itself, no matter what the costs to the relationship with the British. US defence secretary Bob Lovett wrote to Dean Acheson calling for immediate US action to prevent Iran turning communist. The British had failed, forcing the Americans to take primary responsibility in Iran, he said. They should act now regardless of the cost to America's relations with its closest allies.

Acheson's response was caustic. 'The problem in Iran does not lend itself to any facile solution,' he said bluntly. 'You say that events have forced primary responsibility for Iran on the United States regardless of our wishes or those of the British. It has seemed to us for some time that an even broader problem faces us.' It was not that the British did not have the ability to deal with the problem, it was that both the US and the UK needed each other, their joint efforts amounting to far more than either side's did on their own.

'Our policy should take into account the strength as well as the weakness of the British position in the area,' Acheson said. 'It is only by correlating our efforts with the British that the limited resources available to us can be employed with any lasting effectiveness in developing stability and a capability of defence in the Middle East.' Lovett's proposals also ignored the fact that 'the United Kingdom is the most important element of strength in the Western alliance outside of the United States', Acheson said. If America were to act without recognising understandable British sensitivities over the issue it 'could do deep and lasting harm to our alliance'.[31]

The US oil companies were also watching from the sidelines with interest, and while the larger ones regarded Iran under Mossadeq as a problem they did not need and preferred to watch and wait, the smaller US companies saw the possibility of taking over from the AIOC as an easy killing. 'Some moderate-sized oil companies are becoming restive and it is possible that combinations of the purchase and transport of substantial quantities of Iranian oil may be made unless there is direct and strong objection by the US government,' the CIA reported, before warning that 'the British would probably regard any arrangement between US oil companies and Iran, in the absence of British concurrence, as a serious breach of US–UK solidarity'.[32]

The plan to get rid of Mossadeq began to come together in a serious way with talks between the CIA and MI6 in Washington at the

beginning of February 1953, shortly after the Eisenhower administration took over. MI6 Chief Sir John Sinclair and JIC chairman Sir
Patrick Dean discussed Boot with Kim Roosevelt, Frank Wisner and
Allen Dulles, who had just replaced 'Beetle' Smith as CIA director.
They agreed to work up a joint plan to remove Mossadeq, replacing
him with General Zahedi. Since MI6 had no one on the ground, it
was agreed Roosevelt should take charge.[33]

A few weeks later, Roosevelt, Young, Roger Goiran and Norman
Darbyshire held talks in Cyprus, to work out contingency plans
for how to respond to a possible Soviet-backed coup in Iran. The
discussions were given added impetus by an attempt by Mossadeq,
a few days earlier, to force the Shah into exile and effective abdica-
tion, leading to a further recognition in Washington of the flaws in
their policy of sticking with Mossadeq. Dulles told the NSC that the
Iranian prime minister was 'out to finish the Shah'. Mossadeq had
accused him of conspiring against him, blamed him for an attack by
Bakhtiari tribesmen on government forces in Khuzestan a few days
earlier, and demanded he hand over his land to the government and
give up control of the army. The Shah had 'capitulated', Dulles said,
leaving a dangerous power vacuum.[34]

The Cyprus talks focused on setting up stay-behind movements
of CIA and MI6 agents, the establishment of a 'free government'
under Zahedi—who was at the time under arrest accused of seeking
to overthrow Mossadeq—and the creation of a guerrilla resistance
movement using the southern tribes. The meeting 'established the
guiding principles of Anglo-American cooperation, at both the
policy and intelligence levels'. Immediately afterwards, Roosevelt
flew to Beirut and caught a bus to Baghdad from where he and a CIA
colleague drove across the border into Iran.[35]

The Rashidians, Jalali and Keyvani set to work rallying support
for the Shah while Loy Henderson spoke to him by telephone,
passing on a message from Anthony Eden urging him not to leave
the country. Eden had been on board the *Queen Elizabeth* on his
way to Washington when he sent his message, leading to a bizarre
misunderstanding in which the Americans mistakenly told the
Shah that the appeal had come from the Queen herself. Ultimately,

the misunderstanding proved irrelevant. The popular outrage at Mossadeq's attempts to get rid of the Shah drove people out onto the streets around the palace—their numbers no doubt bolstered by the activities of Jalali, Keyvani and the Rashidian brothers—convincing the Shah that he should not leave and forcing Mossadeq to back down.[36]

At a meeting of the NSC in early March, the demands that America should sideline the British in order to solve the crisis resurfaced, with Eisenhower's secretary of state, John Foster Dulles, the brother of Allen Dulles, complaining that America was 'constantly slowed up by the British, French, and other of our allies, in actions which we feel it is vital to take in many parts of the world'. Eisenhower's new defence secretary, Charlie Wilson, backed the UK, pointing out that America was 'in partnership with the British' in Iran, with the UK as the senior partner, and Eisenhower agreed, telling John Foster Dulles that they had to respect 'the enormous investment the British had in Iran'. The US should do what it thought necessary in Iran, 'but we certainly don't want a break with the British'. When Iran came up again at the following week's NSC meeting, Dulles revisited the issue, pointing out that while ensuring they kept the British on side, the US administration must now usurp them as the senior partner in the relationship. Eisenhower simply nodded.[37]

By mid-April, the CIA's Iranian desk had produced an outline for a coup based on a number of fundamental assumptions, the most important of which were: Mossadeq must go, the CIA's covert assets should be directed towards his overthrow, and US policy and financial aid should support his successor. Zahedi was deemed the only possible candidate to succeed Mossadeq.[38]

Under MI6 instructions, General Mahmoud Afshartus, the Iranian chief of police and a supporter of Mossadeq, was abducted in Tehran on 20 April 1953. Six days later, his body was found about 20 miles from Tehran. Darbyshire later insisted that his death was never part of the plan. An Iranian army officer who was guarding him had shot him for insulting the Shah. Zahedi was among a number of retired army officers and politicians implicated in the murder of the police chief and a warrant was put out for his arrest, but Ayatollah Kashani gave him asylum in the Majlis, where he could not be touched.[39]

The final plan for the coup was drawn up in three stages. The first took place at the British military base in Nicosia, which was to be the forward operations base for Operation Boot, or Project Ajax as the Americans dubbed it. The coup operation was to be kept separate from the MI6 station, which was just outside the Cypriot capital and doubled as the service's regional headquarters. The CIA was not to be allowed into the station, in part to protect those sources like OMAR who had not been shared with the Americans, but also to allow Darbyshire to continue to have conversations with the Rashidians to adjust the brothers' actions if the plan went wrong.[40]

The first stage of the plan was put together in Nicosia by Darbyshire and Donald Wilber, a Princeton academic who was a specialist on Iran and was employed by the CIA as a contract consultant. Darbyshire let Wilber take the lead. They shared similar views on the personalities and dynamics in Iranian politics and the MI6 officer knew that the real plan would not evolve until at least the next stage of the process, a meeting of CIA officers in Beirut, with the third and final stage taking place between Roosevelt and senior MI6 officers in London.[41]

Wilber disclosed that the relationship between the Rashidians and Goiran was less than perfect, with the CIA station chief regarding them as 'far overstated and oversold', possibly because, despite instructions from Woodhouse, they had not hidden the fact that while pro-British they were violently anti-American. Darbyshire broke off the discussions for several days to fly to Geneva for talks with Assadollah Rashidian. 'He not only briefed Darbyshire on the situation but was able to give comprehensive answers to a number of specific questions,' Wilber said. He was no doubt also firmly warned that the CIA team was indispensable and if he and his brothers wanted Mossadeq gone they would have to set aside their differences with the Americans.[42]

During the latter part of the planning, Darbyshire and Wilber were joined by George Carroll, who had served with the OSS in southern France and, as the new deputy head of station in Tehran, was to coordinate the military aspects of the coup. Once the draft plan was agreed, Wilber took it to Beirut where he, Roosevelt, Goiran and Carroll were to work on it. Meanwhile, Darbyshire took it to London, stopping off in Geneva for further consultations with Rashidian.[43]

Two weeks later, Roosevelt and Carroll flew to London to finalise the plans with Darbyshire and Paddy Flynn, the MI6 desk officer with responsibility for Iran. They recast the Beirut draft to make it more acceptable to the Foreign Office, agreeing to split costs, with the British paying around a third of the estimated total of $422,500 ($4 million in today's terms), much of which would be paid out by the Rashidians, Jalali and Keyvani in bribes to key players.[44]

The Shah's constitutional ability to replace the prime minister made it vital to obtain his backing, so the plan contained a series of measures 'designed to rid him once and for all of his pathological fear of the "hidden hand" of the British' and assure him that both the US and Britain saw him as the future for Iran. His 'forceful and scheming' sister Ashraf, who spent most of her time living the high life in Paris or the south of France, was to be recruited to persuade him to back the coup. US brigadier-general Norman Schwarzkopf,* who having led the Iranian Gendarmerie during the war was close to the Shah, would also be sent in to reassure him that it would work.

The plan was complicated unnecessarily by Carroll's concerns over the military side to the coup. 'He was the CIA's paramilitary expert, commando type,' Darbyshire recalled. 'His line was "I'd just hang the bastards." He was all for doing wild and peculiar things. Very wild indeed.' But despite his intervention, the plan to undermine Mossadeq remained largely focused on the bribes already being paid out by the Rashidians, and by Jalali and Keyvani, to politicians, newspaper editors, senior army officers and influential mullahs. The Shah was to leave the capital immediately before the coup. Multiple bribes would be used to get as many people out onto the streets in a pro-Shah, anti-Mossadeq protest as possible, at which

---

* Schwarzkopf's son of the same name was the US general who led the allied forces in the 1991 operation to remove Iraqi forces from Kuwait.

point Zahedi and his supporters would call the army out and take over the government in the name of the people.

It was this final part of the plan—the means by which Zahedi was to take control—which had the greatest potential to go wrong. Woodhouse in his original plan for Operation Boot had envisaged the Shah issuing two royal decrees, or firmans, one sacking Mossadeq and a second appointing Zahedi as his replacement; the Majlis would then get an opportunity to confirm him as prime minister. This would have ensured that, despite it having been a coup engineered by the CIA and MI6, the change of prime minister would appear to be completely legal and in accordance with the constitution. Carroll insisted that they did not have sufficient control over the army, so the Shah should issue one firman naming Zahedi as head of the armed forces and a second appealing to the military to carry out Zahedi's orders. At the beginning of July, Sir John Sinclair, Eden and Churchill signed the plan off, and Eisenhower and the Dulles brothers followed ten days later, handing the CIA station in Tehran $1 million ($9.6 million in today's terms) to fund the coup.[45]

In public, the Americans were making very clear to Mossadeq that their patience with his attempts to play them off against the British was wearing thin. Eisenhower waited a month before responding to a plea from Mossadeq for more financial support, telling him Americans would find it difficult to understand why their taxes should support a country which only had to negotiate fairly to see its oil being sold and producing the necessary funds.[46]

Meanwhile, Assadollah Rashidian flew to France to persuade Princess Ashraf to take part. She refused until Darbyshire and CIA officer Steve Meade visited her in Paris, eventually persuading her to fly to Tehran. 'We made it clear that we would pay expenses, and when I produced a great wad of notes her eyes alighted and she said she would just have to go to Nice for a week to clear things up,' Darbyshire recalled. 'Eventually, we said here is your first-class ticket and you are booked for the day after tomorrow and this time I did let her get her hands on the money. She was quite a flighty woman and Steve, who fancied anything, fancied her.'[47]

Soleiman Behdudi, the MI6 agent inside the palace, facilitated a series of meetings between the Shah and the various emissaries sent in to persuade him to take part. Princess Ashraf, who was unpopular in Iran, caused a degree of controversy by flying in to Tehran, but she did her job, persuading the Shah to go along with the coup. Rashidian then went to see the Shah to tell him that, in the absence of diplomatic relations, he represented the British government, giving him a choice of wording to be used at midnight on 30 July on the BBC Persian Service to confirm this was true. He also alerted the Shah to Schwarzkopf's arrival. The Shah was so scared the meeting with the US general might be bugged that he insisted they sit at a small table in the centre of the room. Schwarzkopf tried to persuade the Shah to sign the firman appointing Zahedi as army chief, but he refused on the basis that he had given up his right to do so to Mossadeq.

Rashidian and Roosevelt had a number of meetings with the Shah to persuade him to come on board and eventually it was the Iranian who succeeded in doing so, albeit only after Roosevelt agreed that they should revert to Woodhouse's original plans for two firmans that the Shah felt happy to sign, one removing Mossadeq and another appointing Zahedi in his place. Rashidian then saw the Shah again and persuaded him to tell key senior army officers that he had personally chosen Zahedi as his prime minister. He also agreed to leave Tehran for his holiday home at Ramsar on the Caspian Sea. Behdudi then prepared the firmans and Colonel Nematullah Nasieri, the head of the Palace Guard, took them to Ramsar for the Shah to sign.[48]

The coup began to go wrong two days before it was due to take place following an ill-judged meeting between Carroll and senior army officers, some of whom were communist sympathisers. Reports of a planned coup appeared in newspapers that backed the Tudeh Party on 14 August. Nevertheless, the next evening Nasieri delivered the signed firmans to Mossadeq's house, as scheduled. He was immediately arrested along with other army officers who backed the coup. The next day the Mossadeq government announced that an attempted coup had been put down. The Shah and Queen Soraya flew to Baghdad while Mossadeq began talks with the Tudeh Party to set up a republic, agreeing to hold a referendum to determine 'the will of the people'.

Both the Foreign Office and the State Department responded by calling the coup off, but none of the key players – Roosevelt, the Rashidians, Jalali and Keyvani, and Darbyshire in Cyprus – was prepared to give up. It was largely the actions behind the scenes by the Rashidians, directed remotely by Darbyshire—and those of Jalali and Keyvani, frequently acting on their own initiative—that provided the psychological impetus for the coup and ensured the right circumstances were created for its eventual execution. They continued to spread rumours and worked to ensure that as many people as possible were prepared to come out onto the streets to oppose Mossadeq and support the Shah. *New York Times* correspondent Kennett Love and his Associated Press counterpart Don Schwind were taken to the hills north of Tehran to be shown the decree signed by the Shah appointing Zahedi prime minister to demonstrate that Mossadeq was no longer prime minister and was holding onto power illegally.[49]

On the evening of Monday 17 August, Roosevelt and Carroll held a four-hour 'council of war' with Zahedi, two of his military allies and the Rashidians, who were all smuggled into the embassy compound. The mullahs had agreed to use Friday prayers to denounce Mossadeq and urge their followers onto the streets. But with the executions of the arrested officers scheduled for a Thursday, the coup could not afford to wait. It would have to begin the following day.[50]

Jalali and Keyvani fabricated an interview with Zahedi calling on the people to back the legal government and had it published in a number of newspapers alongside the firmans sacking Mossadeq. On 18 August, they paid a large crowd of fake Tudeh demonstrators to come out onto the streets of Tehran, calling for the replacement of the monarchy by a republic. The demonstration soon gathered genuine Tudeh Party supporters unaware it was a 'false flag' operation. Mossadeq ordered the army to clear the streets, but in a sign things were turning against him, police and soldiers chanting pro-Shah slogans beat the Tudeh demonstrators.[51]

The key intervention came from the Rashidians, directed from Cyprus by Darbyshire. Early the next morning, 19 August, a large group of several thousand people, organised and paid for by the Rashidians, took to the streets in the poorer districts in the south of Tehran and began to march on the city centre. They were led by members of the zurkhanehs, the 'houses of strength' or gymnasiums which were largely owned by the criminal gangs who provided protection for the bazaars. Many of the sportsmen who frequented the zurkhanehs were popular idols, so large numbers of people came out onto the streets to watch. The brothers had dispersed their men in among the throngs to whip up opposition to Mossadeq and support for the Shah. 'It was the Rashidians who provided people to infiltrate the demonstrations,' Darbyshire recalled. 'I was personally giving orders and directing.' The march was a contingency plan worked out by Darbyshire and Assadollah Rashidian in Geneva in the event that the first coup attempt failed.

'With the army standing guard around the uneasy capital, a grotesque procession made its way along the streets leading to the heart of Tehran,' one of those watching said. 'There were tumblers turning handsprings, weightlifters twirling iron bars and wrestlers flexing their biceps. As spectators grew in number, the bizarre assortment of performers began shouting pro-Shah slogans in unison. The crowd took up the chant and there, after one precarious moment, the balance of public psychology swung against Mossadeq.'

As the procession closed in on the city centre, making its way through more affluent areas, large numbers of the middle classes began to join the demonstrators and, rather than stop them, the police escorted the procession, leading Mossadeq to order the army to send in tanks. The orders were initially ignored by the junior ranks and even when they were enforced, many of the soldiers joined the crowds chanting 'Long live the Shah' and 'Death to Mossadeq the traitor'. The offices of the newspapers which backed the government or the Tudeh Party were ransacked and at 2.30 in the afternoon, Tehran Radio was captured by Zahedi's followers.[52]

The new prime minister then went on the air to announce his appointment and promise change. Most government offices were taken over with very little resistance and as the afternoon wore on demonstrators attacked Mossadeq's house. They were driven back by machine-gun fire, with several hundred killed or wounded, but pro-Zahedi troops brought in tanks to bombard the house. Mossadeq and members of his cabinet escaped over the garden wall, but were arrested the next day. Zahedi ordered all political prisoners to be set free and assumed power. The Shah returned to Tehran on 22 August and broadcast to the nation, thanking the people for their support and for their 'valiant rising' in defence of their country. He would gladly give his life for the people who had shown 'such magnificent loyalty'.[53]

The US administration saw the success of the coup as the opportunity they needed to reverse the British/American position in the Middle East. Eisenhower told Roosevelt to pass the Shah a personal message from him alone. America was the dominant partner. America had executed the coup. America should take the glory and, more importantly, control the aftermath. The CIA told its stations in London and Tehran that Churchill was not in any way to affiliate himself with the message. Nor should he make any reference to Eisenhower's message in his own. This instruction should be passed on to the British 'in the most diplomatic way possible'. While it was important to avoid 'unduly impairing' relations with the UK, this 'should not inhibit vigorous unilateral action on our part to exploit the current fortunate turn of events'.[54]

The CIA and Roosevelt were only too happy to claim the success of the coup as their own, but the reality was that the initial attempt carried out according to the Beirut plan had failed—in large part as a result of Carroll's clumsy interventions—and had only been rescued by the contingency plan devised in Geneva by Darbyshire and Rashidian. The CIA – or Iranian military intelligence – agents Jalali and Keyvani had played a vital role. But it was the skilful way in which the demonstrations led by the popular athletes were orchestrated by the Rashidians, using their influence across the board in Iranian society from the mullahs to the criminal bosses of the zurkhanehs, that ensured the success of the coup. In his post-operational report, Wilber stressed that it would not have been a success without the British secret service and its agents in Iran. 'The lesson here is clear,' he said. 'As in the larger world picture, US–UK interests and activities must be coordinated. A great deal is to be gained by direct coordination in special fields of activity once both parties have recognised that their aims are really identical.'[55]

While there is no doubt that many within the CIA recognised the truth of that argument, an increasing number of its officers—some of whom had no experience of the cooperation between MI6 and the OSS during the Second World War—felt that the British had played on their experience in the spying game for far too long and saw the coup as evidence of CIA dominance over their British counterpart. 'It was part of this new pattern of policy that the CIA claimed total responsibility for the disposal of Mossadeq,' Monty Woodhouse said. 'This did not displease the Foreign Office, which would not have liked it to be suggested that British inspiration had anything to do with it. But the CIA became increasingly confident that it no longer needed British expertise.' The willingness of the CIA to claim responsibility for operations that owed their success to MI6 would become a feature of the relationship between the two services.[56]

Certainly, within the wider US administration, there were very few who thought they owed anything to the British. American interests were far more important. In the negotiations over the future of Iran's oil supplies, US companies acquired substantial rights they would never have enjoyed as a result of their own efforts in Iran. The AIOC, renamed as the British Petroleum Company (later BP), acquired 40 per cent of the rights to Iranian oil. The main American companies – Esso, Mobil, Gulf, Standard Oil of California and Texaco – took another 40 per cent between them, with the Anglo-Dutch company Shell and Total of France sharing the rest.[57]

10

DRAGON LADY

Britain's ability to provide bases for the Americans was to be a key feature, and for successive US administrations a major advantage, of the Special Relationship. These were located not just in overseas territories but, in significant numbers, in the UK itself. During the 1948 Berlin Blockade, the USAF sent seventy B-29 nuclear bombers to Britain, in what was a very firm warning to Moscow — given that, as a result of America's refusal to share its atomic secrets, the UK still had no nuclear weapons of its own. Despite concerns within the Attlee cabinet that the Americans were 'trying to go too far too fast in this business of securing bases for themselves on the national territories of their allies' and that allowing them to base nuclear bombers in the UK would make Britain 'a primary target for any Russian atomic attack', the Labour government decided that the arguments in favour of doing as much as possible to keep America committed to defending Europe made an 'overwhelming' case for allowing US forces to stay in the UK.

The US nuclear bombers were initially based at several airfields in eastern England but these were deemed to be too vulnerable to attack and, in January 1949, the Americans asked for bases in central England which would be better protected. They were moved to Brize Norton and Upper Heyford in Oxfordshire, to Fairford in Gloucestershire, and eventually to Greenham Common in Berkshire, with a number of other nuclear bomber units rotating through Mildenhall on the western borders of Suffolk.

They also based fighter units at Lakenheath in Suffolk and Manston in Kent to provide protection for the nuclear bombers.

The US bases in Britain were the largest USAF presence outside the United States itself. Over the next few years, more
than twenty US bases were set up in the UK. They included
the CIA analysis and communications base at RAF Croughton
in Northamptonshire and a major signals intelligence base at
Chicksands in Bedfordshire. A second signals intelligence base in
the UK was agreed in 1952. It was eventually set up at Menwith
Hill, near Harrogate in North Yorkshire, in 1956, becoming fully
operational three years later.[1]

In intelligence terms, the most important USAF and RAF operations out of the UK were reconnaissance missions along the borders
of eastern Europe and the Soviet Union. Amid serious concern over
Russian intentions, demand for both signals and imagery intelligence
was extremely high. For much of the Second World War, the British
and Americans had operated a joint imagery intelligence centre, the
Allied Central Interpretation Unit, at Medmenham near Marlow
in Buckinghamshire, and approaches were made to Washington as
early as August 1944 to continue these close links in peacetime. The
Americans were keen—not least because Britain provided an ideal
starting point for reconnaissance flights across eastern Europe and
the Soviet Union and had access to a number of strategic airfields
elsewhere, in the Mediterranean, the Middle East, the Indian sub-
continent and south-east Asia.

The British and Americans had a good start in their efforts
to obtain aerial photography of the Soviet Union thanks to the
Germans, who had accumulated large stocks of pictures taken by
Heinkel photo-reconnaissance aircraft during the campaign on the
Eastern Front. In an operation codenamed Dick Tracy, large numbers of Luftwaffe aerial photographs were rescued by British and
US airmen sent into Germany to collect them. One particularly
valuable haul was collected at Berchtesgaden in south-east Bavaria
only hours before a Russian team arrived to try to prevent it falling into Allied hands. Other operations collected similar material
from Oslo, Vienna and Berlin, taking up to a million photographs
back to the UK. German wartime aerial photography of the Soviet
Union continued to turn up for a number of years. As late as 1954,

photographs of areas not covered by the Allies' archives were purchased from 'two gentlemen in Vienna' for an undisclosed sum.

The German photographs filled a large gap in the Allies' imagery intelligence archives. At the end of 1945, the RAF had begun a large-scale aerial reconnaissance operation, taking stock photographs first of the whole of western Europe, then of the Middle East, and later of north Africa. The USAF meanwhile was covering south-east Asia and the Americas. Neither side was prepared to overfly eastern Europe or the Soviet Union, for fear of offending the Russians.

But in August 1946, the RAF started making a limited number of flights over Soviet-occupied Europe, 'in order that the present shortage of factual intelligence should, in some measure, be remedied'. The risk of detection was slight, the JIC was told. The Russians had limited radar facilities and the British aircraft—their undercarriages camouflaged pale blue—were invisible from the ground. Even if they were spotted, there was no Soviet aircraft capable of intercepting them at that time. The RAF photo-reconnaissance aircraft were based initially at RAF Benson in Oxfordshire and then, from 1953, at Wyton in Cambridgeshire. RAF flights over the southern Soviet Union were flown from bases in Crete, Cyprus and Iraq.[2]

USAF and RAF aircraft were also used as signals and electronic intelligence (ELINT) platforms, intercepting communications intelligence and radar emissions. The first attempts to intercept communications from aircraft were made during the Second World War. By 1947, RAF Lancaster and Lincoln bombers, modified to include communications intercept and radar monitoring equipment, and with onboard photo-reconnaissance cameras, were patrolling the border between the Soviet and British zones of Germany. The flights triggered the Soviet air defences, allowing operators on board the aircraft and on the ground at RAF Gatow in the western sector of Berlin to record reaction times and build up a picture of the Soviet air defence locations and capabilities. Similar operations took place elsewhere on the borders of the Soviet Union with signals intelligence operations carried out by RAF Lincolns and Washingtons based at Watton in Norfolk.

The British and Americans flew almost continuous aerial

reconnaissance flights along the periphery of the Soviet Union. But as the Soviet air defences were built up, the dangers inherent in such flights became clear. The first loss of an allied aircraft came in April 1950 when a US Navy PB4Y-2 Privateer with ten men on board, six of them signals intelligence operators, was shot down over the Baltic, 20 miles off the Latvian coast, by Soviet MiG-15 fighter aircraft, with the loss of all those on board. All US reconnaissance flights were suspended for a month. Nevertheless, President Truman authorised penetration flights of the Soviet Union shortly afterwards, albeit with severe limitations which prevented the aircraft from fulfilling their goals.[3]

As a result, with the agreement of the Attlee government, RAF pilots, based alongside their American colleagues, flew missions over eastern Europe and the Soviet Union from the USAF base at Sculthorpe in Norfolk in US RB-45 Tornado aircraft repainted with RAF insignia. The missions, codenamed Operation Jiu-Jitsu, used night radar photography to fly the routes which RAF and US nuclear bombers would take to attack targets in the Baltic states, Moscow and central southern Russia, the location of a number of key Soviet ballistic missile sites. The first flights took place in 1952 and were followed by further missions in 1954. There was concern over the capability of the increasingly effective Soviet air defences. The flights would not only collect imagery of all the Soviet surface-to-air missile sites along the route; the aim was to test their reactions.

'There were three routes,' said Wing Commander Rex Sanders, who as navigator on one of the flights was also taking the photographs. 'One was through Germany to the Baltic states. The second was south of that, through Germany towards Moscow, and the third was south of that, going down through the centre of Russia and then arcing down south on the way out. There was a fear, of course, that they might think this was something more serious than just reconnaissance. It did cross our minds that the Soviets might think we were attacking.'

All three flights collected the imagery they were tasked to take and returned safely to the UK, but the RAF reconnaissance flights were not immune to Soviet attack. In March 1953—amid confusion and in-fighting in Moscow over who would succeed the recently deceased Stalin—two RAF Lincolns strayed off course during flights over East Germany, leaving the established air corridors from West Germany to Berlin which non-Soviet aircraft were obliged to use. The first was escorted out of East Germany by Soviet MiG-15 fighter aircraft. The second was shot down by three MiG-15s with the loss of all seven crew. The Russians said the second Lincoln had strayed outside the northern air corridor which non-Soviet aircraft were obliged to use and was shot down after opening fire on the Soviet fighters. The RAF board of inquiry said the Lincoln had no weaponry.

A few hours before the two incidents, a British European Airways (BEA) airliner was buzzed by Soviet MiG fighters after briefly straying out of the southern air corridor. Given that the government-owned BEA and its transcontinental counterpart, British Overseas Airways Corporation (BOAC), were both prepared, using ex-RAF pilots and in secret operations hidden even from their aircrew, to assist the intelligence services, this may well have been a deliberate coordinated attempt to test Soviet air defences and trigger Soviet radar and communications links. The British flag carrier's aircraft also routinely carried cameras which photographed areas below their approved routes that could not be reached by RAF surveillance aircraft. This was not an isolated practice. The CIA carried out similar operations using pilots from a number of allied countries who flew commercial airliners over Eastern Bloc countries to collect intelligence.[4]

An RAF Canberra—a new British-built aircraft capable of flying at 65,000 feet, far higher than the Soviet fighters—carried out a reconnaissance mission over the Soviet Kapustin Yar missile test site, 60 miles east of Volgograd in south-west Russia, in 1953. The earliest information on the site had come from Lieutenant-Colonel Grigori Tokaev, the first post-war Soviet defector obtained by MI6. Tokaev, an expert on missile and jet propulsion who was based in the Soviet sector of Berlin, was a scientific adviser to the Soviet state commission for the development of long-range rockets. His job in Berlin was to track down any German scientists who had worked on the Nazis' German V-2 rocket technology, which formed the basis for Soviet missile technology at that stage. 'Stalin and the Politburo are working hard and on an enormous scale to perfect long-range rockets,' Tokaev told 'Biffy' Dunderdale, who led his MI6 debriefing. 'Stalin demands the production of larger rockets with a range of up to 6,000 kilometres [3,700 miles].'* More detail had come out over the years from those German scientists who had been taken by the Russians to the Soviet Union to help to create the Soviet missile programme before returning home, where they were debriefed by the CIA or MI6. But with that source having dried up and continuing restrictions on USAF penetration missions of the Soviet Union, the RAF was asked to collect up-to-date details of the installations at the site. A specially modified Canberra equipped with the latest US high-resolution camera flew over the site and then headed south to land in Iran. The Russians detected the aircraft and came close to shooting it down, riddling part of the fuselage with bullet holes.

'When we first heard of the Russian missile centre, at Kapustin Yar on the Volga, we demanded that we get photographs of it,' said Bob Amory, then CIA deputy director of intelligence. 'We just can't ignore it. This is going to be a major new thing, this whole missile development, and we've got to get on top of it in the beginning.' The USAF said it could not be done, he recalled. 'The British actually did it for us with the Canberra all the way from Germany to the Volga and down into Persia, a risky thing but they got some fair pictures. And then we said, "Well, this is fine." But the British said, "God, never again." The whole of Russia had been alerted to the thing, and it damn near created a major international incident.'[5]

Nevertheless, six months later, an RAF RB-45 Tornado aircraft, with a maximum altitude of 36,000 feet, repeated their previous runs along the nuclear bomber routes. By now, five US reconnaissance aircraft and the RAF Lincoln had been shot down by Soviet fighter aircraft and for Sanders and John Crampton, the captain of his aircraft, the flight was worryingly dangerous. 'Our "targets"

---

* During the 1960s, Tokaev was invited to America to advise on the Apollo programme to put a man on the moon.

were ICBM [inter-continental ballistic missile] sites and similar strategically important areas,' Crampton recalled. 'Timing was critical because our intelligence agencies would be listening for Soviet reaction to our penetration of their airspace and had certain diversionary exercises for keeping them clear of our routes.

'We were, of course, to fly without navigation lights and maintain R/T (radio transmitter) silence, although we would have an OMG ("Oh My God") frequency for desperate emergency. The intelligence people briefed us carefully: there might be some surface-to-air missiles but no radar-equipped night fighters, [and] although there was a ground control radar system which would enable them to track us and position a fighter within visual range this was not thought to be likely. The one comforting thought was that we should be too high and too fast for any anti-aircraft fire.'

As a result, Crampton was not overly worried when, as they flew across Ukraine, he saw reflections of flashes from the ground on the clouds below them. Given the absolute certainty of the intelligence briefing that there would be no effective anti-aircraft fire, Crampton dismissed it as an electrical storm. It would have no impact on them. Sanders was very happy with the photographs they were taking, just occasionally calling for slight changes of direction as they flew between the various target sites. Crampton saw absolutely no need for concern.

'My reverie was rudely interrupted by the sudden heart-stopping appearance of a veritable flare path of exploding golden anti-aircraft fire, dead ahead and at the same height as we were,' he recalled. 'My reaction was instinctive—throttles wide open and haul the aircraft round on its starboard wing tip until the gyro compass pointed west. The early attempts had all misjudged our height and thank God, the Kiev defences had misjudged our speed; they had chucked everything up a few hundred yards ahead of us. Poor old Rex piped up, "Hey, what about my photos?" I replied succinctly and requested a course to steer to Fürstenfeldbruck [in West Germany], our declared alternative in an emergency.'[6]

The Soviet destruction of two more US reconnaissance aircraft in late 1954 led to a major rethink. A US Navy P-2V Neptune was shot down in the Sea of Japan in September 1954 with the loss of all ten men on board and a USAF RB-29 Superfortress was brought down two months later in the same area with the loss of one crew member (ten others survived). There were now large gaps in allied intelligence coverage of the Soviet Union caused by the inability of the NSA and GCHQ to break the high-grade Soviet ciphers, the difficulties of human intelligence operations on the ground, and the limitations on what could be done with aerial reconnaissance given presidential nervousness over how the Soviet leadership might react and the potential impact on US public opinion of the increasing number of shootdowns. The main concern was over Soviet nuclear weapons, Allen Dulles recalled, particularly long-range bomber and guided missile capability. 'Without a better basis than we had for gauging the nature and extent of the threat from surprise nuclear missile attack, our very survival might be threatened.'[7]

A joint MI6–CIA conference in London in November 1954 revealed that British estimates of Soviet missile technology were 'relatively close' to those of the Americans, which were marred by 'serious deficiencies' on current Soviet capabilities. Dulles decided that the only way to obtain that intelligence was through deep penetration of Soviet airspace by reconnaissance aircraft, which President Eisenhower opposed on the basis that it might provoke a war. The CIA boss encouraged the service intelligence chiefs to work with him to persuade Eisenhower that the US could develop an aircraft which could fly undetected above the Soviet air defence radar.

At a lunch hosted by US air secretary Hal Talbott, Dulles questioned Kelly Johnson, chief engineer at Lockheed's legendary 'Skunk Works', about a lightweight 'jet-powered glider' he was known to have designed. Could it be made capable of carrying imagery cameras and electronic intelligence equipment at 70,000 feet, so high it would be impossible for the Soviet air defence systems to detect and destroy? Johnson said he saw no problem in adapting his designs. A few days after the lunch, Dulles and the service intelligence chiefs signed a memo to the president warning him of 'serious gaps in our intelligence covering the Soviet Bloc areas, particularly in relation to our ability to determine the capabilities of the Soviet Union to launch nuclear attacks against the US and to detect indications of their intentions to do so' and of their belief that only overflights could provide the solution.[8]

The following day, Dulles sent Eisenhower a memo asking the president to authorise the resumption of US overflights of the Soviet Union. 'You are familiar with the large gaps in our intelligence coverage of the Soviet Union,' the CIA boss said. 'You are familiar, too, with the current and growing difficulties in the way of filling those gaps by the more classic means. In my considered judgement, as well as that of the other members of the Intelligence Community, there is not the prospect of gaining this vital intelligence without the conduct of systematic and repeated air reconnaissance over the Soviet Union itself. We are all agreed that the requirement is an urgent one and that with suitable direction and support, it is feasible of accomplishment with minimum risk.'

The USAF could follow the RAF's lead and modify their own Canberra aircraft to fly up to 65,000 feet, Dulles said. 'At such an altitude now, the expectation that it would be detected is very low indeed, and the possibility that it would be intercepted and shot down is practically nil.' At the same time, he asked the president to authorise Project Aquatone, a joint programme with Lockheed to produce 'thirty special high-performance aircraft at a cost of about $35 million'. Eisenhower agreed.[9]

The new aircraft, designated U-2 and nicknamed Dragon Lady, made the first of a number of test flights over the US in August 1955 and by April 1956 two production models were ready to make their first operational flights. They were CIA-controlled, with some of the pilots being air force veterans supposedly employed by Lockheed as 'flight test consultants' while others were serving USAF pilots attached to the CIA on 'special duties'. Initially, Anthony Eden, who had replaced the ailing Winston Churchill as British prime minister, gave permission for the flights to take off from Lakenheath, but the embarrassing publicity surrounding Operation Claret, a botched MI6 undertaking in which Buster Crabb, a veteran British diver, was killed in Portsmouth harbour while investigating the hull of the Soviet cruiser *Ordzhonikidze*—on which Soviet leader Nikita

Khrushchev had arrived on a state visit to the UK—led to a change of mind.[10]

It also led to an end to Royal Navy submarine signals intelligence missions to the Soviet Northern Fleet bases around Murmansk in north-west Russia. Operation Defiant had begun in March 1954 with the first of a number of dangerous missions by Royal Navy submarines, fitted with state-of-the-art communications and electronic intelligence suites, to track Soviet warships and submarines. There were an average of two missions a year, each lasting six weeks, four weeks of which was spent in the Barents Sea. The Americans had been happy for the British to carry out the commitment and share the product, and the cancellation left GCHQ 'deeply embarrassed' that it was coming to an end.

Commander John Coote, who had led a number of the Operation Defiant missions—and had spent time with the US Navy submariners carrying out similar missions against the Soviet Navy in the Pacific—was sent to Washington to brief the US Navy on the best ways to carry out the operations in place of the British. The Royal Navy missions resumed in early 1957 as part of a coordinated joint programme with the US Navy. Royal Navy signals intelligence operators also monitored the operations of the Soviet Baltic Fleet from shore locations at Cuxhaven and Kiel in northern Germany, using the British Baltic Fishery Protection Service, which, while ostensibly protecting British trawlers, carried out close-range interception of Soviet naval communications from converted German E-boats.[11]

The initial U-2 missions were flown from Wiesbaden in West Germany. The highest-priority targets were the threats to mainland America and western Europe: guided missiles with nuclear warheads and long-range nuclear bombers. 'The decision to proceed with the U-2 programme was based on considerations deemed to be vital to our national security,' Dulles said. 'We required the information necessary to guide our various military programmes and particularly our missile programme. This we could not do if we had no knowledge of the Soviet missile programme.' Other high-priority targets included air defence sites which might threaten a US attack on the Soviet Union, atomic energy installations, naval bases and shipyards, industrial complexes, and military barracks and exercise areas.

The U-2 had a range of 4,600 miles, capable of reaching deep inside the Soviet Union. The first three flights, one on 20 June 1956, and the other two on 2 July, covered East Germany, Poland and the Balkans, but never penetrated Soviet airspace. The first actual overflight of the Soviet Union took place on 4 July 1956, covering the Baltic states and Leningrad with the main target being the city's seven naval shipyards. It was 'driven' by Hervey Stockman, a former Second World War US pilot. For security reasons, the pilots were always called 'drivers' and the individual aircraft were known as 'articles'.

An internal CIA history recorded that 'it was hoped that cover age of these shipyards would shed light on the construction of submarines, including possible evidence of any that might be nuclear-powered or armed with missiles'. The next day a U-2 overflew Moscow, photographing the factory where the Myasishchev M-4 Bison bomber, the Soviet equivalent to the US B-52 Stratofortress nuclear bomber, was built; the nearby airfield from which the Bisons took off for their new bases; the Kaliningrad missile plant; and the Khimki rocket engine plant. Some of the imagery obtained from the first five flights, which also included a highly productive flight over Crimea, was 'little short of spectacular'.[12]

Despite the belief that the flights would not be detected, Moscow accused the US of 'gross violations' of Soviet airspace, correctly naming the dates of some of the flights but inaccurately describing the flight paths, clearly demonstrating that they were unable to track the U-2 once it reached its cruising altitude of 13.5 miles, at which point the 'driver' could see almost 300 miles in every direction. It was also obvious that the Russians had no way of knowing for sure that the aircraft were American rather than British and had no tangible evidence of their existence. The US government claimed no knowledge of the flights, but they were suspended temporarily.[13]

The most immediate impact of the U-2 imagery came in the dismissal of the so-called 'bomber gap': the USAF claim, founded on a Soviet deception of the US air attaché in Moscow, that the Russians had far more long-range bombers than the Americans did. The five missions covered nine separate long-range bomber bases. 'Not one Bison was present at any of the nine long-range airfields,' the internal history said. 'This was a datum that did not go unnoticed by the foes of the Air Force. It was not long before the so-called "Bomber-Gap" was proven a myth.'

But the most important discoveries were related to guided-missile launch sites although—aside from imagery of the Kapustin Yar test site, which was already well known in the West—the full extent of the missile sites covered was not realised at the time, largely because it was the first time any US analysts had seen such installations. The most interesting and 'perplexing' of these was a site, captured in just two images, which was near the town of Mozhaisk, 75 miles west of Moscow. The photographs showed two large earth-covered domes, around 200 feet in diameter and 85 feet high, each with a cap on the top of the dome. The CIA imagery analysts were convinced it must be a nuclear site but had no evidence to confirm this. A number of consultants and experts were called in to look at the images, including Nobel Prize-winning US physicist Luis Alvarez and Wernher von Braun, the designer of the Nazi V-2 rocket, who had moved to America to help lead the US post-war missile and space technology programmes.

Braun thought the installation might be intended to launch long-range nuclear-powered missiles. Alvarez agreed that the domes looked like launch sites for long-range missiles, but conventionally powered rather than nuclear because they were less than a mile away from housing for the workers, who would have been dangerously exposed to radiation if the missiles were nuclear-powered. Ultimately, Alvarez was proved correct but not until many months later when collateral evidence confirmed they were launcher sites for intermediate-range missiles. The speculation by both Braun and Alvarez that they might be launch sites for even longer-range ICBMs caused 'considerable agitation' among those US officials who were privy to the top secret assessments, the CIA internal history noted. 'The result was to conjure up, in the minds of those concerned, a vision of clouds of Russian missiles raining down on Western

Europe and/or the United States following any refusal by Western powers to submit to Russian blackmail.'[14]

The fifth flight, over Crimea, had turned up two further missile sites. The first, a pair of large circular pads on a bluff overlooking the Black Sea 5 miles south of Sevastopol, was found to be a cruise missile test site. The second missile launch site photographed by the U-2 was also on high ground overlooking the Black Sea, but further east on the Kerch peninsula.[15]

Following the Soviet protest over the first five missions, Eisenhower insisted on personally checking the flight plans and setting the time limits for each U-2 operation. Over the next twelve months, there was only one U-2 overflight of the Soviet Union, on 20 November 1956, when an aircraft took off from İncirlik in eastern Turkey covering the Caucasus region and flying as far as Baku, the capital of the Azerbaijan Soviet Socialist Republic. The penetration flights returned in earnest on 19 June 1957, with more than a dozen missions over the Soviet Union that summer, including coverage of the Soviet Far East by flights flown from Eielson in Alaska—or on one occasion from Atsugi in Japan—and flights over the Murmansk headquarters of the Soviet Northern Fleet which were flown from Giebelstadt in Bavaria.

The internal CIA history notes that at this point 'U-2s were crossing the Russian border with impunity all the way from Finland to the Pacific coast of Siberia'. Most of the U-2 missions originated from İncirlik, but some were flown out of Lahore and Peshawar in Pakistan as part of Operation Soft Touch, which penetrated areas of Soviet Central Asia that flights out of Germany, Turkey or Alaska could not reach, providing 'sensational' intelligence on missile test sites, nuclear plants and suspected biological warfare facilities, none of which had previously been known to exist.[16]

The abrupt end to the British and American codebreakers' ability to break high-grade Soviet ciphers caused by William Weisband's treachery forced them to look for other ways to get back into the Soviet systems, with the Americans in particular looking hard at computer technology. The British codebreakers at Bletchley Park might have led the way during the Second World

War with Colossus, but it was their US counterparts—with access to far greater funding—who broke new ground in the search for technological advances that would help unravel the increasingly sophisticated machine ciphers introduced by the world's major powers. Howard Engstrom, the man described by Frank Raven as 'the father of the US Navy operation against Enigma' and the main architect of the more sophisticated US Bombes, was to become one of the leading pioneers in the field.

At the end of the Second World War, with many members of the armed forces being demobilised, Joe Wenger was concerned that the wealth of talent he had assembled to break the German and Japanese codes would be lost. He suggested that Engstrom and others, who were leaving Op-20-G and hoping to forge civilian careers, look at producing a computer which would help the codebreakers crack the more complex Russian ciphers. '[Wenger] came up with the idea of having them form an independent, private organisation which would keep them together,' recalled Howie Campaigne, who having worked on Colossus while stationed at Bletchley, was one of the team developing ideas for how the US codebreakers could use computers. 'They talked about this idea to a considerable extent and [how] the Navy would help them stay together and they'd be available there anytime an emergency arose.'

As a result of these discussions, Engstrom and Bill Norris, who had also worked on the U-boat ciphers, left the navy—taking with them a number of people who had been involved in the US Bombe programme—and set up a company called Engineering Research Associates, more generally known as ERA, to explore ways of using computer-type machinery to help break the Russian codes. 'They set up business in St Paul, Minnesota, and for a long time, almost the only business they had was with the navy,' Campaigne said. 'Wenger was satisfied with that arrangement, but other people in the Navy looked at it askance because, you know, it looked like Wenger was just feeding his favourites and they didn't like it.'

ERA was forced, albeit successfully, to look for work else-where, but Norris and Engstrom retained a contract with the US Navy codebreakers, which allowed Joe Eachus, the former US

Navy liaison officer at Bletchley Park who was now in charge of Op-20-G's move into computers, to assign them projects. Towards the end of 1947, Eachus gave ERA 'Task 13', an order for the code-breakers' first fully programmable high-speed computer. Both Campaigne and Eachus, who was to go on to become one of the leading lights of the US computer industry, worked 'very closely' with the ERA technicians to produce what would become Atlas I, Campaigne recalled. 'In fact, I designed the arithmetic unit, and the rest of it. We gave the logical design to them and they copied it. I only remember one change.'[17]

The Atlas I computers, the first of which was delivered in December 1950 and cost just under a million dollars each (£12.8 million at today's values), were valve-driven electronic computers with drum memories. They employed a number of processors working in parallel to perform basic arithmetic processes and were able to modify their own programs to suit the task in hand. Atlas I was a major step forward not just for the US codebreakers but for computing in general, turning ERA into one of the world's leading pioneers in computer technology.

A year later, ERA produced a commercial version, the ERA 1101, a designation based on the binary representation for 13, which is 1101, in a nod to its navy origins in 'Task 13'. It was so successful that in 1952 ERA was bought by Remington Rand and from then on, the commercial version of Atlas I was sold as the highly successful UNIVAC 1101. Although the Atlas I was extremely efficient at performing the tasks it was programmed to carry out, its operational capability was nothing like that of a modern mobile telephone. Its memory was the equivalent of 48 kilobytes, compared to a modern iPhone's 6 gigabytes, and it was significantly larger in size. The entire Atlas I system was 38 feet long, 20 feet wide and 7 feet high, weighed more than 8 tons, and took up more than 1,000 square feet of floor space.

There were two Atlas I computers, the second of which was installed in May 1953. Both machines were moved to the NSA's new headquarters at Fort Meade, set up in 1957 midway between Washington DC and Baltimore, and continued in service until

November 1959. Perhaps their most important role was one of their first, helping to break the Venona ciphers—in the operation that unveiled so many of the Soviet agents within the US and British governments, including the Cambridge spy ring—by searching for streams of text that were identical or similar in different messages. The old ERA team, in its new Remington Rand persona, also produced the successor, Atlas II, which had additional memory, giving it greater capacity and enabling it to operate much faster. There were two Atlas II computers built for the NSA, the first installed in October 1953 and the second, which used ground-breaking magnetic cores for high-speed memory, in November 1954. It was sold commercially as the UNIVAC 1103.[18]

At the same time as the navy codebreakers were using ERA to produce the first Atlas machine, their army counterparts, led by Solomon Kullback, yet another Bletchley veteran, were working in-house to build their own electronic digital computer. The Abner used serial processing, in which each task is completed one at a time in sequence. Its memories were supplied by an outside company, Technitrol (now Pulse Electronics), and its magnetic tape drives by Raytheon.

Abner became operational in April 1952. A second Abner computer was commissioned from Technitrol and installed three years later. Neither of the two Abner machines was as reliable as Atlas, but they laid the foundations for future developments in computer technology. By October 1953, with two Atlas computers and one Abner, the NSA already had the largest computer installation in the world. The addition in the same year of an IBM 701, which was very similar to the Atlas II and also used parallel processing, followed by two more Atlas machines and the second Abner, brought the agency's computer capability to what at the time was an internationally unrivalled seven machines.[19]

Major-General Ralph Canine, the first head of the NSA, was extremely proud of the agency's computer capabilities, providing GCHQ with an Atlas II machine in 1958 in appreciation of the way in which the British codebreakers seemed able to answer any question US policy makers asked him no matter how difficult, very often when finding the answers himself would have cost NSA a disproportionate amount of money. Canine visited the UK on a number of occasions and had Eric Jones, his GCHQ counterpart, over in America on a reciprocal basis.

'I went to England, oh, several times,' Canine recalled. 'But I got Eric Jones over here pretty often. And you know, they do twice as much as we do with one-third of the people and I found out that Eric could answer a good many of my requirements without any further build-up of his outfit.' The British had made various updates to the two Colossus computers they kept in the wake of the Second World War in order to work on Soviet teleprinter cipher systems and also bought one of the first Ferranti Mark 1 computers. But they had nothing like the Atlas II machine which Canine gave them. They codenamed it Effigy and almost immediately repaid the gift by swiftly using it to solve a cipher that had eluded the NSA codebreakers.[20]

Jones decided, shortly after taking over in 1952, that the title of the BRUSA agreement was too dismissive of the Australian, Canadian and New Zealand codebreakers who were playing an important role in the alliance and told John Tiltman, still the senior UK liaison officer at the NSA, to ask Canine to agree to a change from BRUSA to UKUSA, a decision which was implemented on 17 November 1953. Quite how the change recognised the contribution of Australia, Canada and New Zealand is unclear but from that point on, the agreement between the British and American codebreakers became known as the UKUSA Accord.[21]

The continuing inability of GCHQ and the NSA to break the highest-grade Soviet ciphers like Albatross, and its replacement the Fialka (Violet) M105 cipher machine, which was introduced in 1956 and proved just as impenetrable, made them heavily reliant on plain language communications—like the microwave links used by the Soviet Union and its communist allies to carry telephone conversations between party officials—and traffic analysis of Warsaw Pact armed forces. The British and US military used bases around the periphery of the Soviet Union to intercept Soviet and eastern European army and air force communications, with British and American servicemen and women analysing and reporting on the results, assisted by direction-finding and radio-fingerprinting techniques which helped to locate individual target units and keep track of them. Enciphered teleprinter communications and radio messages sent in Morse code were relayed back to GCHQ and the NSA for cryptanalysts to attempt to break them.[22]

The frontline signals intelligence sites were in Germany, where a Soviet attack was most likely in the event of war, with the highest priority given to Group Soviet Forces Germany (GSFG), the Soviet armies based in East Germany, led by the elite 3rd Shock Army, which was expected to bulldoze its way through to the English Channel within days in the event of war. Traffic analysis provided a wealth of information on the Warsaw Pact order of battle, with every unit's location tracked down and its communications with other units followed religiously on a day-to-day basis. Their closeness to the target units just across the inner German border allowed British and US operators to monitor the shorter-range VHF communications used during training exercises in the field, providing extensive details of Soviet military tactics and, in the case of large-scale Soviet Bloc exercises, each unit's specific role in the event of war.

While the British units in northern Germany and West Berlin focused on GSFG and—from their creation in 1956—East German forces, the Americans in the south monitored Soviet, East German, Polish, Hungarian, Czechoslovak, Romanian and Bulgarian armed forces communications, with the US Army and Air Force stations in West Berlin also covering GSFG, East German and Polish armed forces. A US intercept operation at Aviano in north-eastern Italy monitored Yugoslav and Albanian communications.[23]

British and American signals intelligence sites were also based in the Middle East, to cover the southern Soviet Union, Bulgaria and Romania. The most important were the British base at Ayios Nikolaos near Famagusta in eastern Cyprus, and the US operations in Crete and at Sinop on the most northern edge of Turkey's Black Sea coast, where Soviet missile tests were a key target.

Covert British signals intelligence teams, posing as archaeologists or under cover of commercial communications operations by companies like the British government-owned Cable & Wireless, were used in areas bordering on the Soviet Union, such as northern Iran. Perhaps the most surprising US intercept operation covering the southern and central Soviet Union was at Asmara in what was then Ethiopia, partly a result of the peculiarities of propagation of HF radio signals, which bounce off the ionosphere and then return to earth, but more importantly because of its ability to monitor Soviet missile test and space missions. The Soviet Far East and China were monitored by the British and Australians from Hong Kong and by US operations in Alaska, Japan, South Korea, Taiwan, the Philippines and, from 1956 onwards, Hawaii.[24]

Substantial intelligence on the locations, equipment and order of battle of GSFG and later the East German armed forces also came from British and US military missions set up in the wake of the occupation of Germany to liaise with the Soviet military commander-in-chief. The British mission, BRIXMIS, and the US Military Liaison Mission, along with the reciprocal Soviet missions to the British and US sectors, swiftly became intelligence-gathering operations.

BRIXMIS was formed in mid-1946 with a staff of around thirty, including interpreters, drivers, radio operators and 'four fairly high-ranking intelligence officers representing all three services plus a technical expert to collect technical intelligence, scientific intelligence and economic intelligence'. The US mission, the subject of a later agreement with the Russians, was smaller and more restricted than BRIXMIS. Both had qualified freedom of travel throughout East Germany but were banned from military training areas, which were designated as permanent restricted areas, and temporary restricted areas were frequently imposed to cover an exercise or secret deployment of Soviet forces.

BRIXMIS spent much of its time making covert expeditions into the restricted areas to gather intelligence on military installations and equipment or to monitor military exercises. As a result, its members were frequently attacked by the Russians or the East Germans. Their vehicles were forced off the road, they were beaten up, and on occasion they were even shot at. Nevertheless, they produced endless photographs of new pieces of Soviet equipment that had never been seen before and managed to steal a lot of extremely useful Soviet or East German documents, including signals instructions and hand cipher systems, which were passed to GCHQ and the NSA. But BRIXMIS produced some of its best intelligence by tapping into Soviet landline terminals to intercept high-level plain language telephone conversations.[25]

The use of telephone taps to compensate for the inability of US and American codebreakers to read the high-grade Soviet ciphers had been pioneered by MI6 in 1949 in occupied Vienna, which, like Berlin, was split into separate sectors each controlled by one of the four victorious Allies, the Russians, the British, the French and the Americans. Operation Silver was set up by the MI6 head of station, Peter Lunn, a former captain of the British Olympic skiing team whose grandfather Henry owned Sir Henry Lunn Travel, one of the companies MI6 had used to collect intelligence from the Soviet Union in the early years of the Cold War.

The British had discovered that some of the underground landlines that serviced Vienna's Imperial Hotel, the Soviet Red Army headquarters, ran through their zone. The British excavated tunnels at several points to gain access to the communications cables. As cover for one 70-foot tunnel, the house from which it led was turned into a shop selling Harris tweed, recalled Andrew King, who was put in charge of Operation Silver. But the shop became so popular with the local populace and US servicemen that MI6 officers found themselves spending more time attending to customers than monitoring Soviet telephone calls and the cover was abandoned.[26]

Simon Preston, a young Royal Marines officer attached to MI6, was involved briefly in digging one of the tunnels:

In late 1952, I was sent up to Vienna for a week because they wanted someone to help in pretending to dig the road up. We were actually listening in on the Russian communications, which had to go through that part of our sector. We dug a hole, and a long way down there was a chap with earphones on tapping the Russian telephone lines. My job was simply steering people on the surface away—police, curious passers-by—and that went on every day for a week. I was working with an MI6 character in his mid-thirties. He and I were put up by an eccentric landlady in the south end of Vienna, and every day we used to come back covered in mud. For some reason he had told her that he played football, and she used to ask, quite incredulously, '*Wieder Fussball spielen, Herr Oberleutnant? Wieder Fussball spielen?*'*[27]

The British brought the Americans into Operation Silver in 1951 and the tapping of Soviet communications links continued until 1955, when the wartime Allies withdrew from Austria, by which time it had provided substantial intelligence, including details of the Soviet order of battle as well as vital intelligence on Soviet intentions towards Yugoslavia. Bob Steers, one of the young Intelligence Corps servicemen who monitored the telephone calls on one of the tunnels, recalled that it was often very boring work. 'The only light relief was in the early morning between 0100 and 0300 hours when the female Austrian telephonists would phone their opposite numbers in Prague, Budapest, Sofia and Bucharest and discuss their intimate love lives, which was an unusual education for us 18- to 20-year-olds.'

The tapes were sent back to London to be transcribed by Russian émigrés recruited by MI6 and produced a great deal of intelligence on Soviet policy, armed forces and equipment. 'They were important operations and the customers became very excited about them, particularly the defence establishment,' King recalled. 'They really thought they were in on something. It was a tremendous operation. It was shared with the Americans—the CIA finance went to I should think about 75 per cent of the thing – and there was enormous manpower put into it on processing the results, which were brought back on tapes. We had something like fifty or sixty Russian émigrés going through all these tapes.'[28]

The British suggested to the Americans when they brought them into Operation Silver that there should be a second joint operation

---

* 'Playing football again, Lieutenant? Playing football again?'

in Berlin. Around the same time, the US Army codebreaker Frank Rowlett, who had become unhappy at the NSA, having clashed repeatedly with General Canine, was chatting to Bill Harvey, a friend in the CIA. He was bemoaning the role of William Weisband, who had recently been found to have been the cause of 'Black Friday' and the loss of the high-grade Soviet cipher systems.

Rowlett told Harvey that he had obtained a map of pre-war Germany's telecommunications systems, which showed that Berlin was the hub for much of eastern Europe's landline communications. It also revealed that the cables running under the German capital were only a couple of feet underground. Could the CIA not tap the landlines under Berlin and listen into the Soviet communications, making up for the NSA's, and GCHQ's, inability to break into the Soviet high-grade cipher systems? Harvey, a hard-drinking, straight-talking Texan, and something of a legend of the early Cold War, was intrigued by the idea. He persuaded Allen Dulles that it was worth taking up. Realising that they would need someone with communications intelligence expertise to make the best of tapping the Soviet landlines, they poached Rowlett from the NSA and he was put in charge of the intercept side of Operation Gold.[29]

It was a joint British–American operation from the start. Harvey was posted to Berlin as CIA head of station, with Peter Lunn as his MI6 counterpart to ensure the project had the complete backing of the people in charge. Rowlett took the lead role for the Americans in the discussions with the British, pushing the case for cooperation. 'Most of the people at CIA had not come from the technical end of the business,' Rowlett recalled. 'They didn't quite understand what was required in terms of a cryptanalytic organisation and what was important to pick up and how much, how deeply, they should go in the liaison with the [British] on these third-party deals, and this was kind of my role.' The scheme was not undertaken lightly. It took four years to bring it to fruition and from very early on there was an order from Dulles that as little as possible should be committed to paper with a need-to-know policy strictly enforced, a move which ultimately kept the operation going for far longer than would otherwise have been the case.[30]

A series of meetings in Washington and London led initially to a CIA operation to infiltrate the East German Post and Telecommunications Office to obtain samples of the sort of traffic that might be intercepted by the tunnel and work out which cables would be most productive. Two sites were selected as possibilities for the tunnel, one in the British zone and one in the US sector. The latter was ultimately ruled the better option, largely because of the considerable expanse of land which was available there. In December 1953, Dulles and MI6 Chief Sir John Sinclair gave the project the go-ahead and in a meeting in London shortly afterwards a joint CIA–MI6 team began deciding the technical processes that would be required to make it work.

Given his vast experience of dealing with intercepted communications, and liaison with the British, Frank Rowlett was the obvious man to lead the US delegation. The MI6 team was extremely high-powered, including George Kennedy Young, now director of requirements, and in a lesser role George Blake, the former MI6 head of station in Seoul, who had been taken prisoner by the North Koreans and unbeknown to MI6 had offered to spy for the KGB. Blake, who was chosen to take the British minutes of the London planning meetings, handed them over a few weeks later to his KGB contact Sergei Kondrashev.[31]

The biggest problem at this stage for the MI6–CIA team seemed to be how to dig the tunnel, and remove the earth from the site, without the Russians or East Germans noticing what was going on. Amid the discussions, one flippant idea was that they dig a hole to put the earth in. Despite the deliberately ridiculous nature of the suggestion, one of those involved realised it was the answer to their dilemma. They should build a two-storey 'warehouse', the lower floor of which would be underground, on the wasteland close to the edge of the US sector. They could then dig the tunnel through from the lower floor, simply leaving the earth inside the warehouse.[32]

There was a complex double bluff of a cover story for the construction of the building, in which the German contractors who built it were told it was merely a standard quartermaster's storage warehouse, information that was bound to be leaked to the Russians.

Then antennas specifically designed for the collection of electronic intelligence were installed on the roof to give the impression it was a top secret intercept facility targeted at the Soviet sector. The CIA agreed that it would pay the construction costs for the warehouse and main tunnel, which was to be dug down through the warehouse floor and then under the boundary between the US and Soviet sectors for 1,476 feet, to the point directly below where the cables were to be tapped. British engineers developed a unique technical system to construct the vertical shaft up to the cables and MI6 technicians installed the necessary monitoring equipment, including a specialised amplification process.[33]

The warehouse was finished in August 1954 and the construction of the tunnel, by US Army engineers, began the following month. It was 6 feet in diameter and lined with 125 tons of steel. It was finished in February 1955, by which time 3,100 tons of earth and sand had been deposited in the warehouse.

At one point, the US engineers decided they needed a reference point of known size in the Soviet zone, so they arranged a baseball game with the aim of hitting the ball over the border. Unfortunately, the plan was stymied by the friendliness of the East German border guards, who kept returning the ball. The most difficult part of the whole enterprise was excavating the vertical shaft to reach the cables, which were just 2 inches in diameter and little more than 2 feet below the surface of the main road leading to East Berlin's Schönefeld airport. This required precision work and the shaft was constructed by British Army Royal Engineers, with the busy road likely to collapse into the hole at any moment. 'This was the most delicate and tedious job in the entire process,' one of the CIA officers involved recalled. 'The vertical shaft was carved out using a "window blind" shield. A slot was opened and about an inch of soil was removed; then that slot was closed and the next one opened. This was repeated until the target cables were reached, a process that required extreme patience and skill.'[34]

The MI6 technicians placed wiretaps on the three target cables in May 1955 and the tapes began running immediately. The voice conversations were recorded by a bank of 150 tape recorders located in the 'warehouse'. The 'tap chamber' was sealed off from the tunnel by a heavy steel door emblazoned with the words 'Entry is forbidden by order of the Commanding General' in both Russian and German to make the tapping operation look like an official Soviet or East German facility and make anyone who stumbled across it hesitate before entering. A microphone linked to the warehouse enabled those on duty to monitor any activity inside the tap chamber. A four-person intelligence section was maintained on site to monitor the conversations as they came through, to report any flash intelligence and provide daily round-ups of what had been heard. The tapes of the voice conversations were flown back to London to be transcribed by the Russian émigrés assembled to deal with the 'take' from the Vienna tunnel. The teleprinter tapes, most of which were enciphered, were sent back to CIA headquarters in Washington.[35]

By now, George Blake had been posted to the MI6 station in Berlin, which was kept separate from Operation Gold, so he had no further knowledge of what was happening with the tunnel. But he had already passed on most of the important details, and Blake's initial KGB contact, Sergei Kondrashev, later said he had told them about the warehouse, and messages intercepted by the wiretaps in the tunnel subsequently confirmed the KGB interest in what was going on there. When Blake was finally exposed as a Soviet spy— by Michał Goleniewski, a Polish intelligence officer who spied for the CIA before defecting to the US in 1961—there were questions asked as to why the Russians allowed Operation Gold to go ahead.

The reason was simple. The KGB was obtaining too much intelligence from Blake to risk giving him away by revealing their knowledge of the tunnel. His new position in Berlin was even more useful than his role in London. All of the MI6 networks in East Germany were being rolled up one by one as a result of the intelligence he was passing on, and he seemed likely to go on to higher things, potentially providing a high-level source inside MI6 to compensate for the loss of Kim Philby.

The teleprinter communications were enciphered and telephone conversations between senior party and military officials were scrambled, as were important KGB communications. The British and Americans could not possibly have access to that information. All that was left was routine conversations between lower-ranking armed forces officers and party officials. The KGB did not underestimate the amount of intelligence which could be derived from that. A security team was sent in and a clampdown ordered on loose talk, but it made little difference. Soviet and East German officials talking over telephone landlines realised their own security people might be listening into them but they never imagined that the British and Americans were as well.

What the KGB did not know, because—as a result of the strict need-to-know policy imposed by Allen Dulles—Blake himself did not know, was that a CIA technical expert had discovered a flaw in a Soviet teleprinter system that rendered its encrypted traffic exploitable. The teleprinter tapes sent back to CIA headquarters in Washington were deciphered by special processors designed to exploit the flaw in the Soviet system, a fact that was known to only a select few in London and Washington. The secrecy surrounding Operation Gold was so tight that, to Ralph Canine's fury, the CIA did not even tell the NSA about the tunnel until a month after it began processing the 'take'. If the KGB had known that the enciphered teleprinter messages were being read, they would have been forced to find a way to stop the operation. Instead, they decided to bide their time.[36]

Curiously, the security surrounding the tunnel revived the use of the wartime Bombes. The East German police, the Volkspolizei, were the only people who continued to use the Enigma cipher after the demise of Nazi Germany. So, the US Army, which was responsible for monitoring the Volkspolizei communications, used two old US Navy Bombes to continue breaking the police traffic in order to warn the British and Americans if the East Germans or the Russians showed any sign of detecting the tunnel. The East German police never found it, but it was uncovered by Soviet forces in April 1956. Frank Rowlett later specified that the tapes had kept running for '11 months, 11 days and 11 hours' before the tunnel's demise.[37]

Heavy rains had caused a number of short circuits in the cables and East German and Soviet telecommunications engineers were out in force to fix the faults, providing the perfect cover for the 'discovery' of the tunnel. Khrushchev was keen to milk the propaganda value of the Soviet success in uncovering the tunnel and a detailed plan was instituted to expose and condemn this 'illegal and intolerable action by the American military authorities'. The Soviet military authorities in East Berlin telephoned every news correspondent in both East and West Berlin to invite them to visit the exposed section of the tunnel inside the Soviet sector. But with Khrushchev's state visit to Britain imminent, the Soviet leader ordered that 'despite the fact that the tunnel contains English equipment' any suggestion of British involvement in the tunnel should be dismissed. Very few of the journalists on the spot were fooled. The Berlin correspondent of *The Times* reported that 'the roadside on the way to the east Berlin airport this afternoon resembled an archaeological site after exciting new finds, with benevolent Russian officers acting as guides to the curious'. He noted that the main control for the tap, the fluorescent lighting, fire extinguishers and other equipment all bore British trademarks 'but the Russians . . . maintain that the whole tunnel is recognisably American work'.[38]

The tunnel and its wiretaps could no longer be used but so much material remained to be processed that Operation Gold continued for another two-and-a-half years until the end of September 1958. The London 'Main Processing Unit' received so much material it was forced to increase its staff to more than 300 people. They transcribed nearly half-a-million telephone conversations, most of which were in Russian but with 75,000 in German.

The 'Technical Processing Unit' in Washington employed 350 people at its peak and dealt with 18,000 six-hour tapes of Soviet teleprinter traffic and 11,000 six-hour German tapes. Given that as many as eighteen different systems were using each cable at any one time, a single six-hour tape could contain 216 hours of teleprinter messages. The intercepts produced a wealth of intelligence of a type not seen since the loss of the Soviet high-grade ciphers on Black Friday.[39]

The intelligence 'take' included details of Khrushchev's denunciation of Stalin at the 20th Soviet Communist Party Congress and the knock-on effects of that decision, including measures to suppress activities by leading Soviet scientists who mistakenly took the Soviet leader's attack on Stalin as a sign of greater liberalisation. It provided early warning of plans to create the Warsaw Pact as a counter to NATO, ensuring greater coordination between the operations of the eastern European armed forces and those of the Soviet armed forces, and the creation in March 1956 of East Germany's National People's Army. Despite the KGB's confidence that their communications were all safe, the 'take' produced detailed information on several hundred intelligence officers in East Germany and in Moscow as well as the operations and tradecraft of both the KGB and the GRU, Soviet military intelligence. It also swept up an enormous amount of information on the relationships between high-ranking senior Soviet officials, including the political manoeuvring which would lead to the fall from grace of Soviet defence minister Marshal Georgi Zhukov.

The extensive nature of the intelligence from Operation Gold had knock-on effects across the US and UK intelligence communities, providing a far more detailed picture of the orders of battle of the Soviet armed forces and their allies than was previously available and significantly enhancing the British and American knowledge of what was happening behind the Iron Curtain. Just as importantly, much of the intelligence could be followed up by aerial reconnaissance and targeted intercept operations to collect even more detail.

Operation Gold supplied significant intelligence on Soviet atomic weapons and energy programmes, including locations, which could be targeted by U-2 overflights, lists of several hundred of the more prominent personalities involved, and improved nuclear air-to-ground missiles for GSFG. There was unprecedented detail of the order of battle of the Soviet armed forces in East Germany and other satellite countries, and full details of the organisation of the headquarters of the Soviet Baltic Fleet and Soviet naval bases in the Baltic republics.[40]

None of this extremely valuable intelligence would ever have been acquired had Allen Dulles not insisted on the extremely tight 'need-to-know' security policy which surrounded the entire tunnel project—in stark contrast, it has to be said, to the careless lack of security he displayed, until MI6 intervened, with his operations in wartime Berne. He had obviously learned his lesson. Blake had no need to know about the flaw in the Soviet teleprinter system, so he was not told about it and as a result was unable to warn the KGB that the Soviet teleprinter ciphers were being read. The level of trust between the two sides was at an all-time high but the Special Relationship was about to face what was possibly its greatest challenge.[41]

11

'WALTZING OVER SUEZ
WHILE HUNGARY BURNS'

The Eisenhower administration had been elected on a platform of liberating the Warsaw Pact states from Soviet control—the so-called 'rollback' policy—but in the ten years since the end of the Second World War, the Russians had considerably strengthened their hold over eastern Europe. All reports from inside the satellite states spoke of high levels of dissatisfaction, but East German riots in June 1953 had been brutally put down by Soviet troops with more than fifty rioters killed, and the presence of 800,000 Soviet forces based in eastern Europe suggested there was little hope that any similar revolt was likely to succeed.[1]

The CIA had stepped up its covert operations in eastern Europe in the mid-1950s, training the 'Red Sox' teams of Polish, Hungarian, Czechoslovak and Romanian émigrés for covert action inside their home countries. MI6 was also in close contact with dissident elements inside Hungary, spiriting them across the border into the British zone of Austria for resistance training in preparation for any uprising. Paul Gorka* was one of a group of Hungarian students recruited in the early 1950s to gather intelligence on Soviet activity inside Hungary and equipped with 'enough weapons to shoot our way across the border'. They were sent 'coded messages from Vienna asking us for information about Russian troop movements, index numbers of military vehicles, so that a picture could be built up of

---

* Gorka's son Sebastian was briefly, in 2017, an aide to President Donald Trump.

details of Russian occupation units. We replied with information written in invisible ink in innocuous letters to special addresses.'

But Gorka and his fellow students developed the unfortunate habit of meeting in a popular Budapest coffee bar to discuss their activities and were swiftly rounded up. 'I was interrogated for seven weeks, sometimes in the presence of a Soviet major. I was tortured several times. Sometimes I was left in my cell with both feet immersed in icy water, other times I was hung from a beam by my arms, handcuffed together. When I was cut down after several hours, my hands were black and so swollen that it was impossible to remove the handcuffs. Under torture, I confessed and after a brief trial was sent to prison for 15 years.'[2]

MI6 put plans in place to support resistance fighters in both Hungary and Czechoslovakia. The service's representatives in Prague and Budapest went out into the woods burying stay-behind packs for the eastern Europeans to use in uprisings against communist control. Some Hungarian dissidents were smuggled across the border for resistance training, rendezvousing with their contact in true Cold War fashion, often quite literally under a certain lamp post in a back street of a border town.

Michael Giles was one of those training the dissidents for resistance work.

> I had this battered old Volkswagen and I was picking up agents on the Hungarian border. We were taking them up into the mountains and giving them a sort of three- or four-day crash course. I would be told to pick somebody up from a street corner at a certain time of night in the pouring rain. Graz was our staging point. Then, after we'd trained them – explosives, weapons training – I used to take them back. This was in 1954, two years before the uprising. But we knew it was going to come. We were training agents for the uprising.

The expectation that an uprising would take place in Hungary seems overstated, even if that was the hope. Certainly, the circumstances that led to it could not have been anticipated by either MI6 or the CIA.[3]

Khrushchev's attack on Stalin at the Communist Party Congress in February 1956, the details of which slowly leaked out in newspapers in both eastern Europe and the West, led to unrealistic expectations of a liberalisation of policy across the Warsaw Pact. Daphne Park, now the MI6 head of station in Moscow, wrote a number of influential reports on what had occurred and the Berlin Tunnel added more detail, but the speech was intended to be confidential and for party members only. The aim was to push them into a more realistic approach towards what could be achieved by the Soviet state, but the Western intelligence services were swift to try to track down details, with the Israeli intelligence service Mossad first to get a full transcript, which they passed to the CIA. Allen Dulles persuaded Eisenhower that the text should be made public and it was passed to the *New York Times*.[4]

As the news of Khrushchev's denunciation of Stalin leaked out across eastern Europe, the Stalinist hardliners who had taken over from less dogmatic national leaders came under intense pressure, particularly in East Germany, Czechoslovakia, Poland and Hungary. The CIA reported that in Hungary pressure was mounting from 'nationalist elements' in the Communist Central Committee to rehabilitate former prime minister Imre Nagy, who had been expelled from the party the previous year over his reformist programme. Dulles briefed the NSC that 'developments in the satellites present the greatest opportunity for the last ten years both covertly and overtly to exploit the situation', with Hungary and Poland being the countries where there were most likely to be problems for the Soviets.[5]

Riots broke out in the East German city of Dresden in May, leading the British and American intercept sites in West Germany to be put on high alert to monitor any reaction from East German or Soviet forces. On 17 May, Dulles told the NSC that Poland had been 'most seriously affected' by the de-Stalinisation campaign and 'the United States should take particular pains to see what it could do to exploit developments in Poland in our national interest'. Six weeks later, rioting broke out in the Polish city of Poznań following a strike over poor pay and conditions at the Stalin Locomotive

Works, with 100,000 people coming out onto the streets in what was initially a peaceful demonstration.

At the start of the day, the marchers took communion and were blessed by priests, but the protests turned into near insurrection with the city's jail stormed, prisoners freed and weapons seized, and the communist party headquarters were occupied by protestors. British and US Army signals intelligence sites in West Germany and the British and American sectors of Berlin reported three Soviet divisions, close to 50,000 troops, moving out of their barracks in East Germany and stationing themselves at convenient entry points along the border with Poland, where the imposition of a temporary restricted area prevented their activities from being observed by BRIXMIS and its US counterpart.

Polish defence minister Marshal Konstanty Rokossowski, who had served in the Red Army during the war, demanded that the Politburo allow him to deal with 'adventurists who attack state insti tutions'. A total of seventy-three people, eight of them Communist officials, were killed and many hundreds wounded when Polish troops and security police opened fire on the demonstrators. The East German newspaper *Neues Deutschland* accused Allen Dulles of being the 'mastermind' behind the revolt.[6]

Dulles specifically pointed to Hungary as the next satellite to be affected, claiming that the country's leader, Mátyás Rákosi, was 'trembling in his boots' on account of his tenuous hold on his 'power-hungry job'. With students leading calls for change, the ruling communist party set up a discussion club within its youth wing in an attempt to create a harmless pressure valve which would allow debate without having any real effect. But the Petőfi Circle, named after the nineteenth-century Hungarian poet Sándor Petőfi, attracted huge crowds to its meetings, spreading and amplifying opposition criticism of the Rákosi regime rather than dampening it down. The communist party newspaper *Szabad Nép* conceded in early July that, as a result of the Khrushchev speech, workers across the country were criticising 'the faults of party work and the short-comings of the state and economic administration ever more boldly', adding that 'it cannot be accidental that these opportunist, harmful and anti-Party views were voiced by those who still maintain a close and systematic contact with Imre Nagy, who has been expelled from the Party because of his anti-Marxist views'.[7]

The US legation in Budapest had been warning for weeks that 'Rákosi's Stalinist background, his unsavoury record and his current political acrobatics make him an extremely vulnerable target' for the Kremlin and was ultimately proven correct. Khrushchev was not prepared to gamble on Rákosi's ability to keep control, and in July the Hungarian party leader was forced to step down and went to Moscow 'for medical treatment'. He never returned but was replaced by his deputy Ernő Gerő, who as another Stalinist was unlikely to placate the Hungarian reformers.[8]

The Soviet authorities were extremely concerned by the situation in Hungary, ordering army chiefs to draw up plans for the 'restoration of order'. Soviet troops in East Germany, Hungary and Poland remained on high alert throughout the summer, with the divisions in Hungary on near-permanent exercise from mid-July onwards. Meanwhile, Moscow began looking for a political solution that might placate the Hungarian population. Soviet ambassador Yuri Andropov—a future head of the KGB and later Soviet leader—held a series of talks with Nagy in which the question of what he would require to return to the party was at the top of the agenda. Nagy proved difficult, determined to clear his name, and the Russians were wary of him, realising that like many Hungarians, he saw Tito's Yugoslavia as the model for his country's future. But they recognised that his widespread popularity made him the only Hungarian communist with a chance of restraining the opposition.[9]

In the wake of the Poznań riots, the Polish authorities had instituted a number of reforms aimed at placating the population, including promising the return of Władysław Gomułka, who had been sacked as party leader in 1948 for 'rightist-nationalist deviation'. The Soviet authorities provided the Polish government with a $25 million loan in an attempt to bolster the regime run by party leader Edward Ochab, who invited Gomułka back into the fold in an attempt to appease the rioters. The decision rattled the Kremlin.

Shortly before Gomułka was due to be confirmed as Ochab's

replacement, Soviet troops based in Poland left their barracks for a joint exercise with their Polish counterparts, their movements monitored and tracked by US and British signals intelligence sites in West Germany and Berlin. At the same time, Khrushchev flew to Warsaw accompanied by a high-powered delegation of senior Soviet leaders, in an attempt to pressure Gomułka into offering full allegiance to Moscow. In the event, the Soviet leader had to be content with an assurance that while the new regime would adopt a distinctively Polish approach to communism it would take its lead from Moscow. A few days later, the troops returned to their barracks. The independence displayed by Gomułka in what became known as the 'Polish October' only encouraged the reformers and opposition in Hungary.[10]

On 4 October 1956, Moscow provided the new regime in Budapest with a similar $25 million loan. Gerő had been in Crimea holding talks with Khrushchev and the money was seen as a way of alleviating Hungary's economic problems and thereby bolstering his regime. The CIA reported that it was nowhere near enough to solve Hungary's economic problems and predicted 'anti-Russian' demonstrations in the next few days as the regime held a ceremonial funeral procession for the remains of László Rajk, a former communist minister executed in 1949 for being a 'Titoist deviationist' and US spy.

Rajk had been rehabilitated following the Khrushchev condemnation of Stalin. As a former secret police chief, responsible for numerous deaths, his rehabilitation might not seem to be an ideal cause for celebration by the Hungarian opposition. But the date of the funeral procession, 6 October, was traditionally observed in pre-communist Hungary as a day of mourning for thirteen Hungarian generals executed in 1849 when the country's rebellion against the Habsburg Empire was put down by Austria, largely as a result of Russian intervention. The resonance was clear.

'The public, which has not been involved so far in the party's disputes, may use the occasion to demonstrate its dislike for the Communists and the Russians,' a CIA report warned. Some 200,000 Hungarians took part in the procession, most of them apparently individual members of the public, many of them holding flowers. In a sign that he expected to be rehabilitated, Nagy was one of the most prominent mourners, openly embracing Rajk's widow Julia. Two days earlier, he had written to the party central committee demanding 'clarification' of his own status and uncompromisingly criticising party policy. At the same time, one of his reformist allies in the Politburo, István Kovács, had warned that senior party officials who opposed liberalisation would have to go. Although the procession was attended by senior party leaders—but not by Gerő, who was in Moscow receiving instructions—it was clearly the demonstration against communism the CIA analysts had predicted.[11]

In many ways—despite the intelligence warnings of what might happen in Hungary—London and Washington were more focused on the events in Poland than they were on the series of student meetings in Hungary that provided the spark for the 1956 revolution. They began on 20 October in the southern city of Szeged, the last redoubt of the 1848 revolutionary government, where students published a list of twelve demands, including the appointment of Nagy as prime minister, the withdrawal of Soviet troops, free elections, sweeping changes in conditions for workers and a return to freedom of expression and freedom of the press.

Over the next forty-eight hours, meetings in Budapest and other major cities expanded the list of demands to sixteen, including the removal of the statue of Stalin from the capital's central park, the Városliget. At the same time, the Soviet armed forces began carrying out the contingency plans devised in July for a 'restoration of order'. They built pontoon bridges across the Tisza River that separated Hungary from the Soviet Union to ensure that, if necessary, Soviet troops based in the Carpathian Military District in Ukraine, on the other side of the river, could take part in the suppression of the Hungarian opposition. Elements of the Soviet 17th Motorised Rifle Division left their barracks in the Székesfehérvár area to the west of Budapest in readiness to advance on the capital, while Soviet Army units based in Romania ordered the recall from leave of officers who spoke Hungarian.[12]

The Hungarian Writers' Union planned to lay a wreath at the statue in Budapest of General József Bem, a Polish freedom fighter who had been one of the heroes of the 1848 Hungarian revolution, on the afternoon of 23 October. The wreath-laying was a show of solidarity with those agitating for more freedom in Poland, but thousands of students, workers and even Hungarian soldiers joined the silent protest. After the wreath-laying, their sixteen demands were read out to the crowd, which crossed the Danube to join demonstrators outside the parliament building.

By the early evening, around a quarter of a million people had gathered there chanting for Imre Nagy, who briefly came out onto a balcony to address the crowd, albeit without any of the inspiration the situation seemed to demand. He urged the people to bide their time and to be patient over the pace of reform, and ended by asking them to sing the national anthem and then go home. They were in no mood to listen and, with increasing numbers coming out onto the street, large crowds were forming in various parts of the city. Many had moved on to the radio station waiting for an address by Ernő Gerő which was due to be broadcast at 8 p.m. on Budapest Radio.

Gerő and other party leaders had just returned from a visit to Yugoslavia and there were hopes that he might hint at a more independent path for Hungary, similar to that taken by Tito. But instead, he attacked the calls for reform and reports suggested he spoke of a 'fascist rabble'. That may have been an exaggeration, but his tone was certainly contemptuous, which only incited the crowd. At the city park, another large crowd fulfilled one of the sixteen demands on their own, toppling the giant statue of Stalin, while at the radio station, student leaders went into the building to try to persuade the director to broadcast the sixteen demands. As the crowd waited for the delegation to return, it began to get restless and angry, a mood not helped by a rumour that one of the students inside had been shot. At around 9 p.m., in an apparent attempt to disperse the crowd, the ÁVH secret policemen guarding the building threw tear gas canisters out of the windows and a few minutes later opened fire on the demonstrators.

Red Cross ambulances arrived but when they turned out to be manned by secret police, the anger overflowed. Parts of the crowd attacked them, stealing their weapons. When the Hungarian Army was called in, the soldiers sided with the crowd. Meanwhile, workers from outlying districts drove into the city centre, obtaining weapons from friendly soldiers and a weapons factory. It is not clear how many weapons were obtained from secret caches hidden by MI6 and the CIA, but it is unlikely that they were ignored. Intermittent exchanges of gunfire between armed demonstrators and the secret police around the radio building continued into the night and, by midnight, Budapest Radio reported that firefights were taking place at 'various points' across the capital.

Shortly after that broadcast, Russian linguists based at the US Army intercept station at Bad Aibling in southern Bavaria, which covered Warsaw Pact operations in Hungary, began picking up unusual activity by the Soviet 2nd Guards Motorised Rifle Division, which was based in Kecskemét, 50 miles south of the capital. The unit showed no respect for the normal radio silence that would have routinely accompanied a move out of barracks or indeed for any kind of communications security, with 'nearly continuous transmissions' revealing that the division was on its way to Budapest to deal with the rioters and officers telling the troops to go faster because they were needed urgently.[13]

Meanwhile, the communist party's central committee met in emergency session, appointing Nagy prime minister, in what was an attempt by both Moscow and Gerő to try to persuade people to leave the streets, rather than a real commitment to change. Gerő told the meeting that he had spoken to Yuri Andropov and asked that Moscow send troops in to intervene. The first Soviet tanks arrived on the city's streets at around 2 a.m. on 24 October. The US site at Bad Aibling intercepted orders from the divisional headquarters to Russian tank commanders to fire their main guns to dispel the rioters. Martial law was imposed and all telephone contact with the outside world cut. Budapest Radio announced that Soviet troops had been called in by the authorities in response to 'the dastardly armed attack of counter-revolutionaries'.

The following morning, the Bad Aibling field station intercepted the radio conversations of elements of the Soviet Army's 32nd Motorised Rifle Division as they moved out of their barracks in the western Romanian city of Arad and crossed into Hungary, heading for Budapest. Moscow Radio claimed that the 'enemy adventure' in Hungary, which had 'obviously been in preparation for some time', had been 'liquidated'. But over the next five days, small groups of 'freedom fighters' armed with rifles and Molotov cocktails made hit-and-run attacks on the Soviet tanks, with sporadic firefights taking place in other cities.

While it was clear that some of the Soviet troops normally based in Hungary were hesitant to open fire, most simply obeyed orders. In one of the worst individual instances, on 25 October, Soviet tanks defending the parliament building opened fire on demonstrators, most of them unarmed, killing a substantial but undocumented number of people. Many Hungarian servicemen defected to the 'freedom fighters', with one of the main army units based in the centre of the city repeatedly fighting off attempts by Soviet troops to take its barracks in a series of battles which cost the lives of more than sixty Soviet soldiers. Meanwhile, the communist party reformers sacked Gerő, who had asked Moscow to send in the troops, together with a number of other hardliners.[14]

Both MI6 and the CIA would have wanted to have people on the ground independent of their embassies to ensure that the arms caches were used by the right people and to work with their agents to collect intelligence. The CIA's presence in the US legation was in any event limited, but how many people it actually had inside Hungary is not clear. Although there were clearly very productive agents providing detailed plans of Soviet military sites, Allen Dulles certainly felt that the Agency should be doing more, telling Frank Wisner: 'These are dramatic days and we must weigh carefully all our actions. However, I'm not one of those who believes we should be hindered by undue caution.'[15]

MI6 certainly had several former members of the service very quickly on the ground. Anthony Cavendish, who had left MI6 in 1953 to become a journalist, subsequently complained that the spy writer Chapman Pincher 'did us no favours' when he wrote in one of his books that MI6 officers 'never lose contact with their organisation when they retire'. But it was certainly the case that Cavendish remained in contact with former colleagues when he became eastern European correspondent of the United Press. He was in Poland when the Hungarian rebellion broke out and flew into Budapest with another former MI6 officer, Basil Davidson of the *Daily Herald*, on a Red Cross aircraft carrying blood supplies.

Davidson's first job in MI6, in December 1939, had been to set up a 'news agency' in Budapest to collect intelligence on supplies being shipped down the Danube to the Germans and disseminate propaganda. Another of the British journalists with links to British intelligence sent to Budapest to cover the uprising was Sefton Delmer, a colleague of Pincher's on the *Daily Express*. Delmer had led some of the more successful British wartime propaganda operations and Cavendish openly admitted introducing him to his friend Maurice Oldfield, a senior MI6 officer, so that Delmer could 'do intelligence a few more favours'.

Peter Kemp, who had helped organise the MI6 operations in Albania, was also in Budapest, nominally on behalf of the Catholic newspaper *The Tablet*, and subsequently smuggled several students across the border into Austria. Cavendish himself was briefly arrested as 'a spy' by the KGB as he was about to leave Hungary, probably because of his continuing links to the British secret service. He was subsequently told by Oldfield that a senior KGB officer had been on his way from Moscow to Budapest to interrogate a journalist 'on whom they had records' and MI6 believed it to have been Cavendish.[16]

A few days into the uprising, Dulles told the NSC that it constituted the most serious threat yet to continued Soviet control of the satellites. 'It confronted Moscow with a very harsh dilemma,' he said. 'Either to revert to a harsh Stalinist policy, or to permit democratisation to develop in the satellites to a point which risked the complete loss of Soviet control.' Opposition forces across Hungary set up 'revolutionary councils' to replace the regional communist party authorities and 'workers' councils' which took over the running of local industries. By 30 October, a ceasefire was in place across the country. Nagy went on Budapest Radio to announce that the one-party system was being abolished and that a coalition government of the parties which existed before the communists took control would be set up pending free elections. He asked the nascent 'revolutionary councils' to stay in place, acting as regional governments, and told the 'freedom fighters' to remain armed since they would become part of a new National Guard.

In a move apparently agreed in advance with Soviet Communist Party second secretary Mikhail Suslov, who had flown to Budapest that day, the Hungarian prime minister appealed for Soviet troops to withdraw from the capital immediately and said his government intended to negotiate the ultimate withdrawal of all Soviet armed forces from Hungarian territory. That night, Soviet defence minister Marshal Zhukov told Chip Bohlen, the US ambassador in Moscow, that 'the order has already been given' for Soviet forces to withdraw from the Hungarian capital. The next day, the Soviet party newspaper *Pravda* confirmed the withdrawal, together with Moscow's willingness to negotiate on the presence of Soviet troops on Hungarian soil. Eisenhower, in the middle of a presidential election, welcomed the move, adding that 'the fervour and the sacrifice of the peoples of these countries, in the name of freedom, have themselves brought real promise that the light of liberty soon will shine again in this darkness'.

When the NSC met again on the morning of 1 November, there was a clear sense of shock in the briefing that Dulles provided on Hungary. 'In a sense, what had occurred there was a miracle,' he said. 'Events had belied all our past views that a popular revolt in the face of modern weapons was an utter impossibility.'

Having spent a decade working for 'rollback', MI6 and the CIA seemed close to achieving their aim, with the real possibility that Soviet troops might start withdrawing from the eastern European satellite states. But although it was clear to the US intercept site at Bad Aibling that Soviet troops had indeed withdrawn from Budapest, it was also clear from 'direction-finding' of the radio communications of the 2nd Guards Motorised Rifle Division and the 17th Motorised Rifle Division by US and British intercept sites in West Germany—which provided the NSA and GCHQ with their precise locations—that they had not returned to their barracks. Nor was the 32nd Motorised Rifle Division showing any signs of returning to Romania.[17]

Nevertheless, both the British and the Americans were distracted by other matters. On 29 October, Israeli paratroopers began landing on the eastern banks of the Suez Canal and the Gulf of Aqaba while reconnaissance elements of six Israel Defense Forces brigades raced across the Sinai Desert to join them. The attack was part of a joint British, French and Israeli response to Egypt's nationalisation of the canal.

Under a plan agreed in secret talks at Sèvres, south-west of Paris, a few days earlier, Israel would invade Egypt. Britain and France would then call for an immediate ceasefire and demand both sides move 10 miles back from the canal. When the Soviet-backed Egyptian president Gamal Abdel Nasser refused, as he was bound to do rather than cede Egyptian territory to the Israelis, British and French forces would move in, ostensibly to separate the two sides in order to protect the Suez Canal, but in fact to create a situation in which they could force Nasser to quit.[18]

Nasser's announcement on 26 July 1956 that he was nationalising the Suez Canal had played well across the Middle East but infuriated Anthony Eden, who only eighteen months earlier, following dinner with the Egyptian leader in the British embassy in Cairo, had declared himself 'impressed by Nasser who seemed forthright and friendly'. Ironically, the Egyptian leader had originally been manoeuvred into power by the CIA, with Kim Roosevelt leading the way, in a ham-fisted attempt to create a Western-orientated leader of the Arab world.

Nasser's willingness to sign an $80 million arms deal with Moscow in September 1955 changed that perception, although even then the CIA seemed to believe it could still keep the Egyptian leader on side. As British ambassador Humphrey Trevelyan arrived at the Presidential Palace to protest against the deal, Roosevelt and his colleague Miles Copeland hid in an upstairs room, having just advised Nasser to argue that the weapons were from Czechoslovakia, not the Soviet Union. Copeland later claimed to have wondered aloud to Roosevelt how Trevelyan would react if they went downstairs and said: 'Excuse me, Gamel, but we're out of soda.'

The US administration took a different view, agreeing with the British that if Nasser did not distance himself from Moscow he would have to go. Eden was not even prepared to give the Egyptian leader that much leeway, at one point shouting at a junior Foreign Office minister: 'What's all this nonsense about isolating Nasser or "neutralising" him? I want him murdered, can't you understand?' Nigel Clive, head of the MI6 Special Political Action group, looked for ways to engineer a coup against Nasser. Julian Amery was drafted in to find dissidents who could be counted on to form a pro-British government. A senior MI6 officer, Nicholas Elliott, was sent to Tel Aviv to liaise with the Israelis.

George Kennedy Young led the way in attempting to follow the Eden directive to the letter. Various schemes were devised to assassinate the Egyptian leader: an exploding electric razor; poison gas in the ventilation system; or even a straightforward hit squad. Dick White, who had replaced Sir John Sinclair as MI6 Chief in the wake of the Buster Crabb fiasco, vetoed them all. Young laughingly told one planning meeting that 'thuggery is not on the agenda'. It was. While the collusion with Tel Aviv was known to only a few, the suggestion that Nasser should be killed was widespread. After a meeting with one senior Treasury official, Trevelyan complained: 'High officials in the Treasury seem to have been very free with their proposals on what to do with Nasser, which included the most extreme solutions.'[19]

MI6 activities on the ground in Cairo were not as good as they should have been given Britain's long-standing presence there. The service recruited a senior Egyptian Air Force officer, Squadron Leader Assam ul-Din Mahmoud Khalil, handing him valuable intelligence on Israel as cover for meetings with his controllers. Khalil turned out to be a double agent who apparently kept Nasser completely informed of what the Egyptian leader later dubbed 'the Restoration Plot'.

There was an element of irony in this failure, since Egyptian intelligence held MI6 in such high regard that its training school used

James Bond books as textbooks in tradecraft. 'The Egyptians had a thing about 007,' former MI6 officer Michael Whittall recalled. 'Their representative in London in the days of Nasser was instructed to go and buy every book by Fleming on James Bond because they wanted to have it as compulsory reading for the training course for their intelligence service. At that time, we happened to have a good connection with the Egyptian intelligence service of which they were not aware, and indeed this chap went and bought them all and was congratulated on subsequent visits to Cairo for having done so.'[20]

Eisenhower had spent his presidency carefully changing the dynamic of British and American decision-making in the Middle East and had in fact done so in a remarkably tactful fashion, frequently restraining his secretary of state, John Foster Dulles, who distrusted British foreign policy and disliked Eden. The US president had always insisted that while the United States must take the lead in the region, its British allies should be consulted at all times. He was shocked to find the British colluding with the French and the Israelis behind his back and doing so in direct contravention of his repeated insistence that there could be no military solution to the Suez question.

In his conversations and correspondence with both Eisenhower and John Foster Dulles, Eden had never made any secret of his determination that Nasser 'should not be allowed to get away with it' and that military action to remove him offered the only real solution, but the US president genuinely saw Eden as having 'double-crossed' America. He was perhaps understandably naïve about Eden's willingness to carry out such an act behind his back, but no one reading the intelligence he was receiving from the CIA and the NSA should have been surprised. Dulles, while less naïve, was far more disingenuous in his response, infuriating his brother Allen by insisting that 'the actual attack occurred without our knowledge and came as a complete surprise to us'.[21]

The suggestion that it was surprising that Britain and France might respond militarily, and that France at the very least was prepared to bring in Israel as part of the plan, was nonsensical. Not only had Eden, his foreign secretary Selwyn Lloyd, and French premier Guy Mollet and his foreign minister Christian Pineau made it very clear on a repeated basis that they believed that only a military solution would suffice, both the CIA and the NSA had produced substantial evidence to show that Britain, France and Israel were working together as part of a military response. The intelligence was incontrovertible.

At the end of August 1956, CIA U-2s had carried out four reconnaissance flights over Syria, Lebanon, Jordan and Egypt, which were passed to the British by Art Lundahl, the head of the CIA's Photo-Intelligence Division. But from September, the U-2s concentrated exclusively on the French and British build-up of troops in the Mediterranean. Bob Amory set up a special team, including NSA analysts, to report on the activities of the French, Israeli and British forces, while Frank Wisner told John Foster Dulles that the British and French were going all out, or as he put it, 'pulling the throttle open', for a military solution. All eight U-2 flights over the region in September, some from Giebelstadt in Germany and others from İncirlik in Turkey, sprawled across the Mediterranean from the French naval base at Toulon via the British bases in Malta and Cyprus, to highlight the creation of a major invasion force. One flight from İncirlik on 3 October passed over Israel, spotting sixty new French Mystère IV fighter aircraft at Lod airfield, more than double the number the French government had told the Americans it was selling to the Israelis.[22]

The CIA-controlled Intelligence Advisory Committee (IAC), supervised by Bill Bundy, who having left signals intelligence following his wartime exploits in Hut 6 at Bletchley Park was now a senior CIA official, was particularly prescient in its predictions. It concluded on 12 September, in a clear reaction to the build-up of forces exposed by the U-2 flights, that there were 'strong indications' that Britain and France were about to launch military action against Egypt. A week later, it produced a Special National Intelligence Estimate on the likelihood of British and French military action which reported that their forces in the Mediterranean were 'in a high state of military readiness and can initiate military action at any time', adding that there was very little America could do to stop them.

Both London and Paris were convinced that 'the elimination of Nasser' was essential to the preservation of vital Western interests in the Middle East and north Africa. By mid-October, CIA officers in the region were reporting a 'decidedly acute estrangement' from MI6, which was clearly hiding something from them. Kim Roosevelt, now deputy director plans, reported confidential information from an old contact which backed up the CIA suspicions. The IAC's clearest warning, issued the day before the Israeli invasion, not only accurately predicted that it would happen but added that it was probably designed 'to provide a diversionary threat against Egypt to afford greater freedom of action for France and the UK in the Suez situation and to relieve Egyptian pressures on France in North Africa'.[23]

The NSA response was hampered by the fact that it was in the throes of the move out of its Washington headquarters to Fort Meade, north-east of the capital on the road to Baltimore. There was a small USAF intercept site on Crete, but it and other US sites in Turkey were targeted at the southern Soviet Union, so the Americans relied heavily on the British for their coverage of the Middle East. Despite the political tensions, there was no pause in the intelligence exchange between GCHQ and the NSA, with the British sharing the results of their interception of the Egyptian diplomatic messages between Nasser's government in Cairo and the embassy in Moscow as well as intelligence gleaned from the heavy increase in diplomatic messages between the Quai d'Orsay in Paris and the French embassy in Israel.

GCHQ and the NSA also shared the results of their intercepts of the communications of both the Israeli and Egyptian armed forces by 2 Wireless Regiment, the British Army signals intelligence base at Ayios Nikolaos, 4 miles west of Famagusta in Cyprus, and by the US Army intercept site in Asmara, which dropped its coverage of the Soviet Union to concentrate on Egyptian and Israeli military operations. Both sides kept strictly to the letter of the UKUSA Accord, the official NSA history of the Suez crisis notes, adding that 'such a strong alliance could not be torn asunder by Suez'.[24]

There were inevitable tensions in the MI6 relationship with the CIA but it nevertheless remained remarkably strong, as evidenced by Art Lundahl's sharing of the imagery intelligence (IMINT) from the U-2 flights over Egypt and Israel with his British colleagues. By chance, a U-2 aircraft overflew al-Maza airfield north-east of Cairo shortly before British and French planes launched their first attacks on Egypt on 31 October. The U-2 passed back over the airfield after the British aircraft had dropped their bombs, providing perfect 'before and after' images which were passed to the RAF. Its imagery analysts were receiving similar photographs from their own Canberra PR9 reconnaissance aircraft flying out of Akrotiri in Cyprus but responded gratefully to the U-2 material, saying: 'Warm thanks. It's the quickest bomb damage assessment we've ever had.' Shown the imagery, and told the story, forty-eight hours later, Eisenhower admired the product but insisted that no further imagery was to be shared with the British until the crisis was over.[25]

America led the calls within the UN for an immediate ceasefire and the formation of an emergency force to separate the Israeli and Egyptian forces, but there were mixed messages coming out of Washington. Despite Eisenhower's anger at Eden's decision to join the French and Israelis in military action, US officials made clear that if the British and French acted quickly they would stand aside. Indeed, the Joint Chiefs of Staff believed the British and French were right to attack, arguing that 'if Nasser's expropriation and nationalisation of the Suez Canal are permitted to stand, related reactions may well develop which will jeopardise US military, political and economic interests throughout the world'. John Foster Dulles believed that if the British did go in, they should certainly not stop until they had finished the job. Bob Amory phoned Chet Cooper, the CIA liaison with MI6, and said: 'Tell your friends to comply with the goddamn ceasefire or go ahead with the goddamn invasion. Either way, we'll back them up. What we can't stand is their goddamn hesitation, waltzing while Hungary is burning.'[26]

Hungary might not have been burning, but it was certainly being torn apart. The Soviet Union had used the Western attention on Suez to completely reverse its original suggestions of a more liberal approach to the eastern European satellite states. With hindsight, the first indication that the promise to withdraw was not all it seemed came in a statement carried by the Soviet news agency TASS at midday on 31 October, which said the withdrawal would take place 'as soon as the Hungarian government considers it appropriate'. Given that Imre Nagy had made it perfectly clear that his government wanted them to leave, it was obvious something was wrong.

A few hours later, reports began to come in from Záhony on the eastern border with Ukraine that elements of the Soviet 23rd Tank Division, normally based in the Ukrainian city of Uzhgorod, were crossing the border into Hungary. Forward elements of the Soviet 35th Motorised Rifle Division, normally based at Košice in eastern Czechoslovakia, had also begun crossing the border into northern Hungary, joining the three Soviet divisions already poised around Budapest. Nagy called in Soviet ambassador Yuri Andropov and protested at the arrival of more Soviet troops and the failure of the two divisions normally based in Hungary to return to barracks.

Moscow claimed the new troops were only relieving those already there, but shortly afterwards Soviet forces occupied Hungarian air force bases to allow more troops to fly in. Nagy told Andropov that his government was giving immediate notice of termination of its membership of the Warsaw Pact and that Hungary was now a neutral state. By early evening, there were reports from the borders with Romania, Ukraine and Czechoslovakia of Soviet troops 'pouring into Hungary'. A total of eight Soviet divisions were soon inside Hungary and ready to put down the revolution once and for all, sending out a powerful message to the other eastern European satellite states.

Operation Whirlwind began in the early hours of 4 November. Hungarians manned the barricades and attacked the Soviet troops with Molotov cocktails, but they were pinpricks against such overwhelming force. The US Army intercept site at Bad Aibling was overloaded with Soviet communications and reinforcements were sent out from America. But by the time they arrived, the revolution was over. Nagy had been arrested by Soviet forces and taken out of the country, his government replaced by one led by party leader János Kádár, who for much of the crisis had been working behind the scenes with Andropov and Moscow to return the country to communism. Around 6,000 Hungarians were estimated to have died in the revolution. Nagy was later returned to Budapest, put on trial and hanged for treason.[27]

On 5 November, the day after the Soviet crackdown in Budapest, British and French paratroopers landed in northern Egypt, swiftly taking Gamel airport and Port Fuad and advancing on Port Said. The following day, with sterling under intense pressure and the US refusing to allow Britain to borrow funds from the IMF to help the Bank of England keep the pound pegged at $2.80 on the foreign exchanges, the British government agreed to the UN ceasefire, leaving the French no option but to follow suit. It was an undoubted humiliation for Britain and is still widely seen as the end of the country's post-war aspirations to remain a major world power. Eden, plagued by ill health, was ordered by his doctor to go on holiday, staying at Ian Fleming's Jamaican holiday home, Goldeneye, and eventually returning home to resign.[28]

The anger of the old hands in MI6 at the way Britain had been treated by America was epitomised by George Kennedy Young, who a year later would go on to become vice-chief of the service. While Russia was invading Hungary, to put down an uprising for which both the CIA and MI6 had spent a decade preparing, the US president had not only blocked CIA plans to drop arms and supplies to the Hungarian rebels, he had prevented his country's closest ally from carrying out military action which even the US Joint Chiefs of Staff saw as justified and necessary. 'Although for ten years the United States government had always hoped for, even where it had not tried to propagate, a spirit of active resistance to Communism behind the Iron Curtain, when the moment came, it was not prepared to lift a finger,' Young said. 'When its own allies acted in pursuance of what they believed to be in their national interests, the United States government took the lead in preventing them.'[29]

Nevertheless, the traditional image of Suez as the Americans ruthlessly casting the British aside is vastly overdone. Eisenhower, having just won the November 1956 presidential election by a landslide, made a point of reminding his colleagues that they should not lose sight of the fact that 'the Bear is still the central enemy' and even in the middle of the crisis, the US president reached out to Eden to reassure him that America's relationship with Britain would not suffer lasting harm. 'No matter what our differences in the approach to this problem,' Eisenhower said, 'please remember that my personal regard and friendship for you, Harold [Macmillan], Winston and so many others is unaffected. On top of this, I assure you I shall do all in my power to restore to their full strength our accustomed practices of cooperation just as quickly as it can be done.'[30]

At the end of November, Eisenhower received a personal message from his wartime friend and colleague Lord 'Pug' Ismay, who was now NATO secretary-general. The central thrust of the message, which the US president felt was 'very desperate in tone', seemed to be 'that we deserted our two friends in their hour of trial'. Coming from a man with whom he was 'the best of friends', this dismayed Eisenhower such that he felt compelled to issue a statement stressing that the Anglo-American differences over Suez 'should in no way be construed as weakening or disrupting the bonds which have for so long joined us together', and in a personal message to Ismay, he insisted: 'I have never lost sight of the importance of Anglo-American friendship and the absolute necessity of keeping it strong and healthy in the face of the continuing Soviet threat.' A day later, Eisenhower expanded on that sentiment, telling *Newsweek* that 'our friendship with the people of Great Britain and Western Europe must be maintained and must be strengthened. It represents a priceless asset of which I have never, for one moment, lost sight.'[31]

Eisenhower knew the value of the Special Relationship in terms of intelligence cooperation better than anyone. At the end of the Second World War, he had written to Stewart Menzies, the then Chief of MI6, praising the intelligence produced by Bletchley Park, which he said had been of 'priceless value' and had made a 'very decisive' contribution to winning the war and saving thousands of British and American lives. He was pleased when Harold Macmillan took over as prime minister from Eden. The two had worked very closely together during the war when Macmillan was British minister resident at Algiers, reporting directly to Churchill as a member of the cabinet.

Eisenhower told his aides that the new British prime minister was 'a straight, fine man . . . the most outstanding' of the Britons he served with during the war. The US president suggested a conference 'to restore confidence in the Anglo-American relationship' in the wake of the Suez disagreements and to ensure that Britain remained 'an important and effective ally'. Macmillan opened the conference in Bermuda in March 1957 by stressing that while Britain recognised it was the junior partner in the relationship it was determined 'to stay in the game' and cooperate with its American allies. Eisenhower for his part thought it the most successful international meeting he had attended since the end of the Second World War, noting in his diary 'the atmosphere of frankness and confidence', which he put down to the fact that he and Macmillan were 'old wartime comrades and friends of longstanding'.

The conference ended with a Declaration of Common Purpose, representing the 'interdependence' of the two countries, but nothing went further towards restoring the Special Relationship than a secret agreement—proposed by Eisenhower and kept out of the official communiqué—that Britain and America should 're-establish their intimate wartime cooperation, including joint intelligence and planning systems, to meet international problems'. The discussions on the subject led to an agreement to establish joint intelligence and planning groups in various locations around the world, the *New York Times* reported, adding that the new arrangement would ensure the US was 'better informed on developments in Communist China' where, unlike America, Britain maintained a diplomatic mission. In reality of course, the agreement was largely formalising looser arrangements between MI6 and the CIA that were already in place.[32]

One of the first moves to expand the existing intelligence exchanges was Eisenhower's decision, a few weeks after the Bermuda conference, to invite the British to take part in the U-2 operations. He was of course well aware of the extent of Britain and America's joint aerial reconnaissance operations during the Second

World War and the value of the British contribution, in particular the photographic interpreters based at Medmenham, as he was of the value of British signals intelligence operations. He also remained concerned that the CIA's U-2 overflights of the Soviet Union might cause an international incident, with the potential for a clash with Moscow to spiral out of control. Dick Bissell, the senior CIA officer running the U-2 programme, hoped that bringing the British into the operation would increase the American ability to deny involvement if an aircraft were to be shot down, thereby reducing the political risks and making it easier to persuade Eisenhower to sanction the missions. Following a series of Soviet nuclear tests at the Semipalatinsk test site in Kazakhstan, and amid increasing concern over the number of missiles the Russians were believed to have available, Allen Dulles persuaded the president to approve British participation in the U-2 programme.[33]

Dulles began consultations with Dick White and RAF intelligence chiefs on a joint programme, codenamed Chalice, and officials from the CIA's Photo-Intelligence Division liaised with their opposite numbers at the British Joint Air Reconnaissance Intelligence Centre (JARIC) at RAF Brampton in Cambridgeshire, to work out a system of requirements, analysis and reporting. Given that the Soviet nuclear tests had persuaded Eisenhower to back a new series of overflights, there was less urgency on British pilots joining the system until authorised flights came to an end in late 1957. The CIA then began pressing for the British to provide pilots who could be trained to take part. The first four RAF pilots arrived for training at Laughlin Air Force Base in Texas in the summer of 1958; one died in a training accident, but the other three were sent to İncirlik in November to form a small British contingent.[34]

The RAF U-2 pilots were attached to MI6, which also paid their salaries. They spent most of the next eighteen months conducting reconnaissance flights over the Middle East, a total of twenty-seven in all, but they carried out two overflights of the Soviet Union—at a time, in late 1959 and early 1960, when Eisenhower was refusing to allow the CIA to carry out any at all. On 6 December 1959, in Operation High Wire, an overflight authorised by Macmillan

Operation High Wire

First British U-2 Overflight of the USSR, 6 December 1959

Source: CIA

rather than Eisenhower, Squadron Leader Robert Robinson flew from Peshawar across Soviet Uzbekistan and the Aral Sea, over the 'closed city' of Kuybyshev (Samara), where he changed direction, flying south-west past the main Soviet heavy bomber base at Engels-2 airfield, near Saratov, then diverting over the Kapustin Yar missile test range before landing at İncirlik.

The second, and only other, RAF overflight ordered by Macmillan took place a couple of months later. In Operation Knife Edge, Squadron Leader John MacArthur took off from Peshawar on 5 February 1960, overflew the Tyuratam missile test range, which was also the home of the Russian space programme, then continued heading north-west to the city of Kazan, where he obtained the first photographs of the experimental Tu-98 Backfin supersonic bomber, sat on the Borisoglebsk military air base. He then headed south, photographing long stretches of the rail network, since any important sites would need to be close to the railway and the Soviet ICBM network in particular was heavily dependent on the railways for transportation.

Three months later, on 1 May, Gary Powers, the most experienced of the CIA pilots, took off from Peshawar for the final overflight authorised by Eisenhower. The flight plan for Operation Grand Slam was designed to take in as many ICBM sites as possible in order to ease concerns over the so-called 'missile gap', the false belief, fuelled by Khrushchev's jingoistic rhetoric, that the Soviet Union had far more ICBMs than the United States. His first target was the Tyuratam test range. He then changed direction slightly more towards the north and flew to Chelyabinsk, just south of Sverdlovsk (Yekaterinburg), then over Kyshtym, the source of substantial radiation following an accident at a nuclear plant only three years earlier. From Sverdlovsk, he was due to fly north-west, then over the ICBM launch sites at Yur'ya and Plesetsk, the Soviet Northern Fleet nuclear missile submarine construction site at Severodvinsk and the naval base at Kandalaksha, and north to Murmansk, before crossing into Norway to land at the Bodø air base. Powers never made it past Sverdlovsk.

An SA-2 Guideline missile, one of a number fired from a site which the Americans had not known to exist, exploded close enough to his aircraft to disable it. Powers was forced to eject and parachute to the ground where he was arrested. Khrushchev fully exploited the propaganda value of the loss of the U-2 and the capture of its pilot, threatening 'retaliatory measures' in the event of any further overflights.

Moscow accused Britain of being involved but only on the basis that when the U-2s overflying the Soviet Union flew from İncirlik to the start point at Peshawar they stopped at a British base in Bahrain to refuel and were checked over by RAF technicians before continuing to Pakistan. The British contingent had been immediately removed from the İncirlik air base when Powers failed to return and the Russians seemed unaware of its existence. A four-man RAF U-2 contingent was subsequently stationed at Edwards Air Force Base in southern California until 1974 but there were no further British U-2 overflights of the Soviet Union.[35]

Throughout the 1950s, beginning with a 1951 RAND report on 'Utility of a Satellite Vehicle for Reconnaissance', the Americans had been investigating the potential of satellites to provide aerial photographs of the Soviet Union, eastern Europe and China and collect signals intelligence. The launch of the Soviet Sputnik satellite in October 1957 had been a traumatic moment for the United States, reinforcing the false belief that the Soviet Union's technological capabilities might be superior to those of America and galvanising its own space programme. Less than two months after Powers was shot down, on 22 June 1960, the US launched its first intelligence satellite. The GRAB (Galactic Radiation and Background) satellite, later renamed Poppy, collected electronic intelligence, tracking radar systems of Soviet warships and pinpointing air defence systems, all of which was shared with the British.

Two months later, on 18 August 1960, the first Corona photographic reconnaissance satellite was launched. It returned to earth a day later and the imagery taken by its KH-1 Keyhole camera included photographs of the Kapustin Yar missile test site and the Sarova nuclear weapons research and development centre, 250 miles south-east of Moscow. It also produced 'good to very good' imagery of sixty-four Soviet airfields and twenty-six previously unidentified surface-to-air missile sites. Subsequent satellites soon photographed the ICBM launch site at Plesetsk and the main Soviet shipyard for the construction of ballistic missile submarines at Severodvinsk that Powers had been due to photograph but had never reached.

Dick Helms recalled that the Corona programme produced intelligence very few agents, no matter how well placed, could begin to supply. 'Although the superbly detailed photographs taken from outer space could not show what foreign policy-makers were thinking or discussing among themselves, the data on foreign capabilities were outstanding,' Helms said. 'A good agent in the right place can be expected to produce intelligence that cannot be duplicated by any amount of overhead photography, but no spy can hope to reveal the mass of data that were such easy pickings for the unmanned satellites. The fact that this material could be produced without any compelling diplomatic or political bothers is also a significant advantage.'[36]

The KH-1 camera could detect objects from on average 20 to 30 feet in size. Ground resolution was considerably improved by subsequent cameras, with the KH-4B, introduced in 1967, able to photograph anything over 5 feet. In order to analyse the imagery, the CIA Photographic Intelligence Division was combined with its armed forces counterparts to create the National Photographic Interpretation Center (NPIC) inside the CIA and run by Lundahl. NPIC worked extremely closely with its British counterpart, JARIC, so closely in fact that when he retired Lundahl, who had ensured the British received U-2 imagery intelligence during the Suez crisis, was awarded an honorary knighthood by the Queen.[37]

The efforts by Macmillan and Eisenhower to rebuild the Special Relationship also extended to lifting many of the restrictions on cooperation on nuclear weapons that had been enshrined in the 1946 McMahon Act. The UK government initiated an independent nuclear weapons programme in January 1947, testing its first atomic device in October 1952, and went on to develop a hydrogen bomb, with a number of successful tests beginning in May 1957. This persuaded Eisenhower to ask Congress to amend the McMahon Act and led in July 1958 to the UK–US Mutual Defence Agreement, which ensured Britain and America could share the details of their respective nuclear weapons programmes. It did not allow for the transfer of nuclear warheads, but Britain had shown itself perfectly capable of building its own.

This persuaded Eisenhower to promise that, from 1965, America would supply the RAF with the US Skybolt stand-off air-to-ground missile, which was then under development, to extend the life of its V-Bomber nuclear strike force, with the British fitting their own Red Snow warheads to the missiles. In return, the US Navy was permitted to base its nuclear submarines carrying Polaris ballistic missiles at Holy Loch in Scotland, significantly reinforcing a relationship which was about to be tested by the greatest crisis of the Cold War.[38]

I 2

THE CUBAN MISSILE CRISIS

President John F. Kennedy's key advisers were far more sceptical of the Special Relationship than most of their predecessors and determined to present a new image of an idealistic, more intellectual presidency than the 'muddling and moralising' Eisenhower administration with its 'self-righteousness and sermonising . . . Cold War clichés'. Mac Bundy, Kennedy's national security adviser, had briefed senior officers on the ULTRA intelligence during the D-Day landings, but most of his colleagues had no such experience or understanding of the value of the transatlantic intelligence exchange. They regarded Harold Macmillan's desire to join the European Economic Community (EEC) as an opportunity to transform the Special Relationship between Britain and America into a closer relationship with Europe as a whole and they saw absolutely no point in an independent British nuclear deterrent. Fortunately, the president himself was far more in tune with the spirit of the Special Relationship. Not only did he not share his father's obsessive Anglophobic tendencies, he enjoyed a good rapport with Macmillan from the start.

During the handover period, Eisenhower had gone out of his way to brief Kennedy on the close relationship between the CIA and MI6, and on the even closer UKUSA exchanges between the NSA and GCHQ. He pointed out that since Macmillan would be receiving the same intelligence, Kennedy would find him a highly experienced and valuable sounding board. Eisenhower also had Art Lundahl and Dick Bissell, now deputy director plans, brief the president-elect on the Keyhole satellite and U-2 imagery.[1]

Kennedy was, famously, a fan of James Bond. He had dined with Ian Fleming—who no doubt took the opportunity to mention his own involvement in the creation of the transatlantic intelligence relationship—and *From Russia with Love* had appeared in a list of the new president's top ten books. He was impressed with Allen Dulles, Bissell and Lundahl and, from the very beginning, preferred the reports he received from the CIA to the much longer, highly detailed State Department briefing papers. Kennedy had briefly served in naval signals intelligence, working on low-level communications systems, where the obsession with minor details bored him to tears. But the information the CIA provided for him was hard-hitting and to the point, in stark contrast to the State Department briefings. 'By gosh, I don't care what it is, but if I need some material fast or an idea fast, CIA is the place I have to go,' Kennedy said. 'The State Department is four or five days to answer a simple yes or no.'

Bob Amory recalled that Kennedy's enthusiastic reaction to the briefings he received from CIA officers had an extremely positive impact on those writing the intelligence reports. 'We tried very hard to live up to his high views of us,' Amory said. 'I don't mean just at the high level. This had a very good morale effect all down the line in the analytical side of the CIA establishment. People were willing to work long hours and to come in at 3 o'clock in the morning because they knew damn well what they produced was read personally by the President immediately upon its delivery to the White House. There was a good feeling, a good rapport between the Agency and the President. I would say that this had a lot to do with Kennedy's relatively unquestioning acceptances of the Bay of Pigs proposal.'[2]

The ill-fated Bay of Pigs invasion, a CIA-run operation in which 1,400 Cuban exiles landed on the south of the island intent on setting up a beachhead with its own airstrip in order to kick-start guerrilla operations against the Castro government, was hamstrung from the start by the need to avoid any indication of US involvement. The operation, codenamed Zapata, was a hangover from the Eisenhower administration, which in March 1960 had ordered the CIA to look at ways of removing Fidel Castro from power. The plan was stepped up shortly before Kennedy came to power as a result of a break in relations between the US and Cuba.[3]

The CIA plan is frequently misrepresented as aiming to incite an immediate revolution that would remove Castro from power. It was in fact far less ambitious. The invasion force was to hold the beach-head for 'two weeks, possibly as long as thirty days', allowing time for members of a 'provisional government'—made up of leading Cuban refugees selected by the CIA – to fly in, providing a tangible symbol of resistance inside the country. The anti-Castro guerrillas and the provisional government would then move out into the countryside, mounting hit-and-run attacks on government installations to create 'a set of affairs describable as continuing civil war'.[4]

Arthur M. Schlesinger Jr, a Harvard professor—and former OSS intelligence officer—appointed by Kennedy as his special assistant, was one of a number of key members of the administration who opposed the idea, but he nevertheless found Bissell's briefings on the operation impressive. The CIA deputy director plans, had an 'unsurpassed talent for lucid analysis and fluent exposition', Schlesinger recalled. 'We all listened transfixed, fascinated by the workings of this superbly clear, organised and articulated intelligence, while Bissell, pointer in hand, would explain how the invasion would work or discourse on the relative merits of alternative landing sites.'[5]

One key problem with the plan was that, as with the Albanian operations, the émigrés involved could not keep their mouths shut. Throughout March 1961 and into April, Havana Radio daily accused America of preparing 'invasion units' to attack Cuba. Just over a week before Operation Zapata was due to take place, the New York Times reported that it was common knowledge in Miami—'a city of open secrets and rampaging rumours'—that the anti-Castro guerrillas already infiltrated into Cuba 'will be followed next week by professional men and intellectuals who are to be concentrated at an undisclosed spot to prepare to serve as military government officials if the revolutionaries gain a foothold on Cuban soil. The proclaimed objective of the Revolutionary Council . . . is to gain a beachhead in Cuba to set up a government-in-arms.'[6]

Bill Bundy, having left the CIA, was now assistant under-secretary for national security and the Pentagon's representative in the discussions on Operation Zapata. As such, he sat in on all of Bissell's major briefings for the president and his advisers. Both Dulles and Bissell were clear from the outset that there were no guarantees there would be any revolt against Castro, Bundy recalled. But the Joint Chiefs gave Kennedy a misleading impression of the likelihood of success because they wanted the Cuban leader gone.

'I don't think there was enough weight given to the military possibilities of failure,' Bundy said. 'I remember senior officers in the Pentagon saying they didn't suppose it really had more than a 30–40 per cent chance of succeeding, but they still thought it ought to be done. That kind of feeling—the feeling that we just had to do something about Castro, which was very strong in the Pentagon—may have contributed to the judgements not coming through to the President as forcefully as they might have done.'

An operation with only a limited chance of success, not least due to the lack of surprise, was dealt a fatal blow by the insistence of Adlai Stevenson, the US ambassador to the UN, and Dean Rusk, Kennedy's secretary of state, that air strikes by US B-26 bombers to destroy Castro's air force could not take place since they would be seen as American in all but name, despite the fact that the aircraft would have been flown by Cuban pilots and repainted with the colours and insignia of an independent Cuban air force, the Fuerza Aérea de Liberación.

That anyone who had gone through the Second World War could believe that the Cuban rebels could land and hold a beachhead under fire from the Cuban Revolutionary Air Force with no air support of their own beggars belief. But Stevenson and Rusk, a former US Army colonel who should have known better, persuaded Kennedy to cancel the strikes at the very last minute, when it was too late to stop the actual landing, with inevitable results. The exiles held out under sustained air attack for more than two days before surrendering with the ultimate loss of more than 100 men. The operation inflicted irreparable damage to the reputation of the CIA that lingers even now.

The new president's faith in the CIA was momentarily knocked by the Bay of Pigs failure and he questioned whether he had been right to keep Dulles on as head of the CIA. 'Dulles is a legendary figure and it's hard to operate with legendary figures,' he told Schlesinger over lunch in the White House. 'It is a hell of a way to learn things, but I have learned one thing from this business. That is that we will have to deal with the CIA. [Robert] McNamara has dealt with Defence. Rusk has done a lot with State. But no one has dealt with the CIA.'

It was agreed that both Bissell and Dulles should step down, but out of respect for their abilities and substantial achievements, neither was to be forced out immediately, creating a 'bleak period' when the most senior CIA officials found it difficult to gain access to the White House. The only useful consequence of this lack of communication was that it led to the creation of the 'President's Checklist', the forerunner of the 'President's Daily Brief', which has been provided to every US president since. Dulles retired in November 1961 and Bissell left the CIA a few months later.[7]

While the British agencies looked on in horror, they had their own failings to deal with. Michał Goleniewski, who had defected to the CIA in January 1961, identified fourteen MI6 files that had been passed to the KGB, and the only possible suspect with his name on the distribution list of every one of the documents was George Blake. He was responsible for the deaths of large numbers of MI6 agents, many of them in extensive and valuable networks inside East Germany. Macmillan was furious, not least because he felt obliged to inform Kennedy personally about Blake, who was swiftly put on trial in camera and sentenced to forty-two years' imprisonment.[8]

A summit between the leaders of the world's two undisputed superpowers, the United States and the Soviet Union, took place in Vienna on 2 and 3 June 1961. Khrushchev felt able to bully Kennedy on the basis of the younger man's inexperience in the job and the failure of the Bay of Pigs invasion. The main topics of discussion were Berlin—where Khrushchev believed that by signing a peace deal with East Germany, he could force the Western powers out of the former German capital—and Laos, where the US was supporting the right-wing monarchy over the Soviet-backed communist guerrillas. Little was agreed between the two sides and although the US media reported the summit favourably in terms of what Kennedy got out of it, in truth neither side came out of it with any real success. Worse, Kennedy felt he had been bettered by the older man, hitting his confidence. He sent Rusk to Paris to brief President Charles de Gaulle and Assistant Secretary of State Foy D. Kohler to Bonn to brief Chancellor Konrad Adenauer.

Kennedy himself flew to London to discuss the way forward on what had become known as the Berlin crisis with Macmillan, confessing to fears that any concessions on the status of West Berlin would be seen as the allies having lost a key battle in the Cold War. The president and the prime minister got on well.* So much so that they spent two hours together discussing Berlin and other issues without any of their advisers present. 'K looks like being a good friend to me,' Macmillan noted in his diary. 'He has some old prejudices (perhaps a little of the Irish tradition) about us. But he lives in a modern world.' Two weeks later, in what was a far more potent symbol of who was winning or losing the Cold War than Khrushchev's bullying approach at the Vienna summit, the Russian ballet dancer Rudolf Nureyev defected to the West.[9]

Not only was Kennedy fostering a good personal relationship with the British prime minister, his administration was tempering the stance taken by John Foster Dulles and Eisenhower with regard to the joint US and British position in the Middle East. When Iraqi dictator Abdul Karim Qasim declared in June 1961 that Kuwait was part of Iraq and appeared to be moving forces to the border, Britain sent in troops to ward off any Iraqi invasion. Gulf Oil called for US military intervention to protect its 50 per cent share in the Kuwait Oil Company (British Petroleum held the other 50 per cent), but Rusk insisted that America 'in no repeat no way wishes to undercut British position in Kuwait'. He subsequently told the US ambassador to Kuwait that the administration supported the 'paramount UK

---

* A distant family relationship between the British prime minister and Kennedy, whose deceased sister Kick had been married to Macmillan's nephew, also engendered trust, with Kennedy even occasionally calling Macmillan 'Uncle Harold'.

position in the Persian Gulf', adding that 'western interests must be preserved primarily by UK actions and programmes . . . US role should remain essentially one of consultation, encouragement, and support'.[10]

Meanwhile, thousands of East Germans were fleeing to West Berlin because they feared Khrushchev would force the pace and cut East Berlin off from the West, and on 13 August 1961 the East German authorities did just that. Barbed wire was rolled out to prevent East German citizens from crossing into West Berlin. A few days later, construction of the Berlin Wall began, effectively preserving the western sector's status as an island of capitalism inside the Eastern Bloc. Many still tried to cross into West Berlin, and some even succeeded. Those who did not were killed, shot in the back by automatic weapons fire. Nevertheless, the construction of the wall would eventually put an end to the crisis, with Kennedy confiding to aides: 'It's not a very nice solution, but a wall is a hell of a lot better than a war.'

Allen Dulles was replaced as CIA director by John A. McCone, the chairman of the US Atomic Energy Commission. McCone appointed Dick Helms as deputy director plans and Ray Cline as deputy director intelligence. Cline had worked briefly on Japanese codes in naval intelligence during the Second World War before transferring into the OSS. After joining the CIA, he worked at the London station as liaison to the JIC. A senior representative of the CIA's London station, often the station chief himself, sat in on the first half of the JIC's weekly meetings, discreetly leaving halfway through to allow the committee to discuss issues that were 'UK Eyes Only'. So Cline was well aware of the value of the close relationship with MI6.

'The wartime partnership was still paying off handsomely,' Cline recalled. 'The British, recognising the importance of keeping the United States actively engaged in an effort to contain Soviet disruptive thrusts, were extraordinarily open and cooperative with Americans in intelligence matters. They provided not only most of their highest-level joint intelligence estimates but also supplied the station chief in London with most of their clandestine intelligence reports. It was in London, the hub of the closest intelligence exchange in history, that I perceived very early what vast benefits our allies provided in the way of good intelligence. Without them the alliance system itself could not function effectively. By roughly dividing the world between them and exchanging the materials recorded, the United States and Great Britain have always saved themselves a great deal of money and trouble and continue to do so.'[11]

One of the most important collaborations between the CIA and MI6 had begun just as Kennedy was coming to power. In August 1960, Oleg Penkovsky, a colonel in the GRU, Soviet military intelligence, who had been attempting to contact the CIA for a number of years, saw a group of American language students on a train. A few days later, back in Moscow, he spotted two of the group in Red Square and gave them an envelope containing a letter offering his services as a spy and asked them to hand it to the US embassy. They passed it on. Penkovsky was a member of the State Committee for the Coordination of Scientific Research, which set up visits to the West by delegations of Soviet scientists and electronics experts, an ideal platform for the GRU to obtain intelligence on Western technology. He had invaluable access to Soviet secrets. The CIA attempted repeatedly to get in touch with him. They were unable to do so.[12]

Fortunately, the British had become aware of Penkovsky's attempts to contact the West. Dickie Franks, a senior MI6 Russian specialist who would later become the service's Chief, set up an operation to contact the GRU officer and run him as a British agent-in-place. From its creation in 1909, MI6 had been adept at using patriotic businessmen to help gather intelligence. One of those it had used in the past for work inside the Communist Bloc was Greville Wynne, a business consultant who helped British companies sell their products across eastern Europe.

Franks took Wynne to The Ivy, an expensive art deco restaurant in London's West End, and suggested that once again he do his bit for Queen and country. A few months later, Wynne was part of a delegation hosted by Penkovsky's committee in Moscow. He did not have to approach the GRU officer; Penkovsky singled him out, going out of his way to persuade a reluctant Wynne to take some intelligence material back to the UK and suggesting that his new friend organise a Soviet delegation to London to meet British electronics companies.[13]

Meanwhile, restricted in their own operations in Moscow and unaware that MI6 was already in touch with Penkovsky, the CIA asked the British for help in contacting him. MI6 revealed that they had already made contact and the operation became a joint one. When Penkovsky's delegation arrived in London, Franks told Wynne to send the Russian to a room at the Mount Royal Hotel, close to Marble Arch, where two MI6 officers and two CIA officers were waiting to debrief him. The GRU officer arrived with a demonstration of his own good faith, two packages of handwritten notes on Soviet secret military programmes and intelligence operations in the West. During this first meeting, on 20 April 1961, information poured out of the Russian, but the most important intelligence he had to offer concerned Soviet long-range missiles.

During the Second World War, while serving in Ukraine, Penkovsky had been assigned to the staff of General Sergei Varentsov, who was in charge of all artillery forces in the region. Six months later, Varentsov was wounded and brought back to Moscow. He spent four months in hospital while Penkovsky looked after his wife and daughter, ensuring they had sufficient food. The general's daughter from a previous marriage died while he was in hospital and Penkovsky sorted out the burial arrangements. 'I sold my last watch and went down to Lvov to bury the girl, purchasing a black dress and her coffin,' Penkovsky said. 'After I returned to the front and he knew what I had done, he said: "You are like a son to me."'

In a move that was critical to Penkovsky's value as a spy, Varentsov became his lifelong friend and mentor. By the time Penkovsky offered to spy for the West, Varentsov was in charge of all Soviet military missile systems and one of a small select group of officers privy to the problems the Russians were experiencing with missile technology, in particular with electronic guidance systems. Penkovsky was a frequent visitor to Varentsov's home,

and at the weekend to his *dacha*, and since the GRU man's respon-
sibilities focused on missile technology, they frequently discussed
the subject.

Penkovsky was adamant that the missile gap argument was nonsense. He revealed at the first meeting that the Soviet Union had no
working ICBMs at all. The programme to build the R-16 missile, the
first Soviet ICBM, had stalled spectacularly the previous October
when the fuel in one missile ignited ahead of a test launch, killing
scores of those watching, including the head of the Soviet missile
programme, Chief Marshal of Artillery Mitrofan Nedelin. The
Americans had far more and far better missiles than the Russians,
who were pouring money into missile programmes, scrambling to
catch up.[14]

There were a series of meetings during that first visit to the UK
in April and May 1961. The MI6 and CIA officers followed the
delegation around as it travelled from London to Birmingham and
Leeds, and back to London. Penkovsky was trained to use a Minox
spy camera and given a series of intelligence targets: details of GRU
operations and agents in the West, particularly the 'illegals', agents
working under unofficial cover and living in the community. Had
the Russians broken the British and American codes, and if so which
ones? And missiles: continuous updates of the Soviet strategic missile systems. How many did they have? Which ones worked? Which
ones did not? How accurate were they? Where were the bases? What
were their targets? How many atomic warheads did the Russians
have? Where were they stored?

Despite the quality and detail of the information Penkovsky provided, there was some resistance in the CIA to the idea that he was
genuine. The British, by contrast, were absolutely convinced and
determined to push ahead no matter what. Penkovsky had provided
them with too much valuable intelligence, much of it highly damaging to the Russians. Maurice Oldfield, another future 'C', who was
the MI6 head of station in Washington, and Jack Maury, head of the
CIA's Soviet division, had to fight hard to ensure the joint operation
went ahead, with Jim Angleton, one of the original OSS officers
based in London and now in charge of CIA counter-intelligence,

convinced that Penkovsky was a KGB plant. At one point, after a fractious discussion of the case, Maury felt compelled to put his thoughts on record. During the meeting, he had shown Angleton one of Penkovsky's comments and asked him how he thought revealing this particular piece of intelligence could possibly have helped the Russians.

'After reading the source comment, he confessed he could see no way in which it would be to the Soviet interest to give us this line,' Maury said. 'However, Mr Angleton then took off on the notion that Penkovsky was an anarchist or a crank and for some obscure reason was trying to get us into war with the Russians. I frankly do not know what he was talking about in this regard and doubt very much that he did.'

Maury and Oldfield ensured that, despite Angleton's intervention, the CIA came on board. Angleton was a particularly difficult character, having become convinced, in the wake of the Philby revelations, that the Western intelligence services were heavily infiltrated by Soviet agents-in-place. But the row was symptomatic of the difficulties inherent in the relationship between MI6 and the CIA, which was never as closely integrated as that between GCHQ and the NSA. 'Joint operations are usually to be avoided for reasons ranging from petty to profound,' Dick Helms said. 'Methods are different. Egos clash. Routine procedures tangle. The Penkovsky operation was an exception. Harnessed in tandem, our combined facilities were much enhanced. The extraordinary value of Penkovsky's reporting smoothed the few kinks that developed.'[15]

Running Penkovsky in Moscow was fraught with danger and, in the wake of several CIA espionage problems in the Soviet capital, the US ambassador refused to countenance any Agency operations from his embassy, leaving Penkovsky's handling to MI6 head of station Ruari Chisholm. He devised a system of collecting the GRU officer's intelligence based on a long-standing MI6 tradition of giving wives of officers serving abroad a role in agent-handling operations, particularly in countries like the Soviet Union where the MI6 officers themselves were likely to be under constant surveillance. Chisholm's wife Janet, a former MI6 secretary, would meet

Penkovsky on a Sunday afternoon stroll in a park with her children, one of whom was young enough to be pushed in a pram. Penkovsky would put the Minox cassettes and any messages into a box of sweets 'for the children' and drop them in the pram as he passed.[16]

Penkovsky was an inveterate collector of top secret documents with no apparent fear of being caught. During the eighteen months that he was run by MI6 and the CIA, he handed over 110 cassette films, including photographs of 8,000 pages of documents. The Penkovsky 'product' was extraordinarily valuable, none of it more so than during the Cuban missile crisis.

The first sign of Moscow supplying arms to Castro's regime had been picked up in July 1960, through British intercepts of the messages sent to and from Soviet ships travelling to Cuba from Baltic and Black Sea ports. The GCHQ listening post at Scarborough in Yorkshire—which under the UKUSA coordinated coverage of the world was the only station tasked to track all Soviet merchant shipping travelling out of the Baltic and across the Atlantic—noted a large increase in the number of Soviet merchant ships using sophisticated cipher communications. There were clear differences between their manifests as declared to Lloyd's List and plain language messages reflecting military cargoes.

The Scarborough intercepts were supplemented by communications from ships sailing from the Black Sea monitored by the British signals intelligence site at Ayios Nikolaos in Cyprus. They also intercepted a highly unusual coordination of communications with the ships and their controllers in the Baltic and Black Sea ports including a major communications exercise of the kind more normally carried out by the Soviet Navy.[17]

By the beginning of 1961, USAF bases in Germany were intercepting the communications of Cuban pilots being trained to fly MiG fighter aircraft at the Trenčín air base in central Czechoslovakia. Interception of Cuban armed forces communications, previously limited to a US Navy site at Sabana Seca in Puerto Rico and an army site at Vint Hill Farms at Warrenton, Virginia, was rapidly expanded. A US Army special forces signals intelligence unit based at Fort Bragg, North Carolina, began tracking the communications of Cuban Army and paramilitary forces, building up a detailed picture of the order of battle.

In December 1961, the US Navy ordered the Sabana Seca site to impose blanket coverage of shipping movements in and out of Cuban ports and sent the USS *Oxford*, fitted with a complete communications and electronic intelligence suite and more than twenty operator positions, to circumnavigate the island carrying out an audibility survey of everything that could be intercepted, including Soviet ships unloading supplies at the northern port of Mariel, 25 miles west of Havana. Amid evidence of an increasing number of Soviet military advisers arriving on the island, an army signals intercept site at Fort Clayton in the Panama Canal Zone was tasked to monitor all Russian communications emanating from Cuba.[18]

The first few months of 1962 saw an unprecedented increase in intelligence operations against Cuba, so much so that, according to Bruce Clarke, the then director of the CIA's Office of Strategic Research, 'the build-up of analytical capabilities just barely kept pace with the influx of information. One of the problems that kept coming unsolved throughout the pre-crisis period was how to cope with the vast volume of reporting.' In February 1962, the CIA set up a Caribbean Admissions Center at Opa-locka in Miami to debrief all refugees and defectors arriving from Cuba. The NSA based a 'target exploitation' team in the centre to interrogate refugees who might have knowledge that would help them to intercept Cuban communications. U-2 flights over Cuba were doubled from one a month to two and, from March 1962, the CIA Office of Current Intelligence began to publish a Daily Summary devoted entirely to Cuba.[19]

The US Army special forces intercept battalion at Fort Bragg was overwhelmed with work as the Soviet advisers set about a complete reorganisation of the Cuban armed forces, including communications security. 'Cuban Ground Forces were in constant state of reorganisation, re-subordination and relocation,' the battalion's intelligence analysts recalled. 'Identification of units became increasingly difficult when the Cubans reverted to landline and microwave communications.' In an attempt to improve reception, the battalion moved from Fort Bragg to Homestead Air Force Base, on the southern tip of Florida, 200 miles across the Florida Straits from Havana. Evidence of radar systems associated with Soviet MiG-17 and MiG-19 fighter aircraft began appearing on Cuban communications systems in late spring and, at the beginning of May, Soviet air controllers were intercepted talking to Cuban fighter pilots in heavily accented Spanish, occasionally reverting to Russian to speak to other Soviet Bloc pilots or controllers.[20]

Despite all the evidence of Warsaw Pact military assistance, it was not until late May that plans to place Soviet missiles in Cuba were finalised. At Khrushchev's request, the Soviet General Staff put together a plan to base a complete group of Soviet forces, with every element represented, in Cuba. 'The Soviets had ambitious plans for their military presence in Cuba,' Clarke said. 'Basically, they intended to export a miniature of the Soviet military establishment at home, with everything from motorised infantry to strategic missiles, with a total of at least 26,000 personnel. The first Soviet arms carriers connected with the build-up began to arrive in Cuba in late July 1962. We knew the ships were coming in, and we identified them as arms carriers. We didn't know, however, what the arms were or that this was just the beginning.'[21]

In mid-July, in response to the increase in military equipment arriving in Cuba, the *Oxford* was stationed in the waters north of Havana 'as a matter of the highest intelligence priority' in order to complement Scarborough's coverage of the cargo ships. By the middle of August, more than ninety Soviet vessels had docked in the ports of Havana or Mariel with many of them hiding the true content of their cargo behind nebulous words such as 'varied' or 'general' which the Russians had previously used to disguise military equipment.[22]

Following the break in relations between Cuba and the US in January 1961, the British embassy had agreed that its staff would collect intelligence for the Americans on what Castro's government was doing. This was a major departure from routine British diplomatic behaviour, in which ambassadors frequently refused to allow British intelligence officers to use their missions for espionage operations, although inevitably MI6 would pay lip service to such demands while in reality ignoring them. But Bill Marchant, the British ambassador in Havana, had spent the war as the deputy head of Hut 3, the main Bletchley Park intelligence-reporting operation, and as a result was much more amenable to US requests for assistance. Indeed, in the spring of 1962, KGB officials warned the Cuban intelligence services that British embassy staff were 'most actively supporting American intelligence'.

The extent of the intelligence the British diplomats were collecting was revealed in the President's Checklist for 23 August 1962, which noted: 'We now have several reports from the British Embassy whose people have been out looking.' They had focused on a camp at Lourdes just west of Havana where there were a large number of Russians and where a large antenna field suggested, not least to Marchant's expert eye, the presence of a communications intercept operation. That assessment was correct. The newly constructed antenna field was the beginnings of a major Soviet signals intelligence base which monitored US communications for the next forty years. As for the military equipment that was being delivered to the camp, the embassy suggested that 'an expert might consider the possibility of anti-aircraft rockets and radar', a conclusion that was echoed in intercepted radio conversations and reports coming in from recently arrived refugees debriefed at the Opa-locka admissions centre.[23]

Six days after the British embassy reports, a CIA U-2 photographed SA-2 Guideline surface-to-air missiles—the type of missile that had brought down Gary Powers—at eight locations. They were capable of hitting targets as high as 80,000 feet out to a distance of 25 miles. The cameras also picked up SA-2 missiles, transporters and radars at assembly areas south of Havana, and at Banes in the far north-east of the island, as well as eight Komar guided-missile boats equipped with the Styx anti-ship missile, which had a range of 50 miles. Two weeks later, an SA-2 target acquisition radar was intercepted searching for aircraft, confirming that at least some of the surface-to-air missiles were operational and capable of taking out a U-2.[24]

At this stage, the consensus view within the CIA and the US

administration itself was that the SA-2 missiles, the relatively short-range Styx missiles and the Soviet MiG fighters, which a U-2 flight on 5 September had revealed now included the more up-to-date MiG-21, were all legitimate, if unwelcome, defensive measures designed to deter a US invasion. Nevertheless, there were still concerns that Khrushchev might base surface-to-surface missiles in Cuba. President Kennedy decided to send the Soviet leader a clear message warning him not to place 'offensive weapons' capable of being used to attack the US on the island.[25]

While rejecting claims from his Republican opponents in the coming Congressional elections of 'offensive ground-to-ground missiles, or of other significant offensive capability either in Cuban hands or under Soviet direction and guidance', Kennedy warned that 'were it to be otherwise the gravest issues would arise'. He made it very clear that 'the Castro regime will not be allowed to export its aggressive purposes by force or the threat of force. It will be prevented by whatever means may be necessary from taking action against any part of the Western Hemisphere.'[26]

The 'groupthink' that it would not be in Khrushchev's interest to put surface-to-surface missiles on Cuba because the Russians 'evidently recognise that the development of an offensive military base in Cuba might provoke US military intervention and thus defeat their present purpose' was reflected in a CIA Special National Intelligence Estimate released on 19 September 1962. Placing surface-to-surface missiles on Cuba would undoubtedly give Moscow 'considerable military advantage', dramatically increasing the deterrent effect of its nuclear missile capability, but this 'would be incompatible with Soviet practice to date and with Soviet policy as we presently estimate it. It would indicate a far greater willingness to increase the level of risk in US–Soviet relations than the USSR has displayed thus far.'[27]

John McCone, who was away on honeymoon on the French Riviera, was most passionate in his disagreement with his own analysts, making his opinion very clear in a series of messages which came to be known as the 'Honeymoon Cables', including one which deliberately dissociated him from the 19 September Special National

Intelligence Estimate. He was not alone. The NSA, GCHQ and the newly formed US Defense Intelligence Agency (DIA) agreed, although among Kennedy's key advisers the complacent consensus ruled. McCone rightly reasoned that the surface-to-air missiles were not there to protect 'the workers in the sugar cane plantations'. There must be something more important they were there to prevent the CIA U-2 aircraft from finding and he firmly believed that this must be surface-to-surface missiles capable of attacking the US.

Bill Casey, the wartime OSS officer who would go on to become CIA director, recalled that McCone immediately questioned the arrival of the SA-2 missiles: 'What are they there to protect, he wondered. There are no targets there now, he concluded, so they must intend to bring something there which will need to be attacked and hence will need to be defended. When Cuban refugees reported that large missiles were being brought in and installed, McCone considered this confirmation of his tentative forecast, while most others in Washington dismissed them on the basis that the Soviets would never do anything so foolish.'[28]

The Soviet delivery of military supplies continued throughout the summer so that by the end of September more than 160 ships had docked in Cuba, the vast majority of which were carrying Soviet military equipment or personnel. 'The programme which had begun to shape up in August—both in Cuba itself and in the eyes of US intelligence—really got rolling in September,' Bruce Clarke recalled. 'The SA-2 programme was well underway, other conventional weapons were coming in, and the heart of the Soviet programme—the strategic missiles—began to arrive.'[29]

The first report of Soviet surface-to-surface missiles came on 27 September from the debriefing of a refugee who had just arrived in Miami. 'After dark on 12 September 1962, I was driving east on Avenida 23, Marianao, Havana, when I observed and counted 20 Soviet trucks towing 20 long trailers going west on Avenida 23,' he said. 'The trailers, the longest I have ever seen in Cuba, were two-axle, four-wheeled. They were about 65 to 70 feet in length and about eight feet in width. I believe the transport trailers were carrying large missiles, so long that the tail end extended over the end of the trailer. I would guess that the missiles were a few foot longer than the trailers. The missiles were covered with wood and canvas.' However, when pressed, the refugee could not be certain that there were missiles under the canvas covering. It was an interesting but as yet unconfirmed piece of intelligence.[30]

Then a few days later, a low-level CIA agent inside Cuba, a farmer recruited as part of Operation Mongoose, a covert US operation to destabilise the Castro regime, claimed to have seen missiles being taken to an area near San Cristóbal, 55 miles west of Havana, where 'very secret and important work' was going on. 'At first the report seemed like another well-meant but not very closely observed collection of bits and pieces,' Dick Helms recalled. 'After extensive examination, the agent's information proved to square with other reports from the area—notably considerable military traffic, and long, canvas-cloaked trucks moving like scythes, toppling telegraph poles along narrow street corners before disappearing into restricted areas in the nearby countryside.'[31]

Four further U-2 flights, at the end of September and beginning of October, picked out twenty-five SA-2 sites with missiles ready to fire. They also captured a ship unloading crates known to be custom-built to carry sections of Il-28 Beagle medium-range bombers, an aircraft capable of attacking the US capital from airfields on Cuba. Given the threat posed to U-2 aircraft by SA-2 surface-to-air missiles, attempts were made to use the Corona satellites to collect photographs of potential missile sites, but cloud cover led to unsatisfactory results. Amid concern that the shooting down of a CIA U-2 would create a scandal similar to the Powers incident—with media reports bound to link it to the CIA's role in the Bay of Pigs disaster—Kennedy ordered that USAF pilots take over the U-2 flights, albeit using the more up-to-date CIA aircraft.[32]

Early on the morning of Sunday 14 October 1962, Major Richard Heyser's U-2 crossed Cuba on a route from the south to north around 70 miles west of Havana. In the six minutes he spent over the island, he took 928 images covering an area 75 miles wide. His main target was the suspected missile site at San Cristóbal. No sooner had he landed at McCoy Air Force Base near Orlando in

Florida, than the film was transferred onto another aircraft and flown to Art Lundahl's NPIC photographic interpreters just outside Washington. The prints were developed and, throughout the following day, photographic interpreters struggled to work out what they were looking at. They knew the missiles at San Cristóbal were Soviet surface-to-surface missiles; they were just not certain which type of missile they were and therefore what targets they could hit. What they did now know for sure was that McCone had been right all along.[33]

Ray Cline had spent that afternoon at the first of what would become an annual MI6–CIA Methods of Intelligence conference, which that year was being held at CIA headquarters in Langley. He returned to his office at half past five to find a group of Lundahl's analysts waiting to show him the images of the Soviet missiles. 'They were all agreed that they had just identified a base for missiles of a range upwards of 330 miles,' Cline said. 'I reviewed their evidence and was obliged to concur. About 2130 that evening, my intelligence officers checking out the evidence on the site reported somewhat cryptically by phone that they had agreed on a report identifying offensive missile systems probably in the 700-mile and possibly in the 1,000-mile range. I instructed them to complete a written report and stand by for action early the next morning.'

Cline briefed Mac Bundy, who decided the president should not be disturbed until a full report was available the following day. The next morning, Cline, Lundahl and Sid Graybeal, the CIA's top Soviet missiles expert, went to Bundy's office. 'I told him the story,' Cline recalled. 'He also brought in the Attorney-General [the president's brother Bobby], whom I also briefed. His initial comment was one four-letter word.'[34]

Bundy and Marshall 'Pat' Carter, the deputy head of the CIA, briefed the president later that morning. Further analysis of the imagery, in tandem with the documents supplied by Oleg Penkovsky, had convinced them the missiles were SS-4 Sandal medium-range ballistic missiles which had a range of around 1,000 miles, capable of hitting much of the south-eastern United States from Houston, Texas, in the west across to the US Navy's main base

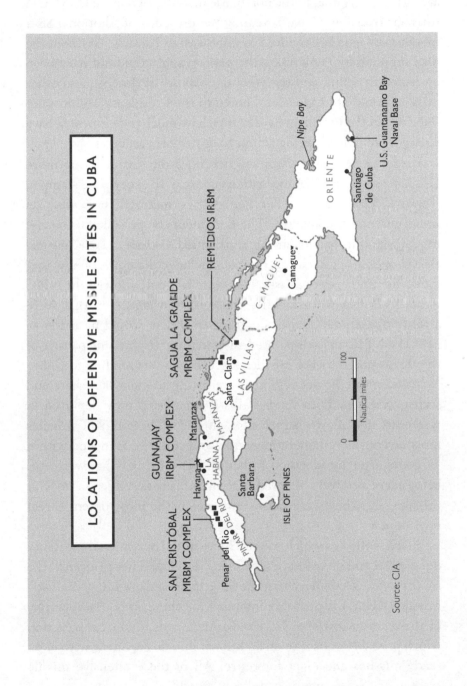

LOCATIONS OF OFFENSIVE MISSILE SITES IN CUBA

Nipe Bay

U.S. Guantanamo Bay
Naval Base

ORIENTE

Santiago
de Cuba

REMEDIOS IRBM

SAGUA LA GRANDE
MRBM COMPLEX

CAMAGUEY

Camaguey

Santa Clara

LAS VILLAS

100

Nautical miles

0

GUANAJAY
IRBM COMPLEX

Matanzas

MATANZAS

LA
HABANA

Havana

Santa
Barbara

ISLE OF PINES

SAN CRISTÓBAL
MRBM COMPLEX

Penar del Rio

PINAR DEL RIO

Source: CIA

at Norfolk, Virginia, in the north. Meanwhile, two more USAF U-2 missions overflew Cuba, revealing the presence of additional SS-4 missiles at Sagua la Grande, 150 miles east of Havana. 'Without the data supplied by Penkovsky, the photographs could not have been evaluated in detail, and the precise capability of the SS-4 and other missiles could not have been known to the President,' Helms said. 'Nor would the President have known how much time he might have to negotiate before taking action to destroy the missiles.'[35]

Over the next two days, assessments from half a dozen more U-2 flights led to a CIA evaluation report with every page stamped Ironbark, the codename for Penkovsky's material, indicating its importance to the analysis. The documents he provided on Soviet missiles, and in particular a manual titled *Methods of Protecting and Defending Strategic Rocket Sites*, which included diagrams of how various different types of missile sites were laid out, allowed the NPIC photo interpreters to identify those missile launchers that were already operational and estimate when others would be ready to fire. The NPIC analysis painted an even more frightening picture of the threat posed by the missiles Khrushchev was sending to Cuba.

'At least one Soviet regiment consisting of eight launchers and sixteen SS-4 medium range ballistic missiles is now deployed in western Cuba at two launch sites,' it said. 'These mobile missiles must be considered operational now and could be launched within 18 hours after the decision to launch.' U-2 images that were still being examined were believed to show as many as sixteen more SS-4 missiles. But they were not by any means the most potent threat to America.

'Fixed, soft sites which could achieve initial operational capability during December 1962 are now being developed near Havana,' the report said. 'We believe that the SS-5 Intermediate Range Ballistic Missile (IRBM) is probably intended for these sites. Photography of these sites show[s] eight, fixed launch pads under construction which probably equate to an additional missile regiment with eight ready missiles and eight for refire. All of these offensive missile systems are Soviet manned and controlled.'

Further imagery showed a third 'soft site' being prepared for SS-5 missiles at Remedios, 190 miles east of Havana, with Penkovsky's documents indicating that standard Soviet practice suggested there would eventually be two sites there. The SS-5 Skean had a range of 2,300 miles, making it more than capable of hitting the majority of America's major cities, including Washington.

The layout of the surface-to-air missile defences at these 'soft sites' and the rigid nature of Soviet military doctrine indicated that the Russians intended to place sixteen SS-5 missiles on Cuba, providing 'a significant strategic strike capability against almost all targets in the US'. The deployment of the missiles was 'no token show of strength', the report concluded. The Russians intended to turn Cuba into 'a prime strategic base' that would supplement their ability to target America 'in a significant way . . . with some of their most effective guided missile systems'.[36]

The following day, the MI6 officers attending the MI6–CIA conference were briefed on the evidence, which was still restricted to a very tight inner circle. Sherman Kent, then director of the CIA's Office of National Estimates, recalled that only the president, a small number of senior intelligence officers and the members of the National Security Council's executive committee, or ExComm, knew of the missiles. Kennedy had not even mentioned them in talks with Soviet foreign minister Andrei Gromyko in the White House the previous day. 'Until the President was ready to act, the Russians must not know that we knew their secret,' Kent said. 'And when we were ready to act, our allies should know our chosen course before our adversaries.'

Throughout that week, members of the ExComm spent many hours discussing various scenarios ranging from immediate air strikes to a full-scale invasion without any prior warning—an option ruled out by the president, who likened it to the Pearl Harbor attack and said it was not the sort of thing that America had ever done or indeed ever would do. By the time the NSC met on Saturday 20 October, the US response had come down to one of two options: a series of pre-emptive air strikes to take out all of the known missiles or an unequivocal warning to Khrushchev that the missiles must be removed and the imposition of a blockade to stop the twenty-eight Soviet ships that were on their way to Cuba—some of them carrying the longer-range SS-5 missiles. Crucially, one of the key pieces of intelligence provided by Penkovsky was the time it would take for missiles to be operational after being shipped to a new location. This persuaded Kennedy he had time to pursue a negotiated settlement rather than order immediate air strikes.[37]

The US president decided to write to Khrushchev on Monday 22 October, warning him that the missiles must be removed, and to address the American people at 7.00 that evening on the situation, repeating his demands that the missiles be removed and announcing a US 'quarantine' of Cuba, effectively a blockade preventing the Russians from bringing in any more. The leaders of Britain, France, West Germany and Canada would be personally briefed ahead of time, with Macmillan to be told some time before any of the others, in keeping with Kennedy's determination to maintain a much closer relationship with the British prime minister.[38]

In fact, as a result of the briefing to MI6 officers in Washington on the Friday, Macmillan had already been informed by Sir Dick White, the MI6 Chief, while Kennedy sent the British prime minister a personal message on the Sunday, the day before other NATO leaders were briefed, outlining the key issues and specifically making clear that he would keep in close contact with him via their encrypted telephone link, discussing any issues that arose. 'It is a source of great personal satisfaction to me that you and I can keep in close touch with each other by rapid and secure means at a time like this,' Kennedy said, 'and I intend to keep you fully informed of my thinking as the situation evolves.' He also invited the British ambassador, David Ormsby-Gore, a close personal friend, to the White House to discuss the options and to seek his advice.

'I had a pretty good idea of what was already happening,' Ormsby-Gore recalled. 'We had had various indications of it from the CIA but I didn't know precisely and he just filled me in on exactly what the picture was that these U-2 flights had shown up; the existence of the missiles; that they had then checked on them and there was now no doubt about it that they were offensive missiles and that they had a certain capability and that there would be this number by such and such a date and what the estimates were and what was the United States to do about it.

'He posed to me alternative policies without indicating which policies he was in favour of and he said which do you think would be right and I said that I thought an immediate strike would not be understood in the rest of the world and that some form of blockade was probably the right answer.' Ormsby-Gore sent a full report of their discussions to London before returning to the White House that evening with his wife for dinner with the Kennedys, after which the president, Bobby Kennedy and Ormsby-Gore continued to discuss the crisis into the night.[39]

The next day, Chet Cooper, now Ray Cline's assistant for policy support, accompanied David Bruce, the wartime head of the OSS London office and now US ambassador to the UK, to brief Macmillan personally. 'It was evident that the Prime Minister had some advance general knowledge of the developing situation in Cuba,' Cooper recalled, 'as indeed he should have since we had briefed various members of the British intelligence community several days before in Washington. However, Mr Macmillan obviously had no idea of the extent or precise nature of Soviet offensive capabilities in Cuba. After my recitation of the present Soviet offensive strength in Cuba, Mr Macmillan said that, if the President were convinced that a meaningful offensive capability was present, "That was good enough for him." He did not spend more than a few seconds on the photographs.'

Cooper briefed White that evening and the JIC on the following day. 'There was, naturally, considerable speculation as to Soviet motives,' he recalled. 'To the extent that there was any consensus in the JIC, it was very much along the line propounded by Sir Dick the previous evening . . . namely: that the Soviet aim was to confront the President late in November with a *fait accompli* in Cuba, a vantage point from which Khrushchev could bargain for a definitive settlement of the Berlin question and the question of US foreign bases in general.'[40]

By now imagery from a U-2 flight on 19 October had shown that the first of the four SS-4 sites at San Cristóbal was already operational with four launchers and missiles aimed at the US and ready to fire. A second site had two of its four launchers already in operational position and was deemed to have emergency, rather than full, operational capability. There were two other sites at San Cristóbal with launchers and missiles but they were not yet operational. One of the two further SS-4 sites at Sagua la Grande had three of its four launchers in place and was already operational. The missiles at the second site were not yet ready to fire. Construction at the sites for the longer-range SS-5 missiles was in its early stages. There were no missiles at any of those sites and none were expected to become operational before December.[41]

After making his address to the nation, the president rang Macmillan, the first of a number of telephone conversations with the British prime minister that week. 'He seemed rather excited but very clear,' Macmillan noted in his diary. 'He was grateful for my messages and for David Gore's help. He was rather vague about the blockade (it is clear that all kinds of plans have been all day under discussion). He is building up his forces for a *coup de main* to seize Cuba should that become necessary.'

The close relationship the president had with Macmillan and Ormsby-Gore and the number of times during the week when he telephoned them, or in the British ambassador's case invited him to the White House to discuss the crisis, have led at least two leading US historians of the crisis to conclude that 'Macmillan and Ormsby-Gore became de facto members of the ExComm'. While this is something of an exaggeration, Ormsby-Gore later recalled that the phone calls between Macmillan and Kennedy were 'very much an exchange of views and I would say that the initiative came about equally from each side. I saw the president four times during the course of the week,' the British ambassador said. 'On three of those occasions for long periods. I also had a number of telephone conversations with him.'[42]

Early on the morning of 23 October, the GCHQ listening post at Scarborough reported 'very urgent' messages being sent to Soviet merchant ships on their way to Cuba, one of which informed them that their orders would now come direct from Moscow rather than

Odessa or Murmansk. By the following day, it was clear from locations given by a number of Soviet ships, intercepted at Scarborough,
that they were heading back to the Baltic or the Black Sea.

'Twelve of the 25 Soviet ships heading for Cuba had turned around
and were not going to risk running the US quarantine line,' Bruce
Clarke said. 'The messages went back and forth between Moscow
and Washington as Khrushchev tried to get out of his predicament.'
The ships that had turned around included four that—on the basis of
their distinctive communications with their Soviet controllers, dis-
crepancies in their manifests, and the cargo visible on deck—were
confidently believed to be carrying the longer-range SS-5 missiles.
The knowledge that the GCHQ reports of ships turning around
reached the White House Situation Room before any provided by
the US Navy made that evening's telephone call from Kennedy to
Macmillan particularly satisfying for the British prime minister.[43]

Despite his orders that the ships turn around, Khrushchev
responded belligerently to Kennedy's imposition of the quarantine,
accusing the US of 'banditry' towards Cuba and issuing his own
warning that the Soviet Union 'will not simply be bystanders with
regard to piratical acts by American ships on the high seas'. Given
that there were four Soviet Foxtrot-class attack submarines armed
with nuclear-tipped torpedoes known to be on their way to Cuba,
this could not be taken as a vain threat. If US warships tried to stop
Soviet ships from docking in Cuba, 'we will then be forced on our
part to take the measures we consider necessary and adequate in
order to protect our rights,' Khrushchev said. 'We have everything
necessary to do so.'[44]

The US president might have lost the mind games in Vienna, but
he was not prepared to lose them now. He confidently brushed aside
Khrushchev's threats, knowing that Oleg Penkovsky had told his
MI6 and CIA contacts at their very first meeting that the Russians
simply did not have enough missiles to play fast and loose with the
Americans. 'Kennedy should be firm,' Penkovsky told his MI6 and
CIA handlers. 'Khrushchev is not going to fire the rockets. He is not
ready for war.' The US superiority in missile strength gave Kennedy
the confidence he needed. His response to the Soviet leader's

bombast was a calm but very clear repetition of the US position. Any Soviet ships carrying military cargo to Cuba would be stopped and Khrushchev must order all of the surface-to-surface missiles that were already on the island to be removed.[45]

As part of the preparations for air strikes if Khrushchev refused to back down, the president approved a series of low-level reconnaissance flights over the missile sites and other potential targets. The flightpaths were designed to replicate those of the aircraft poised to attack the missile sites in order to disguise any real air strikes and catch the defences off guard.[46]

On Friday 26 October, the President's Checklist noted that the latest U-2 flights had shown 'no slackening in the pace of construction work at the missile sites'. Both SS-4 sites at Sagua la Grande were now fully operational. Three of the SS-4 sites at San Cristóbal also had full operational capability. Only the fourth site at San Cristóbal had no capability whatsoever. But a further U-2 flight on 26 October revealed that was no longer the case. All six of the SS-4 sites had full operational capability. Soviet surface-to-surface missiles, based on Cuba, little more than 100 miles from Florida, and already pointed at their targets, could hit a large swathe of the south-eastern US mainland.[47]

The same day Aleksandr Fomin, the KGB's top man in Washington, called John Scali, the diplomatic editor of ABC News, and asked to meet him for lunch. 'It's very important,' Fomin said. Could Scali be at the Occidental Restaurant, a short distance from the White House, in ten minutes? When Scali arrived, Fomin was clearly agitated. 'The situation is very serious,' he said. 'Something must be done.' The waiter had no sooner taken their orders than Fomin proposed a way of resolving the crisis. The Russians would dismantle the missile sites and take the missiles back to the Soviet Union, with the UN overseeing the process. Castro would pledge never to allow such missiles on Cuban soil again. In return, the US would promise that it would never invade Cuba. Did Scali think the Americans would accept this as a way out of the crisis? Scali had no idea but rushed off to the State Department to put the proposals to Dean Rusk.

The secretary of state consulted with the White House before giving Scali a handwritten note. 'I want you to go back to this man and tell him this,' Rusk said. Scali met Fomin in the Statler Hilton, just around the corner from the Soviet embassy. Sticking precisely to the script, he said: 'I have reason to believe that the US government sees real possibilities in this and supposes the representatives of the two governments could work this matter out with [UN secretary-general] U Thant and with each other. My impression is, however, that time is urgent.' Fomin asked Scali: 'Does this come from the highest sources?' When Scali insisted it did, Fomin rushed back to the embassy to contact Moscow.[48]

Shortly afterwards, Kennedy received a long, rambling letter from Khrushchev which briefly skirted around the proposals that Fomin had asked Scali to put to the administration. 'If assurances were given by the President and the Government of the United States that the USA itself would not participate in an attack on Cuba . . . the question of armaments would disappear,' the Soviet leader said, 'since, if there is no threat, then armaments are a burden for every people. Then, too, the question of the destruction, not only of the armaments which you call offensive, but of all other armaments as well, would look different.'[49]

It was shortly after ten o'clock in the morning in Washington on Saturday 27 October, when Moscow Radio, routinely listened to and reported on by the BBC Monitoring Service at Caversham Park, 50 miles west of London, began broadcasting another personal letter to President Kennedy from the Soviet leader. The BBC Russian monitors in the ground floor 'listening room' worked in tandem to transcribe small sections of the letter, like members of a relay team passing the baton on to their colleagues, so the text was sent as swiftly as possible via a Lamson vacuum tube system up to the CIA's Foreign Broadcast Information Service (FBIS) offices on the first floor of the building and telexed immediately to the White House Situation Room, where it was ripped off for President Kennedy to read. Khrushchev made a firm offer. If the US withdrew its Jupiter surface-to-surface missiles from Turkey and pledged never to invade Cuba, the Soviet Union would remove the surface-to-surface missiles from Cuba and make a similar undertaking that it would not invade Turkey.[50]

The demand that the US withdraw the Jupiter missiles from Turkey raised problems, since they were part of the NATO defences and their removal would have to be agreed by the alliance as a whole. The ExComm met later that day to discuss how Kennedy should respond. The debate was in full flow when General Maxwell Taylor, the chairman of the Joint Chiefs, received a report that a U-2 aircraft had been shot down and the pilot, Major Rudolf Anderson, killed. Amid fears of a US invasion, a nervous Cuban SA-2 team had fired the missile which brought the U-2 down, but this was not known at the time and it appeared to be a Soviet escalation of the crisis.[51]

Ordinarily, it would have been the role of the US secretary of state to call in Soviet ambassador Anatoli Dobrynin to complain, but Rusk suggested the president's brother Bobby might have more impact. The attorney-general asked the Soviet ambassador to come to his office in the Justice Department and—exaggerating the willingness of the Joint Chiefs to take out the SA-2 missile site that had shot down the U-2—told him the generals were 'itching for a fight' and his brother was struggling to hold them back. If the Russians or the Cubans fired on another US reconnaissance aircraft the United States would respond. He told Dobrynin to contact Khrushchev and 'have a commitment from him by the next day to withdraw the missile bases under United Nations supervision'. This was not an ultimatum but unless the missiles were removed, there would inevitably be 'drastic consequences', he said.

The Soviet ambassador raised Khrushchev's demand that America remove the Jupiter missiles from Turkey, Bobby Kennedy recalled. 'I said that there could be no quid pro quo or any arrangement made under this kind of threat or pressure. However, President Kennedy had ordered their removal some time ago, and it was our judgement that, within a short time after this crisis was over, those missiles would be gone.'[52]

The following day, Sunday 28 October, at four minutes past nine in the morning Washington time, just as the US president and his family were getting ready to go to church, Moscow Radio began broadcasting Khrushchev's response. The first flash signal from the FBIS station in Caversham arrived five minutes later, followed

Bill Friedman (left) and John Tiltman, the leading US and British codebreakers who were the founding fathers of the close relationship between the British and American codebreakers.

Prescott Currier, one of the four Americans who arrived at Bletchley Park in February 1941 and became a close friend and colleague of John Tiltman.

Bill Bundy, the US Army codebreaker who worked at Bletchley Park during the Second World War and went on to become a key member of the Kennedy and Johnson administrations, but still saw his time at Bletchley as 'the high point' of his career.

Barbara Eachus, who served the first Americans to arrive at Bletchley Park with sherry, and future husband US Navy liaison officer Joe Eachus, who played a key role in NSA's move into computers.

A US codebreaker working in Hut 6 where the German army and air force Enigma ciphers were broken.

Stewart Menzies, who as 'C' was in overall charge of both MI6 and Bletchley Park throughout the Second World War.

William 'Wild Bill' Donovan, the First World War hero and Wall Street lawyer who created and led the Office of Strategic Services (OSS), the Second World War forerunner of the CIA.

John Godfrey, the British wartime director of Naval Intelligence, who worked closely with Menzies to create a US equivalent of MI6 with the Anglophile Donovan at its head.

Ian Fleming, the author of the James Bond books who, as personal assistant to Godfrey, played a key role in helping to create a US equivalent of MI6. Fleming is pictured at his home in Jamaica, named 'Goldeneye' after a Second World War operation he devised.

Sterling Hayden, the US movie star whose pre-war work sailing rich Americans around the Caribbean led not only to his Hollywood career but to successful OSS operations ferrying weapons and supplies across the Adriatic to Tito's Partisans in wartime Yugoslavia.

Harry Hinsley (left), Edward 'Jumbo' Travis, the head of Bletchley Park, and John Tiltman visit America to negotiate post-war cooperation between GCHQ and its US counterparts.

Harold 'Perks' Perkins, a wartime SOE officer who at the start of the Cold War was put in charge of MI6 special operations behind the Iron Curtain.

Sam Barclay (left) and John Leatham, the two former Royal Navy officers who ferried the 'pixies' into Albania on board the *Stormie Seas*.

The NSA's groundbreaking Atlas I computer that was used to help to break the VENONA ciphers which led ultimately to the exposure of the Cambridge Spy Ring.

The Automatic Computing Engine (ACE), one of the first computers built in Britain, was designed by former Bletchley Park codebreaker Alan Turing.

Monty Woodhouse, the MI6 station chief in Tehran who planned the MI6-CIA coup which removed Iranian prime minister Mohammad Mossadeq from power in 1953, pictured here during his time with SOE working with the Greek resistance.

Kermit 'Kim' Roosevelt, the former OSS officer who ran the CIA operations on the ground in Tehran during the 1954 coup.

Iranians demonstrating on the streets of Tehran during the tempestuous period that led to the 1954 coup.

A Russian officer examining the inside of the MI6-CIA tunnel used to intercept Soviet communications in post-war Berlin.

Art Lundahl, who as head of the CIA's imagery intelligence operations ensured the British received U-2 images during the Suez Crisis and was awarded an honorary knighthood.

U-2 Dragon Lady signals and imagery intelligence spy plane.

A US U-2 photograph of al-Maza airfield before it was bombed by the RAF during the Suez Crisis supplied to the British on Lundahl's orders.

A US U-2 photograph of al-Maza airfield shortly after the RAF bombing raid again supplied to the British on Lundahl's orders.

Hungarian protestors on a Soviet tank waving the Hungarian flag during the 1956 invasion.

President John F. Kennedy with CIA
Director Allen Dulles.

Bill Marchant, former deputy head of
Bletchley Park's Hut 3 intelligence centre,
who as British ambassador to Cuba
used embassy staff to collect intelligence
during the missile crisis.

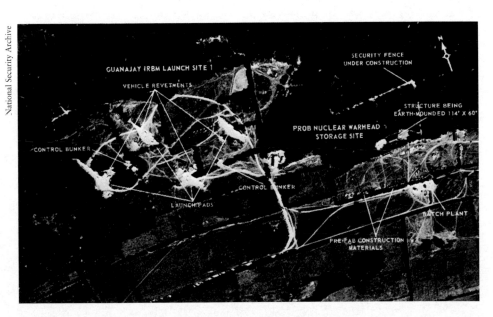

U-2 photograph of one of the Soviet missile sites under construction in
Cuba during the 1962 missile crisis.

A US Navy low-level reconnaissance photograph
of the San Cristobal missile site.

Harold Macmillan and President Kennedy during
the 1962 Nassau summit at which the British
Prime Minister secured Polaris missiles to ensure a
continued independent nuclear deterrent.

Lou Conein and the South Vietnamese generals who mounted the coup in which South Vietnamese president Ngô Đinh Diem was murdered.

Rob Judges

Daphne Park who trained OSS officers during the war, including Bill Colby, a future CIA Director, and went on to become a senior MI6 officer, working in a number of foreign capitals including Moscow and Hanoi.

John Colvin

The British Consul-General's residence in Hanoi which had formerly been a brothel.

Bill Colby, a wartime OSS officer who was trained by Daphne Park and went on to become CIA Director.

John Tiltman (left) and Prescott Currier in the late 1960s when both men were members of NSA's team of troubleshooters breaking the codes that others could not break.

BRIXMIS operators load pieces of the crashed Yak-28 Firebar onto a barge to be handed back to the Russians minus the latest Soviet radar system.

Czechoslovak protestors confront Soviet tanks during the 1968 invasion.

British Prime Minister Ted Heath (right) with Henry Kissinger, who as National Security Advisor twice ordered a break in intelligence cooperation with the British only for NSA to refuse to comply.

The Gross Gusborn intercept site in northern Germany used to monitor East German party officials' telephone calls.

The British signals intelligence base at Ayios Nikolaos which provided vital information on the Middle East and the southern Soviet Union throughout the second half of the twentieth century and remains an essential cog in the intelligence relationship between Britain and America.

GCHQ

John Tiltman (right) of GCHQ with Lou Tordella, the NSA deputy director who orchestrated close liaison with the British from the late 1950s until the mid-1970s and on his retirement was awarded an honorary knighthood.

Bobby Ray Inman, the CIA deputy director who vociferously fought off suggestions from within the Reagan administration that the US should back Argentina during the 1982 Falklands conflict.

Bucky Burruss, the Delta Force chief executive whose close relations with the SAS led him to supply them with Stinger surface-to-air missiles and satellite communications systems before it was officially authorised.

Oleg Gordievsky, former MI6 agent-in-place inside the KGB, briefing President Ronald Reagan on how to negotiate with Soviet leader Mikhail Gorbachev.

Getty Images

Ahmed Shah Masood, the Afghanistan
Northern Alliance leader who was
a long-term contact of MI6 but was
murdered by al-Qaeda terrorists
shortly before the 9/11 attacks.

Graeme Lamb (left), former British
Director Special Forces, who worked
closely with his US counterparts in
occupied Iraq to bring Sunni rebels
into the reconciliation process known
as 'the Awakening'. Seen here with
former British Army chief General
Sir Mike Jackson.

David Whittaker-Smith

US Navy photo by Petty Officer 1st Class Mark O'Donald

Stan McChrystal, US special
operations chief in Iraq who worked
closely with Lamb on reconciliation
and, as commander allied forces in
Afghanistan, asked him to try to
persuade the Taliban to join a similar
process there.

by small sections of the Soviet leader's address that were telexed through as the BBC monitors translated them, each handed to the president as it was torn off one of the Situation Room teleprinters. The key passage began half a dozen sections into the Soviet leader's message to Kennedy. Given the US assurance that it would not invade Cuba or allow its territory to be used to invade Cuba, 'the Soviet Government, in addition to earlier instructions on the discontinuation of further work on weapons construction sites, has given a new order to dismantle the arms which you described as offensive, and to crate and return them to the Soviet Union'. The crisis was at an end.[53]

By the following Sunday, 4 November, the equipment from the surface-to-surface missile sites had shown up at the Cuban ports, Bruce Clarke recalled.

At Mariel, we counted four launch stands, 17 missile erectors, and various trucks and vans. One of the U-2 aircraft took a picture of its own shadow as it flew over a Soviet freighter with six missiles on their transporters lashed on the open deck, and personnel lined up waiting to go aboard. The Soviets did not have any large hatch ships available to take the missiles back right away, so they loaded them aboard anything they had in Cuban waters. By Saturday 10 November, the last of the surface-to-surface missiles delivered to Cuba before the quarantine were on their way out.

The British intelligence contribution to the resolution of the crisis was substantial, in particular the material collected in Janet Chisholm's pram. Both Dick Helms and Ray Cline later recalled that without Oleg Penkovsky's intelligence, Art Lundahl's photo interpreters could not have analysed the images on the U-2 photographs in such detail, and the precise capability of the SS-4 Sandal missiles and the preparations for the arrival of the much longer-range SS-5 Skeans would not have been known. 'Nor would the President have known how much time he might have to negotiate before taking action to destroy the missiles,' Helms said. 'This information was without question a fundamental part of the data that permitted

President Kennedy to make the decisions that avoided the possibility of a nuclear showdown and perhaps war.'[54]

Cline agreed that Penkovsky's reports 'proved invaluable to US intelligence analysts during the Cuban missile crisis'. Nevertheless, 'this reporting may have been his undoing', Cline said. 'Somehow, he was discovered, arrested on 22 October 1962 [just hours before Kennedy broadcast to the American people] and a few months later tried and shot.' Even in his demise, Penkovsky assisted in the resolution of the crisis, with his interrogation revealing that Kennedy knew that all Khrushchev's talk of Soviet missiles and their capabilities was just bluster.[55]

Once it was all over, Sir Dick White called his staff together at Century House, the then MI6 headquarters, a few hundred yards away from London's Waterloo station. 'I have been asked by the CIA to let you know of the absolutely crucial value of the Penkovsky intelligence we have been passing to them,' he said. 'I am given to understand that this intelligence was largely instrumental in deciding that the United States should not make a pre-emptive nuclear strike against the Soviet Union, as a substantial body of important opinion in the States has been in favour of doing. In making known this appreciation of our contribution, I would stress to all of you that, if proof were needed, this operation has demonstrated beyond all doubt the prime importance of the human intelligence source, handled with professional skill and expertise.'[56]

13

'THE LADY'S VIRGINITY
HAS BEEN QUESTIONED'

The reaction in Britain to the missile crisis reflected the secrecy surrounding the extensive conversations between John F. Kennedy, Harold Macmillan and David Ormsby-Gore, with the Labour opposition and the media condemning a supposed lack of consultation and questioning the legality of the blockade. 'The opposition (supported by some of the press — especially the columnists and gossip writers) have been making out that the Americans not only failed to consult us but have treated us with contempt,' Macmillan complained in his diary. They were also claiming that 'the Special Relationship no longer applies, that we have gained nothing from our position as a nuclear power, that America risked total war in a US/USSR quarrel without bothering about us or Europe'. There were a number of reasons for this attitude, he noted, including 'a desire to injure and denigrate me personally' but largely 'ignorance of what really happened'.[1]

There was further supposed humiliation in early December when Dean Acheson—who as Truman's secretary of state had been a steadfast supporter of the British position as America's closest ally, even lauding 'the genuineness of the Special Relationship'—gave a speech at the US Military Academy at West Point in which he suggested that Britain had yet to find its place in the post-war world. 'Great Britain has lost an empire and not yet found a role,' Acheson said. 'The attempt to plan a separate power role – that is apart from Europe—a role based on a "special relationship" with the United

States, a role based on being the head of a Commonwealth which has no political structure, no unity or strength, this role is about played out. Great Britain attempting to work alone and to be a broker between the United States and Russia has seemed to conduct policy as weak as its military power.'

The main thrust of Acheson's speech was completely in line with the Kennedy administration's policy of backing the Macmillan government's attempts to join the EEC, thereby extending the strength of the Special Relationship into Europe. The administration did not see the British entry into the EEC as ending the close relationship between the US and Britain. It regarded UK membership as being in America's interest. Not only would it tie the US closer to continental Europe, it would ensure Britain retained 'a distinctive world-wide role and would permit a continuation of the Anglo-American relationship and Commonwealth ties'. But given the domestic claims of lack of consultation over the missile crisis, Acheson's argument that Britain had 'lost an empire and not yet found a role' provoked fury in London and further ridicule of Macmillan. Given that Acheson was a special adviser to the president, which linked the criticism to the administration, Kennedy ordered officials to brief *The Times* and the *New York Times* that the 'White House emphatically does not share the view of US–UK relations seemingly indicated in press reports of Acheson's speech'.

The president personally oversaw a briefing paper which said: 'US–UK relations are not based only on a power calculus, but also on a deep community of purpose and long practice of close cooperation.' It pointed out that examples of that close collaboration were legion, including on nuclear affairs, Berlin and the Cuban missile crisis, 'where President and Prime Minister were in daily intimate consultation to a degree not publicly known'. The term 'Special Relationship' might not be a perfect way of expressing such close cooperation, 'but sneers at Anglo-American reality would be equally foolish'. The officials were authorised to point out on behalf of the White House that Acheson had also been critical of Kennedy himself in the wake of the Bay of Pigs operation. 'The President has survived and expects that US–UK relations will too.'[2]

Macmillan, who had laid out his view of Britain's role in the world to President Eisenhower five years earlier—as a junior partner to America but its strongest and closest military ally in the West—was realistically nonchalant about the comments. 'Acheson was always a conceited ass, but I don't really think he meant to be offensive,' the British prime minister noted in his diaries. 'We ought to be strong enough to laugh off this kind of thing.' He was far more concerned about preparing for what he anticipated would be difficult talks with Kennedy in Nassau over the British nuclear deterrent. Robert McNamara had warned Ormsby-Gore and British defence secretary Peter Thorneycroft that the Americans were likely to cancel the Skybolt missile programme on the grounds of cost and reliability, leaving the UK without an effective nuclear weapon.[3]

During talks in London with Thorneycroft, McNamara had refused to provide a categorical assurance that the US was in favour of the independent British nuclear deterrent. The Americans were suggesting several options. The production of the British Skybolt missiles could go ahead on its own. Or the UK could buy the existing US Hound Dog stand-off air-launched missile, which would not fit on the RAF's nuclear bombers. Alternatively, Britain could participate in a jointly owned and manned NATO sea-launched ballistic missile system, using the US Polaris missile system, thereby losing the independent element of the British nuclear deterrent. Given the technical failings of the Skybolt missile, none of these options was acceptable to Macmillan. He wanted an independent British nuclear deterrent that would be available both to him and to any future British prime minister.[4]

Although it was repeatedly denied by Washington, Mac Bundy, Dean Rusk and McNamara all hoped to use the Skybolt cancellation to get rid of the independent British nuclear deterrent. Ahead of McNamara's visit to London, Rusk had warned that the resentment in France and Germany over 'the US–UK special military relation' had only been kept in check by American assurances that they would not support an independent British nuclear deterrent beyond the life of the RAF's nuclear bombers. Given that improvements to Soviet air defences revealed by the US spy satellites meant the bombers could not get through, this made a stand-off air-launched missile system like Skybolt the only possible option. The Kennedy administration had always taken the position that it would not allow Britain to acquire next-generation missiles like Polaris.

'If we were now to reverse this policy and extend the special relation, the continental reaction would be immediate and highly critical,' Rusk said. 'Existing continental objections to admitting the UK to membership in the Community on the grounds that its special relation with the US is incompatible with that membership would be heightened; the difficulties of bringing EEC negotiations to a successful conclusion might be significantly enhanced. Resentment in France, where the US–UK special nuclear relation is a standing irritant, would be particularly strong.'[5]

It is often suggested that Macmillan was reduced to pleading with Kennedy in order to get Polaris, but in fact Kennedy had overruled Rusk's arguments at a meeting in the White House a few days before the Nassau conference and, despite rejecting the British request for Polaris during his talks in London, McNamara had changed his position. The US aspiration for a jointly owned and manned NATO nuclear deterrent was not going to happen. Most of the Europeans could not afford it. The US defence secretary said it was 'time to move on to a more realistic arrangement and one which would better serve our own interests'. The British desire to buy Polaris offered the perfect answer. They should be sold the missiles and their fire control, launch, guidance and navigation systems, with the British providing their own submarines and warheads, but on the proviso that their nuclear force be wholly committed to NATO.

Far from taking his advisers' view that this was a perfect way of ending the British nuclear deterrent—as claimed by a British press still wedded to the idea that the US president had ignored Macmillan during the missile crisis and that Washington was now riding roughshod over its closest ally—Kennedy believed he had a moral responsibility to stick to the original agreement and provide the British with their own nuclear deterrent. 'The President clearly recognised the complexity of the problem which appeared to involve grave political risks for Mr Macmillan if we should not help him, and serious risks also for our own policy in Europe if we should help him too much,' Mac Bundy said. Kennedy approved McNamara's Polaris proposals as a fall-back option—'which reflected both the desire to be helpful to the British and respect for our European allies'—should Macmillan reject the US offer to produce Skybolt missiles for the British alone.[6]

There was no 'pleading' from Macmillan when the Nassau summit opened on 19 December; indeed from the outset, he adopted a consistently uncompromising stance. Opening the talks as the host, the British prime minister paused only briefly to praise Kennedy's handling of the missile crisis before making clear that he was only really interested in one issue and launching into a passionate portrayal of the route to a British independent nuclear deterrent.

Since he was probably the oldest of those present, he knew the story of British and American atomic weapons research from its very beginnings, he said, pointing out that it was British scientists whose research kick-started the Allied wartime programme, which had taken place in America only because the UK was too small to host atomic tests. After the war, Congress had passed the McMahon Act, removing Britain from the research process it had itself started and given freely to America. Relaxations of the act under the Eisenhower administration had led to an agreement to buy Skybolt and in return Macmillan had agreed that the US Navy could base its Polaris submarines on Holy Loch. Now Skybolt was being cancelled, potentially leaving the UK without an independent nuclear deterrent. There were many in the UK who thought it should not have its own nuclear weapons, but the British were not prepared to have this imposed on them by the US.

Forced onto the back foot, Kennedy conceded there was a danger that some might think that cancelling Skybolt was an attempt to get rid of the British nuclear deterrent but that was not the case. The US was prepared to continue the Skybolt programme in order to provide British nuclear missiles and to cover the vast bulk of the cost of building them. Macmillan was not interested. The damage done to Skybolt's reputation during McNamara's visit to London—when he pointed out that all five test trials had failed—was terminal, with

Macmillan acerbically noting that 'the virginity of the lady has been questioned'. If the Americans did not want Skybolt because it was unreliable, he was certainly not going to suggest to the British public that they should rely on it as the main plank of their defence against a Soviet nuclear attack.[7]

David Bruce, who as ambassador to Britain attended the summit, noted in his diary the difficulty of reaching agreement. 'Meetings, meetings and meetings, with and without the British,' he wrote. 'The personal relationships are delightful but the bargaining is tough and realistic. I have never seen the President in action before. His mind is acute, quick and comprehensive. He expresses his thoughts easily and with polish. The Prime Minister, of course, dominates his delegation. His style is different to the President's, not at all staccato.' Macmillan was almost hesitant at times, Bruce said, 'at others eloquent, sentimental, and, when he wishes, steely'.[8]

It took two sessions of discussion entirely on Polaris on the first day of the summit and another on the morning of the second day before Macmillan had reached a position he was prepared to accept. He knew Kennedy well enough from their discussions on Khrushchev and Berlin, from the previous year's summit in Bermuda, and from their daily discussions during the missile crisis to know the approach to take. There had been 'a gentleman's agreement' with Eisenhower who had asked for the Holy Loch base in return for the US missiles. He had taken a political risk by saying 'Yes'. As a result, there were those who accused him of putting Britain in peril of Soviet attack without having any control over the way in which the US missiles would be used. But even if he and Kennedy could not agree on a deal for Polaris, he would not react in a petty fashion; the Americans would continue to be allowed to base their submarines on Holy Loch.

What he was not prepared to accept was a situation in which not just the British prime minister but the Queen herself could not call upon the use of a nuclear deterrent for which Britain had paid, and on the submarines and warheads its own workers had constructed, if they were required to defend British interests. He was completely candid that the UK was 'in a period of history between two worlds: the world of independence and the world of interdependence'. It was happy to go to the expense of paying for Polaris and developing its own submarines and warheads and indeed to commit them to NATO, but it must have the ability, if necessary, to use them itself.[9]

Macmillan rejected the strangled language initially suggested by the Americans, that Britain would use its own nuclear deterrent 'only in the event of a dire national emergency—an emergency which we might have to face alone, which we, happily, cannot envisage, and which we must all trust will never occur'. He was sorry, but if the US insisted on such language, he would prefer to have no agreement at all. It would look as though the US was just trying 'to keep the little boys quiet'. Britain did not want much. It accepted its position as a junior partner to America, its most important ally, but it must be accorded respect. It was still America's most powerful ally in the West. It could not be treated as a satellite. It must 'remain something in the world'. If that were not possible, he would walk away.

After three sessions of negotiation, on the afternoon of the second day of the summit, Kennedy agreed to Macmillan's far less restrictive wording that Britain's Polaris missiles would be assigned to NATO but could be withdrawn when 'supreme national interests are at stake'.

The British prime minister had no illusions that his tough negotiation would be lauded, 'but I have reserved absolutely the right of HMG to use it indefinitely "for supreme national interest"', he noted in his diaries. 'These phrases will be argued and counter-argued, but they represent a genuine attempt (which the Americans accepted) at interdependent defence, while retaining the ultimate rights of a sovereign state.' Despite the scepticism of the UK media and the opposition parties, the subsequent agreement was the basis for the continuing independent British nuclear deterrent, and the close nuclear relationship between Britain and America which has remained in place to the current day.[10]

The success of the summit did little to help Macmillan politically. President de Gaulle used the Polaris decision as an excuse for the veto on Britain joining the EEC that he had always intended to deploy and the British media were little kinder. The false perception that Kennedy had ignored Macmillan over both Cuba and Skybolt, a series of spy scandals culminating in the defection of Kim Philby to Moscow and—most destructively—the Profumo affair left the impression of a prime minister at the mercy of events over which he had no control. The lurid sexual elements of the Profumo scandal, in which secretary of state for war John Profumo lied to Parliament over his affair with Christine Keeler, a call-girl who was also sleeping with the Russian naval attaché, dominated the British media throughout the summer of 1963, gripping the attention of the British public. The scandal even dragged in David Bruce, who as a friend of Profumo had dined at his London home, afterwards dancing the twist with the war secretary's actress wife, Valerie Hobson, and the Queen Mother. He and his wife had also attended a poolside party at Cliveden, the home of Viscount Astor, at which Keeler and her friend Mandy Rice-Davies were present.

Although there was no doubt that Macmillan was regarded as a decent man, Bruce noted in a sympathetic dispatch back to Washington, the damage done to his reputation was beyond repair. 'Few people believe that Macmillan, whose private integrity has not been questioned, would have connived at a clumsy attempt to avoid an almost inevitable disclosure if he had known that Profumo had lied,' Bruce said, but 'a sacrifice is increasingly demanded here, and the appointed lamb for the altar is the Prime Minister, who must already have appreciated the sad truth that no ingratitude surpassed that of a democracy'.[11]

It was not just the damage to the Macmillan government which interested the US administration. An internal CIA history of John McCone's time as the Agency's director notes that he declared the Profumo affair to be a 'matter of great concern to highest authority', a CIA euphemism for the president. McCone's own 'inordinate interest' was said by his executive assistant Walter Elder to be caused by 'some of John Kennedy's private indiscretions before he was elected president' when he was reported to have had a liaison with Suzy Chang, a close associate of Keeler. 'As it unfolded, the scandal revealed deep anxiety about its potential for compromising secrets and embarrassing the Kennedy administration,' the internal CIA history says.

When the story began to leak out in mid-June 1963, there was a series of meetings between McCone, McNamara, FBI director J. Edgar Hoover and DIA director Lieutenant-General Joseph Carroll to discuss how to deal with the issue. A week later the *New York Journal-American* linked one of 'the biggest names in American politics – a man who holds a very high elective office' to the Profumo affair. Bobby Kennedy 'summoned the *Journal-American* reporters to his office to confirm that they were referring to his brother . . . and to demand that they reveal their sources', the CIA internal history notes. 'They refused. Soon after, the attorney-general threatened the paper with an anti-trust suit and it dropped its coverage of the affair.'[12]

Harold Macmillan stepped down as prime minister on 18 October 1963 on the grounds of ill health. One of the undoubted high points of the Special Relationship was at an end.

Given the US irritation, and occasional fury, at the UK's refusal to send troops to take part in the Vietnam War, it is something of a paradox that the US military initially rebuffed British attempts to help counter the Việt Cộng fighters who were infiltrating South Vietnam from the communist north. The British were concerned that US military advisers in South Vietnam were wedded to conventional warfare techniques that had no chance of beating the communist guerrillas, and as a result offered to share the lessons learned during the Malayan emergency of 1948–60, which saw the first use of the intelligence-led 'hearts and minds' policy that was to be a key factor behind a number of British post-war counter-insurgency successes.

The British victory in Malaya was based on an intensive intelligence campaign, closely integrating military intelligence (both the British Army Intelligence Corps and the SAS) with MI5 and the Malay Police Special Branch. The 'hearts and minds' policy—known early on as 'political pacification'—was devised by General Sir Harold Briggs, the British Army's director of operations in Malaya, but was carried out by his successor, General Sir Gerald Templer. An ex-director of military intelligence, Templer was dispatched to the colony in early 1952, following the assassination by Chin Peng's communist insurgents of Sir Henry Gurney, the British high commissioner. He brought with him MI5 officers intended to revitalise their Malay counterparts.

MI5 was in charge of both security and intelligence collection in the post-war British colonies and good intelligence was fundamental to Templer's plans. 'What was lacking was information about the terrorist organisation and order of battle and their supplies,' one former British military intelligence officer said. 'Our main task was to track them down by means of every kind of intelligence—informers from the towns and villages where supplies were obtained, captured documents from camps overrun by our patrols, prisoners and aerial photographs. At the start of the year, we knew where Chin Peng had been four months before and when I left, we knew where he had been six weeks before. Eventually, they got so close on his tail that he fled over the border into Thailand.'

Templer laid out the plan to win the 'hearts and minds' of the population from the very start. 'Any idea that the business of normal civil government and the business of the Emergency are two separate entities must be killed for good and all,' he said shortly after arriving in Malaya. 'The shooting side of this business is only 25 per cent of the trouble and the other 75 per cent is getting the people of this country behind us.'

The SAS set about denying local support for the communist guerrillas, identifying and eliminating causes for discontent with the British to win over the 'hearts and minds' of the local population. In a carefully staggered operation, inhabitants of more than 400 villages were moved to specially constructed 'new villages' away from the insurgents. The 'new villagers' were given work, or plots of land to farm, and provided with decent medical facilities and schools for their children. They were also given free radio receivers to listen to Radio Malaya, which under Templer's control systematically pumped out propaganda messages about how life for all Malayans, and in particular the ethnic Chinese population, was improving. As each area became free of insurgent influence it was declared 'white' and emergency restrictions were lifted, thereby providing more incentive for other areas to cooperate and become 'white'.[13]

The first South Vietnamese Army officers were sent to the British Jungle Warfare Training School in Malaya in August 1959. It was clear from their performance that the training they had received from the US Military Assistance Advisory Group (MAAG) was in conventional combat rather than countering guerrilla warfare. South Vietnamese president Ngô Đình Diệm, who had been educated in Malaya, visited Kuala Lumpur in February 1960 and was briefed by Robert Thompson, the permanent secretary for defence, on how the British had defeated the communist insurgents. Diệm was so impressed that on his return to Saigon he asked the British government to supply him with an expert who could explain the strategy in detail.

The British Foreign Office was very keen to push the 'hearts and minds' policy, not least as a way of trying to steer the US approach to Vietnam away from conventional warfare towards an approach better suited to dealing with guerrilla warfare, so Thompson was sent to Saigon in April 1960 as head of a three-man Malayan mission. Its conclusions led Diệm to invite Thompson to become his personal adviser on counter-insurgency, but he declined to do so unless it was under the umbrella of either the UN or the British government. Thompson's visit was followed by a stream of Malayan and British counter-insurgency experts, including Templer himself. The State Department was very interested in the British offer to help, but the US military was adamantly opposed from very early on, with the head of the MAAG, General Haydn Williams, complaining that too 'many back-seat drivers without any responsibility like to give advice'.[14]

The British concerns that the South Vietnamese Army was not being trained in guerrilla warfare were shared by US ambassador Eldridge Durbrow – who was ostensibly in charge of US policy on the ground – by the CIA, and by the Saigon government itself. A senior CIA officer who visited South Vietnam in early 1960 reported back that the MAAG was drilling the South Vietnamese troops in divisional and corps manoeuvres more suited for a major land war than a counter-insurgency campaign.[15]

The idea of sending Thompson in to advise the South Vietnamese on how to win 'hearts and minds' was backed at the highest levels of the Kennedy administration. When Thompson's plans to create Malayan-style 'new villages' was explained to Kennedy's deputy national security adviser Walt Rostow, who had served as an OSS intelligence officer in London during the war, he jumped to his feet enthusiastically, describing it as 'the first time I have heard a practical suggestion as to how we should carry out our operations in Vietnam'. Thompson arrived in Saigon in September 1961 as head of the British Advisory Mission to Vietnam (BRIAM), with a remit to 'strategise' the intelligence operations of the Diệm government.[16]

As part of an attempt to forestall sending US combat troops to Vietnam, Roger Hilsman, director of the State Department's Bureau of Intelligence and Research, put together 'A Strategic Concept for South Vietnam', essentially a plan for civil pacification, under which 'strategic hamlets', defended by civil guards and local self-defence forces, would be set up to perform the same role as Malaya's 'new villages', with areas to be cleared of Việt Cộng in a step-by-step process. Each of the hamlets would have access to government advisers providing funding for farmers, education and medical care. The cleared areas would be protected by a perimeter of 'defended villages' patrolled by both civil guards and the South Vietnamese Army. US Army senior NCOs would train and oversee the local defence forces. Hilsman even suggested that around 100 Malayan-British advisers be involved to ensure the plan was properly implemented.

Hilsman made it absolutely clear that his concept of strategic hamlets was heavily based on Thompson's own plans, even mirroring some of the key phrases the BRIAM chief had used. Hilsman also used his own experience as a member of the OSS working alongside the British in Burma during the Second World War to help explain how the plans would work. The Việt Cộng were largely avoiding the trap of 'conventional warfare' with the US-trained South Vietnamese Army, gradually extending their control of the villages outside the main South Vietnamese centres of population. They were proceeding slowly 'in order to consolidate, regroup, and extend their control throughout the countryside', Hilsman said. The villages they controlled were the guerrillas' main source of supplies and manpower. 'The struggle for South Vietnam, in sum, is essentially a battle for control of the villages,' he said. 'This struggle cannot be won merely by attempting to seal off South Vietnam from the North. It must be won by cutting the Việt Cộng off from their local sources of strength, i.e., by denying them access to the villages and the people. The objective is to cut the Việt Cộng off from their sources of supplies and recruits.'

The plan, adopted by the South Vietnamese at the beginning of 1962 and operated in tandem with the CIA, was initially successful, encouraging those rehoused in the new hamlets to provide substantial amounts of intelligence on the Việt Cộng. Unlike the US military, which from the top down dismissed Thompson's ideas, the CIA backed them to the hilt. Bill Colby, now CIA head of station in Saigon, admitted to minor differences with Thompson over the implementation but stressed that 'we so closely agreed on the necessity of a village-based approach over the military one that we remained the closest of friends and collaborators'.

During a meeting with President Kennedy in early April 1963, Thompson praised the strategic hamlet programme, which had 'gone much better than anyone had expected', providing the rural population with an unprecedented degree of security. If progress continued at the current rate, by the summer it should be possible to declare one or two provinces 'white', enabling a reduction in the number of US military advisers, which would demonstrate that the US strategy was winning. In a subsequent meeting with Kennedy's advisers on counter-insurgency, he stressed that it was important to move slowly and methodically so as not to leave even the smallest area under Việt Cộng control. No area should be declared 'white' until all the Việt Cộng guerrillas had been eliminated, Thompson warned. The only valid benchmark for US success in Vietnam would be 'when we reach the level of having sufficient control of the population to deny their accessibility to actions by the Việt Cộng'.

In his conversations with both Kennedy and the president's counter-insurgency advisers, Thompson made clear that for the strategic hamlets to work it was essential that President Diệm, who was far more popular in the provinces than he was in Saigon, should stay in place. There was no other candidate capable of taking the rural population with them. If Diệm were to disappear 'there would be a risk of losing the war within six months'. This mirrored Hilsman's assessment that 'the Việt Cộng's preferred strategy is one of political denouement, preparing for conventional warfare, but hoping for a non-communist coup against Diệm that would create confusion and an opportunity for them to take over the country by political-guerrilla action'.[17]

A few weeks later, a senior CIA officer told the President's Special Group for Counter-Insurgency that the creation of the strategic hamlets had led to an increase in 'spontaneous intelligence' provided by people out in the countryside which had brought a major improvement in operations against the Việt Cộng. 'The big success story in Vietnam is the strategic hamlet programme,' he said. 'Out of a total population in Vietnam of about 16 million, some 8 million have been moved into strategic hamlets, resulting in one of the biggest population moves in history.' But he warned that Diệm's determination to push ahead with the programme as fast as possible risked overextending it and leaving Việt Cộng inside the areas that had supposedly been cleared. 'Unless we clear out these Việt Cộng pockets we may provide the Việt Cộng with an opportunity to concentrate against the overextended Vietnamese armed forces.'[18]

The warnings to keep Diệm in place were no doubt triggered by the growing belief in Washington—long entrenched within the State Department, though resisted by the Pentagon—that not only was President Diệm dispensable but that getting rid of him, and his unpopular brother Nhu and the brother's wife, 'Madame Nhu', would improve the government's relations with the people and, as a result, the chances of beating the Việt Cộng.[19]

A crackdown on celebrations by South Vietnam's Buddhists of Buddha's birthday in May 1963 spiralled out of control, with riot police killing a number of demonstrators, including children. Buddhist monks responded by self-immolation, which attracted worldwide criticism of Diệm, which was only increased by Madame

Nhu's reference to the monks 'putting on a barbeque show'. President Kennedy, who had been one of Diệm's most prominent Congressional supporters in the 1950s, went on US television to say that unless the government in Saigon did more to win popular support, the war could not be won and called for 'changes in policy and personnel', a clear reference to the need to get rid of Diệm's brother and sister-in-law. A tour of America by Madame Nhu—during which she castigated the US military advisers, who now numbered more than 12,000, as 'little soldiers of fortune' and accused the American media of being 'worse than the communists'—did nothing to help Diệm's cause.[20]

The State Department had a limited perspective which saw the lack of support for Diệm among Saigon's educated middle classes as a crucial factor. It was not. The key support was out in the countryside, where the Việt Cộng were active. The rural peasants who strongly supported Diệm had wholeheartedly bought into the strategic hamlet programme. Thompson argued strongly that the US must back Diệm, as the only civilian with the support among the rural communities to fight off Việt Cộng influence. The Diệm government was pushing rapidly ahead with the strategic hamlets and as a result was literally 'winning hearts and minds'. The war was going well. There was no need to change the regime. Indeed, to do so would be a serious mistake.

In late September, Mac Bundy asked David Ormsby-Gore to have Thompson produce a report for President Kennedy on what he saw as the way forward. Thompson came down firmly in support of Diệm. The Buddhist protests had not been handled well but 'the achievements of the last 18 months have been remarkable and progress is still being made', he said. It would perhaps take as much as two years, but by then there would be 'decisive progress' that would allow the US to make substantial cuts to the number of military advisers. But Thompson was adamant. In order to make that progress, Diệm had to be kept in place. 'This is not the moment for upheaval.' Thompson's report never reached Kennedy. Gordon Etherington-Smith, British ambassador to Vietnam, who had decided that Diệm must go, demanded that the Foreign Office hold it back.[21]

In what would represent the death knell for the attempts to use the strategic hamlets programme to push back the Việt Cộng, a number of key generals in the South Vietnamese Army had decided that both Nhu and Diệm must go and had begun planning a coup. They did not want or need active American support, but they did need to be sure that the US would not thwart them and there was only one American they trusted enough to act as a go-between.[22]

Lou Conein, the OSS Jedburgh sent into France in 1944 as a direct result of Daphne Park's efforts, was now serving in Vietnam and on 2 October coincidentally bumped into General Trần Văn Đôn at Saigon airport, in a moment that would be critical for the progress of the war. After his exploits in France, Conein had served with the OSS fighting the Japanese in Vietnam in 1945 and had worked with a number of Vietnamese Army officers. He had been particularly close to Đôn, who told him he had been trying to get in touch with him for some time and asked if he could meet him in the coastal resort of Nha Trang that evening for a 'private discussion'. Amid persistent rumours of a coup, Conein knew immediately what the discussions would be about. He responded in a non-committal way and reported the approach to the CIA station. The embassy backed the meeting on the proviso that Conein said nothing that might encourage or discourage a coup. He was to confine himself to finding out as much as he could about what was going on.

At the meeting in Nha Trang, Đôn outlined the bare bones of the plans but, questioned by Conein on who was involved and how and when it would take place, cited security concerns for not expanding further. Dean Rusk and Henry Cabot Lodge Jr, the new US ambassador, who had just arrived in Saigon, agreed that Conein's talks must be deniable with no active US promotion of the coup. There was concern in Washington that Conein, a hard-drinking womaniser with a reputation for having a short fuse, might be the wrong man to deal with such a sensitive subject, but Lodge was rightly adamant that Conein was the only American the generals would talk to. They had known him for eighteen years, Lodge said, and Đôn 'has expressed extreme reluctance to deal with anyone else. I do not believe the involvement of another American in close contact with the generals would be productive.' Nevertheless, as a protective measure, CIA deputy station chief Dave Smith ordered Conein to 'go on the wagon' for the duration of the talks.[23]

During a series of conversations with Đôn, most of which were held in a Saigon dentist's surgery, Conein managed to solicit encouraging details of the coup committee's plans, if not the full extent of their support or precisely how and when it would go ahead. Đôn would only say that it would happen before 2 November.[24]

Meanwhile, the White House remained keen to see Thompson's report, but when Ormsby-Gore asked where it was the Foreign Office said they had not sent it because it contradicted Etherington-Smith's view. Ormsby-Gore pointed out that Kennedy was not interested in the British ambassador's opinion, he wanted Thompson's view and the report should be sent immediately. The Foreign Office prevaricated. The following day the president met with key advisers to discuss whether the coup should be allowed to go ahead.

The US military were not the only ones who shared Thompson's concerns. John McCone, backed by Bobby Kennedy, warned that a failed coup would be a disaster while a successful coup would seriously damage the war effort, effectively echoing Thompson's argument. The CIA director also warned that neither Dave Smith nor Conein believed that either Nhu or Diệm would survive a coup. But despite having been one of Diệm's strongest Congressional supporters through the mid-to-late 1950s, President Kennedy was persuaded by the majority view that blocking the coup would put America on the wrong side of the generals, damaging the war effort. Had he read Thompson's report, blocked by the Foreign Office, he might well have decided differently.[25]

Shortly before 2 p.m. Saigon time on 1 November, Đôn telephoned an aide to US commander General Paul Harkins to tell him that the coup was about to begin. Although there was some fighting, including air attacks on the presidential palace, it was backed by the vast majority of army units and was carried out relatively quickly. At first the only real problem seemed to be the bloody demise of Diệm and Nhu, who were hauled out of a church in which they had taken refuge and shot dead. When Conein went to army headquarters to ask that they be allowed to leave the country, he was told the brothers, devout Catholics, had committed suicide in the church, to which he replied that the generals had 'better put a better story together than that'.[26]

The next day, both Lodge and Smith reported on the success of the coup and the positive reaction on the streets of Saigon. 'Believe the very great popularity of this coup should be stressed,' Lodge said. 'Every Vietnamese has a grin on his face today.' The acting CIA station chief confirmed the elated atmosphere, reporting that people had 'poured into the streets in exhilarated mood'. But the deaths of Nhu and Diệm dampened the mood in Washington. When news of their 'suicides' emerged during a meeting in the White House that morning the president 'leaped to his feet and rushed from the room with a look of shock and dismay on his face which I had never seen before', recalled General Max Taylor, who was by now chairman of the Joint Chiefs. 'He had always insisted that Diệm must never suffer more than exile and had been led to believe or had persuaded himself that a change in government could be carried out without bloodshed.' By the end of the month, the news from Vietnam had been overshadowed by Kennedy's own assassination and Vice-President Lyndon Johnson had been sworn in as president.[27]

Meanwhile, the results of the coup were already proving Thompson correct. The impact on the battle against the Việt Cộng in the provinces was immediate, reinvigorating their operations. The strategic hamlet programme fell into disarray. Two weeks into his presidency, Johnson's daily intelligence checklist reported that in the wake of the coup, and orders from Hanoi to step up the fight 'on all fronts', many strategic hamlets in Long An province just south-west of Saigon had been seized by the Việt Cộng. 'The province, along with two neighbouring ones, bore the brunt of the intensified communist effort following Diệm's ouster,' the checklist said.

By early February 1964, it was reporting 'Việt Cộng activity is on the upswing. Their tactics suggest greater self-confidence. In the past few weeks, they have stepped up the number of ambushes of regular army units, cut numerous telephone and electric power

lines, and shelled or raided sections close to the provincial and district capitals. In government-held areas of the central and northern
coast, they have also entered a number of Strategic Hamlets, ter-
rorised inhabitants and kidnapped hamlet officials.' They had taken
over the hamlets and renamed them 'Combat Hamlets', imposing
village administrations that were controlled by Việt Cộng officials.[28]

At the end of May 1964, Bill Bundy, now assistant secretary of
state for Far Eastern affairs, flew to London to brief British foreign
secretary Rab Butler on the US view of where America was going
with Vietnam. 'Bill made a thorough and brilliant exposition of
present American thinking on the subject,' David Bruce noted in
his diary. 'It is apparent that the United States will have to reach
a definite decision as to whether or not it is prepared to intervene
militarily in Laos and North Vietnam. We cannot afford any longer
to be considered a "paper tiger". The President is considering this
weekend whether, if necessary, to use force in these countries.'

Over the next two months, Johnson made a number of changes
designed to prepare for a more extensive engagement in the war,
including sending Max Taylor to Saigon as ambassador, in order to
ensure closer relations between the ambassador and the military. He
replaced Harkins with Lieutenant-General William Westmoreland
and increased the number of US troops to 21,000. It was clear the
administration had decided it had a choice, to withdraw ignomini-
ously in a way which would throw doubt on its ability to stand up
to communism or go all out to win.

The CIA advice was overwhelmingly negative on the prospects of
winning the war. Asked by the State Department for an assessment
of what 'possible carrots' the US could offer Hanoi that might induce
it to accept a settlement of the conflict, the Agency's response was
blunt. While there were undeniably 'doctrinal differences' within
the leadership—with Hồ Chí Minh primarily a nationalist while
party leader Lê Duẩn was a pro-Chinese communist—they were
all determined to reunify the country however long, and whatever, it took.

'Hanoi is probably under little present compunction to settle for
half a loaf, even temporarily,' the analysts noted. 'Though the idea of

canvassing our imaginations to develop positive inducements capable of giving North Vietnam some reason to stop its insurgent activities in Laos and South Vietnam is worthwhile, we think it unlikely that any inducements can be evolved which could be really tempting to the north and not be counterproductive for the US.'[29]

A conference of key US officials, including Rusk, McNamara, McCone, Taylor, Lodge, Westmoreland and Bill Bundy, in Honolulu in early June discussed the planned escalation of the US role in the war and noted the need to keep the British informed of what was going on. 'We must continue to work closely and urgently with the British,' Bundy noted in an account of what he regarded as the most important decisions made in the Honolulu discussions. 'They hold a large share of the key to successful diplomacy and standing firm concerning Laos, and they almost certainly have serious doubts about the basic question of wider action, on which they have now been fully informed. We should also cut in the Australians and perhaps the New Zealanders, probably to the full extent that we have done with the British.'[30]

On 2 August, the US destroyer *Maddox*, which had an NSA intercept unit on board and was patrolling the coast of North Vietnam collecting intelligence, was attacked by North Vietnamese patrol boats. Signals intelligence suggested that the attack was a mistake which the authorities in Hanoi had tried to prevent and Rusk went out of his way to play down the incident. But at the same time the president made it very clear that if there were any further attacks, the US Navy would not just ward off the attackers, it would destroy them.

Two days later, a report from a US Marine Corps intercept site at Phu Bai, about 50 miles south of the demilitarised zone between North and South Vietnam, warned of a possible North Vietnamese naval operation against the *Maddox* that night. A form of hysteria seems to have set in with crew members on the *Maddox* and another US destroyer, the *Turner Joy*, reporting supposed attacks by North Vietnamese vessels, an inflated experience exacerbated by radar problems that threw up extraneous evidence of enemy boats which subsequently disappeared without trace.

Although Captain John Herrick, the senior officer on board the *Maddox*, expressed serious doubts that there had been an actual attack, the president ordered 'retaliatory' attacks on the North Vietnamese patrol boats. He used the alleged attacks to persuade Congress—supported by worryingly selective and highly prejudicial NSA signals intelligence—to pass the so-called Gulf of Tonkin Resolution, backing whatever support was required 'to promote the maintenance of international peace and security in South-East Asia', an act used to support any new measures deemed to be required to win the Vietnam War.[31]

The rapid build-up from an advisory role to that of full-blown combatant led to increased opposition in western Europe, and not just among student protestors. Mid-October 1964 saw three crucial events in Cold War politics. Nikita Khrushchev was forced from office, with Leonid Brezhnev taking over as party leader and Aleksei Kosygin becoming Soviet premier; China became the fifth country to explode an atomic bomb; and Labour leader Harold Wilson became British prime minister with a limited majority of just four seats and a large number of MPs who were on the left of the party and vociferously opposed to US involvement in Vietnam. The Special Relationship was about to enter a new, far more complex era, severely testing the resilience of the close ties built up in the immediate post-war years.

A CAPITALIST RUNNING
DOG'S VIEW FROM HANOI

The new British prime minister's largely successful attempts to manage the left of the Labour Party led initially to a strained relationship with President Johnson. Harold Wilson saw Britain's co-chairmanship, with the Soviet Union, of the 1954 International Control Commission on Indo-China (ICC), which divided Vietnam into the communist north and the French-controlled south, as a means by which he could work for a negotiated peace that would give the US a way out of an increasingly difficult problem while at the same time maintaining the support of his own MPs.

Wilson sensibly avoided the term 'Special Relationship'—he preferred to speak of 'the close relationship' between Britain and America—but nevertheless believed as strongly as any of his post-war predecessors that Britain should remain America's staunchest ally in the Cold War fight against communism and, as a result, he consistently backed the US approach in Vietnam. None of this impressed Johnson, who, according to David Bruce, swiftly developed a distinct 'antipathy' towards Wilson, regarding British attempts 'to insinuate themselves into Vietnamese affairs as irrelevant and impertinent' while the prime minister's public support for the administration's position in Vietnam was simply 'taken for granted' in the White House.

At the first meeting between Johnson and Wilson, at the White House on 7 December 1964, the discussions were dominated by Britain's crippling £800 million balance of payments deficit, and the potential knock-on effects for its defence commitments across the globe, but the addition of British troops, even as a token force, to the war in Vietnam was the most important issue for the president. He took Wilson into his private office to press him on the issue, but the British prime minister declined to contribute any military forces to the war, in part on the basis that, as co-chair of the ICC, Britain should remain neutral, an argument that Johnson subsequently dismissed as a 'fig leaf'.

When the president took Wilson for a walk in the Rose Garden to try to persuade him, Wilson responded by arguing that the UK was already making important contributions through the Thompson mission, the training of South Vietnamese soldiers in guerrilla warfare, and the provision of medics. Johnson's response was that 'the only effective contribution Britain could make would be soldiers on the ground'. A British presence would, as much as anything else, reassure the American public that they were not alone. Could he not send the Black Watch? 'Even a few pipers would be better than nothing.' Wilson apparently did not respond.[1]

What is not clear is whether there was any discussion between Johnson and Wilson of the highly secret role being played by British intelligence with regard to Vietnam. The UK was in fact providing a considerable amount of support for US operations there, albeit behind the scenes. British and Australian radio operators based at the GCHQ sites in Hong Kong were intercepting Vietnamese communications, as well as those between China and the Soviet Union and their respective embassies in Hanoi. This was supplemented by signals intelligence supplied by Royal Navy Oberon-class submarines operating out of Singapore with intercept operators trained in Vietnamese on board.

Meanwhile, RAF reconnaissance aircraft back-filled in eastern Europe and the Soviet Union for the US aircraft that were committed to collecting intelligence over Vietnam. Most interestingly, a couple of months before the Washington talks, the consul-general in Hanoi, who at that time was a career diplomat, was replaced by MI6 officer Myles Ponsonby, almost certainly at the direct request of

John McCone, who had visited London in September for discussions with senior British officials.[2]

'In September 1964, I was told that I had been selected to take the post of consul-general in North Vietnam,' Ponsonby recalled. 'The consulate in Hanoi was at the time when I arrived three individuals: the consul-general – myself, a vice-consul and a male clerk. That was it. The position of HMG was that we recognised the government of South Vietnam but did not recognise the government of North Vietnam but because of the Geneva agreements, which were signed in 1954, it was felt important to have the position in the north however difficult it might be for the incumbent. So, the North Vietnamese regime tolerated the British presence but we were not given any diplomatic status whatsoever. We were regarded as privileged foreigners.'[3]

Ponsonby was not the first MI6 officer to take up the post. At the end of the Second World War Arthur Trevor-Wilson was head of the British military mission to the Chinese occupying forces in French Indo-China and very close to Hồ Chí Minh, leader of the Việt Minh resistance, whom he met on a weekly basis. Trevor-Wilson's previous MI6 post had been in Section V in wartime London where he and his colleague the novelist Graham Greene had become great friends. Indeed, it was a visit by Greene to see him in early 1951 that inspired *The Quiet American*.

Trevor-Wilson was by all accounts an extremely intuitive intelligence officer, with good access both among the French and, as demonstrated by his friendship with Hồ, among the Việt Minh. He also had close links to the CIA, which by the early 1950s was already operating in both Hanoi and Saigon. But the French were highly suspicious of him, and by extension of his friend and former MI6 colleague Greene, assuming, with some justification, that they were both spying on them, and in late 1951, Trevor-Wilson was declared *persona non grata* with a knock-on effect on Greene himself. 'My friendship with Trevor has mucked things up for me here completely,' he wrote in a letter to his mistress Catherine Walston. 'The French imagine all kinds of sinister motives and very politely all doors are closed.'[4]

Trevor-Wilson was replaced by a career diplomat, and although a number of MI6 officers were part of the much larger Hanoi consulate during the 1950s, when Britain was heavily involved in charting the post-war situation in Indo-China, Ponsonby's appointment as consul-general was unusual by that stage and was probably triggered by last-ditch CIA attempts to place its own agents inside the North Vietnamese capital. This had proven far more difficult than it had elsewhere in the world. Very few North Vietnamese officials travelled abroad, making it extremely difficult to recruit influential agents, but McCone and the chief of the CIA's Far East Division, Bill Colby, were trying hard to reactivate those agents who had been sent into the north at various times in the past. Given that the Americans had no presence in Hanoi themselves, they would need some way of keeping in touch with them. An MI6 officer trained to deal with secret contacts in hostile environments would have been the best option available.

McCone had just asked a number of CIA officers with previous experience in Vietnam to try to renew their old contacts, Lou Conein among them. At the end of the Second World War, Conein had been sent to Germany where he led the recruitment and running of CIA agents inside the eastern sector. He returned to Vietnam in 1954 to set up a network of agents in the north ahead of the anticipated decision by the ICC to split Vietnam into the north, which was already dominated by Hồ Chí Minh's communist Việt Minh, and the French-controlled south. Conein's agents were covertly exfiltrated to the south for training before being returned to the north where, according to one of those he worked with, they 'became normal citizens, carrying out everyday civil pursuits, on the surface'.[5]

Conein ran a number of these agents for some time and it is possible that one or more had resurfaced. He certainly remained active himself in Saigon for much of this period. Alternatively, more recent attempts to infiltrate individual intelligence agents into the north might have been successful. The operations had begun in the early 1960s when Colby was station chief in Saigon and continued after he returned to Langley.

Both Kennedy and Johnson were more interested in sending

special operations forces in to set up guerrilla operations, 'to do to them what they do to us'. Colby's deputy station chief in Saigon, Bob Myers, argued against these plans, but Colby himself believed that if teams of trained Vietnamese fighters were dropped into lightly populated areas they might be able to create secure bases from which to carry out attacks against the North Vietnamese military. Colby seems to have taken inspiration from his OSS service in Nazi-occupied Europe. 'He thought it was like Norway,' Myers said. None of the teams sent in survived, their members ending up in prison with their radios turned back against the CIA in North Vietnamese deception operations.

Nevertheless, a number of so-called 'singleton' agents were sent in with the sole mission of collecting intelligence, with their targets to be assigned 'once the agent is in place, depending on the access he turns out to have', and it was possible that some of those had survived. By September 1964, Colby was focusing on obtaining 'ten good high-level penetration agents, going through as many as 100 or 200 real cases to get them'. If any of these agents turned up, they would need someone to collect their intelligence and pass on orders and requests. But servicing a pre-determined dead letter drop would almost certainly have been the most that even an experienced MI6 officer would have been realistically confident or indeed capable of doing. 'It would have been virtually impossible for an obvious Caucasian to have run agents in Hanoi,' one former MI6 officer said. 'Especially during that time when there were so few foreigners there and they would have stood out like a sore thumb. Moreover, Ponsonby was very tall, so would have been even more visible than most.'[6]

In March 1965, the Americans had begun an escalated bombing campaign codenamed Rolling Thunder to try to force the North Vietnamese to halt the flow of Việt Cộng into the South, and it could have been that the CIA wanted an experienced intelligence officer in place to report on the impact of the bombing. But when Ponsonby's term came to an end in January 1966, he was replaced not by another MI6 officer but by a career diplomat, who like his predecessors continued to file reports on what was happening in

Hanoi. This seems to suggest that McCone was not simply looking for an intelligence officer's take on life in Hanoi, rather than that of a diplomat, and that if any CIA agents did resurface, they did not last very long.[7]

Whatever the reason for his presence in Hanoi, Ponsonby's reports were gratefully received at Langley and frequently landed on President Johnson's desk, not least because, although aerial imagery and diplomatic intercepts provided occasional intelligence about the situation in Hanoi, the British consul-general provided a rare view from the ground which revealed how the regime was coping with and reacting to the US escalation of the war. Disappointingly for the Johnson administration, Ponsonby detected no sign of any diminution in the North Vietnamese determination to win the war whatever the cost.

In February 1965, the President's Daily Brief, as it was now known, reported that 'the British Consul-General in Hanoi believes that the North Vietnamese leaders were not so impressed by the air strikes as to attempt to restrain the Việt Cộng'. Ponsonby felt that Hồ Chí Minh and Lê Duẩn 'might not be able to restrain them even if they wanted to, since the Việt Cộng now scent victory'. He also argued that the North Vietnamese leaders were 'quite prepared to suffer further air strikes, even ones wiping out major industrial installations in the Hanoi–Haiphong area' because they were 'viciously self-confident' and so 'thoroughly convinced by their success against the French that nothing can prevent them from gaining complete victory'.[8]

A month later, Ponsonby's analysis again made its way into Johnson's Daily Brief. During a visit to Saigon, the MI6 officer told CIA station chief Peer de Silva that the Rolling Thunder bombing had made 'no significant impact' on the Hanoi government. 'He [Ponsonby] does not believe that the strikes will make a real impression until they start hitting the Hanoi–Haiphong area,' de Silva told Langley.

There were inevitable tensions between what the Americans wanted and what the Foreign Office were happy for them to see. When Ponsonby found a map that had military locations marked on it, a simple request from the Americans for anything more like that led to a spiky response from the Foreign Office that 'any task of this kind, particularly if it involved Ponsonby in a perceptible departure from his daily routine could be dangerous to him personally and could jeopardise the value for other purposes of keeping him in Hanoi'. Given that Ponsonby was briefing de Silva in detail during his visits to Saigon, it seems unlikely that much, if anything, was kept back from the Americans and his reports were so well regarded in both London and Washington that when he left he was appointed CBE.[9]

Johnson had ruled out any air strikes within a 35-mile radius of Hanoi, but by early 1966 he was beginning to accept that, as suggested by Ponsonby's reporting, this limited their impact. US bombing of the North Vietnamese capital would present a problem for Harold Wilson, who would be forced to condemn it, a move that previously would have led Johnson to lose his temper with the British prime minister. A year earlier, Wilson had woken up in the early hours of the morning to discuss Vietnam with the president and was left in absolutely no doubt that his advice was not welcome. Johnson, who had just been told that the Việt Cộng had carried out a bomb attack on a hotel housing US troops in the South Vietnamese town of Qui Nhơn, killing twenty-three US servicemen, responded furiously, shouting down the phone at Wilson: 'I won't tell you how to run Malaysia and you don't tell us how to run Vietnam.'[10]

But since that conversation, the relationship between Johnson and Wilson had undergone a sea change. Ahead of talks in December 1965, Johnson had asked David Bruce why the British prime minister was so keen to come to Washington given that he was attacked so regularly from within his own party for his support of US policy in Vietnam and frequently accused by British media commentators of having turned his country into the '51st State'. Bruce explained that Wilson was 'anxious to establish something like the close relationship—or its appearance—which existed between Harold Macmillan and President Kennedy'. Johnson subsequently told aides that the December talks with Wilson had been 'the most satisfactory he had ever had with a foreign president or prime minister', even though the British prime minister had warned him that if the Americans bombed Hanoi, he would be forced to condemn them. Johnson, who was never a man to stand on ceremony himself, evidently respected Wilson's blunt response.

By the spring of 1966, the US ambassador was noting that the tone of the 'almost daily' messages passing between Johnson and Wilson was 'cordial to the point of being on both sides effusive', with the president at one point noting that Palmerston had once said that Britain had no permanent friends, only permanent interests. 'With due respect to that illustrious British statesman, I must disagree,' Johnson said. 'For Americans, Britain is a permanent friend, and the unbreakable link between our two nations is our permanent interest.'[11]

A measure of the improvement in the relationship between the two men came when Bruce visited Washington in May 1966 for discussions on the French decision to withdraw from NATO. Johnson called him in for a one-to-one conversation. 'He said he felt he would soon have to order the bombing of North Vietnamese oil installations near Haiphong and Hanoi,' Bruce noted in his diary. 'He wishes me to tell Harold Wilson as soon as possible that this might be done but that he would send him a message before it is ordered.' On his return to London, the US ambassador passed on Johnson's message to Wilson, assuring him that the president understood his position and would warn him before any attacks on Hanoi took place.[12]

Johnson's subsequent decision to bomb Hanoi and Haiphong led to a change of policy in London, with Ponsonby's successor replaced after only five months by another MI6 officer, John Colvin, who had the expertise to provide far better intelligence on what was happening on the ground in Hanoi, including expert bomb damage assessment of the results of the US air raids.

The son of an admiral, Colvin had served in the Royal Navy during the Second World War and had been seconded to the SOE, leading a group of Việt Minh fighters in Vietnam and, as the senior British officer in Saigon, accepting the swords of the Japanese commanders when they surrendered. Asked in later life by his nine-year-old grandson whether he had shot any Japanese, he replied: 'No. But I garrotted quite a few.'

Recruited into MI6 after the war, Colvin made his name in Vienna by obtaining the soiled pages of a copy of the Soviet order of battle, rescued by one of his agents in Czechoslovakia from the lavatories in a military barracks where they had been used as toilet paper. He was subsequently posted to Malaya, organising counter-insurgency operations against Chin Peng's communist guerrillas, before returning to London to work on intelligence against Indonesia, which was then involved in an undeclared war—the so-called 'Confrontation'—with Britain over the creation of Malaysia. His knowledge and understanding of the region was therefore impeccable.[13]

He arrived in June via the ICC's air link between Saigon and Hanoi—an ageing propeller-driven Stratoliner aircraft which stopped over in the Laotian capital, Vientiane—in time to report on the first US raids, which took place at the end of that month. The consulate-general buildings, which had been taken over only two years earlier, consisted of the offices, with an apartment occupied by the vice-consul, and the consul-general's residence, a curious looking multi-storeyed house that had formerly seen service as a brothel.

'The British residence, a square, box-like structure, cream and brown with blue shutters, stood in a garden off a quiet, tree-lined road running, at one extremity, to the Red River, and at the other, into the relative bustle of downtown Hanoi,' Colvin recalled. 'Under the covered entrance, Monsieur Dong, butler, "boy", factotum and genial incompetent, lightly clad in singlet and white ducks, shifted nervously from foot to foot before, with an uncertain smile of welcome, opening the car door and, head bowed, seizing my hand in both of his. The office of the Consulate-General, some two hundred yards round the corner, was a low building almost entirely hidden in trees, directly opposite a factory, the purpose of which I never determined but which appeared to hold ancient vehicles and mechanical parts of every description. On the rare occasions the gates were opened the place resembled both repair shop and junk yard.'[14]

Colvin was there to answer President Johnson's persistent

questions to Dick Helms, who had taken over as head of the CIA: 'Are the US bombing raids working? Are they having an impact on the regime? Are they worth risking the lives of our air crew?' The president held weekly Tuesday lunches in the White House attended by key aides such as Rusk, McNamara, Walt Rostow, the new national security adviser—who as an OSS officer in war-time London had been in charge of working out the priorities for bombing targets inside Nazi Germany—and Helms himself, who was trusted by Johnson in a way his predecessor had never been, in part because John McCone had felt obliged to point out repeatedly during discussions of the administration's policy that the CIA believed the North Vietnamese were determined to fight on until North and South were united as an independent country.

Helms recalled one Tuesday lunch where General Earle 'Bus' Wheeler, the chairman of the Joint Chiefs, outlined the success of USAF aircraft in taking out the power station supplying electricity to the North Vietnamese capital. The president had only reluctantly authorised the raid. Helms said that after the lunch, Johnson took him to one side. 'He put his hand on my shoulder. "If as 'Bus' just said, the bombers demolished the grid and destroyed the generators, am I right in assuming that the lights must be out in downtown Hanoi?" He took another few steps before saying: "Let me know about that tomorrow."' The resultant telex Helms sent to the chief of station in Saigon asked a very simple question: 'Are the lights on in Hanoi?'

Colvin and his vice-consul, Geoffrey Livesey, were in a perfect position to answer that question, having personally witnessed the raid from the balcony of the vice-consul's apartment. Livesey had just given Colvin a drink when the air raid sirens sounded. 'We walked out onto the balcony,' Colvin recalled. 'As we stood there seven or eight United States Thunderchief jet fighter-bombers, flying at scarcely more than roof-top height and no more, it seemed, than 100 yards away, shot across our vision at what appeared—so tight was the space in which the whole incident was framed between houses and sky—enormous speed. They had come on us suddenly out of nowhere, in superb formation at 600 mph, disappearing for an instant behind the trees and buildings that lay between us and the thermal power plant less than one mile to the south, and then quickly climbing clear and away. As they hurtled past, so close it seemed we could almost touch them or call to the pilots, we had seen the rockets fired from the pods under their wings. Almost simultaneously, such lights as were on in the apartment went out, the fan stopped turning, and a column of dust, smoke and flame rose from the direction of the power station.'

Despite the risk of being accused of 'target-spotting' for the Americans, Colvin and Livesey felt compelled by the importance of the situation to go to the power station to see the damage for themselves. 'The flames had died down by the time we approached it, but the dust still rose from fallen masonry,' Colvin recalled. 'The building had repeatedly been struck by high explosive: the chimneys had collapsed, and the whole structure, gaping with holes caused by the rockets, seemed also to be listing drunkenly to one side. There was in our opinion, no hope for it at all.'

The next day, as the US bombing raids continued, Colvin sat down to compose a report on the events of the past twenty-four hours. 'Having described the raid on the city, the condition of the power plant and its consequences, I concluded that there was no possibility known to me of restoring any electric services,' Colvin said. He then handed the report to Livesey to encipher. 'At that moment, the lights went on. The fans started to turn and the rattle of the box air conditioner began. Across the street, the repair factory was once again brightly lit. There were no more means then than there are today of determining how that happened. The lesson, however, was of the astonishing preparedness and resourcefulness of the North Vietnamese. Only continual air attacks of a kind that Rolling Thunder had not yet initiated would surmount those qualities.'

Unsurprisingly, the North Vietnamese seem to have been in no doubt that the British were spying on behalf of the Americans. Colvin recalled how his strong suspicion that the consulate-general was bugged was confirmed by two Vietnamese 'post office' workers, one male, one female, who turned up claiming that Colvin had reported that his phone was not working properly. 'I had naturally taken for granted that all the telephones were tapped,' Colvin said. 'I was therefore delighted rather than surprised when the male official seized the telephone, removed the base plate, extracted two presumably worn-out devices, which he asked me to hold, and replaced them with new objects from a broken spectacle case held by his giggling assistant. The whole incident was endearing and, in its naïveté, reassuring.'[15]

Colvin reported frequently on the remarkable way in which the population were reacting to the war, repeatedly making the point that the American bombing only seemed to stiffen their resolve and noting that the attitude of the locals seemed 'weirdly similar' to that of Londoners during the Blitz. 'Mr Colvin believes that American bombing is indecisive in so far as attainment of American objectives is concerned,' one British official noted. 'He believes that the peasant population is comparatively indifferent to the damage being done to the possibility of developing a consumer-goods economy and that consequently their leaders are willing to see a degree of disruption that would be unthinkable in a more advanced country.'[16]

There was a problem at the beginning of 1967 when Colvin's regular reporting of the damage caused by the US bombing was outed in the British and US media but, despite his concerns that he might be expelled, the North Vietnamese simply called him in and harangued him. By March, he was reporting the destruction of the main North Vietnamese steel works north of Hanoi by repeated American air raids and composing a long description on the city's emergence from winter for George Brown, the foreign secretary, who had told him during a visit to London that he enjoyed reading his reports from Hanoi in bed with a tumbler of whisky in hand. Colvin went into some detail of how the population refused to be cowed by the impact of the war.

'There has been a change in the atmosphere of this city in the last six weeks,' Colvin reported. 'Not only does the populace seem more cheerful and light-hearted, but the numbers of shops half-open has noticeably increased. Now that the winter is over and they have removed the hideous sweaters, ear-muffs and padded coats in which they encased themselves, they are certainly more attractive. The short, slit, waisted tunic coats worn by the girls over black silk trousers, the habitual pigtails and the occasional high heels offer small competition to their Saigon siblings, but at least the effort to appear presentable is maintained. Neither do the men, in their off-duty moments, neglect their appearance, and if their double-breasted suits are more reminiscent of a Paris *banlieue* than W1, that is to be expected. Greetings and smiles are almost invariably returned with, I think, warmth and the politeness that is a characteristic of this people. It is difficult to account for this. I think myself that the lifting of tension may be due to . . . an impression, in short, that spring has come, the war may not continue forever and, even if it does, they can take it.'[17]

Colvin was appointed CMG, the more normal honour for a member of the British secret intelligence service, for his work in Hanoi. He was replaced in September 1967 by Brian Stewart,* another MI6 officer with experience in Malaya and an experienced Far East hand who had served in both Shanghai and Beijing.

Shortly before Colvin left, he, or possibly Livesey, referred by mistake in a plain text telegram to a report of the extent of the US bomb damage which had been sent previously in cipher, leading the North Vietnamese to rescind permission for the consulate-general to send enciphered telexes. This forced Stewart and his successors to use the Canadian diplomatic bag to send their intelligence, delaying its arrival in London by as much as a week, although it normally reached Saigon the following day. The MI6 officers also continued periodically to make their own bag runs via the ICC flight to Saigon, where there were briefings for the US and British ambassadors and the CIA chief of station, before flying on to the regional MI6 headquarters in Singapore for a debriefing session with the Controller Far East, whose cover was as political adviser to the commander-in-chief, UK Forces.[18]

The new consul-general did not let the fresh restrictions prevent him doing his job. Shortly after his arrival, Stewart interviewed two recent travellers to Haiphong, gathering useful intelligence

---

* Stewart was the father of the writer and former Conservative politician Rory Stewart.

on the effect of the US bombing of the port and its industrial area. Citing 'an intelligent and experienced non-Communist Western observer' who had just travelled from Hanoi to Haiphong and back, Stewart reported:

> Traffic was moving between Hanoi and Haiphong from dark (about 1830) until midnight. Journey was done in bright moonlight and road surface near Haiphong appeared to consist of a mass of bomb craters, either repaired or under repair. Whole town area had the air of European city which had suffered general bombardment during last war: in some residential quarters it looked as if 80 per cent of houses had been destroyed.
>
> Lorries moved within town during daytime but it seemed as if most movements to and from docks was done under cover of darkness. Despite heavy frequent bombing, population looked unperturbed and cheerful as if they had become accustomed to living in front line and adjusted their philosophy accordingly. Cinemas, shops and restaurants continued to operate. In Hanoi, there was no evidence of panic or fear. Main river between Hanoi and Haiphong was bridged by pontoon which would serve whichever of the three roads was in best state of repair at any particular time. According to Vietnamese, repair work on roads and railways was being made more difficult by use of bombs with delayed action fuses using varied time patterns.

The reporting was backed up by an interview with 'another experienced Western observer of Communist sympathies who visited Haiphong on 11–12 October' providing a less detailed account. 'His general impression was that town was in state of almost perpetual alert, population was standing up to bombing with great fortitude and stores were moving effectively.' Stewart had not omitted the age-old intelligence-gathering process of train-watching, noting that 'Long goods trains (60 wagons at one count) continue to arrive in Hanoi railway station from North. Open wagons are piled high with boxes and sacks under tarpaulin covers.' He summarised the two accounts by noting that they tallied and that while on the face of it the US bombing of Haiphong was creating difficulties for the North Vietnamese authorities, these were 'not decisive' and the port continued to operate.[19]

Some Foreign Office officials were sniffily dismissive of the value of Stewart's reports, surprisingly including those on the effectiveness of the US raids. The Americans were less dismissive and in late October Stewart made his first entry into the President's Daily Brief in reporting of the US bombing of the capital, the most intensive raid to have taken place up to that point. The Paul Doumer Bridge had been badly damaged with two spans dropped, and ferries had to be used to transport goods coming in from Haiphong across the river. But despite the intensity of the bombing, the population retained the resilience noted by Colvin earlier that year.

'Although the bombing has adversely affected the lives of the North Vietnamese, they do not seem to be disheartened,' Stewart said. 'They appear resigned to a prolonged war and fully confident of ultimate victory.' A few weeks later, the consulate-general was hit by a US air raid, suffering only limited damage but enough to make a more personal entry into the President's Daily Brief, followed not long after by a report on the way in which Stewart's ability to do his job was being steadily cut back following his arrest for entering a heavily bombed area, albeit ostensibly only on his way to church. Nevertheless, the CIA analyst assured the president that despite the harassment, 'the US embassy in London feels that as long as the Consul-General is able to make use of the Canadians to get his reports out the British will maintain the mission'.[20]

Stewart's observations during his walks around Hanoi frequently made their way onto President Johnson's desk in their original form, as sent to the Foreign Office. They included the sighting of anti-aircraft batteries hidden away in 'shabby peasant huts of wood and leaves' in the city's Thống Nhất Park and a moment when a visit to the zoo put him in the perfect position to watch a US air strike on the Paul Doumer Bridge and the response by the North Vietnamese air defences, in which elderly anti-aircraft guns proved surprisingly more effective than modern surface-to-air missiles, in North Vietnamese hands at least. Stewart watched as five US aircraft were shot down, reporting that at least two of the aircrew had parachuted to the ground. Sightings of US prisoners of war were naturally of major interest to the US authorities, as were reports of any signs of mass recruitment which might signify an impending major offensive.[21]

At the beginning of a long and assiduous dispatch to George Brown, in late 1967, recording the situation in the North Vietnamese capital in colourful detail for the benefit of the foreign secretary's night-time reading, Stewart outlined 'four types of valid evidence available in Hanoi from which one is entitled to draw some conclusions: The physical signs of increasing military and civil defence measures in and around the city; direct conversation with official and unofficial Vietnamese contacts; the press and other propaganda media; and the comments of the diplomatic corps', who often had access to officials who would never speak to the UK consul-general.[22]

Stewart remained in Hanoi for a year and, despite the restrictions—against which he railed with some ferocity in his com munications with the Foreign Office—he nevertheless felt that the intelligence produced in his extremely regular 'Hanoi Observations' was worthwhile. 'I am convinced that we more than earned our keep in this post, supplying a perspective on North Vietnam which was not available to our allies,' he wrote. 'It was a very privileged position to have. Western capitalist running dogs of the American imperialists were not, in general, welcome. Our movements were severely restricted, so our choice of sources was small indeed. But we were on the ground, and so had a view denied to the embassies in Saigon. We could see the people and the shops, draw conclusions about the food situation, health and morale. This direct experience was a valuable ingredient for assessors struggling to put together an intelligence mosaic. I am sure that even if our assessment was gloomy, the US was grateful for our moral support.'[23]

The intelligence picture on North Vietnam provided in the President's Daily Briefs during the war backs up Stewart's judgement on the value of the MI6 reporting—however limited it might have seemed at times to the officers themselves. Occasionally, the Foreign Office intervened, invoking the 'Guard' UK Eyes Only

precautions to prevent the Americans seeing the MI6 officers' criticism of US policy, or even what officials in London deemed to be
'uncorroborated' evidence that might encourage more bombing,
but by and large the reports from the British consul-general were
passed to the CIA uncensored, providing intelligence from the
ground in the North that was unmatched by any other source during
that period. Stewart left Hanoi in September 1968, collecting an
undoubtedly deserved CMG.

He was replaced by Gordon Philo, a Russian specialist who had
worked on the copious amounts of intelligence supplied by Oleg
Penkovsky. Stewart had returned to Century House, the dowdy
1960s London headquarters of MI6, halfway through his tour in
Hanoi to find that no one had been selected to replace him. At
the behest of the MI6 personnel department, he allegedly sold the
posting to Philo as one of constant sunshine, a deceit for which he
was apparently never forgiven. Stewart went on to become the MI6
Controller Far East, by then based in Hong Kong, before returning
to London as Director Technical and Support Services, frequently
standing in for the then 'C', Sir Maurice Oldfield.[24]

Philo's fluency in Russian allowed him to develop a good relationship with diplomats at the Soviet embassy and he obtained
useful intelligence from a Soviet assistant military attaché who
went on a tour of the northern provinces in December 1967. The
officer returned to Hanoi complaining that 'he was obliged to
obtain a pass from Chinese military officials to travel to certain
areas and had been stopped several times for his pass to be checked
by Chinese soldiers'. This was interesting evidence of the control
carried out by Chinese troops inside Vietnam—particularly given
the rift between Moscow and Beijing and the uncertainty over the
Vietnamese position—and provided Philo with an early appearance
in the President's Daily Brief.

Another report from Philo on the construction of air raid shelters
deep underground also landed on President Johnson's desk. 'Large-
scale underground construction is under way at two sites in the city,'
the Daily Brief noted. 'A Vietnamese source is quoted as stating that
many more deep and strong shelters are under construction but are

not normally noticeable to persons above ground as access to them is from the inside of buildings.' Philo described the slow progress of efforts to clean up after previous US air raids and reported the training of workers at a factory near the consulate-general in drill, camouflage and small arms, although this seemed 'designed primarily to keep the population alert and active rather than serving any real military role'.[25]

The good relationship with the Soviet embassy built up by Philo may have been the reason that his successor in September 1969 was Daphne Park, who had been head of station in Moscow in the mid-1950s. She built on Philo's contacts with the Soviet embassy. Julian Harston, one of her MI6 successors in Hanoi, recalled that she had a particularly good relationship with the younger members of the Soviet embassy, whom she met at their regular film evenings. 'She spoke Russian as taught by White Russian émigrés in Paris, which for the young Soviets was fascinating,' he said. 'A voice from history was how one young second secretary described it.'

From the start, Park set out to ensure that the Foreign Office understood the difficulties of the posting, which until she arrived was not accorded the status of 'hardship post' that would have ensured that she and her vice-consul received extra pay. She repeated the evidence in a number of telegrams to London, all of which made much of the residence's previous history as a brothel, the earlier ones also pointing out that there was a bidet in each room. The evidence was reprised in a valedictory telegram widely admired by colleagues in both MI6 and the Foreign Office.[26]

'The Residence was formerly a house of ill-fame,' Park wrote. 'Handkerchiefs are boiled in the saucepans, other dirty clothes in the dustbin. When the household cat disappeared, opinion was divided whether she had been eaten by the neighbours or the rats. When even more water than usual flooded the bathroom floor, and even less (though more noisome) water came from the tap, and the plumbers eventually came, they withdrew for three days to attend cadre meetings before removing the dead rats they found in the pipes. No rodent extermination service exists because, officially, rats have been eliminated. Unfortunately, the rats do not know this.

The major domo of the Residence has been at some earlier time an
inmate of a mental institution; the misfortune is that he was ever
released.'[27]

The restrictions imposed by the North Vietnamese prevented her
from visiting the diplomatic club, shop and swimming pool, and
other government facilities to which most diplomats based in Hanoi
were allowed access. This severely limited the amount of routine
intelligence that would normally be available from diplomat chatter.
Park reacted by inviting various foreign diplomats, including the
influential Soviet ambassador, Ilya Shcherbakov, to her residence
where she wined and dined them, engaging them in conversation
over whisky or brandy into the early hours as the water dripped into
the buckets and bowls strategically placed around them.

They spoke to her with a good deal of candour, in part a result
of the brandy but also because, as a woman who in her own words
'always looked just like a fat missionary', her chauvinistic male
drinking partners rarely saw her as a threat. Those who joined her
for the sessions over brandy ranged from Shcherbakov to the Hanoi
representative of the Provisional Revolutionary Government, which
the communists claimed to have set up in the South. As word of the
pleasant drinking sessions spread, she was even joined by a member
of the Communist Party Politburo who turned up uninvited and
spent six hours chatting on her veranda, a meeting that would
have provided unparalleled intelligence of the views of the North
Vietnamese leadership. 'We have agents in every ministry and every
village in the south,' he claimed. 'In that case, why do you find it
necessary to hang village headmen?' Park asked. She later recalled
her chill at his unnerving response: 'Because we are Leninists and
Lenin believed in revolutionary terror.'[28]

Like her predecessors, Park was also able to make her own
observations of life inside the city centre, providing further useful
intelligence. 'I went for a walk every day,' she said. 'And in the
middle of the war, there's a lot you can see.' Harston recalled that
'the de visu reporting that could be done in Hanoi itself was all
fresh for our US cousins, and despite being limited to two square
kilometres, there were key places that could be visited. Passing the

rubbish bins outside the military hospitals could give a good estimate of the number of soldiers being recruited just by counting the
used syringes used for inoculations.'[29]

Park's wartime service alongside the OSS was particularly useful
in her relations with the Americans. By now, Bill Colby was back in
Saigon, heading up the pacification programme, so on her journeys
out of Hanoi she could meet him along with the CIA station chief,
Ted Shackley. The fact that, when Colby was a young OSS officer,
Park had trained him in communications security would provide a
useful entrée throughout her MI6 career, particularly when he later
went on to become the CIA director. 'I found it very useful to be
able to say casually to a CIA officer who mightn't perhaps be being
totally helpful to me, although they usually were. I had very good
relations with the Americans. I would mention Bill Colby quietly
and he would say: "Oh." I would say: "Yes I taught him you know.
He's an old pupil of mine." It was very useful indeed and Bill was
very amused when I told him about it. I said: "I take your name in
vain sometimes." Very useful.'

Colby was not the only one of her former charges still operating
in the region, as she discovered during one visit to MI6 regional
headquarters. 'I was out of Hanoi being debriefed in Singapore,'
she recalled. 'And suddenly there was a sort of roar from across the
room and somebody rushed up to me and embraced me tenderly and
it was Lou Conein, who had been one of the officers who'd come
back from Algiers and extracted me from General Gubbins.'[30]

Park got on surprisingly well with the very few North Vietnamese
officials who dealt with the consulate-general, because she always
treated them as if they were trying to be helpful even when they
clearly were not. 'If things go wrong, I assume that their only
wish in life is going to be to help me solve the problem,' she said.
'Looking somewhat surprised, they occasionally do, even according
a certain amused respect to my tactics. I have found a certain satisfaction in not noticing harassment when it happens.'

The most dangerous point in her time in Hanoi came when
Ellsworth Bunker, the US ambassador in Saigon, held a dinner for
journalists and repeated some of Park's more amusing accounts of

life in Hanoi, including her attempts to obtain a bicycle. When the authorities refused to let her have one, claiming it was too risky, she suggested she get a tandem with her driver occupying the front saddle. When this failed, she proposed a trishaw pedalled by a North Vietnamese security officer. This was accepted but withdrawn after she turned up to a function at the Soviet embassy with a Union Flag draped across the handlebars.

Bunker also referred to her previous presence in the Congo along-side her great friend Larry Devlin, then CIA station chief in Kinshasa but by this time well known to the journalists covering south-east Asia as the Agency's man in the Laotian capital, Vientiane. Bunker's loose remarks—not the first or the last time that a US official's inju-dicious comments to the press jeopardised an MI6 operation—risked a disastrous linkage between the British consul-general's position and the CIA. They led to an inaccurate but potentially damaging story in *Time* magazine which claimed Park had produced a report on the Vietnamese economy containing 'adverse comments on North Vietnamese economic capacity'. The dinner also led to a request from the *Daily Express*'s south-east Asia correspondent, Ian Brodie, for a 'human interest' interview on Park's work in the Congo and Vietnam. Brodie's request was refused but the story of the tandem did make it into the *Express*, albeit with the background on Park's role removed at the request of the Foreign Office.[31]

At the end of her tour, in October 1970, Park remained convinced that the post was worthwhile retaining so long as the consul-general continued to have access to the Canadian diplomatic bag or some other means by which intelligence could be sent out in a reasonably timely fashion. Her valedictory dispatch to the new Conservative foreign secretary, Sir Alec Douglas-Home, clearly demonstrated that she looked back on her time in Hanoi with some affection. 'When I arrived here, 13 months ago, buffaloes grazed on the grass in front of the Consulate-General,' Park wrote. 'The factory defence militia practised unarmed combat and grenade throwing, an occasional *cyclo-pousse* creaked past carrying a family and its chattels, and at night the bats swooped and the cicada were noisy. None of this has changed. But the sentry outside the Algerian Embassy has planted a garden round his sentry-box, Hanoi is full of new lorries, the shape of Hồ Chí Minh's mausoleum is under debate, and the State Plan for 1970 has allowed the Residence roof to be mended; my successor will not need to catch the drips in the drawing room. A new kitten appeared at the Residence this month and may one day kill rats, if it survives. We have moved a few steps out of Limbo for we have been allowed to travel, and perhaps even hell is a little less hot than before. The children are back from the country and Hanoi is a year further from the war. I do not yet know, and neither do the Vietnamese, whether that means they are a year nearer to peace.'[32]

Park went on to become Controller Western Hemisphere, the first woman to reach such a position. She was replaced as consul-general in October 1970 by yet another experienced MI6 officer, John Liudzius, who was the son of Lithuanian émigrés and a veteran of the failed post-war operations in the Baltic republics. The way in which the British government was prepared to send so many highly experienced MI6 officers to Hanoi—at a time when it refused to back the Americans militarily, even publicly condemning the US bombing raids on North Vietnam—in order to ensure that the Johnson and Nixon administrations were aware of the impact of those same attacks was a remarkable moment in the real Special Relationship, the extensive sharing of intelligence between Britain and America.

By 1973, with the Paris peace accords signed and the North Vietnamese returning US servicemen captured during the war, Julian Harston was consul-general. The end of the war led to far greater access to diplomatic and government facilities, and by extension occasional contact with more interesting members of the North Vietnamese leadership.[33] 'On one of the rare occasions that we were allowed out of Hanoi for a weekend, we went to a government rest house in Hạ Long Bay,' Harston said. 'On the Saturday evening, I heard Glenn Miller's *String of Pearls* being played in the room below. I went onto the balcony and looked down. On the balcony below was an elderly Vietnamese in military uniform. He looked up and I asked him in French whether he liked American Big Band music. He replied that he did not. I asked him how long he had disliked it and he said, with a very mischievous smile: "Since about 1945." I had recognised him as soon as he looked up. It was General Võ Nguyên Giáp, victor over the French [at Điện Biên Phủ] and well on his way to defeating the US.'[34]

PACKING A PUNCH

The Labour government's plans to withdraw the majority of Britain's armed forces from 'east of Suez'—a substantial reduction in the UK's global presence forced on it by the dire state of the British economy—were bitterly opposed by the Americans, who saw themselves being left to fight communism alone in the Far East. The withdrawal from the Persian Gulf and south-east Asia, which would include the loss of signals intelligence bases in Singapore and the Maldives, caused far more concern in Washington than Harold Wilson's refusal to take part in the Vietnam War.

Despite the proposed cuts, first mooted in 1966, there was no let-up in intelligence-sharing. The mid-1960s saw the US Navy expand its top secret anti-submarine intelligence operations to involve the Royal Navy on an equal intelligence-sharing basis. During the Second World War, US scientists had discovered that low-frequency sound travel great distances along the bottom of the world's oceans. In the early 1950s, the US Navy developed arrays of sonar sensors along America's Atlantic and Pacific coasts, and around Hawaii, that were designed to pick up the sounds given off by the engines or other working parts on Russian submarines. The arrays of sensors, or 'hydrophones', were linked to shore stations by underwater cables and the low-frequency sounds were then analysed using spectrograms which provided a visual image of all the frequencies in each sound. The system was so highly classified that even its title, SOSUS, an acronym of Sound Surveillance System, was designated top secret.

The US coastal system was initially limited in its capabilities—it did not pick up its first Soviet submarine until 1962—and the British remained sceptical of its use against the quieter nuclear submarines that were replacing the noisy diesel submarines of the early Cold War. The situation changed in the early 1960s when the submarines of the Soviet Northern Fleet based in Murmansk began entering the North Atlantic in large numbers. At this point, the US Navy set up an array of sensors in the Norwegian Sea linked by cable to a new processing centre at Keflavík in Iceland. The success of the new array convinced the Americans it was worth expanding, and they approached the British with a view to creating a joint array which would cover most of the eastern Atlantic, picking up Soviet submarines heading into the ocean as well as those which were transiting on their way to the Mediterranean. The array was to terminate at a new regional evaluation centre at Brawdy in Pembrokeshire, south Wales.

Despite the earlier British concerns, the system was highly successful, not only at picking up the sounds from Russian submarines but in coordinating multiple arrays to locate the submarines down to a 50-mile radius using a sound-ranging process that narrowed down their location by means of cross-bearings in a similar way to that used by GCHQ and NSA direction-finding systems. As operators developed their skills, they began to identify specific types of submarines from the distinctive sounds of their individual engines or, in the case of nuclear submarines, their reactor pumps, and at times even individual boats were named. This acoustic intelligence (ACINT) was coordinated with signals intelligence to produce a reasonably comprehensive picture of Soviet submarine activity in the waters around the UK and out into the Atlantic.[1]

During the mid-1960s, British naval intelligence and MI6 mounted a joint operation, codenamed Hornbeam, in which the skippers of trawlers based in Hull that regularly fished in the Barents Sea were commissioned to take photographs of the ships of the Soviet Northern Fleet. Commander John Brookes, a retired naval officer attached to MI6, recruited a number of trawler skippers who were specially trained and provided with high-specification cameras and a recognition manual for Soviet warships. They were told to stick to their normal fishing areas and wait for Soviet warships to come into view before taking their photographs rather than go looking for them. If they were boarded by Soviet crews, they were to place the camera, film and any other incriminating evidence in a weighted bag and drop it over the side of the ship.

Mason Redfearn was one of the trawler skippers recruited by Brookes to take photographs of Soviet ships while fishing off the islands of Kildin and Novaya Zemlya in the Barents Sea. 'Every cruiser, destroyer, submarine (conventional or nuclear) which I saw, were all captured on film,' he recalled. 'In the early years, it was possible to go within three miles of the Russian coast. This was later extended to 12 miles. There were times while fishing off Kildin, I could strike it lucky. I would watch on my radar the activity of the warships coming down from Murmansk and forming up behind Kildin in preparation for manoeuvres early in the morning and there I would be waiting to photograph them. There was one occasion when I was particularly fortunate, and it happened when we were fishing off Cape Cherny [on Novaya Zemlya]. This resulted in my obtaining photographs of one of the first Russian aircraft carriers, complete with escorts, undergoing her sea-trials.'

The photograph which Redfearn recalls taking off Cape Cherny was apparently one of the best images obtained during the relatively brief life of Operation Hornbeam. It was in fact the new Soviet helicopter carrier *Moskva*, the first of two such warships built specifically to counter US and UK Polaris nuclear submarines, and capturing it on film was something of a coup.[2]

Obtaining photographs of the latest Soviet military equipment, or even examples of the equipment itself, was an extremely important part of the role of British naval, military and air force intelligence and one where, despite the impending cutbacks, they could make an extremely useful contribution to the relationship with the Americans. One of the greatest and most skilfully engineered of these coups came as the result of swift coordination between RAF signals intelligence operators and members of BRIXMIS in the British sector of Berlin.

On 6 April 1966, RAF intercept operators based at the joint

US–UK intercept site on top of Teufelsberg, a man-made hill constructed with the rubble from the wartime destruction of Berlin, were tracking a pair of Soviet Yak-28 Firebar ground attack aircraft. The Firebar was of particular interest because it had the latest Soviet technology, including a Skip Spin radar, which could look up and down as well as straight ahead. As the aircraft approached Berlin, the British intercept operators heard one of the pilots telling his ground controller that he had lost power in one of his engines and was struggling to keep the aircraft under control. He was ordered to land at Schönefeld airport in East Berlin but, unable to regain control of the aircraft and desperately avoiding apartment blocks, he crashed into the Stössensee, a lake in the British-controlled sector of West Berlin. Both the pilot and navigator failed to eject and were killed outright.

Brigadier David Wilson, the head of BRIXMIS, was playing squash when the aircraft came down. A quarter of an hour later, still in his shorts, he was already coordinating an extraordinary operation to remove and examine the top secret Skip Spin radar without the Russians realising what was happening. British military police cordoned off the scene and a BRIXMIS interpreter was sent to the lakeside, where Russian troops based at Spandau prison in the British sector to guard Hitler's former deputy Rudolf Hess were trying to assume control of the crash site. Their commander, General Vladimir Bulanov, was told by the interpreter that he had no authority in the British sector and must back away.

Bulanov and his men watched as Squadron Leader Maurice Taylor, the BRIXMIS operations officer, rowed to the wreckage to take photographs, while divers went down to see if it was possible to recover the bodies of the Soviet pilot and navigator. At the same time, the RAF was flying technical experts from the Royal Aircraft Establishment at Farnborough in Hampshire out to Berlin to inspect the wreckage and determine which parts should be examined. A pontoon ferry with a crane to lift wreckage from the bottom of the lake was moved to the crash site. While the British told the Russians they were trying to find ways to recover the bodies of the pilot and navigator, they in fact removed the two engines and the various parts of the radar system under water, placed them in protected containers, attached them by wire to a small launch and dragged them to a jetty out of sight of the watching Soviet troops where they were removed from the water and flown back to Farnborough to be examined.

The Russians, under pressure from their superiors and frustrated by their lack of ability to witness what exactly was happening, fumed on the sidelines. At one point, Bulanov accused the British of having soldiers ready to shoot any Russian who approached the site. When Major Jonathan Backhouse, the BRIXMIS interpreter, denied this, Bulanov ordered a platoon of Soviet soldiers to march down a track towards the lakeside. 'We hadn't gone a dozen yards when suddenly two riflemen jumped out of the dark,' Backhouse recalled. Both sides clicked off their safety catches and there was a long pause as the British officer frantically thought of a way to defuse the situation. Hoping the British infantryman would back up his claim that there was no attempt to stop the Russians finding out what was going on, he asked: 'Are you authorised to let this Soviet officer pass?'

'Not on your fucking life, sir,' the British soldier replied.

That blunt response broke the tension. Bulanov roared with laughter and ordered his men back down the track before turning to Backhouse with the parting shot: 'I think, Major, Russian intelligence is superior to yours.' The next day, the pilot's and navigator's bodies were handed over and the British said they could now start to recover the aircraft itself. Meanwhile, having been dissected, measured, photographed and thoroughly examined at Farnborough, the engines and the main Skip Spin radar unit — but not the antenna, which was still being examined—were carefully returned to the Firebar's wreckage. Over the next few days all of the wreckage was loaded onto the ferry and on 13 April, a week after the crash, it was taken to the Soviet sector and handed back to the Russians, who complained that something was missing.

'We are at a loss to understand why, in an accident of this sort, one significant item seems to be missing while the other, surrounding parts are all intact,' the Russians said. The British, playing ignorant, replied that they did not understand what they were talking about. If something was missing it must be buried in the mud at the bottom of the lake. 'The Soviets were not going to say exactly what part they were talking about just in case we hadn't got it,' one of those involved in the operation said. 'We had nicked it and couldn't return it because it was a very intricate item.' The operation allowed the British and Americans to devise electronic counter-measures to deceive the new Soviet radar system.[3]

'The BRIXMIS mission was one of the great success stories of UK intelligence-gathering after the Second World War,' one senior RAF intelligence officer recalled. 'It was an important source of information on the deployment and use of new Soviet military equipment in GSFG, including Soviet tank divisions massing under cover of darkness with total radio silence. Sometimes it was Washington that sent congratulations directly back to the Mission, rather than going via Whitehall where there was a tendency to look for collateral from GCHQ, which was not always available.

'BRIXMIS also had the right to fly a light aircraft (officially, to maintain the flying skills of any pilots stationed there) within a defined area—although those area definitions were frequently ignored by the aircrew. This light aircraft, a Chipmunk, provided unique opportunities to observe and photograph activities of many quite different types normally military but some of the aerial photography included personal civilian images – at one particular address in East Berlin the residents often played table tennis in the garden, with mixed doubles and no clothes.'[4]

By the end of 1966, the focus had switched to the Middle East where fedayeen fighters from the Palestinian group Fatah, led by Yasser Arafat, were infiltrating Israel from Syrian territory to carry out terrorist attacks with the backing of the newly installed left-wing government in Damascus. Clashes broke out along the Syrian border with the two sides exchanging tank fire. The primary source of information for British and US intelligence on the day-to-day operations of the Israel Defense Forces (IDF) and the Syrian and Egyptian armies was the British Army's 9 Signal Regiment at Ayios Nikolaos in Cyprus and the RAF's 33 Signals Unit at nearby

Pergamos. The only really effective US signals intelligence coverage
of the region came from reconnaissance aircraft, with one senior
NSA officer candidly admitting that the Americans were 'primarily
dependent' on their British colleagues.[5]

The situation along the Israeli–Syrian border began deteriorating
rapidly in mid-January, with the British intercept operators reporting that the Israelis had moved tanks and artillery up to the border
together with a rapid reaction force capable of launching a retaliatory
raid into Syria. After conversations with his IDF contacts, the US
defence attaché in Tel Aviv confirmed that assessment, with the Daily
Brief warning President Johnson that the situation was 'explosive' and
an Israeli attack 'could come with little warning and be either a limited ground attack or a ground-air raid'. Israeli foreign minister Abba
Eban, who had served as a British Army intelligence officer during
the Second World War, warned Damascus that Israel had reached
the limit of its 'restraint' in the face of Fatah's cross-border attacks,
adding: 'We have the strength and will to make them stop.'[6]

A CIA assessment in late March, entitled 'Syria: A Center of
Instability', reported heightened tensions both between the Arabs
and Israel and among the Arab states themselves, with Syrian
support for Fatah's commando raids into Israeli territory—often
through Israel's softer borders with Jordan and Lebanon—hampering the efforts of both those more moderate states to avoid being
drawn into confrontation with the Israelis.[7]

On 7 April 1967, Syrian troops opened fire on Israeli tractors
cultivating fields close to the village of Haon on the eastern bank of
the Sea of Galilee and inside the demilitarised zone. When Israeli
troops fired back, the Syrians upped the ante, responding with tank
and mortar fire. The border clashes were monitored by Arabic- and
Hebrew-speaking intercept operators at 9 Signal Regiment, while
the RAF specialists at 33 Signals Unit listened in as Israeli Mirage
III fighters took on the Syrian Air Force's Russian-made MiG-21
Fishbed fighter aircraft. The dogfights extended as far as the Syrian
capital of Damascus, 70 miles to the north-east of the border, the
Israeli pilots shooting down six Syrian MiG-21s, nearly a quarter of
the Syrian Air Force attack aircraft, with the loss of none of their

own Mirage III fighters.[8]

The Israeli superiority was not solely due to the ability of the pilots on either side and certainly not to the aircraft themselves, with the MiG-21, which was also flown by the Egyptian Air Force, supposedly a superior aircraft to the Mirage III. It was in large part the result of a remarkable operation by the Israeli intelligence agency Mossad that would have stretched the imagination of a Hollywood screenwriter.

A 1958 coup in Baghdad had brought a pro-Soviet government to power, leading the Russians to sell the MiG-21 to Iraq. But in 1963, a pro-Western government came to power in Baghdad and started to build military links with the US, which initiated a training programme for Iraqi Air Force pilots. Mossad's Operation Diamond, an attempt to unravel the capabilities of the MiG-21, began with the seduction by female Mossad agents of four Iraqi MiG-21 pilots who were on a staff course in San Antonio, Texas. All four were picked up in local bars and one by one they were asked to defect to Israel taking a MiG-21 with them. The first Iraqi refused, at which point the lights went out in the bar, a shot rang out, and when the lights came back on, the Iraqi officer was lying dead on the floor with a bullet hole in his head, killed by an unknown assailant.

The second was followed to Baghdad by his seductress who met him in a hotel for sex before asking him to defect. When he turned down the offer, a male Mossad officer who had been listening into the conversation in the next room walked in and shot him dead. The third initially agreed and was invited to West Germany to discuss the logistics of the operation and what he would get in return. But he made the fatal mistake of suggesting to his Mossad contacts that if he did not get what he wanted he could tell his bosses in Baghdad and that would be the end of any chance the Israelis had of obtaining a MiG-21. The response was brutal. He never returned to Iraq to talk to his bosses, he was thrown from a speeding train in Germany, leaving just one remaining MiG-21 pilot of the four seduced in America by the Israeli agents.

Perhaps unsurprisingly, Munir Redfa agreed to defect and on 16 August 1966 he took off from Tammuz air base west of Baghdad on

a high-altitude training mission, taking a circuitous flight devised
by the Israelis to disguise his intentions until it was too late to stop
him crossing briefly into Jordanian airspace and, after a 500-mile
flight, landing at Hatzor air base, east of the Israeli coastal town of
Ashdod. The Israelis therefore had a unique opportunity to examine
a MiG-21 and question a pilot who had been trained in how to fly
the aircraft by Soviet instructors. This made a dramatic difference
when they first came up against the aircraft in air-to-air combat
during the cross-border confrontation.[9]

The day after the 7 April clash, the President's Daily Brief
reported that a repeat was unlikely in the short term since the
Israelis, having shot down six of the Syrians' MiG-21s, had compre-
hensively demonstrated their superiority in the air and Damascus
would be unwilling to risk losing any more of their limited stock of
only twenty remaining MiG-21s. But by 9 April, the CIA was telling
President Johnson that the situation along the Syrian–Israeli border
was looking 'more ominous'. The exchanges of tank fire over the
past two days were far more dangerous than the previous sporadic
cross-border small-arms fire. 'Thus far no Israelis have been killed,'
the Brief said. 'But if there are fatalities, a reprisal could be mounted
with little or no warning.' Nevertheless, at this stage the CIA analysts stuck to the belief that, given neither side really believed that
war would solve anything, 'the chances are good that the threat of
great power intervention will prevent an attempt by either side to
resolve the problem by military force'.[10]

But by late April, with Israeli troops moving into the demilitarised zones on the banks of the Sea of Galilee in some strength,
rumours of an imminent attack began to sweep Damascus and UN
officials monitoring the border areas were 'becoming alarmed' over
the potential for a relatively minor breach of the border on either
side to escalate into war.[11] The President's Daily Brief remained
focused on Vietnam throughout this period, even during the first
part of May when, lower down the list, it began warning that the
April clashes had failed to stop the Fatah attacks on Israel and that
pressure was building internally for Israel to retaliate. Meanwhile,
in accordance with his ambitions to be seen as the leader of the

Arab world, Gamal Abdel Nasser was taking a number of apparently aggressive measures, including openly mobilising Egypt's armed forces in support of Syria. The Daily Briefs made clear that he was not looking to start a Middle East war, indeed he was 'anxious to duck a fight'; he was simply posturing to win over 'the Arab street'.

In accordance with a deliberate policy of tailoring the Daily Briefs to the preferences of the sitting president, those presented to Johnson used language that was often colourful. Nasser was taking 'a gigantic gamble', one warned. 'If he is lucky and there is no major outbreak, he will be crowing about how he deterred Israeli aggression.' The problem was that the Egyptian president did not 'control all the players' in the game. Fatah had put itself in a position where simply by mounting an attack that killed Israelis, it could spark a full-scale war. 'Nasser must be hoping desperately that there will be no need for him to fight the Israelis,' the CIA brief noted. 'He probably feels, however, that his prestige in the Arab world would nose-dive if he stood idly by while Israel mauled Syria again.'[12]

Nasser's request the following day for the withdrawal of UN forces protecting access to the Gulf of Aqaba, through which 90 per cent of Israel's oil was transported, led to growing concern in London and Washington. Pat Dean, now UK ambassador to the US, contacted Walt Rostow to share the concerns of the British JIC and the Wilson government that if Nasser closed the Gulf of Aqaba, war was inevitable. For the first time that year, the Middle East crisis knocked Vietnam off the top of the President's Daily Brief. 'The situation is explosive and the Syrians hold the match,' it said. 'If Syrian terrorists kill any Israelis, Israel is quite likely to strike fast and hard.' Meanwhile, the government in Tel Aviv ordered a partial mobilisation and Israeli troops began reinforcing the borders with Syria and Egypt.[13]

'For a moment, intelligence from the rest of the world slipped down the roster of events demanding immediate attention,' Dick Helms recalled. Late on Monday 22 May, Nasser announced that he was closing the Straits of Tiran, the only passage into the Gulf of Aqaba navigable by oil tankers. The Middle East was by far the most important item for discussion at Johnson's 'Tuesday breakfast' on

23 May, with Helms describing the Egyptian closure of the Gulf of Aqaba as 'a very serious turn' for the worse. Neither Israel nor the Arab nations really wanted a war. The problem was that none of the main players 'want peace badly enough to stop a war'.

Nasser must know that Israel regarded the closure of the Gulf of Aqaba as a *casus belli*, Helms said. Under the circumstances, war could come at any time as a result of 'accident, incident, or miscalculation'. Those attending the meeting were handed a CIA assessment that Israeli overall superiority was such that it could easily win a quick war but would struggle if it went on too long because the Arab states had twice as many troops. As a result, the Israelis would go all out for a swift victory and the war would probably be over within ten days. This agreed with the judgement of the British JIC, that overall Israeli superiority, particularly in terms of equipment and training, would ensure an Israeli victory within 'a week plus'.[14]

'LBJ read our estimate and asked if all present had read it,' Helms recalled. 'We had. After one more glance at the report, the President, peering over his reading glasses, went around the table again, asking each of us in turn if we agreed with the assessment. We did. LBJ then ordered General Wheeler* and me to review the assessment and, in his words, "scrub it down". There was only one change in our "scrubbed" assessment. After checking the original data and the latest reports, we shaved three days from the original estimate and concluded that the war might end within seven days. There remained another critical question: when would the war begin?'[15]

That question was answered, in general terms at least, a few days later when Meir Amit, the head of Mossad, visited Langley for talks with Helms. 'As I reported to President Johnson the following morning, my visitor had hinted that Israel could no longer avoid a decision,' Helms said. 'Israel's restraint, he felt, was the result of US pressure and might have cost Israel the advantage of a surprise attack. Such an attack, he seemed to suggest, was likely to come

---

* General Earle 'Bus' Wheeler, chairman of the Joint Chiefs of Staff.

quite soon. In passing this information to the President, I added my own conviction that this visit was a clear portent that war might come at any time, with no advance warning.' Asked how long a war would last, Amit said: 'Seven days.'[16]

There were extensive conversations between British and American officials throughout the crisis. The planned British 'east of Suez' defence cuts were a particular cause of tension within the relationship at the time, but both Johnson and Rusk expressed gratitude for the way in which Britain had raised the idea of joint measures—including a British proposal for a US–UK naval task force to enforce freedom of navigation in the Gulf of Aqaba—rather than leaving the Americans to take the initiative and appeal for help. Whatever the stress among the allies over other issues, it was 'of particular importance that our unity on fundamentals be reaffirmed', Rusk said.

Johnson was effusive in his gratitude to Harold Wilson for his willingness to step up to the base. 'I must say that the initiative you have showed [sic] in this crisis thus far has been greatly appreciated here where our capacity to act hinges so greatly on some of us at least being able to move together,' the president said at the end of their initial correspondence on the crisis. Cooperation was enhanced by a steady stream of British officials crossing the Atlantic to work on ways of ending the crisis, culminating in a pre-planned official visit to Washington by Wilson himself.[17]

Given the limited ability of even the US president, let alone Wilson, to influence the situation, the more vital discussions were inevitably those behind the scenes between intelligence officials including MI6 and the CIA, particularly the individual stations in the region, and GCHQ and the NSA on coverage of the situation. Pat Carter, who had left the CIA to become NSA director, was a confirmed Anglophile. He believed very strongly in the UKUSA relationship between GCHQ and the NSA. He also got on extremely well with his GCHQ opposite number, Joe Hooper, who like his predecessors had been a senior codebreaker at Bletchley Park, and they routinely discussed how to split up coverage of various parts of the world.

Carter recalled that when they first started working together, Hooper had 'somewhat of a supplicant viewpoint, an apologetic viewpoint' because the NSA was far better funded and as a result could provide much of the coverage of the world, outside Europe and the Middle East. Hooper felt 'that the British really weren't putting into it anything on the order of magnitude that we were', Carter recalled. 'But on the other hand, I was able to convince him that without them we were helpless in a large number of areas and we needed them. We were all in bed together. This was truly a joint operation between the US and the British and the magnitude of effort isn't something that we could measure by number of people or amount of money, and I think he accepted this as my viewpoint and operated on that basis that we were co-equal.'[18]

A crisis in the Middle East was a good example of where the British were capable of more than pulling their own weight in terms of production, but even so, with the British intercept sites in Cyprus reporting a steady build up of Egyptian forces in the Sinai Desert, it was clear that in the event of a full-scale war they would be overwhelmed by Arab and Israeli radio communications. Nor could Carter afford for political reasons to have US policy makers see the NSA relying heavily on its British partners for intelligence on a major world crisis. So, he sent the USS *Liberty*, sister ship to the USS *Oxford*, which had been so productive during the Cuban missile crisis, to the Mediterranean with orders to position itself north of the border between Israel and Egypt in order to cover the area where the bulk of the fighting would be taking place.[19]

Throughout the first four days of June, intercept operators at the British Army base at Ayios Nikolaos on Cyprus, who were monitoring Syrian, Jordanian, Egyptian and Israeli military communications, logged regular radio checks and situation reports with army units from all four countries reinforcing their respective borders. The only sign of fighting came in the early hours of 2 June when Israeli troops clashed with a small Syrian patrol a mile inside Israel just north of the Sea of Galilee. The resultant firefight left one Syrian commando and two Israeli soldiers dead, but it was an isolated incident and neither side showed any interest in retaliating.[20]

The next few days continued in similar fashion, with radio checks punctuated by occasional troop movements but no sign of any fighting. The first indication of any change came in the early hours of 5 June. Although the Arab radio operators continued their routine communications, the Israeli military radio operators disappeared from their normal frequencies and, despite extensive searches of the airwaves, could not be tracked down.

Shortly before eight o'clock in the morning, 33 Signals Unit began picking up signs of large numbers of Israeli Mirage attack aircraft preparing for take-off. Shortly afterwards, all hell broke loose on the airwaves as the Israelis launched pre-emptive strikes on all three fronts, albeit primarily focused on Egyptian forces in the Sinai peninsula, with Israeli tanks racing across the desert while the Israeli Air Force launched wave after wave of attacks on the Egyptian airfields in Sinai, and in Cairo, Alexandria and Port Said, as well as on the main Syrian and Jordanian airfields. The attacks destroyed most of the Egyptian, Syrian and Jordanian combat aircraft on the ground, giving the Israelis air superiority, and therefore dominance of the battlefield, for the rest of the war.[21]

With the Liberty still on its way to the region, the first US sources to report on the fighting were the Arabic monitors at the FBIS Mediterranean Bureau at Kyrenia in the north of Cyprus, who just before 10 a.m. (3 a.m. Washington time) reported that, according to Israel Army Radio, 'fierce fighting' had broken out between Israeli and Egyptian armoured units confronting each other in the Sinai Desert. Later that morning the teleprinter 'hot-line' between Washington and Moscow, set up in the wake of the Cuban missile crisis, was used for the first time when Premier Kosygin contacted Johnson to attempt to coordinate efforts to end the fighting. It was the first of twenty hot-line exchanges between the two men over the course of that week.[22]

The Liberty was just south of Italy on its way to the eastern Mediterranean when war broke out. It did not arrive in position, about 30 miles north of the eastern Egyptian town of al-Arish and 45 miles west of the lowest point of the Israeli coast, until the early morning of 8 June when it immediately began intercepting and processing Egyptian communications. The ship had a 125-man signals intelligence team, including nine Arabic specialists, three of whom were NSA civilians, and a couple of dozen US Navy intercept operators trained to take down messages sent in Morse code, with the head of the unit, Commander Maury Bennett, who was also an Arabic linguist, the NSA civilians and some US Navy intelligence personnel analysing what was happening and compiling the intelligence reports.

'We were to monitor specifically Egypt,' recalled Bob Wilson, one of the three NSA civilian Arabic specialists. 'That was what we were after, any military communications, especially air and air defence communications, and report back on anything significant that we got. Besides being linguists, we were all three also experienced reporters and analysts, so we, in effect, could handle just about everything.'

But by now much of the fighting had taken place and the Egyptian Air Force had been destroyed by the initial Israeli air attacks, so there were very few Egyptian Air Force communications to be intercepted. 'The Israelis were the only ones in the skies at the time because they had complete air superiority at that point,' Wilson said. 'They were dominating the airwaves.' There were no Hebrew linguists on board because the NSA had so few available. Wilson and his colleagues recorded some of the Israeli Air Force radio communications and focused on Egyptian military communications.

Meanwhile, the Joint Chiefs of Staff had concerns that, given that the US ambassador to the UN, Arthur Goldberg, had stated unequivocally that no US ships were within 400 miles of the war zone, the *Liberty* was far too close, while the NSA pointed out that it needed to be reasonably close to intercept the radio communications used by both the Egyptian and Israeli aircraft and individual military units on the ground. A decision was taken to withdraw the ship to at least 100 miles from any of the combatant countries and several different messages were sent to the *Liberty* ordering it to withdraw, but due to a bizarre series of coincidental foul-ups none of those messages would arrive in time.

Shortly before nine o'clock on the morning of 8 June, two Israeli

Air Force Mirage aircraft circled the *Liberty*, which was flying the US flag and the US Navy ensign. The incident was reported to the 6th Fleet, which had responsibility for all US Navy vessels in the Mediterranean, but it was not thought to have been of major concern. A couple of hours later, an Israeli Navy Nord-2501 Noratlas maritime reconnaissance aircraft also circled the *Liberty*. Wilson remembered not being worried about the aircraft at all. 'It was obvious that it was Israeli,' he said. 'I didn't think much of it. They were just out there checking us out. That's what I would do too.' Israel was America's ally. It was not seen as a threat.

At two o'clock that afternoon, two Israeli Mirage III aircraft flew straight towards the *Liberty*, one firing a series of missiles into the areas around the bridge, while armour-piercing tracer bullets fired by both aircraft ripped through the *Liberty*'s hull. For around five minutes, the two aircraft made criss-cross attacks on the ship at about one-minute intervals, hitting it with rockets and machine-gun fire more than 800 times, setting much of the ship ablaze. Within twenty minutes, the ship was under attack again, this time from three Israeli torpedo boats which opened fire with machine cannons and fired two torpedoes, one of which hit the *Liberty* just forward of the bridge and a few feet below the water line, tearing a 40-foot hole in the side of the ship and ripping the technical operations centre apart.

'It hit with tremendous force,' Wilson said. 'It blew a hole in the floor beside me. The entire third deck was flooded out and that's where all of our intercept material, equipment, recording facilities were. So, after the attack we had no capability at all.' Al Blue, one of Wilson's NSA civilian colleagues, was among the twenty-five crew members and signals intelligence operators killed when the torpedo hit the ship.[23]

Vice-Admiral William Martin, the commander of the US Navy's 6th Fleet, which was just south of Crete, dispatched four A-4 Skyhawk and four A-1 Skyraider attack aircraft to defend the *Liberty*, providing Washington with a major problem. US aircraft operating in the war zone could lead to conflict with Egyptian aircraft and claims that the Americans were intervening on the side of Israel.

Johnson sent Kosygin an immediate hot-line message explaining why US aircraft were on their way to the region. The Soviet premier responded within the hour to acknowledge the message and say that he had also explained to Nasser why the aircraft were there and that they were not hostile to Egypt.[24]

The USS *Liberty* limped back to Malta. A total of thirty-four members of the crew died in the attack, for which Israel immediately apologised. It insisted it was a mistake rather than an attempt to prevent the ship monitoring Israeli communications, and there were undoubtedly similarities between the shape and structure of the *Liberty* and an Egyptian Navy transport vessel. Inevitably, a number of conspiracy theories emerged, claiming that the attack was deliberately targeting the Americans, but there remains little real evidence to suggest that was the case. British intercepts of communications between the Israeli helicopters dispatched to assist the ship after the attacks revealed that the Israelis were still uncertain as to the ship's identity, believing it was Egyptian. Whatever the reason behind the attack on the *Liberty*, its late arrival and subsequent loss left the US heavily dependent on the much larger British intercept operations on Cyprus, which according to the internal NSA history provided the 'most timely and authoritative' information on what was happening on the ground.[25]

The war came to an end on 10 June and a ceasefire was signed the following day. The war had lasted one day less than the promised seven days, vindicating the intelligence provided by the British and American agencies in full. But if the intelligence picture provided to President Johnson and Harold Wilson for the Six-Day War was regarded as a major success on both sides of the Atlantic, the same could not be said for the next major world crisis, which was little more than a year away.

16

THE PRAGUE SPRING

The 1968 Soviet invasion of Czechoslovakia, in response to the political and economic reforms of what became known as the 'Prague
Spring', was widely seen as a major intelligence failure on both sides
of the Atlantic and from the British perspective it certainly was. The
arguments in the case of the US agencies are far less persuasive. The
NSA warned the US intelligence community that Soviet and other
Warsaw Pact forces were about to invade Czechoslovakia more than
twenty-four hours ahead of time, and that warning was repeated to
President Johnson and other key members of the National Security
Council by CIA boss Dick Helms. Given the comprehensive
intelligence-sharing process GCHQ enjoyed with the NSA—and
the key role of various British military teams in West Germany—it
is clear that the UK's lack of warning was a failure of analysis by
the relevant British authorities rather than a lack of sufficient intelligence collection.

The push for more political and economic freedom in
Czechoslovakia had been building up since the mid-1960s, with
economists arguing that the country should be building closer economic ties with neighbouring West Germany, and the Czechoslovak
people, including a substantial number of members of the
Communist Party itself, making increasing demands for democratic
reform, freedom of speech and the right to criticise the decisions
of those in authority, something unthinkable under Soviet-style
communism. In October 1967, the pressure for reform led to student protests, followed at the end of that month by attacks on party
leader Antonín Novotný at a meeting of the country's leadership,

the Communist party presidium. Three months later, Novotný was forced to resign and was replaced by the more reform-minded Alexander Dubček. Although the Soviet leadership was initially concerned by Novotný's removal, it was actually reassured by Dubček's appointment. He was not regarded as a problem. He was seen as a loyal Moscow-trained communist, 'Our Sasha', a man who would not rock the boat.

It soon became clear that Dubček had been elected with the clear intention of doing precisely that. He pushed ahead with reforms, while carefully making clear that there could be no change to the leading role of the Communist Party within society. But even inside the party itself, there were calls for change that ran ahead of what the new regime planned, many of which began to appear in the press, which felt increasingly free to discuss sensitive issues like relations with the USSR and Soviet responsibility for the 1948 killing of Czechoslovak foreign minister Jan Masaryk, issues that were bound to raise concerns in Moscow. There were even suggestions that Czechoslovakia should unilaterally establish diplomatic relations with West Germany, which at the time refused to have diplomatic relations with any state that recognised East Germany.*

These moves led inevitably to widespread concern within the Eastern Bloc and Dubček was called to a meeting of party leaders in Dresden on 23 March at which he was harangued by the East German leader, Walter Ulbricht, who was incandescent over the possibility of diplomatic ties between Prague and Bonn. Pressure was put on Dubček to allow Warsaw Pact troops to stage a major combined-forces exercise in Czechoslovakia. He said the timing was 'not convenient' and asked that it be postponed to later in the year and downgraded to a command post exercise involving only headquarters staff from the various Warsaw Pact countries. Immediately following the meeting, East Germany publicly accused the leading Czechoslovak reformers of assisting West German attempts to undermine communism. Meanwhile, the Soviet media referred to

---

* The Soviet Union was an exception. Bonn established diplomatic ties with Moscow in 1955 in exchange for the repatriation of German prisoners of war.

the problems in Czechoslovakia for the first time, with Moscow Radio claiming Western 'imperialists' were trying to detach it from the Soviet Bloc and a comment article in the party newspaper *Pravda* by 'I. Aleksandrov', the covername used for articles written by leading party members, accusing the West of stirring up trouble in Czechoslovakia.[1]

The monitoring of Soviet and Czechoslovak broadcasts of the respective politicians' speeches and newspaper commentary like the 'Aleksandrov' article, carried out by the BBC Monitoring Service at Caversham and the FBIS's London-based Press Monitoring Unit, and shared by both sides in an open-source intelligence exchange relationship which mirrored that of the NSA and GCHQ, was to play as important a part in the British and US intelligence analysis of the build-up to the Soviet invasion of Czechoslovakia as it had during the Cuban missile crisis.

The chairman of the CIA's Office of National Estimates, Abbot Smith, played down the idea of Soviet intervention while covering himself by warning it was nevertheless possible. The situation both inside the Eastern Bloc and in the outside world had changed considerably since the 1956 suppression of the Hungarian revolution, he said. Czechoslovakia was not Hungary. Moscow was committed to détente with the West. An invasion would inevitably bring delays if not an end to that process, and while conservatives like chief party ideologue Mikhail Suslov might want a military crackdown, the more rational response, given that Prague said it had no intention of ditching communism, was to wait and see.

'It is not too difficult to imagine Suslov, invoking doctrine and counselling an immediate and immoderate approach, in opposition to Kosygin, examining the facts and advising a measure of patience,' Smith said. The Soviet premier was likely to prevail. But if things got out of hand in Prague, the Politburo would face the tough choice of whether or not to intervene militarily, and 'though they would be even more reluctant to do so than they were in 1956, in the end they would probably decide that they could not tolerate such a setback and would intervene'. The British JIC took a less nuanced view, concluding that, given Kosygin's clear commitment to détente and the inevitable damage an invasion would do to the Soviet Union's international reputation, Moscow was unlikely to take military action.[2]

The KGB, led by Yuri Andropov, who as Soviet ambassador in Budapest in 1956 had played a key role in the invasion of Hungary, began a top secret 'active measures' campaign, codenamed Operation Progress, to undermine the reformers, sending in a number of 'illegals', agents operating under non-official cover—in this case as Western students, journalists, businessmen and women, or tourists—with orders to infiltrate key organisations and create provocations that might put the regime under pressure to haul back reforms or, if necessary, help to justify a Soviet invasion. Those targeted included prominent Czech activists, including the novelist Milan Kundera, and journalists in senior editorial positions within the Czechoslovak media.[3]

The attacks from Moscow and East Germany did not deter Dubček from introducing a promised 'Action Plan' of reforms—both economic and political and including freedom of the press—which were designed to create 'socialism with a human face'. The Czechoslovak government also announced an investigation into the circumstances surrounding Masaryk's death, including the claims of Soviet involvement. Meanwhile, reformers and economists continued pushing for closer ties with West Germany.

In late April, the CIA concluded that both Moscow and the West had been caught napping by what was effectively a 'bloodless revolution' in Prague. It nevertheless agreed with the JIC that there was no real threat of a Soviet invasion. 'Moscow would presumably have to believe itself directly threatened before it would intervene militarily,' the CIA report said. 'This belief would only result from a drastic action on the part of the Czechoslovaks, such as renunciation of their alliance with the USSR. The caution that the Dubček regime has demonstrated thus far indicates that this is not a likely possibility. The outlook therefore is for a continuation of the present state of mutual suspicion and caution.'[4]

On 4 May, the President's Daily Brief noted that Dubček had suddenly been called to Moscow for a 'short comradely meeting' with Soviet Communist Party leader Leonid Brezhnev following criticism of Soviet and East German policy towards West Germany in the Czechoslovak Communist Party paper, *Rudé Právo*. 'This kind of talk obviously is not going down well in Moscow,' the Daily Brief said. The talks were described by a Soviet spokesperson as 'frank and friendly', which indicated serious differences but not yet serious enough to fall out over.[5]

Immediately following the talks, US and British military signals intelligence units based in West Germany, primarily the 319th US Army Security Agency Unit at Rothwesten, north of Kassel, and 13 Signal Regiment, a British Army signals intelligence site at Birgelen on the Dutch–German border, reported that Group Soviet Forces Germany was on a high state of alert, with a number of divisions moving out of their barracks and heading south towards the Czechoslovak border. The continuing inability of GCHQ and the NSA to break the Soviet military ciphers limited intelligence production to traffic analysis, but the information this produced was still sufficient to provide substantial intelligence on what the troops were doing, while the interception of telephone systems in both the Soviet Union and East Germany often added useful detail.

East German officials talking on the ruling Socialist Unity Party's internal telephone network, which was relayed by a series of microwave radio transmitters located around the country and monitored by US and British Army intercept units in West Germany, were also heard discussing substantial movements of Soviet troops out of their barracks and towards the Czechoslovak border on manoeuvres. An East German soldier who was also taking part told his wife on the parallel military telephone circuit that he expected to leave East Germany at some point.[6]

A few days later, Warsaw Pact forces assembled in Poland and East Germany on the borders with Czechoslovakia began what was said to be a routine command post exercise, which would not normally require the deployment of many troops on the ground. It was soon clear that this particular command post exercise was anything but routine. Three days in, US and British intercept operators monitored new communications links being set up between the forces taking part in the exercise and Soviet ground forces headquarters.

The NSA also noted two Soviet divisions based in Ukraine moving south towards Czechoslovakia and another to Kraków in Poland, again close to the border with Czechoslovakia.[7]

A temporary restricted area was imposed on the East German border with Czechoslovakia, preventing BRIXMIS and its US counterpart from observing what was happening there. But touring the Soviet barracks in the unrestricted areas further north allowed them to determine which were deserted and which were still occupied, providing precise details of the units taking part in the Soviet-led operation and clearly demonstrating that this was no ordinary command post exercise. There were far more troops involved than would be normal for such an exercise while *de visu* observation of those still on the move showed that they clearly expected to be in the field for some time, with substantial amounts of personal effects designed to improve their comfort during downtime piled high on their tanks and armoured vehicles.[8]

Meanwhile, Walter Ulbricht, his Polish counterpart Władysław Gomułka, and the Hungarian and Bulgarian party leaders, János Kádár and Todor Zhivkov, flew to Moscow for what the President's Daily Brief said 'looks very much like an urgent conclave over what to do about Czechoslovakia'. Soviet patience was 'wearing thin', it said. 'Moscow clearly does not accept at face value Dubček's assurances that he can control the pace and scope of democratisation. We know the leaders in Prague were worried late last month that the Soviets may feel obliged to intervene more forcibly in Czechoslovakia. Yesterday's gathering in Moscow will surely heighten these fears.'[9]

The following day, during a Liberation Day celebration in Prague, Marshal of the Soviet Union Ivan Konev, who had led the suppression of the 1956 Hungarian revolution, pointedly reminded the Czechoslovak leadership of Soviet military capabilities. In a speech monitored by the BBC at Caversham Park and circulated to the CIA, British intelligence and the Foreign Office, Konev said Soviet troops were 'standing guard' over Czechoslovakia's frontiers 'always in a state of full combat readiness'. While ostensibly celebrating the country's liberation from German occupation by Soviet troops and the protection they continued to provide the country, Konev inevitably made that 'protection' sound far more like a threat than a promise.[10]

Over the next two days, US and British signals intelligence units based in West Germany and the western sectors of Berlin reported a continuing movement of Soviet troops in East Germany and Poland towards the Czechoslovak border. Attempts by the US and British defence attachés based in Warsaw to travel to the border area were stopped by Polish security officers, an extremely unusual occurrence in a country that normally allowed foreign diplomats relative freedom of movement.

The President's Daily Brief noted that Soviet and East German forces in East Germany were on a high state of alert. 'It appears that the Soviets may be thinking of a show of force designed to pull the Czechoslovaks back toward orthodoxy,' it said. 'The Soviets probably would not intervene outright without a call for help from some segment of the Czechoslovak party.' Unbeknown to the Western intelligence agencies at the time, and only revealed later by a defector, Soviet defence chiefs had also ordered a mobilisation of troops in western Ukraine, the only part of the Soviet Union which bordered on Czechoslovakia. What had begun a few days earlier as a simple command post exercise had evolved to a point where Soviet troops were now lined up along the entire northern and eastern borders of Czechoslovakia.[11]

At this stage, both the CIA and the JIC saw the Soviet military manoeuvres as part of a war of nerves, designed to bully the Czechoslovak leadership into clamping down on the media and limiting any reforms to those acceptable to Moscow, a view that was whole-heartedly endorsed by the State Department and the Foreign Office, both of whom were focused on détente. Talks between the US and Vietnam were under way in Paris. The long-awaited ratification of the Nuclear Non-Proliferation Treaty (NPT) was due to take place on 1 July. They were anxious not to see anything disrupt that process or indeed the strategic arms limitation talks that were being negotiated with Moscow. Johnson and Kosygin were already discussing fresh talks that were expected to be announced after the NPT was signed.[12]

There were some influential voices in Washington who were not convinced that détente made Moscow reluctant to intervene, even within the State Department. But very few in London, where the spring of 1968 had seen the JIC develop a strong pro-Foreign Office bias. Reforms to the British intelligence-reporting system saw Dick White step down as MI6 Chief to become the first UK intelligence coordinator, overseeing the entire system of reporting to government. The JIC's analytical capability was expanded with the creation of a Joint Assessments Staff to analyse the intelligence, but the system was still bedding in when the crisis began. The JIC was chaired by Denis Greenhill, a high-flying Foreign Office mandarin, while Foreign Office manoeuvring and Labour Party suspicions of Britain's spies had seen White replaced as MI6 Chief by Sir John Rennie, a Foreign Office insider with no experience in intelligence collection.

Senior MI6 officers who had expected White to be replaced by the MI6 vice-chief, Maurice Oldfield, White's friend and anointed successor, were furious and Rennie found himself outflanked during the early months of his tenure, confined to a largely administrative role while the flow of intelligence passed through Oldfield. This and Rennie's instinctive tendency to think in the same way as his former Foreign Office colleagues led to the JIC—the main interface between the British intelligence services and government—being effectively subverted by the Foreign Office viewpoint.

The situation was not helped by a reactionary GCHQ dismissal of media speculation over the Warsaw Pact exercises on Czechoslovakia's borders as simply due to a lack of understanding of routine Soviet military training. Furthermore, the Defence Intelligence Staff (DIS) representative on the JIC's current intelligence group shared the Foreign Office view that military intervention was unlikely, despite the fact that the bulk of evidence pointing towards preparations for an invasion was coming from BRIXMIS and US and British military signals intelligence units in West Germany and Berlin.[13]

Kosygin flew to Prague on 17 May, ostensibly to take the waters in the Czech spa town of Karlovy Vary, but in fact for talks with

Dubček and Czechoslovak prime minister Oldřich Černík aimed at persuading them to rein in the reforms. At the same time, Soviet defence minister Andrei Grechko arrived to inform Czech defence chiefs that they were to host a major Warsaw Pact exercise, simulating an invasion of their country, during which the Czechoslovak Army would provide the 'defending forces'. The exercise was code-named Šumava, a pointed reference to the Šumava mountains in western Czechoslovakia, which, along with Germany's Elbe River, were always cited by Moscow as the frontline against imperialism. Kosygin left four days early, having reached what he hoped was a modus vivendi with Dubček and Černík, albeit without the end to freedom of the press that might have made it acceptable to the hardliners in Moscow.[14]

Nevertheless, the talks with Kosygin seem to have left Dubček believing he could still manage a way through the crisis. A meeting of the Czechoslovak Communist Party's Central Committee at the end of May removed Antonín Novotný from its membership and voted to elect a new Central Committee at an extraordinary party congress that September. In a nod to Moscow, Dubček went out of his way to attack the 'anti-communist and anti-socialist tendencies' that had emerged during the reforms, albeit dismissing criticism from other Soviet Bloc countries as 'hysteria'.

The President's Daily Brief interpreted the speech as 'an attempt to satisfy the party's liberals while at the same time mollifying the party's conservatives and the Soviet Union'. The talks with Kosygin had left Czechoslovak leaders believing 'they could salvage most of their liberalisation programme but that they would have to meet a number of Soviet demands', the Daily Brief reported. 'As a result, they partially revved-up the party's opposition to the Catholic Church and to new non-Communist political groups.' Most importantly of all, Kosygin had persuaded them that they had to find a way to control the media to stop it taunting Moscow, although it was unclear how that could now be done without reimposing censorship.[15]

Meanwhile, the Soviet military cranked up the psychological pressure, with the first contingent of Soviet troops due to take part in the Warsaw Pact exercise entering Czechoslovakia two weeks ahead of schedule. A few days later, at a meeting of 6,000 party activists, Dubček attacked Novotný and his fellow conservatives with what the Presidential Daily Brief described as 'unprecedented vehemence'. He admitted some 'anti-communists' existed but insisted the party would remain in charge. The Daily Brief noted that 'his remarks have a self-confident ring, leaving the impression that he no longer expects the Soviets to line up behind the conservatives'.[16]

The Warsaw Pact 'command post exercise' began on 20 June, yet again with far more troops and tanks on the ground than would normally be the case for such an exercise. There was no doubting the significance of the manoeuvres, however, with Marshal of the Soviet Union Ivan Yakubovsky, the supreme commander of Warsaw Pact forces, flying in to take command. The actual troops operating in Czechoslovakia—apart from the home country's military, who were providing the 'defending forces'—were solely Soviet and Hungarian troops, with the Polish troops taking part remaining on Polish territory. There were East German and Bulgarian military observers involved in order to give the impression of a full Warsaw Pact representation, but for understandable historical political reasons and fear of inflaming reaction from Czech nationalists no actual East German units crossed the border into Czechoslovakia itself.[17]

The Czechoslovak media reported on Friday 28 June that the exercise would come to an end that weekend and the Soviet forces would go home. The following Monday, the government in Prague said the exercise was over and the Soviet troops were about to leave. They did not leave. The following day, the Soviet news agency, TASS, retracted a previous statement that the exercise was over. Some of the Soviet forces which formed the frontline of the Warsaw Pact defence in East Germany did return to barracks, but more than 6,000 would remain in Czechoslovakia. GCHQ noted that their communications had taken on a 'distinctly suspicious appearance'.

The signing of the NPT and the announcement of Kosygin's acceptance of further talks on strategic arms limitation went ahead as agreed but by now, the CIA was beginning to see the Warsaw Pact troop movements as more than intimidation. An intelligence assessment of the crisis noted that 'the force that is in Czechoslovakia, even if only a token force, is a reminder of Moscow's readiness to involve itself militarily and to intervene in force'.[18]

The CIA concerns were heightened by reports that Yakubovsky was unhappy with how the exercise had gone and keen for a rerun. The President's Daily Brief noted that 'Prague rightly sees more than military training in this request and the issue has been sent to the highest Soviet and Czechoslovak levels for resolution'. Leonid Brezhnev, clearly aligning himself with the hardliners in the Soviet Politburo, made three speeches within the space of a week complaining about the West's attempts at 'ideological subversion' of eastern Europe. 'Although neither side wants to push the dispute to the point of military conflict, they are skating on thin ice,' the President's Daily Brief reported, adding that 'Moscow's unwillingness to remove its troops is particularly disturbing'.[19]

On 11 July, with Soviet troops still in Czechoslovakia, *Pravda* carried another 'Aleksandrov' article accusing the leading reformers of having 'embarked on the course of overthrowing the existing system and restoring capitalist ways'. Given that it was written by a senior member of the party, almost certainly a Politburo member, this ought to have made the JIC realise that the writing was on the wall, not least because for the first time it directly linked what was going on in Czechoslovakia to Hungary in 1956. The Czechoslovak reformers were making the same false claims that their reforms adhered to socialist principles as their Hungarian predecessors, the author said, but they were doing so in an 'even more sophisticated and perfidious' fashion.[20]

Unsurprisingly, given the clear message that what was happening in Czechoslovakia was worse than the reforms that precipitated the 1956 invasion of Hungary, the article caused a stir across the Soviet Bloc, not least in Moscow itself. The section on Czechoslovakia in the Presidential Brief for the following day was entirely redacted by the CIA ahead of its public release. This was almost certainly because it included reaction among senior Soviet officials heard discussing the article on their car radio telephones. The conversations were intercepted by a top secret CIA–NSA signals intelligence operation codenamed Gamma Guppy based on the tenth floor of the US embassy in Moscow and by a similar GCHQ intercept team inside the British mission.[21]

By now, the view in Washington about the likelihood of invasion was beginning to change. In a personal memo to Dick Helms, written late on 12 July, Abbot Smith warned that 'the chances for a violent Soviet intervention have sharply increased'. He was not alone in his concerns. Influential figures among the US administration's security specialists, including national security adviser Walt Rostow, David McManis, an NSA official who was deputy chief of the White House Situation Room, and Chip Bohlen, the US ambassador in Moscow during the invasion of Hungary and now a senior State Department official, were convinced the Russians would invade Czechoslovakia unless the reforms were reversed. The slow realisation within the State Department that things might go wrong led a few days later to the production of a contingency paper which accepted there would be little America and its NATO allies could do militarily and instead discussed options for dealing with any Soviet intervention through the UN.[22]

On 14 July, Brezhnev and Kosygin met the party leaders of East Germany, Poland, Hungary and Bulgaria in Warsaw to discuss the crisis. Both Walter Ulbricht and Władysław Gomułka were extremely concerned that the Prague Spring was encouraging calls for reforms in their own parties. The communist leaders agreed a joint letter to their Czechoslovak counterparts which was uncompromisingly blunt and again ought to have left little doubt that military intervention was on the agenda.

In what was effectively an enunciation of what would become known as the 'Brezhnev doctrine'—under which the Soviet Union reserved the right to invade any country which appeared to be slipping out of its orbit—the Warsaw participants described the situation as 'completely unacceptable'. Attempts by 'enemy forces' to restore capitalism in Czechoslovakia threatened to unravel the entire communist system across the Soviet Bloc. They warned Prague that 'this is no longer your affair alone. The frontiers of the socialist world in Europe are situated along the Elbe and the Sumava

Mountains. We shall never accept that the historic achievements of socialism and the independence and security of our peoples are threatened. The peoples of our countries would never forgive us our indifference and carelessness in the face of such danger.'[23]

Although the JIC continued to argue that the Soviet leadership's focus on détente and arms talks meant that it would try very hard to avoid an invasion, the Wilson government acknowledged that it remained a risk. During discussions in cabinet shortly after details of the letter from the Warsaw meeting became known, Michael Stewart, who had succeeded George Brown as foreign secretary, repeated the Foreign Office and JIC argument that 'the Soviet Union was clearly hoping to intimidate the present Czechoslovak Government or to promote its overthrow. Only if these tactics failed might they feel obliged to resort to armed force.' This remained the JIC line and while it allowed for the possibility of an invasion, the 'might' ensured it was taken to mean that it would not happen. The cabinet agreed that even if it did 'there could be no question of military intervention by the Western Powers'.[24]

The following day, the Soviet Politburo demanded a meeting with the Czechoslovak leadership either in Moscow or 'if more convenient for the Czechoslovak colleagues' in the Ukrainian cities of Kiev or L'vov. It coincided with the emergence in Moscow of some of the results of the KGB's attempts to undermine the Czechoslovak reformers. *Pravda* revealed the discovery of a cache of US-made weapons 10 miles west of the Karlovy Vary spa, close to Czechoslovakia's border with West Germany, and quoted from a US military document on CIA operations to train East European 'insurgent elements' in sabotage and revolution.

At this point, Andrei Grechko and Ivan Yakubovsky were recalled to Moscow for consultations and, unbeknown to Western intelligence, Brezhnev asked fellow Politburo member Petro Shelest, who as Ukrainian Communist Party leader was not based in Moscow and was therefore less high-profile, to make contact with conservatives in the Czechoslovak Communist Party with a view to securing an invitation for Moscow to intervene to prevent 'the imminent danger of counterrevolution'. With the assistance of János Kádár,

Shelest met Vasil' Bil'ak, a relatively conservative member of the Czechoslovak party presidium, at Kádár's *dacha* at Balatonfüred, a party retreat on the shores of Lake Balaton, south-west of Budapest, and along with a number of other conservatives persuaded him to request military assistance.[25]

Meanwhile, the CIA noted that while the build-up of troops in early May and the exercise in June had looked very much like psychological pressure rather than preparations for invasion, from mid-July onwards Soviet military activity had intensified in ways that went far beyond simple intimidation. On 23 July, the Soviet military announced a two-week rear-services 'mobilisation and logistics' exercise, codenamed Nyeman, throughout the western Soviet Union, from Latvia in the north to Ukraine in the south. Reservists were recalled, large amounts of civilian transport were requisitioned and military equipment that had been mothballed was restored to use in what the CIA described as 'an unprecedented move in peacetime'.

At the same time, British and US military signals intelligence sites intercepted the communications of a significant number of Soviet troops based in East Germany and Poland leaving their barracks and moving south to reinforce those already lined up along the Czechoslovak border. The exercise communications control station moved to the Soviet military's command bunker at Legnica in Poland, just 30 miles from the Czechoslovak border, from where Marshal Yakubovsky was to direct the exercise and the subsequent invasion.[26]

The President's Daily Brief for 24 July described the announcement of the 'massive military exercise' near the Czechoslovak border as having 'all but put a gun on the table' ahead of talks between the two countries' leaderships. The concerns about the possibility of a Soviet invasion of Czechoslovakia were raised later that day at President Johnson's Tuesday lunch, but were shot down by Dean Rusk, who remained focused on the agreement with Kosygin on strategic arms limitation, what would become the so-called SALT talks. The Czechoslovak dispute was nearly over, he said. 'The real crisis has subsided. We don't want to spoil the deal.'[27]

Two days later, with more Soviet divisions moving south, the CIA reported that Poland was under pressure to prepare for an invasion, with five Polish Army divisions in the Silesia area bordering on Czechoslovakia placed at a state of high readiness. Meanwhile, British and US military signals intelligence units reported that three East German Army divisions had moved into the temporary restricted area covering the border with Czechoslovakia. The USAF deployed a number of SR-71 Blackbird reconnaissance aircraft to gather imagery of the Warsaw Pact troops lined up along the border between West and East Germany.[28]

That same day, Chip Bohlen wrote to Rusk expressing his own grave concern. As a Soviet expert and a former ambassador, he found the tone of the Soviet media far 'shriller' than normal, which given his presence in Moscow during the Hungarian invasion ought to have carried some weight. *Pravda*, the party newspaper and clearly closest to the Soviet leadership's thinking, was talking of 'counter-revolution' taking place in Prague and insisting 'action is necessary to forestall this coup', and the Soviet Army newspaper, *Krasnaya Zvezda*, was reporting the combat readiness of the Soviet military increasing 'day by day and hour by hour'. Meanwhile, more Soviet divisions were moving south towards the Czechoslovak border. 'I find the military preparations somewhat excessive for a war of nerves,' Bohlen said, adding that it looked as if the Soviet forces were 'making final preparation for a move into Czechoslovakia'.[29]

The Soviet Politburo and its Czech equivalent, the Czechoslovak Communist party presidium, met over five days beginning on 29 July in the local railwaymen's club in the town of Čierna nad Tisou on the border with Ukraine for what were tough talks. They began angrily on the Soviet side and ended with agreement that some of the domestic reforms could continue so long as the Czechoslovak media stopped publishing articles critical of the Soviet Union and other members of the Warsaw Pact. The Russians also agreed to remove the remaining 6,000 troops, but only after demanding the right to station Soviet troops in western Czechoslovakia permanently to protect the border with West Germany.[30]

Despite the apparent agreement, the President's Daily Brief noted that 'the Soviet military build-up opposite Czechoslovakia continues relentlessly'. As the two leaderships met, the temporary restricted area along East Germany's border with Czechoslovakia was expanded to close off the entire south-east corner of East Germany to BRIXMIS, its US counterpart and foreign visitors, while the Soviet authorities announced that the rear-services exercise had been extended to include East Germany and Poland.

Soviet forces based in Hungary moved into assembly areas close to the border with Czechoslovakia while troops based in the Baltic republics and Byelorussia began moving into Poland. The CIA also reported that the Soviet SS-4 Sandal medium-range ballistic missiles which lined the western border of the Soviet Union were in an increased state of readiness, an obvious contingency measure in case of any Western military reaction to an invasion. Len Parkinson, a senior officer in the Agency's Office of Strategic Research, said the analysts were able to detect that the SS-4 crews were 'performing certain critical work' to prepare for a potential attack only as a result of operational detail revealed in Oleg Penkovsky's Ironbark material seven years earlier.[31]

The meeting in Čierna nad Tisou was followed by a further meeting in Bratislava which included the East German, Polish, Hungarian and Bulgarian party leaderships. Bil'ak slipped out of the meeting for a pre-arranged visit to the lavatory during which he surreptitiously passed an invitation to the Soviet leadership to intervene 'with all the means at your disposal' to a waiting KGB officer. Shelest then made his own visit to the lavatory so the KGB officer could pass the invitation on to him, later recalling that when he took Leonid Brezhnev aside at the end of the day's talk to hand him the letter, the Soviet leader 'took it with his hands trembling and his face pale'.[32]

When 'Nyeman' came to an end on 10 August, it was immediately followed by a 'Staff and Signals' exercise, essentially yet another command post exercise which had no need for large numbers of troops on the ground, let alone the thirty-odd Warsaw Pact divisions that were now in place. Grechko and Yakubovsky toured the troops to ensure that everything was going according to plan. Nevertheless, even at this late stage, the JIC explanation for the exercises and what was by any standards an unprecedented peacetime build-up of Warsaw Pact forces, naïvely remained that they were 'part of the psychological warfare being waged against Czechoslovakia'.

Apparently satisfied with what he had seen, Grechko flew back to Moscow, calling Brezhnev immediately his aircraft landed. 'When he arrived back at Moscow airport, we were able to intercept a telephone call Grechko made to Brezhnev,' a former US intelligence officer said. 'The problem is they were no fools and spoke in a word code—the moon is red or some silly phrase—and we didn't have the faintest idea whether that meant the invasion was on or off.'[33]

The military exercises were not simply intimidation. Ultimately, they were rehearsals for an invasion, in case Dubček and his colleagues did not fall back into line, testing all the systems to ensure they worked, and when Grechko flew back to Moscow his telephone call to Brezhnev was to say that the troops were in place should the Soviet leadership decide to invade.[34]

The Politburo met to make a final decision as to whether to invade on 18 August. That morning, Pravda had carried a third 'Aleksandrov' article setting the stage for intervention. It portrayed Czechoslovakia as being in a state of anarchy with 'fresh, vicious attempts by right-wing, reactionary forces aimed at undermining socialism, discrediting the party and separating Czechoslovakia from the socialist community'. That night the communications among the Warsaw Pact divisions on the border and between those divisions and the command bunker at Legnica went quiet, maintaining total radio silence for the next forty-eight hours. The following day, the NSA issued an alert to the US intelligence community warning that it appeared the Soviet Union was about to invade Czechoslovakia. In the White House Situation Room, David McManis sent Walt Rostow a brief note to say the invasion they were both expecting was imminent.[35]

It is unclear how much of the intelligence collected by the CIA was passed to MI6, although in a situation like this it is likely to have been the large bulk of it, as indeed would be the case in terms of sharing the other way. But under the joint collection and exchange arrangements between the US and British signals intelligence operations, GCHQ should have been seeing exactly the same material as the NSA. It is therefore far from clear why its reporting did not persuade the JIC's current intelligence group to change its assessments.

The official GCHQ history notes that there were problems at the time due to the NSA's switch to computerised communications logs and a move to consolidate the centre for all US military signals intelligence operations at Augsburg in Bavaria, both issues confirmed by the internal NSA history. There also seems to have been a surprising scepticism by at least one senior GCHQ official over the importance of 'radio silence'. The DIS rightly concluded that, given that in normal operations the Soviet military could not avoid using radio communications, radio silence would betray that something was afoot. But the senior GCHQ official dismissed this suggestion. The UK 'must put this whole business of "radio silence" in context,' the official said. 'Frankly—so far as the Soviet Army is concerned—we have no real evidence of any attempts to put such a concept into practice.' Unless his or her claim referred solely to the Soviet troops gathered on the border with Czechoslovakia at some specific moment before Yakubovsky ordered radio silence on 18 August, it did not reflect reality on the frontline of signals intelligence collection and might explain why GCHQ did not take the same course as the NSA.[36]

On the morning of 20 August, the UPI news agency reported that the entire Politburo was back in Moscow for an emergency meeting, not realising that it had already taken place a day earlier. It pointed out that a Politburo meeting at the height of summer when the Soviet leadership would normally be at their holiday homes on the Black Sea was highly unusual. Bruce Clarke, the CIA director of strategic research, and Richard Lehman, the head of the Agency's Current Intelligence staff, briefed Dick Helms about the UPI report ahead of the president's Tuesday lunch. The three of them agreed that given the NSA warning and the fact that the Warsaw Pact forces were clearly on high alert, the Politburo meeting was almost certainly to give the go-ahead for the invasion.

When Helms arrived in the White House, Johnson and Rusk were deep in conversation away to one side but when the lunch finally got going, Helms told the president about the Politburo meeting and pointed out that all the signs were that it was to order the invasion of Czechoslovakia. 'The President cut me short,' Helms later recalled. '"Dick, that Moscow meeting is to talk about us." I hadn't the slightest idea what the President meant but kept my peace.'[37]

Johnson and Rusk had already decided in pre-lunch conversation that the Politburo meeting was to discuss an announcement due the next day that Johnson had been invited to Leningrad in October for a summit meeting to kick-start the SALT talks, in what would have been the first-ever visit by a US president to the Soviet Union. Johnson was stepping down in January 1969 and saw the initiation of the SALT process as an important legacy.

Later that same day, Soviet ambassador Anatoli Dobrynin asked to see the US president to inform him that at the request of the government in Prague, Warsaw Pact troops had entered Czechoslovakia to end the 'conspiracy of the external and internal forces of aggression against the existing social order'. Johnson called an emergency meeting of the NSC at which 'Bus' Wheeler, chairman of the Joint Chiefs, lamented that 'there is no military action we can take. We do not have the forces to do it.'[38]

The first signals intelligence of the actual invasion came from aircraft carrying Soviet airborne forces who were to take control of Prague airport and other key sites. Brian Tovey, the then head of Soviet reporting at GCHQ, noted that until they took off from their home bases in Vitebsk in northern Byelorussia and Panevėžys in Lithuania and headed for Czechoslovakia, 'none of us could point to any firm SIGINT indication of imminent invasion'. Even then, the aircraft might have been on training runs. The CIA concluded that twenty-five of the more than thirty Warsaw Pact divisions* lined up along Czechoslovakia's northern and eastern borders took part in the invasion, most of them Soviet troops but including four Polish divisions and one Hungarian division, while as many as eight divisions

---

* The final JIC estimate appears to have been twenty-seven Warsaw Pact divisions. A CIA post-mortem put the figure at thirty-three.

were held in reserve, including the three East German divisions, kept out of the action for the same historical political reasons as during the Šumava rehearsal.[39]

Oliver Kirby, the NSA's assistant director of production during the crisis, agreed with Tovey that there was no definitive confirmation from signals intelligence that the Soviet troops were preparing to invade although he added that the number of divisions waiting on the border was a fairly good indicator. 'We saw the build-up of troops beforehand and watched what happened there,' he said. 'It wasn't real clear until the blow fell, but you had a pretty good idea, because of the reserve that was built up, what was going to happen. It was a case where SIGINT would give you an indication of something about to happen, but there's nothing you can do about it.'[40]

Despite the advent of the Keyhole satellites, the vast bulk of the intelligence came from signals intelligence. A satellite was tasked to collect imagery of Czechoslovakia and the region in early to mid-August but its canister was not collected until after the invasion had taken place. When it was, and NPIC was able to analyse the imagery, it showed a massive build-up of military aircraft at Soviet air bases in East Germany, Poland and the western Soviet Union, extending as far north as the Baltic republics, and white crosses painted on the roofs and sides of all of the vehicles of the Warsaw Pact forces waiting on the border to distinguish them from the identical Czechoslovak Army vehicles, an analysis which as the CIA said 'could have permitted a better assessment of a Soviet intent to intervene as opposed to the continuation of a war of nerves'.[41]

The satellite imagery and Brezhnev's manoeuvring to obtain an invitation from Vasil' Bil'ak and his fellow conservatives to justify military intervention was the only intelligence not available to the US and UK agencies at the time. There was some imagery intelligence from SR-71 Blackbird flights, and RAF and USAF reconnaissance aircraft flying along the air corridors from West Germany to Berlin. But the vast majority came from signals intelligence, most of it American, for purely geographical reasons—the US Army's signals intelligence units in West Germany were based in the south, much closer to Czechoslovakia, while the British were in the north. All of this intelligence was shared between the NSA and GCHQ. As was the photographic evidence between the respective imagery analysis bodies, NPIC for the US and JARIC for the UK. Much of the rest was either intelligence gathered by BRIXMIS and its US counterpart, or open-source intelligence produced by the BBC Monitoring Service at Caversham Park, and in both cases also shared between the British and the Americans.[42]

Douglas Nicoll, a former Bletchley Park codebreaker who had gone on to become deputy director of GCHQ, was asked to produce a study of how well British intelligence and the JIC in particular had done in assessing and reporting to government on a number of acts of aggression by foreign governments, including the 1968 invasion of Czechoslovakia. As a former head of GCHQ's 'Z' Division, which distributed the UK SIGINT reports, and with a lifetime of experience in signals intelligence, Nicoll was well qualified to make such judgements. He noted that from March 1968, when it decided 'that intervention was probably a politically unacceptable option for the Russians' right through to the invasion itself on 20 August, the JIC 'consistently took the view that the USSR was unlikely to invade Czechoslovakia because of the effect a move would have on world opinion (not least in the world Communist movement) and on détente'.

Certainly, there was no point in the crisis when it was possible to say that the Russians were definitely going to invade, but the weight of the intelligence available during the month before the invasion was such that the JIC judgement that the second and third extended command post exercises were just 'part of the psychological warfare being waged against Czechoslovakia' seems perverse. With GCHQ and the NSA unable to break the Soviet military ciphers, only an unlikely CIA or MI6 agent-in-place within the highest levels of the Soviet political or military leadership could have produced advance intelligence that a decision to invade had been taken.

Nicoll made a similar point to that made by Chip Bohlen and the CIA analysts who had revised the Agency's position a month before the invasion. The Šumava exercise inside Czechoslovakia in late June, and the slow withdrawal of the troops, bore all the hallmarks of a war of nerves, but what happened from mid-July onwards did not. If the aim was purely psychological pressure, two command post exercises requiring few if any troops scarcely made the most of the formidable military power sat on the other side of the border. As Nicoll said: 'The Czechs could not possibly have had any idea of the size of the build-up around them.'

Nicoll pointed to two major failings that affected the JIC's judgement that the Soviet Union was unlikely to invade. Firstly, 'mirror imaging'. The committee had overestimated 'the value placed by the USSR on world opinion' and made a judgement more in line with what constraints a British government might consider in a similar position. 'The JIC analysts reasoned that the Soviet Union would hold back from such crude direct intervention given the international condemnation that would inevitably follow,' said Sir David Omand, who subsequently sat on the JIC over a period of seven years, first as GCHQ director and then as UK intelligence and security coordinator. 'That verb "reasoned" carries the explanation of why the analysts got it wrong: they were reasonable people trying to predict the actions of an unreasonable regime. When they put themselves in the shoes of the decision makers in Moscow, they still thought exclusively from their own perspective.'

Secondly, the JIC had fallen into the trap of 'perseveration', sticking with an initial judgement long after the facts that led to that judgement had changed. And given the disproportionate influence the Foreign Office had over JIC decision-making it is hard not to suspect that there was a third element, of believing, in much the same way as President Johnson, that what it wanted to happen would happen. As one of the world's five nuclear powers, and with both France and China having refused to be a party to the NPT, détente had given Britain a prominent role on the world stage which the Foreign Office was reluctant to lose.[43]

THE LOWEST POINT

The early 1970s were undoubtedly the worst period of the post-war relationship between Britain and America with Conservative prime minister Ted Heath deliberately distancing himself from the Nixon administration in order to prevent a third French veto of Britain's entry to the EEC. Heath, a passionate pro-European who had negotiated the first failed attempt by the Macmillan government to join the 'Common Market' and watched as opposition leader when Harold Wilson's 1967 attempt suffered the same fate, was determined that the UK should gain entry. He was so intent on distancing himself from the US that he told French president Georges Pompidou 'there could be no special partnership between Britain and the United States, even if Britain wanted it'.

After taking over the leadership of the Conservative Party in 1965, Heath had set out in a series of lectures at Harvard his belief that Britain's post-war role should be as a prominent member of the European 'community' rather than as a subordinate partner of America. This tallied with the view of the State Department, which, as Bill Stephenson, the MI6 wartime representative in America, had suggested back in 1942, was determined to ensure that Britain should not emerge from the Second World War as anything other than a means for the US of maintaining strong links to, and thereby control of, Europe in the post-war world. But Heath was not interested in being America's means of controlling Europe. Indeed, he was determined that this should not be the case because he was concerned that it would poison the well and prevent the other EEC leaders from trusting him.

Shortly after becoming prime minister, amid the forcible removal of the population of the Indian Ocean island of Diego Garcia to create a strategic Anglo-American naval and signals intelligence base, Heath ordered a comprehensive examination of what Britain got out of allowing America to use so many bases in the United Kingdom and throughout the Commonwealth. He had to be persuaded by Alec Douglas-Home, his foreign secretary, and Lord Carrington, the defence secretary, that the intelligence and assistance on updating and testing of nuclear weapons that the British received in return more than compensated for allowing the Americans access to the bases. Carrington went on to explain that since key US and British decision makers were working from the best available intelligence that in its totality was available only to them, the British prime minister was the only other world leader with whom the US president could have 'a meaningful exchange on matters of common interest from a basis of common intelligence'.[1]

Richard Nixon saw great value in the Special Relationship, frequently referring to it in positive fashion, and even expressing his regret that the US reaction to the Suez crisis, when he was vice-president under Eisenhower, had diminished the position of America's greatest and most powerful Western ally to the detriment of US interests. Both he and his national security adviser Henry Kissinger were dismissive of the views of the pro-Europeans within the State Department, which under Nixon found itself sidelined and its position on Europe ignored. Kissinger recalled that Heath's determination to end the Special Relationship left the US president feeling like 'a jilted lover'.[2]

Nixon's support for the UK 'gave no little pain to many of the European integrationists' in the State Department, Kissinger said. 'The advocates—almost fanatics—of European unity were eager to terminate the Special Relationship with our oldest ally as an alleged favour to Britain to smooth its entry into the Common Market. They felt it essential to deprive Britain of any special status with us lest it impede Britain's role in the Europe they cherished. I considered the attacks from within our government on the Special Relationship as petty and formalistic. Severing our Special Relationship—assuming it could be done—would undermine British self-confidence and gain us nothing. Even if desirable, which I doubted, this was impractical.

'The Special Relationship with Britain was peculiarly impervious to abstract theories. It did not depend on formal arrangements. It derived in part from the memory of Britain's heroic wartime effort. It reflected the common language and culture of two sister peoples. It owed no little to the superb self-discipline by which Britain had succeeded in maintaining political influence after its physical power had waned. When Britain emerged from the Second World War too enfeebled to insist on its views, it wasted no time in mourning its irretrievable past. British leaders instead tenaciously elaborated the Special Relationship with us.

'This was, in effect, a pattern of consultation so matter-of-factly intimate that it became psychologically impossible to ignore British views. Above all, they used an abundance of wisdom and trustworthiness of conduct so exceptional that successive American leaders saw it in their self-interest to obtain British advice before taking major decisions. It was an extraordinary relationship because it rested on no legal claims. It was formalised by no document. It was carried forward by successive British governments as if no alternative were conceivable. Britain's influence was great precisely because it never insisted on it.'[3]

Certainly, there was no single political agreement covering the relationship and Kissinger was right in describing the determination of a succession of British prime ministers and senior civil servants to regard it as being heavily in the UK's interest to maintain the Special Relationship, but there was one formal agreement which, from its signing in 1946 right up to the present day, has played as fundamental a role in keeping the Special Relationship alive as any of the politicians on either side. The UKUSA Accord, and the shared intelligence it produced, combined with what was predominantly a shared liberal, democratic worldview throughout the Cold War, formed the real basis for the close relationship between Britain and America.

The reactions of the governments in London and Washington to various world events in the Soviet Bloc and the Middle East during

the late 1960s and early 1970s only served to show how close, and
how important, the intelligence exchange between Britain and
America had become, in particular with regard to signals intelligence. On occasion, US interests would override UK judgements
but, for the most part, the way in which not just the intelligence
itself but coverage of the world was shared between the NSA and
GCHQ, and human intelligence freely exchanged between the CIA
and MI6, inevitably led US presidents and UK prime ministers to
come to similar conclusions on how to react and what might be the
most sensible way forward.

The MI6 reports from Hanoi, which frequently made their way
into the President's Daily Brief, always cited the British consul-
general and so were obviously supplied by the UK, but that was
extremely unusual. More often, policy makers on both sides of the
Atlantic were completely unaware as to whether the intelligence
they were receiving came from US or British sources, or indeed
both, with one qualifying or confirming the other, making the NSA
and GCHQ, and to a lesser extent the CIA and MI6, dependent on
each other and perpetuating the Special Relationship in a way that
the State Department had never envisaged.

The relationship between GCHQ and the NSA, already close,
developed exponentially during Joe Hooper's time as GCHQ
director, in part as a result of his own friendship with NSA deputy
director Lou Tordella, who was himself a passionate supporter of
the UKUSA relationship. Tordella controlled the NSA's liaison with
the British codebreakers from the late 1950s to the mid-1970s and
made it very clear that it could not simply be a question of sharing
intelligence. It was a joint intelligence production programme and
GCHQ would have to produce the goods across the board if the
British were to remain at the top table, particularly in the future
when NSA officials with no memories of wartime cooperation began
to take charge.

Michael Herman, a senior GCHQ official, recalled that Hooper
'took the maintenance of the UK–US alliance to be the keystone of
intelligence policy and supported a variety of joint UK–US operations', while in return, Tordella provided funding to help Hooper

resist Treasury attempts to force GCHQ to focus solely on producing the intelligence the UK itself required. Hooper would later
point to that funding as one of the reasons the British and Americans
were so closely bound together. 'I know I have leaned shamefully
on you, and sometimes taken your name in vain, when I sometimes
needed approval for something at this end,' Hooper told then NSA
director Pat Carter. 'Between us, we have ensured that the blankets
and sheets are more tightly tucked around the bed in which our two
sets of people lie and, like you, I like it that way.'*

The Americans had the money to cover areas GCHQ simply could
not reach, in particular with satellites, pioneering radio technology
and computers. But the different approaches by the codebreakers on
either side of the Atlantic still meant that, just like their wartime
predecessors at Bletchley Park, the British could often break ciphers
which the NSA could not, provide a different perspective on a piece
of intelligence, and indeed correct the errors that inevitably resulted
from rushed analysis. The NSA was under constant pressure to provide intelligence fast, whereas the British tended to take more time
analysing the detail, often providing a more accurate result.

'The US continues to value the UK's contribution, in spite of
our smaller resources,' Hooper said after a trip to the NSA's Fort
Meade HQ. 'They will assist us when opportunities occur in which
they can see advantages to themselves but not otherwise. We cannot
expect them to respond to positive requests for assistance solely
in order to contain or reduce our own expenditure or resources.
They will gladly discuss with us means of achieving greater interdependence but will wish us to retain independent capabilities in
areas where independent judgement and skill can contribute to the
partnership as a whole for that is one of our major values to them.'⁴

Even within the Foreign Office there was often a lack of
understanding among quite senior officials of the extent to which
intelligence was exchanged with the Americans, and the value the
US agencies put on British analysis and reporting. At one point,

---

* After his retirement, Tordella was appointed an Honorary Knight Commander of the Most
Excellent Order of the British Empire in gratitude for his work with GCHQ.

James Cable, head of the Foreign Office Planning Staff, complained that the Defence Intelligence Staff was paying far too much attention to 'intelligence and analysis concerning areas of the world where the British armed forces are never likely to play a significant part'.

Derek Tonkin, a senior official in the Foreign Office Permanent Under-Secretary's Department, which coordinated with the intelligence services, went out of his way to explain why it was important for political reasons that UK intelligence collection and analysis was not limited solely to information the British themselves were likely to need. 'There are very real British interests, more of a political than an intelligence nature, which make it most desirable that our contribution to the Anglo-American intelligence exchange should not diminish significantly,' he noted. 'The balance of advantage in this intelligence exchange is overwhelmingly in our favour. If the Americans were to withdraw their contribution, we would lose much extremely useful intelligence, including certain very important lines of intelligence which only the Americans can supply.

'The Americans need us, both for the intrinsic value of our contribution—especially our assessments—but also because they find it extremely useful, particularly in times of crisis, to have a sounding board against which they can judge their own assessments. The intelligence exchange with the Americans is perhaps the last bastion of the "Special Relationship". But it is still very active and very effective. This is accepted by those of influence in the American administration and the relationship pays us very useful dividends. The relationship gives us an *entrée* to American political thinking in a way that no other country is able to benefit.'[5]

The relationship was by no means one-sided. Where both the British interest and its capability were strong, the Americans were happy to save money by relying on them, as for example with the signals intelligence base at Ayios Nikolaos in Cyprus. Although ostensibly a British Army base, it also had Royal Navy personnel and a number of GCHQ operators and analysts, while Soviet and Middle East air targets were monitored by the RAF's 33 Signals Unit a short distance away at Pergamos. The combined GCHQ-controlled operation had an astonishing reach, not just in the Middle

East and the Mediterranean but across the Black Sea and deep into the Soviet Union, including the missile test sites at Kapustin Yar and Tyuratam. As a result, much of the US signals intelligence from the region was actually collected by the British, tying the NSA and GCHQ together like Siamese twins. An internal history of the NSA noted that by 1970 the British and American intercept and code-breaking operations 'had become virtually inseparable'.[6]

'Collaboration remained almost total,' it said. 'The key decisions that kept the two countries closely tied related generally to advances into new technological realms. At each bend of the road, NSA made a conscious decision to remain engaged. Each country lived with the foibles of the other. The American tendency to leak everything significant to the press was counterbalanced in England by the Official Secrets Act, by which the government tried, often unsuccessfully, to stop publication of material regarded as "sensitive".

'GCHQ employees were unionised from an early date, and this introduced some interesting twists to the relationship. Politically, the Left in England was stronger than in the US, and they employed some novel techniques to attempt to wreck the intelligence business. One such was the device of "public footpaths", a mediaeval concept by which, under British common law, paths that had been used by walkers in previous centuries were required to be kept open. Diligent British researchers discovered footpaths across [the NSA bases at] Chicksands and Menwith Hill and would endeavour, at least once a year, to walk them to maintain the concept. Having walkers wandering through signals intelligence antenna fields was not what a typical base commander had in mind.'[7]

Where there were political difficulties between the two sides, they tended to be caused not by Ted Heath's determination to demonstrate his belief in Britain's European future at the expense of the Special Relationship, but by the personalities of the three major players, himself, Nixon and Kissinger. All three men were swift to take offence in a way that sometimes risked descending into petulance. Nixon was distrustful of the US establishment, the outsiders' outsider, and anxious to maintain control at all times. Kissinger was no less controlling, deliberately sidelining the State

Department, and overseeing all of the intelligence that reached the president.[8]

During Nixon's first meeting with Heath at Chequers, the prime minister's official country residence, in October 1970, the US president stressed how keen he was that they establish 'a close personal communication' between them. 'If anything comes up, please call it right,' Nixon said. 'The need for communication has never been greater. We will continue to face major problems in the Middle East. SALT is quite undetermined. Tell us where you disagree. We will feel free to ask your advice. We do not want to be the only country making foreign policy.'[9]

Heath soon came to see the reality as somewhat different. He was irritated that, despite discussing Britain's relationship with China in some depth with Nixon, the US president did not confide in him over Kissinger's negotiations with the Chinese for his state visit to China, a prelude to establishing diplomatic relations, until four days before the visit was announced in July 1971. A month later, Heath was furious when Nixon gave him no warning of the US cancellation of the Bretton Woods Agreement, under which the major world currencies, including the pound, were tied to the dollar. At the Bermuda summit in December that year, Nixon and Kissinger went out of their way to explain the reasoning behind both decisions and the president sought to reassure Heath that he was keen to hear his views. 'We'd like to keep you informed on a personal basis,' he said. 'We must have better communications. We feel that you should take an active role in world affairs. We should reach some sort of agreement on general objectives.'[10]

Even so, in reality, contact between Nixon and Heath was limited, albeit initially at least on friendly terms, with the US president particularly grateful for the British prime minister's support over the bombing of Hanoi—alone among America's closest allies; even Australia condemned it—and for his expression of sympathy over the Watergate crisis, passed on via Kissinger, along with an assurance that so far as the British prime minister was concerned his dealings with the White House would continue to be 'business as usual' no matter what.

But interaction between the two men was largely controlled behind the scenes by back channels, initially between Kissinger and the British ambassador, Lord Cromer, and from July 1972 onwards via the cabinet secretary, Sir Burke Trend. Kissinger's often tempestuous personality and his blanket control over the intelligence Nixon received, and just as importantly how it was presented, is frequently blamed for doing more harm than good to the Special Relationship, but the records of his top secret talks with Trend suggest this is vastly overplayed. In a letter to Heath briefing him on the first set of talks, in July 1972, the British cabinet secretary stressed how helpful and friendly Kissinger had been. 'One always has to take what he says with several grains of salt,' Trend said. 'But I have little doubt that he is speaking sincerely and in earnest when he assures us—as he assured me several times—that, so far as the President and he himself are concerned, there is the maximum of basic goodwill towards the United Kingdom within the necessary limits imposed by United States interests and the realities of domestic politics.'

At any event, Kissinger's accumulation of power over US foreign policy meant not only that he spoke for the president but that he was the only person in the administration the British needed to speak to in order to determine US positions on foreign and defence policy, even before September 1973 when he took a joint role as secretary of state as well as national security adviser. The talks between Trend and Kissinger covered every area of foreign policy in great detail, including the negotiations with the Soviet Union on reducing the numbers of forces and nuclear weapons.

Kissinger also reassured the British cabinet secretary that the Nixon administration was committed to helping the UK keep its own nuclear forces up to date and would not agree to a limitation on transference of nuclear technology as part of the SALT talks, a key British fear at the time. For the most part, Kissinger had an extremely good working relationship with the impeccably correct and measured Trend, who, despite Heath's initial doubts over his previously close relationship with Harold Wilson, was completely trusted by the British prime minister. As a result of managing the intelligence budget, the so-called Secret Vote, during his time in the Treasury, Trend also had substantial experience of dealing with GCHQ and MI6 and understood their value to the relations with the US.[11]

The late 1960s and early 1970s were a time of mass computerisation, with the NSA, which had substantially more funding than its British partners, forging ahead in the number of computers it used. NSA director Pat Carter later recalled that during his time in charge, in the late 1960s, the NSA's computers occupied 240,000 square feet of the agency's Fort Meade headquarters.

The limited capabilities of the early British post-war computers led GCHQ to rely largely on US computer technology, with GCHQ's own specialists understanding the technology and future possibilities in a way the UK computer industry could not match. In addition to Ralph Canine's gift of 'Effigy', the Atlas II computer he presented to Eric Jones, the Americans funded GCHQ's computer development to the tune of 10 per cent of the UK service's annual budget over a nine year period between the mid-1950s and mid-1960s, giving GCHQ the largest number of computers of any organisation outside the US.

The most important development in computing technology in relation to the work of the NSA and GCHQ came in 1976 with the creation of the Cray-1 supercomputer. The NSA secretly acquired the first Cray-1, using it to break back into the high-grade ciphers employed by the Soviet Foreign Ministry to talk to its ambassadors abroad. Given this spectacular success, GCHQ purchased its own Cray-1, allowing it to use the same bespoke Folklore operating system as the NSA and further enhance the close working relationship between the two agencies. It came at a price. A Cray-1 cost $8 million (around £112 million at today's values). It was 6 feet high and 9 feet in diameter. Its processing speed was 80 megahertz, compared to the 3.1 gigahertz of an iPhone 12, and it had an 8.39 megabyte memory as opposed to the iPhone's 4 gigabyte memory.

During the 1970s, GCHQ more than doubled the number of American IBM computers it had to the point where they took up 26,000 square feet of space, still only a fraction of the NSA's 5 acres but sufficient for most complex tasks. While lower funding forced

GCHQ staff to patch and adapt their computers, rather than buying in new technology as the NSA was prone to do, that process helped ensure that their computer expertise developed rapidly to match, and in some areas better, that of their US colleagues, with GCHQ employees James Ellis, Clifford Cocks and Malcolm Williamson secretly developing the public key cryptography system, now commonly used for secure internet exchanges such as purchasing goods, in the early 1970s, several years before it was developed independently by US computer scientists Whitfield Diffie, Martin Hellman and Ralph Merkle.[12]

The early 1970s was also a period which saw a considerable rise in international terrorism, in particular that relating to the situation in the Middle East, led by the Palestinian Liberation Organization (PLO), a coalition of various Palestinian guerrilla organisations based in Jordan, Syria, Lebanon and Egypt, of which the two leading groups were Yasser Arafat's Fatah and the Popular Front for the Liberation of Palestine (PFLP). The Israeli occupation of the West Bank during the Six-Day War forced large numbers of Palestinian *fedayeen* fighters to move to Jordan, from where they mounted cross-border attacks on Israel—which inevitably led to retaliation—and undermined the control of the Jordanian authorities.

Meanwhile, the PFLP had begun a series of terrorist 'spectaculars' designed to attract attention to the plight of the Palestinians. In early September 1970, it hijacked four international airliners, flying three of them to Dawson's Field, a former RAF air base near Zarqa in north-west Jordan. Eventually all the hostages were released unharmed but King Hussein ordered a crackdown on the Palestinians, forcing the PLO to move its fighters to Lebanon. 'Black September', the name the Palestinians gave to the Jordanian response, was subsequently used as the banner for the Fatah terror attack on the 1972 Munich Olympics in which eleven Israeli athletes and one German police officer were killed.

As a result of these atrocities, the PLO became a major target for the US and UK agencies, with the British signals intelligence base at Ayios Nikolaos intercepting communications between the group's bases in a number of Arab states and monitoring its activities in Lebanon and Syria intensely. The NSA was slower off the mark and during the 1970s relied heavily on the British. There was also concern within the UK and US agencies over the level of support the Palestinian terrorists were receiving from Moscow, albeit that it was provided only reluctantly and largely limited to supplying arms for attacks on Israel.[13]

The 1973 Yom Kippur War was undoubtedly one of the worst intelligence failures of the UKUSA intelligence partnership. Throughout the spring of 1973, Egyptian president Anwar Sadat, who had come to power in October 1970 after Gamal Abdel Nasser's death from a heart attack, adopted an increasingly tough approach towards Israel over its occupation of the Sinai peninsula. The hard-line rhetoric coming out of Cairo, in which Sadat went so far as to say the time had come for 'all-out confrontation', was accompanied by a number of moves suggesting preparations for war, including the transfer to Egypt from Libya and Iraq of combat aircraft, preparations for civil defence, blood donor drives and increased cooperation by both Egypt and Syria with other Arab states, with Moroccan and Iraqi troops moving to Syria to supplement its armed forces.[14]

Nevertheless, in view of the Israeli military superiority demonstrated in the Six-Day War, the CIA concluded in April 1973 that these measures were not signs that Sadat was preparing an invasion. 'They do, however, seem to indicate an element of bluff, to suggest the intention to either increase pressure on Israel, or the United States, to be more responsive to Egyptian wishes in connection with a peaceful settlement of the Middle East problem, or to divert Egyptian public opinion from focus on dissatisfaction with conditions in Egypt, or both,' the CIA analysts said. 'Given the weak Egyptian military capability against Israel, any military move by Sadat would be an act of desperation. We see no evidence that he is that desperate at present.'[15]

The British took a different view. The MI6 station in Cairo was running a secret back channel to the Egyptian presidency via Ashraf Marwan, a billionaire businessman married to Nasser's daughter Mona. Marwan, who was also talking to Mossad, had passed his MI6 contact 'a tough message . . . to the effect that President Sadat intended to start some attack before long'. This appeared to be backed up by major Egyptian Army exercises on the west bank of the Suez Canal, simulating an invasion of the Sinai peninsula. They were monitored in full by the British signals intelligence base at Ayios Nikolaos. The JIC concluded accurately that Sadat was planning 'a limited attack' across the Suez Canal which would catch the Israelis off guard and recapture Sinai, with the intention of leading the UN, US and USSR to call for a ceasefire to which Sadat could acquiesce, thereby returning the borders to their pre-1967 position.[16]

In early May, Kissinger had a meeting with the Israeli ambassador in Washington, Simcha Dinitz, who asked what information the Americans had on Sadat's plans. Kissinger, who was about to fly to London for talks with his UK counterpart, Alec Douglas-Home, asked the CIA for an assessment of Egyptian and Syrian intentions. The resultant report looked at the build-up of Egyptian and Syrian forces and concluded that it was designed to put psychological pressure not just on Israel but also on the US and the Soviet Union ahead of a UN debate on the Middle East due to take place the following month. In what was to be a recurrent theme of US intelligence assessments ahead of the war, the CIA analysts pointed out that Israeli intelligence shared their view. Sadat would not start a war he could not possibly win. 'Both Sadat and his advisers are aware that their military prospects are poor at best,' the CIA report said. 'A fresh disaster might well sweep away Sadat's regime rather than rescue him from his dilemma.'[17]

During their talks in London, Douglas-Home shared the Marwan message with Kissinger, and Anthony Parsons, head of the Foreign Office Middle East and North Africa Department, told the US national security adviser that Sadat 'seemed to be under an illusion that he could start a limited war and get away with it'. Parsons said that 'the fact was that the roof would fall in on him if he fired a shot at the Israelis' and the British had tried repeatedly to persuade the Egyptians of this, but the response was always that 'if they took action, it would not get out of hand'. Kissinger had a good relationship with his Egyptian counterpart, General Hafez Ismail, Sadat's national security adviser, but their discussions had focused on what

Egypt would accept in terms of a peace deal rather than whether Egypt was prepared to go to war.[18]

As a result, the MI6 intelligence from Marwan led to a demand from Kissinger for a fresh CIA assessment, resulting in a memorandum produced by the Agency's Middle East specialists which, while repeating the previous stance, included a caveat that 'knowledgeable Egyptian observers . . . now believe Sadat is serious and that to consider that he is bluffing is unrealistic and naïve'. It seems likely Marwan's information for MI6 had been shared with the Agency, either at the time or at the very least following its disclosure to Kissinger. The CIA analysts were nevertheless careful to point out that 'the source conceded' that Sadat's preference was for a diplomatic solution albeit that he would resort to hostilities should diplomacy fail.[19]

In a National Intelligence Estimate released three days later, the CIA accepted that Sadat's threats of renewed hostilities were consistent with both preparations to go to war and a campaign designed to push the US and the Soviet Union into producing a peace settlement, but again came down heavily on the side of psychological bluff. 'The Egyptians believe deeply that progress toward solution of the Arab–Israeli problem on terms tolerable to Egypt can only come about through actions of the Great Powers,' the estimate said. 'If Sadat is once again disappointed, the temptation to resort to military action in order to force the US hand might prove irresistible.'

It was possible that Sadat's own rhetoric might raise expectations to the point where a failure on his part to take military action 'would seem to him more dangerous to his own hold on power than attacking and taking the consequences'. But if Egypt did attack Israel 'it will do so in spite of the military consequences, rather than in hope of military gains'. If Sadat decided to go to war, it would end as swiftly as it began, 'with small, brief Egyptian commando raids or Egyptian artillery barrages, and then massive Israeli retaliation'.[20]

Ray Cline, now director of the State Department's Bureau of Intelligence and Research, begged to differ, if only marginally, arguing that the bureau was 'inclined to state the case on the risk of hostilities for a political purpose with a little more urgency' than the CIA. Sadat had no illusions he could beat Israel militarily, Cline said. But if the UN debate did not produce any convincing movement in the Israeli–Egyptian impasse 'our view is that the resumption of hostilities by autumn will become a better than even bet'. The debates at the UN ended with the US vetoing a resolution which 'strongly' condemned Israel's continuing occupation of Arab territory taken during the Six-Day War, leading Sadat to accuse America of being part of 'a conspiracy' designed 'to bring the Arabs to their knees and force them to negotiate with Israel'.[21]

What was not known by the British and US intelligence agencies at that time was that in October 1972 Sadat had ordered his defence chiefs to plan an attack designed to catch the Israelis by surprise, with the intention—as the JIC had correctly suggested—of retaking the territory lost in the Six-Day War. Sadat would then accept the inevitable ceasefire calls from the UN, US and Soviet Union, thereby establishing himself as a worthy successor to Nasser for having recovered the lost territory. These plans led to the creation in January 1973 of a joint Egyptian–Syrian planning group and four months later to the major military exercises monitored by the British signals intelligence base in Cyprus. But although Sadat had hoped that by June the Egyptian forces would be ready to carry out the invasion, they were not and he postponed the attack.[22]

Meanwhile, at the end of July, the goodwill that had been a feature of the Kissinger–Trend conversations fell apart amid differences between America and Europe, and particularly France, which left Britain caught in the middle. The problem was fundamentally caused by Ted Heath's somewhat schizophrenic desire to maintain a strong private bilateral relationship with the US—with Kissinger being completely open with the UK over the SALT talks and the negotiations with Moscow on a deal over 'mutual and balanced force reductions'—while refusing to help push better US relations with Europe without first consulting his EEC colleagues.

Kissinger was furious, telling Trend that it was 'insulting' coming from an ally with which 'we've been more open than any other' and that the relationship between Britain and the US would inevitably be 'severely affected'. Kissinger had in fact already decided to find a way to make Heath realise there were consequences to siding with Europe against the US, telling colleagues that the British were 'behaving shitty' and it was time to 'shoot one across the bow to them brutally now'.[23]

Ten days later, in a response which only served to emphasise that the intelligence relationship was so close it was often impossible to know who had produced what, Kissinger ordered the NSA, CIA and DIA to stop cooperating with their British counterparts. 'I'm cutting them off from intelligence special information they are getting here,' he told Nixon. 'If they are going to share everything with the Europeans, we can't trust them for special relationship.' While this certainly made Kissinger's point in London, he had picked the wrong time to make it.

Bill Bonsall, newly appointed as GCHQ director and the last of the Bletchley Park veterans to take up that post, flew to Washington to try to prevent any break in the relationship. But he had no need to worry; the NSA had already decided that the UKUSA relationship was a contractual agreement that could not legally be broken. This was not, and had never been, the case but with the intelligence agencies focused firmly on the crisis in the Middle East, and the British signals intelligence base in Cyprus the main source of information, the NSA knew US decision makers would lose far more than their UK counterparts as a result of Kissinger's 'brutal' shot across the bows. Nor would the enforced break have affected many CIA stations around the world. A majority of CIA station chiefs would have built up a good relationship with their MI6 counterparts, knowing that it ensured neither side missed important intelligence. Kissinger's orders would not have affected any of the discreet, private exchanges carried out by many of the CIA and MI6 stations in foreign capitals. Nor indeed would it have affected those where there were no such exchanges, which were only rarely the result of reluctance on the part of the local MI6 head of station. Anti-British prejudice has regularly prevented some CIA station chiefs from seeking such a relationship, particularly among those who had Irish forebears, a common occurrence given 10 per cent of Americans claim Irish origins.

'There was one CIA station chief I just couldn't get through to,' one MI6 station head recalled. 'He was Irish American and clearly despised me not for who I was but for what I represented. It was that hatred of the Brits that was instilled in him along with his mother's milk. It was in both our interests that we talked, but he wasn't interested. I'm not a difficult man to get along with but he simply wasn't interested and there was nothing I could do to change that.'

But given that the CIA station chiefs who harboured those prejudices were never going to exchange information anyway, the Kissinger order made no difference one way or the other. The DIA, under somewhat firmer direction from the administration, reacted more resolutely, halting the flow of real-time imagery intelligence collected by the U-2 and SR-71 Blackbird reconnaissance aircraft to the UK, as did the CIA's NPIC, which controlled the satellite imagery. As a result, imagery intelligence was by far the most important data that was lost, albeit briefly, as a result of Kissinger's petulant intervention.[24]

Despite its relative lack of impact on the actual exchange of intelligence, the break in the intelligence exchange inevitably caused concern in London, with the JIC meeting four times to discuss what it meant for the future. It was undecided but the reality was nothing much at all. The UKUSA signals intelligence exchange, the most important element of the relationship, continued unabated. In those relatively few areas where the break was imposed it was only brief and did not affect the ultimate product, it merely delayed its arrival. Nevertheless, the threat led Heath to write a contrite message to Nixon making it clear that 'so far as I am concerned, there is certainly no question of the relationship between your country and mine becoming one of adversaries: and it is very far from my intention that there should be any loosening of the close ties which have bound us together in so many fields for the whole of the post-war period'.[25]

Meanwhile, Sadat had approved the invasion plans and the readiness of the troops in August, with the attack planned for early October. Egyptian preparations for military action were first detected on 22 September by the British Ayios Nikolaos signals intelligence base, which was soon monitoring major military activity that seemed to replicate the previous major exercises carried out on the western bank of the Suez Canal three months earlier. Nevertheless, the JIC had changed its view in the wake of the military activity of May and June and decided that since nothing happened then, it had simply been a training exercise which was now being repeated. It concurred with the views of the Israelis and the Americans that Sadat knew that defeat was inevitable and had therefore decided it was too risky to go ahead.

The Yom Kippur War was one of the international incidents that former Bletchley Park and GCHQ officer Douglas Nicoll looked at in his assessment of how well the JIC had performed in its prediction of international acts of aggression. He suggested it might be that having predicted an invasion that had not taken place in May and June, the JIC had been concerned that repeating that prediction would make its customers in Whitehall suspect that it was 'crying wolf'.

'It may well be that this underlay the committee's reluctance to accept the evidence from Sadat's preparations in September/October 1973 after his failure to move in June,' Nicoll concluded. 'Had the evidence for Egyptian preparations for war in March to June 1973 been collated in detail, I have little doubt that the phenomena of late September/early October would have been identified as a virtual repeat of preparations of April to June 1973 and earlier and more positive warning of the Arab attack would have been given.'[26]

Much like the JIC, Ray Cline's State Department Bureau of Intelligence and Research had backtracked on its earlier belief that Sadat might mount an attack if the UN debates failed to produce movement on the Israeli occupation of Egyptian territory. Examining a claim by Israeli defence minister Moshe Dayan that Syria had massed tanks and artillery behind the Golan Heights, the bureau took the same view as the CIA. If Israel really believed Syria was 'in an advanced state of military preparation' it would already have approached America 'with considerable alarm' to ask for assistance, the bureau said. Since it had not, there was in its view 'no evidence to connect the increased readiness of Egyptian air and air defence units, which went into effect on September 26, with any Syrian military moves'.[27]

Only the analysts in Cyprus, and at the NSA and GCHQ, who

were reading the mass of signals intelligence material on Egyptian and Syrian military preparations, believed that war was imminent. But the JIC was unconvinced by GCHQ's arguments and the NSA found it impossible to persuade the CIA and DIA that this was the case. It was precluded by the national security directive under which it was created from writing 'finished intelligence' reports and so had to go cap in hand to brief Samuel Hoskinson, the CIA's national intelligence officer for the Middle East and the Islamic World, who dismissed its arguments. According to an internal NSA history, Hoskinson said 'the political climate was not right for an attack' and argued that the mass of signals intelligence intercepted on Cyprus was simply 'heightened exercise activity', a repeat of other exercises such as those earlier in the year.[28]

By 5 October, the Israeli intelligence assessment had changed as a result of a warning from Ashraf Marwan to Mossad that Egypt and Syria were about to attack. Israeli prime minister Golda Meir ordered a mobilisation of Israeli reservists and contacted Kissinger, asking him to talk to the Arab and Soviet leaders to say that if the build-up was a result of concerns over Israeli intentions to attack Syria or Egypt they were misplaced. If on the other hand Syria and Egypt were to make an unprovoked attack on Israel, 'it would be important to make it clear to them in advance that Israel will react militarily, with firmness and in great strength'. Kissinger telephoned Egyptian foreign minister Mohammed Hassan Zayyat to pass on the message direct and spoke to Anatoli Dobrynin, the Soviet ambassador in Washington, asking him to pass the message on via Moscow. He also sent personal messages to King Faisal of Saudi Arabia and King Hussein of Jordan asking them to pass the same message to Sadat and his Syrian counterpart, Hafiz Assad.[29]

Even as Kissinger was making these calls, the CIA was reporting that while the exercises monitored by the British in Cyprus 'may be on a somewhat larger scale and more realistic than previous exercises . . . they do not appear to be preparing for a military offensive against Israel'. The DIA was similarly inclined to ignore the evidence, dismissively reporting the Egyptian 'mobilisation of some personnel, increased readiness of isolated units, and greater communication security' as being part of a routine exercise. 'There are still no military or political indicators of Egyptian intentions or preparations to resume hostilities with Israel,' it said in a report released on the morning of 6 October 1973, around the same time as the first shots began to be exchanged across the Suez Canal.

Robert Gates, a future CIA director, was an intelligence adviser to the US delegation to the SALT talks in Geneva at the time. He recalled receiving the daily Central Intelligence Bulletin that morning and taking it into Paul Nitze, one of the delegation's senior officials. The bulletin dismissed the idea that either side was 'bent on initiating hostilities' and went on to state unequivocally that it made no sense whatsoever for Egypt to commence another round of hostilities, 'which would almost certainly destroy Sadat's painstaking efforts to invigorate the economy'. Nor would Assad want to participate in any attack on Israel, the bulletin said; 'a military adventure now would be suicidal, and he has said so'. Gates handed the bulletin to Nitze. 'He looked up at me from his desk and asked if I spoke French and listened to the radio. I replied "No" twice and Nitze proceeded to inform me that had I answered "Yes" I would have known that war had already broken out—because he had found out from the radio news. I slunk out of his office. It was my worst personal intelligence embarrassment.'[30]

Yet even then, with the fighting already taking place, and Egyptian forces advancing across the Suez Canal, the Watch Committee of expert analysts from all of the US intelligence agencies met in special session to discuss what was happening. They concluded in what, given the weight of evidence already flowing in from the British base in Cyprus, must be one of the most bizarre intelligence assessments in history, that 'we can find no hard evidence of a major, coordinated Egyptian/Syrian offensive across the Canal and in the Golan Heights area, rather, the weight of evidence indicates an action–reaction situation where a series of responses by each side to perceived threats created an increasingly dangerous potential for confrontation'. It was a classic case of perseveration. So far as Hoskinson and his fellow committee members were concerned, it was simply not possible that their previous assessments were wrong.

'It is possible that the Egyptians or Syrians, particularly the latter, may have been preparing a raid or other small-scale action,' they concluded. So far as the committee members were concerned, the fighting was a coincidental series of clashes into which both sides had inadvertently stumbled.

A CIA post-mortem concluded that there was no lack of intelligence pointing to an invasion, only a lack of common sense. 'Community analysts were provided with a plenitude of information which should have suggested, at a minimum, that they take very seriously the threat of war in the near term,' the post-mortem said. 'Certain substantive preconceptions, reinforced by official Israeli interpretations, turned the analyst's attention principally toward political indications that the Arabs were bent on finding non-violent means to achieve their objectives and away from indications (mainly military) to the contrary. Whatever the rationale, the principal conclusions concerning the imminence of hostilities reached and reiterated by those responsible for intelligence analysis were quite simply, obviously, and starkly, wrong.'[31]

The sixth of October was chosen because it was Yom Kippur, the Day of Atonement and the holiest day in the Jewish calendar, which it was assumed would make the invasion even more of a surprise. In the event, since many Jewish males spent most of the day in the synagogue, mass mobilisation was made easier. The war began with Egyptian forces gaining ground in the Sinai, but the position was soon reversed with Israeli forces crossing the Suez Canal and seizing a substantial bridgehead. With Kissinger working with the Soviet Union to negotiate a UN ceasefire, the US needed aerial reconnaissance imagery to monitor the movement of the battle.

The USAF had previously used the British air base at Akrotiri in western Cyprus as a forward operations base for its U-2 aircraft. But given that Moscow had provided both the Egyptians and the Syrians with the same SA-2 Guideline air defence missiles that had shot down Gary Powers's aircraft, the USAF planned to use the faster, higher-altitude SR-71 Blackbird reconnaissance aircraft instead, albeit still operating from Akrotiri. It also wanted to use the base to ferry ammunition supplies and combat aircraft to the Israelis.

This provided major problems for Ted Heath. Notwithstanding his previous conciliatory message to President Nixon, the prime minister was desperate to ensure that the UK took a neutral stance in the war in order to ensure the continued flow of oil from the Arab states on which the UK depended for its energy supplies. Heath would later claim that he banned the US from flying out of Cyprus, but in fact British officials simply placed a series of bureaucratic obstacles in the way, with the demand that the intelligence gathered by any SR-71 missions not be shared with the Israelis probably the most decisive. The USAF complained bitterly of 'consistently unhelpful behaviour' by the British, who were 'rolling barrels in our way', until it became easier to adopt the alternative plan of flying the aircraft direct from the United States. The first mission took place on 13 October, flying out of Griffiss Air Base in central New York state, refuelling in the Gulf of St Lawrence, passing over the eastern Atlantic north of the Azores, and finally coming in south of Crete.[32]

Although the British did authorise a flight from Akrotiri to monitor the ceasefire lines, the USAF deemed the associated restrictions too odious to bother with and the two ceasefire-related SR-71 missions also flew out of Griffiss Air Base. Kissinger was predictably furious over the restrictions, describing the British as 'jackals', and once the war was over, he looked at a wide range of ways to punish the UK in order 'to demonstrate our dissatisfaction with their performance as an ally'. These ranged from supporting the Spanish position on Gibraltar to putting pressure on the other eight EEC members to stop providing subsidies to depressed areas of the UK such as the Midlands, Wales and Scotland.

He was backed by the new CIA director, Bill Colby, who, despite his wartime Anglophilia, said: 'They can't have a special relationship with us and do what they are.' Kissinger ultimately fell back on another break in the intelligence exchange, which had exactly the same limited real impact as before and unsurprisingly, given the continuing importance of the product of the British intercept base at Ayios Nikolaos, had no effect whatsoever on the constant 24-hour exchange between the NSA and GCHQ.[33]

The petulance was not all one-sided. Heath was furious when, amid attempts to enforce a ceasefire, and without any consultation with the British, Nixon and Kissinger put US nuclear missiles worldwide on high alert—a show of force to prevent the Soviet Union intervening to help Egypt. This might not have gone against the strict letter of the agreements surrounding US bases in the UK, which demanded consultation only before an attack was launched, and none was planned, but it certainly appeared to be a breach of the spirit of the relationship Nixon had claimed to want with Heath. In fact, while Nixon had not consulted Heath personally, Kissinger had informed Lord Cromer several days earlier, with Britain the only US ally warned ahead of time, but for some reason the UK ambassador had not passed the information back to London. Nevertheless, such an escalation of Cold War tension was an extraordinary move for Nixon to take without consulting America's NATO allies, who would inevitably have been drawn into any conflict.[34]

At the end of 1973 and into early 1974, Heath's position as prime minister was undermined by a battle with Britain's trade unions, and in particular the National Union of Mineworkers, which led to the British being forced to work a three-day week and urged to restrict their use of energy supplies. In an attempt to obtain a clear mandate for government over the power of the unions, Heath called a general election in February 1974 with the slogan 'Who governs Britain?', but despite winning the most votes, the Conservatives lost seats to Labour, with Harold Wilson returning as prime minister and appointing Jim Callaghan as foreign secretary.

One of Callaghan's first instructions to senior Foreign Office staff was that 'the highest priority was to be given to close relations with the US', which had reached such a low under Heath that Nixon joked that the former prime minister had achieved the improbable in turning him and Wilson into 'good friends'. Whether or not this was true, it had little impact since six months later Nixon resigned over the Watergate scandal and was replaced by his vice-president, Gerald Ford. With Britain's economy in a dire state, there were US concerns about the Wilson government's determination to pursue further defence cuts that were so drastic that even the Polaris nuclear missile upgrade and—astonishingly given its importance in terms of the UKUSA intelligence exchange—the Ayios Nikolaos intercept site in Cyprus were listed among potential cuts.[35]

Although there was a relatively swift decision made to proceed with the Polaris upgrade, the future of the Ayios Nikolaos base remained uncertain until November and heated discussions with visiting British officials in which Kissinger and Colby made the US anger over the possibility that the base might go extremely clear. In doing so, they displayed an understanding of its importance that senior British officials and politicians had clearly failed to grasp.

Ford wrote to Wilson explaining that while he understood the economic factors behind the defence cuts he was unhappy at the potential loss of the British signals intelligence base on Cyprus. 'We are concerned that current plans for eliminating UK capabilities on the island will diminish future Western flexibility to react to unpre dictable situations in the Eastern Mediterranean, and beyond,' he said, adding that Callaghan would shortly receive a more detailed letter from Kissinger outlining the concerns. Wilson replied within days assuring the US president that 'I have noted very carefully what you say about Cyprus' and the announcement of the defence cuts in early December 'will cause you no problems in this respect'. Astonishingly, it had taken a US intervention to prevent British politicians removing one of the UK's most important contributions to the transatlantic intelligence relationship and return it to a stable footing. The most spectacular MI6 operation of the Cold War was about to take it to an even higher level.[36]

18

THE GREATEST OF THEM ALL

The 1970s may have been the lowest point in relations between the British and US administrations, but it was also the period when MI6 acquired the most valuable and productive agent available to any of the Western intelligence agencies during the Cold War. Oleg Gordievsky was brought up within the Soviet intelligence establishment, his father having been a member of the NKVD, a predecessor of the KGB, and in the early 1960s the young Oleg joined the Russian intelligence service himself.

The turning point in his career came with the 1968 invasion of Czechoslovakia, when he was based at the Soviet embassy in Copenhagen. He and his wife Yelena, also a KGB officer, had discussed the Prague Spring and the promise of reform of the Soviet communist system that it offered and he was bitterly disappointed that it had been so brutally suppressed.

Knowing that the Danish security and intelligence service, Politiets Efterretningstjeneste (PET), was likely to be monitoring his apartment's telephone, Gordievsky called his wife and raged against the decision to invade Czechoslovakia. It was a deliberate, if tentative, message to Danish intelligence that he was unhappy with his bosses in Moscow and therefore a potential agent for the West inside the KGB. His *cri de coeur* went unheard and no one responded. But the seed of betrayal had been sown in his mind. 'My soul was aching,' he said. 'It was that dreadful event, that awful day, which determined the course of my own life.'[1]

Gordievsky was posted back to Moscow in 1970 but, although his telephone rant had been missed, an MI6 officer reading the file on an

Eastern Bloc defector who was an old friend of Gordievsky's found a suggestion that he was disenchanted with Soviet-style communism and might well be amenable to an approach from a Western intelligence service. The MI6 officer looked through the records for other mentions of Gordievsky and found that surveillance by PET, which included a search of his apartment, had led the Danes to conclude that he was almost certainly a KGB officer. The MI6 officer gave him the codename SUNBEAM and his file was flagged for attention should he resurface in the West, which he soon did. He and Yelena were posted back to Copenhagen in October 1972.

The MI6 head of station, warned in advance when the Russians applied for Gordievsky's Danish visa, began the necessarily careful process of making contact ahead of recruitment, initially merely chatting to him at diplomatic receptions, placing himself in line of sight. The operation proceeded cautiously and it was more than a year after Gordievsky returned to Denmark that the defector who had first named him as a possible recruit was sent in to test the waters. When he reported back that Gordievsky retained his dissident views, the MI6 head of station made a more confident approach, eventually recruiting the Russian as an agent-in-place inside the KGB. In January 1975, Gordievsky was handed over to another MI6 officer, who was to be his initial handler, and the intelligence operation began.

Once a month, they met in a safe house in the Copenhagen suburbs and Gordievsky would explain how the KGB's foreign intelligence service, the First Chief Directorate, operated. His new handler seemed to harbour suspicions, so Gordievsky explained it in extensive detail in order to leave no shadow of a doubt that he was a genuine agent-in-place rather than a KGB attempt to infiltrate MI6. Prior to returning to Denmark, Gordievsky had worked in the Third Department, which dealt with the UK and Scandinavia—a combination that stemmed from the period immediately following the Bolshevik Revolution when British intelligence ran its agents inside Russia from Stockholm and Helsinki. As a result, Gordievsky had a substantial amount of intelligence to provide. Eventually, he was taken over by a new handler, the MI6 officer who had originally spotted his potential in the defector's debriefing. With the relationship on a far firmer footing, the operation began to become more productive.

All correspondence between the KGB centre in Moscow and the *rezidentura* in the Soviet embassy arrived on microfilm. If a swift method of copying it could be devised, Gordievsky might be able to briefly intercept the microfilm before it left the registry to be cut up and distributed to the various recipients and then, under the guise of going out for lunch, walk to a local park and surreptitiously slip it to his MI6 handler in a process known as a 'brush pass'. The MI6 officer would copy it before reversing the process to hand it back to Gordievsky, who could then replace it on his return to the registry.

But it took time and therefore ran the risk of discovery. So the MI6 technical support section at Hanslope Park in Buckinghamshire, the equivalent of James Bond's 'Q', was tasked with producing something that would allow the MI6 officer to copy the microfilm with a minimum of fuss and delay. The result was a small hand-held device, the size of a modern mobile telephone, through which the microfilm was fed and copied. Gordievsky would smuggle the microfilm out of the *rezidentura* and make his way to a pre-determined location. The MI6 officer would pick it up, take it to a safe house, copy it and return it to Gordievsky. The process became so refined that it could take little more than half an hour, ensuring that the microfilm was returned before anyone noticed its absence.

Gordievsky was undoubtedly the best and most productive Western agent inside the KGB in the Cold War era. Neither he nor MI6 had any doubt that he was putting his life at risk and might be detected at any time. Were that to happen, he would have been taken back to Moscow for a show trial, followed by the standard KGB execution—a bullet to the back of the head.

Agents of Gordievsky's calibre need to be nurtured carefully, made to feel that their handlers care about them. As part of that process, Maurice Oldfield wrote to Gordievsky in green ink, a classic MI6 tradition and the legacy of Mansfield Cumming, the naval officer who created Britain's secret intelligence service; like the captains of all Royal Navy ships, he wrote all of his personal letters in green ink. Cumming also signed his memos and reports with a large green 'C', another tradition of which Gordievsky as a UK expert would have been very well aware. His MI6 handler described the letter, handwritten in green ink and signed by C, as 'a way to reassure Oleg that we took him seriously and put it on a formal footing, to establish a personal connection and show Oleg that he was dealing with the organisation itself. That all helped to settle him down and marked the maturity of the case'.

Gordievsky's intelligence was shared with the Americans in a very controlled fashion. Unlike the relationship between the NSA and GCHQ, which with only a few exceptions is all-encompassing, the relationship between MI6 and the CIA is extremely pragmatic, a barter process whereby important intelligence that affects both countries is routinely shared, but some intelligence is held back or redacted for any number of reasons, of which the most frequent is the need to protect the source. If one service provides one valuable piece of intelligence, the other is indebted and seeks to provide another piece of intelligence of similar value in response. Inevitably with the Americans, there tends to be a competitive edge.

Nevertheless, protecting the source is a predominant factor in this exchange. The US agencies have always been less secure in their dealings with politicians and the media, sometimes deliberately so, even gaining political capital by claiming an operation that was MI6-led as their own. The 1970s were also a period when the US Congress was determined through two separate inquiries to unmask CIA and NSA secrets in an effort to prove that the US intelligence agencies were 'rogue elephants' rampaging out of control, and with a number of American politicians either not understanding or not caring about the need to protect intelligence sources, that process inevitably revealed information that damaged British sources.

Pat Carter, the former NSA director and deputy CIA director, recalled that the British were 'very badly burned' by Congressional inquiries into US intelligence, adding: 'I don't blame them a god-damned bit quite frankly for being in-house as much as they possibly can.' Protecting Gordievsky was paramount. The CIA was inevitably inquisitive about the source of the astonishingly authoritative intelligence it was receiving on the Soviet Union but, unlike Oleg Penkovsky, Gordievsky's identity was not to be revealed to the Americans. He had to be protected at all costs, so much so that when he returned to Moscow in 1978, it was decided that there should be no contact with him at all. KGB surveillance of MI6 officers based in the Soviet capital was too extensive. It was simply not safe. Gordievsky would continue to collect intelligence but hold it back until he was next posted abroad. 'Oleg was too good to jeopardise,' his MI6 handler said. 'We had something so precious that we had to exercise restraint.'

Before he left the UK, an MI6 Soviet specialist devised a plan codenamed Pimlico under which, if Gordievsky's bosses inside the KGB realised he had been working for the British, he could be exfiltrated from the Soviet Union. It was encased in cellophane and sealed behind the endpaper of a hardback edition of Shakespeare's sonnets which he took with him to Moscow.[2]

Although the CIA had no one who was quite as well placed and productive on the Soviet Union as Gordievsky, it did have an extremely valuable source inside the Warsaw Pact command structure. Ryszard Kukliński's father was a war hero who had lost his life fighting the Nazis as a member of the Home Army, the Polish resistance. The family were committed socialists and Ryszard joined the Polish People's Army, rapidly climbing up the ranks. But like Gordievsky, he was bitterly disillusioned by the 1968 invasion of Czechoslovakia.

Kukliński was a senior staff officer working with Soviet colleagues on plans for the invasion of western Europe. These 'unambiguously offensive' plans involved the use of tactical nuclear missiles and accepted that the inevitable response by NATO would lay waste to his homeland. When an outbreak of protests in the 1970s in Poland was brutally crushed—with around forty people shot dead by troops and militia—he decided to act.

He proposed to his bosses that he and some colleagues take a sailing trip by yacht along the German, Danish, Dutch and Belgian coasts. It would look like a holiday but would actually be a spying mission. So far as his bosses were concerned, Kukliński and a few colleagues would be collecting intelligence and photographing naval bases and NATO warships. But Kukliński's sole aim was to contact the Americans to offer his services as a spy.

When they docked in Wilhelmshaven, Kukliński posted a letter written in halting English to the 'USA Ambassy Bonn' in which he said he was a serviceman 'from Communistische Kantry' and wanted 'to meet secretly with US Army Officer'. Kukliński gave a number of days when the yacht would be in Holland and said he would telephone the US embassy in The Hague. When he rang, he was given directions for a meeting at the city's main railway station, where two CIA officers took him to a hotel. Expecting a simple seaman of limited use, they were stunned to learn he was a colonel on the Polish Army's general staff, liaising with senior Soviet officers on top secret Warsaw Pact war plans. Kukliński laid out his motives. He was no traitor. He would take no money for what he was doing. He was a patriotic Pole fighting for his country's freedom from Soviet rule.

The case was deemed so important that it was controlled from CIA headquarters at Langley by David Forden, a former head of station in Poland who spoke Polish well enough to hold regular meetings with Kukliński at safe houses in West Germany. The Polish officer knew Forden only as 'Daniel'. Kukliński's own codename was GULL, an allusion to his love of the sea. Using Minox cameras supplied by the CIA, he photographed every document that came across his desk, more than 30,000 in all over the nine years during which he was in play. Routine exchanges were carried out by the local CIA station. A car would meet him on a Warsaw back street at night so he could hand over the unprocessed film and his reports. There were numerous fall-back plans to avoid surveillance and even if 'casuals'—civilians with no link to the Polish authorities—were spotted, the car would drive round the area and make repeated passes of the location until the officer was absolutely certain no one could see the exchange take place.

Kukliński delivered regular updates of the latest Soviet plans for the invasion of western Europe, details of Soviet deception operations designed to fool the US spy satellites, and the specifications and photographs of every new piece of Soviet military equipment as it was introduced—including the T-72 tank and the SS-20 Saber intermediate-range missiles based in Poland and East Germany and targeted at western Europe. He also supplied a complete breakdown of how every Warsaw Pact unit would be deployed in an attack on the West.

For one of the most dangerous decades of the Cold War, the US—and therefore the UK—had unprecedented detail of Soviet military capabilities and plans, intelligence which led to major changes in the locations, size and operational plans for NATO forces in Germany and western Europe. Had a war been fought, NATO commanders would have known precisely what Warsaw Pact forces would do at every turn, allowing them to pre-empt or counter their plans easily.[3]

Kukliński's role as a long-term CIA agent-in-place was brought to an end by a wave of unrest which swept across Poland in the spring of 1980 and led to the creation of Solidarność (Solidarity), an independent (and therefore illegal) trade union. In an attempt to defuse the situation, the Polish communist party leader, Edward Gierek, sanctioned a deal which allowed the formation of independent trade unions, the right to strike without repercussions and 'freedom of expression'. The Russians reacted predictably, ousting Gierek and replacing him with the hardline Stanisław Kania. But even before the agreement with the independent unions was put in place, the Polish Ministry of Defence and the Internal Affairs Ministry had begun planning to send in the troops. In late October, Kukliński reported that he was part of a small five-man team drafting plans to introduce martial law.[4]

The agreement permitting free trade unions failed to take the sting out of the unrest while pay rises intended to buy off striking workers only led to more strikes by others demanding more money. When Polish railway workers voted to strike, potentially leaving Soviet forces unable to move in the event of war, it was deemed by Moscow to be a step too far. In late November, with unusual numbers of Soviet and East German troops carrying out a joint exercise close to the East German–Polish border, a temporary restricted area was set up all along the border, preventing BRIXMIS and other

Western observers from monitoring troop movements in precisely the same fashion as had occurred ahead of the Soviet invasion of Czechoslovakia.

Two days later, after a meeting of Warsaw Pact defence ministers, Kukliński reported that the Polish delegation had backed a plan to allow Soviet, East German, Czechoslovak, Bulgarian and Hungarian forces to intervene under cover of carrying out military manoeuvres. They had to be ready to invade on 8 December, he said, adding: 'I very much regret to say that although everyone who has seen the plans is very depressed and crestfallen, no one is even contemplating putting up active resistance against the Warsaw Pact action.'[5]

NSA and GCHQ monitoring of the situation was disrupted midway through the crisis by a catastrophic leak of their ability to read Soviet communications systems. Ronald Pelton, a senior NSA Soviet specialist, who had been forced to resign as a result of financial problems, contacted the Soviet embassy in Washington offering to provide details of a number of extremely successful US and UK secret signals intelligence operations against the Soviet Union. The KGB had an agent inside GCHQ for much of the 1970s, a former RAF Russian linguist called Geoffrey Prime, but he was relatively low-level and as a result the intelligence he could provide was limited. Pelton had access to all NSA and GCHQ operations against the Soviet Union and had written the internal NSA manual on how to decipher a number of complex Soviet ciphers. As a result of his information, the Russians replaced or changed all of the communications systems the British and Americans were monitoring, dramatically reducing intelligence on the Soviet Union and forcing the NSA and GCHQ to fall back on traffic analysis.[6]

In the early hours of 7 December, the day before the Soviet invasion was due to take place, an East German Army vehicle recovery team entered the restricted area along the Polish border to pick up a broken-down truck. With senior US officials expecting the Kremlin to send in the troops, and frontline intelligence units under intense pressure to report any sign of an invasion, US Army signals intelligence operators at Augsburg in Bavaria completely misread the brief communications between the recovery team and its base and sent out a flash signal reporting that an entire East German motorised rifle regiment had moved into the restricted area, suggesting that the invasion by Soviet and Warsaw Pact forces was about to begin.

The report went to all possible recipients, including the White House Situation Room and Downing Street. The resultant full-scale alert was only called off after the main British signals intelligence base in Germany, 13 Signal Regiment at Birgelen on the Dutch border, sent out a similar flash signal—to precisely the same recipients—explaining that there was no other movement than a broken-down lorry being taken back to its base, and appending a 'technical summary' providing the dates and times of the East German communications and the actual German text so that no one could be in any doubt as to what was happening. The overreaction by the US analysts was an extreme example of a regular phenomenon induced by pressure on US intelligence to process reports as quickly as possible and one of the reasons the NSA remained grateful for the often more measured assessments provided by the British.[7]

In the event, a hot-line exchange between US president Jimmy Carter and Leonid Brezhnev, and a very public warning of 'most negative consequences for East–West relations in general and US–Soviet relations in particular', led the Kremlin to step back and Kukliński reported that the invasion had been 'postponed for the indefinite future'. By January, he was reporting contingency plans for the introduction of martial law. At the same time, he provided the latest Warsaw Pact plans for an invasion of western Europe, giving the full details for two options, one using a combination of conventional forces and nuclear strikes from the very first, the second initially using conventional weapons prior to a staged transition to the use of nuclear weapons.[8]

In mid-February 1981, with no end in sight to the industrial unrest, Moscow ordered the appointment of the Polish defence minister, Wojciech Jaruzelski, as prime minister and Kukliński reported hurried preparations for the introduction of martial law and the arrests of key Solidarność activists. Police harassment of trade unionists was stepped up and, in late March, the trade union staged a strike in protest. It was a major show of strength at a time when large numbers of Soviet troops were carrying out a joint exercise with Polish troops on Polish soil. In a clear threat to the strikers, Jaruzelski announced that, at his request, the manoeuvres were being extended by a week.[9]

The unrest continued through the summer of 1981, with a million Solidarność members taking to the streets in August to protest against the combination of rising prices and low wages. In early September, Kukliński reported that he and his team had been ordered to draw up a new decree that would allow the rapid introduction of martial law.[10] The following month, he reported that martial law was about to be introduced and handed over a document detailing how it was to be implemented.

Shortly afterwards, he and three colleagues were called to an urgent meeting. The KGB had found out from an agent inside the Vatican that the CIA had a copy of the plans for martial law. The four of them were the only ones with access to the plans. There were only two copies of the plans and one of them was always kept in Kukliński's safe. On his way home, he spotted surveillance. He knew then that he had no choice. He needed to get out.[11]

Using a short-burst transmitter designed to go undetected by Polish security systems, Kukliński sent a message to the CIA Warsaw station warning them that he had been compromised. 'Everything is pointing to the end of my mission,' he said. 'I have a choice of taking my life, early arrest, or the help which was once offered to me.' The response was swift. David Forden ordered the immediate exfiltration of Kukliński and his family. On 7 November 1981, hidden in boxes in an embassy van protected by diplomatic plates, they were driven across the border to West Berlin and flown to America.[12]

Martial law was imposed at midnight on 12 December 1981 under the control of the Military Council of National Salvation, with the Polish Army and security services arresting 6,000 trade unionists and secret police units suppressing any resistance. With the country locked down, the BBC Monitoring Service at Caversham Park became the main source of information on what was going on. Its Polish team was doubled in size and Polish television was monitored in Berlin and fed back to Caversham. The BBC material, passed up to the CIA/FBIS station on the floor above, was the only real source of information for the US administration, and indeed the British government, on what was going on for some months, and continued to be a primary source right through to the end of martial law in July 1983, yet again demonstrating the value of open-source intelligence to the transatlantic intelligence exchange.[13]

In early 1982, the head of the MI6 Soviet intelligence section received some exceptionally good news. The Soviet Foreign Ministry had applied for a visa for a new counsellor at its London embassy. The name on the application was Oleg Gordievsky. It was a stunning coup for MI6. It was about to acquire a well-placed source inside the KGB *rezidentura* in Kensington Palace Gardens. He did not arrive until June but had spent much of the previous three months going through the KGB files on the UK and memorising details of the agents run by the political intelligence section of the London *rezidentura*.

A few days after flying into the UK, Gordievsky passed all of their names and details to his new MI6 handler along with evidence confirming that John Cairncross was the so-called 'Fifth Man' in the Cambridge spy ring, and that former MI5 director-general Sir Roger Hollis was not a Soviet agent. He also described the contents of the dossier on Michael Foot, the then Labour leader, who was classified by the KGB as an 'agent of influence'. Given that an election might bring Foot to power, this was an extremely difficult issue. Only a very few senior civil servants were informed, including MI6 Chief Colin Figures, the director-general of MI5, John Jones, and cabinet secretary Sir Robert Armstrong. At this stage no politician, not even the prime minister, Margaret Thatcher, was told.[14]

The head of the Soviet section had been due to take up a new post overseas but given the importance of the intelligence that Gordievsky would be able to produce, and the need to have someone who understood the territory inside out overseeing the case, he agreed to stay in the UK to act as the KGB officer's handler and take charge of the intelligence assessment and reporting. Gordievsky was given a new codename, NOCTON, and a safe house was set up in Belgravia where, initially once a month, but increasingly more frequently until it was once a week, he would meet the former head of the Soviet section to be debriefed over a lunchtime session which he could hide from his bosses as time spent on a meeting with a contact. Every session was recorded and—with Gordievsky's existence kept on a very tight hold—transcribed personally by his new handler. From the very beginning, the KGB officer was such a productive source that the meetings often resulted in as many as twenty different reports.

As with Kukliński and Forden, the handling of the operation was a key reason for the extent of its success. Gordievsky and his MI6 controller got on extremely well. 'I had been carefully briefed and he was exactly what I had expected,' the MI6 officer said. 'Young, vigorous, on the ball, disciplined, focused. I never had any suspicions of him. Not a squeak. It's hard to explain, but you just know what to trust and what not to trust. You exercise your judgement. Oleg was completely reliable, honest and driven by the right emotions.'

The respect was mutual, with Gordievsky describing the MI6 officer as 'brilliant, the best minder I have ever had. He was a first-class intelligence officer, but also truly kind, full of emotion and sensitivity, honest both personally and in his ethical principles. As the expression goes in Russian, he had a fine structure of the soul. Tremendously quick to take the point and to understand my problems, he was forever analysing things and looking for new solutions.'[15]

One of the key problems Gordievsky had was that, from the very beginning of his time in the London *rezidentura*, he was seen as an outsider and did not get on with any of his bosses, not least the KGB head of station or *rezident*, Arkadi Guk. 'The animosity within the building was so strong that I felt it immediately, on my first day,' Gordievsky said. 'Guk disliked me from the start. Although not clever, he was well served by instinct and seemed to feel that there was something different about me. He cannot have had any inkling I was working for the British. Rather, he saw a man entirely different from himself, a man with intellectual interests, who read books as well as magazines and newspapers, the only one in the station whose radio was tuned to play classical music.'

Given the antagonism from Guk, the extent of the backstabbing within the *rezidentura* and the fact that the contacts left to him by his predecessor were all people with little or no access to anything that could be remotely described as useful intelligence, Gordievsky soon found himself under fire, with colleagues accusing him of not being up to the job. The response of his MI6 handler was to pass him 'chickenfeed', genuine information that did not give away any secrets but would begin to improve his reputation. He was also put in touch with an influential female member of the Conservative Party, who had no idea he was working for the British but, under instruction from MI5, provided him with substantial gossip and inside information on government policy.

'There was nothing sensitive,' Gordievsky said. 'They could not pass me anything classified, but they could always come up with something worthwhile. One young officer typed out very good little summaries about, for instance, current problems in South Africa, or the state of the Anglo-American relationship. Each was about three-quarters of a page, which I could take back with me, translate into KGB language, embellish with a few extra details, and hand in my contribution. By this means, I slowly pushed up my rating.'[16]

But MI6 did not stop there. Having improved Gordievsky's status by providing him with intelligence that significantly enhanced his reputation both with the *rezidentura* and at Moscow Centre, it had his immediate boss, the head of the political intelligence section, declared *persona non grata* and sent back to Moscow. It also had two GRU officers expelled at the same time in order to disguise the real objective, which was to have its own man promoted to a more prominent position with even greater access. All the time, Gordievsky was informing MI6 of the latest KGB operations in the UK and of the questions that Moscow Centre was asking, revealing what the Russians did not know—and by extension what they did know—about every aspect of Britain's government apparatus and secret policy, including the military and intelligence services themselves. With Gordievsky already a rising star, an unforeseen event provided what initially seemed like a threat but was ultimately an opportunity to have his position within the *rezidentura* advanced even further.

and the subsequent measures to prepare the country for a nuclear war would enable us to increase the so-called period of anticipation essential for the Soviet Union to take retaliatory measures,' it said. 'Otherwise, reprisal time would be extremely limited. For instance, noting the launching of strategic missiles from the continental part of the USA and taking into account the time required to determine the direction of flight leaves roughly 20 minutes' reaction time. This period will be considerably curtailed after the deployment to West Germany of the Pershing-2 missile, for which the flight time to long-range targets in the Soviet Union is calculated at 4-6 minutes.' A Pershing-2 missile based in West Germany would have needed to fly to the furthest edge of its 1,100-mile range to hit Moscow and the flight time was wrong, but even a more accurate fifteen minutes' warning would not have given the Soviet leaders much time to respond.[20]

Completely unaware of the fears in Moscow, the US administration continued to pile on the pressure. In March 1983, Reagan used a speech to Evangelical clergymen in Florida to denounce the Soviet Union as an 'evil empire'. He dismissed the idea of freezing the number of nuclear weapons on either side, insisting that the West 'must find peace through strength'. Two weeks later, he announced the 'Star Wars' initiative, under which a ground- and space-based laser system would destroy Soviet nuclear missiles before they could reach the US, provoking an incendiary response from Andropov, who accused the US president of 'devising one option after another in the search of the best ways of unleashing nuclear war. This is not just irresponsible,' the Soviet leader said. 'It is insane.'[21]

By August 1983, Vladimir Kryuchkov, the new KGB chief, was insisting all overseas stations concentrate entirely on 'signs of any secret measures which, in conjunction with other factors, may point to a decision being taken to begin immediate preparations for a nuclear missile strike against the USSR'. Three weeks later, relations between Moscow and Washington plummeted to a new low with the shooting down of a Korean Airlines Boeing 747 airliner, flight KAL007, on its way from New York to Seoul, killing all 269 passengers and crew. The Soviet air defence system, the

Protivovozdushnaya Oborona Strany, had recently been reorganised and Western spy planes had been testing it to build up a picture of how it worked. When KAL007 inadvertently strayed off course while flying over the north Pacific, entering Soviet airspace, not once but twice, it was misidentified as a US spy plane.

The second time it flew into Soviet airspace, three Su-15 Flagon fighter aircraft were sent up to intercept it. One of the aircraft fired two missiles which disabled the aircraft's operating systems. The pilot briefly managed to keep it in the air, but it eventually spun out of control, breaking up in mid-air with the loss of all those on board, sixty-one of whom were US citizens. Bob Gates, one of the CIA's leading Russian experts and by now the Agency's deputy director, told US secretary of state George Shultz: 'It is probably true that US–Soviet relations are as pervasively bleak now—and prospectively—as at any time since Stalin's death. I believe bilateral relations will be in a deep freeze until 1985 when the US will be in a position to seize the initiative.'[22]

Gates's assessment was confirmed by an official statement from the Soviet leader at the end of September in which he attacked Reagan personally over his anti-Soviet rhetoric and the plans to deploy the cruise and Pershing-2 missiles. Responsible leaders had an obligation 'to do everything possible to prevent a nuclear catastrophe,' Andropov said. 'Any other position is not just short-sighted, it is suicidal.'[23]

Despite Gordievsky's reporting of the incessant demands from Moscow Centre for any information of virtually any kind that might give an indication of preparations for a pre-emptive nuclear strike, it was not until a major NATO exercise in November 1983 that the full extent of the problem was understood. The annual command post exercise known as Able Archer was designed to test the use of the West's nuclear forces in the event of a war with the Soviet Union.

Able Archer 83, which took place between 2 and 11 November, was a step up from previous exercises. The procedures and message formats were all new, which would have been immediately apparent to the Soviet signals intelligence units monitoring the exercise com-munications, and although it remained a command post exercise, with no troops involved, some US aircraft in West Germany did simulate nuclear warhead handling procedures, taxiing out of hangars onto the runways carrying realistic-looking dummy warheads. Exercise planners initially envisaged Reagan, defense secretary Caspar Weinberger and General Jack Vessey, the chairman of the joint chiefs, taking part in the decision-making on when to fire the nuclear missiles, an idea that fortunately was eventually dropped.

All NATO exercises, and in particular those dealing with nuclear weapons procedures, were heavily monitored by Warsaw Pact military intelligence organisations. But from the very start, it was clear that the Soviet reaction to Able Archer 83 was unusual in the extreme. On the day it began, RAF intercept operators at 26 Signals Unit on Teufelsberg in West Berlin reported that all Soviet Air Force units based in East Germany and Poland had gone onto full-scale alert, with all base command posts and supporting command-and-control elements brought up to full wartime strength, and more than 100 strike aircraft fully loaded and ready to take off at any moment. One Soviet Air Force squadron based in East Germany was subsequently monitored requesting, and receiving, permission to jettison a jamming device because the additional bombs it was carrying were causing weight and balance problems, suggesting the aircraft were carrying full war-conditions payloads.[24]

The Soviet Air Force and Navy conducted more than thirty-six intelligence flights, far more than in previous such exercises, flying over Scandinavia and the Baltic and Barents Seas, looking for any sign of NATO naval forces operating in support of Able Archer. Meanwhile, all other Soviet aircraft were grounded for the extent of the exercise, almost certainly to ensure that as many aircraft as possible were available for combat should they be needed.

While those measures were known at the time as a result of allied signals intelligence operations, there were even more serious precautions taking place which only emerged later. During normal NATO exercises in West Germany, 10 per cent of Soviet SS-20 intermediate-range ballistic missiles were sent forward to their operational positions, but during Able Archer 83, some 50 per cent were deployed into the field and, in an unprecedented operation, nuclear warheads were ferried forward by helicopter. Indeed, while the Able Archer exercise planners had decided that Vessey's involvement was unnecessary, Marshal Nikolai Ogarkov, the chief of the Soviet General Staff, spent the entire exercise controlling the Warsaw Pact reaction from the Soviet military command bunker outside Moscow.[25]

A week into Able Archer 83, Moscow Centre sent out a flash signal warning that the exercise appeared to be cover for a pre-emptive nuclear attack. Gordievsky reported this immediately to MI6, providing the caveat that he had difficulty in taking the warning seriously. But alongside the signals intelligence reporting demonstrating the extent to which the Soviet armed forces were preparing for an attack, it was clear to MI6 and the JIC that a situation was developing under which it was possible that mixed signals might lead the Soviet leadership to believe they were under threat and persuade them to order their own pre-emptive strike.[26]

MI6 briefed the CIA head of station in London on Gordievsky's reporting of excessive Soviet reaction to the exercise, still without identifying him but pointing out the corroborative evidence from signals intelligence of increased readiness among Soviet forces in East Germany and Poland. The reporting reached the president within a week of the exercise coming to an end, with Reagan noting in his diary that he could not understand how the Soviet leadership could be 'so paranoid about being attacked'.[27]

The US president was not alone. The tight restrictions protecting Gordievsky at all costs left the provenance of his intelligence unclear, leading the US intelligence community and key NSC members to reject the idea that Moscow seriously believed the US would mount a pre-emptive nuclear strike on the Soviet Union. A CIA memo written in response to the British concerns suggested MI6 was taking Soviet rhetoric too seriously, concluding unequivocally that 'Soviet leaders do not believe their own war danger propaganda and are not likely to base policy on it'. John Lenczowski, who as the NSC's chief Soviet analyst was the man national security adviser Bud Mcfarlane relied on for his advice to the president, dismissed the claims as 'preposterous'. The suggestion that Soviet leaders feared a US pre-emptive nuclear strike was a 'fundamental misinterpreta-tion' of the situation, Lenczowski said. 'The Soviets are not, and in the post-war period never have been, "paranoid" about the United States.'[28]

With MI6 deeply concerned at the US response, there were more talks with the CIA station chief, who had himself been involved in JIC discussions over its recent report on 'Soviet Union Concern about a Surprise Nuclear Attack'. He produced an eleven-page document outlining the MI6 reporting which Bill Casey, now CIA director, took to the president, but with Mcfarlane backing Lenczowski's line, it was difficult to persuade senior US officials of the danger. Nevertheless, and despite his own scepticism, Mcfarlane later believed that the report from the CIA's London station chief must have had an impact on the president, who in contrast to his hardline image had always been extremely concerned over the pos-sibility of a nuclear war devastating the world. 'For him to see that,' Mcfarlane said, 'with this deep-seated worry about Armageddon, and to see that the Russians might even think we could set it off, I'm sure generated very serious thought on his part about how he could relieve that concern.'[29]

Whether or not Reagan was more convinced than his advisers, the UK government remained concerned at the US attitude. At the end of April, Margaret Thatcher, her deputy, Willie Whitelaw, and foreign secretary Geoffrey Howe —all of whom were now fully briefed on the Gordievsky intelligence—discussed the need to per-suade the Americans that it was genuine. A few weeks later, Howe flew to Washington and briefed George Shultz, who asked the CIA for a Special National Intelligence Estimate on the British concerns.

Despite the extensive evidence provided by Gordievsky to MI6 clearly demonstrating the concern in Moscow, the US experts claimed to have 'inadequate information about the current mindset of the Soviet leadership', although notwithstanding this supposed lack of knowledge of the view in the Kremlin, their conclusions were unequivocal. 'We believe strongly that Soviet actions are not inspired by, and Soviet leaders do not perceive, a genuine danger of imminent conflict or confrontation with the United States,' they said, in what must rank—given the strength of Gordievsky's evidence and the dangers of Soviet miscalculation and overreaction—as one of the worst failures of analysis and assessment of the Cold War period. 'On the basis of what we believe to be very strong evidence, we judge that the Soviet leadership does not perceive an imminent danger of war.'[30]

Although there were undoubtedly a number of people within the US intelligence community, including Casey, who believed that there might be truth in the British reports, the majority of US Soviet experts 'didn't want to admit that we had badly misread the state of mind of the Soviet leadership', Bob Gates said. Further British pressure led to a second National Intelligence Estimate in August 1984 which simply repeated the earlier conclusions.

But by now, while the US scepticism remained irritating, it was largely irrelevant. Yuri Andropov, the main proponent of the 'war scare', had died the previous February and, as a result, the tension between Washington and Moscow had significantly dissipated. The new Soviet leader, Konstantin Chernenko, was not a well man and clearly an interim leader, with Mikhail Gorbachev expected to replace him at any moment.

In September 1984, Thatcher visited MI6 headquarters at Century House where, among other issues, she was briefed in extensive detail about Gordievsky and his reporting. With Gorbachev due to arrive in Britain for a visit that December, Gordievsky had been asked to provide briefing points for the prime minister on how best to handle the meetings. The Russians needed reassurance, he said. The economy was in trouble and they could not afford to keep up with the Americans in an arms race. Yet they craved an acceptance that they were equal to the Americans in terms of being a superpower. They were paranoid that the US was intent on destroying the Soviet system, if necessary, by a pre-emptive nuclear strike. The Soviet leadership needed to feel that its nuclear arsenal matched that of the US. Arms limitation was the obvious way forward.

At the same time, Gordievsky, as head of the London *rezidentura*'s political intelligence section, was also being asked by Moscow Centre to provide advice on how Gorbachev should deal with the

British prime minister, putting MI6 in a unique position to man-
oeuvre the situation in the West's favour. The Gordievsky advice to
both sides was extremely valuable, ensuring that Thatcher's talks
with Gorbachev were highly successful, leading her to say, both in
public and in her subsequent private conversations with President
Reagan: 'I like Mr Gorbachev. We can do business together.'[31]

The success of the talks had what appeared to be a knock-on effect
for both Gordievsky and MI6. In January 1985, he was summoned
to Moscow to be told he was to be the next KGB *rezident* in London.
It was a stunning success for both him and his MI6 handlers, promising untold intelligence riches. But the euphoria did not last long.
Gordievsky took over as London *rezident* on 28 April. Twelve days
earlier, Aldrich Ames, a senior CIA officer in charge of counter-
espionage operations against the KGB and GRU, had walked into the
Soviet embassy in Washington and handed over an envelope offering
his services as an agent-in-place inside the CIA for an initial payment
of $50,000. As an example of what he could produce, he named a
number of Soviet officials who were working for the Americans.

The first meeting between Ames and Viktor Cherkashin, the
deputy *rezident* in the embassy, took place on 15 May. Cherkashin
said they were prepared to pay him the money but not for the
names he had already given them. He must be holding something
bigger back. What was it? At that point, it seems, Ames informed
Cherkashin that MI6 had an agent-in-place inside the KGB. The next
day, Gordievsky was recalled to Moscow where he was suspended,
drugged, interrogated and accused of being a spy. But crucially he
was not arrested, suggesting Ames had provided sufficient evidence
for him to become the focus of Moscow Centre's suspicions, but
not enough to identify him definitively as the MI6 agent-in-place.[32]

His escape was the stuff of fiction. Avoiding his KGB watchers,
he followed the instructions hidden behind Shakespeare's sonnets
to warn MI6 that he needed to be exfiltrated. The signal was to
stand on a designated street corner, holding a Safeway carrier bag.
It would be acknowledged by an MI6 officer carrying a Harrods bag
and chewing a chocolate bar as he walked past. On 16 July 1985,
Gordievsky went to the street corner at the designated time and

waited. It was more than twenty minutes before he saw a man 'with an unmistakably British look' carrying a Harrods bag and eating a Mars bar. The man briefly glanced at him before taking another bite out of the Mars bar and walking straight ahead. Three days later, following his instructions to the letter, Gordievsky took the overnight train to Leningrad.[33]

He was heading for a rendezvous 50 miles from the border with Finland, a lay-by easily identified by the large rock that lay behind it on the edge of a forest. Arriving in Leningrad shortly after five in the morning, he took a taxi across the Neva River to the Finland Station, boarding a train towards the border, getting off 30 miles later and then travelling the rest of the way to the rendezvous by bus. Arriving several hours early, with his nerves frayed, he made what he later admitted was an at best ill-considered trip into the local town that could have led to his arrest before hitching his way back to the rock and hiding in the undergrowth.[34]

Eventually, two cars pulled into the lay-by. Expecting Gordievsky to be with his family, the MI6 head of station, Raymond Asquith, had decided he needed two cars for the operation, one his own, the other that of his deputy, the man with 'an unmistakably British look' who had acknowledged Gordievsky's original signal. In the long MI6 tradition of using the wives of officers as a means of dispelling suspicion—as with Janet Chisholm collecting Oleg Penkovsky's intelligence in her baby's pram—the cover for Operation Pimlico was that the wife of the deputy head of station needed medical treatment in Finland. So both wives plus the Asquiths' baby daughter were in the cars, reinforcing the idea that this was simply friends combining a medical appointment in Finland with a short break away from Moscow.

Gordievsky was swiftly placed in the boot of the deputy's car and they moved on towards the border, the deputy in the lead with the Asquiths' car behind protecting the Russian from any attempt by a KGB car to ram them. There were sedatives and water for Gordievsky in the boot, together with a bottle in which he could urinate, and a space blanket with which he was to cover himself to protect against infra-red heat detectors. When they got to the border, and guards with sniffer dogs approached the cars, Clare Asquith fed the dogs crisps and then, in a move not anticipated in the plan, she improvised. Taking advantage of her baby daughter having soiled her nappy, she placed her on the boot of the deputy's car to change her and then dropped the dirty nappy beside the nearest dog, completely overriding the scent of sweat and urine emanating from the boot and ensuring their safe passage across the border.[35]

When he arrived back in the UK, Gordievsky was taken to Fort Monckton, the MI6 training base near Gosport in Hampshire. He was given a new codename, the rather apt OVATION, and the debriefings began. Whereas in the past, with the need to protect its agent paramount, MI6 had been very careful about distributing any of his reporting, particularly among foreign intelligence services—including the CIA—now it could share the massive intelligence haul widely where appropriate. Bill Casey was briefed on the case and flew to the UK to talk to Gordievsky. Reagan was due to meet Gorbachev for a summit in Geneva a few weeks later and Casey wanted Gordievsky's advice on how the president should deal with the Soviet leader.

A few months later, Gordievsky was flown to Washington for the first of a number of meetings with CIA officers. 'I liked most of the people I met in the CIA,' he recalled. 'The intellectual standard struck me as lower than in the British service. Yet often they showed a high degree of brilliance.' Nevertheless, there remained resistance to the idea of what had become known as the 'Soviet war scare', he said. 'One senior intelligence officer with responsibility for Soviet affairs cast doubt on all my information about Operation RYaN. His theory was that it was no more than a deception exercise by the Soviet leadership.'[36]

Gordievsky had a number of meetings with Margaret Thatcher to advise her on how to deal with Gorbachev and in 1987 was invited to the White House to brief President Reagan on the Soviet leader. Nevertheless, the sceptical US response to the 'Soviet war scare' continued until the President's Foreign Intelligence Advisory Board re-examined the evidence in 1990.

After looking at all the intelligence and interviewing CIA and

MI6 officers who had been involved at the time, the board was scathing of the conclusions of the 1984 Special National Intelligence Estimates. It was 'deeply disturbed' by the reaction to the MI6 evidence from within the US intelligence community, which 'did not at the time, and for several years afterwards, attach sufficient weight to the possibility that the war scare was real'. The Soviet experts who prepared the estimates had 'invited failure' by displaying 'some of the worst analytical hazards' such as playing it safe, mirror-imaging, and a bias towards their own previously held views.

'The problem was compounded by what the British call "perseveration", an unreadiness to alter earlier views even when evidence requiring them to be revised becomes available,' the board said. 'There is little doubt in our minds that the Soviets were genuinely worried by Able Archer. We may have inadvertently placed our relations with the Soviet Union on a hair trigger.' The more considered and far better-informed British approach had been proven correct, even if it had been ignored, further underlining the value of the British contribution to the Special Relationship.[37]

'DO WE STILL NEED THE BRITS?'

Despite the close cooperation between the CIA and MI6 over Oleg Gordievsky and Ryszard Kukliński, there was one key area where there was virtually no cooperation at all. A communist coup in Afghanistan in April 1978 brought in a Soviet-backed government under Nur Muhammad Taraki which imposed policies that ran counter to traditional Afghan society, leading to a series of tribal revolts. By early 1979, the Soviet Union had begun sending in military advisers and equipment, including Mi-24 Hind helicopter gunships, to help suppress the rebels. Amid concern that Afghanistan was being taken into the Soviet fold, President Jimmy Carter asked the CIA to come up with a plan for covert action against the Taraki regime. CIA director Stan Turner proposed a range of measures from black propaganda to a coup, but the most viable covert operation was deemed to be funding the rebels. In a move which would handicap the CIA's ability to control who received the funding, it was to be channelled via Pakistan's Inter-Services Intelligence (ISI) with no Americans involved in frontline operations.[1]

Throughout the summer of 1979, Soviet forces took on an increasing role in fighting the rebel *mujahideen*, sending ever more troops and equipment into Afghanistan. At the same time, the NSA picked up signs of several Soviet Army divisions based on the border with Afghanistan carrying out extensive preparations for what appeared to be an invasion, as well as the creation inside Afghanistan of a nationwide Soviet Army command-and-control communications network. By mid-September, both the NSA and the CIA had concluded that Soviet leaders were on the verge of ordering an invasion designed to shore up the Taraki government and bring Afghanistan firmly into the Soviet orbit. When Taraki was overthrown by his hardline henchman Hafizullah Amin, a Soviet invasion became inevitable.[2]

Three days before Christmas 1979, NSA director Bobby Ray Inman rang national security adviser Zbigniew Brzezinski and US defence secretary Harold Brown to tell them signals intelligence had revealed that an invasion would take place 'within the next 72 hours'. On Christmas Eve, US intercept operators at Chicksands in the UK detected Soviet transport aircraft taking off from bases in the western Soviet Union ferrying two airborne divisions to Afghanistan. Inman rang Brzezinski and Brown again to warn the invasion would come 'within 15 hours'. Early on Christmas Day, CIA deputy director Frank Carlucci issued an alert that large numbers of Soviet troops had crossed the border into Afghanistan. Three days later, Carter signed a Presidential Finding authorising the CIA to begin sending weapons to the rebels. Over the next decade, some $3 billion worth of weaponry was poured into Afghanistan, most of it to Islamic fundamentalist fighters.[3]

While the CIA worked with the ISI, which favoured the Pushtun groups in the south, MI6 opted to back Ahmed Shah Masood, the leading guerrilla leader in the mainly Uzbek and Tajik north. The operation to help Masood began in the early summer of 1981 when two MI6 officers, accompanied by three SAS soldiers, officially 'retired' to take part in the operation, flew into the small northern Pakistani town of Chitral before heading north over the Hindu Kush and down into Masood's stronghold in the Panjshir Valley.

They met Masood near his home in one of the side-valleys of the Panjshir and—claiming to work for a right-wing European foundation, a very light cover that would not need to last long—told him they wanted to help him fight the Russians. They agreed to provide him with weapons, explosives and a secure communications system to stop the Russians eavesdropping on his conversations with his commanders. His forward observation post overlooking the Soviet air base at Bagram used the radios to warn him whenever Soviet aircraft were taking off to bomb the Panjshir, allowing him to withdraw his men to safety. Masood also sent his best fighters to the UK around ten at a time for training in guerrilla tactics and the use of explosives.[4]

Although both the Americans and the British viewed support for the *mujahideen* as the best way forward, there was little agreement on anything else. Despite their own dependence on the ISI, the CIA officers in charge of operations in Afghanistan had a dismissive attitude to their MI6 counterparts. 'They probably thought they knew more about Afghanistan than we did and they could play Athens to our Rome,' one senior CIA officer said, in a comment which typified the often patronising approach. 'There was a certain desire to be involved. They didn't want to be missing out.'

The ISI's control of the distribution of the arms meant that the majority went to the Islamist fundamentalist Hezbi-i-Islami (Islamic Party), led by Gulbuddin Hekmatyar, a divisive figure who frequently attacked Masood's men and plundered his supply lines. MI6 warnings to the CIA about Hekmatyar were ignored. The CIA officers involved felt his effectiveness against the Russians more than made up for his failings, and at any event they had little respect for Masood or the views of their MI6 counterparts.[5]

Yet in reality, the CIA was hamstrung by its obligations to the ISI whereas MI6 officers could operate on the ground inside Afghanistan. US spy satellites, NSA intercept sites in Pakistan and remote-controlled signals intelligence radio receivers smuggled into Afghanistan, which intercepted Soviet radio transmissions and sent them back live via satellite to GCHQ or the NSA, meant the vast bulk of intelligence on the Soviet occupation was signals intelligence. The CIA station in Islamabad had a small number of Afghan agents, but a substantial part of its human intelligence was supplied by the ISI with an inevitable emphasis on what the Pakistan authorities wanted the Americans to know.

The British provided Masood with a number of weapons, many of them highly effective, one of them completely useless. One former MI6 officer referred to Blowpipe shoulder-held surface-to-air missiles, supplied to Masood so his men could shoot down the Soviet helicopter gunships, as 'little more than a suicide note' because they

426 THE REAL SPECIAL RELATIONSHIP

were so inaccurate that all they did was alert the Russians to the *mujahideen* positions. In 1985, with Soviet commanders using the Hinds to pursue a scorched-earth policy that was overwhelming the *mujahideen*, the US began supplying them with Stinger heat-seeking surface-to-air missiles, a simple-to-operate shoulder-held device that required nothing more from the Afghan guerrillas than to point it at the helicopter and fire.

'The effect of these events on the *mujahideen* was electric, and within days the setbacks for the Soviet forces were snowballing, with one or two aircraft per day falling from the skies at the end of the Stingers' telltale white plumes,' recalled Milt Bearden, the then CIA station chief in Islamabad. 'When the snows melted in the high passes for the new fighting season of 1987, it had become clear not only to Gorbachev and his negotiators but also to his generals in the field that there would be no let-up in Afghanistan, and that the time to consider disengagement had come.'[6]

Despite the dismissive attitude of some of their CIA colleagues, MI6 officers on the ground, working with supposedly 'retired' members of the SAS or with 'contract labourers', members of the so-called 'Circuit' of former special forces for hire, had far more success than the Americans gave them credit for, using the close ties to Masood to collect intelligence on Soviet activity across the north-east and as far south as Kabul. They also worked with prominent members of rival *mujahideen* groups to overcome the numerous 'blood feuds' between the various tribal factions and stitch together more effective alliances, operations which provided MI6 officers with a number of key contacts and agents who were to be very useful in the future. One group of 'contract labourers' even managed to smuggle a Hind helicopter that had been shot down out of Afghanistan, taking out the various pieces on the backs of packhorses.

Daphne Park described the MI6 operations in Afghanistan as

the most wonderful opportunity for acquiring knowledge of, and in some cases possession of, a large range of the most up-to-date Soviet equipment. And when our forces came to fight the Iraqis in the Gulf War, the Iraqis were of course armed with those very Soviet weapons, and because of that activity in Afghanistan—which is one of the arguments for being global, you never know when things are going to turn up that are going to be very useful—they knew in great detail what they were up against.

Paradoxically, the next conflict to test the relationship between British and US intelligence involved not Soviet but Western weaponry, a good deal of it supplied by the Americans.[7]

On 19 March 1982, a group of forty-eight Argentinians landed on South Georgia, a British dependency in the South Atlantic, ostensibly to clear scrap metal from an old whaling station. They raised the Argentine flag and shots were fired in the air, leading to adulatory publicity in the Buenos Aires press. At the time, it was widely seen as a typical but effectively meaningless Argentine display of braggadocio over territory they claimed as their own. The British protested and demanded that the Argentinians and the ship on which they had arrived must leave. On 22 March, the British base commander on South Georgia reported that they had left and for a brief moment that seemed to be that. There was little immediate evidence to suggest that it was intended to be, or indeed was, a prelude to what would become known as the Falklands Conflict.

The arguments between Britain and Argentina over sovereignty of the Falklands, a small group of islands in the South Atlantic, 300 miles east of Argentina, and the dependencies of South Georgia and the South Sandwich Islands a thousand miles further east, date back nearly two centuries. Negotiation designed to find a solution to the issue had been taking place since the mid-1960s, but with Buenos Aires demanding full sovereignty regardless of the wishes of the islands' inhabitants, almost all of whom were British, the exchanges, although generally cordial, made little progress. Fresh talks in February 1982 were more difficult, with Robin Fearn, the head of the Foreign Office South American Department, warning that the Argentine delegation was 'clearly uninterested' in discussing anything other than an early transfer of sovereignty.

Immediately following the talks, the Argentine Foreign Ministry issued a communiqué warning that unless 'an early solution' was agreed, Buenos Aires would end discussions and 'choose freely the procedure which best accords with her interests'. The ruling *junta*, led by army chief General Leopoldo Galtieri, began making increasingly belligerent noises, and while the Argentine government's official, and utterly mendacious, position remained that it wanted to resolve the issue peacefully and was not going to invade the islands, it was clear from articles in the Buenos Aires media that the Argentine Navy and the Foreign Ministry were briefing selected journalists that military action was indeed an option. If there was no handover of sovereignty in the next three to four months, the sources said, an invasion would follow.[8]

MI6 had warned in early 1982 that there were clear signs of Argentina's willingness to invade the Falklands but, according to George Kennedy Young, its reports were ignored because of a dislike within Whitehall of 'hard facts which would conflict with its preference for soothing description'. MI6 was not alone in its warnings. Two weeks before the landings, the British defence attaché in Buenos Aires, Colonel Stephen Love, warned of military action to take the Falklands which might begin with the establishment of a 'naval research' station on an outlying island. The Argentine Navy had set up such a station on Southern Thule in the South Sandwich Islands in late 1976 and it was still in place 'occupying' the island. Love suggested that the occupation of another island would be followed by an invasion of the Falkland Islands.[9]

His warnings, sent to the Foreign Office Latin American Department and the Defence Intelligence Staff (DIS), were not seen as worrying—despite indications from a conversation two weeks earlier between Lord Buxton, a private British citizen, and the Argentine foreign minister, Nicanor Costa Méndez, of a possible Argentine landing on South Georgia, and a previous JIC warning that South Georgia might face a similar 'occupation' to that of Southern Thule.

The JIC report, in November 1977, had ruled that military action was unlikely unless the British stopped negotiating seriously on the islands' future. The latest JIC report, circulated in

July 1981, repeated that assessment, and went on to warn that if the Argentinians concluded that there was no hope of a peaceful transfer of sovereignty, there was a high risk they would turn to military action without warning, using a variety of measures up to and including an invasion and occupation of the Falkland Islands. The DIS issued a minute, triggered by Love's report, in which it said that current intelligence confirmed that Argentine Navy chief Admiral Jorge Anaya was pushing for military action and was behind the menacing media reports, but neither the army, led by President Galtieri, nor the air force would be prepared to back an invasion.[10]

There was substantial evidence that the landing of the 'scrap metal workers' in 1982 was a deliberate provocation ordered by Anaya. The ship that brought the workers to South Georgia was the Argentine Navy transport *Bahía Buen Suceso*. The Royal Navy ice patrol vessel *Endurance*, which had a team of navy signals intelligence operators on board, intercepted a message from the Argentine Navy on 23 March congratulating the captain of the *Bahía Buen Suceso* on his successful mission and ordering him to bring the workers back to Buenos Aires. In addition, the staff of the British Antarctic Survey reported around a dozen men dressed in white military-style Arctic warfare uniforms who were not involved in salvage work and did not leave. They were Argentine marines and were reinforced a few days after the salvage workers left by around a dozen more landed by an Argentine Navy support vessel, the *Bahía Paraíso*. All of this led Foreign Office officials to conclude that the landings had been 'undertaken with the full knowledge and probable guidance of the Argentine Navy'.[11]

Nevertheless, the JIC retained its long-standing position that an invasion was unlikely without a long period of escalating diplomatic tension between the two sides, albeit warning that if Britain's response was too heavy-handed it might well be used by the *junta* as a pretext for military action. David Omand, then principal private secretary to British defence secretary John Nott, later recalled that since no one in the British government was considering a heavy-handed response, the JIC assessment was interpreted in Whitehall as 'reassuring'. GCHQ had intercepted a number of Argentine Navy signals suggesting attempts to use the incident to put pressure on the British, but none of them pointed to the sort of intense military preparations that would be needed ahead of an invasion. The UK government dispatched two nuclear submarines to the South Atlantic but held off from ordering the *Endurance* to remove the remaining Argentinians from South Georgia amid concern it might inflame the situation.[12]

In what with hindsight was an unfortunate coincidence, Doug Nicoll's report on the failure of the JIC to predict a series of invasions, including Czechoslovakia and the 1973 Arab invasion of Israel, landed on prime minister Margaret Thatcher's desk just as the deliberations over South Georgia were taking place, with an assurance from the JIC—which was still arguing that there was no likelihood of any imminent military action by the Argentinians—that it had absorbed Nicoll's criticisms and learned the lessons of the past.

On the afternoon of 31 March, Omand was in Nott's office in the House of Commons when a DIS officer rushed in with three files of GCHQ intelligence, the covers of which all bore the words 'Top Secret UMBRA', the latest equivalent codeword to Bletchley Park's ULTRA. 'The folders contained decrypted intercepts of Argentine naval communications,' Omand recalled. 'The messages showed that an Argentine submarine had been on covert reconnaissance around the Falklands capital Port Stanley and that the Argentine fleet, which had been on exercises, was reassembling. A further intercept referred to a task force said to be due to arrive at an unstated destination in the early hours of Friday 2 April. From their analysis of the coordinates of the naval vessels, GCHQ had concluded that its destination could only be Port Stanley.'

Omand and Nott immediately rushed down the corridor to Thatcher's office to show her the GCHQ reports and the intercepts on which they were based.

'This is very serious, isn't it?' she said to Omand.

'Yes, Prime Minister,' he replied, 'this intelligence can only be read one way: the Argentine Junta are in the final stages of preparing to invade the Falkland Islands, very likely this coming Saturday.'[13]

Thatcher's relationship with Ronald Reagan was famously close, certainly as close as that between Kennedy and Macmillan. They had shared philosophies and, more importantly perhaps, instincts on all the main issues of domestic and foreign policy. But the previous year had brought the first of a number of potential problems when the Reagan administration announced that it would be ditching the Trident 1 (C-4) system which the British had opted for in favour of the more sophisticated, and more expensive, Trident 2 (D-5) missiles.

The unilateral US decision had all the makings of a rerun of the Skybolt crisis, made even more politically difficult by the fact that the veteran anti-nuclear campaigner Michael Foot was Labour leader. Britain would be left operating a system the Americans had abandoned with all the problems that would cause in terms of maintenance. But the close relationship between Thatcher and Reagan ensured that Britain was able to buy Trident 2. The wording of the deal mirrored that of the arrangement which she had agreed with Jimmy Carter for the C-4 missile system, substantially easing the £7.5 billion cost of Trident 2. The agreement was signed just one week before the forty-eight Argentinians landed on South Georgia.[14]

Thatcher's immediate reaction to the GCHQ intelligence was to send Reagan an urgent personal message asking him to intervene with Galtieri to prevent any hostilities, warning that while Britain would not seek to escalate the dispute 'we could not acquiesce in any Argentine occupation'. Meanwhile, Omand ensured that all the relevant intelligence was sent to Sir Nicholas Henderson, the British ambassador in Washington, who took it to Al Haig, Reagan's secretary of state, and set out 'in some detail' the threat to the Falkland Islands. Henderson described Haig's reaction to the intelligence as 'electric'. Although the intercepts had come from sources shared by GCHQ with the NSA, US officials had failed to put the various pieces of intelligence together to assemble a complete picture of what was happening.

It was far from clear at this point that America would take Britain's side. Attempts by the British over the previous months to get the Americans to push for restraint had met with opposition from the US embassy in Buenos Aires and from Tom Enders, the

US assistant secretary for inter-American affairs, who insisted the Americans should not get involved. Enders and the US ambassador to the UN, Jeane Kirkpatrick, were the leaders of the so-called 'Latino Lobby' within the Reagan administration and saw Argentina as a major ally in the US attempts to counter communist influence across Latin America.

Enders had spent a week in Buenos Aires that February discussing ways in which the *junta* might help, while Kirkpatrick was so close to Argentina's military regime that on the evening of the invasion the Argentine embassy in Washington was hosting a dinner in her honour, which to the consternation of the British and a number of senior members of the US administration, she insisted on attending. Henderson dismissed her as a 'tactless, wrong-headed fool' while Bill Casey, the wartime OSS officer who was now CIA director, even went so far as to suggest to the British ambassador that Kirkpatrick or Enders, possibly both, had encouraged the *junta* to believe that, in return for its assistance in opposing communism, the US would not take sides in any clash over the islands.[15]

A few days after the invasion, during a meeting of key officials in the White House Situation Room, Kirkpatrick's pro-*junta* stance led to a major row with Bobby Ray Inman, who was now CIA deputy director. Kirkpatrick insisted that Argentina was 'an all-important partner in hemisphere solidarity' and that the administration must force Thatcher to back down. 'We simply cannot let the UK call the shots,' she said. Inman angrily disagreed. As a former director of the NSA, he knew the value of the relationship with the British better than anyone else in the room. Two years earlier, Inman had stood alongside his GCHQ counterpart, Sir Brian Tovey, paying tribute to a man who over the space of the preceding forty years had become a potent symbol of the close relationship between British and US intelligence.

John Tiltman, who had met the four US codebreakers who arrived at Sheerness dockyard in February 1941 at the very beginning of that relationship, had finally retired from service in August 1980. Having been rushed to America in 1949, in the wake of the Weisband betrayal, to try to get back into the Soviet cipher systems, Tiltman had spent five years as senior UK liaison officer, nurturing the UKUSA relationship before returning to GCHQ in 1954. At that point, he had reached the official retirement age for British civil servants, but his ability as a codebreaker was such that GCHQ kept him on for another ten years, sending him back to the NSA as senior liaison officer in 1958 and only forcing him to retire in 1964 at the age of seventy.

Despite his age, his codebreaking skills were so good that the NSA recruited him as the leading light in their troubleshooting team—examining codes and ciphers that others had been unable to break —where his colleagues included his close friend Pres Currier, one of those four US codebreakers on the dockside at Sheerness. In a ceremony marking Tiltman's retirement, Inman and Tovey presented him with a scroll which acknowledged the 'uncountable contributions and successes in cryptology which attest to his technical brilliance, leadership, and inspiration'.

As a result, Inman was in no doubt as to the importance of the relationship with Britain and was furious at the careless fashion in which Kirkpatrick was happy to discard it for her Argentine friends. At the end of the meeting in the Situation Room, with officials anxious to hurry off to their next appointments, he stood up and delivered an impassioned speech, described by one of those present as both 'eloquent and compelling', which was testimony to the depth of a relationship forged over forty years of intense cooperation.

'I want to reiterate, as emphatically as I can, my opposition to Jeane Kirkpatrick's point of view,' Inman said silencing the hubbub. 'It's the most wrongheaded thing I have ever heard. I am here to say we have no alternative but to back our British allies to the hilt. I am not evoking just the historic ties of bloodlines, language, law, alliance, culture, and tradition, central as these are. I want you to remember the overwhelming importance of our shared interest in the strategic stakes, the depth and breadth of our intelligence cooperation, the whole gamut of global Cold War concerns we have riding on close interaction with the UK.' Given Kirkpatrick's abrasive personality, and her response behind the scenes to Inman's criticism, it was no coincidence that a couple of weeks later he decided to retire, citing a 'lost zest' for bureaucratic battles.[16]

While the British assembled the Operation Corporate task force to retake the islands, and Falklands fervour gripped the UK, the US administration adopted a determinedly neutral public position as 'an honest broker' attempting to negotiate a way out of the crisis. Haig embarked on an extensive bout of ultimately hopeless shuttle diplomacy. Although at times the seeming US lack of understanding of the British position infuriated Thatcher, the apparently endless peace efforts served only to underline the Argentine intransigence, leading at the end of April to the US decision to unequivocally back Britain. 'He [Haig] really was always on our side,' Henderson recalled. 'He kept saying to me, he said this so many times, "We will never do another Suez on you. But we have to show the American people and Congress that the Argentinians are not prepared to have any negotiated settlement that is reasonable."'[17]

In fact, from the beginning of the crisis both the Pentagon and the NSA had provided the British task force with everything it needed. The NSA, as part of its close cooperation with GCHQ under the UKUSA agreement, switched a Vortex signals intelligence satellite away from some of its programmed targets to provide better coverage of the South Atlantic and the Falkland Islands. Meanwhile, the Pentagon interpreted existing memoranda of understanding between the UK and the US over the use of satellite communications so broadly that it deprived US forces of channels they wanted to use in order to ensure that the UK task force had all the communications links it needed. There was a similar flexibility over Britain's use of the US Wideawake air base on Ascension Island.[18]

'The Americans could not have denied us the use of this base without infringing the terms of the agreement under which it had been set up,' Henderson said. 'But nothing in the agreement bound them to be as cooperative as they were.' When the US realised it could not deliver sufficient fuel to Ascension Island in time to keep the British task force on track, the Wideawake base commander was ordered to refuel RAF aircraft out of his war reserve stock until fresh supplies arrived in order to ensure that the British could operate 'without any reduction in tempo'.

The US defence secretary, Caspar Weinberger, insisted

throughout that the British must be given every assistance possible. 'I was in frequent touch with Mr Weinberger and on the few occasions Pentagon officials queried our requests he overruled them,' Henderson recalled. Even within the State Department, where backing for Argentina was at its strongest, Larry Eagleburger, the deputy secretary of state, ensured the UK's opponents were sidelined. Rick Burt, one of Eagleburger's most senior aides, made the case for helping the British very clear.

'An unsuccessful UK would gravely weaken the integrity of the Atlantic Alliance,' Burt said. 'We could well lose the Special Relationship and Britain's unique ability to bridge, and at times, heal differences across the Atlantic. The US must be prepared to do what is necessary to see the UK prevail and must be seen to be doing so.' UK requirements for US assistance would be considerable, he said. But no decision on how to respond, on public statements or negotiating tactics was to be made 'without reference to our long-term undeniable objective of seeing Britain come out of this crisis with its confidence and close ties to the United States intact'.[19]

Henderson subsequently recalled a conversation at the height of the crisis with US senator Joe Biden, then a member of both the Senate Foreign Affairs Committee and its Intelligence Committee. When the British ambassador suggested that the US was supporting the UK because it believed that aggression should not be allowed to succeed, Biden dismissed the idea. 'Do you think that if the Falkland Islands had belonged to Brazil rather than you, and Argentina had invaded them, the US would have reacted in the way they have done?' Biden asked. 'It is because you are British, with all that means in this country, that we have supported you.'

As a result of the US determination to help the British win—assisted in great part by Reagan's respect and admiration for Thatcher, and by the British prime minister's willingness to react bluntly to the slightest sign of US obfuscation—the task force received vital signals, imagery and submarine intelligence; satellite communications; meteorological data; millions of gallons of fuel; submarine detection devices; limpet mines; communications equipment and cipher systems; helicopter engines; 4,700 tons of airfield matting to allow the rapid reconstruction of Stanley airfield; and numerous types of weapons systems, including the latest version of the Sidewinder air-to-air missile for the Harrier aircraft and Stinger shoulder-held surface-to-air missiles for British special forces—the last of which had been surreptitiously dispatched to the SAS ahead of time by their US counterparts, in anticipation of an authorisation later made direct from Buenos Aires by Haig, apparently 'in disgust' at the Argentine response to negotiations.[20]

Within days of the invasion, the CIA's NPIC had provided its British counterpart, JARIC, with imagery of Argentina and the Falkland Islands which dated back to late 1981 and early 1982. The first contemporaneous US imagery the British received, almost certainly collected by a single USAF SR-71 flight, was of South Georgia. The intelligence it provided was used by a combined SAS–SBS force which recaptured the island on 25 April in Operation Paraquet. GCHQ intercepts had warned that the Argentine Navy's best-equipped submarine, the *Santa Fe*, was standing by to protect the Argentine marines left on South Georgia. The *Santa Fe* was disabled by missiles fired from Royal Navy helicopters, allowing the British special forces to capture a number of valuable documents, including recent operational messages and signals instructions which helped to explain the Argentine Navy's callsign systems. This provided invaluable assistance to the GCHQ traffic analysts who were producing much of the intelligence on the Argentine forces.[21]

The bulk of the British intelligence on the Falklands was provided by GCHQ, mainly collected by its listening station on Ascension Island, by the NSA, which included the satellite intercepts, and by Royal Navy teams on board a large number of the task force ships and submarines. There were also two small ground forces signals intelligence detachments, one from the British Army and one from the Royal Marines.

Incredibly, given that the main threat to the British forces came from Argentine aircraft, Air Chief Marshal Sir Michael James Beetham, the then chief of the air staff, refused to send an RAF team of Spanish-speaking signals intelligence specialists, holding them back in Gibraltar, a decision that was only revoked in the wake of the loss of the Royal Navy destroyer *Sheffield* to an Exocet missile fired by an Argentine Navy Super Étendard attack aircraft. The RAF team did not reach the task force until 25 May, the day the destroyer *Coventry* and the container ship *Atlantic Conveyor* were also lost to attacks by Argentine aircraft.[22]

While British Army signals intelligence operators spent much of the Cold War in static intercept sites in Germany and the Middle East, they had also provided signals intelligence for the SAS in a series of 'small wars'—most recently in Oman in the 1970s and Zimbabwe in 1980. They had a unit based at the former Second World War intercept site at Woodhouse Eaves in Leicestershire ready to provide a small rapid reaction team to any trouble spot worldwide. It was immediately activated to be part of the task force.

While the teams had slotted easily into relatively small-scale conflicts overseas, the extreme secrecy surrounding the very existence of signals intelligence and the number of people involved in the Falklands campaign created unprecedented security issues. Major Dave Thorp, a veteran of Cold War signals intelligence operations in Germany and Cyprus, was in charge of the seven-man detachment of army Spanish linguists and intelligence analysts sent south with the task force. He found that neither the Royal Navy officer coordinating signals intelligence for the task force nor the ground forces intelligence cell was aware of his team's presence until they started receiving his reports, with the intelligence cell so ill-informed that it asked him how on earth he knew what the Argentinians were saying.[23]

The Argentine armed services used the Crypto AG machine cipher systems to which the British and Americans had access as a result of surreptitious agreements made between Bill Friedman on behalf of NSA and Crypto's owner Boris Hagelin going back to the mid-1950s, allowing GCHQ to break their systems with ease. Commander Robert Denton Green, an intelligence staff officer at the Royal Navy's Fleet Headquarters in Northwood, north-west London, recalled that GCHQ had no problem in reading the Argentine messages. 'We got a lot of very high-quality planning-type intelligence of battle plans,' he said. 'But they first of all had to be broken, then they had to be translated and then they were sent to us for assessment. So, you had a delay of something between 12 and 24 hours. You were always trying to extrapolate from this to come up to date. But it was good intelligence. On balance we had a reasonable picture of what was going on in the minds of the main commanders.'[24]

As a result of the ability to read the Argentine ciphers, GCHQ knew at the end of April that the Argentine Navy had been told to penetrate the 200-mile exclusion zone the British had imposed around the islands and was authorised to use its weapons 'without restriction'. On 1 May, Admiral Anaya ordered the Argentine naval commanders to commence 'offensive operations' with complete freedom of action. All ships were to mount 'a massive attack' on the task force. The aircraft carrier *Veinticinco de Mayo*, with seven A-4 Skyhawk fighter bombers on board, was to 'deploy by night to launch a daytime air attack'. The light cruiser *General Belgrano* was ordered to use its escorts to carry out missile attacks on the British task force.

The next day, the *Veinticinco de Mayo* was waiting inside the northern edge of the exclusion zone and ready to launch a surprise attack which never went ahead due to poor weather. The *General Belgrano* was inside the southern edge of the zone preparing to attack the British ships as the second pincer of the ambush. When the *Veinticinco de Mayo* was spotted by a Harrier aircraft, it withdrew from the zone temporarily to prepare for a second attempt. The *General Belgrano* similarly withdrew, albeit also only temporarily and in order to ready itself again for the attack.

The Royal Navy nuclear submarine *Conqueror* had the *General Belgrano* in its sights but its commander was concerned he might lose it. Contrary to subsequent claims, it was not withdrawing to the mainland. The GCHQ intelligence demonstrated unequivocally that it was preparing to carry out its orders and attack the task force. The British first sea lord, Admiral Sir Henry Leach, consulted the war cabinet, which authorised the *Conqueror* to attack it. It fired two torpedoes which sank the *General Belgrano* with the loss of 323 lives. From that point on, the Argentine Navy stayed in port but the sinking was highly controversial, largely because, in order to protect the all-important GCHQ signals intelligence source, the orders to carry out 'a massive attack' on the British task force could not be revealed.[25]

There was no active US imagery satellite available during the early days of the conflict. It was not until a US KH-9 Hexagon satellite was launched on 11 May 1982 that there was any current satellite imagery of the South Atlantic. Even then, given that the southern hemisphere late autumn had covered the Falklands in cloud, the initial pass produced just eleven images of Argentine armed forces bases in the Buenos Aires region. It was sufficient to show that a number of military aircraft, including the ten Argentine Air Force Canberra bombers, had moved to airfields in southern Argentina, closer to the Falklands, but was nevertheless of only limited importance, leaving the DIS briefly questioning whether there would be any loss if the Americans decided not to share their satellite imagery.[26]

The DIS pessimism was unfounded. A break in the weather on 28 May produced extensive images providing a detailed picture of the Argentine defensive positions on the Falkland Islands themselves. Although NPIC's analysis of the imagery of East Falkland was relatively cursory, noting the extent to which the Argentine forces had begun to dig themselves in and the strengthening of defensive positions around Port Stanley itself, JARIC understandably pored over the imagery in far more extensive detail to produce a comprehensive picture of precisely where all the Argentine forces, and their ammunition and fuel dumps, were located.[27]

The arrival of the US satellite imagery was timely. Although the Nimrod maritime surveillance aircraft flying out of Ascension provided good aerial reconnaissance of Argentine threats to the task force while it sailed south, there was very little tactical intelligence of the islands themselves from imagery produced by UK aircraft. Nor was GCHQ able to provide much useable intelligence to assist the British troops on the ground. The best tactical intelligence came from SAS and SBS teams inserted onto East Falkland three weeks ahead of the main attacks.

When the US satellite imagery arrived in the UK, the British

troops were breaking out of the San Carlos bridgehead and Goose
Green to advance eastwards across the island. The JARIC interpretation of the imagery identified a number of targets for the RAF
and Fleet Air Arm Harrier aircraft that were providing air cover for
the British troops and—combined with GCHQ traffic analysis of
the Argentine order of battle and locations of key commanders—
reassured British commanders that they were facing no significant
opposition and ensured that they knew precisely which enemy forces
were dug in on a succession of military objectives culminating in
Port Stanley. It was liberated on 14 June 1982, leading the Argentine
forces to surrender.[28] While there is no doubt that GCHQ signals
intelligence, supplemented by the NSA satellite intercepts, provided
the vast bulk of the intelligence that ensured British troops won
the battle, it is difficult to argue that the comprehensive picture of
Argentine defensive positions produced by that one set of US satellite imagery did not provide some of the most important, and indeed
reassuring, intelligence available to British commanders during the
advance on Port Stanley.[29]

MI6 did not provide substantial intelligence during the conflict,
either in its own right or through its relationship with the CIA, but
it did play a key role in stopping Argentina's supply of the Exocet
air-to-surface missiles that were the main threat to the British
warships. Long-standing MI6 agent Tony Divall, who as 'Herr
Stephan' had created and run the Goldfinger operation to obtain
illicit roubles in post-war Berlin, was now a freelance arms dealer
based in Hamburg. He persuaded Captain Alfredo Corti, the head
of the Argentine arms procurement team, that he was in a position
to provide thirty Exocets at a cost of a million pounds apiece from
Iraq and Libya. By committing Corti to the sale and then stringing
him along until the British had recovered the islands, Divall ensured
that the Argentinians' supply of Exocets dried up.[30]

Despite their close relationship, there were several intense disagreements between Thatcher and Reagan, most notably over the
US invasion of the Caribbean island of Grenada in October 1983, in
the wake of a left-wing coup in which the Marxist prime minister,
Maurice Bishop, was murdered. The island, a British colony until

1974, was a member of the Commonwealth with the Queen still its head of state. The British prime minister was furious that, despite firm promises from Reagan that he would consult her before making a final decision on whether or not to invade, and the delicate constitutional position of the Queen, she was deliberately not informed until the very last moment, by which time it was too late to call off the invasion. Unsurprisingly, she made her irritation clear in a fraught telephone exchange with the US president.

Bud McFarlane, the then national security adviser, was in the Oval Office listening to Reagan trying to calm Thatcher down. 'It was not a happy conversation,' McFarlane recalled. 'The President was very disappointed. Not angry. His respect for her was too deep for him ever to become angry with her but he was disappointed.' The Americans understood Thatcher's anger at the deliberate decision not to consult the British, with State Department officials who were in frequent consultation with the embassy also kept out of the loop. But they had difficulty understanding that since the Queen was technically Grenada's head of state, it was deeply embarrassing that her own government had no idea that the invasion was about to take place.[31]

There was, to be fair, a mutual lack of understanding. Even Larry Eagleburger, one of the most pro-British members of the US administration, felt betrayed by Thatcher's public criticism of the invasion, complaining that the UK's 'strident and persistent' complaints had done the British cause 'a good deal of harm'. Nevertheless, the damage was more than repaired by Thatcher's decision to allow US F-111 bombers based in the UK to attack Libya in the wake of the bombing by Libyan-backed terrorists of a West Berlin discotheque in which a US serviceman died, by Thatcher's support and advice in Reagan's dealings with Gorbachev, and by the UK's role as America's most prominent ally in the 1991 Gulf War.[32]

The Iraqi invasion of Kuwait and the subsequent Gulf War led to an evolution in another key element of the Special Relationship, the close cooperation between UK and US special operations forces. This had begun when Charlie Beckwith, a US Army Green Beret, did a tour with the SAS in the 1960s. He returned to America convinced the US Army needed a similar elite special operations team and in late 1977 set up what became known as Delta. In order to ensure that those he recruited had the same mental toughness he had seen in the SAS, Beckwith had sent Bucky Burruss, his executive officer, to the UK to undergo SAS selection. Graeme Lamb, a future UK director of special forces, was a young lieutenant on the same course.

'Bucky Burruss was sent across, literally from a cold start, and we did selection together,' Lamb said. 'Then he went back to Delta and used what he'd learned to create not exactly a mirror image of the SAS selection course but an adapted format where they brought in psycho-metric testing and analysis, which we now use. So, the genesis of the Delta selection was all part of the 1970s experience which then created something that was not dissimilar from the SAS.'

By the time of the Gulf War, Delta was part of the US Joint Special Operations Command (JSOC), along with the US Navy's SEAL Team Six and a number of specialist support units, but it was regarded by many senior US officers as a dedicated counter-terrorist unit and so, unlike the SAS, was not included in the plans for the war. Lamb, now a lieutenant-colonel, was sent out to the Gulf to act as special forces adviser controlling the operations of the SAS.

Iraq was known to be planning to respond to any attack by firing Scud surface-to-surface missiles at Israel, with the clear intention of dragging it into the war and fracturing the anti-Saddam coalition, which included Syria, Egypt and a number of other Arab countries. So, the SAS was sent into western Iraq at the start of the air war, six weeks before other ground forces were deployed, to hunt down the Scuds. But the British did not have the capabilities that their US counterparts possessed, so Lamb asked that they be sent in to work with them.

'They came in and they had the longer reach, more technically capable equipment, which we didn't,' Lamb said. 'Those two forces, British and US, complemented each other on the battlefield with their forces and capabilities.' The close links between British and American special forces developed during the Gulf War became a vital and highly valued component of the Special Relationship between Britain and America.[33]

*

Although the collapse of the Soviet economy had been predicted by both US and British intelligence throughout the 1980s, with suggestions that one or more of the Warsaw Pact countries, most likely Poland, might break away, leading to a domino effect in which other communist states split from Moscow, no one expected the swift end to communist rule which followed Mikhail Gorbachev's attempts to reform the system, leading to democratic elections across the Eastern Bloc and, in December 1991, to the dissolution of the Soviet Union.[34]

The collapse of the communist satellites and the economic chaos across the former Soviet Union provided a number of intelligence coups, notably the capture of every major Russian cipher machine and a number of defectors. One of the first of these was Vladimir Pasechnik, a Soviet microbiologist who, during an official trip to France in the summer of 1989, walked into the British embassy in Paris and asked to speak to the MI6 head of station.

Pasechnik ran the Institute of Ultra-Pure Biochemical Preparations in Leningrad, part of an organisation known as Biopreparat which had eighteen laboratories scattered around the Soviet Union ostensibly doing biological research to assist in the treatment of disease, but in fact developing a range of viruses for use as biological weapons. They included anthrax, ebola, Q-fever and smallpox. Pasechnik's laboratory was working on Yersinia pestis, the plague bacterium that caused the Black Death, which wiped out a third of the population of fourteenth-century Europe. 'I couldn't sleep at night, thinking about what we were doing,' Pasechnik told David Kelly, the British biological weapons expert who led his MI6 debriefing.

The Pasechnik intelligence was shared with the Americans, leading President George Bush and Margaret Thatcher to apply joint pressure on Gorbachev to open up the Biopreparat operation to Anglo-American weapons inspectors. When the Soviet leader finally agreed, in early 1991, the weapons inspectors were met with obvious attempts to cover up what had been going on. 'This was clearly the most successful biological-weapons programme on earth,' Kelly said. 'These people just sat there and lied to us, and lied, and lied.'[35]

The best of the post-Cold War 'walk-ins' was Vasili Mitrokhin, another KGB officer who had become disenchanted by the Soviet system. A member of the KGB's foreign intelligence division, the First Chief Directorate, Mitrokhin was removed from a frontline operations role and transferred to the archives. For more than a decade, he carefully copied out files, compiling a secret archive of Soviet agents and operations in the West. Mitrokhin made detailed notes which he stored in his waste-paper basket until the end of the day when he retrieved them and smuggled them out of the directorate's offices at Yasenevo, south-west of Moscow. Once home, he hid the notes under his mattress and, every weekend, took them to a *dacha* 20 miles outside Moscow where he typed them up and concealed them in a milk churn under the floorboards. By the time he retired in 1984, he had also filled a tin clothes boiler, two tin trunks and two aluminium cases.

In March 1992, Mitrokhin travelled to Latvia and went to the US embassy in Riga, where he was told they were too busy and he should come back later. Instead, he went to the British embassy, where he received a more encouraging response. A female Russian-speaking diplomat examined the samples he had brought with him, made clear that she understood the importance of what he had to offer and told him to come back in early April with more.

A team of MI6 Russian experts were flown in to question him during the second visit, when he brought around a dozen envelopes containing over 2,000 closely typed pages of details from the KGB records, including the names of 645 KGB agents in the West, from 1917 right up to 1984 when he retired. Two months later, he brought the rest of his archive to the Riga embassy, before travelling to the UK to help the MI6 officers examining his notes to understand what he had written. He was debriefed at a series of safe houses and, after deciding to defect, was infiltrated back into Russia to collect his family. A few weeks later, they boarded a train to Latvia and from there were taken to the UK.

MI6 shared the documents on America with the CIA and FBI, and intelligence officers on both sides of the Atlantic trawled through the Mitrokhin archive looking for KGB agents who were still in place and ways of turning that knowledge to the best possible advantage. One FBI officer described it as 'the most complete and extensive intelligence ever received from one source'. Inevitably, some details of the Mitrokhin archive leaked into the US media, a persistent problem in liaison with the Americans. But the leaks caused little real damage and simply left the SVR, the new Russian foreign intelligence service which had replaced the KGB's First Chief Directorate, struggling to work out which of its agents and operations were blown. The disruption caused to Russian intelligence operations abroad was incalculable, representing a major coup for MI6.[36]

John Major's time as prime minister was even more difficult in terms of relations between Britain and America than Ted Heath's. In a clear attempt to distance himself from his predecessor, he banned the use of the term 'Special Relationship' and made it clear to those around him that the priority was the British partnership with Europe. The election of Bill Clinton led to a tense relationship, with the incoming president believing the Conservatives had actively worked to get Bush re-elected. Ray Seitz, the US ambassador to the UK, recalled flying to Washington in February 1993 to prepare for Major's first meeting with the new president. 'The British press was almost ghoulish in its anticipation of rancour,' Seitz said. 'Just before the Prime Minister arrived at the White House, Clinton was sitting with a few aides in the Oval Office. "Don't forget to say Special Relationship when the press comes in," one of them joked. "Oh, yes," Clinton said. "How could I forget? The Special Relationship." And he threw back his head and laughed.'[37]

Shortly before stepping down as US ambassador to the UK, Seitz warned against a 'careless' approach to the 'important strategic relationship' between Britain and America. His concerns were shared by Major's defence secretary, Malcolm Rifkind, and by his foreign secretary, Douglas Hurd, who circulated a paper which tellingly began by making clear that it was not his intention to argue that relations with the US were more important than those with France and Germany. Hurd stressed that defence and intelligence were 'the central planks of the Anglo-American relationship', which remained 'critical to our interests worldwide', but expressed concern that it 'may have suffered some neglect because of our necessary pre-occupation with Europe'. The expressions of concern from Hurd and Rifkind fell on stony ground in Downing Street. Major had only a limited grasp of the real value of the transatlantic intelligence cooperation with America and what was being put at risk.

The transatlantic tension was not helped by serious disagreements over the war in Bosnia. Two years after his initial paper, with relations as strained as ever, Hurd warned of 'a real risk' that Britain and America 'could gradually drift apart', with 'indifference and disagreement' replacing the previous 'instinctive understanding and cooperation'. His suggestions on how to renew the relationship were dismissed as 'piffle and guff' by a relatively junior Downing Street official, who had, astonishingly, been seconded from the Foreign Office and who even went so far as to block attempts by John Kerr, the British ambassador in Washington, to discuss the issues Hurd had raised with Clinton's national security adviser, Anthony Lake.[38]

The dangers pointed out by Seitz and Hurd were not overstated. Even the real Special Relationship between British and US intelligence was strained. By the mid-1990s, with the departures of wartime intelligence officers like John Tiltman, Pres Currier, Daphne Park and Bill Colby, and the rapid promotion across the Atlantic of younger intelligence officers, questions were beginning to be asked, even within the NSA, as to whether they really needed 'the Brits'. So much so that the senior NSA liaison officer to GCHQ felt compelled to write an impassioned defence of the UKUSA relationship, pointing out that it was 'the most important and productive one we have'; indeed, it was 'so broad and so important' that it was 'neither possible nor desirable' to cut it back.

The past few years had been a watershed marked by the collapse of the Soviet Union and Warsaw Pact on the one hand and the emergence of internet communications on the other, the liaison officer said. 'The reality of the one and the eventuality of the other have had and will continue to have a significant impact on NSA operations and on our approach to dealing with GCHQ.' He pointed out that while 'peace dividend' budget cuts would have a profound effect on the NSA's capabilities, GCHQ had reacted to the end of the

Cold War by buying a share in the US spy satellite system, paying the £500 million cost of one of the satellites, and recruiting ever more IT specialists. As a result, it had some 'very talented technical people' who promised much for the future. The UK also retained key dependencies around the world which provided intercept sites in areas the Americans could not reach, and while GCHQ had less money it had far greater financial flexibility, which allowed it to step in at short notice to cover targets that the NSA could not. The emergence of the internet would require even closer cooperation with GCHQ, not less.

The announcement in April 1999 by Major's successor, Tony Blair, of the European Defence Initiative led to concerns at the NSA that the British were continuing the tilt away from the US towards Europe and a feeling that they could no longer be trusted with everything the Americans had. 'They were convinced that Britain had taken a sort of strategic decision to alter course away from America, away from the Atlantic Partnership and towards Europe,' Sir Francis Richards, the then GCHQ director, said. 'They started to think that they must rely less on co-operation with Britain, and we started to see, in all sorts of contacts with the Americans, doors beginning to close, access being denied to our embedded personnel in America. They would find themselves not being shown stuff.'

On 24 January 2000, the main signals intelligence processing computer at the NSA's Fort Meade headquarters crashed and, despite frantic efforts to get it working, could not be patched back together for four days, leading to a complete blackout. For seventy-two hours, with the NSA unable to send out any intelligence, GCHQ stepped in to keep the intelligence flowing to the NSA's US customers. 'We covered the whole thing for them,' one GCHQ official said, 'to their acute embarrassment.' No one at the NSA ever asked if they still needed 'the Brits' again.[39]

AMERICA'S AVENGING ANGELS

On the morning of 11 September 2001, al-Qaeda terrorists hijacked four passenger aircraft on domestic flights across the United States of America. The first aircraft, with ninety-two people on board, was flown into the north tower of New York's World Trade Center and, with TV news channels around the world showing events as they happened, a second aircraft with sixty-five people on board was flown into the south tower. Both towers caught fire and collapsed. A third aircraft with sixty-four people on board was flown into the Pentagon. The fourth was apparently headed for the White House or the US Capitol building in Washington, but the passengers fought back and it crashed into a field near Shanksville, Pennsylvania, with the loss of all forty-four people on board. A total of 2,996 people, including the nineteen terrorists, died in what remains the worst terrorist attack in history. They included 2,605 US citizens and sixty-seven Britons, in both cases the most ever killed in a single act of terrorism.

It was a cataclysmic moment, sparking a widespread belief that if this could happen to the world's most powerful nation, Islamist terrorism was now capable of wreaking havoc across the Western world. Support for America from Britain was immediate and unequivocal, emotionally, politically, and in terms of the intelligence relationship. The day after the attacks, British prime minister Tony Blair telephoned President George W. Bush to offer the UK's assistance in any response, telling him that Britain stood 'full square alongside the US' in the fight against terrorism. At the same time, MI6 Chief Richard Dearlove, GCHQ director Francis Richards and MI5 deputy director-general Eliza Manningham-Buller flew to Washington, exempted from a ban on any aircraft entering US airspace, to talk to CIA director George Tenet.

'We flew past the still burning Twin Towers with an F-15 on each wingtip to keep us out of trouble and went straight out to Langley,' Richards said. 'It was an extremely emotional meeting which was primarily an expression of solidarity and an offer on our part to spare nothing in supporting our American counterparts. I think all doubts in America about our commitment to the transatlantic intelligence relationship were stilled at that point.'

At the same time, Graeme Lamb, now the UK's director of special forces, flew to US Central Command in Tampa, Florida, which was responsible for US military operations in the Middle East and south Asia. 'There was a need to get a better understanding of America's state of mind and what it might do,' Lamb recalled. 'I had gone to America with the clear support from the Prime Minister that we the Brits were up for absolutely supporting the idea of how to bring bin Laden and al-Qaeda to account. It was clear that we would have a part in it. I needed to get to America and talk to various people before what America intended to do was overly fixed.'

From Tampa, he went up to North Carolina, to Fort Bragg, the headquarters of JSOC, to see his American counterpart, General Dell Dailey, then to Langley to discuss the options with the CIA, and on to Washington to talk to the Pentagon's operations chief before flying back to the UK. 'I was the first guy back, so I went straight up to Chequers and gave a debrief to the Prime Minister. America was simply a nation at war. They intended to avenge what was a murderous act of significant proportion. The Taliban would comply or they would just be in the way. So, the idea in those early stages was to remove the Taliban, mortally wound al-Qaeda and bring its leadership to account.'

Tenet told the British intelligence chiefs that the CIA had been ordered to 'take the war against the terrorists to their sanctuaries and those that provide them'. The Bush administration was determined to bring down any regimes that supported terrorists. 'While the emotional reaction to the attacks is still vivid the US has a window of public support for a major act of retaliation' even if it were to include 'significant collateral damage', Tenet told the British intelligence chiefs. 'The gloves are off.'[1]

It will become increasingly difficult at such a distance from the events for those who were very young or not born at the time to imagine the widespread shock and horror across the Western world at television footage of people jumping from the top floors of the Twin Towers rather than be burned alive and the collapse of the buildings with so many people, including rescue workers, still inside. The sympathy and support for America displayed across Britain itself was extraordinary. The day after the attacks, the Queen ordered the music for the Changing of the Guard to be changed from the national anthem to the 'Star-Spangled Banner', while the following day she was shown on American TV singing the US national anthem at a memorial service in St Paul's Cathedral.

On the Saturday following the attacks, the traditional Last Night of the Proms concert, normally a fervent celebration of British patriotism, was turned into what was both a memorial to the victims of 9/11 and a vociferous expression of British support for the American people as a whole. 'God Save the Queen' was followed by a rousing rendition of the US national anthem led from an auditorium awash with Britons waving the Stars and Stripes. By coincidence, the orchestra was conducted for the first time in the history of the Proms by an American, Leonard Slatkin, and the reflective music that replaced 'Rule Britannia', 'Land of Hope and Glory' and other British classics included Samuel Barber's *Adagio for Strings*, which is traditionally played at US memorial services, and Michael Tippett's arrangements of classic US spirituals from his oratorio *A Child of Our Time*. The concert was broadcast for the first time across America on 300 National Public Radio stations and on the BBC America television channel. There was a minute's silence for the 9/11 victims and Slatkin praised the British response to the attacks which had demonstrated the close bonds between the two countries. 'It's not for me to speak on behalf of the American public,' he said. 'But all of us are so moved by everything you have done over these last four horrific days.'

While the scale and the sheer audacity of the 9/11 attacks were a shock to British and US intelligence, the fact that al-Qaeda was targeting America was no surprise at all. Five years before the attacks, Osama bin Laden had moved his operations to Afghanistan and begun training his followers to carry out attacks on the West. The CIA created a specialist unit, the 'Alec Station', to monitor his activities. In February 1998, al-Qaeda issued a *fatwa* imposing a religious duty on all believers to attack US and allied targets around the world, and at a news conference a few months later bin Laden talked openly about 'bringing the war home to America'. On 7 August 1998, al-Qaeda terrorists used trucks full of explosives to destroy the US embassies in the Kenyan capital, Nairobi, and the Tanzanian capital, Dar es Salaam, killing 224 people, including 12 Americans, and injuring 5,000 more.[2]

While the CIA had largely ignored Afghanistan in the period after the 1989 Soviet withdrawal, MI6 had continued to keep in touch with Ahmed Shah Masood and its other Afghan contacts, initially simply maintaining the links, later for intelligence on the drugs trade, which had risen up the service's list of post-Cold War priorities. But in the wake of bin Laden's arrival in Afghanistan, intelligence on his activities and whereabouts was at a premium.

The CIA's Counterterrorist Center had developed a plan to send special operations teams into Afghanistan to abduct the al-Qaeda leader, taking him back to the US. British contacts provided intelligence that might allow the Americans to capture him and MI6 passed it on to the CIA. Ultimately it was not good enough for the operation to go ahead with any certainty that bin Laden would be captured without being killed, at the time a prerequisite for presidential authorisation, but the existence and reliability of the British sources led the CIA to send a six-man team into the Panjshir Valley to make its own contacts with Masood, who was now head of the Northern Alliance, a group of mainly Tajik, Uzbek and Hazara forces who were holding out against the Taliban government.[3]

Over the next two years, there was an intensive focus on al-Qaeda, with both the NSA and GCHQ monitoring its followers' mobile and satellite telephones as well as their internet communications, while MI6, the CIA, the FBI and MI5 worked with allies, particularly Saudi Arabia and the Gulf states, to obtain intelligence on al-Qaeda operations. By the spring of 2001, there was acute concern at the amount of 'chatter' on the terrorist networks monitored by the NSA and GCHQ about an impending attack, with America or Israel seen as the most likely target.

At the annual intelligence conference between the CIA and MI6 in June 2001, 'considerable anxieties' were raised at the lack of specific intelligence on an attack which everyone knew was coming. The British JIC reported in July 2001 that a major al-Qaeda attack, probably against US or Israeli interests, was in its final stages of preparation. Neither the British nor the US intelligence services had any idea what the attacks would be—although MI6 obtained intelligence suggesting plans to hijack civilian aircraft which it shared with the CIA. Just over a month before the 9/11 attacks, the Agency warned, in a report in the President's Daily Brief entitled 'Bin Laden Determined to Strike in US', of an attack similar in intention to the 1993 failed attack on the World Trade Center and revisited the MI6 report of potential hijacking. But there was certainly no expectation among intelligence chiefs on either side of the Atlantic that the terrorists were capable of killing several thousand people in an attack on mainland America itself.[4]

On Saturday 15 September, as Slatkin and the BBC Symphony Orchestra rehearsed for that evening's Last Night of the Proms, Bush and his war cabinet were sat around a large table in the wood-panelled Laurel Lodge at Camp David, working out the US response to the attacks. Tenet put forward an imaginative plan entitled simply 'Going to War' which envisaged members of the CIA's Special Activities Division and small teams of special operations forces going into Afghanistan to coordinate attacks by the Northern Alliance and calling in close air support from US aircraft or Predator drones armed with Hellfire missiles.[5]

It was not a new idea. Two weeks earlier, having spent years dismissing Masood's usefulness, the CIA had received authorisation to spend up to $200 million a year arming the *mujahideen* leader's Northern Alliance in a joint operation with MI6. Bin Laden was under no illusion about the threat posed by Masood and just two days before the 9/11 attacks sent a two-man team into the Panjshir Valley. Disguised as a Belgian television crew looking to interview Masood, they killed him by detonating a bomb hidden in their equipment.

A week later, the first CIA officers, known as the Northern Alliance Liaison Team, went into Afghanistan to link up with Masood's men, now led by Mohammed Fahim, who was very keen to take the fight to the Taliban. The CIA officers brought with them a large metal suitcase containing $3 million in $100 bills for what were effectively bribes to bring or keep various Afghan tribes and factions on side, a traditional Afghan way of uniting otherwise fractious groups to achieve victory. MI6 sent its own team of eight officers, with a far smaller amount of money, to contact its own agents on the ground, collect intelligence on bin Laden's where-abouts and persuade tribal groups who might otherwise support the Taliban to join its opponents.[6]

Operation Enduring Freedom, the ousting of the Taliban, began on 7 October with an extensive US and British air campaign. The combination of proxy forces and US and British special operations teams, with the CIA and MI6 bribing opposing forces to join the anti-Taliban coalition, swept across Afghanistan, capturing Kabul on 13 November and finally overpowering the Taliban stronghold at Kandahar on 6 December. Large numbers of al-Qaeda fighters were among the first on the frontlines and lost their lives in the fighting, while those who fled were hunted down by US and UK special operations forces backed up by allied air attacks. But bin Laden and some of his key lieutenants managed to escape across the border into Pakistan.

By now, the US administration was already turning its attention to Iraq. Donald Rumsfeld, the US defence secretary, had raised the possibility of removing Saddam Hussein from power the day after the 9/11 attacks, arguing that Iraq was a key supporter of terrorism and a much easier target for US forces with a detailed plan ready and waiting on the shelf. Bush was initially, and rightly, determined to concentrate on bin Laden and Afghanistan first, but the swift success against the Taliban allowed senior members of the administration, and in particular Vice-President Dick Cheney, Rumsfeld and his deputy Paul Wolfowitz, to argue that Iraq should be next, based on what was perceived to be its continued chemical, biological and nuclear weapons programmes and its support for terrorism.

There were also repeated claims of links between Saddam Hussein and al-Qaeda, despite a complete lack of any reliable evidence. When the CIA dismissed the reports, an aide to Wolfowitz set up the Policy Counterterrorism Evaluation Group in the Pentagon to cherry-pick intelligence that seemed to suggest links between Iraq and al-Qaeda. A senior Foreign Office official described US 'scrambling' to tie Iraq to al-Qaeda as 'frankly unconvincing', and Richard Dearlove, the MI6 Chief, who had just returned from discussions with Tenet in the US, told a meeting of Tony Blair's war cabinet in July 2002 that in Washington 'the intelligence and facts were being fixed around the policy'.[7]

A series of US and British inquiries into the intelligence used to justify going to war subsequently exposed extensive flaws in the intelligence. Iraq was a 'hard target'. Both MI6 and the CIA struggled to recruit human sources with access to the Iraqi weapons of mass destruction (WMD) programmes. The intelligence services on both sides of the Atlantic were also acutely aware of how successfully Saddam had concealed his nuclear weapons programme ahead of the 1991 Gulf War. International Atomic Energy Authority (IAEA) inspectors who went into Iraq after the war discovered that it had been on course to produce a nuclear bomb by 1993, two years earlier than previously believed. For most of the 1990s, intelligence on Iraqi WMD programmes was based on reports by the UN weapons inspectors, albeit 'significantly boosted' in 1995 by the defection of Saddam's son-in-law Hussein Kamal. But after the weapons inspectors left in 1998, intelligence on the programmes was scarce.

Updated reports were difficult to obtain and not always reliable. The JIC assessment in the period leading up to the publication of a British government dossier on Iraq's WMD in September 2002 was dominated by two MI6 agents. They had produced authoritative intelligence on a number of subjects that had proven to be correct, but both relied on other contacts, albeit well placed in Baghdad, for their intelligence on WMD. As a result, the JIC noted in early

September 2002 that the intelligence was 'limited' but it did conclude that 'Iraq has a chemical and biological weapons capability and Saddam is prepared to use it'.[8]

There was no evidence from any of the available intelligence of an active nuclear weapons programme, but a visit by an Iraqi official to Niger in 1999 and GCHQ intercepts related to the visit led the JIC to make a cautious note in December 2000 that 'unconfirmed intelligence indicates Iraqi interest in acquiring uranium'. In 2002, the then French security service, the DST (Direction de la Surveillance du Territoire), which was responsible for the security of the French nuclear industry, including the uranium mines in its former colony Niger, passed MI6 documentary evidence that the Iraqi official had asked about the possibility of purchasing uranium ore.

It was not evidence of the existence of a nuclear programme but it was evidence of a continued interest in developing one and as a result the JIC assessed that Iraq had 'sought significant quantities of uranium from Africa, despite having no active civil nuclear power programme that could require it'. That assessment, which subsequently appeared in the British dossier, was to become highly controversial when President Bush cited it in his State of the Union address of 28 January 2003, saying: 'The British government has learned that Saddam Hussein recently sought significant quantities of uranium from Africa.'

MI6 had shared the DST intelligence with the CIA, but under the terms of its intelligence-sharing agreement with the French, it was not allowed to give the Americans the documentary evidence that backed it up. The DST even refused to allow MI6 to say who had provided the intelligence, which would have given it far more credibility. All MI6 could tell the Americans was that the intelligence had come from 'a foreign liaison service'. Unfortunately, at the same time, fake evidence originating in Italy of an Iraqi attempt to obtain uranium ore from Niger had discredited the idea and, unaware of the DST evidence, the CIA assumed that the MI6 report was from similar sources and therefore unreliable.

Nevertheless, in a National Intelligence Estimate entitled 'Iraq's Continuing Programs for Weapons of Mass Destruction' published in October 2002, US intelligence went considerably further than the JIC, noting that Iraq was 'reconstituting its nuclear weapons programme' and had begun 'vigorously trying to procure uranium ore'. Both the Butler Review of Intelligence on Weapons of Mass Destruction and the UK Parliament's Intelligence and Security Committee inquiry into the intelligence on Iraqi WMD backed the JIC reporting of the Iraqi attempt to obtain uranium from Niger, with Butler noting that its assessment and, by extension, the president's claim were 'well-founded'.[9]

Notwithstanding the extensive problems with the intelligence used to support the war in Iraq, the most immediate issue was that the war not only squandered the 'emotional . . . window of public support' around the world that the sheer horror of the 9/11 attacks had undoubtedly produced—and the US administration had been so eager to harness in order to destroy al-Qaeda—but also deflected attention and vital resources away from operations in Afghanistan, and led to the radicalisation of Muslims, providing al-Qaeda with an increased number of recruits, many of them coming from the UK. Sir David Omand, the then intelligence and security coordinator, recalled that from October 2002 onwards, the JIC was warning that an invasion of Iraq would radicalise increasing numbers of British Muslims. 'We pointed out that AQ would use an attack on Iraq as "justification" for terrorist attacks on western or Israeli targets,' he said. 'We pointed out that AQ was already in their propaganda portraying US-led operations as being a war on Islam and that, indeed, this view was attracting widespread support across the Muslim community.'

In the weeks before the war began, the JIC again warned that it would increase the worldwide threat from al-Qaeda and other Islamist terrorist groups. Al-Qaeda and its affiliates posed 'the greatest terrorist threat to the UK' with some attacks likely to be carried out by 'lone wolf' individuals. The committee also warned that once the war was over terrorists linked to al-Qaeda would in all probability carry out attacks against coalition forces in Iraq, and just days before the invasion it reinforced that warning with a suggestion that al-Qaeda might have set up 'sleeper cells' in Iraq to attack allied forces during the post-war occupation.[10]

Eliza Manningham-Buller, who was now MI5 director-general, would later point out that the British participation in the Iraq War had indeed spurred some young British Muslims with family links to Pakistan to turn to terror and 'through those links al-Qaeda gives guidance and training to its largely British foot soldiers here on an extensive and growing scale'. Within months of the invasion, MI5 discovered a group of British-born Pakistani Muslims who had travelled to Pakistan for training in the use of weapons and explosives and on their return to the UK had begun planning a series of bomb attacks. MI5's Operation Crevice involved many months of surveillance. The bombers were arrested shortly before they were due to begin their attacks and five of those involved were subsequently jailed for life. MI5 went on to prevent a number of other attacks but Manningham-Buller warned in the summer of 2004 that it was 'only a matter of time' before a serious attack went undetected.

On 7 July 2005, three British-born Pakistani Muslims and a young Briton born in Jamaica who had converted to Islam detonated explosives-filled backpacks on the London transport system, three of them on Underground trains which had just left King's Cross station and one on a double-decker bus, killing a total of fifty-two people. Al-Qaeda's sponsorship of the attacks was confirmed when bin Laden's deputy Ayman al-Zawahiri released videos made before the attack by two of the bombers, both of whose names had come up during the Operation Crevice investigations, although neither had at that time appeared to pose a terrorist threat.[11]

MI5 had liaised closely with both the FBI and the CIA on counter-espionage throughout the Cold War, and from the early 1970s onwards on Middle East and Irish terrorism, with MI5 officers seeing a tour in the British embassy in Washington as an important part of any successful career, and FBI and CIA officers based in London building close relationships with their MI5 colleagues. But that relationship grew exponentially in the wake of the 9/11 attacks with particular emphasis on al-Qaeda. MI5 set up a Joint Terrorism Analysis Centre, including GCHQ and MI6 personnel, at its Westminster headquarters. MI6 provided 10 per cent of the intelligence officers working on UK counter-terrorism operations, including specialist agent recruiters and handlers, and conducted substantial 'disruption operations' against Islamist terrorists operating overseas. It also stepped up its focus on Britons travelling abroad, in particular to Pakistan and Afghanistan, while GCHQ reallocated resources to provide direct support to MI5 counter-terrorist operations.[12]

The first operation on which this multi-agency cooperation had a major impact was a substantial success for the intelligence relationship between Britain and America, albeit providing evidence of the problems of working with the US agencies. Operation Overt had begun with a tip-off from a member of the public suspicious of a young British-born Pakistani Muslim. Abdulla Ahmed Ali had been radicalised in his teens and in the wake of the Iraq War had volunteered to work as an ambulance driver for a British Islamic charity in Afghanistan. While there, he met Assad Sarwar, who had been trained in Pakistan by al-Qaeda as a bomb maker. At Sarwar's suggestion, Ali crossed into Pakistan himself to meet up with Rashid Rauf, another UK British-born Pakistani Muslim, who had trained other Britons to carry out terror attacks, including the 7/7 bombings.

British intelligence officers monitored Ali's repeated visits to Pakistan, with MI6 carrying out surveillance when he arrived and watching who he met. When he returned from one of his visits in June 2006, MI5 had his baggage searched. It contained large numbers of AA batteries and orange soft drink powder, leading to fears that he might be looking to mix the powder with liquid explosive to disguise a bomb as a bottle of soft drink.

MI5 obtained a warrant to track and monitor his mobile phone and internet communications. They also put him under 24-hour surveillance, a huge operation involving large numbers of MI5 and Metropolitan Police officers, along with a team of MI5 lawyers who monitored the surveillance operations to ensure the intelligence obtained could be used as evidence in court. Surveillance officers spotted Ali meeting Sarwar at the latter's home in High Wycombe, 30 miles west of London, and passing over what were subsequently found to be various components for liquid bombs which Sarwar then buried in a nearby wood.

GCHQ was monitoring Ali's calls to Pakistan, in which he and his contacts normally used a 'veiled speech' code system to give the impression that he was just calling family, addressing Rauf as 'Papa' whenever they spoke. Then in February 2006, Ali was heard talking about plans to bomb civilian airliners in mid-air over the Atlantic. The British immediately briefed the Americans and Prime Minister Blair spoke to President Bush to persuade him to stop the CIA from intervening to have the Pakistanis arrest Rauf, in order to allow MI5 to continue to collect the evidence it needed to bring Ali and his fellow terrorists to court.

As part of the surveillance operation, MI5 planted a hidden video camera and a bug in a two-bedroom flat at 386a Forest Road in Walthamstow, north-east London, which Ali had bought for £138,000 in cash. They were able to watch as members of Ali's terrorist cell, which included Sarwar and a number of friends from their time in Afghanistan, talked about their plans and set about making bombs and suicide videos. On 3 August 2006, the camera caught Ali and a co-conspirator drilling a hole in the bottom of a soft drinks bottle so they could replace its contents with a mixture of explosive hydrogen peroxide and orange drink powder while leaving the seal on the cap unbroken. They planned to use disposable cameras and batteries, the contents of which had been replaced by explosive, as detonators. Three days later, the MI5 team tracking Ali followed him to an internet café where he looked up details of seven transatlantic flights all leaving the UK within a three-hour timeframe, copying them onto a data stick. They included flights to Chicago, Washington, New York, San Francisco, Toronto and Montreal.

'The British cell was planning to smuggle those liquid bombs onto planes and blow up seven airliners heading to North America, with at least 1,500 people onboard,' said Mark Kelton, then chief of the CIA's European Division. 'That would have made it the biggest loss of life since 9/11 and if the bombs had gone off over a populated area, the casualties would have gone up exponentially.' The British estimated the number of people likely to die at around 5,000.

On 9 August, one of the bombers arrived at the Walthamstow flat and asked Ali: 'What's the time frame anyway?' The response was 'a couple of weeks'. MI5's lawyers still wanted more time to collect additional evidence. 'They would have wanted things to develop a little more, and for the evidence to manifest itself a little bit more before trial,' Kelton said. But when the Pakistani authorities said they were in a position to arrest Rauf, CIA chiefs decided they were not prepared to take any chances and told them to go ahead, forcing the British to end the operation and arrest Ali and Sarwar along with more than twenty other suspects.

Jose Rodriguez, the then head of CIA clandestine operations, defended the decision to arrest Rauf. 'To me, the most dangerous point that basically told me that this was an imminent operation that was going to happen was when the plotters started to select flights,' Rodriguez said. 'Some of these terrorists had already recorded suicide videos.' Kelton agreed that it was the right decision. 'There are always operational differences of opinion. That's the nature of the intelligence business. I think it was the right move. They made the best call with the information they had at the time.'[13]

The CIA decision to have Rauf arrested in Pakistan meant that it took four years to bring those involved to justice, but there were far more problematic legal difficulties in working so closely with the Americans. President Bush ruled that the Geneva Conventions did not apply to the conflict with al-Qaeda, leading to the arrest and forcible rendition of numerous terrorist suspects and the widespread use of torture at various secret sites around the world. In the immediate aftermath of the 9/11 attacks, a senior US official even told MI6 that the president had authorised the CIA to detain and arrest any terrorist target wherever he or she might be, including in the UK. MI5 refused to allow this to happen, with Eliza Manningham-Buller going to the extent of warning one intensely irritated CIA officer that, if he tried to do so, she would have *him* arrested.

The invasion of Afghanistan led to the incarceration of numerous al-Qaeda militants and as MI6 had far more expertise in Arabic than its US counterparts, and with the UK seen as a likely target for any future al-Qaeda attacks, it was heavily involved in interrogating the Arab militants captured during the operations that led to the demise of the Taliban regime. By early 2002, British intelligence officers had been present when suspected terrorists held by the Americans were interrogated in Afghanistan, Iraq and Guantanamo Bay.

British intelligence chiefs had known for some time, certainly before Bush became president, that the Americans were prone to dealing with terrorist suspects in ways that did not accord with British human rights policy. Nevertheless, both MI5 and MI6 insisted that initially they had no knowledge that the CIA made extensive use of extraordinary rendition and torture on the suspected terrorists it captured, and they defended their cooperation with the Americans on the basis that the intelligence it produced was saving British lives. When they did find out what was going on, they modified their own operations to ensure that nothing British intelligence officers did was complicit with any mistreatment of terrorist suspects.

'We have received intelligence of the highest value from detainees, to whom we have not had access and whose location is unknown to us, some of which has led to the frustration of terrorist attacks in the UK or against UK interests,' Manningham-Buller said. 'We do a lot of exchange of highly sensitive intelligence in a very trusting way, but we now all of us, including the Americans, have a clear understanding of the legal constraints on that exchange. So, when you are talking about sharing secret intelligence, we still trust them, but we have a better recognition that their standards, their laws, their approaches are different, and therefore we still have to work with them, but we work with them in a rather different fashion.'

The problems with the US use of torture and extraordinary rendition had an additional impact on the transatlantic intelligence exchange as the result of a series of cases brought through the UK courts by British citizens or residents held by the Americans and alleged MI5 or MI6 complicity in their torture or rendition. Binyam Mohamed, a UK resident, had been interviewed by an MI5 officer while held by the Pakistani authorities before being taken to a secret CIA site in Morocco where he was allegedly tortured. The Appeal Court ruled in 2010 that classified intelligence on Mohamed which the US had shared with the British must be given to his lawyers, leading the US to reassess what intelligence it was prepared to pass to the British on UK citizens. 'We were concerned that some of the sensitive information that we had shared would be released,' a former senior CIA officer said. As a direct result, the UK government decided to settle such cases out of court rather than take the risk that, in order to protect its sources, the US might withhold vital intelligence from MI5.

But while there was alarm within the CIA and the US National Security Council that intelligence passed to the British might come out in the UK courts, there was less about the limits on what MI6 could do, the former senior CIA officer said. 'As far as the UK courts impacting our ability to cooperate on the ground with MI6 in counter-terrorism operations, it was immaterial because we didn't do a single rendition operation in coordination with MI6, and to my knowledge other than to Guantanamo, I'm not aware of any visits by UK intelligence to any of our black sites. So, it didn't matter on the ground.'

Even so, there was undoubtedly ill-feeling among some CIA officers at the limits on operational cooperation. 'It would be unfair to say that there wasn't any anger or frustration with the restrictions the Brits were operating under,' the former senior CIA officer said. 'At the senior levels we kind of understood. It never bothered me, and I dealt with those guys all the time. But if you were chief of station in Pakistan, for example, and you were doing all this tough stuff working 24/7 and really not getting a lot of help from anybody and at the same time Langley is sending you messages saying, "Hey, is it OK to release this to the Brits?" you might say: "Jesus. Why the hell would you wanna do that?" But you're so focused on the war you're not seeing the big picture stuff. There was a lot of other stuff going on with our British colleagues, counter-proliferation, counter-intelligence. We in the Agency had a lot of tunnel vision on counter-terrorism, but the more senior you get the more you understand that there is other stuff in play too that is not going away, and you can't let what's happening in one theatre of operations get in the way of other stuff that's going on.'

Nevertheless, concerns within MI6 over the damage done to its relationship with the CIA reached such levels that in early 2010, MI6 Chief Sir John Sawers flew to Washington with two of his most senior directors for a clear-the-air meeting with CIA bosses. They arrived on Wednesday, 17 March, and with much of America wearing green to mark St Patrick's Day, all three sported green shamrock ties, in a tacit nod to the other issue that had done so much over the years to hamper liaison between individual CIA and MI6 officers. The former senior CIA officer played down the long-term damage. 'There was never any question about the operational competence of MI6 or the depth of the relationship. There's no question we are tighter with MI6 than any other service.'[14]

In the wake of the removal of Taliban control in Afghanistan, UK troops there initially did well supporting reconstruction in the relatively peaceful north-west. The British operations were based on joint US–UK provincial reconstruction teams in Mazir-i-Sharif and Meymaneh, with small, lightly armed teams of soldiers successfully reaching out to local leaders, discussing problems within the community and for the most part finding ways to solve them, while USAID and the British Department for International Development set up local projects such as a silkworm farm run by local women to produce silk cloth. But the British military's time in Afghanistan, and indeed the final assessment of what they achieved, was to be dominated by the eight years spent in the far more perilous southern province of Helmand.[15]

Tony Blair agreed in 2004 to a request from President Bush that Britain should send more troops into Afghanistan and take charge of NATO forces there in order to allow US troops to focus on the insurgency in Iraq. The UK government announced in late 2005 that 16 Air Assault Brigade, as the most experienced and battle-hardened of the NATO troops, would take charge in the traditional Taliban stronghold of Helmand. Intelligence reports which warned that there were rising levels of violence associated with both the Taliban and drug-trafficking in the province were only reinforced by the reports from MI6 and special forces reconnaissance carried out ahead of the mission. It was to be more than six months before the British troops arrived.[16]

The warning that the Taliban were given of a substantial British arrival, and their resultant ability to prepare for it, combined with

Operation River Dance—a poorly planned US counter-narcotics operation in the spring of 2006 to destroy the opium crop along the Helmand River on which the local population relied for their income—ensured that British plans for a Malaya-style hearts-and-minds operation never got off the ground. 'We had a year to get ready and we studied what Templer did in Malaya,' said General David Richards, the British general in charge of NATO forces in Afghanistan. 'We wanted to develop an area where governance, development and the economy would flourish, and people outside of that area might be resentful, but they'd see what was happening and want it for themselves, and they would slowly be drawn to our side.'[17]

The UK government put a strict limit of 3,500 on the number of troops it was prepared to deploy to Helmand, which was never likely to be enough to conduct stabilisation operations in an area the size of Wales. The problem was exacerbated by the demands of Mohammed Daoud, the governor of Helmand, that the British defend key administrative centres to ensure that the Afghan flag remained flying. With the Taliban pouring into the province, supported by drugs barons and a hostile population which had lost the bulk of its income as a result of Operation River Dance, the British were immediately forced onto the back foot.

Daoud's demands that British commander in Helmand, Brigadier Ed Butler, send troops to defend the administrative centres in the northern towns of Sangin, Musa Qala, Nowzad and Kajaki provided targets that drew in the Taliban fighters, while severely restricting what Butler and his forces could do elsewhere. Richards opposed the decision to deploy troops to what became known as the British 'platoon houses', where significant numbers of British troops would die. Butler, a former SAS officer, had a stand-up row with Daoud over the issue, but when President Karzai stepped in to back the governor, he felt he had no choice but to comply.

'We were under not inconsiderable pressure from the Afghan government to go in and stop the district centres falling to the Taliban,' Butler said. 'If the leader of a pro-western Islamic state that has adopted democratic government asks for your support, you're in an awkward position to say no.' The British effort in Helmand never recovered and Richards's hopes of replicating Templer's hearts-and-minds operations swiftly faded. When US general Dan McNeill took over in early 2007, he was dismissive of Richards's attempts at engagement of the local population and insistent on a more aggressive approach that left the British with no chance of success.[18]

The differences in emphasis between Richards and McNeill were reflected in the fluctuations in liaison between the CIA and MI6 on the ground, which tended to rely very heavily on the relationships between various MI6 officers and individual station chiefs. An MI6 officer who served in Afghanistan recalled that one CIA station chief in Kabul 'thought we were basically a bunch of dicks because we didn't get into what they were doing'.

The CIA had a large station with a lot of paramilitaries from the Agency's Special Activities Division, he said.

> They were chasing after al-Qaeda and put brutally they were killing al-Qaeda. They weren't all that interested in counter-insurgency against the Taliban. They weren't interested in building Afghan institutions. We had a different orientation. We were busy supporting the internal political process. We were supporting reconciliation. We were very keen to stop the Taliban wrecking it all. Some of their station chiefs just thought: 'They don't really bring any hardware to the argument. Every now and then they bring some good intelligence. I don't have time for that in a war zone.' Some would think some of this could help us and embrace us as just another way of solving the problems they wanted to solve. It seemed to be entirely based on predisposition.[19]

If differences between British and American commanders were hampering rather than helping counter-insurgency operations in Afghanistan, the opposite was taking place in post-war Iraq, where the close ties between British and US special operations forces were again in evidence. By mid-2004, civil disobedience had turned into full-scale insurgency, with a mix of Sunni hardliners, former regime loyalists and nationalist patriots fighting in an unlikely alliance alongside the foreign Islamist militants who, encouraged by bin Laden, had flocked to join al-Qaeda in Iraq. By early 2006, the insurgency had turned into a sectarian civil war triggered by the bombing of the al-Askari mosque in Samarra, one of the holiest sites of Shia Islam, with Sunni Iraqis ranged against their Shia compatriots. The coalition response, led by US and British special operations forces, was based on a 'kill or capture' system designed primarily, despite its name, to capture prominent militants in order to obtain intelligence that would lead to more high-profile targets and allow coalition forces to disrupt the insurgents' operations.

Graeme Lamb, now a lieutenant-general, was sent into Iraq in the summer of 2006 as deputy to General George Casey, the US commander in Iraq, with responsibility for reconciliation. He set about 'trying to see whether we could, through conversations with people who were not with us, or were actually against us', persuade Sunni leaders that the alliance with al-Qaeda in Iraq, however loose, was not helping their cause. It was hurting their own communities and strengthening Shia domination of the political apparatus.

'One of the things I did through 2006-2007 was setting the conditions for what then was the Awakening,' Lamb said. 'I brought a small team in, because I had to convince the US special forces to release people who would then carry the message that the Sunni community, who were currently the insurgents who were fighting us, should get real and realise that the enemy was al-Qaeda, not us.'

Stan McChrystal, who was leading the US special operations forces, had worked with Lamb during the 1991 Gulf War. They were old friends. 'Graeme explained the concept of establishing a cell that would pursue strategic reconciliation,' McChrystal said. 'Many of the hardline leaders Graeme proposed releasing were those whom my men had spent years of their lives trying to capture, losing limbs and friends in the process. Graeme's programme meant setting them free in the hope that, once convinced, they would be more useful on the outside. I agreed on the spot. I did so in part because I knew and trusted Graeme.'

Lamb saw this as a key factor in the Special Relationship between UK special forces and their US counterparts, that—having worked together over many years on the ground—they knew and trusted each other implicitly. 'Invariably the Special Relationship is on two fronts in the special forces community,' Lamb said. 'One is organisationally and culturally. We're attuned because of our training and the nature of who we choose and how individuals are nationally different, but actually not dissimilar in their independence, in their confidence and their character.

'But the second part of the Special Relationship is so often down to a personal relationship between individuals. The main players in Iraq were all people I'd worked with. Not just trained with but actually been on operations with. Stan McChrystal, when I turned round and said: "I need to release this bad dude who you took some trouble, and damage in your own forces, to arrest. I need to release him free as a bird because he's going to carry the message that al-Qaeda is the enemy and not the coalition," and Stan gives it the old "done".'[20]

Just as the close relationship between GCHQ and the NSA developed out of the mutual trust formed between the Bletchley Park codebreakers and their US colleagues during the Second World War, so too had joint special forces operations in a series of wars in the Balkans, Iraq, Syria and Afghanistan created an unbreakable bond between members of the British SAS and SBS and their US counterparts in Delta and SEAL Team Six. 'Chargin" Charlie Beckwith might have based Delta on the model of the British SAS but more recently the British Directorate of Special Forces has followed the American lead by setting up its own special forces intelligence units and a Ranger Regiment, mirroring both the name and role of Delta's infantry support units, reinforcing the close cooperation.

2 1

THE PIVOT TO THE PACIFIC

Despite all the failings of the war in Iraq, and the intelligence used to justify it, the decision to get rid of Saddam Hussein had contributed to a remarkable success by British and US intelligence. Counter-proliferation had been a central task for the agencies going back to the break-up of the former Soviet Union in December 1991. Although initially the concern had been of Soviet nuclear weapons falling into the hands of 'rogue states' or terrorists, by the late 1990s the principal concern was over the activities of the Pakistani scientist Abdul Qadeer Khan, who had used a network of illicit contacts to obtain the materials to build Pakistan's nuclear bomb and went on to turn that network into a money-making business providing nuclear technology to anyone with the cash to pay for it, including countries like Iran and North Korea.

A small joint MI6–CIA team was set up to target Khan, recruiting a number of agents within his supply network, while GCHQ and the NSA monitored telephone and internet communications between him and his associates. Jim Pavitt, the CIA's deputy director of operations at the time, described it as a mix of 'million-dollar recruitment pitches, covert entries, ballet-like sophistication and a level of patience we are often accused of not possessing'.

The British JIC reported in April 2000 that there were indications as yet unconfirmed that Khan was supplying uranium enrichment equipment to Libya. By now, the joint CIA–MI6 operation had steadily built up the details of Khan's operations. 'Working with British colleagues we pieced together his subsidiaries, his clients, his front companies, his finances and manufacturing plants,' George

Tenet said. 'We were inside his residence, inside his facilities, inside his rooms. We were everywhere these people were.' By July 2002, the JIC assessed that Khan, now based in Dubai, was 'central to all aspects of the Libyan nuclear weapons programme' and in January 2003, it expressed deep concern that, with Khan's assistance, Libya's highly unpredictable leader, Colonel Muammar al-Gaddafi, might very soon get his hands on his own nuclear weapons.

Then in March 2003, out of the blue, a Palestinian intermediary known to MI6 telephoned the service's headquarters at Vauxhall Cross and said that Gaddafi wanted to talk. His son Saif, then studying at the London School of Economics, was to be the immediate go-between. Saif was invited to a Mayfair hotel to meet two MI6 officers, the more senior being Mark Allen, a Middle East specialist and a member of the MI6 'Camel Class', who had studied Arabic at Oxford and MECAS, the Middle East Centre for Arabic Studies, at Shemlan in Lebanon.

Convinced the offer was genuine, Allen and his colleague flew to Libya a few days later to meet Gaddafi himself in his Bedouin-style tent in the Bab al-Aziziya Barracks in Tripoli. Despite its drab green appearance, the tent's interior was extravagantly decorated with beautiful carpets, silk tapestries and cushions embroidered with quotations from the Libyan leader's many speeches attacking the West. During a series of late-night meetings in Gaddafi's tent, Allen coaxed him into agreeing to what he clearly already knew, that he would be better off forgetting his nuclear ambitions and siding with Britain and America. Gaddafi proposed that his intelligence chief, Musa Kusa, take negotiations forward but—clearly concerned that after Saddam's removal he would be next—insisted the Americans had to be a party to the deal.

Shortly afterwards, Richard Dearlove and Allen flew to Washington to brief President Bush and Tenet on the agreement with Gaddafi and the CIA director nominated Steve Kappes, a veteran Middle East expert, to be the Agency's representative in the negotiations. Kappes met with Kusa in Geneva to build up confidence that the US was fully locked into the deal, but it was clear that the Libyans were holding back.

In an attempt to move things forward, Tony Blair sent an emissary to Tripoli with a personal letter assuring Gaddafi that, if he gave up his WMD, Libya would be brought in from the cold. At this crucial point, with Libyan cooperation teetering on the edge, an MI6 agent inside Khan's network revealed that a German freighter travelling from Dubai to Libya was carrying equipment vital to Libya's nuclear weapons programme. The freighter was diverted into the Italian port of Taranto where its cargo was found to be components for centrifuges to produce enriched weapons-grade uranium.

MI6 immediately demanded a meeting with Kusa at which he was asked why, if the Libyans were so keen to negotiate a way out of their nuclear programme, they were still procuring components for nuclear centrifuges. He insisted that it was long-ordered equipment which they had always intended to reveal. As a result of the MI6 concerns, Gaddafi agreed that US and British inspectors should be allowed to inspect Libya's WMD materials, but while there was apparent openness about the chemical and biological programmes it was still clear that the Libyans were holding back information on their nuclear programme.

Kusa was called to a fresh meeting in the UK. During a brief and extremely tense conversation with Allen and Kappes at the Bay Tree Hotel in the Cotswold market town of Burford, he was confronted by the CIA officer with comprehensive details of what the Americans and British knew about Khan's role in providing Libya with nuclear technology. Kappes revealed that the CIA had covertly recorded a long and very incriminating conversation in Casablanca between Khan and the head of the Libyan nuclear weapons programme. The CIA officer handed the Libyan intelligence chief a recording of the conversation, noting that 'the centrifuges and uranium enrichment point to one direction only and that is military and not peaceful purposes'. In order to soften the blow, he also produced a letter from President Bush stressing that America wanted a friendly relationship with Libya. 'The President has not sent any letters lately, so it is a very important decision for him to write,' Kappes said. 'This is the strongest sign for the President to be personally involved.'

The realisation that there was very little that MI6 and the CIA did not know led in early December 2003 to a second, much more open, inspection and, a few days later, to a meeting at the Travellers Club in London's Pall Mall at which details of a deal whereby Libya would give up its WMD, including the precise text of the statement to be announced by the Libyan authorities, were agreed. The following day, Blair telephoned Gaddafi to confirm the deal, the first time the two men had ever spoken. 'Gaddafi was clearly impressed about having a phone call with somebody like Tony Blair,' a senior British official said. 'The Prime Minister said we understood what it meant to be doing this and we admired the way that Gaddafi was doing it, but he did emphasise that clarity was necessary. It was put that bluntly.'

The text of the agreement was to be announced by the Libyans the following evening. BBC Monitoring, as the corporation's monitoring service was now known, was primed to check that they were sticking to the letter of the deal. 'The Foreign Office wanted to see if what the Libyan news agency JANA published was the same as the text of the agreement,' the BBC Arab monitor who dealt with the story said. 'We passed on the JANA statement and the Foreign Office compared it to what was agreed and then announced the agreement, presumably because it was identical to the JANA report.'

As a result of Gaddafi's rehabilitation, Blair flew to Libya in March 2004 to sign a number of trade agreements, including a $900 million oil deal. A month earlier, Khan had confessed on Pakistani TV to having passed nuclear weapons technology to Iran, North Korea and Libya. He was held under house arrest, although for many of his countrymen, as 'the father of Pakistan's nuclear weapons programme', he remained a national hero. He was freed five years later.[1]

Shortly after coming into office in May 2010, David Cameron set up a UK National Security Council and the new post of national security adviser, both mirroring their US counterparts. The creation of the NSC was widely welcomed by the intelligence services on the basis that it would provide a clearer view of how much, or how little, influence their reporting was having on government and an opportunity to shape the arguments. One senior intelligence officer described it as being 'like the lights coming on; because it was very difficult under the previous arrangements to necessarily detect what decisions, if any decisions, were being taken on a number of issues, and the thinking that led to those decisions was even more opaque.'[2]

The new prime minister had made a good start, but it soon became clear that decisions had already been made before the NSC actually discussed the issues. Even before coming to power, Cameron had agreed with George Osborne, his close ally and future chancellor, that they would pull British troops out of Afghanistan. Nevertheless, one of his first acts as prime minister was to hold a 'summit' at Chequers to discuss the options and gain the advice of experts, most of whom were unaware of the agreement with Osborne and assumed that their advice would influence his decision as to whether or not to keep troops in Afghanistan.

One of those invited to attend was Graeme Lamb, who in 2009, having been about to retire, had been persuaded by Stan McChrystal, by then the US commander in Afghanistan, to stay on and talk to the Taliban in an attempt to reprise his success in Iraq during the 'Awakening'. Having spent the nine months leading up to the Chequers summit on the ground in Afghanistan reaching out to the Taliban, Lamb was well aware that they were not interested in discussing anything other than a deal that would see the US, Britain and other NATO forces leave and them taking charge. Quite why he then found his experience being questioned, in an understandably 'testy' exchange, by a friend and contemporary of Cameron from Eton and Oxford with no role in government who had a book on the Taliban about to be published and knew a 'nice man' in that organisation who was all too happy to set up talks with the British—but not the Americans—is impossible to comprehend. Later in the day, the prime minister was himself 'particularly testy' with the service chiefs, including General Sir David Richards, now head of the army, who all argued strongly in favour of remaining in Afghanistan.[3]

A similar approach emerged during discussions over the decision to intervene in the 'Arab Spring' revolution in Libya in an Anglo-French humanitarian operation, reluctantly joined by US president Barack Obama, which swiftly morphed into regime change, despite warnings from Richards and MI6 Chief Sir John Sawers that it would create ungoverned territory in which Islamist militants could wreak havoc. Richards was wary from his time in Afghanistan of the difficulties involved in dealing with a tribal society, but his concerns about Libya's tribes were dismissed by an unidentified expert who said: 'They're not a factor in this campaign.' Richards felt that decisions had already been made in Downing Street, with the NSC there not to provide advice on what to do but just to 'tweak at the edges' of the planning. By the end of 2014, Libya had descended into a long-running civil war with thousands of Islamic State militants taking advantage of the security vacuum to seize control of a number of key cities that would provide bases from which to operate into neighbouring countries.[4]

The Cameron government's approach to China was also at best naïve. Concerns within the intelligence services over Chinese involvement in national infrastructure dated back to 2005 and a deal between BT and Chinese company Huawei to provide core elements of Britain's revamped telecommunications network. Huawei had been set up in 1988, with Chinese government funding, by Ren Zhengfei, former director of the People's Liberation Army's signals organisation.

Repeated warnings from the JIC and GCHQ that the Chinese components could be used to mount attacks on critical services such as power, food and water supplies were ignored by both the Blair and Brown governments. The JIC warned in January 2009 that China could make 'covert modifications' to the BT network or 'compromise equipment in ways that are very hard to detect' and that in the future it could 'remotely disrupt or even permanently disable' critical services such as power and water supplies, food and fuel distribution and the banking system. As a result of those concerns, the government eventually insisted on the creation of the Huawei Cyber Security Evaluation Centre, based in Banbury in Oxfordshire and overseen by GCHQ officials, to monitor and remove any security threats posed by the Chinese technology.[5]

Cameron and Osborne similarly ignored warnings from the intelligence services when they embarked on an ill-judged attempt to usher in a 'Golden Era' of relations with China, inviting Chinese president and Communist Party leader Xi Jinping to Britain in October 2015. Xi was guest of honour at a state banquet at Buckingham Palace hosted by the Queen, drank beer with the prime minister in a Buckinghamshire pub and signed more than £30 billion worth of trade deals including the construction by the China General Nuclear Power Group of a new nuclear power station at Bradwell-on-Sea in Essex. Senior British defence and intelligence officials expressed serious concern over the plans, warning that—as with the Huawei parts in the UK's telecommunications network—the Chinese could place 'back doors' into the power station's computer systems allowing them to shut down a key part of the UK's national infrastructure in the event of any disputes between London and Beijing.[6]

Prime Minister Boris Johnson's decision in January 2020 to allow Huawei to provide limited 'non-core' components for Britain's new 5G mobile telephone networks was based on GCHQ advice that the Banbury cell would be able to guarantee the security of the networks. Nevertheless, it led to intense pressure from US officials who warned that it would damage transatlantic intelligence-sharing. That threat never materialised, but the announcement by the Trump administration of trade sanctions against China, which included a ban on the sale of US microchips, changed the situation completely. GCHQ told Johnson that, if Huawei's microchips were no longer coming from the US, it would not be able to guarantee the security of the company's components in either the BT network or the 5G system. The government immediately ordered the removal of Huawei parts from all UK telephone networks and made clear that Chinese participation in the construction of British nuclear power was most unlikely to go ahead.[7]

There were no such solutions for the egregious damage done by Osborne's decision to end government funding for BBC Monitoring, the organisation which had provided vital intelligence on Germany and Italy during the Second World War and a series of international crises, from the Cuban missile crisis, through the invasion of Czechoslovakia and the Chernobyl nuclear accident to the war in Iraq and the emergence of Islamic State. While the BBC obtained a substantial amount of news from its monitoring service, it was ridiculous to expect it to fund its entire budget when so much of what it produced was open-source intelligence for the JIC, the intelligence services, the Ministry of Defence and the Foreign Office. The loss of the £20 million government funding led inevitably to cuts, both in staff and in coverage of areas of the world that were not important to BBC news editors but were vital for government customers on both sides of the Atlantic, risking the loss of BBC Monitoring's relationship with its US counterpart, the CIA's Open Source Enterprise (formerly FBIS), with which it splits coverage of the world.[8]

The leaks by Edward Snowden, an NSA contractor, of details of GCHQ and NSA use of internet surveillance programmes demonstrated the full extent of their cooperation but led to widespread concern that they were carrying out mass interception, reading the emails of US and UK citizens, delving remotely into their computers and monitoring their telephone conversations. It soon emerged that the techniques revealed by Snowden's material were nowhere near as far-reaching. The two programmes that caused most concern were the NSA's PRISM and GCHQ's Tempora, neither of which carried out mass interception and both of which required warrants, in the case of PRISM authorised by the US Foreign Intelligence Surveillance Court (FISC), and for Tempora by the relevant British cabinet minister, usually the home secretary or foreign secretary.

PRISM, introduced in 2007, is a system under which the NSA can obtain suspicious communications—normally detected by its XKeyscore internet search and analysis programme—from internet companies such as Google, Microsoft, Yahoo, Facebook and Apple. It is not as Snowden suggested a 'back door' into the internet systems run by those companies, as every one of them was swift to point out. There must be a FISC warrant before the company will release the data. PRISM provides a Dropbox-style electronic facility to allow it to be released securely.

The Tempora programme is a far greater technological achievement, vindicating the arguments made two decades earlier by the chief NSA liaison officer to GCHQ that the emergence of the internet and the British codebreakers' technological expertise more than justified the maintenance of the close UKUSA relationship. Introduced in the summer of 2011, it taps into the same transatlantic undersea communications cables which allowed Bletchley Park to use US Bombes to break Enigma. The cables, now fibre-optic, carry internet communications, coming ashore in Cornwall before going on to other parts of the world. Mass interception of everything passing through the cables would be impossible, but millions of internet communications are intercepted every day, and progressively cut down using known constants in the authorised target communications to a few thousand which are only then searched for items of interest.

As with the issues surrounding the CIA's different approach to apprehending and interrogating terrorists, there are protections in place to ensure GCHQ acts legally at all times, a senior official told the parliamentary Intelligence and Security Committee. GCHQ would refuse to accept intelligence from the NSA if it was obtained in a way that would have breached UK law and, since the Americans know this, they would never offer it anyway. Nor would GCHQ agree to collect intelligence for the NSA if doing so breached UK law.

Sir Iain Lobban, the then GCHQ director, said the Snowden leaks would have a 'gradual and inexorable' impact on the agencies' ability to collect intelligence. 'We've seen terrorist groups in the Middle East, Afghanistan and elsewhere in South Asia discussing the revelations in specific terms,' he said. 'We have seen chat around specific intelligence groups discussing how to avoid what they now perceive to be vulnerable communications methods. The cumulative effect will make the job that we have far, far harder for years to come.'[9]

By the spring of 2021, Afghanistan had become America's longest war, outlasting even Vietnam. Joe Biden, who as Barack Obama's vice-president had opposed sending more troops to Afghanistan, came to power on a promise to withdraw all US forces and end the 'forever wars'. His decision to withdraw from Afghanistan, ignoring the advice from his generals that it would be better to keep the remaining 2,500 US troops in place, was entirely understandable in a political context. It was an election promise backed by the

American people. But the way in which the withdrawal was carried out damaged America's credibility around the world. Biden's insistence that the withdrawal would not be conditions-based 'only exacerbated the situation', said Lieutenant-General Sami Sadat, Afghanistan's British-trained former intelligence chief. 'It ignored conditions on the ground. The Taliban had a firm end date from the Americans and feared no military reprisal.'

But the scene had already been set by the Trump administration's February 2020 Doha deal with the Taliban, which excluded the Afghan authorities. From then on, the writing was on the wall and, in a country where switching sides is a commonplace method of survival, it was inevitable that the Taliban would begin picking up far more supporters on the ground than it had up to that point. 'The day the deal was signed we saw the change,' one Afghan special forces officer said. 'Everyone was just looking out for himself.' Biden's announcement in April 2021 that the withdrawal would take place by 11 September that year only led to further defections, with Taliban leaders offering Afghan troops money to hand over their weapons and swap sides.

The problems were exacerbated by the timing of the US withdrawal, in the middle of Afghanistan's traditional fighting season, rather than in the winter when many of the fighters would have gone back to their villages to work on their farms, and even more by the departure of the thousands of US contractors who maintained Afghan aircraft and helicopters. 'By July, most of the 17,000 support contractors had left,' said Sadat, who spent much of 2021 commanding Afghan troops fighting the resurgent Taliban in Helmand. 'A technical issue now meant that aircraft—a Black Hawk helicopter, a C-130 transport, a surveillance drone—would be grounded. The contractors also took proprietary software and weapons systems with them. They physically removed our helicopter missile-defence system. Access to the software that we relied on to track our vehicles, weapons and personnel also disappeared. Real-time intelligence on targets went out of the window. Morale was devastated. Across Afghanistan, soldiers stopped fighting. The Taliban overran many bases; in other places, entire units surrendered.'[10]

Douglas London, the CIA's former counter-terrorism chief for south and south-west Asia, who advised the Biden campaign on counter-terrorism policy, dismissed claims there were no intelligence warnings that Afghan forces might swiftly collapse as 'misleading at best'. The CIA anticipated it as a possible scenario, London said. There had been various possible timeframes suggested depending on the actions of the administration. 'So, was it 30 days from withdrawal to collapse? 60? 18 months? Actually, it was all of the above, the projections aligning with the various "what ifs". Ultimately, it was assessed, Afghan forces might capitulate within days under the circumstances we witnessed, in projections highlighted to Trump officials and future Biden officials alike.'

As the Taliban swept across Afghanistan, largely buying up their opponents in much the same way as the CIA and MI6 had done in ousting them from power two decades earlier, the CIA predicted a far more rapid collapse, albeit that by then it was too late. The situation 'unravelled even more quickly than we anticipated', one CIA officer admitted. 'But we consistently identified the risk of a rapid collapse of the Afghan government and grew more pessimistic about the government's survival as the fighting season progressed.'[11]

Ryan Crocker, the first US ambassador to Afghanistan in the wake of the 2001 removal of the Taliban, was highly critical of Biden's decision to pull out, agreeing with the US generals that keeping 2,500 troops in Afghanistan was 'an affordable status quo that could have lasted indefinitely at a minimum cost in blood and treasure'. The allied objective in Afghanistan had always been clear, he said: 'To ensure that Afghan soil is never again used to plan attacks against the American homeland. You don't end a war by withdrawing your forces, you simply cede the field to others with more patience and more staying power.'

In response to the criticism of the Pakistanis for supporting the Taliban, Crocker said that as ambassador there from 2004 to 2007, he had repeatedly tried to get them to deny the Taliban safe haven across the border. The response was brutally simple: 'We know you. We know you don't have patience for the long fight. We know the day will come when you just get tired and go home. It's what you do. But this is where we live. So, if you think we are going to turn the Taliban into a mortal enemy, you are crazy.'[12]

Biden's failure to discuss the issues with Boris Johnson or take his advice was swiftly assessed by British politicians and media commentators as 'the demise of the Special Relationship', a constant refrain throughout the post-war years whenever the US and Britain appeared to take a different stance on any issue. Biden had certainly not consulted Johnson fully before withdrawal—and would have ignored his advice anyway—but that was largely because his mind was made up many years earlier as Obama's vice-president. Johnson, who is on record as saying that 'we would not have wanted to leave Afghanistan in this way' and was advised by his defence and intelligence chiefs that withdrawal was a mistake, would at best only have given Biden the same advice he had already received from the Joint Chiefs and dismissed. It might have looked better to discuss it with Johnson, but it would have largely been for show and the real Special Relationship has never depended on the state of relations between the two countries' leaders.[13]

Reports of its death were, as ever, greatly exaggerated, as evidenced by the joint announcement two weeks later by Biden, Johnson and Australian prime minister Scott Morrison of an agreement between their respective countries—already close allies as part of the Five Eyes intelligence-sharing pact—under which the Australians would receive US or British nuclear submarines, the main purpose of which was to be surveillance operations in the Pacific. Although for diplomatic reasons China was not mentioned in the announcement, it was clearly the most likely target. The nuclear submarines, whether supplied by the British or the Americans, will be able to stay below the surface for many months at a time—unlike the French boats the Australians had intended to buy—and be far more difficult to detect, allowing them to collect signals intelligence, carry out long-range sonar detection, launch remote-controlled surveillance vessels and, if necessary, insert special forces to gather intelligence on the ground.[14]

Islamist terror will remain a significant threat to the West, and therefore a primary target for both British and US intelligence, for the foreseeable future. Islamic State, also known as Daesh, had a brief moment in which it was able to create a caliphate in Syria and northern Iraq and, despite having seen that destroyed by US and British air power and special forces, it is still a powerful terrorist group; and al-Qaeda, although seriously degraded and having lost its leader in Osama bin Laden, remains extremely resilient with franchises across the Muslim world. Both were undoubtedly handed a boost to their morale and their futures by the US withdrawal from Afghanistan. MI5 director-general Ken McCallum warned that the return of Taliban control would not only have 'emboldened' the terrorists; it would provide them with territory from which to plan further attacks. 'The big concern,' he said, 'flowing from Afghanistan alongside the immediate inspirational effect is the risk that terrorists reconstitute and once again pose us more in the way of well-developed, sophisticated plots of the sort that we faced in 9/11 and the years thereafter.'

The withdrawal also caused substantial damage to Britain's and America's ability to collect intelligence on what was happening in Afghanistan, including any resurgence of al-Qaeda operations, said former MI6 Chief Sir Alex Younger. 'There really is no substitute for being on the ground and being able to generate the intelligence upstream which we need to protect ourselves back here in the UK downstream,' Younger said. 'But al-Qaeda and Daesh are significantly degraded organisations and our counter-terrorism operations and the capability of our networks are several orders of magnitude more powerful than they were in 2001. There is a serious job to do to redesign our approach, but there are lots of tools for us to do that with.'

John McLaughlin, former CIA deputy director, said that moving from 'a close, richly resourced presence to remote operations' would not be easy, particularly with Afghanistan's neighbours far more reluctant to allow allied intelligence and special operations forces to operate out of their territories than they were in the wake of 9/11. 'It will require a robust human and technical intelligence collection, coordinated with capabilities ranging from drones to special operations launched from facilities outside Afghanistan,'

McLaughlin said. 'The reality though is that successful counter-terrorism is almost always the result of rapid detection and rapid response.'[15]

While terrorism remains a constant threat, it is not on the same scale as that posed by aggressive nation states, particularly those with nuclear weapons. Iran's nuclear ambitions, its substantial stocks of ballistic missiles and the malevolent influence across the Middle East of its Islamic Revolutionary Guards Corps pose a continued threat, although in many ways the main concern is a pre-emptive Israeli response to Iranian progress in the production of nuclear weapons. The 2015 Joint Comprehensive Plan of Action, which severely limited Iran's ability to enrich uranium in return for a lifting of sanctions, went some way to easing the problem, but the Trump administration's decision to withdraw from the agreement led Tehran to go back on the deal and resume enrichment to a level close to that required to build a bomb.[16]

The 2022 invasion of Ukraine entirely vindicated the British intelligence services' assessment that Russia under Vladimir Putin was 'an acute and direct threat' to the UK. The aging Russian president was determined to incorporate Ukraine and Belarus into what he and many Russians saw as their true place as part of the 'Historical Russia' of Tsarist times and he had, in the words of former MI6 Chief Sir Alex Younger, gone into 'legacy mode, almost messianic in his determination to be the president that restored Russia to greatness.' On the eve of the invasion, Sergei Karaganov, a key Putin adviser and architect of 'the Putin doctrine', outlined the policy of 'constructive destruction' the Russian president intended to use to dismantle the post-war rules-based international order—widely seen as owing its origins to the Atlantic Charter agreed by Roosevelt and Churchill in August 1941—and replace it with rules of his own.

The West was 'on course to a slow but inevitable decay', Karaganov said. Putin was taking advantage of its decline to 'gradually erase' the rules-based international order 'primarily by refusing to take part in it or play by its obsolete rules'. The aim was to create a completely new relationship between Russia and the West and 'the next critical step—a necessity for Moscow not a whim' was incorporating Ukraine into Russia. In a worrying demonstration of the mindset in the Kremlin, Karaganov argued that 'Russia has gotten ahead, making sure that for the next decade, it will be relatively invulnerable strategically and capable of "dominating in an escalation scenario" in conflicts in the regions within its sphere of interests.' The West had yet to realise that by resisting it was 'only hurting itself', but eventually it would accept reality 'stepping down as the global leader and becoming a more reasonable partner'.

The Russian military intervention in Georgia in 2008—in part to support rebels in South Ossetia, where there is a large Russian population, but more importantly to punish Georgia for its application for membership of NATO and bring it into line—laid down a marker for future Russian unconventional military operations. There was little pushback from the West that might have deterred Putin in the future and his popularity at home soared to unprecedented levels. US and British intelligence services, whose work had been dominated by the Soviet Union throughout the Cold War, subsequently denied that they had taken their eye off the ball. But there was no doubt that the belief throughout the 1990s that Russia was much less of a significant threat, combined with the emergence of Islamist terrorism, had led for example to significant cuts in GCHQ coverage of Russia. During the Cold War, 70 per cent of its work focused on Warsaw Pact targets. By 2006, monitoring of Russian communications had dropped to just 4 per cent of its total effort.

Russia's annexation of Crimea in 2014 and its subsequent incursions into Ukraine made widespread use of Spetsnaz special forces and the same combination of cyber- and information warfare used during the invasion of Georgia. It also saw the emergence of the so-called Wagner Group, mercenary paramilitaries controlled by Russian intelligence. 'The reviews and the discussion around what happened in Crimea really brought minds more to the fore again on Russia,' a senior GCHQ official said. 'That then led us to move in, ramping up again.'

The 2014 intervention in Ukraine, and illegal operations such as the 2006 murder in London of former KGB officer Aleksandr Litvinenko and the attempted murder in Salisbury in 2018 of former

GRU officer Sergei Skripal, showcased Putin's intention of constantly operating in the 'Grey Zone' between peaceful coexistence and outright war and his deliberately disruptive refusal to adhere to the post-war rules-based international order.

'There is this element of recklessness there in the way they go about things,' said MI6 Chief Richard Moore. 'They keep on doing things which are intimidating and not really the behaviour of a responsible power. So, when you get that pattern of reckless behaviour, and of course, you then look at what's happening around Ukraine, it worries us and it's why we coordinate so closely with our allies to make sure we're getting firm messages back to President Putin.'

The invasion of Ukraine on 24 February 2022 demonstrated beyond a shadow of any doubt that mere warnings were not enough. Russian forces had been building up on the Russian and Belarusian borders with Ukraine since the autumn of 2021 with US intelligence warning in early December that as many as 175,000 Russian troops were preparing for an invasion. Bill Burns, CIA director, flew to Ukraine to brief President Volodymyr Zelensky on 'intelligence we had at the time about some of the most graphic and concerning details of Russian planning about Kyiv'.

The joint capability of the British and US agencies to obtain extensive detail of the Russian plans was soon evident with a steady stream of intelligence released by the US and UK governments and intelligence chiefs on both sides of the Atlantic, demonstrating a willingness to release information that in the past would have been held back as part of a blanket source-protection policy. Two weeks after Burns briefed Zelensky, the UK said it had intelligence showing that Russia planned to replace the Ukrainian president with a pro-Moscow politician. In early February, US officials said intelligence showed that the GRU was preparing to stage a false flag operation to provide Putin with an excuse to invade. President Biden warned that intelligence collected by the British and Americans confirmed that Putin had given the invasion the go-ahead and that it would happen within days and the US administration warned the UN that it had 'credible information' that Russian military commanders were 'creating lists of identified Ukrainians to be killed or sent to camps following a military occupation'.

The willingness to share secret information led a number of former intelligence officers to express concern that it might reveal sources and damage important operations. There were undoubted risks, particularly given the long-term expertise of Russian intelligence in 'active measures' and deception operations, but the situation was clearly seen as so exceptionally threatening that making the world aware of what was going on overrode any security concerns, and Burns stressed that it was 'selective declassification' with great care taken to ensure that it caused minimal damage to future operations. 'It is not without risk to declassify information,' the CIA director said. But 'by being careful about this . . . we have had a great deal of effect in disrupting their tactics and their calculations and demonstrating to the entire world that this is a premeditated and unprovoked aggression built on a body of lies and false narratives.'

The Russian intelligence services' use of cyber-warfare to gather intelligence and to disrupt or interfere in the West is also a major threat, as was demonstrated by the extensive GRU and FSB operations during the 2016 US presidential election designed to damage the campaign of the Democrat candidate, Hillary Clinton. Those attacks were accompanied by a sustained influence operation using fake personae on social media to push the US electorate away from Clinton and towards Donald Trump.

Both the GRU and the FSB use criminals to conduct their cyber operations in what MI6 described as a 'very muddy nexus between business and corruption and state power in Russia'. Former NSA director Keith Alexander said the hackers are encouraged to carry out criminal hacking as well as state-sponsored operations in order to blur the distinction between the two and allow Russia to deny responsibility. 'They allow their teams to moonlight,' Alexander said. 'So, these guys use their infrastructure to moonlight to steal money, ransomware and other things.' The disruptive potential of Russian cyber-attacks to damage the US or British national infra-structures remains a major concern for the intelligence services on both sides of the Atlantic, with GCHQ describing it as 'an immediate and urgent threat to our national security'.[17]

Despite Russia's reckless behaviour, the main long-term threat to Britain and America comes from China, which has seen itself throughout history as the world's most important power and, under President Xi Jinping, is determined to supplant US global domination. Strategic patience is embedded in Chinese culture going back to imperial times. China's leaders will always take the long view and always see things through, with Afghanistan only the latest example of the West's failure to do the same. Like Putin, Xi is intent on moving the world away from the post-war, rules-based, liberal democratic order to one which fits his own model of 'authoritarian capitalism'. China is bullying its neighbours, expanding its territory into the South China Sea by building artificial islands 500 miles from its coast and claiming the seas in between as its own, and seeking to restrict the normal rules of freedom of navigation and disrupt international supply lines.

China under Xi has torn up the 'one country, two systems' agreement with the UK on Hong Kong and taken a far more belligerent approach to Taiwan. The threat to regional security is very real, which is why the Obama administration announced in 2011, followed ten years later by the UK, that it was 'pivoting' towards the Indo-Pacific region, and why Britain and America signed the AUKUS pact with Australia, their closest ally within the Five Eyes partnership. Former MI6 Chief Sir John Sawers described China as 'the issue of the 21st century', adding that its role in the pandemic and how it reacted to it ensured that 'some of the scales fell from European eyes about the true nature of China under Xi Jinping'.

The Chinese president is determined that, during his leadership, China will become the dominant world power, in part by using projects like the 'Belt and Road Initiative', under which it has invested in more than seventy countries around the world. This is designed to influence those countries in favour of China and 'authoritarian capitalism' while at the same time establishing a degree of long-term control over them. 'I think we were slow to understand just how much China had changed under Xi Jinping,' Sawers said. 'The

Belt and Road Initiative is a commercial economic project and it's a strategic project at the same time. It wants to tie the economies of countries along the Belt and Road and make them strategically dependent on China.'

Rush Doshi, President Biden's primary adviser on China, was convinced the West had been slow to see the threat from Beijing, partly due to hubris over the end of the Cold War and partly because of the distraction of the 9/11 attacks and the focus on defeating Islamist terrorism. But the Chinese move to displace the old world order dates back to the late 1980s and early 1990s. 'The Tiananmen Square protests reminded Beijing of the American ideological threat; the swift Gulf War victory reminded it of the American military threat; and loss of the shared Soviet adversary reminded it of the American geopolitical threat,' Doshi said. 'In short order, the United States quickly replaced the Soviet Union as China's primary security concern, that in turn led to a new grand strategy, and a thirty-year struggle to displace American power was born.'

As part of its efforts first to catch up with the West following the chaos of the Cultural Revolution, and then to get ahead, China ruthlessly reverse-engineered US electronics, bought out Western companies which had the technical expertise it required, and forced companies that wanted to do business in China to transfer sensitive data. But its primary method of obtaining Western technology has been an extraordinarily pervasive cyber-espionage programme stealing shamelessly from the West. Keith Alexander said the losses suffered by US technology companies due to Chinese theft had reached astonishing levels. 'They're stealing us blind,' he said. 'Some of the numbers go in excess of $500bn a year in intellectual property. When you think about that, that's our national future. We're losing our future.' Another former NSA director, Mike McConnell, said the Chinese could swiftly displace America as the world's dominant power. 'They want to change the world and they say that publicly. So, if we don't figure out a way to keep them from taking the technology that adds to that set of goals, we're going to find ourselves not being the prominent player we've been in the past.'[18]

*

The Special Relationship between America and Britain is feted by politicians on both sides of the Atlantic when it suits their purpose and just as frequently dismissed as a myth, not least by the media, which focuses too much on the personal relationships between transient politicians or the simple and undeniable fact that US presidents will always be inclined to do what they see as being in America's best interests, regardless of how it impacts on any of their allies. Yet the basic truth is that Britain and America are bound together more closely than either is to any other ally. The most obvious ties that bind are a common language and a worldview created by shared beliefs in the rule of law and democracy. The former has resulted in a common cultural heritage and strong trade links, while the latter has led to close military cooperation, with the two countries taking the leading roles in NATO throughout the Cold War and into the post-9/11 joint operations against Islamist terrorists. As a result, Britain has been America's most reliable ally through a series of conflicts from the Second World War right up to the present day.

But the real foundations of that Special Relationship are the ties between the British and American intelligence services, which have been exchanging information that is vital to the security of both countries on a day-to-day basis for more than eighty years. The reason those ties have continued for so long is that each side has always had something to offer that the other did not have. Initially, the British had far greater experience and expertise in codebreaking, human intelligence and counter-espionage than the relatively new US agencies and were very happy to share it, while the Americans had greater technical sophistication and the money to pay for it. The British also had the considerable bonus of bases in former colonies which would give the US intelligence agencies access to parts of the world they would not have otherwise been able to reach and which, despite their inherent animosity towards the British Empire, they were very happy to use. The combined effort was far more effective at collecting intelligence from across the world than either side could ever have managed on its own.

Working together so closely also helped to sustain the partnership, producing warm personal relationships between key individuals that were impossible to break. John Tiltman met Pres Currier on a misty Sheerness dockside in February 1941 at the very start of the Anglo-American intelligence cooperation and forty years later they were still working together in the NSA troubleshooting team that cracked the Cold War codes others could not break. The 23-year-old Daphne Park trained a young OSS officer, Bill Colby—a future CIA director—in wartime London and helped Lou Conein parachute into occupied France, meeting both of them again twenty years later when she was collecting intelligence for MI6, and the Americans, during the Vietnam War. The close relationship and cooperation between GCHQ director Brian Tovey, another Bletchley veteran, and his NSA counterpart, Bobby Ray Inman, during the late 1970s and early 1980s was undoubtedly a factor when Inman, by then CIA deputy director, stood up in the White House Situation Room during the Falklands crisis and tore apart the arguments in favour of supporting Argentina, insisting that those present remember 'the overwhelming importance of our shared interest in the strategic stakes, the depth and breadth of our intelligence cooperation, the whole gamut of global Cold War concerns we have riding on close interaction with the UK'.

Relationships like that are not developed out of nothing. They come from a closeness that has evolved over more than eighty years of British and American intelligence officers working together, often extraordinarily closely, frequently disagreeing vociferously over the rights and wrongs of a particular way forward, and in doing so coming to trust each other, often far more deeply than they trusted some of their national colleagues. 'One of the qualities of the US–UK intelligence relationship is that it runs very, very deep,' John Sawers said. 'Politicians come and go, but the intelligence relationship stays really solid. Cooperation between CIA and MI6 is close, but it is even closer between NSA and GCHQ where there is an integration of effort and division of target together with our Five Eyes partners. So, it is a really close relationship.' Even when Donald Trump was attacking the CIA and accusing GCHQ of tapping his phone, 'the relationship between CIA and MI6, between NSA and GCHQ and between FBI and MI5 remained really, really deep', Sawers said. 'At an operational level, the operational cooperation was as deep at that time as it had been in the past. There was no change.'[19]

When two countries are sharing intelligence on such a scale and also share a very similar worldview, the decision makers and governments receiving the same intelligence, whatever their differences over matters of purely national interest, are always likely to adopt a similar approach to world events and as a result coordinate their responses. That is what keeps Britain and America locked together in step with each other. That is the real Special Relationship.

NOTES

PROLOGUE

1 Author interview with Barbara Eachus, 23 March 1998; Prescott Currier, 'My "Purple" Trip to England in 1941', *Cryptologia*, Vol. 20/3 (1996); NSA OH-2011-66 Capt. Currier Lecture with John Tiltman, 14 September 1969

1. TWO MONGRELS MEET

1 F. W. Hilles, 'The Origin and Development of 3-US, Part II', *Cryptologic Spectrum*, Summer 1977
2 Robert L. Benson, 'The Origin of US–British Intelligence Cooperation (1940-1941)', available at https:// www.nsa.gov/portals/75/ documents/news-features/ declassified documents/cryptologic-spectrum/origin_us_british.pdf (accessed 13 December 2021); NSA website, Early Papers Concerning US–UK Agreements, Kramer to Redman, Cryptanalysis, FBI Activities and Liaison with the British, 8 June 1942; Miles to Regnier, 4 October 1940
3 UKNA CAB 65/7/15, War Cabinet Conclusions, 13 May 1940, Minute 6
4 UKNA CAB 65/7/46, War Cabinet Conclusions, 1 June 1940, Minute 9
5 'June 10, 1940: "Stab in the Back" Speech', Miller Center, University of Virginia, https://millercenter.org/ the-presidency/presidential-speeches/ june-10-1940-stab-back-speech (accessed 13 December 2021)
6 'Our help pledged, President offers our full material aid to Allies', *New York Times*, 11 June 1940
7 The Diaries of Captain Malcolm Duncan Kennedy, 1917-1946, 11 June 1940, Kennedy Collection, Sheffield University Library; 'Our help pledged'
8 NSA Early Papers, Lothian Aide-Memoire, 8 July 1940; Memorandum for the Chief of Staff, 19 July 1940
9 NSA Early Papers, London No 401, Strong to Marshall, 5 September 1940
10 NSA Early Papers, Memorandum for the Chief of Staff, 9 September 1940; Miles to Regnier, 4 October 1940; NARA RG457, Historical Cryptologic Collection (HCC) 2738, Box 940, A Chronology of Cooperation between the SSA and the London Office of GC&CS; UKNA ADM 223/487 C/5038, C to DNI, 28 September 1940; HW 14/45, Menzies to Beaumont-Nesbitt, 22 November 1940, Draft Menzies to Lothian
11 Two Purple Machines see NSA Early Papers, Friedman to Corderman, 8 February 1943; Corderman to Clarke, 10 February 1943
12 NSA Oral History OH-07-78, John H. Tiltman, 17 December 1978;

NSA OH-2011-66, Capt. Currier
Lecture with John Tiltman,
14 September 1969

13 UKNA HW 14/45, Menzies to DMI
Beaumont Nesbitt, copied to Godfrey
and Boyle, 22 November 1940

14 NSA Oral History OH-07-78, John
H. Tiltman, 17 December 1978

15 UKNA HW 14/45, Denniston to
Menzies, 5 August 1941; HW 50/13,
AZ393, Notes for Commander Travis's
Visit to USA, 6 May 1943, p. 1

16 NSA Oral History OH-02-72,
Prescott Currier, 14 April 1972;
UKNA HW 14/45, Weeks to
Denniston, 9 March 1941

17 Ralph Erskine & Peter Freeman,
'Brigadier John Tiltman: One of
Britain's Finest Cryptologists',
Cryptologia, Vol. 27/4 (2003)

18 NARA RG457, HCC 2344, Box 808,
J. H. Tiltman, 'Some Reminiscences',
pp. 8-9; UKNA HW 4/25, History
of the Far East Combined Bureau,
pp. 1-3

19 NSA OH-09-83, Rudolph T. Fabian,
4 May 1983

20 NSA DOCID:3575741, Robert
J. Hanyok, 'Madame X: Agnes in
Twilight – The Last Years of the
Career of Agnes Driscoll 1941-1957'.

21 Ibid.

22 NSA OH-1980-03, Frank Raven,
24 January 1980

23 UKNA PRO HW 25/1, Alexander,
'Cryptographic History of Work on
the German Naval Enigma', p. 20

24 Ibid., p. 30; NSA OH-2011-66, Capt.
Currier Lecture with John Tiltman,
14 September 1969; Ralph Erskine &
Michael Smith (eds), The Bletchley Park
Codebreakers, Biteback, London, 2011,
pp. 169-70

25 UKNA CAB 65/19/20, Minutes
of the War Cabinet Meeting,
19 August 1941, Item 1: Discussions
between the Prime Minister and
President Roosevelt

26 UKNA HW 14/45, Interrupted
Conference with Commander
Safford, 18 August 1941

27 UKNA HW 14/45, CSS to Hastings,
1 December 1941; Denniston to
Hastings, 5 December 1941

28 UKNA HW 14/45, Hastings for CSS
only, 27 November 1941; Hastings for
CSS, 2 December 1941; Denniston to
Hastings, 5 December 1941

29 UKNA HW 14/45 Folio
29(a), Denniston to Hastings
5 December 1941

30 UKNA HW 14/45 CXG127, Hastings
to Denniston, 10 December 1941

31 NSA OH-1980-03, Frank Raven,
24 January 1980

32 UKNA HW 50/12, BRUSA &
Negotiations with America Autumn
1943-Mid-October 1944, p. 100

33 NSA Oral History OH-04-78, John
Tiltman, 1 November 1978

34 NSA Oral History OH-07-78, John
Tiltman, 17 December 1978; OH-04-
78, John Tiltman, 1 November 1978;
NARA RG 457, HCC 1414, Box 579,
Memorandum for the Director of
Naval Communications: History of
the Bombe Project, 30 May 1944

35 UKNA HW 57/9, GC&CS to Navy
Department, T677 from Travis,
13 May 1942

36 UKNA HW 14/46, Report
of Lt-Col. J. H. Tiltman on
his Visit to North America
during March and April 1942,
20 May 1942; HW 57/10, Tiltman,
Enigma Policy, 5 May 1942

2. 'HAVE A RYE, SISTER'

1 UKNA HW 14/46, Statement
by Admiral E. J. King at Press
Conference, 7 June 1942; 'US Navy
knew in advance all about Jap Fleet',
Washington Times-Herald, 7 June 1942;
Hastings to Godfrey, 30 June 1942;
Godfrey to Hastings, No 702,
7 July 1942

2 NARA RG 457, HCC 1414, Box
579, Memorandum for the Director
of Naval Communications: History
of the Bombe Project, 30 May 1944;
UKNA HW 14/46, Tiltman to
Friedman, 29 May 1942; HW 14/47

Folio 367, Captured E Machines,
28 June 1942

3 NSA Oral History OH-17-82,
Solomon Kullback, 26 August 1982

4 UKNA HW 3/193, Captain C.
F. Holden, Memorandum for
Commander E. W. R. Travis,
2 October 1942; HW 50/13 American
Liaison, US Navy Department 1941
to Holden Agreement (Oct 1942),
pp. 11-15; American Liaison, US Navy
Department from Holden Agreement
(Oct 1942) to Wenger's Visit to the
UK (July 1943), pp. 9-13; Ralph
Erskine, 'The Holden Agreement
on Naval Sigint: The First BRUSA?',
Intelligence and National Security, Vol.
14/2 (1999).

5 B. Jack Copeland, *Turing: Pioneer of
the Information Age*, Oxford University
Press, Oxford, 2012, p. 84.

6 UKNA HW 57/9 CXG
788, Washington for Travis,
2 October 1942; HW 50/13, AZ393,
Notes for Commander Travis's Visit
to USA, 6 May 1943, p. 5; NSA Oral
History OH-07-78, John Tiltman,
17 December 1978

7 NSA Early Papers, Gen. Geo.
V. Strong to Gen. Marshall,
5 December 1942; Col. Carter
W. Clarke to Gen. Strong,
4 December 1942; Clarke to Strong,
17 December 1942; Clarke to Strong,
21 December 1942

8 NSA Early Papers, Dill to Marshall,
2 December 1942; Marshall to Dill,
9 December 1942; Dill to Marshall,
15 December 1942; Marshall to Dill,
23 December 1942

9 NSA Early Papers, Item 39,
Unsigned British notes responding
to US Army's claims of material not
exchanged

10 See Erskine & Smith, *The Bletchley Park
Codebreakers*, pp. 32-3

11 UKNA HW 14/47 Denniston to the
Director, 24 July 1942; FO 1093/238,
Loxley Minute, 10 April 1942;
NSA Early Papers, Cryptanalysis,
FBI Activities and Liaison with

the British, 8 June 1942; Robert
L. Benson, 'The Army–Navy–FBI
Comint Agreements of 1942',
available at https://www.nsa.
gov/portals/75/documents/news-
features/declassified-documents/
cryptologic-spectrum/Army_
Navy_FBI_Comint.pdf (accessed
14 December 2021)

12 NSA Oral History OH-07-78, John
Tiltman, 17 December 1978

13 NSA Early Papers, Tiltman to Travis,
5 January 1943; HW 50/13, AZ393,
Notes for Commander Travis's Visit
to USA, 6 May 1943, p. 6

14 NSA Early Papers, McNarney to
Macready, 9 January 1943

15 NSA Early Papers, Friedman to
Corderman, 8 February 1943;
Corderman to Clarke,
10 February 1943; Hastings to Strong,
26 February 1943; AZ/232, Letter
Addressed to Field Marshal Sir John
Dill by Chiefs of Staff, 7 March 1943;
UKNA HW 57/23 C/2248,
Memorandum by 'C' on Cooperation
with USA, 10 February 1943;
CXG 190, Hastings to CSS,
20 February 1943

16 UKNA HW 57/23 C/2454, C to
Rushbrooke/Davidson/Inglis/
Travis/Harris, 4 March 1943; NSA
Early Papers, Amembassy London to
MILID, (Personal Private for Strong
only from Kroner), 11 March 1943

17 FO 1093/271 C/3131, Menzies to
Cadogan, 29 April 1943

18 NSA Early Papers, Item 68, TT to
Clarke (undated); Taylor to Clarke,
5 April 1943

19 F. W. Hilles, 'The Origin and
Development of 3-US, Part I',
Cryptologic Spectrum, Spring 1977

20 Friedman to Corderman,
Preliminary Report of Trip to
England, 8 July 1943

21 Stephen Budiansky, *Battle of Wits:
The Complete Story of Codebreaking in
World War II*, Viking, London, 2000,
pp. 233, 298

22 NSA Early Papers, Travis to Clarke,

16 May 1943; UKNA HW 57/23 Agreement Between Government Code and Cipher School and US War Department, 17 May 1943

23 UKNA HW 57/23 Agreement Between Government Code and Cipher School and US War Department, 17 May 1943. For concise overviews of what became known as 'the Enigma Crisis', see Ralph Erskine, 'William Friedman's Bletchley Park Diary: A Different View', *Intelligence and National Security*, Vol. 22/3; Lee A. Gladwin, 'Cautious Collaborators: The Struggle for Anglo-American Cryptanalytic Cooperation, 1943', *Intelligence and National Security*, Vol. 14/1; NSA Website, United States Cryptologic History, Series IV, World War II, Volume 8, Robert Louis Benson, *A History of U.S. Communications Intelligence during World War II: Policy and Administration*

24 Michael Smith, *The Secrets of Station X*, Biteback, London, 2011, pp. 172-4, 177-8; Erskine & Smith, *The Bletchley Park Codebreakers*, p. 66

25 UKNA HW 25/2, The History of Hut 8, pp. 86-92; HW 53/35, Stevens to DD (C), 1 October 1943; HW 8/137, ICY 82, 7 September 1943; Pol 100, 10 September 1943; ICY 93, 14 September 1943; Pol 107, 15 September 1943; ICY 97, 18 September 1943; F. H. Hinsley, *British Intelligence in the Second World War* (abridged), HMSO, London, 1993, pp. 316-17; Erskine & Smith, *The Bletchley Park Codebreakers*, p. 166

26 NSA Oral History, OH-14-83, Howard Campaigne, 29 June 1983

27 Peter Elphick, *Far Eastern File: The Intelligence War in the Far East 1930-1945*, Coronet, London, 1997, p. 399

28 UKNA HW 50/12, BRUSA & Negotiations with America Autumn 1943-Mid-October 1944, pp. 32-6

29 UKNA HW 14/142, Birch to Hastings, 2 July 1944

30 UKNA HW 50/12, BRUSA &

Negotiations with America Autumn 1943-Mid-October 1944, p. 79

31 Interview with Arthur Levenson, October 1998; NSA Oral History, NSA OH-40-80, Arthur Levenson, 25 November 1980

32 F. H. Hinsley & Alan Stripp (eds), *Codebreakers: The Inside Story of Bletchley Park*, Oxford University Press, Oxford, 1993, p. 73

33 Smith, *The Secrets of Station X*, pp. 294-5

3. 'WILD BILL' ENTERS THE RING

1 Gill Bennett, *Churchill's Man of Mystery: Desmond Morton and the World of Intelligence*, Routledge, London, 2007, p. 254

2 Ibid.; UKNA FO 1093/140, C/4503, Menzies to Jebb, 3 June 1940; Cadogan to Lothian, 10 June 1940; Keith Jeffery, *The Secret History of MI6*, Penguin Press, New York, 2010, pp. 438-41

3 Thomas Troy, *Donovan and the CIA* (CIA Internal History), CIA, Langley, VA, 1981, p. 29

4 UKNA FO 1093/238, Telephone Call at 0445/14 from Mr Cordell Hull [in Washington] with Mr Kennedy [in London], 14 June 1940; Troy, *Donovan and the CIA*, pp. 29-34; Jeffery, *The Secret History of MI6*, pp. 442-3

5 Troy, *Donovan and the CIA*, p. 53; UKNA HS 7/74, Report on BSC in the USA, Part 3, Special Operations, p. 92

6 Bennett, *Churchill's Man of Mystery*, p. 369, note 38; Henry Hemming, *Our Man in New York: The British Plot to Bring America into the Second World War*, Quercus, London, 2019, p. 112; Troy, *Donovan and the CIA*, p. 54

7 UKNA FO 1093/238, Cadogan to SoS, 17 December 1940

8 UKNA FO 371/24263, A5194, Martin to Lawford, 18 December 1940; CoS to C-in-Cs Mediterranean & West Africa, 23 December 1940; Jeffery, *The Secret History of MI6*, pp. 442-7; Bennett,

Churchill's Man of Mystery, pp. 257-8; Troy, *Donovan and the CIA*, pp. 52-4; Thomas F. Troy, 'The Coordinator of Information and British Intelligence', *Studies in Intelligence*, Vol. 18/1 (1974), p. 64; Troy, 'The Coordinator of Information and British Intelligence', pp. 51, 72-3, 93-5

9   Troy, *Donovan and the CIA*, pp. 42, 54; Troy, 'The Coordinator of Information and British Intelligence', p. 51

10 Hemming, *Our Man in New York*, p. 126

11 Troy, 'The Coordinator of Information and British Intelligence', pp. 104-6

12 UKNA FO 1093/238, C/6833, Menzies to Hopkinson, 19 June 1941

13 Bennett, *Churchill's Man of Mystery*, p. 257

14 'Donovan will take Information Post', *New York Times*, 9 July 1941; CIA Electronic Reading Room, CREST collection, RDP88G01116R000550009-8, Remarks of William J. Casey, CIA Director, to the OSS/ Donovan Symposium, Washington, 19 September 1986

15 UKNA CAB81/103, JIC (41) 300, 28 July 1941; ADM223/464, History of Naval Intelligence and the Naval Intelligence Department 1939-1945, pp. 115-19; Jay Jakub, *Spies and Saboteurs: Anglo-American Collaboration and Rivalry in Human Intelligence Collection and Special Operations 1940-45*, Macmillan, Basingstoke, 1999, p. 41

16 Troy, *Donovan and the CIA*, pp, 117-18; Jakub, *Spies and Saboteurs*, p. 35; UKNA HS 7/78, SOE Washington, History, 8 February 1944; FO 1093/172, Conclusions come to at a meeting of Sir David Petrie, C and Mr Duff Cooper on 27 September 1943

17 Troy, *Donovan and the CIA*, pp. 115-16

18 UKNA CAB 301/102, C/8684, Menzies to Cadogan, 5 February 1942; Nigel West (ed.),

The Guy Liddell Diaries, Vol. 1: 1939-1942, Routledge, London, 2005, pp. 249-50

19 UKNA FO 1093/170, Butler to Loxley, 26 January 1942

20 West, *The Guy Liddell Diaries, Vol. 1*, pp. 249-50

21 UKNA CAB 301/102, Stephenson to Menzies, 14 March 1942, attached to C/8954, Menzies to Loxley, 15 March 1942; No. 1710, Halifax to Cadogan, 24 March 1942; FO 1093/238, Loxley Minute to PUS, 10 April 1942

22 UKNA HS 8/34, SOE/America/39, American Organizations in Washington with whom British Security Coordination Works, 24 March 1943; Troy, *Donovan and the CIA*, p. 134; Jakub, *Spies and Saboteurs*, p. 113

23 Troy, *Donovan and the CIA*, pp. 136-47

24 CIA CREST, RDP13X00001R000100290001-2: Ellery CV, 5 January 1942; KM Memorandum for File, 8 January 1942; Huntington to Donovan, 6 April 1942; Donovan Telegram, 6 April 1942; Donovan to Huntington, 8 May 1942; 'Ellery Huntington Jr', *New York Times*, 6 July 1987

25 *War Report of the OSS, Vol. 1*, Walker, New York, 1976, pp. 26-7, 84; Troy, *Donovan and the CIA*, pp. 150-2

26 UKNA HS 8/9, Summary of Agreement between British SOE and American SO

27 NARA RG226, Box 251, Folder 739, Relations with the British 1943; Jeffery, *The Secret History of MI6*, pp. 510-11

28 Remarks of William J. Casey, 19 September 1986

29 NARA RG226, Box 251, Folder 739, Relations with the British 1943

30 C. A. Prettiman, 'The Many Lives of William Alfred Eddy', *Princeton University Library Chronicle*, Vol. 53/2 (1992)

31 *War Report of the OSS, Vol. 2: Operations*

in the Field, Walker, New York, 1976, pp. 8-18; Jakub, *Spies and Saboteurs*, pp. 67-8; UKNA HS 3/63, Report of Meeting with OSS Representatives in North Africa, August 1942

32 *War Report of the OSS, Vol. 2*, p. 11; Jakub, *Spies and Saboteurs*, p. 67; Jeffery, *The Secret History of MI6*, pp. 493-5

33 Mieczysław Zygfryd Słowikowski, *Codename Rygor: The Spy behind the Allied Victory in North Africa*, Dialogue, London, 2010, pp. 117-18, 125-9

34 UKNA FO 371/31913, Situation in French North Africa, 27 August 1942

35 Słowikowski, *Codename Rygor*, pp. 256, 314; John Herman, 'Agency Afrika: Rygor's Franco-Polish Network and Operation Torch', *Journal of Contemporary History*, Vol. 22/4 (1987). See also Tessa Stirling, Daria Nałęcz & Tadeusz Dubicki (eds), *Intelligence Cooperation between Poland and Great Britain during World War II*, Vallentine Mitchell, London, 2005, vol. I, pp. 227-8, vol. II, pp. 588-639

36 CIA CREST, RDP13X00001R000100290001-2, Ellery C. Huntington Jr, Report on European Trip – December 24, 1942, to March 21, 1943; Operations in the Field, pp. 13-15; Richard Helms, Remarks during a ceremony on 24 May 1983 to award him the William J. Donovan Award

37 Remarks of William J Casey, 19 September 1986

38 Troy, *Donovan and the CIA*, pp. 179-91; *War Report of the OSS, Vol. 1*, p. x

39 Troy, *Donovan and the CIA*, pp. 190-204; 'Informed sources hint showdown between OSS and OWI', *New York Times*, 19 January 1943

4. SHARING THE TRICKS OF THE TRADE

1 Jakub, *Spies and Saboteurs*, pp. 56-60; UKNA HS 8/34, American Organizations in Washington with whom BSC works, p. 2

2 CIA CREST, RDP13X00001R000100290001-2,

    Ellery C. Huntington Jr, Report on European Trip – December 24, 1942, to March 21, 1943

3 Ibid.

4 CIA CREST, RDP13X00001R000100290001-2, Huntington Diary, 6-10 January 1943; UKNA HS 7/74, Report on BSC in the USA, Part 3, Special Operations, pp. 92-4

5 Huntington, Report on European Trip

6 Huntington Diary, 8 January 1943

7 Huntington Diary, 31 January, 1-4 February, 5 March 1943

8 Huntington Diary, 12 February 1943; UKNA HS 8/5, A841, Cairo to London, 17 February 1943; A1013, Head of SOE Cairo to London, 26 May 1943

9 Huntington Diary, 15 February, 5, 10 March 1943

10 Huntington, Report on European Trip

11 *War Report of the OSS, Vol. 2*, pp. 278-9; NARA RG226, Box 251, Folder 739, Relations with the British 1944; Neal H. Petersen (ed.), *From Hitler's Doorstep: The Wartime Intelligence Reports of Allen Dulles 1942-1945*, Penn State University Press, University Park, pp. 8-12, 183-90, 591; Michael Smith, *The Anatomy of a Spy: A History of Espionage and Betrayal*, History Press, Cheltenham, 2019, pp. 65-73

12 Richard W. Cutler, *Counterspy: Memoirs of a Counterintelligence Officer in World War II and the Cold War*, Brasseys, Washington, DC, 2004, p. 52

13 Smith, *The Anatomy of a Spy*, pp. 116-220; Jeffery, *The Secret History of MI6*, pp. 380-92, 509-12, NARA RG226, Box 251, Folder 739, Relations with the British 1944; *War Report of the OSS, Vol. 2*, pp. 279-80

14 *War Report of the OSS, Vol. 1*, pp. 189-90, 198; *War Report of the OSS, Vol. 2*, pp. 149-56

15 UKNA KV 4/468, Liddell Diaries, 3 March 1946, p. 164

16 UKNA HS 8/5, AD4/903, AD4 to CD, 2 June 1943; Nigel Clive, *A Greek Experience 1943-1948*, Michael Russell, Wilton, 1985, p. 90.

17 Jakub, *Spies and Saboteurs*, pp. 125-6; John Cripps, 'Mihailović or Tito: How the Codebreakers Helped Churchill Choose', in Erskine & Smith, *The Bletchley Park Codebreakers*, pp. 217-39

18 NARA RG226 Box 190, Personnel File of Ellery C. Huntington Jr; UKNA HS 8/5, R8584/14/G, Sargent to Selborne, 11 September 1943; HS 8/7, R10073/5558/G, Cadogan to CD, 13 October 1943; Jeffery, *The Secret History of MI6*, pp. 499-501

19 UKNA HS 8/5, F1049/68/18, Selborne to Eden, OSS in the Balkans, 18 November 1943

20 NARA RG226, Box 205, Folder 47, Messages received from the American Liaison Office with Tito, 13 September 1943; UKNA HS 8/7, Tel 3371, Massingham to London/ Cairo, 9 October 1943

21 UKNA HS 8/1, JCS 155/11/D, Joint Chiefs of Staff Directive, Functions of the Office of Strategic Services, 27 October 1943, p. 1; HS 8/2 London to Cairo, 21 October 1943; No 3110, CD to V/CD for SO [Selborne], 18 November 1943; No 522, V/CD to CD (in Cairo), 20 November 1943; No 3207, Tito from CD, 21 November 1943; HS8/5, Tel No 782, Cairo [CD] to [Stephenson] New York, 21 November 1943; 111 V/CD to CD, 20 November 1943; No 3212, CD to V/CD for SO, 21 November 1943; COS/161/256, Gubbins to CGS, GHQ, MEF (Gen Henry Wilson), 25 November 1943; HS 8/7, Tito from CD, 21 November 43; Notes on meeting held at MO4 at 1500hrs on 17 November 1943

22 UKNA HS 8/2, No 3110, CD to V/CD for SO [Selborne], 18 November 1943; HS 8/7, Tito from CD, 21 November 43; Ian Dear, *Sabotage and Subversion: The SOE and*

OSS at War, History Press, Stroud, 2016, pp. 192-206

23 Jakub, *Spies and Saboteurs*, p. 135

24 NARA RG226, Box 205, Folder 46, London OSS Op-1, Burma: The Beginning

25 NARA RG226, Box 205, Folder 46, London OSS Op-1, APO 885, Heppner to Director OSS, 12 November 1943

26 CIA CREST, RDP13X00001R000100290001-2, Fellers to Donovan, 15 June 1943; John Davies Jr, Comments on Proposal submitted by Major General Cawthorne, 31 May 1943; CIA CREST, RDP13X00001R000100030012-8, John Davies, Anglo American Cooperation in East Asia, 15 November 1943

27 Richard Aldrich, *The Hidden Hand: Britain, America and Cold War Secret Intelligence*, John Murray, London, 2001, p. 79

28 UKNA HS 8/6, Part Played by Britain and America in Helping French Resistance, 3rd draft, 14 November 1944; Extract from VCD/919 of 24 February 1944; MG/2324, Open Address of the London Group, 8 March 1944; SHAEF/17240/Ops, Open Title of SOE/SO Headquarters, 17 March 1944

29 UKNA HS 8/6, Part Played by Britain and America in Helping French Resistance, 3rd draft, 14 November 1944; *War Report of the OSS, Vol. 2*, pp. 199-204; Martin Cox interview with Daphne Park, 21 April 2007; CIA CREST, Doc. No. 0005355248, Wisner to DCI, Major Lucien E. Conein, 25 August 1953; www.plan-sussex-1944.net (accessed 17 March 2022)

30 *War Report of the OSS, Vol. 2*, pp. 204-8; www.plan-sussex-1944. net > anglais > pdf > infiltrations_ into_france—History of WWII infiltrations into France-rev100; John

D. Wilson, 'At Work with Donovan:
One Man's History in OSS', *Studies in
Intelligence*, Vol. 37/3 (1994)
31 NARA RG226, Box 251, Folder 739,
Relations with the British 1943 and
1944
32 Nelson MacPherson, *American
Intelligence in War-time London: The
Story of the OSS*, Frank Cass, London,
2003, pp. 57, 77; Jeffery, *The Secret
History of MI6*, p. 499
33 Patrick Hawker, 'Sussex – The Joint
Project of 1944', unpublished paper
34 *War Report of the OSS, Vol. 2*, pp. 208-
11; Jeffery, *The Secret History of MI6*,
pp. 537-8
35 Remarks of William J. Casey,
19 September 1986; MacPherson,
American Intelligence, pp. 160-81;
Jeffery, *The Secret History of MI6*,
pp. 546-51; UKNA CAB 21/2519,
Guard Procedure, 1 January 1944;
C5535, Menzies to Bridges,
31 January 1944
36 CIA CREST, A Life in Intelligence
– The Richard Helms Collection,
Interview with Richard Helms,
29 September 1982

5. THE COLD WAR BEGINS

1 NARA RG226, Box 251, Folder 739,
Relations with the British, 1944
2 UKNA CAB 308/48, Future
Organization of the SIS, Section IX,
Co-operation with the Secret Services
of Other Nations
3 NARA RG226, Box 251, Folder 739,
Relations with the British, 1944
4 'New deal plans super spy system,
sleuths would snoop on US and
the world', *Chicago Tribune*,
9 February 1945; 'Donovan proposes
super spy system for post-war new
deal', *Washington Times-Herald*,
9 February 1945
5 UKNA HW 57/34, CXG680, Easton
from Duboulay, 1 February 1945;
CXG685, O'Connor to Director,
2 February 1945; GOR G29, GC&CS
to SLU Washington, 3 March 1945
6 NARA RG165, MID, Folder 334,

Memorandum for the Record,
Colonel Park's comments on OSS,
12 March 1945
7 John Ranelagh, *The Agency: The Rise
and Decline of the CIA*, Weidenfeld
& Nicolson, London, 1986; 'OSS is
branded British agency to legislators',
Washington Times-Herald, 18 May 1945;
Christopher Andrew, *For the President's
Eyes Only: Secret Intelligence and the
American Presidency from Washington
to Bush*, HarperPerennial, London,
1996, pp. 149, 156; Troy, *Donovan and
the CIA*, pp. 278-86
8 NARA RG226, Box 203, Allen Dulles
Personnel File, Recommendation for
Medal, 13 November 1945; Cutler,
Counterspy, pp. xx-xxi, 51-2, 87;
Wilson, 'At Work with Donovan';
'On the Front Lines of the Cold
War: Documents on the Intelligence
War in Berlin, 1946 to 1961', CIA
website, https://www.cia.gov/static/
32bfd67a856137968d7c0cc5782214c6/
On-the-Front-Lines-of-the-Cold-War.
pdf (accessed 15 December 2021),
Clay to Chief of Mission, War
Department Detachment (Helms),
20 October 1946; Helms, Targets of
German Mission, 10 January 1947;
Galloway for Vandenberg,
16 January 1947; Ray S. Cline, *The
CIA under Reagan, Bush and Casey: The
Evolution of the Agency from Roosevelt to
Reagan*, Acropolis, Washington, DC,
1981, p. 114
9 Matthew M. Aid (ed.), *Cold War
Intelligence: The Secret War between the
US and the USSR 1945-1991*, Brill,
Leiden & Boston, 2013, http://
primarysources.brillonline.com/
browse/cold-war-intelligence (accessed
15 December 2021): NARA RG38, Box
78, File: 3860/4 Ladd to Shelley, MI6,
Future Relations with, 29 May 1945
10 Aid, *Cold War Intelligence*: NARA
RG38, Box 78, File: 3860/4, Ladd
to Shelley, MI6, Discussion with Sir
Stewart Menzies, 14 May 1945
11 Aid, *Cold War Intelligence*: NARA
RG38, Box 78, File: 3860/4, Ladd

to Shelley, MI6 Liaison, Section IX (Communism), 17 July 1945

12 Aid, *Cold War Intelligence*: NARA RG226, Entry 215, Box 2, Folder 13, Horton to Shepardson, MI6 Plans, 16 August 1945

13 Aid, *Cold War Intelligence*: NARA RG226, Entry 108B, Box 90, Folder 733, Gold to Bross, The Broadway Work Program, 21 August 1945; NARA RG226, Entry 108B, Box 95, Folder 763, Houck to Valk, 25 January 1946

14 CIA CREST, RDP86B00975R000800140001-3, Truman to Donovan, 20 September 1945

15 NARA RG226, Box 251, Folder 739, Relations with the British 1944; Aldrich, *The Hidden Hand*, pp. 83-4; Jeffery, *The Secret History of MI6*, pp. 717-18

16 Cutler, *Counterspy*, pp. 87-8

17 CIA CREST, A Life in Intelligence – The Richard Helms Collection, Interview with Richard Helms, 29 September 1982; Beatrice de Graaf, Ben de Jong & Wies Platje, *Battleground Western Europe: Intelligence Operations in Germany and the Netherlands in the Twentieth Century*, Het Spinhuis, Amsterdam, 2007, pp. 98-9

18 'On the Front Lines of the Cold War', Report on Berlin Operations Base, Chief of Station Karlsruhe to Chief Foreign Branch M, 8 April 1948

19 'A lecture by Sokolovsky', *Marion Star*, 25 November 1947; 'On the Front Lines of the Cold War', Report on Berlin Operations Base, Chief of Station Karlsruhe to Chief Foreign Branch M, 8 April 1948

20 Interviews and correspondence with Tony Divall, April 1995; UKNA FO 1093/473, Halford to Harrison, 24 February 1949

21 UKNA HW 57/34, CXG 664, O'Connor to Director, 28 January 1945; CXG204, Director to McCormack, 5 February 1945; Aid, *Cold War Intelligence*: Robert

Louis Benson & Cecil J. Phillips, *History of Venona*, NSA Center for Cryptologic History, 1995, pp. 8, 13, 20-1; Frank B. Rowlett, Recollections of Work on Russian, 11 February 1965

22 UKNA HW 14/16, Letter to General Tadeusz Klimecki re W/T Operators for Soviet Military and Air interception; HW 14/128, Pritchard to Tiltman, 30 May 1945; Aid, *Cold War Intelligence*: Benson & Phillips, *History of Venona*, p. 30; Michael L. Peterson, *Bourbon to Black Friday: The Allied Collaborative Comint Effort against the Soviet Union 1945-1948*, Center for Cryptologic History, 1995. For more detail of the British work on Russian systems see Michael Smith, 'GC&CS and the First Cold War', in Erskine & Smith, *The Bletchley Park Codebreakers*

23 UKNA HW 57/34, Nicholson to Bromley, 4 April 1945; GOR 200, O'Connor to GC&CS, 24 April 1945; GOR 213, SLU Washington to GC&CS, 26 April 1945

24 UKNA HW 57/34, State of Russian and General Post-War Negotiations with the Americans, 26 July 1945; AZ/2770, Travis to O'Connor, 14 May 1945; GOR 474, SLU Washington to GC&CS, 20 July 1945

25 Matthew M. Aid, '"Stella Polaris" and the Secret Code Battle in Postwar Europe', *Intelligence and National Security*, Vol. 17/3 (2002); C. G. McKay, 'Debris from Stella Polaris: A Footnote to the CIA–NSA Account of Venona', *Intelligence and National Security*, Vol. 14/2 (1999); Aid, *Cold War Intelligence*: Benson & Phillips, *History of Venona*, pp. 50-1; Peterson, *Bourbon to Black Friday*, p. 75

26 NARA RG 457, Box 168, Final Report of TICOM Team I, pp. 10-13, 39-42; Michael Smith interview with Selmer Norland, 11 May 1998; NSA Oral History, OH-14-83, Howard Campaigne, 29 June 1983; Thomas Parrish, *The ULTRA Americans: The US Role in Breaking the Nazi Codes*, Stein &

Day, New York, 1986

27 UKNA HW 57/34, Unidentified memo on TICOM and Russian Baudot Traffic, 26 July 1945; State of Russian and General Post-War Negotiations with the Americans, 26 July 1945

28 Memorandum from Army-Navy Communications Intelligence Board (ANCIB) re: Signals Intelligence, 22 August 1945, available at https://media.defense. gov/2021/Jul/15/2002763682/- 1/-1/0/ANCIB_22AUG45.PDF (accessed 17 December 2021); Aid, *Cold War Intelligence*: Greene to Solomon, History of the Bourbon Problem, 12 March 1946; Naval Communications Activity, Russian Language Section: July 1943-January 1948; Benson & Phillips, *History of Venona*, p. 60

29 Joint Meeting of ANCIB and ANCICC, 15 October 1945, available at https://media.defense.gov/2021/ Jul/15/2002763683/-1/-1/0/JOINT_ MTG_15OCT45.PDF (accessed 17 December 2021); Joint Meeting of Army-Navy Communications Intelligence Board Joint Meeting Summary, 1 November 1945, available at https://media.defense. gov/2021/Jul/15/2002763672/- 1/-1/0/JOINT_MTG_1NOV45. PDF (accessed 17 December 2021); Communications Intelligence, 8 February 1946, available at https://media.defense.gov/2021/ Jul/15/2002763700/-1/-1/0/ COMMS_INT_8FEB46.PDF (accessed 17 December 2021); UKNA HW 80/1, Joint Meeting of Army–Navy Communication Intelligence Board and Army– Navy Communication Intelligence Coordinating Committee, 29 October 1945; HW 80/2, Outline of Draft British–US Communication Intelligence Agreement, 1 November 1945; HW 80/4, British–US Communications

Intelligence Agreement and Outline, 5 March 1946; HW 80/5, Minutes of the Inauguration Meeting British Signal Intelligence Conference, 11-27 March 1946

30 CIA CREST, RDP80R01731R003400110031-3, Central Intelligence Group, Foreign Broadcast Intelligence Service, Future Relations Between FBIS and BBC Monitoring Service, 13 September 1946; RDP80- 00765A000100010125-5, Memo for Director of Central Intelligence, Reciprocal Agreement with BBC Monitoring Service, 10 January 1947; RDP80-00765A000100010122-8, Report on Negotiations Conducted with the British Government Relative to a Reciprocal Monitoring Arrangement between FBIB and BBC, 1 July 1947

31 Matthew M. Aid, *The Secret Sentry: The Untold History of the National Security Agency*, Bloomsbury, New York, 2009, pp. 14-15; Richard Aldrich, *GCHQ*, Centenary Edition, William Collins, London, 2020, p. 78

32 Aid, *Cold War Intelligence*: NARA Aid, RG 38, Box 2742, TI Item #137, NT-1, 4 November 1948, Unprecedented Coordinated Russian Communications Changes; Michael L. Peterson, Beyond Bourbon – 1948. The Fourth Year of Allied Collaborative Comint Effort Against the Soviet Union', *Cryptologic Quarterly*, Spring 1995; Stephen Budiansky, *Code Warriors: NSA's Codebreakers and the Secret Intelligence War Against the Soviet Union*, Vintage, New York, 2017, pp. 110-11; Liddell Hart Centre for Military Archives, King's College London, GB0099 KCLMA, unpublished memoirs of Colonel Leo Steveni, ch. 22, p. 4

6. PLAYING MOSCOW AT ITS OWN GAME

1 UKNA CAB 81/133, Report by Joint Intelligence Sub-Committee,

23 September 1946

2 UKNA FO 1093/447, C to Sargent, 25 June 1948

3 UKNA CAB 301/48, Future Organisation of the SIS, Report of a Committee set up by Sir A. Cadogan on 8 October 1943; SVR Archives, Philby files, Minutes of CSS Committee on SIS Organisation, 21 July 1947, accessed by author in November 1997. See also Nigel West & Oleg Tsarev (eds), *Triplex: Secrets from the Cambridge Spies*, Yale University Press, New Haven, CT, 2009, pp. 120-9

4 Kenneth Benton, 'The ISOS Years: Madrid 1941-3', *Journal of Contemporary History*, Vol. 30/3 (1995)

5 Anthony Cavendish, *Inside Intelligence: The Revelations of an MI6 Officer*, new ed., HarperCollins, London, 1997

6 Interview with Jānis Lukaševics, Latvian Radio, 11 March 1988

7 Tom Bower, *The Red Web: MI6 and the KGB Master Coup*, new ed., Mandarin, London, 1993; Mart Laar, *War in the Woods: Estonia's Struggle for Survival 1944-1956*, Compass, Washington, DC, 1992, pp. 207-16; CIA CREST, CIA/SIS London Talks, May 1952, Operations in the Baltic States, 29-30 May 1952

8 Interview with Kenneth Benton, 3 December 1996

9 CIA CREST, 519697e8993294098d50c29a, CIA and Nazi War Criminals, Chapter 5, Long Experience in the Anti-Soviet Game, pp. 22-5, 31-3

10 Arnold M. Silver, 'Questions, Questions, Questions: Memories of Oberursel', *Intelligence and National Security*, Vol. 8/2 (1993)

11 Michael Smith, *New Cloak, Old Dagger: How Britain's Spies Came In from the Cold*, Victor Gollancz, London, 1996, p. 111

12 UKNA CAB 81/93, Minutes of Joint Intelligence Sub-Committee, 11 September 1945; CAB 81/130, JIC (45) 272 (o), Intelligence on Atomic Energy, 18 September 1945; AB 4/1014, Report by MAUD committee on the use of uranium as a source of power; CAB 104/227, Scientific Advisory Committee: investigations on the use of uranium for a bomb; SVR Archives, Moscow, File of Lista (Liszt – John Cairncross), 83896, Background to No 6881/1065 of 25 September 1941 from London, accessed by author in November 1997; Paul Maddrell, 'British–American Scientific Intelligence Collaboration during the Occupation of Germany', *Intelligence and National Security*, Vol. 15/2 (2000)

13 Henry S. Lowenhaupt, 'On the Soviet Nuclear Scent', *Studies in Intelligence*, Vol. 11/4 (1967); Henry S. Lowenhaupt, 'Chasing Bitterfeld Calcium', *Studies in Intelligence*, Vol. 17/1 (1973); Donald p. Steury, 'How the CIA Missed Stalin's Bomb: Dissecting Soviet Analysis 1946-50', *Studies in Intelligence*, Spring 2005; Maddrell, 'British–American Scientific Intelligence Collaboration'; CIA CREST, RDP67-00059A000200130011-3, Central Intelligence Group, Soviet Capabilities for the Development and Production of Certain Types of Weapons and Equipment, 31 October 1946; *Foreign Relations of the United States* (FRUS) 1947, Volume 1: General: The United Nations, ed. Velma Hastings Cassidy, Ralph R. Goodwin & George H. Dengler, United States Government Printing Office, Washington, DC, 1967, Doc. 450; Michael S. Goodman, *Spying on the Nuclear Bear: Anglo-American Intelligence and the Soviet Bomb*, Stanford University Press, Stanford, CA, 2007, pp. 12-18, 26-32; David E. Murphy, Sergei A. Kondrashev & George Bailey, *Battleground Berlin: CIA vs KGB in the Cold War*, Yale University Press, New Haven, CT, 1997, pp. 13-14; Aldrich, *The Hidden Hand*, pp. 221-6

14 UKNA PREM 8/1279, Perrin

to Rickett, 24 March 1950; KV
2/1250, Folio 443b, Statement
of Michael William Perrin,
31 January 1950; Venona messages:
Moscow evaluates some atomic
bomb information from agent Klaus
Fuchs, 10 April 1945, available at
https://media.defense.gov/2021/
Aug/01/2002818623/-1/-1/0/10APR_
ATOMIC_BOMB_INFO.PDF
(accessed 17 December 2021)
15 Ranelagh, *The Agency*, p. 114;
'Intelligence—III: errors in
collecting data held exceeded by
evaluation weakness', *New York
Times*, 23 July 1948; 'Rumania
accused of affronts to US, envoy
searched at gunpoint', *New York
Times*, 9 December 1947; 'Rumanian
suspects talk', *New York Times*,
29 October 1948; '12 Rumanian
leaders sentenced as spies', *New
York Times*, 3 November 1948;
'Rumania and US each ask recall
of two diplomats', *New York Times*,
12 December 1948
16 UKNA KV 4/467, Liddell Diaries,
28 January 1946; FO 1093/347,
Caccia to Harvey and Sargent,
24 January 1946; C/172, Menzies to
JIC Chairman, 28 March 1946; Caccia
to C, 4 February 1946; C/9970, C
to Caccia, Draft Directive on Special
Operations for the Chief of the Secret
Service, 30 January 1946; Roberts
to Caccia, 2 April 1946; No. 1051,
Caccia to Roberts, 4 April 1946;
Menzies, Instructions to Heads
of Stations abroad, April 1946;
C/423, Menzies to Secretary JIC,
22 June 1946; David Smiley, *Albanian
Assignment*, Sphere, London, 1985,
p. 162; Smith, *New Cloak, Old Dagger*,
pp. 111-12
17 UKNA FO 1093/375, JP (47)
118 Final, Special Operations,
Report by the Joint Planning Staff,
17 December 1947; Stapleton to
Sargent, 23 December 1947; MI6
Paper on the Capabilities of SS in
Peace in Support of an Overall

Political Plan, 20 January 1948;
Hayter to Sargent, 9 March 1948;
Sargent to Bevin, 30 March 1948
18 CIA CREST,
RDP86T00268R000500090034-3,
PPS221, Utilization of Refugees from
the Soviet Union in US National
Interest, 4 March 1948
19 UKNA FO 1093/375, McNeil to
Bevin, 19 April 1948; Balfour to
Hayter, 25 May 1948
20 UKNA FO 1093/375, Balfour to
Hayter, 20 May 1948
21 CIA CREST,
519697e8993294098d50c2a1, CIA
and Nazi War Criminals, Chapter 6,
Common Ground with New Partners,
pp. 2-6
22 SVR Archives, Burgess files 83792,
Burgess to Max (aka Yuri Modin),
6 September 1948, accessed by author
in November 1997
23 FRUS 1945-1950, Emergence of
the Intelligence Establishment, ed.
C. Thomas Thorne Jr & David S.
Patterson, United States Government
Printing Office, Washington, DC,
1996, Doc. 292; CIA CREST, Ref:
519697e8993294098d50c29b, CIA
and Nazi War Criminals, Chapter 7;
RDP86B00269R001100090002-8,
The Central Intelligence Agency
and National Organization for
Intelligence, by Allen W. Dulles,
Chairman, William H. Jackson,
Mathias F. Correa, 1 January 1949,
pp. 131-4; Ranelagh, *The Agency*,
p. 134; Jeffery, *The Secret History
of MI6*, pp. 719-20; 'Our History',
Secret Intelligence Service (MI6)
website, https://www.sis.gov.
uk/our-history.html (accessed
20 December 2021)
24 UKNA FO 1093/375, Sargent to
Bevin, 30 March 1948; FO 1093/477,
A. S. Halford account of meeting
to discuss resuming SIS activities in
Moscow, 12 August 1948
25 CIA CREST,
5166d49199326091c6a6007a,
Directors Log, 15-17 September 1951,

3-4 October 1951, 8-9 October, 28-29 November 1951, 14-15 December 1951, 19-20 December 1951, 26-27 December 1951; Paddy Hayes, *Queen of Spies: Daphne Park, Britain's Cold War Spy Master*, Duckworth Overlook, London, 2016, p. 78

26 Author interviews with Simon Preston, 11 October 1995, and Michael Giles, 25 October 1995

7. VALUABLE OR WORTHLESS?

1 Clive, *Greek Experience*, pp. 176-7; UKNA FO 1093/347 C/423, Menzies to Secretary JIC, 22 June 1946; FO1093/452 Notes on Counter Guerrilla Action in Albania, 30 December 1948

2 UKNA FO 371/71687, Minutes of meeting of Russia Committee, 25 November 1948

3 UKNA FO 371/77623, Minutes of meeting of Russia Committee, 13 February 1949; Nicholas Bethell, *The Great Betrayal: The Untold Story of Kim Philby's Biggest Coup*, Hodder & Stoughton, London, 1984, p. 39

4 CIA CREST, 519a2b76993294098d50f5a5, Memo for PB1, British Counterpart of BGFIEND, 26 July 1949; Smiley, *Albanian Assignment*, p. 165

5 CIA CREST, 519a2b76993294098d50f5a5, Memo for PB1, British Counterpart of BGFIEND, 26 July 1949; CIA CREST, 519a2b76993294098d50f59a, Preliminary Foreign Office reaction to certain aspects of recent OPC–SIS conversations, 13 June 1949; CIA CREST, 519a2b76993294098d50f3f4, Project BGFiend Report, 29 November 1951; Bethell, *The Great Betrayal*, p. 41; Jeffery, *The Secret History of MI6*, pp. 214-15; Association for Diplomatic Studies and Training Foreign Affairs Oral History Project, Interview with James McCargar, 18 April 1995; 'Guerrillas of Albania', *New York Times*, 13 March 1949

6 Bethell, *The Great Betrayal*, pp. 56-63, 127-9

7 Smiley, *Albanian Assignment*, pp. 165-6; Bethell, *The Great Betrayal*, p. 53

8 'Rebels begin spring offensive', *New York Times*, 5 April 1949; 'Greek rebel massing reported', *New York Times*, 9 May 1949; 'Initial successes mark Greek drive', *New York Times*, 12 August 1949; 'Greek rebel units reported fleeing', *New York Times*, 13 August 1949; 'Greek Army cuts rebels' Vitsi area', *New York Times*, 14 August 1949; 'Guerrilla resistance along Albanian border', *New York Times*, 28 August 1949; 'Greek Army captures Grammos', *New York Times*, 29 August 1949

9 Smiley, *Albanian Assignment*, p. 98; Bethell, *The Great Betrayal*, p. 78; CIA CREST, RDP78-001617A000700030002-6, Intelligence Memorandum No. 218, Strengths and Weaknesses of the Hoxha Regime in Albania, 12 September 1949

10 CIA CREST, 519a2b77993294098d50f620, Meeting of the Joint Policy Committee for Operation BGFIEND

11 CIA CREST, 519a2b76993294098d50f3d1, Revaluation of the Project BGFIEND, 29 November 1949; Jeffery, *The Secret History of MI6*, p. 716

12 CIA CREST, 519a2b77993294098d50f5d7, Arms Drops into Albania, 31 January 1950; CIA CREST, 519a2b76993294098d50f3f4, Project BGFiend Report, 29 November 1951; CIA CREST, 519a2b76993294098d50f3ec, Review of BGFIEND, 8 February 1950; CIA CREST, 519a2b7c993294098d5102fe, Fiend Valuable Understanding as of September 1951; UKNA FO 1093/453, Rumbold, Albania: Statement of the Problem, 15 November 1949; Valuable, Liaison Visit to Washington,

12 December 1949; Reilly to Hoyer-Miller, 2 January 1950; Jeffery, *The Secret History of MI6*, p. 716; Nigel West, *The Friends: Britain's Post-War Secret Intelligence Operations*, Weidenfeld & Nicolson, London, 1988, pp. 63-5

13 'West held easing stand on Albania', *New York Times*, 27 March 1950

14 CIA CREST, 519a2b76993294098d50f553. BGFIEND Status Report, 9 January 1951

15 CIA CREST, 519a2b7a993294098d50fe25, Report into incident in summer of 1951 in which US team killed communist officials; CIA CREST, 5166d49199326091c6a6007a, Directors Log 1 September 1951-31 December 1951

16 CIA CREST, 519a2b7a993294098d50fe10, FBIS, Tirana, ATA, 24 October 1951; CIA CREST, 519a2b7a993294098d50fdcc, Seven British-Trained Spies Captured, Tirana, ATA, 25 October 1951; 'Albania reports 17 "spies" killed', *New York Times*, 30 October 1951; CIA CREST, 519a2b7c993294098d51030c, Recapitulation of BGFIEND Operations, 1 January 1952 to 31 December 1952

17 CIA CREST, 519a2b76993294098d50f3ed, Background to Valuable/BGFIEND, 19 November 1952; CIA CREST, 519a2b7c993294098d51030c, Recapitulation, BGFIEND Operations, 1 January 1952 to 31 December 1952; CIA CREST, 19a2b78993294098d50fa07, Recapitulation of OBOPUS Operations, 1 February to 31 December 1953; CIA CREST, 519a2b7c993294098d5102c3, Memorandum of Conversation: Possible Diplomatic Action Relating to Albania, 21 October 1952

18 CIA CREST, 519a2b7a993294098d50fd72, Minutes of the Fiend/Valuable Meeting held

in London 12-13 March 1952; Rory Cormac, *Disrupt and Deny: Spies, Special Forces, and the Secret Pursuit of British Foreign Policy*, Oxford University Press, Oxford, 2018

19 CIA CREST, 519a2b7e993294098d5106b9, OE Review of APPLE Trial, 18 May 1954; 'Albania reports killing 13 spies', *New York Times*, 25 November 1951; CIA CREST, 519a2b7e993294098d5107a8, Valuable Liaison 1 March-30 April, 19 May 1955

20 CIA CREST, 519a2b7e993294098d510793, OBSIDIOUS Mission Briefing for 19-22 June 1955 Infiltration, 14 July 1955; CIA CREST, 519a2b7e993294098d510797, OBSIDIOUS: Debriefing and LCFLUTTER of 19 June Mission, 10 September 1955; CIA CREST, 519a2b7e993294098d5107a9, OBSIDIOUS: Monthly Report for Period 1-30 September 1955; CIA CREST, 519a2b7e993294098d51076d, Project Obhunt Status Report 1-30 November 1955; CIA CREST, RDP-519a2b7e993294098d51075a, Project Oblivious Status Report 1-31 December 1955; CIA CREST, 519a2b7e993294098d510758, Project Obtest Status Report 1-31 December 1955; CIA CREST, 519a2b7e993294098d51075a, Project Obtuse Status Report 1-31 December 1955; CIA CREST, RDP79R01012A010700020001-2, NIE 10-58, Anti-Communist Resistance Potential in the Sino-Soviet Bloc, 4 March 1958

21 CIA CREST, RDP-519a2b7a993294098d50fe15, Liaison with the British in Washington on Projects Fiend and Valuable, 28 August 1951

22 Aid, *Cold War Intelligence*: NSA FOIA, Extracts from Benson & Phillips, *History of Venona*; NSA, Lou Benson, Venona—Summary History, 18 May 1995; Robert L. Benson, *The*

Venona Story, Center for Cryptologic History

23 Benson, *Venona Story*, pp. 10, 59; Christopher Andrew, *The Defence of the Realm: The Authorized History of MI5*, Allen Lane, London, 2009, p. 368; Nigel West, *Venona: The Greatest Secret of the Cold War*, HarperCollins, London, 1999, pp. 27-8, 134-5, UKNA HW 3/1, Paper 91, p. 6; Robert Cecil, 'The Cambridge Comintern', in Christopher Andrew & David Dilks (eds), *The Missing Dimension: Governments and Intelligence Communities in the Twentieth Century*, Macmillan, London, 1983

24 NSA Website, Venona Documents, Evaluation of Material on Enormoz: From CHARL'Z on Funicular and from MLAD, 31 March 1945, available at https://media.defense. gov/2021/Aug/01/2002818558/-1/- 1/0/31MAR_IDENTIFICATION_ MLAD.PDF (accessed 17 January 2022); Moscow evaluates some atomic bomb information from agent Klaus Fuchs, 10 April 1945, available at https://media.defense.gov/2021/ Aug/01/2002818623/-1/-1/0/10APR_ ATOMIC_BOMB_INFO.PDF (accessed 17 January 2022); Roland Philipps, *A Spy Named Orphan: The Enigma of Donald Maclean*, Bodley Head, London, 2018, pp. 218-19; West, *Venona*, pp. 150-2; Cecil, 'The Cambridge Comintern'

25 Andrew, *The Defence of the Realm*, pp. 378-80; NSA Website, Venona Documents, London to Moscow, No. 798, 22 July 1940; Development of the 'G'—Homer (Gomer) Case, 11 October 1951; Report on Information Given by 'Homer', New York to Moscow, No. 1271-1274, 7 September 1944; Washington to Moscow, No. 1788, To the 8th Department. Material of 'G', 29 March 1945; Cecil, 'The Cambridge Comintern'

26 NSA Website, Venona Documents, New York to Moscow, No. 915, 28 June 1944; Philipps, *A Spy Named Orphan*, pp. 50-4

27 UKNA KV 4/473, Liddell Diaries, 1 May 1951, p. 65, 29-30 May 1951, pp. 80-5, 12 June 1951, p. 87; Philipps, *A Spy Named Orphan*, pp. 301-23; Cecil, 'The Cambridge Comintern'; Andrew Lownie, *Stalin's Englishman: The Lives of Guy Burgess*, Hodder & Stoughton, 2015, pp. 227-38; Ben Macintyre, *A Spy among Friends: Kim Philby and the Great Betrayal*, Bloomsbury, London, 2014, pp. 146-51; Stewart Purvis & Jeff Hulbert, *Guy Burgess: The Spy Who Knew Everyone*, Biteback, London, 2016, pp. 255-61

28 Cecil, 'The Cambridge Comintern'; Andrew, *The Defence of the Realm*, pp. 244-8; Macintyre, *A Spy among Friends*, pp. 157-65

29 CIA CREST, 519a2b7a993294098d50fe15, Memorandum for: Chief, EE, Liaison with the British in Washington on Projects Fiend and Valuable, 28 August 1951

30 CIA CREST, 5166d49199326091c6a6007a, Directors Log 1 September 1951- 31 December 1951, 13-14 October 1951, 16-17 October 1951, 20-22 October 1951, 15-16 November 1951

8. THE KOREAN WAR

1 CIA CREST, 0000258388-1, Consequences of US Troop Withdrawal from Korea in Spring 1949, ORE 3-49, 28 February 1949; RDP79-01082A000100020023-3 ORE Far East/Pacific Branch, Intelligence Highlights No 38, 2-8 February 1949; Aldrich, *The Hidden Hand*, pp. 274-6

2 RDP82-00457R002600590002-1, Agreement for Military Aid to North Korea, 15 April 1949; RDP82-00457R002600640001-6, Additional Information concerning

the Soviet–North Korea Military Aid Agreement; RDP82-00457R002700750005-9, Chinese Communist–North Korean Military Agreement, 16 May 1949; RDP82-00457R003100380010-9, Movement of North Korean Munitions and Armor toward the 38th Parallel, 1 September 1949

3 As the first CIA officer to be killed on active duty, Mackiernan is represented by the first star on the CIA Memorial Wall in the Original Headquarters Building at Langley. Boull was eventually released in September 1955. 'Heroes: Douglas S. Mackiernan', CIA website, https://www.cia.gov/legacy/honoring-heroes/heroes/douglas-s-mackiernan/ (accessed 23 December 2021); CIA CREST, 5166d49199326091c6a6007a, Directors Log, 21-22 November 1951, 20-21 December 1951; 'Peiping releases a third American', *New York Times*, 17 September 1955; Ted Gup, *The Book of Honor: The Secret Lives and Deaths of CIA Operatives*, Anchor, New York, 2001, pp. 45-56, 208-14

4 Aldrich, *The Hidden Hand*, p. 306; RDP90-00806R000100200018-9, UPI, Colby addresses Seminar at Caspar College, 2 March 1984

5 Percy Cradock, *Know Your Enemy: How the Joint Intelligence Committee Saw the World*, John Murray, London, 2002, p. 91

6 Johannes R. Lombardo, 'A Mission of Espionage, Intelligence and Psychological Operations: The American Consulate in Hong Kong 1949-1964', *Intelligence and National Security*, Vol. 14/4 (1999); Association for Diplomatic Studies and Training Foreign Affairs Oral History Project, Interview with James McCargar, 18 April 1995; UKNA WO 208/4791, CX Report, FA/iv/999/2, Korean Troops in Manchuria, 20 December 1948; CX Report, FB/iv/1082/2, Korean Troops in Manchuria, 23 December 1948; Christopher Baxter, 'A Closed Book? British Intelligence and East Asia 1945-1950', *Diplomacy and Statecraft*, Vol. 22/1 (2011); Jeffery, *The Secret History of MI6*, pp. 697-705

7 Richard J Aldrich, 'Cold War Codebreaking and Beyond', in Erskine & Smith, *The Bletchley Park Codebreakers*, p. 359; Ian Green, former member of the Hong Kong Special Wireless Centre, letter to the author, 14 March 2003

8 'Post-War Transition Period: The Army Security Agency 1945-1948', p. 127, available at https://media.defense.gov/2021/Jun/30/2002753628/-1/-1/0/ASA-HISTORY-1945-1948-POST-WAR-TRANSITION.PDF (accessed 23 December 2021); Aid, *Cold War Intelligence*: 'On Watch: Profiles from the National Security Agency's Past 40 Years', National Cryptologic School Press, Fort Meade, 1986, p. 24; David A. Hatch with Robert L. Benson, *The Korean War: The SIGINT Background*, National Security Agency, Ford George G. Meade, MD, 2000, pp. 4-5, 8; Thomas R. Johnson, *American Cryptology during the Cold War 1945-1989, Book I: The Struggle for Centralization 1945-1960*, Center for Cryptologic History, National Security Agency, Ford George G. Meade, MD, 1995, pp. 41-3

9 Jeffery, *The Secret History of MI6*, pp. 700-5; CIA CREST, RDP82-00457R004100590009-7, Conscription in North Korea, 20 January 1950; CIA CREST, RDP79-01084A000100090058-6, State Department Office of Intelligence Research to Assistant Director CIA Officer of Reports and Estimates, 24 February 1950; RDP79-01143A000100100017-3, Current Capabilities of the Democratic People's Republic of Northern Korea (ORE 18-50), 22 March 1950;

RDP82-00457R004500740017-7,
Return of Korean Troops from China
to North Korea, 31 March 1950;
RDP82-00457R004700600008-3,
Return of Korean Troops from China,
27 April 1950; Secret Negotiations
between North Korea and the USSR,
9 May 1950; Aldrich, *The Hidden
Hand*, pp. 274-6

10 Hatch with Benson, *The Korean War*,
pp. 2-4; Cradock, *Know Your Enemy*,
p. 90

11 UKNA CAB 129/42, New York
to Foreign Office, No. 1157,
22 September 1950; Derek Leebaert,
*Grand Improvisation: America Confronts
the British Superpower 1945-1957*,
Farrar, Straus & Giroux, New York,
2018

12 SVR Archives, Burgess files 83792,
Burgess note, 25 July 1950, accessed
by author in November 1997

13 UKNA WO 373/119,
Recommendations for Honours
and Awards, S/Sgt Kenneth Reed,
Intelligence Corps, 18 June 1954

14 Johnson, *American Cryptology, Book I*,
pp. 41-3

15 Ibid., p. 44; Aid, *The Secret Sentry*,
pp. 26-7; Budiansky, *Code Warriors*,
pp. 133-4

16 UKNA KV 4/472, Liddell Diaries,
P149, 13 September 1950; 'Policy
clash seen, White House states aims
would merely neutralize island', *New
York Times*, 29 August 1950

17 Leebaert, *Grand Improvisation*, p. 277;
SVR Archives, Burgess files 83792,
Burgess note, undated, accessed by
author in November 1997

18 NSA Website, Friedman Papers,
Folder 387, AFSA-23D3 to AFSA-
02D, Plain Text Exploitation in
the Chinese Military Problem,
18 March 1952; AFSA-23C3,
Necessity of Plain Text in
Cryptanalysis, 28 February 1952

19 Guy Vanderpool, 'Comint and the
PRC Intervention in the Korean War',
Cryptologic Quarterly, Summer 1996

20 CIA CREST,

RDP82-00457R005700660003-1,
Chinese Communist Policy Meeting,
7 September 1950; Vanderpool,
'Comint and the PRC Intervention'

21 Aid, *The Secret Sentry*, p. 30; Cradock,
Know Your Enemy, p. 98

22 Budiansky, *Code Warriors*, p. 134-5;
Johnson, *American Cryptology, Book I*,
p. 44; Aid, *Cold War Intelligence*: 'On
Watch', p. 25; UKNA KV 4/472,
Liddell Diaries, 28 September 1950,
p. 157; Vanderpool, 'Comint and the
PRC Intervention'

23 UKNA CAB 129/42/15, New
York to Foreign Office, No. 1178,
23 September 1950; UN Resolution
376, adopted 7 October 1950

24 CIA CREST,
RDP86B00269R000300040006-8,
Critical Situations in the Far East,
12 October 1950; Andrew, *For the
President's Eyes Only*, p. 188

25 Andrew, *For the President's Eyes Only*,
p. 188

26 CIA CREST,
RDP86B00269R000300040006-8,
Critical Situations in the Far East,
12 October 1950

27 Vanderpool, 'Comint and the PRC
Intervention'

28 UKNA KV 4/472, Liddell
Diaries, 4 October 1950, p. 158,
5 October 1950, p. 159; Cradock,
Know Your Enemy, pp. 96-100

29 CIA CREST, RDP78-
01617A006100020067-6, General
Report, Conflict May develop
over Yalu River Power Plant,
11 October 1950

30 Vanderpool, 'Comint and the PRC
Intervention'

31 Hatch with Benson, *The Korean War*,
p. 9; Aid, *The Secret Sentry*, p. 31

32 Aid, *The Secret Sentry*, pp. 31-2

33 CIA CREST, RDP83-
00764R000300060018-5,
Walter B. Smith, Memorandum
for the President, Chinese
Communist Intervention in Korea,
1 November 1950

34 Vanderpool, 'Comint and the PRC

Intervention'

35 UKNA CAB 129/44/46, Kenneth G.
Younger Memorandum, 'Korea: The
38th Parallel', 10 February 1951; CAB
129/44/65, Younger Memorandum,
'Korea', 1 March 1951; David King &
Mark Lubienski, *The Military Service
of Major-General Charles A. Willoughby*,
private research, 2020

36 Aid, *The Secret Sentry*, pp. 35-6;
Aid, *Cold War Intelligence*: Evidence
for a 'Soviet Puppet Force'
for Korea is inconclusive, CIA
Current Intelligence Review,
12 September 1951; Richard Aldrich,
'GCHQ and Sigint in the Early Cold
War 1945-1970', *Intelligence and
National Security*, Vol. 16/1 (2001)

37 Aid, *The Secret Sentry*, pp. 36-7;
'M'Arthur wants Chiang army on
China mainland, sharp digression
from US policy', *New York Times*,
6 April 1951; 'MacArthur Blamed
British for a "Betrayal" in Korea', *New
York Times*, 9 April 1964

38 Robert Jackson, *High Cold War:
Strategic Air Reconnaissance and the
Electronic Intelligence War*, PSL,
Sparkford, 1998, pp. 40-6; Andrew
Boyd, *British Naval Intelligence through
the Twentieth Century*, Seaforth,
Barnsley, 2020, p. 566; Walter J.
Boyne, 'The Early Overflights',
Air Force Magazine, June 2001;
'Spitfires over China', Spyflight
website, https://spyflight.co.uk/
operations/#Spitfires_China
(accessed 19 January 2022)

39 CIA CREST,
5166d49199326091c6a6007a,
Directors Log, 4-5 September 1951,
19-20 October 1951; Andrew, *For the
President's Eyes Only*, pp. 193-4

40 So little was known about Fecteau and
Downey's whereabouts that at one
point, they were officially declared
dead. Fecteau was freed in 1971 and
Downey was forced to wait another
two years until President Richard
Nixon confirmed he was a CIA officer
in a quid pro quo for his release. CIA

CREST, 5166d49199326091c6a6007a,
Directors Log, 21-22 November 1951;
27-28 November 1951; CIA CREST,
RDP84-00499R000300010009-4,
MIA Cases – Fecteau, Richard G.,
Downey, John T.; 'Chinese release
Fecteau but keep Downey in prison',
New York Times, 13 December 1971;
'Nixon acknowledges American jailed
in China is CIA agent', *New York Times*,
1 February 1973; 'Notes on people',
New York Times, 20 August 1976

41 CIA CREST,
5166d49199326091c6a6007a,
Directors Log, 10-11 December 1951

42 Wendell L. Minnick, review of
Ben S. Malcom, Ron Martz &
John Singlaub, *White Tigers: My
Secret War in North Korea, Journal
of Political and Military Sociology*,
Vol. 25/1 (1997); CIA CREST,
5166d49199326091c6a6007a, Directors
Log, 29 November-1 December 1951;
Jerry L. Thigpen, *The Praetorian
Starship: The Untold Story of the Combat
Talon*, Air University Press, Maxwell
Air Force Base, AL, 2001, p. 5

43 McCann was eventually released
in April 1961 on compassionate
grounds since he was suffering with
terminal cancer. He died a month
later. Redmond was never released,
committing suicide in his cell in 1970.
Gup, *The Book of Honor*, pp. 45-56,
208-14; Maury Allen, *China Spy: The
Story of Hugh Francis Redmond*, Gazette
Press, Yonkers, NY, 1998; CIA
CREST, 5166d49199326091c6a6007a,
Directors Log, 21-22 November 1951;
'Ex-China captive is dead', *New York
Times*, 5 May 1961; 'McCann arrives
in Hong Kong after release by Chinese
Reds', *New York Times*, 6 April 1961

44 CIA CREST,
5166d49199326091c6a6007a,
Directors Log, 28-29 December 1951;
Lombardo, 'A Mission of Espionage'.

45 UKNA KV 4/472, Liddell Diaries,
16 May 1950, p. 86, 30 May 1950,
p. 93, 12 June 1950, p. 103; KV
4/473, Liddell Diaries, 9 August 1951,

p. 138, 13 September 1949, p. 149

46 CIA CREST,
5166d49199326091c6a6007a,
Directors Log, 10-11 October 1951,
25-26 October 1951,
1-2 November 1951,
28-29 December 1951

47 The author is grateful for information
provided by Alan Judge. UKNA
WO 373/118, Recommendations
for Honours and Awards, Sergeant
Clifford Jackson, 8 December 1953;
WO 373/119, Recommendations for
Honours and Awards, Sergeant John
Wells

48 UKNA WO 373/118,
Recommendations for Honours and
Awards, Sgt Alfred Martin Harris,
15 June 1954

49 FRUS 1950-1955, The Intelligence
Community 1950-1955, ed. Douglas
Keane & Michael Warner, United
States Government Printing Office,
Washington, DC, 2007, Doc. 132;
Hatch with Benson, *The Korean
War*, pp. 11, 15-17; NSA Website,
Summary Annual Report of the Army
Security Agency Fiscal Year 1948,
Technical Operations, p. 9

50 FRUS 1950-1955, The Intelligence
Community 1950-1955,
Doc. 29; CIA CREST, RDP-
80B01676R004000130005-1, Report
on CIA Installations in the Far East,
14 March 1952

9. THE IRAN COUP

1 FRUS 1952-1954, Vol. X, Iran
1951-1954, ed. Carl N. Raether &
Charles S. Sampson, United States
Government Printing Office,
Washington, DC, 1989, Docs 2, 6

2 FRUS 1952-1954, Vol. X, Iran 1951-
1954, Docs 5, 9; 15, 22, 34; 'Transcript
of Interview with Norman Darbyshire
for End of Empire, 1985', National
Security Archive, https://nsarchive.
gwu.edu/dc.html?doc=7033886-
National-Security-Archive (accessed
4 January 2022)

3 FRUS 1952-1954, Iran 1951-1954,

Second Edition, ed. James C. Van
Hook, United States Government
Printing Office, Washington, DC,
2018, Document 10; FRUS 1952-
1954, Vol. X, Iran 1951-1954, Doc. 22

4 Liddell Hart Military Archives,
King's College London, GB0099,
Woodhouse 8/1, Iran 1950-53,
16 August 1976, C. M. Woodhouse,
Something Ventured, Granada,
London, 1982, p. 110-11; Darbyshire
Transcript

5 UKNA FO 248/1531, G10105/199/3,
Zaehner Report, 15 May 1952; West,
The Friends, pp. 88-94; Stephen
Dorril, *MI6: Fifty Years of Special
Operations*, Fourth Estate, London,
2000, pp. 569-71; Ali Rahnema,
*Iran: Thugs, Turncoats, Soldiers, and
Spooks*, Cambridge University Press,
Cambridge, 2015, p. 69

6 UKNA PREM 8/1501, British
Embassy Washington to Foreign
Office, 12 May 1951; PREM 8/1501,
British Embassy Washington to
Foreign Office, 17 May 1951; DEFE
6/18, JP (51) 132 (S) T of R, South-
West Persia—Further Military Steps,
12 July 1951; Darbyshire Transcript;
Woodhouse, *Something Ventured*,
p. 111

7 Rahnema, *Iran*, pp. 82-3; Kermit
Roosevelt, *Countercoup: The Struggle for
the Control of Iran*, McGraw-Hill, New
York, 1979, pp. 79-81. Roosevelt's
book, while providing a good general
overview, is extremely unreliable
on the detail, presumably due to an
understandable desire to protect CIA
agents and officers, and a perhaps
unsurprising willingness to have the
Americans receive all the credit,
or blame, for the coup. Roosevelt
inaccurately claims for example that
only one of Jalali and Keyvani was a
journalist, the other being a lawyer.
Jalali did have legal training but was
working as a journalist

8 FRUS 1952-1954, Iran 1951-1954,
Second Edition, Doc. 8; Mark
J. Gasiorowski, 'The 1953 Coup

d'État in Iran', *International Journal of Middle East Studies,* Vol. 19/3 (1987), pp. 268-9; Andreas Etges, 'All That Glitters Is Not Gold: The 1953 Coup against Mohammad Mossadeq in Iran', *Intelligence and National Security,* Vol. 26/4 (2011); Dorril, *MI6,* p. 574; Roosevelt, *Countercoup,* p. 80

9 CIA CREST, 5166d49399326091c6a604bf, Directors Log, 21-22 & 26-27 September 1951; Gasiorowski, 'The 1953 Coup d'État in Iran', pp. 268-9; 'Of local origin', *New York Times,* 25 September 1951

10 FRUS 1952-1954, Vol. X, Iran 1951-1954, Docs 31, 91, 99

11 UKNA FO 371/90932, Cecil Minute, 8 December 1951; A. p. Dobson, 'Informally Special? The Churchill–Truman Talks of January 1952 and the State of Anglo-American Relations', *Review of International Studies,* Vol. 23/1 (1997)

12 'UN body hears Mossadeq assail British "intimidation"', *New York Times,* 16 October 1951; CIA CREST, 5166d49399326091c6a604bf, Directors Log, 8-9 October 1951; Ervand Abrahamian, *The Coup: 1953, the CIA, and the Roots of Modern US–Iranian Relations,* New Press, New York, 2013, p. 75; 'Claude E. Forkner, 92, Internist and Professor', *New York Times,* 29 December 1992

13 Woodhouse, *Something Ventured,* pp. 110, 115

14 FRUS 1952-1954, Vol. X, Iran 1951-1954, Docs 127, 129, 180

15 'Text of the address by Prime Minister Churchill to Congress', *New York Times,* 18 January 1952

16 Gasiorowski, 'The 1953 Coup d'État in Iran', p. 265

17 'Mossadeq out as premier; Ghavam to take Iran helm', *New York Times,* 18 July 1952; 'Hundreds seized in Iranian rioting over Ghavam rule', *New York Times,* 21 July 1952; 'Ghavam quits post in Iranian rioting', *New York Times,* 22 July 1952

18 FRUS 1952-1954, Iran 1951-1954, ed. James C. Van Hook, United States Government Printing Office, Washington, DC, 2017, Docs 101, 107, 102

19 FRUS 1952-1954, Iran 1951-1954, Docs 103, 105, 110, 107, 109, 117; Woodhouse, *Something Ventured,* pp. 115-16; FRUS 1952-1954, Iran 1951-1954, Doc. 160

20 UKNA CAB 159/12, JIC (52) 81st Meeting, Perimeter Review, 24 July 1952; CAB 158/14, JIC (52) 53 (Final), Situation in Persia, 18 August 1952; Gasiorowski, 'The 1953 Coup d'État in Iran', p. 266

21 Woodhouse, *Something Ventured,* pp. 111-14; Dorril, *MI6,* p. 571

22 UKNA FO 800/813, Prime Minister's Personal Minute, No. 17/415/52, to Foreign Secretary, 30 July 1952; Per/52/11, Foreign Office to Washington, No. 3403, Prime Minister to President Truman, 20 August 1952; FRUS 1952-1954, Vol. X, Iran 1951-1954, Doc. 198

23 UKNA FO 800/813, Per/52/17, Foreign Office to Washington, No 3503, 23 August 1952

24 UKNA FO 800/813, Per/52/19, Franks to Foreign Office, Text of Secret and Personal Message from President Truman to Prime Minister, 24 August 1952; Per/52/31, Foreign Office to Tehran, No. 592, 26 August 1952; Per/52/32, Foreign Office to Lisbon, No. 331, Personal for Secretary of State from Prime Minister, 26 August 1952; Per/52/41, Foreign Office to Washington, No. 3596, 28 August 1952; Per/52/49, Middleton to Foreign Office, No. 639, 29 August 1952; Per/52/51, London to Washington, No. 3611, Personal and Secret Message from Prime Minister to President Truman, 29 August 1952; Per/52/56, WSC to Foreign Secretary, M479/52, 11 September 1952; FRUS 1952-1954, Vol. X, Iran 1951-1954, Docs 203, 207, 208, 211-14; 'Mossadeq snubs

Truman, Churchill on joint oil offer',
New York Times, 31 August 1952

25 Woodhouse, *Something Ventured*,
p. 116

26 UKNA CAB 159/12, JIC Minutes,
10 October 1952; Gasiorowski, 'The
1953 Coup d'État in Iran', p. 266

27 Gasiorowski, 'The 1953 Coup d'État
in Iran', pp. 116-17; West, *The Friends*,
p. 90

28 Woodhouse, *Something Ventured*,
p. 118

29 FRUS 1952-1954, Iran 1951-1954,
Second Edition, Doc. 170

30 Roosevelt, *Countercoup*, pp. 107-9;
Woodhouse, *Something Ventured*,
p. 120; West, *The Friends*, p. 92;
Abrahamian, *The Coup*, p. 152

31 FRUS 1952-1954, Vol. X, Iran 1951-
1954, Doc. 234

32 CIA CREST,
RDP79R01012A002500030001-2,
NIE, Probable Developments in Iran
Throughout 1953, 13 November 1952

33 Roosevelt, *Countercoup*, pp. 120-4;
Dorril, *MI6*, p. 582; Gasiorowski,
'The 1953 Coup d'État in Iran', p. 271

34 FRUS 1952-1954, Iran 1951-1954,
Second Edition, Doc. 159

35 FRUS 1952-1954, Iran 1951-1954,
Docs 158, 168, 160, 169; FRUS 1952-
1954, Iran 1951-1954, Second Edition,
Doc. 177; Roosevelt, *Countercoup*,
p. 129

36 FO 800/814, Per/53/11, Foreign
Office to Washington, No. 905,
27 February 1953; FRUS 1952-1954,
Iran 1951-1954, Second Edition, Doc.
166

37 FRUS 1952-1954, Iran 1951-1954,
Doc. 171; FRUS 1952-1954, Iran
1951-1954, Second Edition, Doc. 176

38 FRUS 1952-1954, Iran 1951-1954,
Second Edition, Doc. 192

39 FRUS 1952-1954, Iran 1951-1954,
Doc. 196; Darbyshire Transcript

40 West, *The Friends*, p. 90; Woodhouse,
Something Ventured, p. 117; Donald
Wilber, 'Overthrow of Premier
Mossadeq of Iran, November 1952-
August 1953', March 1954, pp. 22, 77,

available at https://nsarchive2.gwu.
edu/NSAEBB/NSAEBB28/ (accessed
4 January 2022)

41 Woodhouse, *Something Ventured*,
p. 119

42 Wilber, 'Overthrow of Premier
Mossadeq', pp. 5-11

43 Ibid., pp. 5-11

44 Ibid., pp. 13-14, Annex B, p. 1;
Woodhouse, *Something Ventured*,
p. 126

45 Wilber, 'Overthrow of Premier
Mossadeq', p. 18; FRUS 1952-1954,
Iran 1951-1954, Doc. 232; Darbyshire
Transcript

46 FRUS 1952-1954, Iran 1951-1954,
Doc. 230

47 Darbyshire Transcript; Wilber,
'Overthrow of Premier Mossadeq',
pp. 21-3; John Prados, *Safe for
Democracy: The Secret Wars of the CIA*,
Ivan Dee, Chicago, 2006, p. 103

48 Wilber, 'Overthrow of Premier
Mossadeq', pp. 22-6, 35-6; FRUS
1952-1954, Iran 1951-1954, Doc. 260;
FRUS 1952-1954, Vol. X, Iran 1951-
1954, Doc. 340

49 FRUS 1952-1954, Iran 1951-1954,
Doc. 261; FRUS 1952-1954, Iran
1951-1954, Second Edition, Doc.
278; Wilber, 'Overthrow of Premier
Mossadeq', pp. 45-8, 58-60, 64;
Darbyshire Transcript; 'Shah flees
Iran after move to dismiss Mossadegh
fails', *New York Times*, 17 August 1953;
Cutler, *Counterspy*, p. 5

50 Wilber, 'Overthrow of Premier
Mossadeq', pp. 56-7

51 Ibid., pp. 50-2, 62-3

52 Abrahamian, *The Coup*, pp. 191-3;
Darbyshire Transcript; *Saturday
Evening Post*, 6 November 1954,
quoted in Woodhouse, *Something
Ventured*, p. 129; FRUS 1952-1954,
Vol. X, Iran 1951-1954, Doc.
362. This document appears to
contain MI6 reporting, leading to
its Top Secret classification. An
unredacted copy of the original
document can be seen on the
National Security Archive website

at https://nsarchive.gwu.edu/
dc.html?doc=4404301-Document-
1-British-Foreign-Office-Persia
(accessed 4 January 2022)

53 FRUS 1952-1954, Vol. X, Iran 1951-
1954, Doc. 362

54 FRUS 1952-1954, Iran 1951-1954,
Second Edition, Docs 293, 299, 355;
W. Scott Lucas, *Divided We Stand:
Britain, the US and the Suez Crisis*,
Hodder & Stoughton, London, 1991,
p. 19

55 Wilber, 'Overthrow of Premier
Mossadeq', p. 94

56 Woodhouse, *Something Ventured*,
pp. 134-5

57 FRUS 1952-1954, Vol. X, Iran 1951-
1954, Docs 420, 423, 426; 'Oil
flows again from Persia', *The Times*,
1 November 1954

10. DRAGON LADY

1 UKNA AIR 20/8122, Bevin
Memorandum, 10 September 1948;
'Mutual defence agreements
signed in Washington completing
edifice of Atlantic Treaty', *The
Times*, 28 January 1950; 'Proposed
air base at Newbury', *The Times*,
14 March 1951; 'Petition of protest
fails', *The Times*, 11 April 1951; 'US
air arm in Britain status raised',
The Times, 4 May 1951; 'American
bases in Britain', *The Times*,
21 August 1952; Andy Thomas,
'How the US bases came to Britain',
Peace News and Housman's, April 1984;
'Unit History: RAF Fairford', Forces
War Records website, https://
www.forces-war-records.co.uk/
units/582/raf-fairford (accessed
5 January 2022); 'Lakenheath AFB
Factsheets: 1952-1960', Royal Air
Force Lakenheath website, https://
www.lakenheath.af.mil/About-Us/
Fact-Sheets/Factsheet-Display-
Page/Article/297489/1952-1960/
(accessed 5 January 2022); 'RAF
Brize Norton', Royal Air Force
website, https://www.raf.mod.
uk/our-organisation/stations/

raf-brize-norton/ (accessed
5 January 2022); 'RAF Mildenhall
History', Royal Air Force Mildenhall
website, https://www.mildenhall.
af.mil/About-Us/Fact-Sheets/
Display/Article/270389/raf-
mildenhall-history/ (accessed
5 January 2022); Johnson, *American
Cryptology, Book I*, p. 118; *History
of the Army Security Agency and
Subordinate Units, Fiscal Year 1956, Vol.
I: Administration*, National Security
Agency, 1958, pp. 342-6, available
at https://media.defense.gov/2021/
Jun/30/2002753641/-1/-1/0/
ASA-1956-VOL-1.PDF (accessed
5 January 2022)

2 UKNA CAB 79-51-16, Minutes
of the Chiefs of Staff Committee,
6 September 1946; AIR 27/2703, A
Short History of RAF Wyton & A
Short History of No 58 Sqn; Smith,
New Cloak, Old Dagger, pp. 197-8;
Jackson, *High Cold War*, p. 47

3 'Maybe You Had to Be There',
Cryptologic Quarterly, Summer 1993,
pp. 7-9; FRUS 1950-1955, The
Intelligence Community 1950-1955,
Doc. 6; Jackson, *High Cold War*,
pp. 51-3

4 Hansard, HL Deb, 17 March 1953,
vol. 181, cols 23-7; CIA CREST,
5166d49199326091c6a6007a,
Directors Log, 28-29 September 1951;
Boyd, *British Naval Intelligence*,
pp. 565-6; UKNA AIR 19/675,
Prime Minister to Chief of Air Staff,
23 March 1953; Kevin O'Daly,
'Living in the Shadow: Britain and
the USSR's Nuclear Weapon Delivery
Systems 1945-62', PhD thesis,
University of Westminster, 2016;
private knowledge

5 Jackson, *High Cold War*, p. 67; Oral
History Interview with Robert
Amory Jr., John F. Kennedy
Library, 17 February 1966; Gregory
Pedlow & Donald Welzenbach,
*The Central Intelligence Agency and
Overhead Reconnaissance: The U-2
and OXCARTS Programs 1954-1974*,

Central Intelligence Agency, Washington, DC, 1992, pp. 23-4, available at https://nsarchive2.gwu.edu/NSAEBB/NSAEBB434/ (accessed 5 January 2022); UKNA FO 1093/548, EXCISE, Short Summary of Personal Life, 30 December 1047; Hayter to Sargent, 21 November 1947; FO 1093/549, USSR Political, The 'T' Plan, 19 July 1948; Obituary: Professor Grigori Tokaty, *Independent*, 25 November 2003; Boyd, *British Naval Intelligence*, p. 566

6   John Crampton, 'Russian photo-shoot', *Air Pictorial*, August 1997; 'Spies in the Skies', *Timewatch*, BBC 2, 9 February 1994; Jackson, *High Cold War*, pp. 51-3

7   CIA CREST, Doc. OC_0005922737, Office of National Estimates, Post-Mortem of NIE 11-6-54, Soviet Capabilities and Probable Programs in Guided Missiles, 4 October 1954; Allen W. Dulles, *The Craft of Intelligence: America's Legendary Spy Master on the Fundamentals of Intelligence Gathering for a Free World*, Lyons Press, Guilford, CT, 2016, p. 194

8   FRUS 1950-1955, The Intelligence Community 1950-1955, Docs 209, 196; CIA CREST, RDP33-02415A000100430021-9, Memo to DCI, A Unique Opportunity for Comprehensive Intelligence, 5 November 1954; RDP61-00549R000100200023-8-1, IAC-D-81/7, Establishment of a Guided Missile Intelligence Committee, 8 February 1955

9   'Maybe You Had to Be There', pp. 17-19; FRUS 1950-1955, The Intelligence Community 1950-1955, Docs 198, 196, 197, 199; CIA CREST, RDP04T00184R000400070001-5, National Photographic Interpretation Center (NPIC), Vol. I: Antecedents and Early Years 1952-56, pp. 109-11, 188

10 Pedlow & Welzenbach, *The Central Intelligence Agency and Overhead Reconnaissance*, pp. 93-4; Jackson, *High Cold War*, pp. 109, 111-12; Boyd, *British Naval Intelligence*, pp. 566-7

11 Budiansky, *Code Warriors*, p. 175; Boyd, *British Naval Intelligence*, pp. 571-3, 578-9; Dennis R. Mills, 'Signals Intelligence and the Coder Special Branch of the Royal Navy in the 1950s', *Intelligence and National Security*, Vol. 26/5 (2011)

12 Jackson, *High Cold War*, p. 194; Dulles, *The Craft of Intelligence*, p. 194; CIA CREST, RDP04T00184R000400010001-1-1, NPIC, The Years of Project HTAUTOMAT 1956-1958, pp. 18-23; 'Those Daring Young Men and Their ULTRA-High-Flying Machines', *Studies in Intelligence*, Fall 1987, pp. 103-5; Peter W. Merlin, *Unlimited Horizons: Design and Development of the U-2*, NASA, Washington, DC, 2015

13 'Moscow charges US air incursions by military craft', *New York Times*, 11 July 1956; 'Those Daring Young Men', p. 106; Antecedents and Early Years, p. 76

14 CIA CREST RDP04T00184R000400010001-1, National Photographic Interpretation Center, The Years of Project HTAutomat 1956-1958, pp. 23, 84, 87-9, 92

15 Ibid., pp. 59, 136, 138

16 Ibid., pp. 75, 159, 162; 'Those Daring Young Men', pp. 103-4

17 NSA OH-14-83, Oral History Interview with Dr Howard Campaigne, 29 June 1983; Harlan Snyder, 'Atlas and the Early Days of Computers', *The Link, Bulletin of the National Cryptologic Museum Foundation*, Vol. 4, No. 1, Spring 2001; Jim Eachus, *Joe Eachus, Mathematician*, unpublished biography, 29 December 2019, kindly shared with the author by Jim Eachus

18 James V. Boone & James J. Hearn, *Cryptology's Role in the Early Development of Computer Capabilities in the United States*, Center for Cryptologic

History, National Security Agency,
Fort George G. Meade, MD, 2015,
pp. 17, 24-5; Samuel S. Snyder,
'History of NSA General-Purpose
Electronic Digital Computers', 1964,
pp. 8-13, available at https://www.
nsa.gov/portals/75/documents/news-
features/declassified-documents/
nsa-early-computer-history/6586784-
history-of-nsa-general-purpose-
electronic-digital-computers.pdf
(accessed 5 January 2022); Machines
in the Service of Cryptanalysis,
lecture by NSA-82 (Machine Division)
to Director NSA and his Staff,
28 September 1954

19 Boone & Hearn, *Cryptology's Role*,
pp. 18-21; 'Machines in the Service
of Cryptanalysts', Machines Division,
NSA-82 presentation to NSA director
and his staff, 28 December 1954,
available at https://www.nsa.
gov/Portals/75/documents/news-
features/declassified-documents/
friedman-documents/reports-
research/FOLDER_154/
41745979078521.pdf (accessed
5 January 2022); 'Cryptanalytic
Machines in NSA', NSA-34,
30 May 1953, available at https://
www.nsa.gov/Portals/75/
documents/news-features/
declassified-documents/friedman-
documents/reports-research/
FOLDER_107/41743419078275.pdf
(accessed 5 January 2022)

20 NSA OH-2012-81, Oral History
Interview with Lt-Gen Ralph Canine,
Undated (Late 1960s); John Ferris,
*Behind the Enigma: The Authorised
History of GCHQ, Britain's Secret
Cyber-intelligence Agency*, Bloomsbury,
London, 2020, pp. 430-1

21 John R. Chapman, Chief FOIA/PA
Office, NSA, to Kim Scarlet, Privacy
International, 12 September 2018
(letter including John H.
Tiltman to Captain L. H. Frost,
9 December 1953)

22 Anna Borshchevskaya, 'The Soviets'
Unbreakable Code', *Foreign Policy*,

27 April 2019; 'Fialka', Deutsches
Spionagemuseum website, https://
www.deutsches-spionagemuseum.
de/en/sammlung/fialka/ (accessed
5 January 2022)

23 History of the USASA and
Subordinate Units, Fiscal Year
1957, Vol. II, Technical Operations,
pp. 58-102

24 Ibid., pp. 17-23, 31-57, 102-4;
Aldrich, *GCHQ*, p. 112

25 Tony Geraghty, *BRIXMIS: The Untold
Exploits of Britain's Most Daring Cold War
Spy Mission*, HarperCollins, London,
1997, pp. 3-15, 329-31; Michael
Smith, *The Spying Game: A Secret
History of British Espionage*, Politico's,
London, 1993, pp. 343-5

26 Author interview with Andrew King,
10 September 1995

27 Author interview with Simon
Preston, 11 October 1995; Bob
Steers, 'Inside Smoky Joe's', *Special
Forces Club News*, Spring 2012

28 Author interview with Andrew King,
10 September 1995; Steers, 'Inside
Smoky Joe's'

29 NSA OH-1976-1-10, Oral History
Interview with Frank Rowlett,
p. 375; 'Clandestine Services History:
The Berlin Tunnel Operation 1952-
1956', CS Historical Paper No. 150,
24 June 1968, p. 4, available at https://
www.cia.gov/readingroom/docs/
CIA-RDP07X00001R000100010001-9.
pdf (accessed 5 January 2022); David
Stafford, *Spies beneath Berlin*, John
Murray, London, 2002, pp. 38, 51-3;
Murphy et al., *Battleground Berlin*,
pp. 208-9

30 NSA OH-1976-1-10, Oral History
Interview with Frank Rowlett;
Murphy et al., *Battleground Berlin*,
p. 449; 'The Berlin Tunnel
Operation', p. i

31 'The Berlin Tunnel Operation',
pp. 2-4; Murphy et al., *Battleground
Berlin*, p. 449

32 'The Berlin Tunnel Operation',
pp. 7-8

33 Ibid., pp. 10-11; 'Cryptologic

Almanac 50th Anniversary Series: The Berlin Tunnel, Part I: But Did They Call Miss Utility?', 28 February 1998, available at https://www.nsa.gov/portals/75/documents/news-features/declassified-documents/crypto-almanac-50th/Tunnel_1.pdf (accessed 21 January 2022)

34 'Engineering the Berlin Tunnel', *Studies in Intelligence*, Vol. 52/1 (2008); 'The Berlin Tunnel Operation', pp. 14, 18

35 'The Berlin Tunnel Operation', pp. 21, 26

36 'Cryptologic Almanac 50th Anniversary Series: The Berlin Tunnel, Part II: The Rivals', 24 February 1998, available at https://www.nsa.gov/portals/75/documents/news-features/declassified-documents/crypto-almanac-50th/Tunnel_2.pdf (accessed 21 January 2022); Murphy et al., *Battleground Berlin*, pp. 225-6; 'The Berlin Tunnel Operation', pp. 21, 26

37 'Cryptologic Almanac 50th Anniversary Series: The Last Days of the Enigma', https://media.defense.gov/2021/Jun/29/2002751981/-1/-1/0/THE_LAST_DAYS_OF_THE_ENIGMA.PDF (accessed 5 January 2022); NSA OH-1976-1-10, Oral History Interview with Frank Rowlett

38 Murphy et al., *Battleground Berlin*, pp. 227, 232; 'US investigates wiretap tunnel', *New York Times*, 25 April 1956; '"American tunnel" on view', *The Times*, 25 April 1956

39 Murphy et al., *Battleground Berlin*, pp. 25-6

40 Ibid., Appendix B, pp. 2-5; 'The Berlin Tunnel, Part II'; Murphy et al., *Battleground Berlin*, pp. 423-8

41 'The Berlin Tunnel, Part II'

11. 'WALTZING OVER SUEZ WHILE HUNGARY BURNS'

1 Jim Marchio, 'Resistance Potential and Rollback: US Intelligence and the Eisenhower Administration's Policies toward Eastern Europe 1953-56', *Intelligence and National Security*, Vol. 10/2 (1995); Richard A. Bitzinger, 'Assessing the Conventional Balance in Europe 1945-1975', Rand, May 1989, p. 5, available at https://www.rand.org/content/dam/rand/pubs/notes/2007/N2859.pdf (accessed 5 January 2022)

2 'Hungarian ex-spy', *Daily Telegraph*, 28 December 1991; Paul V. Gorka, *Budapest Betrayed: A Prisoner's Story of the Betrayal of the Hungarian Resistance Movement to the Russians*, Oaktree, London, 1986

3 Author interview with Michael Giles, 25 October 1995

4 Dulles, *The Craft of Intelligence*, p. 76; see Footnote 3 to FRUS 1955-1957, Vol. XXIV, Soviet Union, Eastern Mediterranean, ed. Ronald D. Landa, Aaron D. Miller & Charles S. Sampson, United States Government Printing Office, Washington, DC, 1989, Doc. 50; 'Text of speech on Stalin by Khrushchev as released by the State Department', *New York Times*, 5 June 1956; Hayes, *Queen of Spies*, p. 109

5 CIA CREST, RDP79R00890A000700030016-0, NSC Briefing, 20 March 1956; FRUS 1955-1957, Volume XXIV, Soviet Union, Eastern Mediterranean, Doc. 34

6 Tony Kemp-Welch, 'Dethroning Stalin: Poland 1956 and Its Legacy', *Europe-Asia Studies* Vol. 58/8 (2006); NSA, Summary Annual Report of the ASA Fiscal Year 1957, Technical Operations, p. 63; NSA, Summary Annual Report of the ASA Fiscal Year 1956, Technical Operations, p. 69; FRUS 1955-1957, Vol. XXV, Eastern Europe, ed. Edward C. Keefer, Ronald D. Landa & Stanley Shaloff, United States Government Printing Office, Washington, DC, 1990, Doc. 58; CIA CREST, RDP79T00975A002600280001-2, Central Intelligence Bulletin,

30 June 1956; 'Allen Dulles called revolt mastermind', *Atlantic City Press*, 2 July 1956

7 Leader article, *Szabad Nép*, 3 July 1956

8 'Diplomats predict Hungary uprising', *Houston Chronicle*, 5 July 1956; Ferenc A. Váli, *Rift and Revolt in Hungary: Nationalism versus Communism*, Harvard University Press, Cambridge, MA, 1961, p. 220; FRUS 1955-1957, Vol. XXV, Eastern Europe, Docs 53, 82

9 NSA, Summary Annual Report of the ASA Fiscal Year 1957, Technical Operations, p. 72; Váli, *Rift and Revolt*, pp. 249-52

10 Johanna Granville, 'In the Line of Fire: The Soviet Crackdown on Hungary 1956-57', *Journal of Communist Studies and Transition Politics*, Vol. 13/2 (1997); Donald E. Pienkos, 'A Look Back: Poland and the Historic Events of 1956', *Polish Review*, Vol. 51/3-4 (2006); NSA, Summary Annual Report of the ASA Fiscal Year 1957, Technical Operations, p. 72

11 CIA CREST, Doc. 0000119722, Central Intelligence Bulletin, 6 October 1956; RDP79-00927A001000040001-8, Current Intelligence Weekly Summary, 18 October 1956; '200,000 March by Rajk's coffin as Hungary honors ex-"traitors"', *New York Times*, 7 October 1956; Váli, *Rift and Revolt*, pp. 246-8, 250-1

12 United Nations, 'Report of the Special Committee on the Problem of Hungary', Supplement No. 18 (A/3592), New York, 1957, p. 50; Váli, *Rift and Revolt*, pp. 266-7

13 NSA Summary Annual Report of the ASA Fiscal Year 1957, Technical Operations, p. 84; CIA CREST, Doc. 0000119733, Hungary, 25 October 1956

14 NSA Summary Annual Report of the ASA Fiscal Year 1957, Technical Operations, p. 84; CIA CREST, RDP79T00975A002800050001-5, Current Intelligence

Bulletin, 25 October 1956; RDP79T00975A002800060001-4, Current Intelligence Bulletin, 26 October 1956; 'Report of the Special Committee on the Problem of Hungary', pp. 22-3

15 CIA CREST, The 1956 Hungarian Revolution: A Fresh Look at the US Response; Tim Weiner, *Legacy of Ashes: The History of the CIA*, Anchor, New York, 2008, p. 149

16 Cavendish, *Inside Intelligence*, pp. 89-103; Tam Dalyell, 'Anthony Cavendish: intrepid intelligence officer who fought terrorism in the Middle East', *Independent*, 13 March 2013; Alex May, 'Davidson, Basil Craig Risbridger', *Oxford Dictionary of National Biography*, Oxford University Press, Oxford, 2014; Richard Ingrams, 'Delmer, (Denis) Sefton', *Oxford Dictionary of National Biography*, Oxford University Press, Oxford, 2004; Roderick Bailey, 'Kemp, Peter Mant MacIntyre', *Oxford Dictionary of National Biography*, Oxford University Press, Oxford, 2004; M. R. D. Foot, Peter Kemp obituary, *Independent*, 4 November 1993

17 FRUS 1955-1957, Vol. XXV, Eastern Europe, Docs 116, 141, 149, 152; CIA CREST, Doc. 0000119743, To DDI, Situation in Hungary as of 1600 EST, 30 October 1956; Doc. 000119745, The Situation in Hungary 0200 EST, 31 October 1956; RDP81-00280R001300010072-9, Hungary Government Reorganization, 30 October 1956; NSA Summary Annual Report of the ASA Fiscal Year 1957, Technical Operations, p. 84

18 FRUS 1955-1957, Vol. XVI, Suez Crisis, July 26-December 31, 1956, ed. Nina J. Noring, United States Government Printing Office, Washington, DC, 1990, Doc. 373; Alan Campbell, 'Dean, Sir Patrick Henry', *Oxford Dictionary of National Biography*, Oxford University Press, Oxford, 2004

19 UKNA FO 800/776 Eden Memo on dinner with Nasser 20 February 1955; Scott Lucas & Alistair Morey, 'The Hidden "Alliance": The CIA and MI6 before and after Suez', *Intelligence and National Security*, 15/2 (2000); Richard J. Aldrich, 'Intelligence, Anglo-American Relations and the Suez Crisis', *Intelligence and National Security*, 9/3 (1994); Nigel Clive obituary, *Daily Telegraph*, 18 May 2001; Tom Bower, *The Perfect English Spy: Sir Dick White and the Secret War 1935-90*, Heinemann, London, 1995, pp. 191-5; Peter Wright, *Spycatcher: The Candid Autobiography of a Senior Intelligence Officer*, Viking, New York, 1987, pp. 160-1; Keith Kyle, *Suez*, Weidenfeld & Nicolson, London, 1991, p. 101

20 Author interview with the late Michael Whittall

21 FRUS 1955-1957, Vol. XVI, Suez Crisis, July 26-December 31, 1956, Docs 42, 287; NSA, DOCID 4165421, The Suez Crisis: A Brief Comint History, p. 19; 'The Suez crisis: stuck in the canal', *International Herald Tribune*, 29 October 2006

22 CIA CREST, RDP78TO4753A000600010014-2, Mission Coverage Summary Mission 1104, 29 August 1956; RDP78T04753A000600010013-3, Mission Coverage Summary Mission 1105, 29 August 1956; RDP78TO4753A000600010012-4, Mission Coverage Summary Mission 1106, 30 August 1956; RDP78T04753A000600010011-5, Mission Coverage Summary Mission 1107, 30 August 1956; RDP78T04753A000600010019-7, Mission Coverage Summary Mission 1108, 6 September 1956; RDP78T04753A000600010018-8, Mission Coverage Summary Mission 1109, 7 September 1956; RDP78T04753A000600010017-9, Mission Coverage Summary Mission 1301, 11 September 1956; RDP78T04753A000600010015-1, Mission Coverage Summary Mission 1110, 11 September 1956; RDP78T04753A000600010024-1, Mission Coverage Summary Mission 1111, 12 September 1956; RDP61S00750A0002000401, Establishment of Paramount Committee, 12 September 1956; RDP61S00750A0005000601, Paramount Target Nominations, 21 September 1956; RDP78T04753A000600010021-4, Mission Coverage Summary Mission 1108, 14 September 1956; RDP78T04753A000600010021-4, Mission Coverage Summary Mission 1112, 14 September 1956; RDP78T04753A000600010022-3, Mission Coverage Summary Mission 1304, 27 September 1956; RDP78T04753A000600010025-0, Mission Coverage Summary Mission 1305, 3 October 1956; Project HTAUTOMAT, pp. 19, 45-7; 5166d4f999326091c6a60852; Pedlow & Welzenbach, *The Central Intelligence Agency and Overhead Reconnaissance*, pp. 114, 311; Merlin, *Unlimited Horizons*, p. 238; 'Those Daring Young Men'; FRUS 1955-1957, Vol. XVI, Suez Crisis, July 26-December 31, 1956, Doc. 305; Lucas, *Divided We Stand*, p. 181

23 FRUS 1955-1957, Vol. XVI, Suez Crisis, July 26-December 31, 1956, Docs 214, 236, 391, 637: CIA Annex; CIA CREST, RDP61S00750A0002000401, Continuation of Paramount Committee, 16 October 1956

24 Aldrich, *GCHQ*, p. 159; NSA Summary Annual Report of the ASA Fiscal Year 1957, Technical Operations, p. 105; NSA, DOCID 4165421, The Suez Crisis: A Brief Comint History, p. 19

25 Lucas & Morey, 'The Hidden "Alliance"'; CIA CREST, RDP78T04753A000600010037-7, Mission Coverage Summary Mission

1315, 31 October 1956; Pedlow & Welzenbach, *The Central Intelligence Agency and Overhead Reconnaissance*, p. 120; Jackson, *High Cold War*, p. 110

26 FRUS 1955-1957, Vol. XVI, Suez Crisis, July 26-December 31, 1956, Docs 68, 570; Lucas & Morey, 'The Hidden "Alliance"'; Lucas, *Divided We Stand*, pp. 282-3; Aldrich, *GCHQ*, pp. 148-9

27 CIA CREST, RDP80B01676R004000170002-0, Chronology of Recent Events during the Hungarian Revolution 23 October to 4 November 1956; RDP80T00246A04670018000-4, Status of Hungarian and Soviet Forces in Hungary, 9 February 1959; Johnson, *American Cryptology, Book I*, 1995, pp. 232-7

28 UKNA T 273-380-1, Note by Sir Robert Hall on 'The Economic Situation', 28 November 1956; James M. Boughton, 'Northwest of Suez: The 1956 Crisis and the IMF', IMF Working Papers, 1 December 2000

29 George K Young, *Masters of Indecision: An Inquiry into the Political Process*, Methuen, London, 1962, pp. 20-1

30 FRUS 1955-1957, Vol. XVI, Suez Crisis, July 26-December 31, 1956, Docs 499, 542

31 FRUS 1955-1957, Vol. XVI, Suez Crisis, July 26-December 31, 1956, Doc. 618; 'President denies Suez hurts NATO or US alliances', *New York Times*, 28 November 1956; Simon C. Smith, '"America in Britain's Place?": Anglo-American Relations and the Middle East in the Aftermath of the Suez Crisis', *Journal of Transatlantic Studies*, Vol. 10/3 (2012)

32 FRUS 1955-1957, Vol. XVI, Suez Crisis, July 26-December 31, 1956, Doc. 596; FRUS 1955-1957, Vol. XXVII, Western Europe and Canada, ed. Madeline Chi et al., United States Government Printing Office, Washington, DC, 1992, Docs 268, 271, 282; 'US and Britain to pool planning and intelligence', *New York Times*, 26 March 1957

33 FRUS 1955-1957, Vol. XIX, National Security Policy, ed. William Klingaman, David S. Patterson & Ilana Stern, United States Government Printing Office, Washington, DC, 1990, Doc. 115; 'Big nuclear test staged by Soviet', *New York Times*, 19 April 1957

34 Pedlow & Welzenbach, *The Central Intelligence Agency and Overhead Reconnaissance*, pp. 153-7

35 Ibid., pp. 156, 164, 167, 176-7, 181; Russian and US Notes on the Downing of American Pilot in the Soviet Union

36 Richard Helms with William Hood, *A Look over My Shoulder: A Life in the Central Intelligence Agency*, Random House, New York, 2003, p. 166

37 Curtis Peebles, *High Frontier: The US Air Force and the Military Space Program*, Air Force History and Museums Program, Washington, DC, 1997, pp. 5, 14, 15; CIA CREST, 5166d4f999326091c6a60857, Kevin C. Ruffner (ed.), *Corona: America's First Satellite Program*, Center for the Study of Intelligence, Central Intelligence Agency, Langley, MD, 1995, pp. xv, 120; Andrew, *For the President's Eyes Only*, p. 259; Boyd, *British Naval Intelligence*, p. 584

38 FRUS 1958-1960, Vol. VII, Part 2, Western Europe, ed. Ronald D. Landa at al., Doc. 371; House of Commons Library, Claire Mills, SN/IA/3147, UK–US Mutual Defence Agreement

12. THE CUBAN MISSILE CRISIS

1 FRUS 1961-1963, Vol. X, Cuba, January 1961-September 1962, ed. Louis J. Smith, United States Government Printing Office, Washington, DC, 1997, Docs 86, 84; Richard J. Aldrich & Rory Cormac, *The Black Door: Spies, Secret Intelligence and British Prime Ministers*, William Collins, London, 2017, p. 207; Andrew, *For the President's Eyes Only*,

p. 258

2 *JFK Library*, Robert Amory Jr., Oral History Interview, 2 September 1966; David Priess, *The President's Book of Secrets: The Untold Story of Intelligence Briefings to America's Presidents from Kennedy to Obama*, PublicAffairs, New York, 2016, pp. 15-25

3 FRUS 1958-1960, Vol. VI, Cuba, ed. John p. Glennon, United States Government Printing Office, Washington, DC, 1991, Doc. 481; FRUS 1961-1963, Vol. X, Cuba, January 1961-September 1962, Docs 1, 2

4 FRUS 1961-1963, Vol. X, Cuba, January 1961-September 1962, Doc. 27

5 Andrew, *For the President's Eyes Only*, pp. 259-60

6 'The story behind the Cuban statement', *New York Times*, 5 April 1961; 'Cuban intrigue boiling in Miami as Castro foes step up efforts', *New York Times*, 8 April 1961

7 CIA CREST, RDP85G00105R000100040001-9, The Requirements for Intelligence at a National Level, Speech at London Conference on Intelligence Methods, 20 September 1966; Helms with Hood, *A Look over My Shoulder*, p. 185; Arthur Schlesinger Jr, *Journals 1952-2000*, Atlantic, London, 2007, p. 112; Priess, *The President's Book of Secrets*, pp. 15-25

8 Andrew, *The Defence of the Realm*, pp. 489-91

9 FRUS 1961-1963, Vol. XIV, Berlin Crisis 1961-1962, Docs 32, 34; JFK Library, Lord Harlech (William David Ormsby-Gore) Oral History Interview, 3 December 1965; Peter Catterall (ed.), *The Macmillan Diaries, Vol. 2: Prime Minister and After 1957-1966*, Pan, London, 2011, entry for 11 June 1961, pp. 389-90

10 Smith, '"America in Britain's Place?"'

11 Cline, *The CIA under Reagan, Bush and Casey*, p. 147-9; 'Why no questions about the CIA?', *New Statesman*,

29 September 2003

12 CIA CREST, Doc. No. 0000012276, Joseph J. Bulik, Memo for the Record, 31 August 1960; Doc. No. 0000012277, Contact and Debriefing of Henry Lee Cobb on his meeting with Penkovsky in the USSR, 28 September 1960

13 Anthony Verrier, *Through the Looking Glass: British Foreign Policy in an Age of Illusions*, Jonathan Cape, London, 1983, pp. 210-21; 'The businessman who became one of Britain's top spies', *Daily Telegraph*, 29 August 2014

14 CIA CREST, Doc. No. 0000012392, Meeting No 1 (London) at Mount Royal Hotel, 20 April 1961

15 CIA CREST, Doc. No. 5166d4f999326091c6a607ae, John M. Maury, Memorandum for the Record, 13 July 1961; Helms with Hood, *A Look over My Shoulder*, p. 221

16 CIA CREST, Memo for the Record, 6 February 1962; Doc. No. 0000012390, Penkovsky Operational Plan, 1 January 1961; 'Reflections on Handling Penkovsky', *Studies in Intelligence*, undated

17 Ferris, *Behind the Enigma*, pp. 532-3; Gordon Corera, 'Scarborough's role in the Cuban missile crisis revealed', BBC News website, 21 October 2019, https://www.bbc.co.uk/news/uk-50098955 (accessed 7 January 2022)

18 Thomas R. Johnson, *American Cryptology during the Cold War 1945-1989, Book II: Centralization Wins 1960-1972*, Center for Cryptologic History, National Security Agency, Ford George G. Meade, MD, 1995, pp. 318-20; *History of the Army Security Agency and Subordinate Units, Fiscal Year 1960, Vol. II: Technical Operations*, pp. 1, 3, 28; NSA Website Documents: Weekly Comint Economic Briefing, Indications of Soviet Arms Shipments to Cuba, 5 October 1960; Spanish-Speaking Pilot Noted in Czechoslovak Air Activity at Trenčín, 17 January,

1 February 1961; Spanish-Speaking Pilots Training at Trenčín Airfield, Czechoslovakia on 31 May 1961, 19 June 1961; Spanish-Speaking Pilots Training at Trenčín Airfield, Czechoslovakia on 31 May 1961, 19 June 1961; Funnel Messages, 11 April 1962; DIRNSA to CNO, 19 July 1962

19 CIA CREST, RDP85G00105R000100040005-5, Talk by Bruce C. Clarke to London Conference on Intelligence Methods on Role of Intelligence in the Cuban Missile Crisis, 19 September 1966; NSA Website: US Army Security Agency Annual Historical Summary Fiscal Year 1962, p. 3; Judith Edgette, 'Domestic Collection on Cuba', Studies in Intelligence, Fall 1963

20 NSA Website: Reference to Radar Tracking on Russian Equipment in Cuba, 18 April 1962; First Elint evidence of Scan Odd radar in Cuban area, 6 June 1962; Increased flight activity of Cuban Tactical Air Force, 7 September 1962; NSA File: Reflection of Soviet Bloc Pilots/ Technicians in Cuban Air Force Training, 24 August 1962; DIRNSA to JCS, 22 October 1962; US Army Security Agency Annual Historical Summary Fiscal Year 1962, pp. 3, 5, 14; Johnson, American Cryptology, Book II, pp. 317-23

21 CIA CREST, RDP85G00105R000100040005-5, Talk by Bruce C. Clarke to London Conference on Intelligence Methods on Role of Intelligence in the Cuban Missile Crisis, 19 September 1966

22 NSA Website: DIRNSA to CNO, 19 July 1962; Memorandum for the Secretary of the Navy, Navy Participation in Increased SIGINT Program for Cuba, 19 July 1962; Dry Cargo Shipments to and from Cuba in Soviet Ships, 1 January 1962 to 31 March 1962, report dated 2 May 1962; Unusual Number of Soviet Passenger Ships en route

Cuba, 24 July 1962; Further Unusual Soviet/Cuban Trade Relations Recently Noted, 7 August 1962; Status of Soviet Merchant Shipping to Cuba, 23 August 1962; DIRNSA to JCS, 17 September 1962

23 CIA CREST, Doc. OC0005995893, President's Intelligence Checklist for 23 August 1962; Johnson, American Cryptology, Book II, p. 323; James G. Hershberg, 'Their Men in Havana: Anglo-American Intelligence Exchanges and the Cuban Crises 1961-62', Intelligence and National Security, Vol. 15/2 (2000)

24 CIA CREST, RDP89B00569R000700090001-8, Situation Summary Part 1, 5 September 1962; RDP89B00569R000700090016-2, NPIC OPCEN to Army, Navy, USAF, DIA, NSA, 31 August 1962; NSA Website: New Radar Deployment in Cuba, 19 September 1962

25 CIA CREST, RDP85G00105R000100040005-5, Talk by Bruce C. Clarke to London Conference on Intelligence Methods on Role of Intelligence in the Cuban Missile Crisis, 19 September 1966

26 'Kennedy pledges any steps to bar Cuban aggression', New York Times, 5 September 1962; 'Kennedy's Cuba statement', New York Times, 5 September 1962

27 CIA CREST, RDP80B01676R001800050003-7, Special National Intelligence Estimate, Number 85-3-6.2, The Military Buildup in Cuba, 19 September 1962

28 William J. Casey, speech at Brown University, 15 October 1981; Ferris, Behind the Enigma, p. 533

29 NSA Website: Further Information on Soviet Cuban Trade, 31 August 1962; Further Information on Cargo Shipments to Cuba in Soviet Ships, 25 September 1962; Further Information on Cargo Shipments to Cuba in Soviet Ships,

2 October 1962; FRUS 1961-1963, Vol. XI, Cuban Missile Crisis and Aftermath, ed. Edward C. Keefer, Charles S. Sampson & Louis J. Smith, United States Government Printing Office, Washington, DC, 1996, Docs 1, 5; CIA CREST, RDP85G00105R000100040005-5, Talk by Bruce C. Clarke to London Conference on Intelligence Methods on Role of Intelligence in the Cuban Missile Crisis, 19 September 1966

30 David Robarge, *John McCone as Director of Central Intelligence 1961-1965*, Center for the Study of Intelligence, Central Intelligence Agency, Langley, MD, 2015, p. 133

31 FRUS 1961-1963, Vol. XI, Cuban Missile Crisis and Aftermath, Briefing Paper, Doc. 1; CIA CREST, RDP85G00105R000100040005-5, Talk by Bruce C. Clarke to London Conference on Intelligence Methods on Role of Intelligence in the Cuban Missile Crisis, 19 September 1966; Helms with Hood, *A Look over My Shoulder*, pp. 213, 215; Max Holland, 'The "Photo Gap" That Delayed Discovery of Missiles', *Studies in Intelligence*, Vol. 49/4 (2005)

32 CIA CREST, RDP80B01676R001700180032-2, Notes of the Special Group (Augmented) Meeting, 27 September 1962; FRUS 1961-1963, Vol. XI, Cuban Missile Crisis and Aftermath, Doc. 12; CIA CREST, RDP85G00105R000100040005-5, Talk by Bruce C. Clarke to London Conference on Intelligence Methods on Role of Intelligence in the Cuban Missile Crisis, 19 September 1966; Merlin, *Unlimited Horizons*, pp. 217, 219, 221, 239

33 Sherman Kent, 'The Cuban Missile Crisis of 1962: Presenting the Photographic Evidence Abroad', *Studies in Intelligence*, Spring 1972; Helms with Hood, *A Look over My Shoulder*, p. 213; Dino A. Brugioni, 'The Cuban Missile Crisis—Phase I,

The Pi Story', *Studies in Intelligence*, Fall 1972

34 CIA CREST, RDP80B01676R001700140012-8, Memorandum for the Record, Notification of NSC Officials of Intelligence on Missile Bases in Cuba, 27 October 1962; RDP71T00730R000100030002-4, Distribution of the Proceedings of the Second Conference on Intelligence Methods, 27 March 1963; Brugioni, 'The Cuban Missile Crisis—Phase I'

35 Helms with Hood, *A Look over My Shoulder*, p. 216

36 CIA CREST, RDP78T05449A000200030001-8-1, Joint Evaluation of Soviet Missile Threat in Cuba, 8 October 1962; RDP85G00105R000100040005-5, Talk by Bruce C. Clarke to London Conference on Intelligence Methods on Role of Intelligence in the Cuban Missile Crisis, 19 September 1966; FRUS 1961-1963, Vol. XI, Cuban Missile Crisis and Aftermath, Doc. 28

37 CIA CREST, 5077054e993247d4d82b6ac4, The Soviet Missile Venture in Cuba, CIA/RSS/DD/I Staff Study, 17 February 1964; FRUS 1961-1963, Vol. XI, Cuban Missile Crisis and Aftermath, Docs 21, 22, 23, 27, 34

38 Kent, 'The Cuban Missile Crisis of 1962'

39 FRUS 1961-1963, Vol. XI, Cuban Missile Crisis and Aftermath, Docs 37, 39; JFK Library, Ormsby-Gore Oral History Interview

40 Kent, 'The Cuban Missile Crisis of 1962'

41 CIA CREST, RDP78T05449A000200170001-3, Chronology of Events at Cuban Offensive Weapons Sites, 21-30 October 1962, 1 November 1962

42 Catterall, *The Macmillan Diaries, Vol. 2*, p. 510; FRUS 1961-1963, Vol. XI, Cuban Missile Crisis and Aftermath, Doc. 45; JFK Library, Ormsby-Gore

Oral History Interview

43　Corera, 'Scarborough's role in the Cuban missile crisis revealed'; Catterall, *The Macmillan Diaries, Vol. 2*, pp. 511-12; CIA CREST, RDP85G00105R000100040005-5, Talk by Bruce C. Clarke to London Conference on Intelligence Methods on Role of Intelligence in the Cuban Missile Crisis, 19 September 1966; NSA Website: USN22 to Distribution List NWA, SIGINT Readiness Bravo, OWEN Spot Report, 23 October 1962; USN22 to Distribution List NWA, 241638Z, SIGINT Readiness Bravo, OWEN Spot Report, 24 October 1962; Robert J. Hanyok, 'A Reconsideration of the Role of SIGINT during the Cuban Missile Crisis, October 1962, Pt. 2', 24 February 1998, available at https://www.nsa.gov/portals/75/documents/news-features/declassified-documents/crypto-almanac-50th/reconsideration_of_the_role_of_sigint_part_2.pdf (accessed 7 January 2022); CIA CREST, RDP80B01676R001800010020-2, The Crisis, USSR/Cuba, Information as of 0600, 26 October 1962; FRUS 1961-1963, Vol. XI, Cuban Missile Crisis and Aftermath, Docs 57, 58

44　FRUS 1961-1963, Vol. XI, Cuban Missile Crisis and Aftermath, Doc. 61; NSA Website: Jeremy Robinson-Leon & William Burr, 'The Submarines of October, Electronic Briefing Book No. 75, Pt. VI: Chronology of Submarine Contact during the Cuban Missile Crisis, 1 October 1962-14 November 1962'

45　FRUS 1961-1963, Vol. XI, Cuban Missile Crisis and Aftermath, Doc. 68; CIA CREST, Doc. No. 0000012392, Meeting No 1 (London) at Mount Royal Hotel, 20 April 1961

46　FRUS 1961-1963, Vol. XI, Cuban Missile Crisis and Aftermath, Doc. 71; CIA CREST, Doc. No. 0005996003, The President's Intelligence

Checklist, 26 October 1962; RDP80B01676R001800010020-2, The Crisis, USSR/Cuba, Information as of 0600, 26 October 1962

47　CIA CREST, RDP78T05449A000200170001-3, Chronology of Events at Cuban Offensive Weapons Sites, 21-30 October 1962

48　FRUS 1961-1963, Vol. XI, Cuban Missile Crisis and Aftermath, Docs 80, 85; Elie Abel, *The Missiles of October, Twelve Days to World War Three*, new ed., MacGibbon & Kee, London, 1969, pp. 163-5

49　FRUS 1961-1963, Vol. XI, Cuban Missile Crisis and Aftermath, Doc. 84

50　FRUS 1961-1963, Vol. XI, Cuban Missile Crisis and Aftermath, Docs 91, 92; Rosaleen Hughes, 'Attention! Moscow Calling: BBC Monitoring and the Cuban Missile Crisis', available at https://www.iwm.org.uk/sites/default/files/files/2018-11/Attention%21%20Moscow%20Calling%20BBC%20Monitoring%20and%20the%20Cuban%20Missile%20Crisis%20-%20Rosaleen%20Hughes.pdf (accessed 7 January 2022)

51　FRUS 1961-1963, Vol. XI, Cuban Missile Crisis and Aftermath, Doc. 94; National Security Archive, The Cuban Missile Crisis, The Documents, Castro to Khrushchev, 28 October 1962, available at https://nsarchive2.gwu.edu/nsa/cuba_mis_cri/19621028caslet.pdf (accessed 7 January 2022)

52　FRUS 1961-1963, Vol. XI, Cuban Missile Crisis and Aftermath, Doc. 96; Jim Hershberg, 'Anatomy of a Controversy: Anatoly F. Dobrynin's Meeting with Robert F. Kennedy, Saturday, 27 October 1962', *Cold War International History Project Bulletin*, Spring 1995

53　FRUS 1961-1963, Vol. XI, Cuban Missile Crisis and Aftermath, Doc. 102; CIA CREST, RDP83-00586R000300230001-5, Chief

FBIS to Bureau Chiefs, Letter of Information, 19 December 1962; Hughes, 'Attention! Moscow Calling'

54 Helms with Hood, *A Look over My Shoulder*, pp. 216-17

55 Cline, *The CIA under Reagan, Bush and Casey*, p. 222

56 Verrier, *Through the Looking Glass*, p. 193

13. 'THE LADY'S VIRGINITY HAS BEEN QUESTIONED'

1 Catterall, *The Macmillan Diaries, Vol. 2*, pp. 517-18; 'Labour says US action is of doubtful legality, failure to consult regretted', *The Times*, 25 October 1962

2 'Britain's role in world', *Guardian*, 6 December 1962; 'The art of survival', *Daily Mirror*, 7 December 1962; Front page leader, *Daily Herald*, 10 December 1962; John F. Kennedy Library, JFKNSF-170a-009-p0007, White House to Secretary of State, 7 December 1962

3 Catterall, *The Macmillan Diaries, Vol. 2*, pp. 522-3

4 FRUS 1961-1963, Vol. XIII, Western Europe and Canada, ed. Charles S. Sampson & James E. Miller, United States Government Printing Office, Washington, DC, 1994, Doc. 401

5 FRUS 1961-1963, Vol. XIII, Western Europe and Canada, Docs 400, 392, 394

6 'Skybolt fears deepened by London talks', *The Times*, 12 December 1962; 'US views on duty to Britain', *The Times*, 12 December 1962; FRUS 1961-1963, Vol. XIII, Western Europe and Canada, Doc. 401

7 FRUS 1961-1963, Vol. XIII, Western Europe and Canada, Doc. 402; Clare Melland, 'Britain and a New World Role: The Nassau Agreement 1962 and Its Effect on International and Anglo-European Relations, and the Anglo-American "Special Relationship"', MPhil thesis, University of Leicester, July 2010

8 Raj Roy & John W. Young, *Ambassador to Sixties London: The Diaries of David Bruce 1961-1969*, Republic of Letters, Dordrecht, 2009, pp. 87-8

9 FRUS 1961-1963, Vol. XIII, Western Europe and Canada, Docs 402, 403

10 FRUS 1961-1963, Vol. XIII, Western Europe and Canada, Docs 404, 406; John F. Kennedy Library, JFKNSF-230-006, pp. 28-46, Memorandum of Agreement, 28 January 1963 and Annex, 29 January 1963; Catterall, *Macmillan Diaries, Vol. 2*, p. 528; 'After Nassau', *The Times*, 22 December 1962

11 'Philby "Third Man" who warned Maclean now presumed to be behind the Iron Curtain', *The Times*, 2 July 1963; 'British link ex-diplomat to Burgess–Maclean Case', *New York Times*, 2 July 1963; Roy & Young, *Ambassador to Sixties London*, pp. 61-3; FRUS 1961-1963, Vol. XIII, Western Europe and Canada, Doc. 415

12 Robarge, *John McCone*, pp. 316-20; FBI Website, FOIA No. 65-68218-83, R. W. Smith to W. C. Sullivan, 30 June 1963; Hoover to DCI, 1 July 1963

13 Anthony M. Perry, 'The Malayan Effect', *The Rose and the Laurel*, December 1990; Keith Jeffery, 'Intelligence and Counter insurgency Operations: Some Reflections on the British Experience', *Intelligence and National Security*, Vol. 2/1 (1987); Kumar Ramakrishna, '"Transmogrifying" Malaya: The Impact of Sir Gerald Templer 1952-1954, *Journal of Southeast Asian Studies*, Vol. 32/1 (2001)

14 Peter Busch, *All the Way with JFK?: Britain, the US, and the Vietnam War*, Oxford University Press, Oxford, 2003, pp. 66-74; FRUS 1958-1960, Vol. I, Vietnam, ed. Edward C. Keefer & David W. Mabon, United States Government Printing Office, Washington, DC, 1986, Doc. 123

15 FRUS 1958-1960, Vol. I, Vietnam, Docs 109, 111, 110, 141

16 Busch, *All the Way with JFK?*, p. 93;

FRUS 1961-1963, Vol. I, Vietnam, 1961, ed. Ronald D. Landa & Charles S. Sampson, United States Government Printing Office, Washington, DC, 1988, Doc. 80

17 CIA CREST, RDP80B01676R002900280003-0, Hilsman to McCone, 14 May 1963; FRUS 1961-1963, Vol. II, Vietnam, 1962, ed. John p. Glennon, David M. Baehler & Charles S. Sampson, United States Government Printing Office, Washington, 1990, Docs 42, 51; FRUS 1961-1963, Vol. III, Vietnam, January-August 1963, ed. Edward C. Keefer & Louis J. Smith, United States Government Printing Office, Washington, DC, 1991, Docs 77, 78

18 CIA CREST, RDP80B01676R001900150051-2, Minutes for the Special Group (CI) Meeting, 23 May 1963

19 FRUS 1958-1960, Vol. I, Vietnam, Docs 269, 270, 274

20 Chester L. Cooper, *The Lost Crusade: America in Vietnam*, Dodd, Mead, New York, 1970, pp. 208-15; Thomas L. Ahern Jr, *CIA and the House of Ngo: Covert Action in Vietnam 1954-1963*, Center for the Study of Intelligence, Central Intelligence Agency, Langley, MD, 1999, p. 115

21 Busch, *All the Way with JFK?*, pp. 158-61, 167

22 CIA CREST, Doc. No. 0005355248, Wisner to DCI, Major Lucien E. Conein, 25 August 1953; Mike Gravel, *The Pentagon Papers: The Defense Department History of United States Decisionmaking on Vietnam*, Beacon Press, Boston, 1972, pp. 573-83

23 John F. Kennedy Library, National Security Files (JFKNSF) 204-012, pp. 16-17, CAS Message, Saigon 1925; Ahern, *CIA and the House of Ngo*, pp. 192-3, FRUS 1961-1963, Vol. IV, Vietnam, August-December 1963, ed. Edward C. Keefer, United States Government Printing Office,

Washington, DC, 1991, Doc. 216

24 FRUS 1961-1963, Vol. IV, Vietnam, August-December 1963, Doc. 244; JFKNSF-204-012, p. 11, Saigon 1896

25 FRUS 1961-1963, Volume IV, Vietnam, August-December 1963, Doc. 234; Ahern, *CIA and the House of Ngo*, p. 202; Busch, *All the Way with JFK?*, p. 167

26 FRUS 1961-1963, Volume IV, Vietnam, August-December 1963, Docs 251, 252, 253

27 FRUS 1961-1963, Volume IV, Vietnam, August-December 1963, Doc. 270; Ahern, *CIA and the House of Ngo*, p. 214; General Maxwell D. Taylor, *Swords and Plowshares*, W. W. Norton, New York, 1972, p. 301

28 CIA CREST, RDP79T00936A002100170001-5, President's Intelligence Checklist for 11 December 1963; RDP79T00936A002300050001-6, The President's Intelligence Checklist for 5 February 1964; RDP79T00975A007600270001-8, Central Intelligence Bulletin, 18 April 1964; Busch, *All the Way with JFK?*, pp. 169-70

29 FRUS 1964-1968, Vol. I, Vietnam, 1964, ed. Edward C. Keefer & Charles S. Sampson, United States Government Printing Office, Washington, DC, 1992, Doc. 194

30 FRUS 1964-1968, Vol. I, Vietnam, 1964, Docs 188, 189, 193

31 Roy & Young, *Ambassador to Sixties London*, p. 154; 'Red PT boats fire at US destroyer on Vietnam duty', *New York Times*, 3 August 1964; Robert J. Hanyok, 'Skunks, Bogies, Silent Hounds, and the Flying Fish: The Gulf of Tonkin Mystery, 2-4 August 1964', *Cryptologic Quarterly*, Winter 2000/Spring 2001

14. A CAPITALIST RUNNING DOG'S VIEW FROM HANOI

1 Rhiannon Vickers, 'Harold Wilson, The British Labour Party, and the

War in Vietnam', *Journal of Cold War Studies*, Vol. 10/2 (2008)

2 Aldrich, *GCHQ*, pp. 269, 277; Royal Navy submarines and Vietnamese linguists from personal knowledge; Bruce, *Ambassador to Sixties London*, p. 170; Aldrich & Cormac, *The Black Door*, p. 212

3 IWM Interview with Myles Walter Ponsonby, 9 February 1995, Acquisition No. 14929, available at https://www.iwm.org.uk/collections/item/object/80014525 (accessed 7 January 2022)

4 UKNA FO 371/186408, Status of Consulate-General in Hanoi, September 1966; Richard J. Aldrich, 'Britain's Secret Intelligence Service in Asia during the Second World War', *Modern Asian Studies*, Vol. 32/1 (1998); Aldrich, *The Hidden Hand*, p. 516; CIA CREST, 5166d491993260091c6a6007a, Directors Log, Entries for 25-26 October, 13-14 and 19-20 November 1951; Richard Greene, *Russian Roulette: The Life and Times of Graham Greene*, Little, Brown, London, 2020, pp. 205-8, 214-16, 220

5 Gravel, *The Pentagon Papers*, pp. 573-83

6 William Colby with Peter Forbath, *Honourable Men: My Life in the CIA*, Hutchinson, London, 1978, p. 222; Thomas Ahern Jr, *The Way We Do Things: Black Entry Ops into North Vietnam 1961-1964*, Center for the Study of Intelligence, Central Intelligence Agency, Langley, MD, 2005, pp. 9, 14, 31-2, 41, 58, 61; Thomas L. Ahern Jr, *Vietnam Declassified: The CIA and Counterinsurgency*, University Press of Kentucky, Lexington, 2010, p. 259

7 UKNA FO 371/186408, Shepherd to de la Mare, 1 June 1966; Murray to Shepherd, 6 June 1966

8 UKNA FO 371/180562, Discussion on the Post at Hanoi between Mr. Peck and Mr. Ponsonby in Saigon on 31 January 1965; CIA CREST, RDP79T00472A001900010015-5, Memorandum: The Situation in Vietnam, Information as of 0600 23 February 1965

9 CIA CREST, RDP79T00472A001900030014-4, Memorandum: The Situation in Vietnam, Information as of 1600 28 March 1965; RDP79T00936A003600310001-3, PDB, 27 April 1965; Hayes, *Queen of Spies*, p. 229; Supplement to *London Gazette*, 1 January 1966, p. 20

10 UKNA PREM13/692, Record of telephone conversation between Prime Minister and President Johnson, 11 February 1965, at 3.15 in the morning UK time; LBJ Library, Box 228, Bundy to Wright for the Prime Minister, 11 February 1965; Sit Room Report, 10 February 1965, p. 3, both available at http://www.lbjf.org/txt/nsf/cf-vietnam/591194-nsf-co-vn-b228-f7.pdf (accessed 8 January 2022)

11 FRUS 1964-1968, Vol. XII, Western Europe, ed. James E. Miller, United States Government Printing Office, Washington, DC, 2001, Docs 252, 266

12 Roy & Young, *Ambassador to Sixties London*, pp. 233-4, 249, 263-4; FRUS 1964-1968, Vol. XII, Western Europe, Doc. 259

13 UKNA FO 371/186408, Shepherd to de la Mare, 1 June 1966; 'John Colvin', *Daily Telegraph*, 8 October 2003; 'Colourful British diplomat on watch in the world's trouble-spots', *Guardian*, 15 October 2003; 'Diplomat and spy who served in Hanoi during the Vietnam War', *Independent*, 16 October 2003

14 'US, extending bombing, raids Hanoi and Haiphong outskirts', *New York Times*, 30 June 1966; 'Text of McNamara's statement and questions and answers on bombing of Hanoi and Haiphong depots', *New York Times*, 30 June 1966; John Colvin,

Twice around the World: Some Memoirs of Diplomatic Life in North Vietnam and Outer Mongolia, Leo Cooper, London, 1991, pp. 34, 38

15 Colvin, *Twice around the World*, pp. 61-2, 103-7

16 UKNA FCO 15/555, Murray to de la Mare & Wright, 5 June 1967; Murray to de la Mare, 7 June 1967

17 UKNA FCO 15/585, Flash Hanoi to Foreign Office, 6 January 1967; Murray to Colvin, 24 January 1967; Murray to Colvin, 1 February 1967; Hanoi to Foreign Office, 27 March 1967; FCO 15/555, Colvin to Brown, 22 March 1967; 'Damage near Hanoi reported by Briton', *New York Times*, 3 January 1967; 'Britain's man in Hanoi behind "feeling"', *Sun*, 20 January 1967

18 UKNA FCO 15/555, Colvin to Murray, 26 September 1967; Stewart to Murray, 11 October 1967; Stewart to Murray, 17 October 1967; Fyjis-Walker to Murray, 23 November 1967; Stewart to Murray, 8 December 1967; Stewart to Murray, 12 December 1967, The Position of the Consulate-General in Hanoi, December 1967; Stewart to Brown, 4 January 1968, Appendix, Chronology of Attrition 1957-1967; FCO 15/578, Murray to Colvin, 17 August 1967; Nikita Wolf, '"This Secret Town": British Intelligence, the Special Relationship, and the Vietnam War', *International History Review*, Vol. 39/2 (2017)

19 UKNA FCO 15/512, Hanoi telegram No. 28 to Foreign Office, Visits to Haiphong in mid-October, 20 October 1967

20 UKNA FCO 15/481 Waterstone to Fyjis-Walker, 20 November 1967; CIA CREST, PDB, 3 November 1967; PDB, 18 November 1967; PDB, 23 January 1968; UKNA FCO 15/555, Stewart to Murray, Going to Church in Hanoi, 12 December 1967

21 Wolf, '"This Secret Town"'; UKNA FCO 15/524, Hanoi to Foreign Office, Hanoi Observations,

13 September 1968; Hanoi to Foreign Office, Hanoi Observations, 1 August 1968

22 UKNA FCO 15/637 Stewart to Brown, 6 December 1967

23 Brian Stewart & Samantha Newbery, *Why Spy?: The Art of Intelligence*, Hurst, London, 2015, p. 27

24 UKNA FCO 15/585, Foreign Office to Washington, 3 January 1967; Colvin to Murray, 11 January 1967; Stewart to Stewart, Problems of a Protracted People's War, A Hanoi View, 3 September 1968; Murray to Wilford, 9 September 1968; FCO 15/481, Tel. No. 9125, Foreign Office to Washington, 21 August 1967; 'Brian Stewart: MI6 director and China specialist', *The Times*, 9 September 2015; 'Brian Stewart, intelligence officer', *Daily Telegraph*, 28 September 2015; 'Gordon Philo: SIS officer and writer', *The Times*, 18 May 2009

25 CIA CREST, PDB, 27 December 1968

26 Hayes, *Queen of Spies*, pp. 221-2, 228

27 UKNA FCO15/1355, Park to Douglas-Home, Her Majesty's Representative in Limbo: A Valedictory, 25 October 1970

28 Ibid.; 'A licence to kill? Oh heavens, no!', *Daily Telegraph*, 23 April 2003, 'MI6's ladies in the Lords set their sights on beefing up anti-terror law', *Daily Telegraph*, 23 January 2006, 'Labour's cold war rivals opt for a peaceful succession', *Daily Telegraph*, 30 January 2006; 'Baroness Park of Monmouth', *Daily Telegraph*, 25 March 2010; 'More Miss Marple than 007: the true face of British espionage', *The Times*, 16 August 2008; Lady Park of Monmouth obituary, *Guardian*, 28 March 2010

29 'A licence to kill? Oh heavens, no!'; Hayes, *Queen of Spies*, p. 224

30 Martyn Cox interview with Daphne Park, 21 April 2007. I am grateful to Martyn for his transcript of this interview which is available through

the Legasee website at https://www.
legasee.org.uk/veteran/daphne-park/

31 UKNA FCO 15/1355, Park to
Gordon, No Profile in Hanoi,
26 June 1970; Daphne Park's Bicycle,
2 September 1970; 'Tandem tactic',
Daily Express, 28 August 1970; Hanoi
to FCO, 30 August 1970; Wolf,
'"This Secret Town"'

32 UKNA FCO 15/1355, Park to
Douglas-Home, Her Majesty's
Representative in Limbo: A
Valedictory, 25 October 1970

33 'Baroness Park of Monmouth', *Daily
Telegraph*, 25 March 2010; UKNA
FCO 15/1355, Liudzius to Gordon,
20 November 1970; Bower, *Red Web*,
p. 76; Hayes, *Queen of Spies*, p. 224

34 'Lives remembered: Vō Nguyen Giap',
The Times, 7 October 2013

15. PACKING A PUNCH

1 Boyd, *British Naval Intelligence*,
pp. 591-4; Peter Hennessy & James
Jinks, *The Silent Deep: The Royal Navy
Submarine Service since 1945*, Penguin,
London, 2016, pp. 351-4

2 Boyd, *British Naval Intelligence*,
pp. 595-6; Mason Redfearn & Richard
J. Aldrich, 'The Perfect Cover:
British Intelligence, the Soviet
Fleet and Distant Water Trawler
Operations 1963-1974', *Intelligence and
National Security*, Vol. 12/3 (1997)

3 'Britain's secret jet crash Cold
War coup', *Daily Telegraph*,
26 December 2003; Geraghty,
BRIXMIS, pp. 133-42; Rod Saar,
*Brixmis: A Secret Journey behind the Iron
Curtain*, BRIXMIS Association, 2020,
pp. 829-42

4 Correspondence with former senior
RAF intelligence officer, July 2021

5 William D. Gerhard & Henry W.
Millington, *Attack on a SIGINT
Collector, the USS Liberty*, National
Security Agency, Fort George G.
Meade, MD, 1981, p. 6, available at
https://www.nsa.gov/portals/75/
documents/news-features/
declassified-documents/uss-liberty/
chronology-events/attack-sigint.
pdf (accessed 8 January 2022); NSA
Website, OH-20-93, Interview with
Oliver Kirby

6 CIA CREST,
RDP79T00975A009500230001-1,
Central Intelligence Bulletin,
10 January 1967;
RDP79T00975A009500260001-8,
Central Intelligence Bulletin,
13 January 1967; Doc. No.
005968728, PDB, 13 January 1967;
Doc. No. 0005968734,
PDB, 16 January 1967;
RDP79T00826A001600010007-1,
Weekly Intelligence Report,
16 January 1967;
RDP79T00975A009800260001-5,
Central Intelligence Bulletin,
22 April 1967

7 CIA CREST, RDP79-
00927A005700050003-4, Special
Report, Syria: A Center of Instability,
24 March 1967

8 CIA CREST,
RDP79T00826A001800010032-1,
Intelligence Memorandum, No.
0802/67, 7 April 1967

9 Michael Smith, *The Anatomy of a Spy:
A History of Espionage and Betrayal*,
Arcade, New York, 2020, pp. 23-8;
'Iraqi pilot who defected to Israel
finds friendly reception', *Jewish
Telegraphic Agency*, 18 August 1966; 'In
1966, Israeli intelligence convinced
an Iraqi pilot to defect with his
MiG-21 fighter', *National Interest*,
28 August 2016; 'Syrian pilot's
defection in MiG-21 stirs Cold War
memories', *Phoenix Star*, 30 June 2012

10 CIA CREST, Doc. 0005973720,
PDB, 8 April 1967; Doc.
0005968722, PDB, 9 April 1967;
RDP79T00975A009800150001-7,
Central Intelligence Bulletin,
10 April 1967; FRUS 1964-1968, Vol.
XVIII, Arab–Israeli Dispute 1964-
1967, ed. Harriet Dashiell Schwar,
United States Government Printing
Office, Washington, DC, 2000, Doc.
404

11 CIA CREST,
RDP79T00975A009800170001-5,
Central Intelligence
Bulletin, 12 April 1967;
RDP79T00975A009800200001-1,
Central Intelligence
Bulletin, 15 April 1967;
RDP79T00827A000800080005-7,
DCI Briefing for Mahon Sub-
Committee, 21 April 1967;
RDP79T00975A009800260001-5,
Central Intelligence Bulletin,
22 April 1967

12 CIA CREST, Doc. No. 0005973796,
PDB, 11 May 1967; Doc. No.
0005973802, PDB, 15 May 1967;
Doc. No. 0005973804, PDB,
16 May 1967; Doc. No. 0005973808,
PDB, 18 May 1967; Doc. No.
0005973810, PDB, 19 May 1967; Doc.
No. 0005973812, PDB, 20 May 1967

13 FRUS 1964-1968, Vol. XIX, Arab–
Israeli Crisis and War 1967, ed.
Harriet Dashiell Schwar, United
States Government Printing Office,
Washington, DC, 2004, Docs 29, 53;
CIA CREST, Doc. No. 0005973810,
PDB, 19 May 1967; Doc. No.
0005973812, PDB, 20 May 1967

14 Helms with Hood, *A Look over My
Shoulder*, p. 298; FRUS 1964-1968,
Vol. XIX, Arab–Israeli Crisis and
War 1967, Docs 44, 45, 130, 29

15 Helms with Hood, *A Look over My
Shoulder*, p. 299; FRUS 1964-1968,
Volume XIX, Arab–Israeli Crisis and
War 1967, Doc. 72; CIA CREST,
RDP79T00826A002000010049-0,
Joint CIA/DIA Intelligence
Memorandum, 26 May 1967

16 Helms with Hood, *A Look over My
Shoulder*, pp. 299-300; FRUS 1964-
1968, Vol. XIX, Arab–Israeli Crisis
and War 1967, Doc. 124

17 FRUS 1964-1968, Vol. XII, Western
Europe, Doc. 269; FRUS 1964-1968,
Volume XIX, Arab–Israeli Crisis and
War 1967, Docs 29, 31, 53, 62, 66,
68, 130, 154, 168

18 NSA Website, OH-15-88, Interview
with General Marshall S. Carter,

3 October 1988

19 FRUS 1964-1968, Vol. XIX, Arab–
Israeli Crisis and War 1967, Docs 46,
80, 118

20 CIA CREST, Doc. No. 0005973836,
PDB, 3 June 1967; 'Israel–Syria fray
at border kills 3', *New York Times*,
3 June 1967

21 Private information; CIA CREST,
RDP79T00827A000900070001-1,
DCI Briefing, 5 June 1967; Doc. No.
0005973838, PDB, 5 June 1967; Doc.
No. 0005973840, PDB, 6 June 1967

22 CIA CREST, RDP83-
00586R000300260007-6, Letter of
Information, 26 June 1967; FRUS
1964-1968, Vol. XIX, Arab–Israeli
Crisis and War 1967, Doc. 155

23 NSA Website, USS Liberty (USN-
855) (AGTR-5), Chronology of
Events, 8 June 1967; OH-15-RO,
Interview with Robert L. Wilson,
6 May 1980; Gerhard & Millington,
Attack on a SIGINT Collector, pp. 21-32;
Johnson, *American Cryptology,
Book II*, p. 433; CIA CREST,
RDP84B00049R000902350010-7;
Intelligence Memorandum, Attack on
the USS *Liberty*, 13 June 1967; FRUS
1964-1968, Vol. XIX, Arab–Israeli
Crisis and War 1967, Doc. 204

24 FRUS 1964-1968, Vol. XIX, Arab–
Israeli Crisis and War 1967, Docs 207,
209, 212, 213

25 Gerhard & Millington, *Attack on a
SIGINT Collector*; Johnson, *American
Cryptology, Book II*, pp. 429, 437

16. THE PRAGUE SPRING

1 CIA CREST, Doc. No.
5166d4f999326091c6a608d0, FBIS
Special Memorandum, Public
Warning Indicators of the Soviet
Decision to Invade Czechoslovakia,
4 November 1980; 'Czech discount
move', *New York Times*, 10 May 1968

2 CIA CREST,
RDP79R00967A000800010014-8,
ONI Special Memorandum No.
6-68, The USSR and Eastern Europe,
21 March 1968; Douglas Nicoll, Cabinet

Office Report, The JIC and Warning of Aggression, November 1981 (reproduced in Robert Dover & Michael S. Goodman (eds.), *Learning from the Secret Past: Cases in British Intelligence History*, Georgetown University Press, Washington, DC, 2011)

3 Christopher Andrew & Vasili Mitrokhin, *The Mitrokhin Archive: The KGB in Europe and the West*, Allen Lane, London, 1999, pp. 328-30; Radio Prague International, 'UK-held Mitrokhin archives reveal details of KGB operation against Prague Spring', 19 July 2014

4 RDP79-00927A006400050001-8, Weekly Summary Special Report No. 0018/68A, Soviet Reaction to the Changes in Czechoslovakia, 3 May 1968

5 CIA CREST, Doc. No. 0005975730, PDB, 4 May 1968

6 Ferris, *Behind the Enigma*, p. 539

7 CIA CREST, RDP94T00754R000200290008-1, Intelligence Memorandum, The Czechoslovak-Soviet Struggle, 12 July 1968; Johnson, *American Cryptology, Book II*, pp. 454-5; Ferris, *Behind the Enigma*, pp. 538-9

8 UKNA, WO 208/5256, BRIXMIS Quarterly Report 1 July to 30 September 1968, p. iv; Saar, *BRIXMIS*, p. 824; Aldrich, *GCHQ*, pp. 234-5; Geraghty, *BRIXMIS*, p. 159

9 CIA CREST, Doc. No. 0005976138, PDB, 9 May 1968

10 CIA CREST, Doc. No. 5166d4f999326091c6a608d0, FBIS Special Memorandum, Public Warning Indicators of the Soviet Decision to Invade Czechoslovakia, 4 November 1980; 'Hostile intent dismissed', *New York Times*, 11 May 1968

11 CIA CREST, Doc. No 0005976140, PDB, 10 May 1968; Doc. No. 0005976142, PDB, 11 May 1968; RDP78T03194A000300010009-3, Cynthia M. Grabo, 'Soviet Deception in the Czechoslovak Crisis', *Studies in Intelligence*, Spring 1970; 'Russian soldiers said to be on move near Czech line', *New York Times*, 10 May 1968; 'Poles curb Westerners', *New York Times*, 10 May 1968; 'British official skeptical', *New York Times*, 10 May 1968

12 'Johnson flies to address UN', *The Times*, 13 June 1968; 'Moscow ready for missile ban', *The Times*, 28 June 1968; 'US and Soviet agree to parleys on limitation of missile systems', *New York Times*, 2 July 1968

13 FRUS 1964-1968, Vol. XVII, Eastern Europe, ed. James E. Miller, United States Government Printing Office, Washington, DC, 1996, Doc. 60; Nigel Clive, rev Michael Smith, 'Rennie, Sir John Ogilvie', *Oxford Dictionary of National Biography*, Oxford University Press, Oxford, 2004; Aldrich, *GCHQ*, pp. 233-5; Ferris, *Behind the Enigma*, p. 539; Cradock, *Know Your Enemy*, p. 249

14 CIA CREST, Doc. No. 5166d4f999326091c6a608d0, FBIS Special Memorandum, Public Warning Indicators of the Soviet Decision to Invade Czechoslovakia, 4 November 1980; Doc. No. 0005976164, PDB, 24 March 1968; 'Moscow change of mood on Czechs, Kosygin tries reconciliation', *The Times*, 20 May 1968; 'Prague resists Soviet plan to send 10,000 troops', *The Times*, 23 May 1968; 'Kosygin leaves Czechoslovakia for Moscow, cutting visit 4 days short', *New York Times*, 26 May 1968

15 CIA CREST, Doc. No. 0005976176, PDB, 31 May 1968; Doc. No, 0005976180, PDB, 3 June 1968; Doc No. 0005976188, PDB, 7 June 1968

16 CIA CREST, Doc. No. 0005976184, PDB, 5 June 1968; 'Russian tanks in Czechoslovakia, "routine joint exercises"', *The Times*, 7 June 1968

17 FBIS Daily Report, 17 June 1968, Part IV, Page D5, Slovakia *Pravda*, 13 June 1968; Page D9, CTK in English, 1300 GMT, 18 June 1968;

'Russian tanks in Czechoslovakia';
'Controversial East Bloc troop moves
end in Czechoslovakia', *New York
Times*, 1 July 1968

18 CIA CREST, Doc. No.
0005976224, PDB, 28 June 1968;
Doc. No. 0005976227, PDB,
1 July 1968; Doc. No. 0005976229,
PDB, 2 July 1968; Doc. No.
0005976231, PDB, 3 July 1968;
RDP94T00754R000200290008-1,
Intelligence Memorandum, The
Czechoslovak–Soviet Struggle,
12 July 1968; Grabo, 'Soviet
Deception'; Ferris, *Behind the Enigma*,
p. 539; 'Moscow ready for missile
ban'; 'US and Soviet agree to parleys'

19 CIA CREST, Doc. No. 0005976235,
PDB, 5 July 1968; Doc. No.
0005976239, PDB, 8 July 1968; Doc.
No. 0005976243, PDB, 10 July 1968

20 CIA CREST, Doc. No.
5166d4f999326091c6a608d0, FBIS
Special Memorandum, Public
Warning Indicators of the Soviet
Decision to Invade Czechoslovakia,
4 November 1980

21 CIA CREST, Doc. No. 0005976247,
PDB, 12 July 1968; Aid, *The Secret
Sentry*, pp. 143-4

22 FRUS 1964-1968, Vol. XVII, Eastern
Europe, Doc. 66; CIA CREST,
RDP79R00904A001400020011-5,
Memorandum for the
Director, The Crisis in
Czechoslovakia, 12 July 1968;
RDP79B00887A000500010046-1,
National Indications Center,
Memorandum for Chairman
Watch Committee, Czech-Soviet
Confrontation, 12 July 1968; Johnson,
American Cryptology, Book II, p. 458;
Aid, *The Secret Sentry*, p. 144

23 CIA CREST, Doc. No.
5166d4f999326091c6a608d0, FBIS
Special Memorandum, Public
Warning Indicators of the Soviet
Decision to Invade Czechoslovakia,
4 November 1980

24 UKNA CAB 128/43, 36th
Conclusions, 18 July 1968; Cradock,

Know Your Enemy, p. 251

25 Nicoll report, in Dover & Goodman,
Learning from the Secret Past, p. 287;
Shelest's Account of His Secret
Meeting on Lake Balaton with Vasi
Bil'ak, 20-21 July 1968, available
at Wilson Center Digital Archive,
https://digitalarchive.wilsoncenter.
org/document/117113 (accessed
10 January 2022); 'Russians demand
meeting with Czechs', *New York Times*,
20 July 1968

26 CIA CREST,
RDP94T00754R000200290004-5,
Military Developments in the Soviet–
Czech Confrontation, 2 August 1968;
Grabo, 'Soviet Deception'; Johnson,
American Cryptology, Book II, p. 457;
Nicoll report, in Dover & Goodman,
Learning from the Secret Past, p. 280;
Directive of the Ministry of Defence
for Exercise 'Overcast Summer-
68', 27 July 1968, available at
Wilson Center Digital Archive,
https://digitalarchive.wilsoncenter.
org/document/111893 (accessed
10 January 2022)

27 CIA CREST, Doc. No.
0005976267, PDB, 24 July 1968;
RDP79B00972A000100330003-2,
Memorandum for the Record,
Meeting of Working Group
on Strategic Arms Limitation,
10 July 1968; FRUS 1964-1968, Vol.
XVII, Eastern Europe, Doc. 72

28 CIA CREST, Doc. No.
5076e93d993247d4d82b6676,
Strategic Warning and the Role
of Intelligence: Lessons Learned
from the 1968 Soviet Invasion of
Czechoslovakia

29 FRUS 1964-1968, Vol. XVII, Eastern
Europe, Doc. 73; CIA CREST,
RDP94T00754R000200290004-5,
Military Developments in the Soviet–
Czech Confrontation, 2 August 1968

30 CIA CREST, Doc. No. 0005976283,
PDB, 2 August 1968; 'Two sides at
Cierna talks keep their distance;
Russians said to appear angry
after first session', *New York Times*,

31 July 1968; 'Action on Czechs
by Soviets deemed less likely', *New
York Times*, 31 July 1968; 'Optimism
voiced by Czechs as end of parley
nears', *New York Times*, 1 August 1968;
'Czechs will meet Bloc on reforms;
Cierna talks end', *New York Times*,
2 August 1968

31 CIA CREST,
RDP94T00754R000200290004-5,
Military Developments in the
Soviet–Czech Confrontation,
2 August 1968; Doc. No.
0005976279, PDB, 31 July 1968; Doc.
No. 5166d4f999326091c6a6087d,
Len Parkinson, 'Penkovsky's Legacy
and Strategic Research', *Studies in
Intelligence*, Spring 1972; UKNA CAB
128/43/38, Conclusions of Cabinet
Meeting, 22 August 1968; Grabo,
'Soviet Deception'

32 Shelest's Account of the Transfer
of the 'Letter of Invitation',
3 August 1968, available at Wilson
Center Digital Archive, https://
digitalarchive.wilsoncenter.org/
document/117114 (accessed
10 January 2022)

33 CIA CREST, Doc. No.
0005976299, PDB, 12 August 1968;
RDP79T00975A011900020001-7,
Central Intelligence Bulletin
No. 0236/68, 16 August 1968;
RDP79T00975A011900050001-4,
Central Intelligence Bulletin, No.
0239/68, 20 August 1968; Doc.
No. 5166d4f999326091c6a6o8do,
FBIS Special Memorandum, Public
Warning Indicators of the Soviet
Decision to Invade Czechoslovakia,
4 November 1980; Doc. No.
0000126882, Status of Warsaw
Pact Forces in Czechoslovakia,
27 September 1968; Grabo, 'Soviet
Deception'; Nicoll report, in Dover &
Goodman, *Learning from the Secret Past*,
p. 280; Aid, *The Silent Sentry*, p. 144

34 FRUS 1964-1968, Vol. XVII, Eastern
Europe, Docs 81, 85

35 CIA CREST, Doc. No.
5076e93d993247d4d82b651a,

The CIA and Strategic Warning:
The 1968 Soviet-Led Invasion
of Czechoslovakia; Doc. No.
5166d4f999326091c6a6o8do, FBIS
Special Memorandum, Public
Warning Indicators of the Soviet
Decision to Invade Czechoslovakia,
4 November 1980; Johnson, *American
Cryptology, Book II*, p. 457; Aid, *The
Silent Sentry*, p. 144

36 Ferris, *Behind the Enigma*, p. 536

37 CIA CREST, Doc. No.
5076e93d993247d4d82b651a,
The CIA and Strategic Warning:
The 1968 Soviet-Led Invasion of
Czechoslovakia; Helms with Hood,
A Look over My Shoulder, pp. 340-2;
Robert M. Hathaway & Russell Jack
Smith, *Richard Helms as Director of
Central Intelligence 1966-1973*, Center
for Study of Intelligence, Central
Intelligence Agency, Washington,
DC, 1993, pp. 52-4

38 FRUS 1964-1968, Vol. XVII, Eastern
Europe, Docs 80, 81; FRUS 1964-
1968, Vol. XI, Arms Control and
Disarmament, ed. Evans Gerakas,
David S. Patterson & Carolyn B. Yee,
United States Government Printing
Office, Washington, DC, 1997, Doc.
274

39 CIA CREST,
RDP79B00972A000100230002-4,
Military Costs of the Soviet
Invasion of Czechoslovakia,
19 September 1968; Doc. No.
0000126882, Status of Warsaw
Pact Forces in Czechoslovakia,
27 September 1968; Ferris, *Behind the
Enigma*, pp. 539-40; Nicoll report, in
Dover & Goodman, *Learning from the
Secret Past*, p. 280

40 NSA Website, OH-20-93, Interview
with Oliver Kirby

41 CIA CREST, Doc. No.
5076e93d993247d4d82b6676,
Strategic Warning and the
Role of Intelligence: Lessons
Learned from the 1968 Soviet
Invasion of Czechoslovakia;
RDP79B01709A003300060004-7,

Imagery Collection Requirements Sub-Committee of COMIREX, Minutes of Special Meeting, 22 July 1968; RDP78B04549A000400180006-9, Mission 1104-2, 14-22 August, 28 August 1968; RDP78T05929A003200070006-3, Mission 1104, Unusual Transport Aircraft Activity Kaliningrad Area, 22 August 1968

42 CIA CREST, Doc. No. 5076e93d993247d4d82b6676, Strategic Warning and the Role of Intelligence: Lessons Learned from the 1968 Soviet Invasion of Czechoslovakia

43 Michael S. Goodman, 'Avoiding Surprise', in Dover & Goodman, *Learning from the Secret Past*, pp. 265-75; Nicoll report, in Dover & Goodman, *Learning from the Secret Past*, pp. 277-91; 'Douglas Nicoll: Enigma codebreaker at Bletchley Park who warned about gaps in intelligence prior to the Falklands War', *Independent*, 17 November 2015; David Omand, *How Spies Think: Ten Lessons in Intelligence*, Penguin, London, 2020, p. 68; Interview with David Omand, CISI TV, 29 October 2020, https:// fsclub.zyen.com/events/webinars/ how-spies-think-ten-lessons-intelligence-cisi-tv-book-release/ (accessed 10 January 2022)

17. THE LOWEST POINT

1 Edward Heath, *The Course of My Life*, Hodder & Stoughton, London, 1998, p. 370; Aldrich, *GCHQ*, p. 268; Thomas Robb, *A Strained Partnership? US–UK Relations in the Era of Détente 1969-77*, Manchester University Press, Manchester, 2015, p. 34

2 Robb, *A Strained Partnership?*, pp. 24, 30

3 Henry Kissinger, *The White House Years*, Weidenfeld & Nicolson / Michael Joseph, London, 1979, pp. 89-91

4 NSA Website, Center for Cryptologic History, Doc. No. 3575748, Louis W. Tordella; Ferris, *Behind the Enigma*, pp. 355-8; DNB, Michael Herman, 'Hooper, Sir Leonard James (Joe)', *Oxford Dictionary of National Biography*, Oxford University Press, Oxford, 2004; James Bamford, *Body of Secrets: How America's National Security Agency and Britain's GCHQ Eavesdrop on the World*, Century, London, 2001, p. 407

5 UKNA FCO 46/1246, Tonkin to Jackson, Management Review of MOD HQ, 29 August 1975; Richard J. Aldrich, 'The UK–US Intelligence Alliance in 1975: Economies, Evaluations and Explanations', *Intelligence and National Security*, Vol. 21/4 (2006)

6 Johnson, *American Cryptology, Book II*, p. 415; Boyd, *British Naval Intelligence*, p. 624

7 Thomas R. Johnson, *American Cryptology during the Cold War 1945-1989, Book III: Retrenchment and Reform 1972-1980*, Center for Cryptologic History, National Security Agency, Ford George G. Meade, MD, 1998, pp. 157-9

8 FRUS 1969-1976, Vol. I, Foundations of Foreign Policy 1969-1972, ed. Louis J. Smith & David H. Herschler, United States Government Printing Office, Washington, DC, 2003, Doc. 102

9 FRUS 1969-1976, Vol. XLI, Western Europe; NATO 1969-1972, ed. James E. Miller & Laurie Van Hook, United States Government Printing Office, Washington, DC, 2012, Doc. 329

10 FRUS 1969-1976, Vol. I, Foundations of Foreign Policy 1969-1972, Doc. 102

11 UKNA CAB 301/655, Heath to Cromer, 11 May 1973; CAB 301/648, Trend to Kissinger, 31 July 1972; Trend to Heath, Discussions with Dr Kissinger at Washington, 31 July 1972; Robb, *A Strained Partnership?* pp. 29-30; Edward Heath, 'Trend, Burke Frederick St John, Baron Trend',

Oxford Dictionary of National Biography, Oxford University Press, Oxford, 2004

12 NSA Website, OH-15-88, Interview with General Marshall S. Carter, 3 October 1988; Ferris, *Behind the Enigma*, pp. 427-35; Aldrich, *GCHQ*, pp. 350-2; 'The Open Secret', *Wired*, 4 January 1999; Private information

13 CIA CREST, RDP00T02041R000100220001-1, NIE30-71, The Palestinians and *Fedayeen* as factors in the Middle-East Situation, 11 February 1971; RDP79R00967A000800020002-0, Special Memorandum, Moscow and the Fedayeen, 20 November 1968; RDP79R00967A000500030016-0, ONE Memorandum, The *Fedayeen*—Politics of Spoiling, 26 October 1972; Robert J. Hanyok, 'The First Round: NSA's Effort against International Terrorism in the 1970s', 24 February 1998, available at https://nsarchive2.gwu. edu/NSAEBB/NSAEBB278/10.PDF (accessed 10 January 2022); Aldrich, *GCHQ*, p. 263; Andrew, *The Defence of the Realm*, p. 605; Private information

14 CIA CREST, RDP80R01731R002000090003-2, DDCI Address for Army War College, 6 June 1973

15 FRUS 1969-1976, Volume XXV, Arab–Israeli Crisis and War 1973, ed. Nina Howland & Craig Daigle, United States Government Printing Office, Washington, DC, 2011, Doc. 50

16 UKNA CAB 301/655, Record of Conversation between Douglas-Home and Kissinger, 10 May 1973; Nicoll report, in Dover & Goodman, *Learning from the Secret Past*, pp. 279-85; 'Who killed the 20th century's greatest spy?', *The Guardian*, 15 September 2015

17 CIA CREST, LOC-HAK-475-1-15-7, Memorandum of Conversation between Kissinger and Dinitz, White House, 3 May 1973; Memorandum for Dr Henry A. Kissinger, Middle East Military Situation, 5 May 1973

18 UKNA CAB 301/653, Agenda for Prime Minister's Meeting with President Nixon, 16 January 1973, Annex III, Middle-East; CAB 301/655, Record of Conversation between Douglas-Home and Kissinger, 10 May 1973; CIA CREST, LOK-HAK-127-4-1-5, Memorandum of Conversation between Kissinger and Ashraf Ghorbal, Head of UAR Interests Section, 27 June 1972; LOK-HAK-127-6-16-7; Message to Hafez Ismail, 11 April 1973; FRUS 1969-1976, Vol. XXV, Arab-Israeli Crisis and War 1973, Doc. 4

19 CIA CREST, 51112a4a993247d4d8394488, Matthew T. Penney, *Intelligence and the 1973 Arab–Israeli War*, Center for the Study of Intelligence, Central Intelligence Agency, Langley, MD, 2012

20 FRUS 1969-1976, Vol. XXV, Arab–Israeli Crisis and War 1973, Doc. 59; Penney, *Intelligence and the 1973 Arab-Israeli War*

21 FRUS 1969-1976, Vol. XXV, Arab–Israeli Crisis and War 1973, Doc. 65; 'UN measure criticizing Israel vetoed by the US', *New York Times*, 27 July 1973

22 Nicoll report, in Dover & Goodman, *Learning from the Secret Past*, pp. 279-82; CIA CREST, Doc. No. 0001331429, The Performance of the Intelligence Community before the Arab–Israeli War of October 1973: A Preliminary Post-Mortem Report, 20 December 1973

23 FRUS 1969-1976, Vol. E-15, Part 2, Documents on Western Europe 1973-1976, ed. Kathleen B. Rasmussen, United States Government Printing Office, Washington, DC, 2014, Docs 27, 26, 31; Aldrich, *GCHQ*, pp. 274-5

24 FRUS 1969-1976, Vol. E-15, Part 2, Documents on Western Europe 1973-1976, Doc. 31; Ferris, *Behind the Enigma*, p. 381; Aldrich, *GCHQ*, pp. 274-5; Personal knowledge

25 FRUS 1969-1976, Vol. E-15, Part
    2, Documents on Western Europe
    1973-1976, Doc. 32; Aldrich, *GCHQ*,
    p. 274

26 Nicoll report, in Dover & Goodman,
    Learning from the Secret Past, pp. 279-89

27 FRUS 1969-1976, Vol. XXV, Arab–
    Israeli Crisis and War 1973, Doc. 93

28 NSA Website, The Yom Kippur
    War of 1973, Center for Cryptologic
    History, 28 February 2003; Johnson,
    American Cryptology, Book III, p. 184

29 FRUS 1969-1976, Vol. XXV, Arab–
    Israeli Crisis and War 1973, Docs
    97, 100, 101, 102; Omand, *How Spies
    Think*, p. 94

30 CIA CREST, Doc. No. 0001331429,
    The Performance of the Intelligence
    Community before the Arab–
    Israeli War of October 1973: A
    Preliminary Post-Mortem Report,
    20 December 1973; Robert M. Gates,
    *From the Shadows: The Ultimate Insider's
    Story of Five Presidents and How They
    Won the Cold War*, Simon & Schuster,
    New York, 1996, pp. 40-1

31 CIA CREST, Doc. No. 0001331429,
    The Performance of the Intelligence
    Community before the Arab–
    Israeli War of October 1973: A
    Preliminary Post-Mortem Report,
    20 December 1973

32 CIA CREST,
    RDP80B01495R001200080022-0,
    Photographic Capabilities to
    Monitor Middle-East Ceasefire,
    22 October 1973; UKNA PREM
    19/4613, Mallaby to Powell, Mr
    Heath's Alleged Refusal of Use
    of United States Bases in 1973,
    24 April 1986; 'Unhelpful British
    stand rankles in Washington', *The
    Times*, 2 November 1973; 'Why
    Arabists in the Foreign Office are well
    content', *The Times*, 7 November 1973;
    'NATO rift begins to heal',
    Washington Star, 9 November 1973;
    National Security Archive, Office
    of the Historian, Strategic Air
    Command, Chronology 'Middle East
    Crisis', 12 December 1973; Office

of the Historian, Headquarters,
    Second Air Force, Chronology
    of Middle East Contingency,
    6 October-9 November 1973

33 FRUS 1969-1976, Vol. E-15, Part
    2, Documents on Western Europe
    1973-1976, Docs 226, 227; FRUS
    1969-1976, Vol. XXV, Arab–Israeli
    Crisis and War 1973, Doc. 261; Robb,
    A Strained Partnership?, p. 98

34 FRUS 1969-1976, Vol. E-15, Part
    2, Documents on Western Europe
    1973-1976, Doc. 227; Robb, *A
    Strained Partnership?*, p. 95; National
    Security Archive, Office of the
    Historian, Strategic Air Command,
    Chronology 'Middle East Crisis',
    12 December 1973; Office of
    the Historian, Headquarters,
    Second Air Force, Chronology
    of Middle East Contingency,
    6 October-9 November 1973;
    Joint Chiefs of Staff, Operations
    Planners Group, Status of Actions
    Report (OPG), 'Middle East',
    30 October 1973

35 Robb, *A Strained Partnership?*, pp. 128-
    31; FRUS 1969-1976, Vol. E-15, Part
    2, Documents on Western Europe
    1973-1976, Docs 230, 231

36 FRUS 1969-1976, Vol. E-15, Part 2,
    Documents on Western Europe 1973-
    1976, Docs 233, 234; Robb, *A Strained
    Partnership?*, pp. 143-4

18. THE GREATEST OF THEM ALL

1   Ben Macintyre, *The Spy and the Traitor:
    The Greatest Espionage Story of the Cold
    War*, Penguin, London, 2019, p. 36;
    Andrew & Mitrokhin, *The Mitrokhin
    Archive*, p. 341

2   NSA Website, OH-15-88, Interview
    with General Marshall S. Carter,
    3 October 1988; Johnson, *American
    Cryptology, Book III*, pp. 91-8;
    Macintyre, *The Spy and the Traitor*,
    pp. 95-7; Corera, *The Art of Betrayal:
    Life and Death in the British Secret
    Service*, Weidenfeld & Nicolson,
    London, 2011, pp. 256, 270-1;
    Omand, *How Spies Think*, pp. 184-5

3   Douglas J. MacEachin, *US Intelligence and the Polish Crisis 1980-1981*, Center for the Study of Intelligence, Central Intelligence Agency, Langley, MD, 2000; Mark Kramer, 'Colonel Kuklinski and the Polish Crisis 1980-81', *Cold War International History Project Bulletin*, Winter 1998; Mark Kramer, 'The Kuklinski Files and the Polish Crisis of 1980-1981: An Analysis of the Newly Released CIA Documents on Ryszard Kuklinski', Working Paper No. 59, Cold War International History Project, March 2009; Smith, *Anatomy of a Spy*, History Press, pp. 126-35; 'Ryszard Kuklinski, 73, spy in Poland in Cold War, dies', *New York Times*, 12 February 2004; 'David Forden, CIA handler in Cold War intrigue, dies at 88', *New York Times*, 13 February 2019

4   MacEachin, *US Intelligence and the Polish Crisis*, p. 20

5   Kramer, 'Colonel Kuklinski', pp. 50-4; 'German Polish zone closed', *New York Times*, 3 December 1980; 'West's aides visit Polish border', *New York Times*, 11 December 1980; CIA CREST, No. 5076e90a993247d4d82b646c, Polish Ministry of Defense Drafting Plans to Utilize the Polish Military to Implement Martial Law, 23 January 1981; No. 5076e90a993247d4d82b6498, Polish Government Plans for the Possible Soviet Military Intervention and Declaration of Martial Law, 27 February 1981

6   US Justice Department, United States of America v. Ronald William Pelton, Indictment, US District Court for the District of Maryland, 20 December 1985; United States of America v. Ronald William Pelton, US Court of Appeals for the Fourth Circuit, 18 December 1987; 'Agent details Pelton's sale of spy secrets', *Washington Times*, 29 May 1986; 'Pelton spy case chronology', *Washington Post*, 6 June 1986; Aid, *The*

Secret Sentry, pp. 183-5

7   Private information

8   FRUS 1977-1980, Vol. XX, Eastern Europe, ed. Carl Ashley & Mircea A. Muntcanu, United States Government Publishing Office, Washington, DC, 2015, Doc. 42; CIA CREST, No. 5166d4f999326091c6a607e4, VII-328 'Planning, Preparations, Operation and Evaluation of Warsaw Pact Exercises', CIA/DO Intelligence Information Report, 1988 (DOI, 1981)

9   CIA CREST, No. 5076e90a993247d4d82b646e, Polish Government Plans for the Possible Introduction of Martial Law, 11 February 1981

10 CIA CREST, No. 5076e90a993247d4d82b64af, New Draft Decree on Martial Law, 9 September 1981; MacEachin, *US Intelligence and the Polish Crisis*, p. 147

11 CIA CREST, No. 5076e90a993247d4d82b6472, Intelligence Information Special Report, 7 October 1981; Kramer, 'The Kuklinski Files', pp. 48-9; MacEachin, *US Intelligence and the Polish Crisis*, p. 20

12 MacEachin, *US Intelligence and the Polish Crisis*, p. 20; 'Ryszard Kuklinski, 73, spy in Poland in Cold War, dies'; 'David Forden, CIA handler in Cold War intrigue, dies at 88'

13 Kramer, 'The Kuklinski Files', pp. 31-3; CIA CREST, RDP85-00024R000300390005-5, FBIS Coverage of the Polish Situation, 14 December 1981; RDP85-00024R000300390006-4, Foreign Broadcast Information Service, Polish Coverage, 17 December 1981

14 Macintyre, *The Spy and the Traitor*, pp. 111, 122, 141-2, 134-8

15 Oleg Gordievsky, *Next Stop Execution*, Macmillan, London, 1995, p. 253

16 Macintyre, *The Spy and the Traitor*, pp. 157-61; Gordievsky, *Next Stop Execution*, p. 263

17 Gordievsky, *Next Stop Execution*,

pp. 265-70; Macintyre, *The Spy and the Traitor*, pp. 160, 194; 'The MI5 loner who decided the Russians were right', *The Times*, 17 April 1984

18 Christopher Andrew & Oleg Gordievsky, *KGB: The Inside Story*, Hodder & Stoughton, London, 1990, p. 488; Ben B. Fischer, *A Cold War Conundrum: The 1983 Soviet War Scare*, Center for the Study of Intelligence, Central Intelligence Agency, Langley, MD, 1997, pp. 3-5; National Security Archive, Andropov speech to National Consultation Meeting of the KGB Leadership, 25 May 1983, available at https://nsarchive.gwu.edu/document/17306-document-02-kgb-chairman-yuri-andropov (accessed 11 January 2022)

19 Gordievsky, *Next Stop Execution*, p. 261

20 Christopher Andrew & Oleg Gordievsky (eds), *Comrade Kryuchkov's Instructions: Top Secret Files on KGB Foreign Operations 1975-1985*, Stanford University Press, Stanford, CA, 1991, pp. 69-81

21 'Russians attack "bellicose" Reagan', *The Times*, 10 March 1983; Fischer, *A Cold War Conundrum*, pp. 17-18; 'Andropov says US is spurring a race in strategic arms', *New York Times*, 27 March 1983

22 FRUS 1981-1988, Vol. IV, Soviet Union January 1983-March 1985, ed. Elizabeth C. Charles, United States Government Publishing Office, Washington, DC, 2021, Doc. 116; Private information; Fischer, *A Cold War Conundrum*, pp. 19-23; 'Ex-Soviet pilot still insists KAL 007 was spying', *New York Times*, 9 December 1996

23 'Andropov attacks US missile plan as unattainable', *New York Times*, 29 September 1983

24 FRUS 1981-1988, Vol. IV, Soviet Union January 1983-March 1985, Doc. 134, Appendix A

25 National Security Archive, The Soviet 'War Scare', President's Foreign Intelligence Advisory Board, 15 February 1990; National Security Archive, Taylor Downing interview with Colonel-General Ivan Yesin, for *The Brink of Apocalypse*, Flashback Television

26 Andrew, *For the President's Eyes Only*, p. 476

27 Fischer, *A Cold War Conundrum*, pp. 24-6; Douglas Brinkley (ed.), *The Reagan Diaries, Vol. I: January 1981-October 1985*, HarperCollins, New York, 2007, p. 290

28 CIA CREST, RDP85T00287R001400360001-9, Soviet Thinking on the Possibility of Armed Confrontation with the United States, 30 December 1983; FRUS 1981-1988, Vol. IV, Soviet Union January 1983-March 1985, Doc. 156

29 FRUS 1981-1988, Vol. IV, Soviet Union January 1983-March 1985, Doc. 204; Geoffrey Smith, *Reagan and Thatcher*, W. W. Norton, New York, 1991, p. 123

30 CIA CREST, RDP09T00367R000300330001-9, SNIE 11-10-84, Implications of Recent Soviet Military-Political Activities, 18 May 1984; National Security Archive: Charles Powell, PM's Private Secretary, Soviet Union Concern About a Surprise Nuclear Attack, 10 April 1984, available at https://nsarchive.files.wordpress.com/2013/11/document-7.pdf (accessed 11 January 2022)

31 UKNA PREM 19/1635, Thatcher to C, 25 September 1984; FRUS 1981-1988, Vol. V, Soviet Union March 1985-October 1986, ed. Elizabeth C. Charles, United States Government Publishing Office, Washington, DC, 2020, Doc. 125; 'Cordial Gorbachov joins call for peace and goodwill', *The Times*, 17 December 1984; Margaret Thatcher Foundation, TV Interview for BBC ('I like Mr Gorbachev. We can do business together'), 17 December 1984,

https://www.margaretthatcher.
org/document/105592 (accessed
11 January 2022)

32 US Senate Intelligence Committee,
An Assessment of the Aldrich
H. Ames Espionage Case and Its
Implications for US Intelligence,
1 November 1994; Sandra Grimes
& Jeanne Vertefeuille, *Circle of
Treason: A CIA Account of Traitor Aldrich
Ames and the Men He Betrayed,* Naval
Institute Press, Annapolis, MD, 2012,
pp. 168-9, 200; Victor Cherkashin
with Gregory Feifer, *Spy Handler:
Memoir of a KGB Officer,* Basic, New
York, 2005, pp. 15-23

33 Gordievsky, *Next Stop Execution,* p. 10;
Macintyre, *The Spy and the Traitor,*
pp. 259-60

34 Gordievsky, *Next Stop Execution,*
pp. 16-21

35 Macintyre, *The Spy and the Traitor,*
pp. 297-303

36 Gordievsky, *Next Stop Execution,*
pp. 347, 364, 372-3, 376-7;
FRUS 1981-1988, Vol. V, Soviet
Union, March 1985-October 1986,
Doc. 198

37 The Soviet 'War Scare', President's
Foreign Intelligence Advisory
Board, February 15, 1990;
FRUS 1981-1988, Vol. IV, Soviet
Union January 1983-March 1985,
Appendix A

**19. 'DO WE STILL NEED
THE BRITS?'**

1 FRUS 1977-1980, Vol. XII,
Afghanistan, ed. David Zierler,
United States Government Publishing
Office, Washington, DC, 2018, Docs
38, 39, 51, 53, 80

2 FRUS 1977-1980, Vol.
XII, Afghanistan, Docs
59, 67, 62; CIA CREST,
RDP83B01027R000300110001-5,
Special Report for the
President, September 1979;
RDP84B00130R000600010142-2,
Staff Meeting Minutes,
10 September 1979;

RDP83B01027R000300170017-2,
Strategic Warning Staff
Memorandum on USSR–
Afghanistan, 29 October 1979;
RDP86B00269R001100100003-5,
McCaffrey to DCI, A Review
of Intelligence Performance in
Afghanistan, 9 April 1984; Aid, *The
Secret Sentry,* pp. 168-70

3 CIA CREST,
RDP83B01027R000300170018-1,
Director SWS to NIO/W,
12 December 1979; Telegram
from the Embassy in
Afghanistan to the Department
of State, 20 December 1979;
RDP83B01027R000200030005-8,
Turner to NSC, 19 December 1979;
RDP83B01027R000200030004-9,
Carlucci to Vance, Brown,
Brzezinski, General David C. Jones,
25 December 1979; FRUS 1977-1980,
Vol. XII, Afghanistan, Docs 214, 336;
Gates, *From the Shadows,* p. 133; Aid,
The Secret Sentry, p. 170

4 Private information; Corera, *The Art
of Betrayal,* pp. 296-308

5 Private information; CIA CREST,
RDP96R01136R001302260003-3,
Afghanistan: Goals and Prospects
for the Insurgents, May 1983;
RDP96R01136R001302260003-3,
Afghanistan Situation Report,
5 May 1987; Corera, *The Art of Betrayal,*
p. 300

6 Private information; Milton
Bearden, 'Afghanistan, Graveyard of
Empires', *Foreign Affairs,* November/
December 2001

7 Private information; 'We stole secret
guns from the Soviet Army', *Daily
Star,* 24 May 1990; *Panorama,* BBC,
22 November 1993

8 Falkland Islands Review,
HMSO, January 1983; FRUS 1981-
1988, Vol. XIII, Conflict in the South
Atlantic 1981-1984, ed. Alexander R.
Wieland, United States Government
Publishing Office, Washington, DC,
2015, Doc. 14

9 Verrier, *Through the Looking Glass,*

p. 341; 'Frankly speaking', *Daily Telegraph*, 29 December 1987; Cavendish, *Inside Intelligence*, p. xiv; UKNA DEFE 31/227, Col. Stephen Love, Defence Attaché, British Embassy, Buenos Aires to Governor Rex, The Argentine Threat to the Falkland Islands, 2 March 1982

10 Lord Franks, Falkland Islands Review

11 Franks, Falkland Islands Review; FRUS 1981-1988, Vol. XIII, Conflict in the South Atlantic 1981-1984, Doc. 243; UKNA DEFE 31/227, MO5/21, PS SoS (Omand), to PSO/DGI, Falklands, 11 May 1982; D/DIS(CS)21/52, DIS to PS/Secretary of State (Omand), 13 May 1982; SO/DGI, Incident on South Georgia, 12 May 1982; DEFE 68/622, The Argentine Marines. An Assessment of Current Deployment, 11 May 1982

12 Omand, *How Spies Think*, p. 2; Ferris, *Behind the Enigma*, pp. 617-19

13 Omand, *How Spies Think*, pp. 1-2, 122; Ferris, *Behind the Enigma*, pp. 619-20

14 UKNA CAB 128/175, Cabinet Discussions of the UK Strategic Nuclear Deterrent, 21 January 1982; CAB 128/75, Cabinet Discussions of the UK Strategic Nuclear Deterrent, 4 March 1982; 'Britain to buy "bargain" US Trident 2 for £7,500m', *The Times*, 12 March 1982; 'Text of letters on Trident deal', *The Times*, 12 March 1982; 'Trident something of a luxury', *The Times*, 12 March 1982; Smith, *Reagan and Thatcher*, pp. 68-70

15 UKNA DEFE 31/256, Henderson to Pym, US Policy in the Falklands Crisis with some Valedictory Comments on US/UK Relations, 27 July 1982; FRUS 1981-1988, Vol. XIII, Conflict in the South Atlantic 1981-1984, Docs 31, 11, 12, 56

16 FRUS 1981-1988, Vol. XIII, Conflict in the South Atlantic 1981-1984, Doc. 76; James M. Rentschler, *A Reason to Get Up in the Morning: A Cold Warrior Remembers*, Jeffrey Rentschler, New York, 2008, pp. 632-7; '"Lost zest" for bureaucratic battles, Inman says of decision to quit CIA', *Washington Post*, 28 April 1982

17 FRUS 1981-1988, Vol. XIII, Conflict in the South Atlantic 1981-1984, Docs 230, 315, 188, 190; Andrew Dorman, Michael D. Kandiah & Gillian Staerck (eds), *The Falklands War*, Centre for Contemporary British History, London, 2005, p. 36

18 Boyd, *British Naval Intelligence*, p. 661; FRUS 1981-1988. Vol. XIII, Conflict in the South Atlantic 1981-1984, Docs 86, 84, 93

19 UKNA DEFE 31/256, Henderson to Pym, 27 July 1982; FRUS 1981-1988, Vol. XIII, Conflict in the South Atlantic 1981-1984, Docs 108, 143, 205

20 UKNA DEFE 31/256, Henderson to Pym, 27 July 1982; Kathleen Burk, *Old World, New World: The Story of Britain and America*, Little, Brown, London, 2007, p. 636; FRUS 1981-1988, Vol. XIII, Conflict in the South Atlantic 1981-1984, Docs 65, 241, 177, 378, 111

21 UKNA DEFE 70/940, JACRA to NWCRA, UK/US Eyes Only, JAREX 09859/92, 19 April 1982; Ferris, *Behind the Enigma*, pp. 629, 656; 'US providing Britain a wide range of intelligence', *New York Times*, 15 April 1982. The Pentagon subsequently denied an ABC TV report in early April that a US SR-71 aircraft had provided imagery of the Falkland Islands before and after the invasion. Given that there was no KH-9 Hexagon satellite operational at the time it seems likely that the misreported flight was actually over South Georgia.

22 Ferris, *Behind the Enigma*, pp. 630-5; Aldrich, *GCHQ*, p. 369; Boyd, *British Naval Intelligence*, pp. 660-1

23 D. J. Thorp, *The Silent Listener: Falklands 1982*, Spellmount, Stroud, 2011, pp. 61-6, 82-3, 91-2

24 Aldrich, *GCHQ*, p. 373; Imperial War Museum, Oral History, IWM13271, Robert Denton Green

25 Ferris, *Behind the Enigma*, pp. 637-41;
FRUS 1981-1988, Vol. XIII, Conflict
in the South Atlantic 1981-1984, Docs
206, 208

26 UKNA DEFE 31/256, D/DIS
(CS) 21/52, Chiefs of Staff Paper
on Military Contingencies,
21 May 1982; CIA CREST,
RDP82T00709R000101520001-8,
Military Forces Argentina,
12 May 1982

27 CIA CREST,
RDP90T00784R000100230005-5,
Increased Defensive Measures,
Port Stanley Area, Falkland
Islands, 28 May 1982; Dorman et
al., *The Falklands War*, p. 50; Nasa
Space Science Data Coordinated
Archive, STP S81-1, https://nssdc.
gsfc.nasa.gov/nmc/spacecraft/
displayTrajectory.action?id=1982-
041A (accessed 12 January 2022)

28 CIA CREST; UKNA DEFE 72/271
CTTO/25/18/1/OPS, Operation
Corporate: A Worm's-Eye View,
21 July 1982; DEFE 31/227, Point
Brief on Air Power Lessons of
Operation Corporate, 16 June 1982;
DEFE 68/622, TPS Hereford to
RBDEC/CINCFLEET, 18 May 1982,
INTSUM No 1; Ken Connor, *Ghost
Force: The Secret History of the SAS*,
Weidenfeld & Nicolson, London,
1998, p. 244; John Parker, *SBS: The
Inside Story of the Special Boat Service*,
updated ed., Headline, London, 2003,
pp. 241-3; Nasa Space Science Data
Coordinated Archive, STP S81-1

29 UKNA DEFE 31/227, DASB/
CB/22/82, Commanders' Brief
Special Supplement Operation
Corporate September 1982

30 Interviews and correspondence with
Tony Divall, April 1995

31 UKNA PREM 19/1048, T160/83,
Reagan to Thatcher, 24 October 1983;
T161/83, Reagan to Thatcher,
24 October 1983; T162/83, Prime
Minister to President Reagan,
25 October 1983; T163/83, Reagan
to Thatcher, 25 October 1983;

Coles, PS to PM to Fall, PS to
Foreign Secretary, 26 October 1983;
PREM 19/1049, Tel. No. 3225, UK
Ambassador, Washington, to FCO,
30 October 1983; Smith, *Reagan
and Thatcher*, pp. 125-32; 'We'll
Always Have Grenada', *Foreign
Affairs*, November/December 2006

32 UKNA PREM 19/1049, Tel. No.
3404, Thomas to FCO PUS,
11 November 1983; PREM 19/4613,
Washington to FCO, Tel. No. 1185,
Congressional Resolution on UK
Support, 5 May 1986; 'US jets hit
terrorist centers in Libya', *New York
Times*, 15 April 1986; 'While across
the Atlantic, Anglophilia rules', *New
York Times*, 24 April 1986

33 Interview with Graeme Lamb,
20 September 2021; Americans
in Wartime Experience website,
Interview with Lewis 'Bucky' Burruss
Jr.

34 See for example CIA CREST,
RDP83T00233R000200150002-5,
Soviet Union Monthly
Review, April 1982

35 Private information; Vladimir
Pasechnik, *Daily Telegraph*,
29 November 2001; Richard Preston,
'The Bioweaponeers', *New Yorker*,
9 March 1998; James Risen, *State of
War: The Secret History of the CIA and
the Bush Administration*, Pocket Books,
New York, 2006, p. 41

36 Intelligence and Security
Committee (ISC), *The Mitrokhin
Inquiry Report*, June 2000; Andrew
& Mitrokhin, *The Mitrokhin
Archive*, pp. 1-20; 'FBI probing
Soviet spy effort', *Washington Post*,
18 August 1993; 'Hundreds gave data
to the KGB, book says', *Los Angeles
Times*, 18 August 1993

37 Peter Riddell, *Hug Them Close:
Blair, Clinton, Bush and the 'Special
Relationship'*, Politico's, London, 2003,
pp. 54-5

38 Raymond G. Seitz, The Anglo-
American Relationship, Chatham
House, 23 March 1993; UKNA PREM

19/4499, Bilateral Relations with the United States, 25 January 1993; John Pitt-Brooke (MoD) to John Sawers (FCO), 11 February 1993; Hurd to PM, 26 March 1993; Lyne (in Washington) to Sharpe, 19 May 1993; PREM 19/5477, Sharpe to Oakden, 7 November 1995; Oakden to Lyne, 9 November 1995; President Clinton's Visit to the UK, 29 November-1 December 1995, UK/US Bilateral Initiatives

39 Foreign Office Oral History Programme, Recollections of Sir Francis Richards, 4 April 2016; NSA Website, Senior US Liaison Officer London to NSA Executive Director Parks, 23 April 1993 (appendix to NSA to Privacy International, 21 September 2018); ISC Annual Report 1996, February 1997; ISC Annual Report 1999-2000, November 2000; Aldrich, *GCHQ*, pp. 431-4; Aid, *The Secret Sentry*, p. 209; Bamford, *Body of Secrets*, p. 454

20. AMERICA'S AVENGING ANGELS

1 Foreign Office Oral History Programme, Recollections of Sir Francis Richards, 4 April 2016; ISC, Detainee Mistreatment and Rendition: 2001-2010, 28 June 2018; Interview with Graeme Lamb, 20 September 2021

2 House Permanent Select Committee on Intelligence and Senate Select Committee on Intelligence, Report of the Joint Inquiry into the Terrorist Attacks of September 11, 2001, December 2002

3 Private information; ISC, Rendition, July 2007; Michael Smith, *Killer Elite: The Inside Story of America's Most Secret Special Operations Team*, St Martin's Press, New York, 2007, pp. 204-6; The 9/11 Commission Report, pp. 111-15; Henry A. Crumpton, *The Art of Intelligence: Lessons from a Life in the CIA's Clandestine Service*, Penguin

Press, New York, 2012, pp. 127-32

4 Matthew M. Aid, 'All Glory Is Fleeting: Sigint and the Fight against International Terrorism', *Intelligence and National Security*, Vol. 18/4 (2003); House Permanent Select Committee on Intelligence and Senate Select Committee on Intelligence, Report of the Joint Inquiry into the Terrorist Attacks of September 11, 2001, December 2002, pp. 42, 151; ISC Annual Report 2001-2002, June 2002; The 9/11 Commission Report, pp. 128-30, 254-62, 533

5 Bob Woodward, *Bush at War*, Pocket Books, New York, 2003, pp. 50-3

6 Private information; Toby Harnden, *First Casualty: The Untold Story of the Battle That Began the War in Afghanistan*, Welbeck, London, 2021

7 Risen, *State of War*, p. 73; Rycroft to Various, Iraq: Prime Minister's Meeting, 23 July, and Ricketts to Straw, Iraq: Advice for the Prime Minister, 22 March 2002, documents obtained by the author and available at https://www.michaelsmithauthor.com/the-downing-street-memos.html (accessed 12 January 2022)

8 Butler Review of Intelligence on Weapons of Mass Destruction, 14 July 2004

9 Private information; Butler Review of Intelligence on Weapons of Mass Destruction, 14 July 2004; ISC, Iraqi Weapons of Mass Destruction – Intelligence and Assessments, September 2003

10 The Iraq Inquiry, Testimony of Sir David Omand, 20 January 2010, JIC Assessment, International Terrorism: War with Iraq, 10 February 2003

11 Eliza Manningham-Buller, Security Freedom, Reith Lecture, 16 September 2011; Andrew, *The Defence of the Realm*, pp. 816-26; ISC, Could 7/7 Have Been Prevented, May 2009; Bruce Riedel, 'Al Qaeda Strikes Back', *Foreign Affairs*, May/June 2007

12 ISC Annual Report 2006-
    2007, January 2008; ISC Annual
    Report 2008-2009, March 2010
13 'Airliner bomb trial: How MI5
    uncovered the terror plot', *Daily
    Telegraph*, 9 September 2008;
    ISC Annual Report 2006-
    2007, January 2008; Congressional
    Research Service, United States
    Foreign Intelligence Relationships:
    Background, Policy and Legal
    Authorities, Risks, Benefits,
    15 May 2019; Christopher Andrew,
    *The Secret World: A History of
    Intelligence*, Penguin, London, 2019,
    p. 757; 'Suicide bombers convicted
    at end of Britain's biggest terrorism
    investigation', *Daily Telegraph*,
    8 July 2010; 'How the CIA helped
    prevent the next 9/11 – and why you
    can't bring liquids onto planes', *Daily
    Beast*, 25 November 2018
14 ISC, The Handling of Detainees
    by UK Intelligence Personnel
    in Afghanistan, Guantanamo
    Bay and Iraq, March 2005; ISC,
    Rendition, July 2007; ISC Annual
    Report 2009-2010, March 2010;
    ISC Annual Report 2010-
    2011, July 2011; ISC Annual Report
    2011-2012, July 2012; ISC, Detainee
    Mistreatment and Rendition: 2001-
    2010, 28 June 2018; Corera, *The
    Art of Betrayal*, p. 343. Interview
    with former senior CIA officer, 1
    November 2022.
15 Personal knowledge
16 The Iraq Inquiry, Testimony of Gen.
    Sir Richard Dannatt, 28 July 2010;
    Adam Ingram, Armed Forces
    Minister, Written Ministerial
    Statement to the House of Commons,
    14 November 2005; 'Military fears
    big Afghan losses', *Sunday Times*,
    1 January 2006; Theo Farrell,
    *Unwinnable: Britain's War in Afghanistan
    2001-2014*, Vintage, London, 2018,
    pp. 159-60, 233
17 Office of the Special Inspector-
    General for Afghanistan
    Reconstruction, Lessons Learned
    Interview with General David
    Richards, 26 September 2017; Craig
    Whitlock, *The Afghanistan Papers:
    A Secret History of the War*, Simon &
    Schuster, New York, 2021, pp. 179-
    33; Farrell, *Unwinnable*, pp. 167-9
18 Interview with Brigadier Ed Butler,
    15 September 2006; Office of
    the Special Inspector-General for
    Afghanistan Reconstruction, Lessons
    Learned Interview with General Dan
    McNeil
19 Private information
20 Interview with Graeme Lamb,
    20 September 2021; General Stanley
    McChrystal, *My Share of the Task*,
    Portfolio, New York, 2013, pp. 244-6

21. THE PIVOT TO THE PACIFIC

1   Butler Review of Intelligence on
    Weapons of Mass Destruction,
    14 July 2004; ISC Annual Report
    2003-2004, June 2004; Corera, *The
    Art of Betrayal*, pp. 383-6; Gordon
    Corera, *Shopping for Bombs: Nuclear
    Proliferation, Global Insecurity, and the
    Rise and Fall of the A. Q. Khan Network*,
    Hurst, London, 2006, pp. 157-8,
    161-76, 181-94; Private information;
    Remarks by Deputy Director for
    Operations James L. Pavitt, Foreign
    Policy Association, 21 June 2004;
    Interview with former BBC Arab
    Monitor, 29 September 2001; 'Spy
    game that halted Gaddafi WMDs',
    The Times, 1 November 2011;
    'Torture claims raise questions over
    Libya–Britain ties', BBC News,
    5 September 2011; 'Blair May take
    credit, but it was all down to an
    MI6 spy in a Bedouin tent', *Daily
    Telegraph*, 22 December 2003; 'How
    the deal was done', *Sunday Telegraph*,
    21 December 2003; 'No freedom
    for Mr Khan', *New York Times*,
    6 September 2009
2   Dr Jo Devanny & Josh Harris,
    National Security at the Centre of
    Government, KCL Institute for
    Government
3   Anthony Seldon & Peter Snowdon,

Cameron at 10: The Verdict, William Collins, London, 2016, pp. 55-60; McChrystal, *Share of the Task*, pp. 353-4

4 House of Commons Foreign Affairs Committee, Libya: Examination of intervention and collapse and the UK's future policy options, 6 September 2016; Aldrich & Cormac, *The Black Door*, p. 462; David Richards, *Taking Command*, Headline, London, 2014, p. 318; 'Libya doubts were ignored, says former defence chief', *The Times*, 15 September 2016; 'Key facts about Islamic State in Libya', Reuters, 9 December 2016; 'Libya: credible elections – or another failed bid at nation-building', *Guardian*, 29 September 2021

5 Private information; 'Spy chiefs fear Chinese cyber attack', *Sunday Times*, 29 March 2009

6 'Nuclear deal with China is threat to UK security', *The Times*, 16 October 2015

7 House of Commons Defence Committee, The Security of 5G, 8 October 2020; 'Nuclear deal with China is threat to UK security'

8 ISC, Annual Report 2010-2011, July 2011; House of Commons Defence Committee, Open Source Stupidity: The Threat to the BBC Monitoring Service, 20 December 2016

9 ISC, Privacy and Security: A modern and transparent legal framework, 12 March 2015; Gordon Corera, *Intercept: The Secret History of Computers and Spies*, Weidenfeld & Nicolson, London, 2016, pp. 324-6, 338-9; 'Tech companies concede to surveillance program', *New York Times*, 7 June 2013; 'A simple guide to the Prism controversy', *Wired*, 10 June 2013; 'A simple guide to GCHQ's internet surveillance programme Tempora', *Wired*, 24 June 2013; 'Furious spy chiefs warn leaks alert al Qaeda', *The Times*, 8 November 2013

10 'Biden will withdraw all US forces from Afghanistan by Sept. 11, 2021', *Washington Post*, 13 April 2021; 'Senior leaders didn't want to leave Afghanistan', *Military Times*, 28 September 2021; 'Afghanistan and the Haunting Questions of Blame', *New Yorker*, 30 September 2021; 'I commanded Afghan troops this year. We were betrayed', *New York Times*, 25 August 2021; 'Afghanistan's military collapse: illicit deals and mass desertions', *Washington Post*, 15 August 2021; Congressional Research Service, The Collapse of the Afghan National Defense and Security Services, 23 August 2021

11 Douglas London, 'CIA's former counterterrorism chief for the region: Afghanistan, not an intelligence failure—something much worse', *Just Security*, 18 August 2021; 'CIA warned of rapid Afghanistan collapse. So why did US get it so wrong?', NBC News, 18 August 2021; 'Intelligence warned of Afghan military collapse, despite Biden's assurances', *New York Times*, 17 August 2021

12 'Why Biden's lack of strategic patience led to disaster', *New York Times*, 21 August 2021; 'Former administration officials argue over whether keeping troops in Afghanistan would have helped', *Military Times*, 5 October 2021

13 'Afghanistan fallout shows "demise" of "special relationship" between UK and US, says Commons defence chair', *Independent*, 22 August 2021; 'Chaos of Kabul exposes faultlines in UK–US special relationship', *Financial Times*, 19 August 2021; 'Britain's special relationship fantasy has been exposed', *Foreign Policy*, 13 September 2021; 'Barack Obama rebuffs Gordon Brown as "special relationship" sinks to new low', *Daily Telegraph*, 23 September 2009; 'We didn't want to leave Afghanistan this way, Boris Johnson says', *Independent*, 29 August 2021

14 'UK, US and Australia launch pact to counter China', BBC News, 16 September 2021; Pentagon Press Conference with Antony Blinken, Lloyd Austin, Marise Payne and Peter Dutton, 16 September 2021; 'The submarine deal is a real downer for China', *Sunday Times*, 18 September 2021; 'AUKUS', The Lindley-French Analysis, 20 September 2021, https://lindleyfrench.blogspot.com/2021/09/aukus.html (accessed 13 January 2022)

15 'MI5: 31 late-stage terror plots foiled in four years in UK', BBC News, 10 September 2021; 'Former MI6 Chief Sir Alex Younger talks to T&G', Times Radio, 5 September 2021; John McLaughlin, 'Afghanistan's dark end game', *Cipher Brief*, 30 July 2021

16 DNI's Annual Threat Assessment, 9 April 2021; DNI's Annual Threat Assessment Oral Remarks to Senate Intelligence Committee, 14 April 2021; 'Iran accelerates enrichment of uranium to near weapons-grade, IAEA says', Reuters, 18 August 2021

17 The Cipher Brief, Ukraine: The Worst Case Scenario, 24 February 2022; Sergey Karaganov: Russia's new foreign policy, the Putin Doctrine, *RT*, 23 February 2002 https://www.rt.com/russia/550271-putin-doctrine-foreign-policy/ (accessed 10 March 2022); Little Green Men: Modern Russian Unconventional Warfare, US Army Special Operations Command, Fort Bragg, North Carolina; Renewed Great Power Competition: Implications for Defense—Issues for Congress, Congressional Research Service, 10 March 2022; ISC, Russia,

21 July 2020; 'CIA chief William Burns made secret visit to Europe ahead of Secretary of State Blinken's trip as part of effort to drum up support for tough response if Moscow invades Ukraine', *Daily Mail*, 20 January 2022; 'UK accuses Russia of scheming to install a pro-Kremlin government in Ukraine', *Washington Post*, 23 January 2022; 'US accuses Russia of planning to film false attack as pretext for Ukraine invasion', *Washington Post*, 3 February 2022; 'US says Russia has a list of Ukrainians to kill or detain after an invasion', *New York Times*, 21 February 2022; 'Senators praise role of US intelligence in Ukraine as officials detailed looming threats', *Stars and Stripes*, 11 March 2022; Heads of the US Intelligence community testified before the House Select Intelligence Committee https://www.c-span.org/video/?518352-1/house-intel-panel-told-putin-endgame-ukraine (accessed 9 March 2022); National Cryptologic Foundation, Panel Discussion with Six Former NSA Directors, 14 April 2021

18 DNI's Annual Threat Assessment, 9 April 2021; Virtual Briefing with Sir John Sawers, *Cipher Brief*, 9 February 2021; Rush Doshi, *The Long Game: China's Grand Strategy to Displace American Order*, Oxford University Press, New York, 2021, p. 48; National Cryptologic Foundation, Panel Discussion with Six Former NSA Directors, 14 April 2021; Renewed Great Power Competition: Implications for Defense – Issues for Congress, Congressional Research Service, 9 September 2021

19 Virtual Briefing with Sir John Sawers

INDEX

ABOUT THE AUTHOR

Michael Smith is a number one bestselling author and award-winning journalist. He left school at fifteen to join the British Army and after service with the Royal Artillery became a member of the army's Intelligence Corps, monitoring terrorist and Soviet Bloc communications. Smith studied Arabic before working for three years in the Middle East collecting intelligence on terrorists operating in Syria, Iraq and Lebanon. He also took part in Britain's secret war against communist rebels in Oman as part of a small unit providing intelligence for the SAS. Smith then spent four years in Europe, becoming a German interpreter and producing reports on the activities of the East German armed forces.

He left the army in 1982 to join the BBC Monitoring Service, which listened in to radio and television broadcasts from around the world. It was here that he began his career in journalism. He left the BBC in 1990 to become a newspaper journalist, writing on Eastern Europe for the *Financial Times* and the *Sunday Times* before joining the *Daily Telegraph*, where he wrote on defense and security issues and covered a number of conflicts around the world. Smith reported on the 1991 Gulf War and various conflicts in the Balkans—twice going into Kosovo under fire to meet up with the Kosovo Liberation Army during the 1999 war. He also reported extensively on the wars Afghanistan and Iraq for the *Daily Telegraph* and the *Sunday Times*.

He is an expert on special operations and intelligence with extremely good contacts inside Britain's intelligence and special forces community and a track record of breaking stories previously kept top secret. This was graphically demonstrated with the so-called Downing Street Memos, which showed how President George W. Bush and Tony Blair agreed to use military force to bring about regime change in Iraq in April 2002—something that was illegal under international law—and within weeks began bombing Iraqi military installations in an attempt to provoke Saddam into a response that could be used to justify war. All this happened more than six months before votes in either Congress or the UK Parliament authorized the allied invasion.

Smith is the author of numerous books on intelligence and special operations including *The Secrets of Station X: How Bletchley Park Helped Win the War*, which is widely seen as the definitive history of the British wartime codebreaking centre at Bletchley Park; *Killer Elite: America's Most Secret Special Operations Team*, which reveals the secret history of "The Activity," a top secret US Army intelligence unit which works alongside Delta and Seal Team Six to track down terrorists and other threats to America; and *Foley: The Spy Who Saved 10,000 Jews*, which led to Israeli recognition of the former MI6 officer Frank Foley as Righteous Among Nations, the same award granted to Oskar Schindler and Raoul Wallenberg. He has published two previous books with Arcade: *The Emperor's Codes*, which tells the story of how US, British and Australian codebreakers cracked the secret ciphers used by the Japanese during the Second World War, and *The Anatomy of a Spy* which examines a number of cases of espionage, many of them new, to explain the various motives and reasons that lead spies to spy.

Michael Smith lives near Henley-on-Thames in Oxfordshire.